The Amarna Letters

MW01028215

THE AMARNA LETTERS

Edited and Translated by William L. Moran

The Johns Hopkins University Press
Baltimore and London

Originally published as *Les Lettres d'El-Amarna,*
© Les Éditions du Cerf, 1987

English-language edition
© 1992 The Johns Hopkins University Press
All rights reserved
Printed in the United States of America

The Johns Hopkins University Press
701 West 40th Street
Baltimore, Maryland 21211-2190
The Johns Hopkins Press Ltd., London

The paper used in this book meets the minimum requirements of American National Standard for Information Sciences—Permanence of Paper for Printed Library Materials, ANSI Z39.48-1984.

Library of Congress Cataloging-in-Publication Data
Tell el-Amarna tablets.
The Amarna letters / edited and translated by William L. Moran.
p. cm.
Translation of: Tel el-Amarna tablets.
Includes bibliographical references and index.
ISBN 0-8018-4251-4 (alk. paper)
1. Assyro-Babylonian letters—Translations into English.
2. Akkadian language—Texts. 3. Egypt—History—Eighteenth dynasty, ca. 1510–1320 B.C.—Sources. 4. Middle East—History—To 622—Sources. I. Moran, William L. II. Title.
PJ3886.E5M67 1992
492'.1—dc20 91-20570

For Suzie

Contents

Preface

A little more than a century has passed since the discovery of the Amarna letters. At first virtually unique and so extraordinary that even their genuineness was seriously questioned, these letters over the years have gradually acquired context and perspective. As subsequent discoveries made clear, the Amarna letters reflect a cosmopolitan culture, a "cuneiform culture," that throughout most of the second millennium B.C. extended from the mountains to the east of Assyria and Babylonia, across the Fertile Crescent, over into Asia Minor.

Though seen now as only part of a much larger picture, the Amarna letters still remain documents of the highest importance and still form, as one cuneiformist once put it so enthusiastically, "une des collections les plus précieuses du monde." This importance derives mainly from the rich evidence they provide for the social and political history of Syria and Palestine in the fourteenth century B.C. They may, therefore, be read as a kind of preface to biblical history, and it is for this reason, above all, that they have been, and continue to be, the subject of the most diligent inquiry and reflection. Indeed, one can safely predict that as long as the Bible retains in our culture its unique importance, the Amarna letters will command the serious attention of historian and exegete.

Over the years, too, there has been great progress in our understanding of these letters. Collations of the originals by various scholars have yielded a more accurate reading of the text. Grammatical and lexical studies have vastly extended our grasp of the language of the letters. Unfortunately, however, since J. A. Knudtzon's magisterial edition, in 1907–15, of the letters known at that time, the results of all this progress have remained scattered in dictionaries, monographs, dissertations, anthologies, articles, and footnotes. Except to the narrow specialist, they have been practically inaccessible.

A long-standing desideratum, therefore, and one with ever-increasing urgency, has been a translation of the entire corpus that reflects the advances of the last seventy-five years. It was to meet this demand that the present work was undertaken.

A translation: that is my main objective, and, I might almost say, my only objective. The Introduction aims principally at tracing in broad outline the form and the content of the translations that follow. Of the notes accompanying the translations, the primary, if not exclusive, purpose is to indicate the reading of the cuneiform text on which the translation is based and to offer the arguments—grammatical, lexical, and contextual—that support the translation. I regret that considerations of space often made it impossible to give in these notes due recognition to counterarguments and divergent views.

The translation is, in general, what is called literal, with the lack of felicity the term usually implies. It might be added, however, that here *traduttore traditore* seldom, if ever, applies. For the most part, the prose of the Amarna letters is, at best, pedestrian. Where the translation is not literal is in its grammatical correctness, a virtue that conceals the solecisms and barbarisms of the language of so much of the original text. I have also taken a certain liberty in the translation of some particles, often replacing a more literal, paratactic version with a subordinate clause. Those who have confronted the translation of *hinne* in the Hebrew Bible will recognize the option and perhaps sympathize with the inconsistency.

With the support of the American Council of Learned Societies and of Harvard University, which I gratefully acknowledge, I was able in 1973–74 to collate almost all of the letters. Besides those that had disappeared many years before, there were thirteen that eluded me; at the time, they were either destroyed, lost, misplaced, or on loan. My time being limited, the collations were at times not sign by sign, but recognized difficulty by recognized difficulty. This limitation was compensated for to some extent through the generosity of Albert E. Glock, at the time the Director of the Albright Institute in Jerusalem, who very kindly made available to me the results of the collations by the late Edmund I. Gordon of most of the letters housed in London and Cairo. As will become evident to the reader, Gordon's contribution is not a small one.

For granting me access to the Amarna letters, and for all their kind assistance and courtesy, I heartily thank the authorities of the Arkeoloji Müzeleri (Istanbul), the Ashmolean Museum (Oxford), the British Museum (London), the Egyptian Museum (Cairo), the Louvre (Paris), the Metropolitan Museum of Art (New York), the Musées royaux d'Art and d'Histoire (Brussels), the Oriental Museum (Chicago), and the Vorderasiatisches Museum (Berlin). I am most grateful, too, to my colleagues Volkert Haas and Gernot Wilhelm for their contributing, respectively, the translations of the letters written in the Hittite and Hurrian languages.

The present work is a revision of an earlier one that appeared in French, *Les Lettres d'El Amarna* (Paris, 1987). It tries to bring the latter up to date; it also not infrequently corrects and expands. Since the earlier publication three scholars—Shlomo Izre'el, Nadav Na'aman, and Anson Rainey—have put me particularly in their debt, both by their published work and by their unpublished manuscripts they very generously placed at my disposal. As a result, the translation that follows often represents a considerable improvement of my earlier effort. I thank them.

Finally, I am grateful to the Johns Hopkins University Press for making my work available in English and to the editorial staff for their painstaking labors on my behalf. I must mention by name Carolyn I. Moser, my copyeditor. I do not try to describe her contribution, which was enormous, but I do thank her, and most warmly.

Introduction

1. Discoveries and publications

The Amarna tablets take their name from el-ʿAmārna, a plain on the east bank of the Nile about 190 miles south of Cairo. This was the site of Akhetaten, the capital of ancient Egypt for a brief period in the fourteenth century B.C. Akhetaten was founded by Amenophis IV, also known as Akhenaten, one of the most famous of Egyptian kings, most renowned as a religious reformer, often called the "heretic king" and "first monotheist." It was here, among the ancient ruins, that, probably in 1887, natives came upon clay tablets with some writing on them and began clandestine diggings.[1] There are conflicting accounts of the discovery, and we will never know how many tablets may have been found and later lost or destroyed,[2] nor all the ways, perhaps many and devious, by which more than 300 tablets came into the possession of antiquities dealers and private collectors. Eventually, by purchase, gift, or confiscation, most of the tablets made their way to museums: the Vorderasiatisches Museum in Berlin (at first about 160, eventually 202 or 203, besides 3 fragments belonging with British Museum tablets and other unnumbered fragments); the Cairo museum (at first 31, eventually 49 or 50, plus a fragment belonging with a British Museum tablet); the British Museum (at first 81, plus a fragment belonging with a Berlin tablet, eventually 95); the Louvre (1, eventually 7).[3] Remaining in private hands, at least for a while, were the four tablets of the

1. On the various versions of the discovery and dispersal of the tablets, see J. A. Knudtzon, *VAB* 2/1, pp. 1ff.; 2/2, p. 1584. For the corrections of A. H. Sayce mentioned by Knudtzon, see the former's account in *AJSL* 33 (1916–17) pp. 89f. Sayce says that the tablets were found in 1886–87. For the history of the publications, see Anson F. Rainey, AOAT 8², pp. 5ff.

2. Sayce, *AJSL* 33 (1916–17) p. 90, estimated the loss at 150–200 tablets, but the evidence for this high number, which is not supported by other arguments, comes from reports of questionable accuracy.

3. Most of the Berlin and Cairo collections, the Louvre tablet, and the Golenischeff tablets (see below) were published in the cuneiform copies of Ludwig Abel by Hugo Winckler in 1889–90 (WA). The cuneiform copies of the British Museum tablets appeared in 1892 (BB). On the uncertainty as to the eventual numbers in the Berlin and Cairo museums, see n. 12.

merchant Rostovitz Bey,[4] the three of the Russian Egyptologist Vladimir Golenischeff,[5] the one of the American missionary Chauncey Murch,[6] and the one of the French Assyriologist Jules Oppert.[7] In 1896, in their first comprehensive edition, all the known tablets, together with a letter that had been found at Tell el-Ḥesi in Palestine, were transliterated and translated by Hugo Winckler.[8]

When the location of the ruins where the tablets had been discovered was determined, Egyptian authorities explored the site but failed to find more tablets. More fortunate was Sir Flinders Petrie, who found 22 fragments in 1891–92; these went to the Ashmolean Museum in Oxford.[9] In 1903, M. Chassinat, director of l'Institut français d'archéologie orientale du Caire, acquired two more tablets.[10] By 1907, 358 inscribed tablets were known, and in that year—a landmark in the history of Amarna studies—the Norwegian Assyriologist J. A. Knudtzon published the first volume of his magisterial *Die El-Amarna-Tafeln.*[11] Based on painstaking collations of all except the Murch and Chassinat tablets and on an unrivaled knowledge of almost every aspect of the corpus, his readings and translations excelled by far those of all his predecessors, and even today his work remains of fundamental importance.

4. In the British Museum since May 1903 (information from museum authorities); see below, *EA* 28, 82, 230, 292, on the cuneiform copies.

5. Perhaps given to the museum in Moscow in 1911 (Kühne, p. 2, n. 8); see below, *EA* 70, 137, 160.

6. Now in the Oriental Institute in Chicago, after earlier stops in the Art Institute of Chicago in 1894, then on to the Haskell Oriental Museum at the University of Chicago in 1915 (Luckenbill and Allen, *AJSL* 33 [1916–17] pp. 1f.); see below, *EA* 26, of which it is a fragment.

7. A cuneiform copy of this tablet, which seems to have been lost and will probably never be found, was never published; see below, *EA* 260.

8. *Die Thontafeln von Tell-el-Amarna,* in E. Schrader et al., eds., Keilinschriftliche Bibliothek, 5 (Berlin, 1896); English trans. by J. Metcalf, *The Tell-el-Amarna Letters* (New York, 1896). The Tell el-Ḥesi tablet is in the Istanbul Arkeoloji Müzeleri; on the cuneiform copy, see below, *EA* 333.

9. Of these, only seven are relevant here; see below, *EA* 14, 43, 61, 135, 184, 190, 236. Cuneiform copies by Sayce in *Tell el Amarna;* see *VAB* 2/1, pp. 15, 996. One of the fragments was uninscribed; another is part of *EA* 14. Four (*EA* 135, 342, 344, 351) have been lost or destroyed.

10. Now in the Metropolitan Museum of Art in New York (L. Bull, *Bulletin of the Metropolitan Museum of Art* 21 [1926] pp. 169–76); on the cuneiform copies, see below, *EA* 15, 153.

11. *VAB* 2/1. The second volume of commentary by O. Weber and glossaries by E. Ebeling, with additional remarks by Knudtzon, appeared in 1915. *VAB* 2/1–2 (reprint, Aalen, 1964). Knudtzon's numbering of the tablets became standard.

Since 1907 an additional 24 tablets have come to light, one as recently as 1979. Four more have turned up in the Berlin collection, to which two were added by the excavations of the Deutsche Orient-Gesellschaft in 1911–14.[12] The Egyptian Exploration Society discovered one tablet in its excavations of 1921–24,[13] and eight more in the excavations of 1926–37.[14] The most recent to appear perhaps goes back to the explorations under Petrie in 1891–92,[15] and the rest, which eventually were made available to museums,[16] to the first clandestine diggings of the fellahin. With the exception of *EA* 380–82, the "post-Knudtzon" tablets were ably edited by Anson F. Rainey in 1970.[17]

2. *The Archive*

Of the 382 tablets, only 32 are not letters or inventories attached to letters. The content of this small group is quite diverse.[18] Some belong in the Mesopotamian scribal tradition: myths and epics (*EA* 340?, 356–59, 375?), syllabaries (*EA* 348, 350, 379), lexical texts (*EA*

12. Two were published by O. Schroeder, *VS* 11, 179 (now *EA* 360) and *OLZ*, 1917, col. 105f. (now *EA* 361). (In 1914–15 Schroeder published new cuneiform copies of the Berlin collection in *VS* 11–12.) The tablets discovered in 1911–14 are *VS* 12, 193 (now *EA* 359) and *VS* 12, 190 (now *EA* 379; on this number, see P. Artzi, *Or* n.s. 36 [1967] p. 432). *EA* 359 now belongs to the Cairo collection; the location of *EA* 379 I do not know. Finally, H. Klengel, *OLZ*, 1974, col. 262, called attention to VAT 3781 (already noted by Schroeder, *OLZ*, 1917, col. 105f.) and added the "Sammelnummer" VAT 8525 (almost entirely illegible fragments). To these two numbers J.-G. Heintz, *Index Documentaire d'el-Amarna*, I.D.E.A., 1 (Wiesbaden, 1982), p. xvii, n. 25, has given the code numbers *EA* 380 and 381. Hence the number 382 for the most recent discovery (see n. 15).

The numbering *EA* 359ff., based on Knudtzon's *EA* 1–358, was introduced by C. Gordon, *Or* n.s. 16 (1947) pp. 1f.

13. S. Smith and C. Gadd, *JEA* 11 (1925) pp. 230ff.; now in the Ashmolean Museum, *EA* 368 (see E. Edel, *GM* 15 [1975] pp. 11ff.).

14. C. Gordon, *Or* n.s. 16 (1947) pp. 1ff.; now in the British Museum, *EA* 370–77. See below, *EA* 370–72.

15. C. B. F. Walker, *JCS* 31 (1979) p. 249; now in the British Museum. See below, *EA* 382.

16. The Louvre (see below, *EA* 362–67); Musée Cinquantenaire, Brussels (see below, *EA* 369); and the British Museum (see below, *EA* 378).

17. AOAT 8; 2d rev. ed., 1978. An earlier edition by S. A. B. Mercer of the tablets then known (*EA* 1–367, 369), *The Tell El-Amarna Tablets*, 2 vols. (Toronto, 1939), was not successful and is mentioned here as a matter of historical record. For a survey of the Amarna archive, certain characteristic features, and outstanding problems, see D. O. Edzard, in *Biblical Archaeology Today*, Proceedings of the International Congress on Biblical Archaeology, Jerusalem 1984 (Jerusalem, 1985), pp. 69–83.

18. See *HKL* 1, pp. 162, 239f., 478, 493; 2, pp. 88, 132, 258, 264; P. Artzi, in K. R. Veenhof, ed., *Cuneiform Archives and Libraries* (Istanbul, 1986), pp. 210–12.

351–54, 373), a god-list (*EA* 374). On one is a tale of Hurrian origin (*EA* 341); on another (*EA* 368), an unparalleled list of Egyptian words written in syllabic cuneiform with equivalences in Babylonian written either syllabically or logographically.[19] One tablet is perhaps an amulet (*EA* 355). The genres of the other 14 (*EA* 342–47, 349, 360–61, 372, 376–77, 380–81), which are often very fragmentary, remain to be determined.

Of the 350 letters and inventories (*EA* 13–14, 22, 25, 120), our only concern in this volume, it seems that all except one were found in the same place.[20] This was identified by inscriptions as "The Place of the Letters of the Pharaoh." The name, however, may refer to a larger complex, the more extensive part of which was devoted to affairs of state conducted in the Egyptian language, the smaller (the actual find-spot), to those conducted in foreign languages.[21]

In *Die El-Amarna-Tafeln* Knudtzon divided the correspondence into two parts. The first concerns foreign powers that dealt with Egypt more or less on a basis of equality. On a map, the arrangement moves counterclockwise: Babylonia (*EA* 1–14), Assyria (*EA* 15–16), Mittani (*EA* 17, 19–30),[22] Arzawa (*EA* 31–32), Alašia (*EA* 33–40), and Hatti (*EA* 41–44). The other and by far the larger part concerns Syro-Palestine and its various local rulers, most of whom were Egyptian vassals. The arrangement of these letters begins in the north, in central Syria, and moves down, ending in southern Palestine. Knudtzon's assignments, often only on grounds of clay texture and paleography, were remarkably successful, and only occasionally have been proved wrong.[23] Furthermore, throughout, in each dossier (for example, that of Baby-

19. Perhaps an import (Kühne, p. 139). Despite the Babylonian ductus of *EA* 356–58 (Kühne, pp. 138f.), these tablets were hardly written in Babylonia (so Knudtzon, *VAB* 2/1, p. 25), for a Babylonian scribe is not likely to have introduced peripheral features (many plene-writings, syllabary, lexicon); note also the absence of poetic line divisions. This is not to deny that they may also be imports. P. Artzi, in H.-J. Nissen and J. Renger, eds., *Mesopotamien und seine Nachbarn: Politische und kulturelle Wechselbeziehungen im Alten Vorderasien vom 4. bis. 1. Jahrtausend v. Chr.*, Berliner Beiträge zum Vorderen Orient, I (Berlin, 1982), p. 317, maintains that they were written in Egypt.

20. *EA* 371 was discovered in "clerk house no. 43," the find-spot also of *EA* 368. According to Petrie, most of the tablets he found (part of *EA* 14, *EA* 43, 61, 135, 184, 190, 236, 342, 353, 355) were in "two early rubbish-pits" under the building where the other tablets were found and therefore antedating them. For strong reasons to doubt this earlier level, see Kühne, p. 70, n. 345.

21. See Kühne, pp. 2f., n. 12.

22. On *EA* 18, see the note to the letter.

23. See *EA* 63–65, 260, 295, 317–18.

lonia or Jerusalem), Knudtzon also attempted to order the letters chronologically. Here the task was more difficult and the results less firm.

Most of the archive consists of letters received, but a small number were written in Egypt.[24] Two letters (*EA* 1, 5), plus one inventory (*EA* 14), were directed to Babylonia, one to Arzawa (*EA* 31), and the rest to vassals (*EA* 99, 162–63, 190, 367, 369–70). Their presence in the archive probably has more than one explanation. If one may assume that, in general, copies were made only of those letters that bore on matters of considerable importance and required more than some sort of simple record or notation, one would judge that, with the exception of *EA* 162, the letters to vassals are not copies and, probably because of oversight, were not sent.[25] Indeed, letters to vassals seem to have been somewhat infrequent, and even less often such as to demand copies. Hence we should not expect to find many in the archive.[26]

Correspondence with major powers, however, was quite another matter. This was, at times at least, rather regular and often, if not always, dealt with serious issues—for example, marriage negotiations. If Egyptian practice was to make copies of such letters, we must ask why there are so few in the archives.[27] Perhaps the explanation is that usually the letters were first written in Egyptian, and then a translation was prepared.[28] It was the latter that was sent off, though perhaps occasionally the Egyptian messenger may have also carried a copy of the original.[29] The original, if important enough to be saved, would be filed, but in the Egyptian, not the foreign, language section. If so, and

24. On *EA* 12, see the letter, n. 1.

25. See F. Pintore, *OA* 11 (1972) p. 126, n. 145.

26. See M. Liverani, *OA* 10 (1971) pp. 253ff., translated in *Three Amarna Essays*, Monographs on the Ancient Near East, 1/5 (Malibu, 1979), pp. 3ff.

27. On roughly contemporary practice at Nippur, see F. Kraus, *JCS* 1 (1947) p. 112, and R. Biggs, *JCS* 19 (1965) p. 96 and n. 13. At Boghazköy, see *KUB* 3, 24+; KBo 1, 10 and 14. At Ugarit, see *PRU* 3, pp. 4f.; *PRU* 4, p. 294 (probably not a copy); *Ugar.* 5, nos. 21, 24, 28, 32, 34, 36. At Mari, in the Old Babylonian period, copies of letters are common, especially in "the ministry of foreign affairs"; see A. Finet, *Cuneiform Archives and Libraries* (see n. 18), pp. 155, 157.

28. Cf. the "originals" in Hurrian from Mittani (*EA* 24), in Hittite at Boghazköy (H. Otten, *AfO* 19 [1959–60] p. 39; *AfO*, Beiheft 12, pp. 64f.), and perhaps in Ugaritic at Ugarit (*PRU* 5, no. 8). The Egyptians were certainly familiar with the practice, and they seem to have called the translations "copies"; thus, *EA* 27 is a "copy" of a Hurrian original (Kühne, pp. 44f., n. 209).

29. Cf. *EA* 24. A messenger needing an interpreter might prefer to have the Egyptian version available.

assuming that they too were not victims of oversight and simply not sent, then we must consider *EA* 1, 5, 14, and 31 exceptional, being drafts or copies of the translations and filed accordingly in the foreign language section.

3. Language and Writing

The Amarna letters are manifestations of the "cuneiform culture" that was shared in the fourteenth century B.C. throughout the ancient Near East. As it appears in these letters it is largely a provincial and, in many respects, a very heterogeneous culture, the product of a long, complex history, of which we know but a very small part.

In some sense this history begins at least a thousand years before the Amarna period. By the middle of the third millennium B.C. not only had cuneiform writing been introduced into Syria, but already at that early date, as the celebrated discoveries at ancient Ebla have shown, it was being used in a breadth of application and with a sophistication rivaling those of the great centers in Sumer and Akkad.[30] By the first quarter of the second millennium B.C. knowledge of cuneiform writing had spread far and wide, and Babylonian had become the principal language of a cosmopolitan culture.[31] It was the language of international relations, but often, too, of local affairs, both legal and administrative. It was also a language of learning.

In Upper Mesopotamia and the west there developed a regional dialect, a kind of *koinē*, which was also introduced into Anatolia, thus laying the foundations of the Hittite cuneiform tradition.[32] A regional syllabary appeared and took root in Syria. Also discernible are the influences of other traditions and other languages.[33] These were mainly

30. For a general introduction, see P. Matthiae, *Un impero ritrovato* (Turin, 1977), in English as *Ebla: An Empire Rediscovered,* trans. Christopher Holme (Garden City, N.J., 1981); G. Pettinato, *Ebla: Un impero inciso nell' argilla* (Milan, 1979), translated as *The Archives of Ebla: An Empire Inscribed in Clay* (Garden City, N.J., 1981). On the local language and its place within the Semitic family, see L. Cagni, ed., *La lingua di Ebla* (Naples, 1981).

31. See the survey of R. Labat, *Syria* 39 (1962) pp. 1ff.

32. See K. Balkan, *Letter of King Anum-ḫirbi of Mama to King Warshama of Kanish* (Ankara, 1957), p. 27; E. von Schuler, in M. Liverani, ed., *La Siria nel Tardo Bronzo* (Rome, 1969), pp. 113f.

33. As the Mari archives continue to be published, we find sporadic examples of deviations from the standard language that in the Amarna period are common or even the rule: gender of nouns (*ālum,* "city," feminine, *AÉM* 1/2, no. 316:14′; no. 358, note g); confusion of pronouns (*mimma* and *mamma, AÉM* 1/2, no. 535, note d; *mannum* and *mīnum,*

West Semitic and Hurrian, the very forces that would be mainly responsible for the language and writing that we find in the Amarna letters centuries later.[34]

With the exception of *EA* 15 (Assyrian), *EA* 24 (Hurrian), and *EA* 31–32 (Hittite),[35] the language of the Amarna letters is Babylonian, but for the most part it is a Babylonian profoundly different from that of the previous international age. It reflects many of the developments that one finds in the "good" Middle Babylonian language of the letters from Babylonia itself (*EA* 2–4, 6–11).[36] But if the cuneiform culture of the provinces was to some extent up-to-date, it was not infrequently, as is usually the way with provinces, also behind the times. This is true of the writing: a logogram that had been replaced by another logogram centuries before in the scribal schools of Babylonia survives in the provincial culture;[37] an exercise once part of the scribal training but long abandoned in Babylonia is still part of the provincial curriculum;[38] old orthographies are retained, sometimes mixed together with the modern ones;[39] and so on. In the language, too, one finds a similar quaint and archaic quality. The provincial scribes, perhaps at times because of analogues in their own native language, may use old common or dialectal forms that had otherwise disappeared centuries be-

no. 402, note c); morpheme analysis (*kīma i-ia-ti-ia*, "like me," *AÉM* 1/2, no. 314, note e); thematic vowels (*ḫalāqu*, /a/, *AÉM* 1/2, no. 391, note p); lexicon (*inūma*, "that," introducing object clauses, *AÉM* 1/2, no. 523, note k; *arānu*, "to be a sinner/criminal," *AÉM* 1/1, no. 39, note c; 1/2, no. 312, note d; (*w*)aradu, "to serve," *AÉM* 1/1, no. 148, note b; 1/2, no. 377, note b; see *JAOS* 107 [1987] p. 135a). One can speak of "les lettres 'barbares' " (*AÉM* 1/2, pp. 51f.).

34. The main evidence of the Hurrian influence is the syllabary, for which see Labat, *Syria* 39 (1962) pp. 14f. In the letters of Aplaḫanda of Carchemish (*ARMT* 5, 5–11) confusion of gender, often a sign of Hurrian influence, is fairly frequent, especially in *ARMT* 5, 7.

35. On the Hurrian letter, see n. 28. The Arzawa scribe, probably because of incompetence in any form of Babylonian, expressly requests that the correspondence be carried on in Hittite (*EA* 32:24f.). Whether Aššur-uballiṭ's use of Assyrian (*EA* 15) and Hurro-Akkadian (*EA* 16) reflects a conscious avoidance of normative Babylonian is not clear. (On the term "Hurro-Akkadian," see the text below and n. 44.)

36. The modernization of western Old Babylonian, which is not to be understood as a direct development, in an unbroken tradition, is more evident in the north, in the Hurro-Akkadian tradition, just as archaisms of language are more common in the south (see below).

37. See B. Landsberger and H. Güterbock, *AfO* 12 (1937–39) pp. 55ff.; A. Falkenstein, *ZA* 53 (1965) p. 75, discussion of line 107; Güterbock, *Festschrift Heinrich Otten* (Wiesbaden, 1975), pp. 71ff.; W. Moran, *Acta Sumerologica* 5 (1983) pp. 175f.

38. See Nougayrol, *AS* 16, pp. 29ff., on *EA* 350 and parallels at Ugarit.

39. E.g., in *EA* 38 the old writing *a-wa-ta* along with later *a-ma-ta*.

fore.[40] Their lexicon is full of words that by the fourteenth century B.C. had either disappeared completely from the Babylonian language or lived on only in the elevated language reserved for the solemnities of myth, epic, hymns, and prayers.[41] It is this combination of the old and the new that is so typically provincial and so distinctive of the Amarna cuneiform culture.

Equally distinctive, however, are many features that are specifically peripheral and are not found in normal written Babylonian, either in its contemporary or earlier forms.[42] Some few are shared across the entire area;[43] more commonly, one must distinguish two general traditions, northern and southern, within both of which further distinctions are necessary. They divide along a line, roughly, from Ṣumur on the coast to Qaṭna inland.

The northern tradition, which is the more widely diffused, is generally called Hurro-Akkadian.[44] The name indicates the dominant influence of the Hurrians in the formation and the diffusion of both the language and the graphic system in which it was written. It is Hurro-Akkadian that we find in one letter from Assyria (*EA* 16);[45] in the letters from Mittani (*EA* 17, 19–23, 25–30), Hatti (*EA* 41–44), Ugarit (*EA* 45–49), Nuḫašše (*EA* 51), and Qaṭna (*EA* 52–55); and in many of the letters from Amurru (*EA* 156–61, 164–71). Nevertheless, the lan-

40. E.g., dual forms of the pronoun (*BASOR* 211 [1973] pp. 50ff.) and *ti-* preformative in third masculine plural forms of the verb, which is first attested in a language perhaps related to earlier Eblaic (H. Limet, *Syria* 52 [1975] pp. 37ff., esp. p. 48; J.-M. Durand, *MARI* 1 [1982] pp. 81f., lines 21–24; I. Gelb, *Syro-Mesopotamian Studies* 1/1 [1977] pp. 9f.; D. O. Edzard, *Miscellanea Babylonica,* Mélanges M. Birot [Paris, 1985], pp. 85f.). In the latter instance, however, because the preformative is found in later West Semitic languages (Ugaritic), its origins need not go back to the early second millennium B.C. For the Amarna evidence, see S. Izre'el, *UF* 19 (1987) pp. 79ff.

41. E.g., *awīlu,* "man," as a designation of the ruler of a city; *qaqqadu,* "head," in the sense of "self, person"; various adverbs (*anumma, appūna(ma), ašrānu, pānānu*); and the prepositional phrase *ana ṣēr,* "towards." Note also dialectal *gištappu,* "footstool," at Mari, Chagar Bazar, Kumidu (*EA* 195), and Qaṭna.

42. See the survey by Kühne, pp. 5ff.

43. The north seems to influence the south.

44. The Nuzi dialect of the eastern highlands is also Hurro-Akkadian; see G. Wilhelm, *Untersuchungen zum Ḫurro-Akkadischen von Nuzi,* AOAT 9. As a designation of the language as used in the west, Huehnergard, *Akkadian,* p. 20 and n. 34, prefers "Syro-Anatolian," the influence of Hurrian being at times inconsiderable (see below).

45. This suggests that Hurro-Akkadian was socially acceptable even in milieus where one might expect a certain contempt for its provincial character.

guage also differs considerably from site to site,[46] especially so far as the immediate influence of the Hurrian language is concerned.[47] A measure of the complexity of dialectal developments and relationships is, for example, the fact that at the same site the language of the letters may differ considerably from that of the legal documents.[48]

Also belonging to the northern tradition are the letters that are southernmost in origin, the letters from Egypt. The language and writing of these letters are quite unlike what we find just to the northeast along the Egyptian border, in Palestine, and on the Phoenician coast. Their closest ties are farther north, especially in the writing system and, above all, in the sign forms. Many of the latter are typically Hittite, and the relationship can only be one of direct dependence on or derivation from a common source.[49] The language itself, however, lacks many of the more common Hurro-Akkadian features, and so the borrowing must have occurred at a relatively early date.

In the southern tradition the transformation of the Babylonian language and the resulting deviation from normal usage were far more radical than in most forms of Hurro-Akkadian. Indeed, so radical is the transformation that one may ask whether the language of this tradition, even when qualified as "extremely barbarized," should be called Babylonian at all. It is a pidgin in which the Babylonian component is mainly lexical, whereas the grammar is profoundly West-Semitized, most no-

46. In the Amarna corpus, Hurrian influence is most evident in the letters from Mittani and Qaṭna; on the former, see Kühne, p. 9, n. 40, and H.-P. Adler, AOAT 201, pp. 105ff.

47. At Boghazköy A. Kammenhuber, *Or* n.s. 45 (1976) p. 137, sees two traditions, Hurrian and Hittite, plus the influence of direct imports from Babylonia, as formative of Boghazköy-Akkadian. At ancient Emar, D. Arnaud, *AAS* 25 (1979) pp. 87ff., finds both a Syrian and a Syro-Hittite tradition.

48. This is the case at Ugarit; see Huehnergard, *Akkadian,* pp. 220ff., with reference to T. Finley, "*Word Order in the Clause Structure of Syrian Akkadian*" (Ph.D. diss., University of California at Los Angeles, 1979). There is also in the legal texts evidence of an Old Babylonian, North Syrian background; see J. Greenfield, in M. Ellis, ed., *Essays on the Ancient Near East in Memory of Jacob Joel Finkelstein* (Hamden, Conn., 1977), pp. 87ff.

49. This was shown by K. Riemschneider in a paper delivered before the 186th annual meeting of the American Oriental Society, March 16, 1976; see also G. Beckman, *JCS* 35 (1983) pp. 112f., and G. Wilhelm, *Studien zur Altägyptischen Kultur* 11 (1984) pp. 643ff. Note, however, that in the Amarna archive the Egyptian material includes two letters in non-Hittite ductus, *EA* 1 and 369, the former of which manifests a strong preference for verb-subject-object word order, as is the rule in Egyptian and was noted long ago by Böhl, *Sprache,* p. 78. On *EA* 369, see below *EA* 369, n. 1.

tably in the word order and, most important of all, in the verbal system.[50] The language can only be described as an entirely new code, only vaguely intelligible (if at all) to the West Semite because of the lexicon, and to the Babylonian because of the grammar.

It is regrettable that translations either cannot or do not reflect the diversity of language and writing within the corpus itself and the distance of the several dialects from the normative language of Babylonia. They should be read with an awareness of this limitation, correcting so far as possible the impression of a colorless uniformity and grammatical propriety.

4. *The International Correspondence*

The form of the letters is pretty much the same everywhere, though the letters from Alašia (*EA* 33–40) have certain peculiarities.[51] In the usual form, the address, which is directed to the scribe who will read the letter, is usually of the type "Say to PN. Thus PN_2."[52] This form was inherited from the Old Babylonian period, and neither then nor as used here did it carry any implications of the relative social status of the correspondents. Another form, however, "Thus PN: Say to PN_2," appears in two letters from Egypt (*EA* 5 and 31) and in one from Boghazköy (*EA* 41). This is a different usage according to which the sender, if he is the superior or the equal of the addressee, names himself first, and therefore, in this system, the first and more common form

50. This is a subject with a long history of inquiry; see the outline by Kühne, pp. 8f., n. 36, II p-III, and add the work of A. Rainey and his students, most notably S. Izre'el. Rainey has shown that regularly the (preformative) verb base, with no additional marker (*u*-durative, *a*-injunctive), no matter what "tense" (*iparras, iptaras, iprus*), if a statement of fact, has past-time reference (*IOS* 1 [1971] pp. 86ff.; *UF* 7 [1975] pp. 395ff.). The same usage is found in a letter from Tyre a century later; see D. Arnaud, *Syria* 59 (1982) p. 104. Within the southern corpus there are two somewhat erratic blocks, the letters from Jerusalem and those from Abi-Milku of Tyre. On the former, see *Jerusalem Scribe;* on the latter, a dissertation by Cecilia Grave, to be presented to the University of Lund, is in progress (see *OA* 19 [1980] pp. 205ff.; *UF* 12 [1980] pp. 221ff.; *Or* n.s. 51 [1982] pp. 161ff.).

51. For the various forms of address and greeting in Akkadian letters, see the survey of E. Salonen, *StOr* 38, esp. pp. 61ff. on the Amarna letters.

52. In the international correspondence, we retain the conventional translation of *umma* by "thus," except in *EA* 19:3 and 29:2, where it seems that *umma* was understood in the sense of "word, message" (Rainey, *BiOr* 37 [1980] p. 96). The latter meaning seems to have been the rule in the Syro-Palestinian area (see *EA* 144, n. 1), as first noted by W. F. Albright (*BASOR* 87 [1942] p. 33, n. 7), and it was not unknown to Hittite scribes (A. Goetze, *JCS* 2 [1948] p. 224; see also P. Berger, *UF* 1 [1969] p. 218; Izre'el, *IOS* 8 [1978] p. 68; Huehnergard, *Akkadian,* p. 144, n. 112; M. Kossmann, *JEOL* 30 ([1987–88] pp. 38ff.).

noted above ("Say to PN . . .") is employed only by an inferior writing to a superior.[53]

A salutation—which as such was an innovation of the Old Babylonian period—follows, and it consists of two parts. The first is a report on one's own well-being: "For me all goes well." Since it is omitted in the Assyrian letters (*EA* 15–16), it seems to have been optional. The second part, never omitted and therefore probably not optional, is an expression of good wishes for the addressee, usually beginning with "May all go well with you," which is then elaborated and extended to the household, to wives and children, courtiers and troops, even horses and chariots.[54]

The body of the letter is, naturally, much less stereotyped, and formal conventions are few and variable. Two types of letters, especially in combined form, dominate the international correspondence. These are what Jean Nougayrol called *lettre d'envoi* and *lettre d'injonction.*[55] Under the first we should place *EA* 2–3, 5, 21, 31, and 41; they characteristically end with "I (herewith) send. . . ."[56] *Lettres d'injonction* are *EA* 4, 7, 28, and 38–39, and they usually end with one or more injunctives.[57] As I already mentioned, however, most common of all are combinations, which we find in *EA* 6, 8–9, 15–17, 19–20, 23, 26–27, 29, 33–35, 40, and 44.

Occasionally, there is either a double letter (*EA* 12)—i.e., the same person is addressed but by a third party—or a postscript (*EA* 32)—i.e., the writer sends a message to a third party, who in the case in question was the addressee's scribe and whose services, therefore, were needed in

53. See Nougayrol, *Ugar.* 5, pp. 66f. Though "say" (*qibī-ma*) is absent in *EA* 34, this letter probably reflects the same usage. This seems more likely than a survival of the form of the Old Akkadian-Ur III periods (cf. E. Sollberger, *TCS* 1, pp. 2f.).

54. W. von Soden, *AfO* 18 (1958) p. 369, saw in this type of salutation a feature of an official as opposed to a private letter. Characteristic of the Egyptian letters is the addition of a parallel report on one's own household, etc. It seems that, in general, inferiors did not report on the state of their own person (cf. *EA* 12), though this is hardly the explanation of *EA* 15–16. Nougayrol, *Ugar.* 5, p. 67, has noted that the Hittite king and other high-ranking courtiers report only on themselves and do not wish well to their inferiors. (In *Ugar.* 5, no. 33:3′, read *gabbu da*[*n-n*]*iš šulmu.*) Cf. the conclusions of Egyptian letters from the king to vassals (see below, sect. 5). Note that in Hittite usage (cf. *EA* 31:4) ANŠE.KUR.RA.MEŠ may contrast with ÉRIN.MEŠ and mean, not "horses," but "chariot-fighters" (see A. Kammenhuber, *Die Arier im Vorderen Orient* [Heidelberg, 1968], p. 22, n. 30a).

55. *Ugar.* 5, pp. 67f.

56. *EA* 2, rev. 9(?); 3:34; 5:18; 21:38; 31:28; 41:43.

57. *EA* 4:40ff.; 7:80ff.; 28:29ff.; 39:10ff.

communicating and perhaps explaining the message of the letter to his master.[58]

The prevalence of the combination of *envoi* and *injonction* reflects the complex social, economic, and political relationships of the correspondents, and the customs and ideology associated with them. According to the conceptions of the time, the most basic political relationship between the rulers was an alliance of "brotherhood," which made them brothers and members of the same family and household. They were thus united by the bond of love and friendship that befits brothers,[59] and the visible expression of this bond was the exchange of gifts.[60] "From the time my ancestors and your ancestors made a mutual declaration of friendship, they sent beautiful greeting-gifts to each other, and refused no request for anything beautiful" (*EA* 9:7–10). "Send me much gold, and you, for your part, whatever you want from my country, write me so that it may be taken to you" (*EA* 9:16–18). "If your purpose is graciously one of friendship, send me much gold. And this is your house. Write me so what you need may be fetched" (*EA* 16:32–34).[61] Acknowledgment of gifts received, praise of the gifts or

58. In *EA* 42:27f. perhaps the scribe sends a brief message either to the addressee of the letter or to a third party. In the vassal correspondence, too, there are postscripts, all to the Egyptian scribe who will read the letters (*EA* 286–89, 316). In *EA* 170:36ff. both the addressor and the addressees are different from those in the first part of the letter. *EA* 128 is probably a double letter. On these additions to letters, see A. Leo Oppenheim, *AS*, 16, pp. 253ff., and Nougayrol, *Ugar.* 5, p. 67, with references to earlier literature. Other double letters: RS 34.134, *Ugar.* 7, pls. XV–XVI; (the following references from J. Huehnergard) *PRU* 6, no. 7; RS 34.161, *Ugar.* 7, pl. XL; RS 34.171, *Ugar.* 7, pl. LII. *Emar* 6/3 263–64 are double letters; 266 is extraordinary, being four complete letters from the same correspondent. *Emar* 6/3 261 is also unusual; it is sent by two correspondents who, after the greeting, send individual messages, the first being introduced by *umma* (line 10), the second by the logogram INIM, "word" (see above, n. 52).

59. By the Amarna period "love" (*râmu*/*ra'āmu* and derivatives) had become part of the terminology of international relations; see V. Korosec, *Mednarodni odnosaji po klinopisnih porocilih iz el-amarnskega in hetitskega drzavnega arhiva* (International relations according to cuneiform reports from the Tell al-Amarna and Hittite State Archive) (Ljubljana, 1950), p. 340 (English summary, p. 393). It is a favorite term of Tušratta (*EA* 17ff., passim), when he speaks of the relationship between equals, but elsewhere in the Amarna letters it is also used of the relationship between sovereign and vassal (*EA* 53:41; 114:68; 121:61; 123:23; 138:71f.; see *Catholic Biblical Quarterly* 25 [1963] pp. 77ff.). On "friendship" (*ṭābūtu*) and related terms, see M. Weinfeld, *JAOS* 93 (1973) pp. 190ff., and below, *EA* 136, n. 5.

60. See C. Zaccagnini, *Lo scambio dei doni nel Vicino Oriente durante i secoli XV–XIII* (Rome, 1973), which was inspired by Liverani, *OA* 11 (1972) pp. 297ff. (translated in *Three Amarna Essays* [see n. 26], pp. 21ff.).

61. This also belongs to the formal language of treaties: "We are all sons of Šup-

even a frank expression of disappointment, expression of the motivation behind the exchange of gifts, petition of countergifts to respond to the gifts now being dispatched—these and related topics dominate much of the international correspondence.

One of the related topics is marriage, for marriage not only binds the correspondents even closer together, but it also involves the exchange of goods.[62] If in the gifts customarily exchanged the economic value was not always great and symbolic values were often as important, in the case of marriage the economic value was considerable, even staggering.[63]

Apart from declarations of friendship, the discussions of gifts associated with this friendship, proposals of marriage, and lists of goods exchanged at the time of marriage, there is little else in the international correspondence. Tušratta of Mittani tells of the difficulties attending his accession to the throne and makes a passing reference to the Hittites, but he says nothing more about the larger political scene.[64] Burna-Buriaš of Babylonia tells how a predecessor refused to support a coalition of Canaanite kings against Egypt, reveals the dangers of international trade, and implies growing Assyrian truculence and aspirations.[65] In the mention of Mayati, the daughter of Amenophis IV, there

---

piluliumaš and our house is one" (E. F. Weidner, *Politische Dokumente aus Kleinasien: Die Staatsverträge in akkadischer Sprache aus dem Archiv von Boghazköi,* Boghazköi-Studien 8 [Leipzig, 1923; reprint, Hildesheim and New York, 1970], p. 86:8f.). The language goes back at least to the Old Babylonian period. Uruk and Babylon are "one house" (A. Falkenstein, *Baghdader Mitteilungen* 2 [1963] p. 56 ii 1f.), as are their kings (ibid., p. 58:25); Larsa and Eshnunna are also "one house" (*TIM* 1, 26:16; see also A. Zeebari, *Altbabylonische Briefe des Iraq-Museums* [n.p., 1964], p. 72). Išḫi-Addu of Qaṭna wrote to Išme-Dagan of Assyria, "This house is your house. What is missing in your house? Does not a brother give a brother (his) request?" (*ARMT* 5, 20:25–28). Hammurabi of Babylon is quoted as declaring, "From long ago and ever after the city Mari and Babylon have been one house and one finger that cannot be separated (*na-ab'-tu-qí-im*)" (*AÉM* 1/2, no. 449:15f.; see also *ARMT* 1, 2:13′). In the private sphere, see *AbB* 1, 82:7; ibid. 4, 152:20 ("my house is your house and my purse your purse"); *ARMT* 10, 78:27; and Kraus, *BiOr* 22 (1965) p. 289 and n. 8. Cf. also "one man" (*EA* 20:17).

62. See Pintore, *Matrimonio,* esp. pp. 105ff. On dynastic marriages, see also W. Röllig, *RLA* 4, pp. 282ff.; P. Michalowski, *JAOS* 95 (1975) pp. 716ff.; A. Schulman, *JNES* 38 (1979) pp. 177ff.; P. Artzi, in J.-M. Durand, ed., *La femme dans le Proche Orient Antique* (Paris, 1987), pp. 23ff.

63. According to *EA* 14 ii 34, over a half a ton of gold was used on the gifts listed in the previous lines, and according to ii 72, about an eighth of a ton of silver. On *EA* 14 as a list of marriage gifts, see Kühne, pp. 70f.

64. *EA* 7:11–20, 30–38.

65. *EA* 7:73–82; 8:13–42; 9:19–35.

is an opaque reflection of events at the Egyptian court.[66] But all this adds up to little information, and there is not a hint of the religious reforms that make the Amarna period so notable in Egyptian history.[67]

5. *The Vassal Correspondence*

The vassal correspondence[68] reflects the Egyptian administration of its territories in Syria and Palestine.[69] At the time of the Amarna letters, the area was divided into two or three provinces, each under an Egyptian official, who is, in the Amarna letters, without specific title.[70] Probably always a member of the military, he resided in a garrison city, one of a network, and from there he looked after Egyptian interests in the city-states and crown-lands within his territory. One was stationed in Gaza, and his province took in most of Palestine, the Phoenician coast, and, if there were only two provinces, Amurru. If there was a

66. *EA* 11 rev. 26–27.

67. On the alleged request of the Alašian king that the Egyptians form no alliances with the Hittites or Babylonians, see *EA* 35, n. 10.

68. The term *vassal* is used loosely of any ruler subordinate to the Egyptian king, whether or not he was bound by oath and a vassal in the strict sense. It thus includes, for example, Addu-nirari of Nuḫašše (*EA* 51), Aziru of Amurru (*EA* 156ff.), and the rulers of Ugarit (*EA* 45, 49; see A. Altman, *Bar-Ilan* 13 (1976) 1ff., English summary on pp. ix–xi).

69. Albright, *CAH* 2/2, pp. 102ff.; A. Alt, *Kleine Schriften,* 3 (Munich, 1959), pp. 107ff.; M. Drower, *CAH* 2/1, pp. 467ff.; P. Frandsen, in Mogens Trolle Larsen, ed., *Power and Propaganda, Mesopotamia,* 7 (Copenhagen, 1979), pp. 167ff.; R. Hachmann, *ZDPV* 98 (1982) pp. 17ff.; W. Helck, *MDOG* 92 (1960) pp. 1ff.; idem, *Beziehungen²*, pp. 246ff.; K. Kitchen, in Liverani, ed., *La Siria nel Tardo Bronzo* (see n. 32), pp. 80ff.; Liverani, *RA* 61 (1967) pp. 1ff.; M. Abdul Kader Mohammad, *Annales du Service des Antiquités de l'Egypte* 56 (1959) pp. 105ff.; N. Na'aman, *Political Disposition,* esp. ch. 7–8; idem, *IEJ* 31 (1981) pp. 172ff.; M. Several, *PEQ* 104 (1972) pp. 123ff.; R. de Vaux, *Histoire ancienne d'Israël, des origines à l'installation en Canaan* (Paris, 1971), pp. 96ff.; J. Weinstein, *BASOR* 241 (1981) pp. 1ff. Against the once common view that the Amarna letters reflect Egypt's neglect of its territories and the absorption of Amenophis IV in internal matters, especially his religious reforms, see especially Liverani and Several; see also the text below on military operations.

70. Na'aman, *Political Disposition,* pp. 166ff. (cf. *IEJ* 31 [1981] pp. 183f.), argues for only two provinces, whereas Helck (see n. 69), whose views have gained some currency, defends three. The crux is the status of Ṣumur. Donald B. Redford, *Akhenaten, the Heretic King* (Princeton, 1984), p. 26, proposes four provinces. The highest official was usually called "commissioner" (*rābiṣu*), but occasionally so were other Egyptian officials of lesser rank; see the survey of D. O. Edzard and F. A. M. Wiggermann, *RLA* 7/5–6, pp. 449ff., esp. §2.5. All of these officials also shared the designation "magnate" (*rabû;* see O. Weber, *VAB* 2/2, p. 1188, and cf. *EA* 1, n. 3). In *EA* 256:9 and 362:69, *rābiṣu* is glossed by *sú-ki-ni* and *sú-ki-na,* respectively, West Semitic **sôkinu* (Hebrew *sôkēn*), in my opinion "one who provides" (cf. below *sakānu* in the letters from Jerusalem), whereas J.-M. Durand, *Miscellanea Babylonica* (see n. 40), p. 82, n. 10, proposes "Résident," from a West Semitic verb "to dwell" (see *AÉM* 1/1, no. 168, note j; *AÉM* 1/2, no. 316:16′ and note b; no. 519, note d).

third province, its administrative center was Ṣumur and its principal territory Amurru, the borders of which remain ill-defined.[71] Another official was in Kumidu, and he administered an area from Qadeš in southern Syria down to Hazor in northern Palestine, over to the Damascene and down into northern Transjordan.[72]

Subject to these officials, besides Egyptian underlings, were the native local rulers, who are usually referred to as "mayors" (*ḫazannu*) but are also called "rulers" (*awīlu,* lit. "man") or "kings" (*šarru*) or, by the Egyptian term, "princes" (*wr,* lit. "great one").[73] Among their obligations, which may not have been the same in each province, were the payment of tribute, meeting other exactions of goods and personnel, furnishing corvée labor on crown-lands, supplying Egyptian troops in transit and reinforcing them, and protecting caravans.

Six or seven letters in the vassal correspondence are from the Pharaoh (*EA* 99, 162–63, 190?, 367, 369–70; see above, sect. 2). With the exception of *EA* 162, as preserved they are formally very similar. The address, obviously ignoring any implications of social status, always names the inferior first (see above, sect. 4), and would appear to go back to an old tradition.[74] There follows an introduction to the message proper that is peculiar to the Pharaoh's letters to vassals, and it seems to be based on Egyptian models: "He (I?) hereby sends (send?) this tablet

71. The province probably extended from Byblos to an area south of Ugarit, and inland to about the Orontes River.

72. According to Hachmann, *ZDPV* 98 (1982) pp. 18f., the Egyptian official displaced the native rulers; see also *Archéologie au Levant: Recueil à la mémoire de Roger Saidah,* Collection de la Maison de l'Orient mediterranéen, no. 12, serie archéol. 9 (Lyons and Paris, 1982), pp. 133ff.

73. As used in the western periphery in the fifteenth to thirteenth centuries B.C., the *ḫazannu* was usually a royal appointee, and the term as said of the local rulers implied their incorporation within the administration as "fonctionnaires periphériques" (Liverani, in P. Garelli, ed., *Le Palais et la Royauté* [Paris, 1974], pp. 346ff.; on the *ḫazannu* at Boghazköy, see F. Picchioli, *OA* 14 [1975] pp. 93ff.). However, if the place of rule was indicated, one usually did not use *ḫazannu* but *awīlu,* a usage that goes back to the Syrian *koinē* of Old Babylonian times (see *CAD,* A/2, p. 57b). *šarru* was the nonadministrative, non-Egyptian term the city-state rulers used of themselves (Na'aman, *UF* 20 (1988) pp. 182–83, n. 18). Egyptian *wr,* which is used in *EA* only by Abi-Milku of Tyre (*EA* 149:30; 151:39), was applied by the Egyptians to all foreign rulers, not just to vassals; see D. Lorton, *The Juridical Terminology of International Relations in Egyptian Texts through Dynasty XVIII* (Baltimore, 1974), pp. 60ff.

74. The use of *awīlu* to designate the local ruler suggests the Old Babylonian period (see n. 73). These and the following remarks apply also to the king's letters discovered at Kumidu; see D. O. Edzard, *Schriftdokumente aus Kamid el-Loz, Saarbrücker Beiträge zur Altertumskunde* 7 (1970) pp. 55f. (Kumidu 1–2).

to you, saying to you ..." (*EA* 99, 367, 369–70).[75] Three times (*EA* 99, 367, 370), twice ruled off and included in the introductory section (*EA* 367, 370), the message begins with the command to be on one's guard and to guard "the place of the king where you are" (lit. "which is by/near you"), and again there are underlying Egyptian models.[76] The command may be repeated (*EA* 369:14), and along with more specific orders the vassal may be urged to obey without fault or negligence, two injunctions also with close Egyptian parallels.[77] He may also be promised to hear, if he is obedient, an expression of the Pharaoh's approval, "this is good" (*EA* 99:17; 369:21). Finally, all letters end in virtually the same words, following a longer or shorter form, by informing the inferior of the king's prosperity and power.[78]

From these letters, confirmed by letters of the vassals to the king, one sees that the main purpose of the king's writing was to acquire personnel and other goods, to introduce Egyptian officials and secure obedience to their orders, and to arrange for supplies for his troops.

The rest of the vassal correspondence is concerned almost exclu-

75. Cf., in the same position, after the address and immediately before the message, "This letter is brought to you to the following effect" (R. Caminos, *Late-Egyptian Miscellanies* [London, 1954], pp. 4, 7, 13–14), rendering Egyptian *ỉn.tw nk sš pn n ḏd ḥnᶜ ḏd,* followed by injunctions virtually identical with those continuing *EA* 99, 367, and 370. The king usually speaks of himself in the third person (*EA* 99:8f., 11, 17–19, 22; 162 passim; 367:6, 10–11, 16, 18, 20, 22ff.; 369:5, 19; 370:7), but at Kumidu the first person is also attested ("send me": Kumidu 1:5; 2:6), and some of the passages here taken as third person are ambiguous and could be in the first person. It seems likely that *qabê* (*EA* 99, 367, 370; Kumidu 1–2) or *ana qabê* (*EA* 369), lit. "to speak," is meant to correspond to Egyptian *ḥnᶜ ḏd,* lit. "with saying," and therefore to introduce direct quotation. (For the infinitive expressing purpose without *ana,* J. Huehnergard points to *PRU* 4, p. 193:6ff.; *KBo* 1, 3:38f.) "My saying/speech" (Edzard) accords with neither *EA* 369 nor the Egyptian parallel. On *EA* 369 as *extra chorum,* see *EA* 369, n. 1.

76. As first recognized by Liverani, *OA* 10 (1971) p. 258, n. 36, and p. 262, n. 52 (translated in *Three Amarna Essays* [see n. 26], pp. 7, 9), who also established on the basis of Egyptian parallels the meaning of "which is by/near you." See also Liverani, *Vicino Oriente* 2 (1979) p. 68, n. 8.

77. Cf. "lest the king find fault [lit. a crime] in you" (*EA* 367:10f.) and "do not let yourself be found fault with" (Caminos, *Late-Egyptian Miscellanies,* pp. 5, 198); "do not become negligent" (*EA* 367:14) and "slack not" (Caminos, *Late-Egyptian Miscellanies,* p. 7), "be not remiss" (ibid., 198).

78. For the short form, see *EA* 99, 367; for the long form, *EA* 162 and 370, and Kumidu 1–2. The conclusion of *EA* 369 is without parallel. For a brief analysis of the two forms, see J. Wesselius, *UF* 15 (1983) p. 313. Liverani, *Lingering over Words,* pp. 341ff., studies the form and the background of *EA* 99, 367, and 369–70, which he calls "Egyptian spring letters," in his opinion examples of a standard annual procedure. For difficulties with this view, see *EA* 367, n. 1.

sively with letters from subordinate rulers or vassals to the king or high Egyptian officials.[79] Formally, they are very similar, though regional differences are observable. In the address, the vast majority begin either "Say to the king/PN . . . ; Message of $PN_{(2)}$," or simply "To the king. . . ."[80] The exceptions are confined almost entirely to the letters of Rib-Hadda of Byblos, where we also find "Rib-Hadda speaks [17 times]/writes [9 times] to the king . . ."; comparable are *EA* 260 and 317–18.[81] Another unusual form is found in *EA* 126, 129(?), 137(?), and 362. *EA* 100 is unique. The king is almost never addressed by name, only by title, to which are usually added various honorifics.[82] To the identification of himself the vassal regularly adds various expressions of self-abasement.

Salutations are rare. Only once does an inferior report on his own well-being (*EA* 145, to an Egyptian official; see above, sect. 4), and only rarely does he wish his superior well (*EA* 44–45, 49, 59).[83] Again, the letters from Byblos are a notable exception. In letters addressed to the king the desire is expressed that the goddess, the Lady of Byblos, grant power to the king, and in letters to Egyptian officials it is hoped that Aman or the Lady of Byblos, or both, give the addressee honor in the king's sight.[84]

The prostration formula, which in the Byblos letters always precedes the salutation of an official, but always follows the salutation of the king, is omitted only once in a letter to the king (*EA* 44) and once

79. Exceptions: female correspondents (*EA* 48, 50; cf. *EA* 12, 26, and see also 273–74); Egyptian general to vassal (*EA* 96, a copy sent to central archives?). Those sending the letters may be a group of vassals (*EA* 200; cf. 30), the (senior) citizens of a city (*EA* 59, 100), or a vassal's *locum tenens/tenentes* (*EA* 169f.). Letters to Egyptian officials and courtiers: *EA* 62, 71 (cf. 40), 73, 77, 82, 86f., 93, 95, 98, 102, 145, 158, 164, 166f., 169(?), 178, 210(?), 238, 251(?), 256, 333. On postscripts, etc., see the text above at n. 58.

80. On *umma,* "message," see n. 52.

81. Liverani, *Lingering over Words,* p. 344, n. 16, points to the same form in letters written in Egyptian. On *iqbi/ištapar* as examples of *Koinzidenzfall,* see W. Mayer, *Untersuchungen zur Formensprache der babylonischen "Gebetsbeschwörungen"* (Rome, 1976), pp. 195f.; cf. *iqtabi* in *EA* 59:5.

82. The king's name appears in *EA* 53:1; 55:1. It may be doubted that *EA* 210 was addressed to king [. . . ᵐni-i]b-*ḫu-ri*-[ia] (Amenophis IV? Tutankhamun? see below, n. 137), since he would be named without title (see *VAB* 2/1, p. 745, note f) or the homage of proskynesis (see the text below).

83. *EA* 44 is from an independent Hittite prince, 45 and 49 from probably independent rulers of Ugarit, and 59 from the city of Tunip.

84. *EA* 71, 73, 77, 86–87, 95, 102; cf. also 113:32f. in the body of the letter, and, at Kumidu, as a concluding formula (Edzard, *ZA* 66 [1976] p. 64:18–20, with "the gods" as subject; in lines 7, 13, BE is a logogram for *bēlu,* as frequently in *EA*).

in a letter to an official (*EA* 166; also 167?). In letters to officials one simply declares the prostration, but in letters to the king this is usually said to be performed "seven times and seven times," which in Palestinian letters is made even more explicit, with the addition of "(both) on the belly and on the back."[85]

The body of the vassal letters, in both form and content, is quite varied.[86] Most vassals, it seems, wrote neither regularly nor on their own initiative, but rather only in reply to a letter from the king,[87] and very many of the letters begin by acknowledging in different ways that the king's letter has been received: "I have heard";[88] "as to the king's writing/saying";[89] "you have written";[90] "the king ... wrote";[91] "the word(s) ...";[92] "everything/whatever. . . ."[93]

The king's letters are often cited. His command to be on one's guard or to guard oneself,[94] and to guard the place of the king where the vassal is (see above), is frequently quoted[95] and even more frequently alluded to.[96] Associated with this command is at times another, either cited directly[97] or alluded to,[98] to guard (pay close atten-

85. See J. Pritchard, *The Ancient Near East in Pictures* (Princeton, 1954), fig. 5, for the representation of Syrian vassals in both positions. "Seven times" means "over and over." On Egyptian proskynesis, see H. Fischer, *Bulletin University Museum* 20 (1956) pp. 27ff.; ibid., 21 (1957) pp. 35ff.; A. Hermann, *Zeitschrift für ägyptische Sprache* 90 (1963) pp. 52f.

86. On the quality of composition and the general poverty of lexicon, see Edzard, in *Biblical Archaeology Today* (see n. 17), pp. 252f.

87. Campbell, *Chronology*, p. 34.

88. *EA* 141, 192, 196, 213, 216–18, 220f., 243, 246, 253f., 269, 293, 303–5, 364; cf. also 301f., 321, 328f.

89. *EA* 119, 121f., 125f., 130, 222, 224, 252, 306; also *EA* 77 and 95, to Egyptian officials. On epistolary *inūma*, see *EA* 1, n. 9.

90. *EA* 201–6.

91. *EA* 191, 243, 255, 283, 337; cf. also 63, 233, 247.

92. *EA* 267, 275–77; cf. also 65, 225, 239.

93. *EA* 223, 261, 297f.

94. See above n. 76.

95. *EA* 100:14f.; 112:9; 117:84; 119:9; 121:9; 122:10; 123:30f.; 125:9f.; 126:31f.; 130:16ff.; 231:14f.; 292:21f.; 294:9f. For Liverani, *Lingering over Words*, pp. 342ff., in most instances reference to protection indicates a "Syro-Palestinian spring letter," a vassal's reply to an "Egyptian spring letter" (see n. 78).

96. *EA* 63:9f.; 142:11ff.; 221:11ff.; 227:5ff.; 243:10ff.; 304:19ff.; 305:18ff.; 307:3ff.; 314:11f.; 316:10ff.; 320:16ff.; 321:23ff.; 325:10ff.; 326:9ff.; 327:1ff.; 364:14ff.

97. *EA* 292:20; 294:8f.; 317:21.

98. *EA* 216:12ff.; 220:11; 230:9ff.; 303:19ff.; 319:15ff.; 321:15ff.; 322:17ff.; 328:21ff.

tion to?) or listen to the king's commissioner. This may refer to the vassal's general duties, but at times at least it certainly looks to specific missions (cf. *EA* 367, 369; see above).

The command to be on one's guard, etc., was probably never isolated (cf. *EA* 367, 370). There were also orders, for example, "to prepare" (*EA* 99:10ff.), and the best-attested preparations are those of supplies for Egyptian troops in transit (*EA* 367:15ff.).[99] The vassal occasionally cites the actual order (*EA* 141:21–22; 337:8–11), but always, in one way or another, he states his compliance.[100]

The vassals reply to other commands and charges, some cited verbatim,[101] others easily inferred from context, and they do so not always with an unquestioning submissiveness. Thus, it is clear that the king has not succeeded in his attempt to have Aziru rebuild Ṣumur or to get him to come to Egypt (*EA* 156ff.). Lab'ayu does not hesitate to make known his displeasure at certain orders of the king (*EA* 252), and in two other letters (*EA* 253–54) he emphatically denies the serious charges brought against him by others and repeated by the king (cf. also *EA* 256). But the most unusual correspondence as well as by far the longest is that between the king and Rib-Hadda of Byblos, for it goes far beyond the routines that we find in most of the *EA* archive.[102] Rib-Hadda writes and writes. If he is told to guard himself and the city where he is, he does not reply that he will do so; he insists that it is

99. On the background of these preparations, see the text below and nn. 117–18.

100. *EA* 65, 141f., 144, 191, 193, 201, 203–6, 213, 216, 227, 302, 324f., 337; see also 226 and 292:29ff. One is to prepare "before the arrival" (*ana pānī*) of the Egyptian troops. Cf. Caminos, *Late-Egyptian Miscellanies* (see n. 75), p. 198, where the order is to have things ready before the arrival of the Pharaoh; see also p. 199 and p. 202, note. The use of *ana pānī* may reflect Egyptian *r-ḥ3t* (Pintore, *AO* 11 [1972] p. 129, n. 158; Liverani, *Vicino Oriente* 2 [1979] p. 69), but it need not, for in Old Babylonian *ana pānī* has the same temporal meaning; see, for example, M. Stol, *AbB* 9, 63:11; 98:8; 117:5; 137:29; 144:6′, and note too *ina pānī* in F. Kraus, *AbB* 7, 56:26, and the remarks of Durand, *ARMT* 21, p. 413, n. 83. In view of *EA* 5:15–17, its survival in the periphery seems quite probable. The troops in question were the regular army units, "archers" in the literal translation that I have followed, to be distinguished from auxiliaries (*tillatu*) and garrison-troops (*maṣṣartu*, *maṣṣāru*); see Rainey, AOAT, 8^2, p. 87.

101. *EA* 102:15f.; 112:42f.; 129:35; 130:10ff.; 161:31f.; 283:8f.

102. See especially Liverani, *OA* 10 (1971) pp. 253ff. (translated in *Three Amarna Essays* [see n. 26], pp. 3ff.). For the narrative patterns and the self-perception in Rib-Hadda's correspondence, see also Liverani, *Altorientalische Forschungen* 1 (1974) pp. 174ff., and for my criticisms and a somewhat different analysis, see A. Kort and S. Morschauser, eds., *Biblical and Related Studies Presented to Samuel Iwry* (Winona Lake, Ind., 1985), pp. 173ff.

impossible.[103] And he does so not once; to a single letter of the king he sends, it seems, nine letters in reply. Told, too, to send a certain wood, he replies that this also is impossible.[104] The impression that one gets of a tireless and boring correspondent, endlessly reiterating his requests and his complaints, was also shared by the king (the foreign office), who complained that Rib-Hadda wrote to him more than any local ruler.[105] This, of course, gave Rib-Hadda the occasion to insist that he alone was loyal and suffering for his lord.

Some vassals, however, did not simply reply to the various demands of the king. They also reported on their own situation and on anything they thought of possible interest to the crown, frequently on their own initiative, as they were at times urged to do.[106] Such reports are often introduced by "may the king, my lord, know (*idû*) that . . . ," and they tell of the city as "safe and sound,"[107] or threatened,[108] of lost territory,[109] or of other dangers.[110] Letters also end this way, calling attention to something in particular or summing up the letter as a whole.[111]

Unlike the international correspondence, the letters to and from vassals often refer to political events, too often indeed for even the barest summary here. In the north, politics were dominated by two

103. *EA* 112:10ff.; 117:84ff.; 119:10ff.; 121:10ff.; 122:11ff.; 123:30f.; 125:11f.; 126:33f.; 130:19ff.

104. *EA* 126:4ff.; see also 77:7ff.

105. *EA* 124:35ff.; see also 106:13ff.; 117:6ff.

106. *EA* 145:24ff.; 149:54ff.; 151:50f.

107. *EA* 68:9ff.; 74:5ff.; 75:6ff.; 144:10ff.; 226:6ff.; 268:8ff.; see also 100:8ff.; 257:8ff.; 330:9ff. Since the writer may go on to describe the parlous situation of the city that is "safe and sound" (*šalmat*), the meaning must have shifted from the original one of "well-being." *EA* 267:15ff. and 330:9ff., where "safe and sound" is said of "the place of the king, my lord, where I am," and of "the city of the king where I am," respectively, clearly allude to the vassal's duty to guard the place of the king where he is (see the text above) and suggest that "safe and sound" means that the place remains under the loyal protection of the vassal; cf. also *EA* 230:4–22. Already in the Old Babylonian period we find occasional declarations of a city's well-being followed immediately by a report on the strength of the security forces (*AbB* 5, 158:4ff.; *ARMT* 2, 88:6ff.; 3, 12:6ff.).

108. *EA* 72:1ff.(?); 76:7ff.; 78:7ff.; 81:6ff.; 114:6ff.; 116:6ff.

109. *EA* 272:10ff.; 273:8ff.; 279:9ff.

110. *EA* 104:6ff.; 244:8ff.; 249:5ff.; 250:4ff.; cf. also 215, 270, 307.

111. *EA* 147:70f.; 149:81ff.; 230:20ff.; 245:46f.; 273:25f. A virtual synonym of *idû* is *lamādu*, "to learn, be(come) informed," and though used much less frequently, it is otherwise indistinguishable; see *EA* 54:4ff.; 64:8ff.; 79:7ff.; 90:5ff.; 143:36ff.; 238:29ff.; 264:23ff.; 265:14f.; 274:17f.; 281:30ff.; 282:15ff.; 301:21ff.; 308 rev. 2ff.; 309:26ff.; cf. 287:59. The letters referred to in the text fall, in part at least, under what Nougayrol, *Ugar.* 5, p. 68, called "lettres d'information." For Liverani, *Lingering over Words*, pp. 345ff., they

major developments—first, the emergence of a new state, Amurru, and second, the appearance of a new threat to Egyptian power, the resurgent Hittites. The emergence of Amurru—which was achieved by a certain ʿAbdi-Aširta, partly through exploitation of social unrest and disaffection, and then solidified by his able son and successor, Aziru[112]—was the object of unceasing protest by Rib-Hadda of Byblos, who never tired of accusing the rulers of Amurru of disloyalty and treason. Others shared this view of Aziru. As the Hittite threat became evident,[113] Aziru, along with Aitagama of Qadeš, was charged with being a Hittite ally and, with Hittite support, a despoiler of Egyptian territory.[114] Needless to say, in his own letters someone quite different is portrayed.[115]

The vassal correspondence in the south is more insular in its interests and less reflective of international tensions. This correspondence presents a scene of constant rivalries, shifting coalitions, and attacks and counterattacks among the small city-states.[116] A probable exception to the isolation of the south from events to the north and the Hittite threat is seen in those letters that speak of preparations by the vassals before the arrival of Egyptian troops.[117] These preparations seem to reflect plans for a single campaign and the dispatch of Egyptian troops through Palestine to Syria, there to confront the Hittites and former Egyptian vassals supporting them.[118]

---

are mostly "late-summer letters," sent, in his theory, at the time an Egyptian official came to collect the annual tribute. Be it noted, here without comment, that for Liverani the vassal correspondence is shot through with extensive and constant misunderstandings, both linguistic and political; see especially *RA* 61 (1967) 1ff.; *Berytus* 31 (1983) 41ff.; *Lingering over Words*, pp. 343f.

112. On the rise of Amurru and the appeal to the disaffected, see Klengel, *MIO* 10 (1964) pp. 57ff.; Liverani, *Rivista storica italiana* 77 (1965) pp. 315ff.; idem, *RSO* 40 (1965) pp. 267ff. (translated in *Three Amarna Essays* [see n. 26], pp. 14ff.); Altman, *Bar-Ilan Departmental Researches: Bar-Ilan Studies in History* (1978) pp. 1ff.

113. See below, sect. 6.

114. *EA* 55:24, 38–43, 45; 59:21–38; 98:5–20; 140:8–32; 147:68; 149:35ff.; 151:59–62; see also 53:11ff., 35ff., 56ff.; 174–76; 197:31ff.

115. *EA* 156ff.

116. See n. 69, especially Albright and Na'aman.

117. Na'aman, *Lingering over Words*, pp. 397ff., defines the group by their references to subjects mentioned in the Egyptian letter of command (*EA* 367) and/or references to preparations before the arrival of Egyptian troops: *EA* 55, 65, 141–42, 144, 147, 153, 191, 193, 195, 201–6, 216–18, 227, 292, 324–25, 337.

118. This is the more common opinion, most recently defended by Na'aman (see n. 117). Liverani, *OA* 10 (1971) p. 259, n. 41 (*Three Amarna Essays* [see n. 26], p. 7), and *Lingering over Words*, pp. 341ff., sees in the preparation for the troops simply reference to an

6. Chronology

Despite a long history of inquiry, the chronology of the Amarna letters, both relative and absolute, presents many problems, some of bewildering complexity, that still elude definitive solution. Consensus obtains only about what is obvious, certain established facts, and these provide only a broad framework within which many and often quite different reconstructions of the course of events reflected in the Amarna letters are possible and have been defended.[119]

The Amarna archive, it is now generally agreed, spans at most about thirty years, perhaps only fifteen or so. The extremes depend on the number of years, if any, one assigns to the co-regencies of Amenophis IV with Amenophis III, and of Smenkhkare with Amenophis IV. The longer the co-regencies, the shorter the period.

The archive begins about the thirtieth year of Amenophis III and extends no later than the first year or so of Tutankhamun, at which time the court abandoned the site of Akhetaten.[120] The upper limit is suggested, first of all, by the hieratic docket on *EA* 23, which dates the reception of this letter in the thirty-sixth year of Amenophis III. Then, by inference from internal evidence, *EA* 17, 19–21, and 24–25 fit into the previous five years or so. The Babylonian correspondence with Amenophis III also fits well into his last years, and in general, nothing in the archive argues clearly for an earlier date.[121]

---

annual procedure according to which Egyptian troops accompanied an Egyptian official in the late summer in his tour of vassals' cities to collect tribute. See also Pintore, *OA* 11 (1972) pp. 115ff., 130, and *OA* 12 (1973) pp. 299ff., esp. p. 311.

119. See K. Kitchen, *Suppiluliuma and the Amarna Pharaohs: A Study in Relative Chronology* (Liverpool, 1962); Campbell, *Chronology;* E. Hornung, *Untersuchungen zur Chronologie und Geschichte des Neuen Reiches,* Ägyptologische Abhandlungen, Band 11 (Wiesbaden, 1964), pp. 63ff.; D. Redford, *History and Chronology of the Eighteenth Dynasty of Egypt* (Toronto, 1967), pp. 88ff.; Helck, *Beziehungen,* pp. 168ff.; Kühne; R. Krauss, *Das Ende der Amarnazeit: Beiträge zur Geschichte und Chronologie des Neuen Reiches,* Hildesheim Ägyptologische Beiträge (Hildesheim, 1978); William J. Murnane, *The Road to Kadesh,* Studies in Ancient Oriental Civilization, no. 42 (Chicago, 1985), app. 6; G. Wilhelm and J. Boese, in Paul Aström, ed., *High, Middle, or Low? Acts of an International Colloquium on Absolute Chronology Held at the University of Gothenburg, 20th–22nd August 1987,* Part 1, *Studies in Mediterranean Archaeology and Literature,* Pocket Book 56 (Gothenburg, 1987), pp. 74ff., and see the bibliography, pp. 110ff.

120. On *EA* 16, see n. 123.

121. The arguments for an earlier date of the Arzawa correspondence have been refuted by F. Starke, *ZA* 71 (1982) pp. 221ff. (See, however, *EA* 31, n. 2.) Even if one sees in *EA* 31:25–27 reference to events in Hittite history far back in the reign of Amenophis III, this does not imply a date for the writing of the letter; see Wilhelm and Boese, *High, Middle, or Low?* (see n. 119), pp. 103ff.

Within this framework we may locate some of the international correspondence a little more precisely:

Babylonian—the last years of Amenophis III until late in the reign of Amenophis IV, perhaps even as late as the first year or so of Tutankhamun;[122]

Assyrian—late in the reign of Amenophis IV, if not later;[123]

Mittanian—ca. year 30 of Amenophis III until year 4–5 (very short co-regency or no co-regency) or year 14–15 (co-regency of ca. 10 years) of Amenophis IV;

Arzawa—Amenophis III.[124]

Of the Hittite letters, *EA* 41 is addressed to Ḫuriya, who, according to one's reconstruction of Hittite history, is either Amenophis IV, Tutankhamun, or Smenkhkare.[125] The other letters (*EA* 42–44), *non liquet.* The Alašia letters (*EA* 33–40): again *non liquet.*[126]

Since, with few exceptions, the vassals never address the king by name, we lack this valuable evidence for establishing the relative chronology of their letters. The correspondence of the northern vassals, however, presents a fairly clear if rather general sequence of three periods: an earlier and a later Rib-Hadda of Byblos, and one post-Rib-Hadda. To the first are to be assigned *EA* 68–95; in this period ʿAbdi-Aširta of Amurru (*EA* 60–62) was Rib-Hadda's main enemy, and probably Amenophis III was king.[127] In the second period, *EA* 101–38 and

122. The possibility of the later date depends on the identity of the recipient of *EA* 9; see n. 137 and *EA* 9, n. 1.

123. *EA* 15 and 16 were probably separated by a fair interval, since the latter implies, it seems, several exchanges of envoys, any one of which could explain *EA* 9:31–35. If the addressee of *EA* 16 was Aya, the successor of Tutankhamun (see *EA* 16, n. 1), one can only guess how this letter made its way to the abandoned capital.

124. See n. 121.

125. See n. 138 and *EA* 41, n. 1.

126. On the chronology of the international correspondence and for a critical review of earlier opinions, see Kühne.

127. The arguments for placing *EA* 68–70 in the second Rib-Hadda period (Campbell, *Chronology,* pp. 80, 82f.) depend on questionable translations and readings. The assignment of *EA* 83–86 is also not without difficulties (Campbell, *Chronology,* pp. 93ff.). Putting the entire early period in the reign of Amenophis III is not universally accepted; see Campbell, ibid.; Klengel, *Geschichte Syriens im 2. Jahrtausend v. u. Z.*, Teil 2 (Berlin, 1969), pp. 184, 231, n. 4; Kitchen, *Suppiluliuma and the Amarna Pharaohs* (see n. 119), pp. 40ff. Wilhelm and Boese, *Middle, High, or Low?* (see n. 119), p. 86, would assign all vassal letters, or at least the vast majority, to the reign of Amenophis IV. If, however, Rib-Hadda's letters fall in this period, it is very difficult, if not impossible, to explain why the Byblos

362 were written, and Amenophis IV was on the throne. The last period, beginning with the exile and, probably not long afterwards, the death of Rib-Hadda (*EA* 162:7ff.), introduces new protagonists, notably Abi-Milku of Tyre (*EA* 146–55) and Aitagama of Qadeš (*EA* 189), and new synchronisms.[128] Just when this period begins in the reign of Amenophis IV, and whether within it some letters are addressed to his successors, are unresolved issues.[129]

The correspondence of the southern vassals has certain clear sequences and correlations, but its time span is more difficult to determine. One point of reference is the figure of Lab'ayu (*EA* 252–54), who clearly belongs to the earliest level of this correspondence. His death provides a *terminus ante* and *post quem* for a good number of letters. He is

---

ruler, when writing in the Aziru period, recalls (*EA* 108, 117, 131, 132, 362) the success the present king's father, certainly Amenophis III, had in an earlier action against ʿAbdi-Aširta, but when writing in the ʿAbdi-Aširta period, he does not refer to it even once. Why, when Aziru is the enemy, is Amenophis IV urged to do as his father did to ʿAbdi-Aširta, but when the enemy is ʿAbdi-Aširta, and therefore the example of his father even more pertinent, he hears not a word about his father? Different scribes with different arguments are not the explanation; scribes span the two periods (Campbell, *Chronology,* p. 84). Besides, Rib-Hadda did not leave the composition of his letters without his own contribution (Campbell, *Chronology,* p. 83). Had he known at the time of the early letters of a previous defeat and capture of his archenemy, how could he have failed to insist on their being mentioned and mentioned often?

128. Among the contemporaries of Abi-Milku were Zimredda of Sidon (*EA* 144f.; see 146:15; 147:66; 149:49, 57, 68, etc.), Biryawaza of Apu (Upu, *EA* 194–97; see 151:62), Aitagama of Qadeš (*EA* 151:59), Aziru (passim), and Niqmaddu of Ugarit (*EA* 49), as may be inferred from the fact that Abi-Milku wrote *EA* 151:55ff. after the fire in the palace of Ugarit (Liverani, *La storia di Ugarit,* Studi Semitici 6 [Rome, 1962], pp. 27ff.). Aitagama was a contemporary of Akizzi of Qaṭna (*EA* 52–55; see 53:4ff.), Teuwatti of Lapana (*EA* 193; see 53:35ff.), Arsawuya of Ruḫizzi (Ruḫiṣu) (*EA* 191–92; see 53:35ff.), and two kings of Nuḫašše and Ni'i (see *EA* 53:40ff.), who undoubtedly were Addu-Nirari (*EA* 51) and Aki-Teššup, respectively (see Nougayrol, *PRU* 4, pp. 32ff.; cf. *EA* 59:15, 18), in the time of Amenophis IV (*EA* 53:1; see also 140, 363).

129. Rib-Hadda's correspondence with Amenophis IV covered a period of at least five years (Campbell, *Chronology,* p. 88). There is, however, a hiatus in Rib-Hadda's letters during which ʿAbdi-Aširta is captured and eventually dies or is killed. The length of this period is unknown. If Amenophis IV had a long co-regency with his father, Rib-Hadda died about the same time as his master, and the post-Rib-Hadda period would have to be assigned mainly to the reigns of Smenkhkare and Tutankhamun. (Following Krauss, *Das Ende der Amarnazeit* [see n. 119], one would put *ʿnḫ.t-ḫpr.w-rʿ*, Amenophis IV's daughter, Meritaten [Mayati], before Smenkhkare; see the table at the end of the Introduction.) Some letters have been placed in these later reigns on other grounds, apart from the question of co-regency (*EA* 147 and 155, according to Redford, *History and Chronology* [see n. 119], p. 220; *EA* 139, 169, 171, according to Ph. H. J. ten Cate, *BiOr* 22 [1963] pp. 275f.; etc.); on *EA* 210, see above, n. 82, but see Krauss, *Das Ende der Amarnazeit,* pp. 71f.

also a contemporary of Surata of Akka (*EA* 232; see *EA* 245) and of Milkilu of Gazru (*EA* 267–71), to whom a letter was addressed very probably by Amenophis III.[130] He was dead before Rib-Hadda, for *EA* 287 and 289 speak only of Lab'ayu's sons at a time when Pawuru (*EA* 287:45), whom Rib-Hadda survived (*EA* 131, 362), is still alive.

Another correlation between the northern and southern correspondences is probably found in the warnings to a number of vassals, both northern and southern, to make preparations before the arrival of Egyptian troops.[131] If these warnings were all issued at virtually the same time, inspired by the same plans for a Syrian campaign, then not only are the two correspondences linked and a number of synchronisms established, but the relative date is also clear—i.e., shortly after Rib-Hadda's exile and before his death (*EA* 142:15–31).[132]

The major cruces are several. One is the reading of the hieratic docket on *EA* 254, a letter from Lab'ayu: "year 12" or "year 32"? If the first, then it must refer to Amenophis IV and would require a very late date for the entire southern corpus.[133] If the second, then it could refer only to Amenophis III and would put the earliest level of the southern correspondence with comparable levels of the northern and international correspondences, late in this Pharaoh's reign.[134]

Another and, depending on one's interpretation of the letter, a possibly even more serious crux concerns the reading of the hieratic docket on *EA* 27: "[yea]r 2" or "[year] 12"? It raises, on one reading of the letter, the vexing and still unsettled question of the co-regency of Amenophis IV with his father. The letter is addressed to the former, and probably not long after the latter's death. If so, and if the first reading is correct, then a short co-regency remains a possibility, but it would have to be established, not from the Amarna letters, but from

130. In *EA* 369 the king attributes his power to Amun, not to the Aten.

131. See the text above at nn. 117–18.

132. There seem to be few if any southern letters after this time. If the more recent northern correspondence was left behind at Akhetaten, it is perhaps to be explained by the fact that, whereas the southern letters were still relevant for the administration, the profoundly altered situation in the north made letters written there of no practical value.

133. See Campbell, *Chronology,* pp. 69f. "Year 22" is another possibility, epigraphically, but suffers from the same difficulties as the alleged early date of *EA* 31 (see above, n. 121).

134. It would also bring down the date of Rib-Hadda's correspondence.

other evidence. But if the second is right, then a co-regency, and a long one of ten years or so, seems inescapable.[135]

A tissue of problems is the correlation of the data of the Amarna letters with the history of the Hittites and their expansion into Syria. Unfortunately, with the exception of *EA* 170, the Amarna letters speak in rather general terms of Hittite activities, allowing therefore conflicting interpretations, which are only encouraged by the uncertainties afflicting contemporary Hittite history.

Basic to the discussion of the Amarna data is the date of the accession of Šuppiluliumaš to the Hittite throne, for it was under him that the Hittites moved onto the larger political scene and through their ambitions came into conflict with Egypt. Most scholars have put Šuppiluliumaš on the throne ca. 1380 B.C. This would be late in the reign of Amenophis III and provide a broad chronological framework for references to Hittite aggression. This high date, however, has been challenged, with strong arguments assembled in favor of a much later date, ca. 1343 B.C., well into the reign of Amenophis IV. In this view, the Amarna framework collapses to a decade, and the period of possibly relevant Hittite activities is greatly reduced.[136]

Another and urgent problem is whether the Amarna data reflect the six-year Ḫurri war that Šuppiluliumaš waged in Syria late in his reign. On one reading of the evidence no reflection is possible, for it dates an early stage of the war at the time of the death of Tutankhamun; this would be many years after the abandonment of the site of Akhetaten and well out of the Amarna framework.[137] But other readings are

135. See Kühne, pp. 43f.; William J. Murnane, *Ancient Egyptian Coregencies,* Studies in Ancient Oriental Civilization, no. 40 (Chicago, 1977), pp. 124f. Murnane accepts the reading "12" but denies its bearing on the co-regency problem. The way, however, friendship is requested and promised in *EA* 27:9–12, 37–40, 74–78, strongly suggests a period of transition when friendship must be reestablished. Nor does it seem likely at all that after twelve years or more, Tušratta would still be urging that a promise made by Amenophis III be kept now by his son.

136. For the arguments supporting this much later accession date, see Wilhelm and Boese, *High, Middle, or Low?* (see n. 119). This would also make dating the reference to the Hittites in *EA* 75:35ff. more problematic than ever.

137. Early in the war Šuppiluliumaš learned of the death of the Egyptian king Bibḫururiyaš (variant: Nibḫururiyaš) and received the widow's extraordinary request for a Hittite prince to replace him (H. Güterbock, *JCS* 10 [1956] p. 94; A. Goetze, *ANET,* p. 319). As it stands, the name looks like Nibḫurureya (Tutankhamun) rather than Napḫurureya (Amenophis IV) or A(na)ḫururiya (Smenkhkare). If, however, as seems virtually certain, the Ḫurri war is reflected in the Amarna letters, then one either postulates confusion in the Hittite tradition (Albright, *JEA* 23 [1937] p. 194; Redford, *History and Chronology* [see n.

also possible, and indeed more probable. The dead king, whose identity is so important, is in one reading Amenophis IV, in another, Smenkhkare. In either one the Amarna data are most certainly relevant and part of the history of the six-year war.[138]

Absolute dates of kings reigning in the Amarna period cannot be fixed with certainty. The following reflect most recent studies:[139]

Kingdom	*King*	*Dates of reign*
Assyria	Aššur-uballiṭ	1353–1318
Babylonia	Kadašman-Enlil I	(1364)–1350
	Burna-Buriaš II	1349–1323
Egypt	Amenophis III	May 1386–1349 (1390–1352)
	Amenophis IV	1350–1334 (1352–1336)
	(*ʿnḫ.t-ḫpr.w-rʿ*)	(1336–1335)
	Smenkhkare	1336–1334 (1335–1332)
	Tutankhamun	1334–1325 (1332–1323/22)
	Aya	1324–1321 (1323/22–1319/18) or 1324–1319
Hittite	Šuppiluliumaš	1380–1340 (1343–1323/22 or 1319/18)[140]

119], pp. 158ff.; Wilhelm and Boese, *High, Middle, or Low?* [see n. 119], pp. 100ff.) or argues that Nipḫururiya was by a development in the Egyptian language a possible form of the prenomen of Amenophis IV (Krauss, *Das Ende der Amarnazeit* [see n. 119], pp. 99ff.).

138. Krauss, *Das Ende der Amarnazeit* (see n. 119), pp. 54ff., offers an extensive reconstruction of the history, including the Amarna data, on the assumption that the dead king (see n. 137) was Amenophis IV. For criticisms of this view and a reconstruction that assumes the dead king was Smenkhkare, see Wilhelm and Boese, *Middle, High, or Low?* (see n. 119), esp. pp. 96ff.

139. The Assyrian and Babylonian dates are those of J. A. Brinkman, *Materials and Studies for Kassite History: A Catalogue of Cuneiform Sources Pertaining to Specific Monarchs of the Kassite Dynasty*, vol. 1 (Chicago, 1976), p. 31, but lowered by ten years, according to the "low chronology" (see E. Wente and C. Van Siclen, *Studies in Honor of George R. Hughes*, Studies in Ancient Oriental Civilization, no. 39 [Chicago, 1976], p. 249; J. Boese and G. Wilhelm, *WZKM* 71 [1979] pp. 19ff.). The Babylonian dates have a margin error of ± 5 years. The Egyptian chronologies, which are also "low," are those of Wente and Van Siclen, p. 218, and, in parentheses, of Krauss, *Das Ende der Amarnazeit* (see n. 119), p. 202.

140. For the lower dates, see Wente and Van Siclen, *Studies* (see n. 139), pp. 249f.; Wilhelm and Boese, *High, Middle, or Low?* (see n. 119), pp. 107f. Note that, if Aya is addressed in *EA* 16, only the low Assyrian chronology is compatible with the Egyptian chronologies presented here.

Editorial Apparatus

The following symbols are used in the translations and transcriptions:

[ ]	restored text
[. . .]	missing text
. . .	obscure or greatly damaged text
⟨ ⟩	omission by scribe
⟪ ⟫	sign(s) repeated by error
⸢ ⸣	sign(s) partially illegible
( )	word(s) supplied by editor to clarify text

In addition, the following appear in the text:

boldface numbers	line numbers (also in the notes)
paragraph indent	indication of a line of separation traced across the surface of the tablet (a usage that was especially widespread in the North)
italics	translation doubtful (for italics in notes, see below)
centered colon	indication of a gloss (the gloss is translated only if it has a different meaning from the word glossed; glosses in Akkadian are not indicated)

For the transliteration of Sumero-Akkadian passages the following conventions apply:

Sumerian	roman type
Sumerogram	small caps
Akkadian	reading certain: italics
	reading dubious: roman

As always, proper names present problems. I have tried to resolve these in what seemed the simplest, if not always the most consistent, fashion. In general, syllabic writings have been kept; thus, for example, Yapaḫu, and not Yapaʿu. Whenever a logogram has been employed, however, I have given a more exact transcription—for instance, ÌR = ʿAbdu, ^{d}IM = Baʿlu. With the exception of several well-known geographic names (Egypt, not Miṣru; Jerusalem, not Urusalim; etc.), I have retained the ancient forms, and although we know that geographic names are generally in the genitive (the country/the city of + geographic name), the (diptotic) form of the text has usually been kept. In addition, throughout these letters the short form "Ṣumur" has been used rather than the long form "Ṣumuru."

Abbreviations and Short Titles

AAAS	*Annales archéologiques arabes syriennes* (Damascus)
AbB	*Altbabylonische Briefe* (Leiden)
Adler	Hans-Peter Adler, *Das Akkadische des Königs Tušratta von Mitanni,* AOAT 201 (1976)
AÉM	*Archives épistolaires de Mari* (Paris)
AfO	*Archiv für Orientforschung* (Berlin, then Graz)
AHw	W. von Soden, *Akkadisches Handwörterbuch,* vols. 1–3 (Wiesbaden, 1965–81)
AIPHOS	*Annuaire de l'Institut de Philologie et d'Histoire Orientales et Slaves* (Brussels)
AJSL	*American Journal of Semitic Languages* (Chicago)
ANET	J. Pritchard, *Ancient Near Eastern Texts Relating to the Old Testament,* 3d ed. (Princeton, 1969)
AO	Antiquités orientales (the Louvre)
AOAT(S)	Alter Orient und Altes Testament (Sonderreihe) (Kevelaer and Neukirchen-Vluyn)
AoF	*Altorientalische Forschungen* (Berlin)
Arch Anz	*Archäologischer Anzeiger* (Berlin)
ARM(T)	*Archives royales de Mari: Transcriptions et traductions* (Paris)
ArOr	*Archiv Orientální* (Prague)
AS	*Assyriological Studies, The Oriental Institute of the University of Chicago* (Chicago)
Ash	Ashmolean Museum (Oxford)
ATAT	H. Gressmann, ed., *Altorientalische Texte zum Alten Testament,* 2d ed. (Berlin and Leipzig, 1926)
BAM	F. Köcher, *Die babylonisch-assyrische Medezin in Texten und Untersuchungen,* 6 vols. (Berlin and New York, 1963–80)
Barnett, *Illustrations*	R. Barnett, *Illustrations of Old Testament History,* 2d ed. (Bristol and London, 1977)
BASOR	*Bulletin of the American Schools of Oriental Research* (Baltimore, then Cambridge, Mass., then Philadelphia, now Baltimore)
BB	C. Bezold and E. W. Budge, *The Tell el-Amarna Tablets in the British Museum* (London, 1892)
BE	*The Babylonian Expedition of the University of Pennsylvania,* Series A: *Cuneiform Texts,* vol. 1: H. V. Hilprecht, *Old Babylonian Inscriptions Chiefly from Nippur,* pt. 2 (Philadelphia, 1896)
Bi	*Biblica* (Rome)

BiOr	*Bibliotheca Orientalis* (Leiden)
BJPES	*Bulletin of the Jewish Palestine Exploration Society* (Jerusalem)
BM	British Museum
Böhl, *Sprache*	Franz M. Th. Böhl, *Die Sprache der Amarnabriefe,* Leipziger Semitische Studien V/2 (Leipzig, 1909)
Bottéro, *Ḫabiru*	J. Bottéro, *Le Problème des Ḫabiru à la 4ᵉ Rencontre Assyriologique Internationale,* Cahiers de la Société Asiatique, XII (Paris, 1954)
BSOAS	*Bulletin of the School of Oriental and African Studies* (London)
C	Cairo (Egyptian Museum)
CAD	*The Assyrian Dictionary of the Oriental Institute of the University of Chicago* (Chicago and Glückstadt)
CAH	*The Cambridge Ancient History,* 3d ed., vols. 1–2 (Cambridge, 1970–75)
Campbell, *Chronology*	E. F. Campbell, *The Chronology of the Amarna Letters* (Baltimore, 1964)
Campbell, *Shechem*	E. F. Campbell, "Shechem in the Amarna Archive," in G. Ernest Wright, *Shechem: The Biography of a Biblical City* (New York and Toronto, 1965), pp. 191–207
EA	*El Amarna* (refers to the numbering of the letters in *VAB* 2/1 and Rainey, AOAT 8^2)
Ebeling	E. Ebeling, in *ATAT* (q.v.)
Edel, *Brief*	Elmar Edel, *Der Brief des ägyptischen Wesirs Pašiyara an den Hethiterkönig Ḫattušili und verwandte Keilschriftbriefe,* Nachrichten der Akademie der Wissenschaften in Göttingen, I, Philologisch-historische Klasse, No. 4 (Göttingen, 1978), pp. 117–58 = [1–42]
Emar	Daniel Arnaud, *Recherches au pays d'Aštata, Emar* 6.1–4 (Paris, 1985–87)
GAG	W. von Soden, *Grundriss der akkadischen Grammatik, Analecta Orientalia* 33 (Rome, 1952); and *Ergänzungsheft, Analecta Orientalia* 47 (Rome, 1969)
GM	*Göttinger Miszellen, Beiträge zur ägyptologischen Diskussion* (Göttingen)
Gordon	Unpublished notes on *EA* tablets in London and Cairo (see Preface)
Greenberg, *Ḫab/piru*	Moshe Greenberg, *The Ḫab/piru,* American Oriental Series, 39 (New Haven, 1955)
Helck, *Beziehungen*	W. Helck, *Die Beziehungen Ägyptens zu Vorderasien im 3. und 2. Jahrtausend v. Chr.*, *Ägyptologische Abhandlungen,* 2d ed., vol. 5 (Wiesbaden, 1971)
HKL	R. Borger, *Handbuch der Keilschriftliteratur,* vols. 1–3 (Berlin, 1967–75)

HSS	Harvard Semitic Series/Studies (Cambridge, Mass.)
Huehnergard, *Akkadian*	J. Huehnergard, *The Akkadian of Ugarit,* HSS 34 (Atlanta, 1989)
Huehnergard, *Ugaritic Vocabulary*	J. Huehnergard, *Ugaritic Vocabulary in Syllabic Transcription,* HSS 32 (Atlanta, 1987)
Huffmon, *APNMT*	Herbert B. Huffmon, *Amorite Personal Names in the Mari Texts: A Structural and Lexical Study* (Baltimore, 1965)
IEJ	*Israel Exploration Journal* (Jerusalem)
IOS	*Israel Oriental Studies* (Tel Aviv)
Izre'el, *Amurru*	Shlomo Izre'el, *Amurru Akkadian: A Linguistic Study,* HSS 41 (Atlanta, 1991)
JANES	*Journal of the Ancient Near Eastern Society of Columbia University* (New York)
JAOS	*Journal of the American Oriental Society* (New Haven, now Ann Arbor)
JCS	*Journal of Cuneiform Studies* (New Haven, then Philadelphia, now Baltimore)
JEA	*Journal of Egyptian Archaeology* (London)
JEOL	*Jaarbericht van het Voorasiatisch-Egyptisch Genootschap, Ex Oriente Lux* (Leiden)
Jerusalem Scribe	W. L. Moran, "The Syrian Scribe of the Jerusalem Amarna Letters," in H. Goedicke and J. Roberts, eds., *Unity and Diversity* (Baltimore and London, 1975), pp. 146–66
JNES	*Journal of Near Eastern Studies* (Chicago)
JQR	*Jewish Quarterly Review* (Philadelphia)
JSOR	*Journal of the Society of Oriental Research* (Toronto)
JSS	*Journal of Semitic Studies* (Manchester)
KB	H. Winckler, *Die Thontafeln von Tell-el-Amarna,* vol. 5, E. Schrader et al., Keilinschriftliche Bibliothek (Berlin, 1896)
KBo	*Keilschrifttexte aus Boghazköi* (Leipzig)
Knudtzon	See *VAB*
KUB	*Keilschrifturkunden aus Boghazköi, Staatliche Museen zu Berlin, Vorderasiatische Abteilung* (Berlin)
Kühne	Cord Kühne, *Die Chronologie der internationalen Korrespondenz von El-Amarna,* AOAT 17 (1973)
Lingering over Words	T. Abusch, J. Huehnergard, and P. Steinkeller, eds., *Lingering over Words: Studies in Ancient Near Eastern Literature in Honor of William L. Moran,* HSS 37 (Atlanta, 1990)
LTBA	L. Matouš and W. von Soden, *Die lexicalischen Tafelserien der Babylonier und Assyrern in den Berliner Museen,* 2 vols. (Berlin, 1933)
MARI	*Mari: Annales de Recherches Interdisciplinaires* (Paris)

MDOG	*Mitteilungen der Deutschen Orient-Gesellschaft zu Berlin* (Berlin)
MIO	*Mitteilungen des Institut für Orientforschung* (Berlin)
MSL	*Materialien zum sumerischen Lexikon* (Rome)
MUSJ	*Mélanges de l'Université Saint-Joseph* (Beirut)
Na'aman, *Political Disposition*	Nadav Na'aman, "The Political Disposition and Historical Development of Eretz-Israel according to the Amarna Letters," pts. 1–2 (Ph.D. diss., Tel-Aviv University, 1973; in Hebrew)
NABU	*Nouvelles assyriologiques brèves et utilitaires* (Paris)
OA	*Oriens Antiquus* (Rome)
OLZ	*Orientalistische Literaturzeitung* (Leipzig, then Berlin)
Oppenheim, *LFM*	A. Leo Oppenheim, *Letters from Mesopotamia* (Chicago and London, 1967)
Or n.s.	*Orientalia,* nova series (Rome)
PBS	*Publications of the Babylonian Section, University Museum, University of Pennsylvania* (Philadelphia)
PEQ	*Palestine Exploration Quarterly* (London)
PJB	*Palästinajahrbuch* (Berlin)
Pintore, *Matrimonio*	Franco Pintore, *Il matrimonio interdinastico nel Vicino Oriente durante i secoli XV–XIII, Orientis Antiqui Collectio* XIV (Rome, 1978)
PN	personal name
PRU	*Le Palais royal d'Ugarit,* vols. 2–6, Mission de Ras Shamra VI, VII, IX, XI (Paris, 1957–70)
RA	*Revue d'assyriologie et d'archéologie orientale* (Paris)
Rainey, *El Amarna Tablets*	Anson F. Rainey, *El Amarna Tablets 359–379,* AOAT 8, 2d ed. (Kevelaer and Neukirchen, 1978)
Rainey, *Particles*	Anson F. Rainey, *Canaanite in the Amarna Tablets: Morphosyntactic Analysis of the Particles and Adverbs* (forthcoming)
RB	*Revue biblique* (Paris)
RHA	*Revue hittite et asianique* (Paris)
RLA	*Reallexikon der Assyriologie und vorderasiatischen Archäologie* (Berlin and Leipzig, then Berlin and New York)
RN	royal name
RS	Ras Shamra
RSO	*Rivista degli studi orientali* (Rome)
Sayce, *Tell el Amarna*	W. M. F. Petrie, *Tell el Amarna* (London, 1894), cuneiform copies by A. H. Sayce, pls. XXXI–XXXIII
Scheil, *Mémoires*	V. Scheil, O. P., "Tablettes d'el-Amarna de la collection Rostovicz," in *Mémoires publiées par les membres de la Mission archéologique française au Caire,* 6 (Paris, 1892), pp. 297–312

Seux, *Textes du Proche-Orient*	Jacques Briend and Marie-Joseph Seux, *Textes du Proche-Orient ancien et histoire d'Israël* (Paris, 1977)
von Soden	W. von Soden, "Zu den Amarnabriefen aus Babylon und Assur," *Or* n.s. 21 (1952), pp. 426–34
SMEA	*Studi Miceni ed Egeo-Anatolici* (Rome)
SSDB	W. L. Moran, "A Syntactical Study of the Dialect of Byblos as Reflected in the Amarna Tablets" (Ph.D. diss., Johns Hopkins University, 1950)
StBoT	*Studien zu den Boghazköy-Texten* (Wiesbaden)
StOr	*Studia Orientalia* (Helsinki)
TCS	*Texts from Cuneiform Sources* (Locust Valley, N.Y.)
THeth	*Texte der Hethiter* (Heidelberg)
TIM	*Texts in the Iraq Museum* (Baghdad)
UF	*Ugarit-Forschungen* (Neukirchen-Vluyn)
Ugar.	*Ugaritica:* vol. 5, J. Nougayrol et al., Mission de Ras Shamra XVI (Paris, 1968); vol. 7, A. al-Ouche et al., Mission de Ras Shamra XVIII (Paris, 1978)
VAB	*Vorderasiatische Bibliotek,* vol. 2, J. A. Knudtzon, *Die El-Amarna-Tafeln,* Anmerkungen und Register bearbeitet von O. Weber und E. Ebeling, 1–2 (Leipzig, 1907–15; rpt., Aalen, 1964)
VAT	Vorderasiatische Teil (der Staatlichen Museen, Berlin)
VBoT	A. Götze, *Verstreute Boghazköi-Texte* (Marburg, 1930)
VS	O. Schroeder, *Vorderasiatische Schriftdenkmäler der Königlichen Museen zu Berlin,* Hefte 11–12 (Berlin, 1915)
WA	H. Winckler und L. Abel, *Der Thontafelfund von El Amarna,* in *Mitteilungen aus den Orientalischen Sammlungen, Königliche Museen zu Berlin,* Hefte 1–3 (Berlin, 1889–90)
WZKM	*Wiener Zeitschrift für die Kunde des Morgenlandes* (Vienna)
YOS	Yale Oriental Series, Babylonian Texts (New Haven)
Youngblood, *Amarna Correspondence*	Ronald F. Youngblood, "The Amarna Correspondence of Rib-Haddi, Prince of Byblos" (Ph.D. diss., Dropsie College, 1961)
ZA	*Zeitschrift für Assyriologie und verwandte Gebiete;* since 1939: *Zeitschrift für Assyriologie und vorderasiatische Archäologie* (Berlin)
ZAW	*Zeitschrift für die alttestamentliche Wissenschaft* (Berlin, then Berlin and New York)
ZDPV	*Zeitschrift des Deutschen Palästina-Vereins* (Stuttgart)

The Amarna Letters

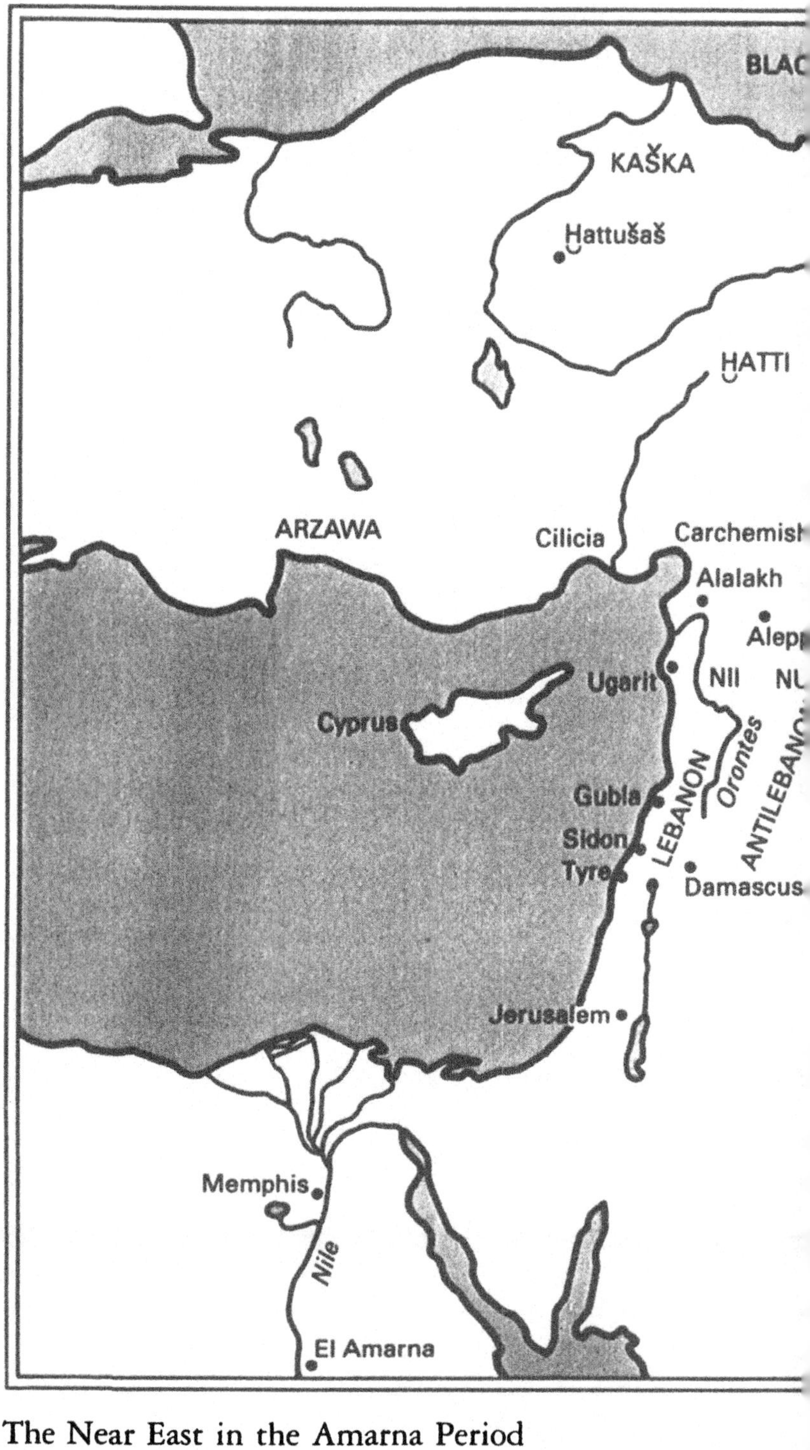

The Near East in the Amarna Period

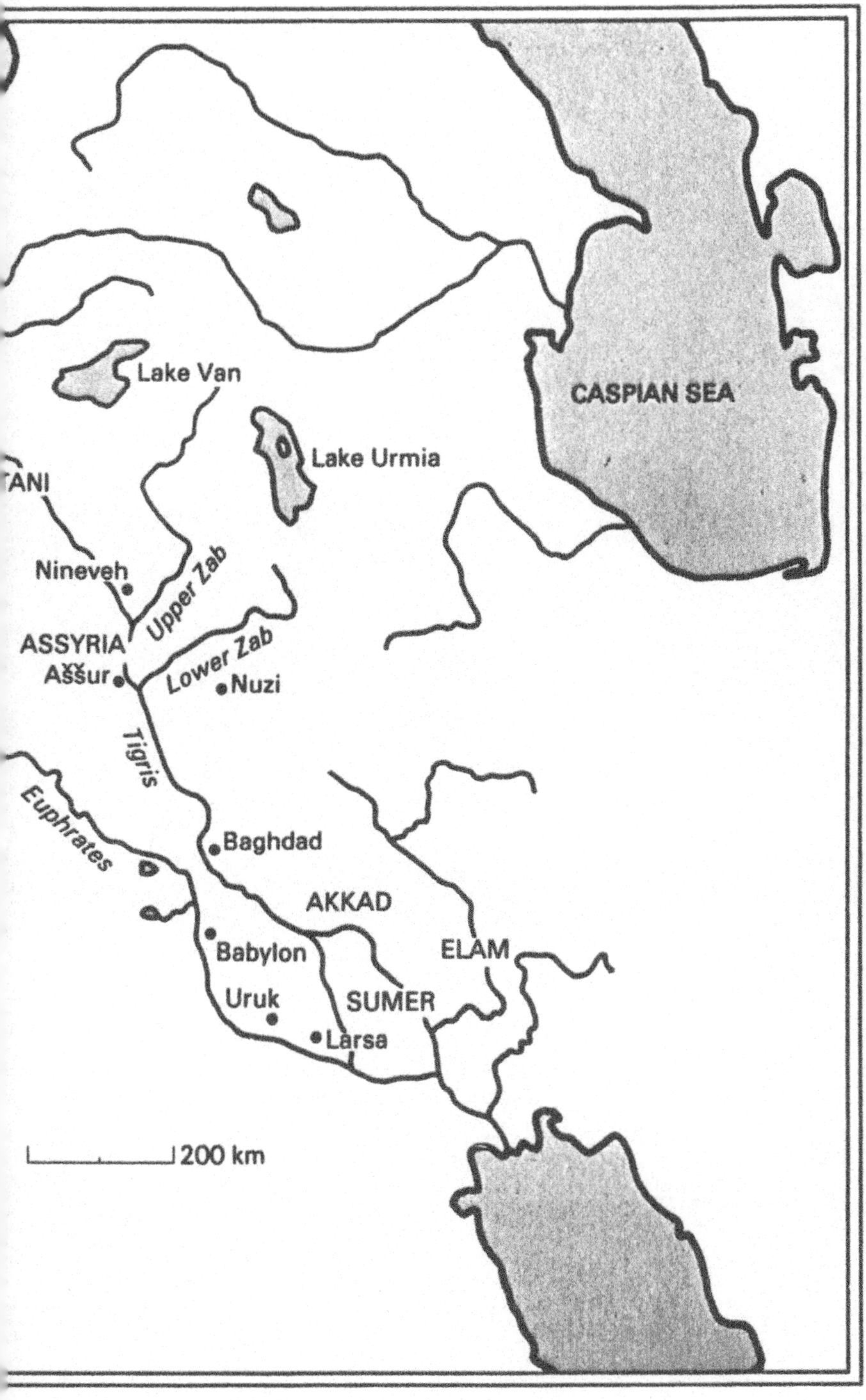

CASPIAN SEA
Lake Van
Lake Urmia
TANI
Nineveh
Upper Zab
ASSYRIA
Aššur
Lower Zab
Nuzi
Tigris
Euphrates
Baghdad
AKKAD
Babylon
ELAM
Uruk
SUMER
Larsa
200 km

EA 1

The Pharaoh complains to the Babylonian king

TEXT: BM 29784.
COPY: BB 1.
PHOTOGRAPH: F. G. Giles, *Ikhnaton: Legend and History* (London, 1970), pl. XI (reverse only).

Say [t]o Kadašman-Enlil,[1] the king of Karadun[i]še, my brother: Thus Nibmuarea, Great King,[2] the king of Egypt, your brother. For me all goes well. For you may all go well. For your household, for your wives, for your sons, for your magnates,[3] your horses, your chariots, for your countries, may all go very well. For me all goes well. For my household, for my wives, for my sons, for my magnates, my horses, the numerous troops, all goes well, and in my countries all goes very well. 10–17 I have just heard what you wrote me about, saying, "Here you are asking for my daughter in marriage, but my sister whom my father gave you was (already) there with you, and no one has seen her (so as to know) if now she is alive or if she is dead." These are your words that you sent me on your tablet. Did you, however, ever send here a dignitary of yours[4] who knows your sister, who could speak with her and identify her?[5] 17–21 Suppose he spoke with her. The men whom you sent here are nobodies.[6] One was the [. . .] of Zaqara, [*the ot*]*her*, an assherder [*fr*]*om* [. . .] There has been no one among the[m *wh*]*o* [*knows her, wh*]*o* was an intimate of your father, and *w*[*ho could identify her*].[7] 21–25 Moreover, the messengers [*who*] . . . [. . .][8] 26–32 And as for your writing me,[9] "You addressed my me[ssen]gers as your wives were standing gathered in your presence, saying, 'Here is your mistress who stands before you.' But my messengers did not know her, (whether) it was my sister who *was at your side*"[10]—*about whom* you yourself have now written me, "My messengers did not know her," and (still) you say, "Who is to identify her?"— 32–36 Why don't you send me a dignitary of yours who can tell you the truth, the well-being[11] of your sister who is here, and then you can believe the one who enters to *see* her quarters and her relationship with the king?[12] 36–42 And as for your writing me, "Perhaps the one my messengers saw was the daughter of some poor man, or of some Ka⟨s⟩kean,[13] or the daughter of some Ḫanigalbatean, or perhaps someone from Ugarit.[14] Who can believe them? *The one who was at your side* . . . , she did not op[en] her mouth.[15] One cannot believe them at all." These are your words. 43–52 But if your [sister] were de[ad], what reason would there be for one's concealing *her de*[*ath,*[16] *and*] our presenting someone [else]? [*May*] Aman [*be my witness*][17] ... [...] 52–62 And as for your writing me, "My daughters who are married to *neigh*[*bori*]*ng* kings, if my messengers [*go*] there, they speak with th[em, and they bri]ng me a greeting-gift. *The one with you* [..."[18] Th]ese are your words. Undoubtedly [*your neigh*]*boring*[19] kings are [*ri*]*ch*[20] (and) mighty. Your daughters can acquire something from them and send (it) to you. But what does she have, your sister who is with me? But should she make some acquisition, I will send (it) to you! It is a fine thing that you give your daughters *in order to acquire a nugget of gold*[21] from your neighbors! 62–77 As for your writing me the words of my father, never mind! you do not cite his (exact) words.[22] Furthermore, "Establish friendly brotherhood between us"—these are the words that you wrote me. Now, we are brothers, you and I, but I have quarreled because of your messengers, since they report to you saying, "Nothing is given to us who go to Egypt." Those who come to me—has a single one of them ever come [*and not*][23] received silver, gold, oil, solemn garb,[24] every sort of finery, [*more than i*]*n* any other country?[25] He does not tell the truth to the one who sends him! The first time the messengers went off to [*y*]*our f*[*ather*],[26] and their mouths told lies.[27] The next time they went off [and] they told lies to you. So I said to myself, "Whether I [gi]ve them anything or do not give them[28] anything, they are going to go on te⟨l⟩ling [l]i[e]s just the same." So I made up my mind in their regard and I did not *gi*[*ve t*]*o them anymore.*[29] 77–88 And as for your writing me, "You said to my messengers, 'Has your master no troops? The girl he gave[30] to me is not beautiful.' "—these are your words, (but) it is not so! Your messengers keep telling you what is not true, (saying things) like this. Whether soldiers[31] are on hand or not can be found out for me.[32] What reason is there for asking about whether there are troops on hand belonging to you, whether there are horses on hand also belonging to you? Please, do not listen to *them*![33] Your messengers, of whom the mouths of both groups[34] are untruthful and whom you sent here, I swear that they have not served you,[35] and so they go on t⟨el⟩ling lies in order to escape your punishment. 88–98 As for your saying to me, "He put my chariots among the chariots of the mayors. You did not *review* them *separately.* You *humiliated* them before the country *where you are.* You did not rev⟨iew⟩ (them) *separately.*" *Whether* the chariots were *here or there, the chariots needed the horses of my* [*coun*]*try—all were my horses.*[36] As for your writing me *in order to aggrandize yourself* (and) to put oil on the *h*[*ea*]*d* of a girl, you for your part sent me one *pr*[*es*]*ent.*[37] *Are we to laugh?*[38]

NOTES

1. ᵐ*ka-dá* (over erasure; also Gordon)-*aš-ma-an-en-líl.* KUR *ka-ra-an-du-n*[*i*]*-še* (Gordon).

2. The exact legal and political implications of the title "Great King," which is confined to the rulers of the major states, are not clear. It appears in the Old Babylonian period, certainly with implications of status and *noblesse oblige* (*ARMT* 5, 20:33), but as used in the fourteenth to thirteenth centuries B.C. it was perhaps an innovation of the Hittites (F. Starke, *ZA* 67 [1977] p. 288). For occurrences, see M.-J. Seux, *Épithètes royales akkadiennes et sumériennes* (Paris, 1967), pp. 298ff.; for the Old Babylonian period, see also M. Rowton, *JCS* 21 (1967) p. 269, A. 7535: 24f., of the king of Elam; D. Charpin, *MARI* 3, p. 110; and K. Veenhof, *MARI* 4, p. 209 and n. 72. That the Babylonian king is here not given the same title need not imply Egyptian claims of superiority or hostility; cf. *EA* 41. The Pharaoh is also addressed as "Great King" by northern vassals; see P. Artzi, *JNES* 27 (1968) p. 165, n. 18. On the West Semitic (at least linguistic) equivalent *mlk rb* in Ugaritic and its later history in Syria and Palestine, see J. Greenfield, *Fourth World Congress of Jewish Studies* 1 (1967) pp. 118f.

3. In the greeting-formula, the term "magnate" (*rabû*, "great one") refers to the highest officials of the palace organization; see Liverani, in Garelli, ed., *Le Palais et la Royauté* (Paris, 1974), p. 343. Cf. *PRU* 4, p. 42:38ff., for a list of the magnates at the Hittite court; in Babylonian sources they are identified as *šūt ekalli,* "those of the palace" (S. Page, *Sumer* 23 [1967] p. 64 ii 13; F. Reschid and C. Wilcke, *ZA* 65 [1975] p. 40:29f.). Lesser kings also had their magnates; for example, the king of Qadeš (see *Ugar.* 5, no. 38).

4. LÚ-*ka* DUGUD (*kabta*; LÚ *ka*-DUGUD?): following Pintore, *OA* 11 (1972) pp. 37f., and Gordon, confirmed by collation (*RA* 69 [1975] p. 156, n. 1); also line 33.

5. *ú-ma-an-di-še* (*AHw,* p. 640; *CAD,* I/J, p. 31).

6. *rīqa,* lit. "empty," contrasting with *kabta* (line 15), "heavy, important," and therefore "nobodies" seems preferable to "simpletons" (Ungnad, *OLZ,* 1916, col. 181; Kühne, p. 53, n. 245) or "idle" (*AHw,* p. 979). "Empty-handed" (Pintore, *Matrimonio,* p. 61) does not fit the context. The figures mentioned were probably proverbial (Ungnad).

7. š]a [i-de$_4$-še š]a *qé-ri-ib* 21 *a-na a-bi-ka ù š*[*a* ú-ma-an-di-še] (cf. lines 16 f.); on *qerib,* for correct *qerub,* see *AHw,* p. 915.

8. Line 22: Knudtzon's *qa,* perhaps the end of a long sign (Gordon). Line 24: the reading *ti-na-din* is quite doubtful, since the prefix appears throughout this letter as *ta-*, never *ti-* (cf. esp. line 61, *ta-na-an-din*). Read šu-ul]-*ma ù* TI (*balāṭa*), "well-being and life," with what goes before, and then *na-din* 25 [x-y] a-[n]a ŠU-*t*[*i*-šu *a*]*-na la-q*[*í*-šu] *a-na um-mi-še,* "[x-y] was given into [*his*] hand [t]o fet[ch *it*] for her *mother*"? Instead of "mother," in context perhaps *ummu* is better taken as "nurse"; cf. the "mother" who accompanies to the Mari court a woman given in marriage (*AÉM* 1/2, no. 298:29 and note f, with references to Durand, *MARI* 4, pp. 414f., and Bardet, *ARMT* 23, pp. 72ff.).

9. Epistolary *inūma* introduces a clause that states the fact of communication, with or without following direct quotation (see also lines 36, 52, 78, 88, 95), and is especially frequent at the beginning of the body of a letter (see above, Introduction, n. 89); cf. epistolary *quod* (*quod scribis*). *kī* is also used this way: *kī aḫīya tašpura mā* . . . . , "As to my brother's having written me, saying. . . ." Cf. perhaps in Ugaritic *w.k.rgm.špš / mlk.rb.bʿly* (*PRU* 2, 18:1f.; see also *PRU* 5, 65 r. 7). Deictic *kī* probably also explains the use of *inūma*; see *Or* n.s. 29 (1960) p. 17, n. 1, and Rainey, *Particles*.

10. *ša* KI(*itti*)-*ka ša anumma*: interpretation very difficult (see also lines 41, 56, 91), but the existence of *kīka* (*AHw*, p. 478, "thus," "she is thus, like this"; *CAD*, K, p. 351, "like her") is very dubious (on *EA* 138:66, see below), and *ša* cannot be the feminine pronominal suffix, which always appears as -*še* in this letter. The assumption of a logographic writing of *itti* is very difficult, though in line 91 "the country where you are" (*māti ša ittīka*) would be very reminiscent of the stock phrase "the place of the king where you are" in the vassal correspondence (*ašru šarri ša ittīka*; see Introduction, sect. 5).

11. Since the main question raised by the Babylonian king concerned his sister's welfare, *šulmāni* (for correct *šulmāna*) seems best taken as "well-being," a meaning well-attested in the Western Periphery (see *AHw*, p. 1268).

12. *ta-qa-ap* (cf. *AHw*, p. 919): the assumption of a short form of *taqabbi* (also lines 40, 42), proposed by Kühne, p. 10, n. 42, does not seem necessary. *a-na na-ma-ra*, for *a-na a-ma-ra* (cf. the common expression *ṭēm* x *amāru*), with *CAD*, N/1, p. 219; otherwise, *AHw*, p. 726.

13. ^{kur}*ga-*⟨*aš*⟩*-ga-ia*: see E. von Schuler, *Die Kaskäer* (Berlin, 1965), p. 81. Cf. *EA* 31:25–27.

14. The sign after *it* is uncertain: KI (Knudtzon), very doubtful; *sa*[*i*]*-ma* (Knudtzon's other proposal), impossible (Gordon).

15. If *ša* a[n-n]i (Knudtzon) is correct, "as to what belongs to an answer"? According to Gordon, there is room only for *ip-t*[*i*].

16. m[u-ta/ut-še].

17. [lu-ú i-de$_4$], end of line 45; end of 46, perhaps *a*-[ḫa-at-ka bal-ṭa-at], "[*your*] *si*[*ster is alive*"; end of 47, [. . . aš-ku-un-še], "[. . . *I have made her*] a mistress of the household"; line 50, "*more than* the wives [*of neighboring kings* . . .]"?

18. On our understanding of *ša* KI-*ka*, one would expect something like *lapnat*, "is poor," *ḫašḫat*, "is in need," or the like; space is small.

19. l[i-me]-⌜ti⌝-[ia], quite probable, was proposed by Kühne, p. 51, n. 237, and also by Gordon.

20. ⌜š⌝a-*ru-ti*: the reading is virtually certain (also Gordon). Perhaps the language is more correct than assumed and the adjectives are attributive rather than predicative; if so, "as to the rich (and) mighty kings. . . ."

21. If LU-*ta* (so Gordon), then either *ra-ši-lu-ta*, "the lucky ones" (cf. *AHw*, p. 961; ". . . you give your daughters to . . ."), or *ṭàb-ta*, "(to acquire) good thing(s)" (Gordon, though, has "to acquire friendship," also possible). However, I could not see the top horizontal that Knudtzon copied (*VAB* 2/1, p. 1001, no. 6), and UR seemed more likely, and therefore *liq-ta* (*CAD*, L, p. 206). This was also Artzi's reading (see *CAD*), but more recently he has favored *ra-ši-lu-ta* (*La femme*

[see Introduction, n. 62], p. 25, n. 15). The venality implied by *liqta* seems more to the point in context.

22. Also possible: "As for your writing me (that) I have gone back on [lit. abandoned] the words of my father, you do not cite. . . ." However, with very few exceptions, the word order is verb-object. Moreover, instead of the expected *tēzib* one must assume a virtual object-clause. The interjection *ezib* seems preferable, even though otherwise unknown in the periphery.

23. [ù la] *el-te-qe*.

24. túgME(MA$_6$/BA$_{13}$).ḪI.A, *nalbašu*, probably a cloak or mantle of some sort ("solemn garb" is a gloss); add this passage and *PRU* 3, p. 183:10, to the dictionaries.

25. 71 [UGU ša i-n]a K[U]R *ša-ni-ti*. Long-established custom required the king to welcome royal envoys to his table as often as their rank demanded, to furnish board and lodging, and to give them gifts; see *ARMT* 21, pp. 506ff., and *AÉM* 1/2, pp. 142f.

26. *a-na a-*[bi-k]a (Gordon).

27. Perhaps the abstract *sarrūtu* (*AHw,* p. 1031), but in line 87 *sà-ra-ti* (*sarrāti*) favors the alternative interpretation, masculine plural adjective.

28. The [z]a "may well be scratches; therefore (*anandinšunu*)-[*ti*] is possible (and no *sà-ru-ti*)" (Gordon). If so, perhaps ⸢*i*⸣-[dá]b-*bu-bu*.

29. *ú-ul ad*-d[i-in a-na m]u-ḫi-*šu-nu*.

30. Or "they gave" (indefinite plural), "that was given."

31. *ḫu-*⸢*ra-t*⸣*a*$_5$ is a possible reading (Gordon).

32. Either *ud-dú-ni* (*CAD,* I/J, p. 30b) or *ut-tu-ni* (*atû,* "to find, discover") is possible.

33. The feminine gender of the suffix is difficult (the things or words said? confusion of gender?). Perhaps better: "do not listen to (any) evil man (*lem-na*)."

34. On the dual suffix, see *BASOR* 211 (1973) pp. 52f.

35. *šumma* is understood as introducing a negative assertory oath.

36. Lines 88ff. are very obscure. I assume that in the Babylonian king's complaint, he speaks of the Pharaoh in both the third and second person. Line 91, *tu-ṭe*$_4$*-pí-il-šu-nu*.

37. *ana šu-ti-ri-ka* (for correct *šu-tu-ri-ka*; a West Semitism): following Pintore, *Matrimonio,* p. 158, n. 88, which I take to imply that the Pharaoh refers to a request by the Babylonian king for an Egyptian girl whom he wishes to have anointed (cf. *EA* 11:17ff.); otherwise, Pintore, *Matrimonio,* p. 27; p. 169, n. 348.

38. Against NI = *šamnu* is the writing NI.ḪI.A in lines 70 and 96, and the impossibility of making any sense of the following *Za-aḫ*. For the assumed first person plural (*niṣâḫ*), cf. *nušezziz* in line 45. Perhaps "we are distressed"; on this meaning of *ṣâḫu,* see Veenhof, *JEOL* 24 (1975–76) pp. 107ff.

EA 2

Proposals of marriage

TEXT: VAT 148 + 2706.
COPIES: WA 2 + WA 5; *VS* 11, 1.

[Say] to Mimmuwareya, the king of Egypt, [my] brother: Thus [K]a[d]aš[m]a[n-En]lil, the king of Kara[duniyaš]. For me and [m]y country all goes very [well]. For you, for [yo]ur wi[ves], for your sons, fo[r your *magnates*], your horses, your chariots, and your entire country, may all go very we[ll].

6–11 With regard to my brother's writing me ab[out *marriage*],[1] saying, "[*I desir*]*e* [*your daughter*],"[2] why should you not marry (her)? [. . .] . . . My daughters are available, [*but their husbands must be a king o*]*r* of royal blood. [*These are the only ones whom I accept for my daughters. No king has ever gi*]*ven* [*his daughters to anyone not of royal blood*].[3]

12–13 [*Your daughters are available. Why have you not* g]iven me (one)?[4] [. . .] . . . [. . .]

Reverse

1–5 [. . .] fine horses [. . .] 20 wooden [. . .] . . . *of gold,* 6–9 *120 shekels* [. . . I send] to you as [your] greeting-[gift]. 60 shekels[5] of lapis-lazu[li I send as the greeting-gift of] my [*si*]*s*[*te*]*r*; [. . .] your wife.

NOTES

1. *a-n*[*a* a-ḫu-za-ti]: following Kühne, p. 55, n. 63.
2. [DUMU.MUNUS-ka a-ḫa-aš-še-e]ḫ: following Kühne, ibid.
3. 9 [mu-tu-ši-na lu-ú LUGAL ù l]u-⌜ú⌝ *ze-er* LUGAL *šu-nu* 10 [šu-nu-ma ša a-na DUMU.MUNUS.MEŠ-ia e-le-eq-qa-a]š-*šu-nu-ti* 11 [LUGAL ma-am-ma a-na la ze-er LUGAL DUMU.MUNUS.MEŠ-šu ul *i*]*d-di-in-ši-na-ti.* These are very conjectural restorations based on the assumption that the Babylonian king wishes to stress the high standards of his own dynasty's customs, while also implying that to demand more would be unreasonable. He would thus lay the grounds for his own request of an Egyptian princess; cf. *EA* 4.
4. [DUMU.MUNUS.MEŠ-ka i-ba-aš-ša-a am-mi-ni la *ta-a*]*d-di-na*: cf. Ungnad, *OLZ,* 1916, col. 181.
5. 1 ŠU GÍN (Gordon).

EA 3

Marriage, grumblings, a palace-opening

TEXT: C 4743 (12210).
COPY: WA 1.

[S]ay [to Nim]u'wareya, the king of Eg[ypt, m]y [brother]: [Thus Kad]ašman-Enlil, the king of Karaduniyaš, your brother. [For me all indeed goes w]ell. For you, your household, your wives, [and for you]r [sons],[1] your country, your chariots, your horses, your [mag]nates may all go very well.

4–12 With regard to the girl, my daughter,[2] about whom you wrote to me in view of marriage, she has become a woman;[3] she is nubile. Just send a delegation to fetch her. Previously, my father would send a messenger to you, and you would not detain him for long. You qui[ck]ly[4] sent him off, and you would also send here to my father a beautiful greeting-gift.[5]

13–22 But now when I sent a messenger to you, you have detained him for six years, and you have sent me as my greeting-gift, the only thing in six years, 30 minas of gold that *looked like silver.*[6] That gold was melted down in the presence of Kasi, your messenger, and he was a witness. When you celebrated a great festival, you did not send your messenger to me, saying, "Come t[o eat an]d drink."[7] No[r did you send me] my greeting-gift[8] in connection with the festival. It was just 30 minas of gold that you [sent me].[9] My [gi]ft [*does not amoun*]*t to what* [*I have given you*] *every yea*[*r*].[10]

23–31 I have built a [*ne*]*w* [*house*].[11] *I*[*n my house*] I have built a [l]arge [. . .]. Your [mes]sengers have see[n *the house and the . . . , and are pleased. No*]*w*[12] I am going to hav[e] a house-opening. Come [*yourself*] to [eat an]d drink with me.[13] [*I shall not act* a]s[14] you yourself did. [25 *men* and] 25 women, altogether 50 *i*[*n my service*],[15] I send [to you *in connection with the house-opening*].[16]

32–34 [. . .] for 10 wooden chariots,[17] [and 10 teams of hor]ses I send to you as your greeting-gift.

NOTES

1. [DUMU.MEŠ-*k*]*a*: following von Soden, p. 427, confirmed by collation (also Gordon).

2. DUMU.MUNUS.A.NI-*ia*: following Ungnad, *OLZ*, 1916, col. 181, with von Soden and also Kühne, p. 54, n. 250; otherwise, Pintore, *Matrimonio*, p. 26. See also *EA* 287:26 for pronominal suffix as part of logogram, as commonly in the Old Babylonian period.

3. MUNUS = *amīltu* or *sinništu*? See *CAD,* A/2, p. 47b, and S, p. 292 (discussion).

4. *ḫa-m*⌜*u*⌝-[*u*]*t*-⌜*t*⌝*a*: Gordon saw all the signs "quite clearly."

5. On lines 9–12 see von Soden, p. 427.

6. Following *AHw,* p. 227, and *CAD,* E, p. 196. Other versions: "of the quality of silver" (Kühne, p. 54); "worked with (KI = *itti*) silver" (Landesberger in Gordon). Egyptian gold had a high percentage of silver, giving it a grayish cast (A. Lucas, *Ancient Egyptian Materials and Industries*[3] [London, 1948], pp. 257ff.).

7. [*akul*] ⌜*ù*⌝ *šiti* (Gordon).

8. *šulmānī,* "my (greeting-)gift": following Kühne, p. 54, n. 252. The festival was undoubtedly one of three *sd*-festivals celebrated by Amenophis III in his thirtieth, thirty-fourth, and thirty-seventh years (Kühne, p. 254).

9. *tu*-[*še-bi-la*]: following von Soden, p. 427.

10. [*šu*]-*ul-ma-ni ša-a e-em* MU.1. [KAM ad-di-na-ak-ku ul ma-ṣi]-*i*: free restoration.

11. [É eš-*š*]*a*: cf. *EA* 5:13, 19. Von Soden, p. 427, proposed [*a-nu-um-ma bī*]*ta,* but there is not enough room for this restoration, and *anumma* is not used in Middle Babylonian. At the end of the line *ina libbi* fits the traces very well.

12. 26 [i-na-an-*n*]*a*. End of line 25, free restoration: *ītam*[*rū*-ma ḫa-du-ú].

13. 27 [ù at-ta] *alkamma ittīya* 28 [*a-ku-ul*] [*ù*⌝ (head of final vertical visible, Gordon) *šiti.*

14. [ul ep-pu-uš *š*]*a*.

15. *a*-š[i-ib maḫrī/pānī-ia): a phonetic spelling, *a*-m[i-li], does not seem likely.

16. [a-na te-ru-ba-ti]: cf. Kühne, p. 55, n. 259.

17. "Wooden chariots" (also *EA* 9:37; 19:84) were perhaps the light two-wheeled battle chariot, as opposed to the heavier four-wheeled wagons that were used for transport and were reinforced with metal fittings; cf. the same distinction in Egyptian and Edel's remarks in Manfred Görg, ed., *Fontes atque Pontes: Eine Festgabe für Hellmut Brunner,* Ägypten und Altes Testament 5 (Wiesbaden, 1983), pp. 104f.

EA 4

Royal deceit and threats

TEXT: VAT 1657.
COPIES: WA 3; *VS* 11, 2.

1–3 . . .[1]

4–22 [*Moreove*]*r,*[2] you, my brother, when I wrote [to you][3] about marrying your daughter, in accordance with your practice of not gi[ving][4] (a daughter), [wrote to me], saying, "From time immemorial no daughter of the king of Egy[pt] is given to anyone." Why *n*[*ot*]?[5] You are a king; you d[o] as you please. Were you to give (a daughter), who would s[ay] anything? Since I was told of this message, I wrote as follows *t[o my brother]*, saying, "[*Someone's*][6] grown daughters, beautiful women, must be available. Send me a beautiful woman as if she were [you]r daughter.[7] Who is going to say, 'She is no daughter of the king!'?" But holding to your decision, you have not sent me anyone. Did not you yourself seek brotherhood and amity, and so wrote me about marriage that we might come closer to each other, and did ⟨not⟩ I, for my part, write you about marriage for this very same reason, i.e., brotherhood and amity, that we might come closer to each other?[8] Why, then, did my brother not send me just one woman? Should I, perhaps, since you did not send me a woman, refuse you a woman, just as you did to me, and *n[ot send her]*?[9] But my daughters being available, I will not refuse [*one*] to y[ou].[10]

23–35 Perhaps, too, when I [*wrote you*] about marriage, [*and*] when I wrote you about the animals, ... [. . .] Now, you *need* not *ac[cept]*[11] the offspring[12] of my daughter whom I shall s[end to you, but] *s[end me]* *any* animals *requested of you.*

36–50 And as to the gold I wrote you about, send me *whatever i[s on hand]*, (as) much (as possible), before your messenger [*comes*] to me, right now, in all haste, this summer, either in the month of Tammuz or in the month of Ab,[13] so I can finish the work that I am engaged on. If during this summer, in the months of Tammuz or Ab, you send[14] the gold I wrote you about, I will give you my daughter. So please[15] send me the gold you [*feel prompted t*]*o.* But if in the months of Tammuz or Ab you do not send me the gold and (with it) I do not finish the work I am engaged on, what would be the point of your being pleased to send me (gold)? Once I have finished the work I am engaged on, what need will I have of gold? Then you could send me 3,000 talents of gold, and I would not accept it.[16] I would send it back to you, and I would not gi[ve] my daughter in marriage.[17]

NOTES

1. The greeting and perhaps several more lines are completely destroyed; lines 1–3 are too fragmentary for translation. That *EA* 4 belongs to the Amenophis III-Kadašman-Enlil correspondence is not completely certain; see Kühne, p. 56.

2. [ap-pu-na-*m*]*a*: [a-nu-um-*m*]*a* (Knudtzon) is not used in Middle Babylonian; see *EA* 3, n. 11.

3. *áš-pu-r[a-ak-ku ta-al/tal-ta-ap-ra]*: first word, with Ungnad, *OLZ*, 1916, col. 181, and von Soden, p. 428. However, since temporal clauses regularly precede, or, as here, are inserted within, the main clause (GAG §169b), the main verb must have followed.

4. *kī lā na-d*[*a-ni-im-ma*]: following Knudtzon and Aro, *StOr* 20, p. 135; otherwise, von Soden, p. 428.

5. *am-mi-ni* l[a innaddin]: beginning of a horizontal wedge visible, and beneath it, a hole, not writing.

6. GAL.M[EŠ ša ma-am-ma]: MEŠ not collated (cf. copy *VS* 11).

7. *ki-*⌜*i*⌝ D[UMU MUNUS-*k*]*a*: following von Soden, p. 428, except for *š*[*a* . . .], for which there is not enough room.

8. Because of the preterite (*ašpurakku*, line 18), lines 17f. must be taken as a question; see Aro, *StOr* 20, p. 81. Either *ul* (line 15) is still felt and understood in this clause, or, as seems more likely, we should read *ù a-na-ku* ⟨*ul*⟩. . . . That *ul* is used rather than *lā* is undoubtedly due to the fact that lines 15–18 are rhetorical questions. On the grammar of rhetorical questions, see also *EA* 11, n. 18.

9. l[a ušebbilši]: following von Soden, p. 428.

10. *a-ka-al-la-a*[*k-ku-uš-ši*]: following ibid.

11. *ta-ṣa-a*[*b-ba-at* ù]: cf. ibid.

12. Literally, "seed"; for a woman's seed, cf. *zēr mārtīya*, "my daughter's seed" (*KBo* 1, 8:31).

13. The fourth (June–July) and fifth (July–August) months of the Babylonian calendar.

14. *tultēbila*[*m*]: following von Soden, p. 428.

15. *ina ṭūbi*: following Ungnad, *OLZ*, 1916, col. 182. Pintore, *Matrimonio*, p. 155, n. 121, sees in the expression as used in line 46 reference to a gift that has not been requested, but the distinction is hard to reconcile with the expression in line 43.

16. Three thousand talents is a huge amount of gold, roughly 100 tons.

17. After a space of three lines, traces suggest additional writing, probably a list of gifts; see *VAB* 2/1, p. 74.

EA 5

Gifts of Egyptian furniture for the Babylonian palace

TEXT: BM 29787 + C (12195).
COPIES: BB 4 + WA 17.

[Thus Nibmuar]ey[a,[1] Great King, the king of Egypt. Say to] Ka[dašman-Enlil, the king of Karadu]niya[š,[2] my brother: For m]e all goes ⟨well⟩. F[or you may all go well. For you]r [household, your] wives, [your sons, yo]ur [magnates], yo[ur] troops, [yo]ur [horses], your [chariots], and i[n your countries, may all go] well. [For me al]l goes well. For my household, [my] wives, [my sons], my magnates, my ma[ny] troops, my [horses], my chariots, and in [m]y [countries] all goes very, very well.

13–33 I have [*just*][3] heard that you have built some n[ew] quarters.[4] I am sending herewith some furnishings for your house. Indeed I shall be preparing everything *possible*[5] before the arrival of your messenger who is bringing your daughter. When[6] your messenger returns, I will send (them) to [yo]u. I herewith send you, in the charge of Šutti, a greeting-gift of things for the new house: 1 bed[7] of ebony, overlaid with ivory and gold; 3 beds of ebony, overlaid with gold; 1 *uruššu* of ebony, overlaid with gold; 1 lar[ge] chair [o]f ebony, overlaid with gold; 5 chairs of [eb]ony, overlaid with gold; 4 chairs of ebo[ny], overlaid with gold.[8] These things, the weight of all the gold: 7 minas, 9 shekels, of gold. The weight of the silver: 1 [mi]na, 8½ shekels, of silver.[9] (In addition), 10 footrests of ebony; [. . .] of ebony, overlaid with gold; [. . .] footrests of ivory, overlaid with gold; [. . .] . . . of gold. [*Total*[10] x] minas, 10 and 7 shekels, of gold.

NOTES

1. [. . . *r*]*e-i*[*a* . . .] (Gordon). Note the form of address (see sect. 4 of the Introduction).

2. Probably not enough room for LUGAL GAL, "Great King," at the beginning of line 3; see Seux, *Épithètes royales akkadiennes et sumériennes* (Paris, 1967), p. 299, n. 162.

3. Restore either *inanna* or *anumma* (cf. *EA* 1:10).

4. É.ḪI.A. GI[BIL]: in line 19, É GIBIL is certain, and the traces here fit GIBIL perfectly.

5. *mimma ma-a-*⌜la⌝: last sign possibly *ad* (so Knudtzon, *VAB* 2/1, p. 76, note n, denied by Gordon) or even *ta*; if *mala,* unusual orthography. Note the stock expression *šūšuru ana pānī,* "to prepare before the arrival," so common in the vassal letters (see the Introduction, sect. 5, and n. 100). *CAD,* E, p. 358a, followed by Durand, *ARMT* 21, p. 456, n. 16: "but now, I will prepare whatever your messenger selects." This gives *ana pānī* a meaning for which I know no parallel. *CAD,* M/1, p. 145a–b, confuses *šūšuru* and *wuššuru,* "to release."

6. Note the use of *šumma* as a temporal conjunction, as at Boghazköy, in a letter characterized by the Hittite ductus and the Hittite form of address.

7. The join with the Cairo fragment begins here.

8. Lines 24–25 are conflated in the WA copy.

9. This is the first reference to silver.

10. [ŠU.NÍGIN . . .]

EA 6

An offer of friendship

TEXT: VAT 149.
COPIES: WA 4; *VS* 11, 3.

Sa[y t]o *Nimmuwarea*,[1] *the k*[*ing of Egypt*], my brother: Thus Burra-Buriyaš, the king of [Karaduniyaš], your brother. For me all goes we[ll]. For you, your household, your wives, [your] sons, your country, your magnates, [yo]ur horses, your chariots, may all go w[ell].

8–12 Just as previously you and m[y] father were friend[ly] to one another,[2] you and I [should] now [be friendly] t[o one another].[3] Between us, anythin[g][4] else whatsoever is not even to be ment[ioned].[5]

13–17 Wri[te me] for what you want from my country so that it may be taken to you, and I will write you for what I want from your country so that it may be taken [to me].[6]

17–19 [. . .] [*I*] will trust yo[u . . .]. Write me so that *it ma*[*y be taken to you*].

20–22 And as [your] greeting-gift [. . .] and 1 [. . .] . . . *I s*[*e*]*n*[*d you*].

NOTES

1. ᵐni-mu-a/wa/ut-re-a/ia: alternative readings; see Kühne, p. 129, n. 642.

2. At the end of line 9, delete *ù*: following von Soden, p. 428.

3. At the end of line 10, add [. . . *lu ṭa-ba-nu*]: von Soden, ibid.; cf. *EA* 8:11f. It must have been written at least partly on the reverse, or perhaps on the line below.

4. a-ma-tu-u[m]: a rare instance of mimation; cf. *EA* 3:12; 4:46; Aro, *StOr* 20, p. 32. *amatum šanītum-ma*, perhaps "a hostile word" (*AHw*, p. 1164).

5. *iq*-[*qa-ab-bi*]: following von Soden, p. 428; see also Schroeder, *OLZ*, 1917, col. 105.

6. *lilqû*-[*ni*]: following von Soden, p. 428.

EA 7

A lesson in geography

TEXT: VAT 150 (not collated).
COPIES: WA 7; *VS* 11, 4.
TRANSLATION: Oppenheim, *LFM*, pp. 113ff.

[Say to Napḫu]rureya,[1] Great King, king of Egy[pt, my brother]:[2] Thus Burra-Buriya[š, Great King, kin]g of Karaduniyaš, [your] brot[her. For m]e and my household, for my horses and [m]y ch[ariots, for] my magnates and my country all goes ver[y well].

6–7 For my brother and his household, for his horses and [his] c[hariots], for his magnates and his country ma[y all go] very [well].

8–13 From the time the messenger of my brother *ar*[*rived here*],[3] I have not been well, and so *on no occa*[*sion*][4] has his messenger eaten food and [drunk] spirits [in my com]pany. If you ask [. . .] . . . ,[5] your messenger, he will [tell you that] I have not been well and that, *as far as my rec*[*overy*] *is concerned,*[6] I am [*still* b]y no means *re*[*stored to health*].[7] 14–25 [Furthermore], since I was not well and my brother [showed me no] conc[ern],[8] I for my part became an[gry][9] with my brother, saying, "Has my brother not hea[rd] that I am ill? Why has he sho[wn] me no concern? Why has he sent no messenger here and *visi*[*ted* me]?"[10] My brother's messenger addressed me, s[aying], "(It) is not a place close by so your brother can hear (about you) and send you greetings. The country is far away. Who is going to tell your brother so he can immediately send you greetings? Would your brother hear that you are ill and still not send you his messenger?" 26–32 I for my part addressed him as follows, saying, "For my brother, a Great King, is there really a faraway country and a close-by one?" He for his part addressed me [as] follows, saying, "Ask your own messenger whether the country is far away and as a result your brother did not hear (about you) and did not send (anyone) to greet you."[11] Now, since I asked my own messenger and he said to me that the journey is far, I was not angry (any longer), I said no [more].[12] 33–41 Furthermore, as I am told, in my brother's country everything is available and my brother needs absolutely nothing. Furthermore, in my country everything too is available and I for my part nee[d] absolutely nothing. We have (however) inherited good relations of long standing from (earlier) kings, and so we should sen[d][13] greetings to each other. It is these same relations that shall be lasting between us. My [greet]ings [*I will send* t]o yo[u, *and your greetings you shall send to me*]. 42–48 [. . .] M[y] greetings [. . .] and your greetings . . . [. . .] 49–62 You no[w, *before es*]*corting* (*him on his way*),[14] have detain[ed] my messenger for two [*years*].[15] I informed your messenger and sen[t him] (on his way). Inform my messenger immediately so he may co[me to me].[16] Furthermore, as I am also told, the journey is diffi[cult],[17] water cut off, and the weather ho[t]. I am not sending many beautiful greeting-gifts. I send to my brother 4 minas of beautiful lapis lazuli as a *routine*[18] greeting-gift. In addition, I send my brother 5 teams of horses. As soon as the weather improves, my next messenger to come I will have bring many beautiful greeting-gifts to my brother. Furthermore, whatever my brother wants, let my brother just write me so it can be taken from the house.[19] 63–72 Being engaged on a work, I write to my brother. May my brother send me much fine gold so I can use it on my work. But the gold that my brother sends me, my brother should not turn over to the charge of any deputy. My brother should make a [personal] check, then my brother should seal and send it to me. Certainly[20] my brother did not check the earlier (shipment of) gold that my brother sent to me. It was only a deputy of my brother who sealed and sent it to me. When I pu[t] the 40 minas of gold that were brought to me into a kiln, not (even) [*10*, I sw]ear,[21] appear[ed]. 73–82 [Furth]ermore, [tw]ice has a caravan of Ṣalmu, my messenger whom I sent to you, been robb[ed].[22] The first one Biriyawaza[23] rob[bed, and] his [sec]ond caravan Pamaḫu, [a *gov*]*ernor* of yours in a *vassalage*,[24] robb[ed]. [*When*] is my brother [going to *adjudicate*] this case?[25] [*As*] my messenger *sp*[*oke*][26] before my brother, (so) [n]ow[27] may Ṣalmu *sp*[*eak*][28] before my brother. His [thi]ngs[29] should be restored t[o him] and [he] should be compensa[ted] for his losses.

NOTES

1. For Amenophis IV as the addressee of this letter, see Kühne, p. 60, n. 292.

2. At the beginning of line 2, restore ŠEŠ-*ia*; for the position, cf. *EA* 6:2. Where Burna-Buriaš calls himself brother, he addresses the Egyptian king in the same way (*EA* 6, 8–9, 11).

3. *ik*-[šu-da] would be less crowded than *ik*-[šu-da-an-ni] (Knudtzon).

4. *a-a-i*-[ka-(am-)ma]: following von Soden, p. 428. Oppenheim seems to emend the text so that Burna-Buriaš says that no foreign messenger, non-Egyptian or Egyptian, had dined with him; see Kühne, p. 61, n. 295. On the banquets for messengers, see *EA* 1, n. 25.

5. von Soden, p. 428, proposes [^{m}Ḫa-a]-*ú*; cf. *EA* 11:19, rev. 13f.

6. *ana na*-a[b-la-ṭi]: if *na*-p[a-aš libbi] (von Soden, ibid.), one would expect to see traces of the vertical (cf., however, *pa* in *EA* 8:22), and the expression refers to mood or sentiment, not to bodily health. Oppenheim: ". . . that I nearly lost my life, and that nothing could help me" (the assumed text is not clear).

7. [a-di-na] *m*[*i*]-*im-ma-ma la uš*-[ta-la/li-mu]; on the assumed *uštalla/imu* rather than *ultalla/imu*, see Aro, *StOr* 20, pp. 37f. Another proposal: [Ú (šammu)] . . . *la uš*-[né-ša-an-ni], "and no medicine has given me any cure" (von Soden, ibid.).

8. *re-e-š*[*i la iš-šu-ú*]: the enclitic *-ma* at the end of the previous clause favors taking the following clause as coordinate, and therefore not *rēš*[*í ul iš-ši*] (von Soden, ibid., following Ungnad, *OLZ*, 1916, col. 182).

9. *am*-[*ta-la*]: not *am*-[*la*] (von Soden, p. 429), for in Middle Babylonian

letters the perfect is the normal form of past narrative, as throughout this letter. In line 32, *amla* because of the negative *ul.*

10. *i-mu-*[ra-an-ni], presumably visit by delegation. If *i-mu-*[ra] is right (Knudtzon), then "*pro*[*vided for me*]"?

11. *ana šulmīka,* "for your *šulmu,*" might also mean "for your health"; probably neither version should be excluded.

12. On the syntax of *girru rūqatu,* see von Soden, p. 429. For a slightly different interpretation, see Veenhof, *JEOL* 27 (1981–82) p. 67, n. 1. *ul am-la as-s*[*a-k*]*u-*[*ut*]: following Gordon.

13. *ni-ša-ap-pa-*[*ra/ar*]: it is not clear why we should create an anacoluthon—"the good relations which we have received from the kings in earlier times, so that we send greetings to each other, these same good relations . . ."—and restore -[ru] (Ungnad, *OLZ,* 1916, col. 182, followed by von Soden, p. 429). Burna-Buriaš prefaces his proposal of continued good relations with remarks that establish how disinterested both parties are. If there are to be greetings with the necessary accompanying gifts, they are not inspired by need.

14. [la-am t]e-*re-ed-du-ú*: following von Soden, ibid. Provision of an escort for messengers was customary. For the Old Babylonian period, at Mari, see *CAD,* A/1, p. 343; *ARMT* 21, pp. 509, 514; *AÉM* 1/2, no. 511:20ff. In *EA,* see 30, n. 2.

15. *ši-it-ta* [šanāti]: following von Soden, p. 429.

16. *li-i*[*l-li-ka*]: following von Soden, ibid. The information is the answer, perhaps quite perfunctory, to the message received; cf. *EA* 29:111.

17. The enclitic in *kī iqbûnim-ma* probably looks back to *kī iqbûni* in line 33, and therefore is rendered by "also." *da-an-n*[*a-at*], with von Soden, ibid., unless the enclitic coordinates clauses (for this possibility, see Römer, AOAT 12, p. 51, n. 5), and then *da-an-n*[*a-tu*$_4$/*tu*] (cf. *rūqatu* in line 32).

18. The gift *ša qāti* seems opposed to the many gifts not sent at the moment; cf. *ša qātim* in Old Assyrian, "normal quality, current quality" (*CAD,* Q, p. 198), and at Mari (*ARMT* 21, p. 252, n. 16; p. 272, n. 28). That the weight of the stone is given implies, according to E. Porada, *AfO* 28 (1981–82) p. 7, n. 18, that the stone was unworked (see also *EA* 8:43; 10:43ff.). Tušratta, therefore, gave only jewelry.

19. Lit. "from their house." Since Burna-Buriaš hardly wishes to say that the gifts will come from others' houses, the suffix must refer to the indefinite plural subject of the verb.

20. *ki-ša* (*kīša*): see the dictionaries; for its influence on tenses, see Aro, *StOr* 20, p. 83.

21. [10 *š*]*a-ar-ru-um-ma*: the asseverative *šarrumma* (Knudtzon) fits the context perfectly (originally, "by the king"; S. Parpola, AOAT 5/2, p. 97) and implies a small number in the break (*10* is only a guess); cf. *EA* 10:19f. Otherwise von Soden, p. 430, followed by *CAD,* B, 113: [KÙ.GI b]a-*ar-ru-um-ma,* "pure gold."

22. *ḫa-ab-t*[*a-at*]: following von Soden, ibid.

23. Written ᵐ*bi-ri-ia-ma-za.*

24. Pamaḫu may be an Egyptian title misunderstood as a personal name; see Albright, *JEA* 23 (1937) p. 200, n. 4, who thought it the Egyptian equivalent of *rābiṣu,* seeing it also in *EA* 162:74. Edel, *JNES* 7 (1948) p. 24, distinguished

between *EA* 7:76 (personal name) and 162:74 (title). Is *ki-iṣ-ri* a mistake for *mi-iṣ-ri*, "[a *pre*]*fect* in your country, the country of Egypt"? An even greater enormity, right under the Pharaoh's nose!

25. [ma-ti] . . . i-[da-an]: following von Soden, p. 430.
26. *id*-[bu-bu]: following von Soden, ibid. Line 80: *li-id*-[bu-ub].
27. [*i-na*]-*an-na*: following von Soden, ibid.
28. See n. 26.
29. [*ú-d*]*e-e-šu*: following von Soden, ibid.

EA 8

Merchants murdered, vengeance demanded

TEXT: VAT 152.
COPIES: WA 8; *VS* 11, 5.
TRANSLATION: Ebeling, pp. 371f.

Sa[y to] Napḫu'rure[ya], the king of Egypt, my brother: Thus Burra-Buriyaš, the king of Kara[duniyaš], your brother. For me all goes well. For you, your country, your household, your wives, yo[ur] sons, your magnates, your horses, your chariots, may all go very well.

8–21 My brother and I made a mutual declaration of friendship, and this is what we said: "Just as our fathers were friends[1] with one another, so will we be friends with one another." Now, my merchants[2] who were on their way with Aḫu-ṭabu, were detained in Canaan for business matters. After Aḫu-ṭabu went on to my brother, in Ḫinnatuna of Canaan, Šum-Adda, the son of Balumme, and Šutatna, the son of Šaratum[3] of Akka, having sent their men,[4] killed my merchants and took away [th]eir money. 22–33 [I] send [. . .] . . . to *y*[*o*]*u post*[*haste*].[5] Inqu[ire from him so] he can inform yo[u. C]anaan is your country, and [*its*] king[s are *your servants*]. In your country I have been despoiled. Bring [them] to account[6] and make compensat[ion] for the money that they took away. Put to death the men who put my servants [to] death,[7] and so avenge their blood. And if you do not put these men to death, they are going to kill again, be it a caravan of mine or your own messengers, and so messengers between us will thereby be cut off. 34–42 And if they try to deny this to you,[8] Šum-Adda, having blocked the passage of one man of mine,[9] retained him in his company, and another man, having been forced into service[10] by Šutatna of Akka, is still serving him. These men sh[ould be] brought to you so you can investigate, inquire [*whether they are de*]*ad*,[11] and thus become informed. 43–47 [As a greet]ing-gift I send you 1 mina of lapis lazuli.

Se[nd off] my [mess]enger immediately so I may kno[w] my brother's [dec]ision.[12] Do not deta[in] my [mess]enger. Let him be off [to me imm]ediately.[13]

NOTES

1. End of line 11, written on reverse, *ṭa-a-bu*; see Schroeder, *OLZ*, 1915, col. 175.

2. The implications of the king's calling them "*my* merchants" are not clear; see Brinkman, in Garelli, ed., *Le Palais et la Royauté* (Paris, 1974), p. 400, n. 34.

3. The scribe, or his informant, interchanged the vowels in the first syllable of the names of the two rulers.

4. LÚ.MEŠ = *amēlī* (also lines 28, 30, 40); cf. von Soden, p. 430.

5. 22 [x-(x)]-x *a-na* pa-[ni-k]a *ki-i* [ka-al-li-e]: at the beginning of the line the very clear [. . .]-*ḫu* of *VS* is misleading; see Schroeder, *OLZ*, 1917, col. 165. The assumption that nothing followed *ki-i* in the rather large broken space at the end of the line is supported by neither the previous nor the following lines, and the resulting sense, "As soon as I send . . . , inquire . . ." (von Soden, p. 430; Aro, *StOr* 20, p. 148), does not seem satisfactory. It seems unlikely that the Babylonian king would put off to some future date sending the messenger who was to provide the Pharaoh with additional information. It is the bearer of the present letter who should have such a role. Cf. *kī kallê* in the Babylonian letters *EA* 10:38 and 11, rev. 18.

6. *su-ni-iq-*[*šu-nu-ti-ma*]: following von Soden, p. 430.

7. *i-*[*du-k*]*u*: following von Soden, ibid.

8. Following Ungnad, *OLZ*, 1916, col. 182; von Soden, p. 430; *CAD*, N/1, p. 165b. Denial can be refuted by two witnesses to the crime who are still available. Aro, *StOr* 20, pp. 144f., postulates a contamination from *šumma-šumma* ("or they will treat you hostilely").

9. Following *CAD*, N/1, p. 179b; cf. *šēpam nakāsum* in *ARMT* 4, 38:7′; 14, 86:27. If the Babylonian's feet had been literally cut off, it would have been an extraordinary indignity and hardly mentioned so casually.

10. *ina rēši kī ulzizzū*: following *AHw*, p. 974a.

11. k[i-i mi]-*tu*: von Soden, p. 431, proposed [amēla ša]-*tu*, but, as he admits, the form of the pronoun is otherwise unattested in the Middle Babylonian period. Besides, one expects a plural—"these men"—not a singular.

12. 44 . . . *ku-*[*uš-ši-da-š*]*u* 45 [*ṭe-e*]*-ma*: following von Soden, ibid. (but not *ṭè-e-ma*; cf. *EA* 7:51, 52; 9:32; 11, rev. 18).

13. *li-it-ta-a*[*l-ka*]: following von Soden, ibid.

EA 9

Ancient loyalties, new requests

TEXT: BM 29785.
COPY: BB 2.
PHOTOGRAPH: BB, pl. 24.

Say to Nibḫurrereya, the king of Egy[pt, my brother]:[1] Thus Burra-Buriyaš, the king of Karad[un]iyaš, your brother. For me all goes well. For you, your household, your wives, your sons, your country, your ma[g]nates, your horses, your chariots, may all go very well.

6–18 From the time my ancestors and your ancestors made a mutual declaration of friendship, they sen[t][2] beautiful greeting-gifts to each other, and refused no request for anything beautiful. My brother has now sent me 2 minas of gold as my greeting-gift. Now, ⟨i⟩f[3] gold is plentiful, send me as much as your ancestors (sent), but if it is scarce, send me half of what your ancestors (sent). Why have you sent me 2 minas of gold? At the moment my work on a temple is extensive, and I am quite busy with carrying it out. Send me much gold. And you for your part, whatever you want from my country, write me so that it may be taken to you.

19–38 In the time of Kurigalzu, my ancestor, all the Canaanites wrote here to him, saying, "C[om]e[4] to the border of the country so we can revolt and be allied [*wi*]*th*[5] you." My ancestor sent them this (reply), saying, "Forget about being allied with me. If you become enemies of the king of Egypt, and are allied with anyone else, will I not then come and plunder you? How can there be an alliance with me?" For the sake of your ancestor my ancestor did not listen to them. Now, as for my Assyrian vassals, I was not the one who sent them to you. Why on their own authority have they come to your country? If you love me,[6] they will conduct no business whatsoever. Send them off to me empty-handed. I send to you as your greeting-gift 3 minas of genuine lapis lazuli and 5 teams of horses for 5 wooden chariots.[7]

NOTES

1. On the addressee, either Amenophis IV or Tutankhamun (so taken here), see Introduction, n. 137. On the end of line 1, see *VAB* 2/2, p. 1585.

2. *ul-te-bi-i-lu-n*[*i*]: following Gordon.

3. *inanna-ma ḫurāṣu mād,* "Right now, (if) the gold is plentiful," is probably possible, but one then expects the same structure in the parallel clause. Hence *inanna* ⟨*šum*⟩-*ma* seems much more likely.

4. ⌜*ku-u*⌝[*š*]-*da-am-ma*: traces support this reading of von Soden, p. 431.

5. [it-t]i-*ka*: despite Knudtzon's correct observations (*VAB* 2/1, p. 90, n. a), this seems the only possible reading. The absence of any sign of the vertical could reflect a form like that in line 29 (*it-ti-ia*).

6. See Introduction, n. 59.

7. See *EA* 3, n. 17.

EA 10

Egyptian gold and carpenters

TEXT: BM 29786.

COPY: BB 3.

PHOTOGRAPH: BB, pl. 10.

[Say t]o [Napḫu]rar[ey]a,[1] the king of [Egypt: T]hus Burra-Buriyaš, the king of Karad[uniyaš]. For me all goes wel[l]. For you, for your household, for your wives, fo[r your *sons*], for your magnates, for your troops, for your chariots, for your horses, and for your country, may all go very well.

8–24 From the time of Karaindaš, since the messengers[2] of your ancestors came regularly to my ancestors, up to the present, they (the ancestors) have been friends. Now, though you and I are friends, 3 times have your messengers come to me and you have not sent me a single beautiful greeting-gift, nor have I for my part sent you a beautiful greeting-gift. (I am one for whom nothing is scarce, and you are one for whom nothing is scarce.)[3] As for your messenger whom you sent to me, the 20 minas of gold that were brought here were not all there. When they put it into the kiln, not 5 minas of gold appeared.[4] [The . . . th]at did appear, on cooling off looked like *ashes.* Was [*the gold ev*]*er identi-fi*[*ed*] (as gold)?[5] [. . .] friends with *e*[*ach other*] [. . .] . . . 25–28 [. . .] 29–42 [. . .] of a wild ox for . . . [. . .][6] when your messenger . . . [. . .][7] let him bring to me. There are skilled carpenters[8] where you are. Let them represent a wild animal, land or aquatic, lifelike,[9] so that the hide is exactly like that of a live animal. Let your messenger bring it to me. But if there are some old ones already on hand, then as soon as Šin-dišugab, my messenger, reaches you, let him immediately, posthaste, *borrow chariot*[*s*][10] and get here. Let them make some n[e]w ones for future delivery, and then when my messenger comes here with your messenger, let them bring (them) here together. 43–49 I send as your greeting-gift 2 minas of lapis lazuli, and concerning your daughter Mayati,[11] having heard (about her), I send to her as her greeting-gift a necklace of *cricket-(shaped)* gems, of lapis lazuli, 1048 their number.

And when your messenger [*comes*] along with Šindišugab, *I will* make [. . .] and have (it) *brough*[*t to h*]*er.*[12]

NOTES

1. [a-n]a [na-ap-ḫu]r-*ra*-⌈*re*⌉ -[i]a/a (Gordon saw more of *ḫur* than I could). Of the *na-ap* in BB, Gordon wrote that there are "no traces of original wedges, completely obliterated by modern pin scratches on rubbed surface of tablet—so confirmed by Mr. Bateman of B[ritish] M[useum] who examined surface under a microscope."

2. DUMU.MEŠ = *mārū*: following von Soden, p. 431.

3. This parenthetical remark stresses the independence of the parties and thereby the symbolism of the exchange of gifts; cf. *EA* 7, n. 13. The usual interpretation—according to which it is stated here that the result of neither one's sending the other party a gift has been "I had nothing precious, and you had nothing precious"—must be rejected; *mimma ana* X (*w*)*aqar* does not mean that "X has something precious" (which would be, rather, *mimma aqru/aqartu ana* X, or X *mimma aqra/aqarta īšu/i*), but that "something is rare/scarce for X." See *AHw*, p. 1460b.

4. Cf. *EA* 7:71–72 and n. 21.

5. [KÙ.GI im-ma-t]i-*ma-a u'-e-du*: *immātīmā*, Landsberger in Gordon; if the verb is *uddû*, one expects *u'-e-du*-[*ú*], but nothing follows (also Gordon).

6. 30 [*ša i*]*r-'i-mu-šu-nu-ti*, "which he presented/with which he presented them" (von Soden, p. 434), is not supported by collation.

7. *il*-q[u-š]i (Knudtzon) is hardly right, especially š]i; see *VAB* 2/1, p. 1001, no. 10. *il*-l[a-k]a (Gordon) is equally difficult.

8. NAGAR.MEŠ: following *CAD*, N/1, p. 114a; so already Landsberger in Gordon.

9. *a*-[*n*]*a* ⌈*p*⌉*i-i balṭi*: following von Soden, p. 431.

10. ^{giš}GIGIR.ME[Š]: the second and third signs are doubtful. If the reading is correct, *narkabta našû* can hardly mean "to load a wagon" (Oppenheim, *Dictionary of Scientific Biography*, 15 [1978], p. 656, n. 39); and "to bring a wagon" (*AHw*, p. 764a) does not seem to fit the context. I understand *našû* in the sense of withdrawing from a supply (*CAD*, N/2, p. 98b) or appropriating (*CAD*, N/2, p. 100). Not expecting to have a shipment of animal figures to bring back to Babylonia, the messenger would have to borrow means of transportation. For *narkabtu* as a means of shipping, cf. *EA* 41:34 and *CAD*, N/1, p. 357b.

11. ^{f}*ma-i-ia*-⌈*a*⌉-*t*⌈*i*⌉: following von Soden, p. 432, and confirmed by collation; correct *CAD*, M/2, p. 74b.

12. 49 [il-la-ka x-x-x] *e-pu-uš-ma ú-še*-ba-l⌈a⌉-a[š]-š[i] (Gordon).

EA 11

Proper escort for a betrothed princess

TEXT: VAT 151 + 1878.
COPIES: WA 6 + WA 218, 225; *VS* 11, 6.

[Say] to Napḫururea, the king of Egypt, [my] broth[er]: Th[us Bur]na-Buriyaš, the king of Karaduniy[aš, your brother]. F[or me all goes w]ell. For you, your wives, you[r] household, [your sons, for yo]ur [horses,] your chariots, may all go very we[ll].

5–8 [*After the wife* of] your father had been mourned,[1] I sent Ḫu'a, [my] mess[enger, and . . . , an interp]reter, [*to you*]. [*I*] wrote [*as follows*],[2] saying, "A daughter of the king who [. . . , *was* (once) ta]ken [*to your father*]. Let [*them take*] another [*to you*]."[3]

9–15 [*And you yourself*][4] sent [Ḫaamaš]ši, your messenger, and [. . . Miḫuni, *the interprete*]*r*, [*saying*, ". . . *the wife of*] my father was mourned[5] [. . .] that woman [. . .] she die[d] in a [pl]ague [. . ." *I*] wrote, saying, "That woman [*may be taken*"].[6]

16–22 [*When*] I presented [*my daughter*] to [Ḫaamašši], your [mess]enger, and to Miḫuni, the inte[rpret]er, they [pou]red o[il] on the hea[d of my] daughter.[7] But as to *the one* tak[ing her] to you,[8] [w]ho is going to take her to you? With Ḫaya there are 5 chariots. Are they going to take her to you in 5 chariots? Should I in these circumstances allow her to be brought to you [*from m*]*y* [*house*],[9] my neighboring kings [*would say*], "They have transported the daughter of a Great King [t]o Egypt in 5 char[iots"].

23–28 [*When my father*] a[llow]ed [*his daughter*] to be br[oug]ht to your father,[10] [. . .] 3000 soldie[rs wi]th him [. . .]

Reverse

1–5 [. . .] . . . [. . . *let*] *them carve* [. . .l]et them brin[g me . . . *l*]*et them carve* [. . . *which look like*] live [. . .][11] let them bring me. 6–12 If old ones in the number required are a[vailab]le, have them brought to me im[mediate]ly.[12] If old ones are not available, let them carve new ones and have Ṣalmu, the merchant, bring them to me. If Ṣalmu, the merchant, has already departed for here, let your messenger that comes to me take them. Trees[13] are to be carved from ivory and colored. Matching plants of the countryside are to be carved, colored, and taken to me.

13–18 As for Ḫaya, your magnate, whom you sent to me, the chariots and soldiers with him are too few. Send here many [char]iots and soldiers so that Ḫaya be the one [to ta]ke[14] the princess to you. Do not send here some other [mag]nate. The princess [on] whose [he]ad oil [has been poured] should not delay here by me.[15] Send them so [*they can take her*] immediate[ly]. [*I*]*f* within this year you intend to sen[d here] chariots and soldiers, [a messen]ger should come out to me posthaste and info[rm me].[16]

19–23 [After][17] your [fa]ther sent [here] to Kurigalzu much gold, what was more lavish than [*the gift*] to Kurigalzu, and so in the palace [of *my ancestor what* wa]s missing?[18] That neighboring kings might hear it said, "The go[ld *is much.* Among][19] the kings there are brotherhood, amity, peace, and [good] relations," [*he*] was rich in stones, rich in silver, rich in [*gold*].[20]

24–34 I s[end] 10 lumps of genuine[21] lapis lazuli as your greeting-gift, and to the mistress of the house [I send] 20 "crickets" of genuine lapis lazuli. [I know] that Mayatu alone[22] did nothing for me *by which* [*I am*] *res*[*tored to health*],[23] and showed no concern for me. As soon as poss[ible][24] let them take to me much gold that is yours alone.[25] Let them take to me [much gold]! By the end of [*this very*] year I wish to bring the work to completion quickly. And . . . [. . .] he must not say, "Your messenger has received a lar[ge and *beautiful*] greeting-gift." He . . . [. . .] how can I send to you? Send me [*much gold*] so that [*I, too, send*] to y[*ou* a] large [greeting]-gift.[26]

NOTES

1. [ul-tu aš-ša-at] *a-bi-ka qu-ub-ba-tu*$_4$: stative subjunctive (cf. *rūqatu, EA* 7:32) of *qubbû*, "to (be)wail" (*AHw,* p. 890; *CAD,* Q, p. 292a); cf. Landsberger in Campbell, *Chronology,* p. 46, and also in Gordon. *CAD,* Q, puts this passage under *qubbātu,* meaning unknown.

2. *al-ta-ap-r*[*a*-ak-ku] 7 [a-ka-an-na al-*t*]*a-ap-ra*; cf. *EA* 4:11.

3. 8 [. . . a-na a-bi-ka il-*q*]*u-ú-ni ša-ni-ta-am-ma li*-i[l-qu-ni-ku].

4. 9 [ù at-ta . . .].

5. *qubbâtu* as in line 5 (see n. 1).

6. *ša*-[a-ši li-il-qu-ni-(ku?)]. Perhaps the girl that had been promised first died and there had been a delay in carrying out the offer of lines 7–8.

7. 17 [DUMU.MUNUS-ti *ki-i*] . . . *qa-qa-*[*a*]*d* DU[MU].MU[NUS-ti-ia] 18 ⌜Ì⌝.[GIŠ *it-t*]*a-du-ú*: following Landsberger, in *Symbolae iuridicae et historicae Martino David dedicatae,* Tomus Alter (Leiden, 1968), pp. 79–80, n. 4. For this first act of betrothal, in *EA* see also 11, rev. 15ff.; 29:22f.; and 31:11ff. See, too, C. Wilcke, *La femme dans le Proche-Orient antique* (Paris, 1987), p. 185, n. 27. At Ugarit, see Pardee, *BiOr* 34 (1977) pp. 3f.; Brooke, *UF* 11 (1979) pp. 69ff.

8. *ša ana muḫḫīka le*-q[u-(ú)-ši]: *ša* . . . *le*-q[í-i/e-ša], grammatically less difficult, is not supported by collation; read ⟨i⟩-*le*-q[u-(ú)-ši]?

9. 21 [i-na É-i]a.

10. 23 [u_4-um a-bu-ú-a-a DUMU.MUNUS-su]. . . .

11. rev. 5 [*ša a-na* . . . M]EŠ *ba-al-ṭú-t*[*i* ma-aš-lu]: following Landsberger in Gordon.

12. *ḫ*[*a-mu-ut-t*]*a šu-bi-i-la*: following Ungnad, *OLZ*, 1916, col. 183; see also Schroeder, *OLZ*, 1917, col. 105.

13. GIŠ.MEŠ = *iṣṣī*: see Ungnad, *OLZ*, 1916, col. 183.

14. [li-il-*q*]*a-ak-ku*.

15. *mārat šarri ša* Ì.GIŠ [*a-na qa-q*]*a-di-ša* 16 [*id-du*]-*ú*: following Landsberger (see n. 7).

16. 18 [DUMU KI]N . . . *li-iq-b*[*a-a*]: following von Soden, p. 432.

17. [ki-i]: following von Soden, ibid.

18. *ina ekal(li)* [a-bi-ia 21 [mi-nu-ú *i*]*n-da-ṭi*: following von Soden, ibid., in the reading of the verb. Being rhetorical questions, *minû ītatir* (line 20) and *minû indaṭi* are probably only apparent exceptions to the rule that in Middle Babylonian letters the perfect was not used in questions (Aro, *StOr* 20, p. 81).

19. [i-na]: hardly enough room for [bi-ri-it] (von Soden, p. 432).

20. [šu-ú(-ma)]: cf. von Soden, ibid.

21. For the distinction between "genuine" (lit. "of the mountain"; see *EA* 9:36 and passim in the inventories) and "artificial" (lit. "of the kiln"), see Oppenheim, *Glass and Glassmaking in Ancient Mesopotamia* (Corning, N.Y., 1970), pp. 10ff. If the qualifier "genuine" is not used, the stone was probably artificial.

22. *fma-ia-tu-ma*: see *EA* 10:44 and n. 11. Lines 26f. are often understood as distinguishing Mayatu from the "mistress of the house" in line 25. The title occurs in the badly broken *EA* 1:48 and *YOS* 13, 90:21; as GAŠAN É in a few Neo-Assyrian texts cited in *CAD*, B, 190b; and as nin é (-e-ke_4) in Sumerian (Civil, *JAOS* 103 [1983] p. 57:156); cf. *bʿlt bhtm* and L. Muntingh, *JNES* 26 (1967) p. 109. The latter is identified either with the famous Nefertiti, Amenophis IV's first wife, or with Ankhsenpaaten, his daughter and last wife; see Pintore, *Matrimonio*, pp. 29f. Two translations have been offered for *kī* in line 26, "whereas," which is without parallel, and "because," which assumes a causal clause after a main clause, a sequence that is extremely rare if not quite without parallel. In either case the line of thought and the implied enthymemes are curious: "I gave so-and-so something, (*a*) whereas so-and-so_2 treated me badly, or (*b*) because so-and-so_2 treated me badly." To abide by conventional usage we must read at the end of line 25 [*ul-te-bi-la i-de*] 26 *ki-i*. . . . This favors the identity of the two figures. By sending the gift (and a small one) to Mayatu under her title it is perhaps suggested that the demands of propriety rather than those of friendship are being met. Cf. Na'aman, *Political Disposition*, *p. 83, n. 20.

23. *šu*-u[l-lu-ma-ku]: cf. *EA* 7:13, n. 7.

24. *ki-i du-lu-uḫ-t*[*i-iš*]: following Kühne, p. 145.

25. *attûkā-ma*: the enclitic seems to stress the identity of the source of the gift, perhaps in contrast to Mayatu, from whom he has learned to expect nothing; cf. *fmayatu-ma* in line 26 and the enclitic "Mayatu alone."

26. *kī lušēbilak*[*ku* KÙ.GI ma-a(')-da *šu-b*]*i-la-am-ma* 34 [a-na-ku-ma *šu-ul-m*]*a-na ma-a-da a-na* k[a-a-ša lu-še-bi-la-ak-ku].

EA 12

A letter from a princess

TEXT: VAT 1605.
COPIES: WA 188; *VS* 11, 7 (tablet now in two pieces).
TRANSLATION: Pintore, *Matrimonio,* p. 61.

Say to my lord: Thus the princess.[1] For you, your chariots, the m[e]n a[nd yo]ur [. . .], may all go well. 6–11 May the gods of Burra-Buriyaš accompany you. March in safety, and safely push on so you will see your house (again). 12–22 In *the pre*[*sence of my lord*] thus [*do I prostrate myself*],[2] saying, "*From* . . . [. . .] my messenger brings (you) colored cloth. For your cities and your household may all go ⟨w⟩ell. *Do no*[*t*] *wo*[*rr*]*y, or* you *will* have made me sad."[3]

23–26 Your servant, Kidin-Adad, . . . I would give my life for you.[4]

NOTES

1. The script is Babylonian, not Egyptian, and so the letter was probably written in Babylonia and sent by a Babylonian princess (lit. "daughter of the king"), perhaps one destined for the Pharaoh's harem. For other views, see Kühne, p. 50, n. 232. Landsberger in Gordon, instead of "to my lord" (*ana* ^{m}*bi-li-ia*), proposed "to Biniya."

2. *i-na pa-*[ni bi-lí-ia] 13 *a-ka-an-n*[*a* ul-ta-ki-in]: Knudtzon could see what looked like u[l], no longer visible. For other and bolder restorations and corrections of the text, see Pintore, *Matrimonio,* p. 167, n. 308.

3. *it-ku-l*[*a*] *tētendanni*: following von Soden, p. 433, but suggesting that the perfect be taken as future perfect (cf. *GAG,* Erg. §80e). The tone of the letter argues against a statement of fact.

4. The second letter (see the Introduction, sect. 4) was added perhaps by the scribe. In line 24, *i ša a*G NI remains unexplained; how it can mean "has decided" (Pintore, without comment) is not clear.

EA 13

Inventory of a dowry

TEXT: VAT 1717.
COPIES: WA 216; *VS* 12, 197.[1]

[. . . *date*]-*stone*[2] of carnelian (with?) *ziminzu*-shaped bead(s).
[. . . *and*] . . .[3] of gol[d].
[. . .] "eye-stones" of genu[ine] *pappardilu*-stone.[4]
[. . .] "eye-stones" of *muššaru*-stone.[5]

[. . .] . . . an alabaster[6] of [*genuin*]*e* [*lapis lazuli*].
[. . .] . . . and . . . [*of gold*].
[. . .] *small ziminzu*-shaped bead(s) of lapis lazuli (and) *m*[*uššaru*-stone].
[. . .] . . .[7] and g[old].
[. . .] . . .[8] "*lentil*" (stones)[9] of lapis lazuli and *muššaru*-stone.
[. . .] . . . and g[old].
[. . .] . . . of lapis lazuli, *muššaru*-stone[10] and g[old].
[. . .] *kakkussu*-stone, lapis lazuli and *muš*[*šaru*-stone].
[. . .] . . . and go[ld].
[. . . *gold*] *leaf,*[11] genuine lapis lazuli and [*muššaru-stone*].
[. . .] . . . and g[old].
[. . . *gold*] *leaf,* genuine lapis lazuli and [gold].
[. . .] . . . lapis lazuli, genuine *mu*[*ššar*]*u*-stone.
[. . .] . . . and gold; in [*the*] center, [*ob*]*sidian.*
[. . .] genuine [lapis] lazuli; mounting and . . . of gold.
A large [. . . of go]ld.
A small [. . .].
[. . .] inlay.
[. . .] inlay.
[. . .]
[. . .] . . . of gold.
A large [. . .].
[. . . *cla*]*sp(s?)*, ivory, of which 1 *clasp* is of ebony.[12]
[. . .] of gold.
[. . .] . . .
[. . .] . . .; mounting of *g*[*o*]*ld.*
[. . .] and . . .
[. . .] and *al*[*aba*]*ster.*[13]
[. . .] . . . [. . .]
[. . .] . . .

Reverse

[. . .] *kamm*[*uššakku*-bed].[14]
[. . . side-bo]ards . . . [. . .].
[*kamm*]*uššakku*-bed . . . [. . .].
[. . .] side-boar[ds *along with* cla]w-feet.
[. . .] . . . *kammuššakku*-bed.
[. . .] . . . *supports* and . . . (*with*) [claw-fe]et of silver.
[. . .] of gold.

[. . . *wi*]*th* its cup, of gold.[15]
[. . . *wash-basin for hands, w*]*ith* their cups, of silver.[16]
[. . . *wash-basin for* f]eet, of silver.
[. . . spr]inkling-vessels of silver.[17]
[. . .] . . . of silver.
[. . .] . . . of silver.
[. . .] of bronze.
[. . . brazi]er of bronze.[18]
[. . . *ch*]*est,* with their *lamp*(s?), of bronze.[19]
[. . . e]wer of bronze.
[. . . *t*]*allu*-jar of bronze.[20]
[. . . *ta*]*llu*-jar of bronze.
[. . . ke]ttle of copper.[21]
[. . .] . . . of bronze.
[. . .] *šalinnu* of bronze.
[. . .] *angurinnu* of bronze.
[. . .] wash-basin for hands, *with* their *cups,* of br[onze].
[. . .] wash-basin for feet, [(. . .) of bronze].
[. . .] . . ., lapis lazuli, . . . [. . .].
[. . . *fl*]*ask* of *dušu*-stone, mounting of gold.[22]
[. . . *fl*]*ask* of lapis lazuli, mounting of gold.

NOTES

1. This inventory, from Babylonia, is apparently the dowry of a Babylonian princess, probably a daughter of Burna-Buriaš. The absence of identifying notation at either the beginning or the end of the tablet suggests that this was one of two or more tablets.

2. ú]-⌜ḫi⌝ -*nu* (cf. *EA* 15:13).

3. Perhaps *be-ra,* "in between" (Gordon); also lines 6 and 19.

4. A type of chalcedony; see Limet, *MARI* 4, p. 511, n. 7.

5. Durand, *ARMT* 21, pp. 224ff., identifies *muššar(r)u* as onyx and cloisonné. The *muš-ša-li* of *Emar* 6/4, p. 127, Annexe V 6′, between *dušû*-stone and *pappardilu*-stone, is pertinent.

6. *šikkatu,* a jar for oil, or an ornament so shaped (*AHw,* p. 1234); see also D. Charpin, *AÉM* 1/2, 294, note a.

7. Gordon proposed ^{na_4}*ta-r*]*a-am-ma-nu,* comparing *tarammanu* in *PBS* 2/2, 120:53 (cf. *tarammu* I, *AHw,* p. 1325); also lines 10, 13, 15, 18.

8. Perhaps [. . . tu-di-it]-*tu* (Gordon); see *EA* 14, n. 11.

9. GÚ.TUR = *kakkû,* "lentil" (or the like)? See also *EA* 14 i 13.

10. Written ^{na_4}MUŠ.GÍR.TAB (von Soden, p. 433); a variety of *muššar(r)u*-stone?

11. [. . . KÚ.GI] *tù-tù-ur-ru*: see *AHw,* p. 1375; Landsberger, *RA* 62 (1968) p. 127, n. 108. Durand, *ARMT* 21, pp. 231f., argues for "granulated."

12. *napādu,* perhaps a type of handle; see Durand, *MARI* 5, p. 186.

13. p[a-ru]-*ti.*

14. Reading in lines 1–6: 1 [. . . *ka*]*m-m*[*u-ša-ak-ku*] 2 [. . . $^{gi\check{s}}$*a-ma-r*]*a-a-tu* x [. . .] 3 [. . . *kam-m*]*u-ša-ak-ku* x [x x (x)] x KÙ.BABBAR 4 [. . . ^{gi}]$^{\check{s}}$*a-ma-ra-*[*tu* a-di *ṣú-up*]*-ri* 5 [. . .] ZUR.MEŠ *kam-m*[*u-ša*]*-ak-ku* 6 [. . .] x *in-di ù* x (10?) ⌜*ṣú*⌝*-up-ri* KÙ.BABBAR. Gordon recognized *kammuššakku* (the double *m* is otherwise unattested).

15. GÚ.ZI = *kāsu*; also rev. lines 9, 24. In view of the feminine suffix (*ina kāsī-ša*) and lines 9 and 24, restore probably [NÍG.ŠU.LUH.HA = *namsītu*].

16. For the restoration of this line and the following one, cf. lines 24–25 below; see also *EA* 22 ii 51, iv 22; 25 ii 53, iv 60. For syllabic writing, see *EA* 14 ii 36; 22 iv 27; 120:12. Unless the plural of *namsû* (*nemsû*) is *namsâtu* (>*namsītu*), at least here and in line 24 the reading of the logogram is *namsītu,* not *namsû* (against *CAD,* N/1, p. 245), as the feminine suffix (*ina kāsī-šina*) makes clear; note, too, the syllabic writings.

17. [. . . *mu-s*]*a-li-ḫa-tu* (*AHw,* p. 1013; *CAD,* M/2, p. 231).

18. [. . . *ḫu-lu-up-pa*]*-aq-qú* (also Gordon); cf. *EA* 22 iv 15.

19. [. . . al-ta]-*pí-pu i-na* IZI.GAR(*nūrī*)*-šu-nu*; cf. *EA* 22 iii 22.

20. ^{dug}*tallu* (also line 19).

21. [. . . $^{(urudu)}$Š]EN = *ruqqu* (Gordon); see also Durand, *MARI* 2, pp. 133f.

22. [. . . mu]-*ša-lu* (Landsberger in Gordon); for the meaning of *mušālu,* see Durand, *ARMT* 21, pp. 356f., and W. Farber, in Francesca Rochberg-Halton, ed., *Language, Literature, and History: Philological and Historical Studies Presented to Erica Reiner,* American Oriental Series 67 (New Haven, 1987), pp. 94f. On *dušû,* "agate" (banded chalcedony), see P. Steinkeller, *ZA* 72 (1982) pp. 249ff.

EA 14

Inventory of Egyptian gifts

TEXT: VAT 1651 + 2711 (+) Ash. 1891.1–41 (415, not collated).

COPIES: WA 28 + WA 209; *VS* 12, 198; (+) Sayce, *Tell el Amarna,* no. 8.

I

[These things *Napḫuru*]rea, Great King, [king of Egypt, s]ent [to his brother, Burna]-Buriyaš, [Great King, king of Karaduniyaš.]

[. . .] . . .[1]

5–7 [. . .] . . .

[. . .] strung with[2] [. . .].

[. . .]

[. . .] . . . , of gold, of the princes.[3]
[. . . , of gl]ass.[4]
[. . . , in]laid.
[. . . , of g]old, (*with*) "*lentil*" (stones)[5] inlaid.
[. . . for the n]eck,[6] of gold, (called) *mašuya*.
[. . .], set with[7] stones, (called) *wizza*.
[. . . , for the n]eck, of gold, set with stones.
[. . . , o]f gold.
[. . .], of gold.
[. . .] . . . , of gold, inlaid.
[. . .] their [. . .].
[. . . , of go]ld, inlaid.

(22–31, broken)

[x *kukkubu*-containers, of gold],[8] filled with "[sw]eet-[oil],"[9] (called) *namša*.
[. . .], of gold, inlaid, (called) *kubu*.
[. . . , of gol]d, inlaid, (called) . . .
[. . . , of gold], inlaid.
[. . . , of] gold, inlaid, (called) *anaḫu*.
[. . .], of copper.
[. . .], for the hand, of gold, inlaid, (called) *šuzuta*.
[. . . , of go]ld, inlaid; in their center, silver and gold.
[. . .], of gold, and 1 small *kukku*[*bu*]-container.
[. . . a pa]il,[10] of gold.
[. . . togg]le pins[11] [(. . .)].
[. . .] . . . , large, (called) *našši*.
[. . .], of gold.
[. . . , of gol]d, and 1 small one.
[. . . , o]f gold, (called) *raḫda*.
[. . .] . . . [. . . fo]r bathing.
[. . . , o]f gold [and of sil]ver, set with gold, (called) *da*[*š*]*i*.
[x goblets of sil]ver (and) go[ld . . .], their [. . .], inlaid, (called) *ḫaragabaš*.[12]

50–54 [. . .] . . .[13]

2 female figurines . . . [. . .], inlaid, *which* . . . [. . .].
15 containers of oil, [*of gold*], inlaid.
1 "cucumber" [*that is*] an oil-container,[14] of gold, inlaid.
1 *ḫubunnu*-container [. . .], of gold.
(*with*) a female figurine [. . .] . . . , silver, standing.
1 *ḫubun*[*nu*-container, o]f gold.

1 small cont[ain]er (of aromatics), of gold,
(with) 1 ibe[x] lying in its center.[15]
8 goblets [. . .] . . . , of gold, (called) *ḫaragabaš*,
[and] 1 s[mall one].[16]
[. . .] . . . , of gold, and 1 small one.
[x] pails, of gold, and 1 small one.
[. . .], of silver and gold, *entirely*; *nam*[*š*]*a* is its name.
[. . .] . . . , which *is studded*[17] with gold and copper in its middle; *zimiu* is its name.
[1] small *kukkubu*-container, for bath[ing], of gold.
[1] small *tallu*-jar, of gold.
[1 con]tainer for eye-paint,[18] of gold, inlaid; *daba'uḫi* is its name.
[x] large finger-rings, of gold.
[x] finger-rings with gold *plating*.[19]
[x] hand-bracelets, of gold, with inlays; *puati* is its name.[20]
19 gold rings for the finger.
3 (pairs of) gold *sandals*.[21]
10 very wide hand-bracelets that are strung with stones; *maḫda* is their name.
3 pairs of foot-bracelets, of gold, strung with stones.
[x] razors, of gold.
[x] razors, of bronze; their handles, of silver and gold.

II

13 gold bowls;[22] *zillaḫta* is its name.
9 necklace-plaques, of gold and . . . -stone.
7 gold tubes,[23] full of eye-paint,
and 3 tubes with gold *plating*.
1 gold box of *ṣippar(r)ātu*-cosmetics.
1 tube for eye-paint,[24] with *kibbu*-ornaments of polished gold, (*called*) *kitini*.
6 knives,[25] of gold, with pomegranates on their top.
1 small container (of aromatics), of gold,
and a stopper of lapis lazuli in the middle.
4 ladles *with claws*, of gold.[26]
1 large statuette that is overlaid with gold, of the king,[27]
and its *pedestal*[28] is overlaid with silver.
1 female figurine, overlaid with gold, of the king's wife.
1 female figurine, overlaid with gold, of the king's daughter.
2 chariots, of *šuššūgu*-wood,[29] overlaid with gold.

2 chariots, of *šuššūgu*-wood, overlaid with gold.
1 ship, of cedar, overlaid with gold, along with all its gear, and 6 small ships that one tows.[30]
1 bed, overlaid with gold; female figurines for its feet.
1 bed, overlaid with gold, 1 headrest, overlaid with gold.
5 thrones, overlaid with gold.
1 throne, overlaid with gold and *šaḫpu.*
2 chairs, overlaid with gold.
1 chair . . . [. . .].
[. . .]
[. . .] . . . of Canaan.
[x hand-bracelets), of "sun"-stone; *puati* is its name.[31]
[hand-bracelets], their [. . .], of gold; *puati* is its name.
[. . .] overlaid with gold.
[. . .]
[. . .] overlaid with gold, delicate work.[32]
[. . .]
[To]ta[l of all the gold]:
1200 mi[nas, x] shekels of gold.
1 [*large*] measuring-ves[sel, of silver].
3 [*large*] washing-bowls, of s[ilver].
1 [*large*] *mabrû,* [o]f silver.[33]
1 (vessel called) "large," o[f silver], its [han]dles *o*[*f* . . .].[34]
10 goblets, of sil[ver . . .] . . . [. . .].
1 lar[ge] pot, [o]f silver.
1 *kukkubu*-container, for [. . . , o]f silver, [al]ong with its cover.
3 s[mal]l measuring-vessels, of silver; *bumer* is its name.
1 *ḫaragabaš,* o[f silv]er.
1 pail, of silver.
1 sieve, of silver.
1 small *tallu*-jar, of silver, for a brazier.
1 "pomegranate," of silver.
1 (female) monkey, with its daughter on its lap, of silver.[35]
1 oblong pot, for a brazier, of silver.
23 *kukkubu*-containers, of silver, full of "sweet-oil"; *namša* is its name.
6 *ḫubunnu*-containers, [and] 1 large *ḫubunnu*-container, also of silver.
1 *upright chest,* of silver, inlaid.
1 ladle, of silver, for an oil-container; *wadḫa* is its name.
11 bowls, of silver, *zillaḫta* ⟨is its name⟩.

29 ladles, of silver, handles of *boxwood* and ebony,
with which one curls the hair.[36]
1 box, of pure silver.[37]
3 (pairs of) *sandals,* of silver.
1 *kukkubu*-container, of silver; its spout, of gold.
[1 box of *ṣ*]*ippar*(*r*)*ātu*-cosmetics, overlaid with silver and gold.
[x ladl]es, for a barber, of silver.
[. . .] . . . , of silver and gold.
3 b[eds, of *pure silver*]; 1 headre[st], of pure silver.
1 [throne], overlaid [with *silver and gold*].
1 mi[rr]o[r, of silver], set with [*ston*]*es.*[38]
1 mi[rr]o[r], of silver and g[ol]d.
18 st[ones . . .], their [m]outh, of gold,
an[d . . .].[39]
1 small *con*[*tainer* (of aromatics), of silver],
and a *st*[*opper in the cen*]*ter,* of *s*[*ilver*].
The to[ta]l of all the silver:
292 [minas], and 3 shekels [of silver].
The tota[l] of all the silver and g[old]:
1500 (+ x) minas and 46½ shekels.
20 mi[rr]ors, of bronze.
12 large mi[rr]ors, of bronze.
The to[tal]: [3]2 mirrors.
80 mi[rrors . . .].
90 m[irrors . . . , o]f bronze.
5 . . . [. . .] . . . , *hand* [. . .]; *našša* is its name.
5 . . . [. . . , o]f bronze.
3 . . . [. . .] . . . , of bronze; *ḫunima* is its name.
5 very long . . . [. . .][40] . . . , of bronze.
3 [*lar*]*ge,* oblong *p*[*ots*], o[f bronze, fo]r a brazier.
2 tall p[o]ts, [o]f bronze.
3 small . . . [. . .], for bathing, of bronze.
2 [. . .] . . . , for a brazier, of bronze; *kuldu* is its name.
20 [. . .], of bronze, *fo*[*r* . . .].

III

2 . . . [. . .].
6 *p*[*ots* . . . , o]f bronze, . . . [. . .].
12 . . . [. . .] . . . mouth, horses.
16 ra[zors, . . . of bronz]e; their [hand]les, of silver.

57 razo[rs, o]f bron[ze].
41 ladles, for a bar[ber], of bronze.
51 ladles, of bronze; their [han]dles, of ebony.
The t[ot]al of the [ob]jects of [bron]ze, all together:
300 [(+ x)] objects. The weight of the bronze:
8[60 m]inas, 20 sh[eke]ls.

---

1 double-sized (piece of) [fine] linen cloth for a festive-garment, byssos (quality).[41]
20 (pieces of) [fi]ne linen cloth; byssos (quality).
20 [s]ma[ll] (pieces of) [fine] linen cloth, byssos (quality).
40 [*large*] (pieces of) [fine] linen cloth, by[ssos] (quality).
35 thin ma[ntl]es, bys[sos] (quality).
3 (pieces of) fine linen cloth, *idru* (quality), in size (equal to) 6 (pieces of) [fine] li[nen cloth].
1 (piece of) fine linen cloth, *idru* (quality), in size (equal to) 2 (pieces of) [fine] linen c[loth].
15 thin mantles, *idru* (quality).
100 large (pieces of) ⟨fine⟩ linen cloth, (for) shawl(s).
150 (pieces of) fine l[in]en cloth, [*adaḫa*] (quality).
100 small (pieces of) fine linen cloth, *adaḫa* (quality).
250 thin mantles, ⟨*adaḫa*⟩ (quality).
250 thin girdles, ⟨*adaḫa*⟩ (quality).[42]
12[0 *t*]*unzu*-cloaks.[43]
5 large [*tu*]*nzu*-cloaks, for the king's bed.
[1] linen cloth, for the *front of the body, decorated with borders.*[44]
[. . .] . . . *of* a robe, *tabarru*-red, not *ami*-red,[45]
[*go*]*ld,* all set with stones.
[x] (pieces of) fine linen cloth, for the *front of the body, decorated with borders,* colored *ami*-red.[46]
6 (pieces of) fine linen cloth, *tabarru*-red.
6½ half *ullu*-cloths(?), of linen cloth,
for their length(wise strips?), *tabarru*-red, *paqa* (quality).[47]
The total of the linen cloth: 1092, and 6½ half ⟨*ul*⟩*lu*-cloths(?):
1 stone *ḫuttu*-jar, full of "sweet oil," (called) *azida.*
19 stone jars, full of "sweet oil"; *kubu* is its name.
20 stone jars, (called) *akunu,* which are full of "sweet oil."
9 *kukkubu*-containers, of stone, full of "sweet oil"; *namša* is its name.
1 "cucumber," of stone, full of "sweet oil."

6 large stone vessels, full of "sweet oil."
[x] *kukkubu*-containers, of stone, full of "sweet oil"; *maziqta* is its name.
[x] jugs, of stone, full of "sweet oil"; *kuba* is its name.
[x] *kukkubu*-containers, of stone, full of "sweet oil"; *kuba-puwanaḫ* is its name.
[x] *kukkubu*-containers, of stone, full of "sweet oil"; *kuiḫku* is its name.
[x j]ars,[48] full of "sweet oil"; *ašša* is its name.
[The t]otal of the stone vessels full of "sweet oil":
[x]000 and 7 vessels.

---

[x] em[pty] boxes, of stone, [. . .].
[1] *kukkubu*-container, of stone; *našša* is its name, [and] 1 small one just li[ke i]t.
[x] onagers, of stone, [and] 1 sm[all one] just like it.
[x] *galdu,* of stone; . . . is its name.
[. . . and × sm]all ones just like them; 35 *ḫaragabaš,* of stone.
A lar[*ge* . . .] . . . , of stone; . . . is its name,
[*and* x smal]l ones, of stone; vessels . . . and 2 . . .
[. . . *along with*] their *stands*; *sabnakû* is its name.[49]
[. . .]; *kuiḫku* is its name.
[. . . , o]f stone.
[. . .]; . . . is its name,
and 1 sma[ll one] *ju*[*st like it*].
21 female figurines, of stone, . . . [. . .].
1 cripple, of stone, with a jar in his hand.[50]
1 *kukkubu*-container, of stone; *šuibta* is its name.[51]
3 jars, of stone; 2 large goblets, of *ḫina*-stone.
3 pails, of stone; 1 sieve, of stone.
1 tall *kanduru*-vessel, of stone.
2 *agannu*-bowls, of stone; 38 *išqillatu*-vessels, of stone.
1 container of oil; *wadḫa* is its name.
3 *kukkubu*-containers, of stone; *namša* is its name.
2 headrests, of stone.
1 headrest, of *dušû*-stone.
1 bowl, of white stone; *zillaḫta* is its name.
9 containers of oil, of white stone; *wadḫa* is its name.
The total of empty stone-vessels:
160 and 3.

117 whetstones, for a barber.
9 boxes, of ebony and ivory, delicate work.[52]
2 boxes, of ebony and ivory, delicate work, (called) *zâ*.[53]

IV

[...] ..., of ebony and ivory, delicate work.
6 (*pairs of*) animal paws, of *stained ivory.*
9 plants, of *stained ivory,* [...] ...
10 *plants,* various sorts, of *stained* ivory.
29 "cucumbers," containers of oil, of *stained* ivory.
44 containers of oil, decorated with apples, pomegranates, dates,[54]
(and) *kurumānu,* of *stained* ivory.
375 containers of oil, of *stained* ivory, [...] (called) [z]*â*.
19 combs,[55] of *stained* ivory.
19 toggle pins, of *stained* ivory.
13 boxes, of *stained* ivory, (called) *upṭa*.[56]
3 headrests, of *stained* ivory.
3 *kukkubu*-containers, of *stained* ivory; *kuba* is its name.
3 oxen, containers of oil, of *stained* ivory.
3 *ibexes*,[57] containers of oil, of *stained* ivory.
1 small container (of aromatics), of *stained* ivory,
and [...] in its center, and 1 ox on top.
[...] ..., of *stained* ivory.
[..., of e]bony, called *maḫan*.
(20–62 scattered signs and phrases)

NOTES

1. For the restoration, see *VAB* 2/2, p. 1586; Kühne, p. 70, n. 342; ibid., p. 71, n. 347 (line 4: "when he (Burna-Buriyaš) gave his daughter to him").

The inventory of *EA* 14 is characterized by the frequent addition of the Egyptian names of the various objects, for which see especially T. Lambdin, *Or* n.s. 22 (1953) pp. 362ff.; Edel, *Brief;* idem, *Studien zur Altägyptischen Kultur* 1 (1974) pp. 105ff., 295; Helck, *Beziehungen,* esp. pp. 370ff.

2. *šukkukat.*

3. Cf. ii 11.

4. [... ^{na_4}*eḫ-l*]*i-pa-ak-ki,* a kind of glass; see Oppenheim, *JAOS* 93 (1973) pp. 259ff.

5. See *EA* 13:9.

6. [... *ša ti-i*]*k-ki*; also i 16. Cf. ii 2 and *ša tikki,* "necklace" (Edel, *Brief,* p. 142).

7. Here and passim, *súm-mu-ḫu* (*AHw,* p. 1017; *CAD,* S, p. 109); cf. *EA* 22 iii 35.

8. [x *ku-ku-bu ša* KÙ.GI Ì DU]G; cf. ii 50.

9. "Sweet oil" (Ì DÙG, *šamnu ṭābu*—cf. *EA* 26:65, Ì *ṭa-a-ba*), in recipes of the Old Babylonian period, contained no oil, but rather the best beer plus a wide range of aromatics, dates, figs, and other substances; see Robert M. Whiting, Jr., *Old Babylonian Letters from Tell Asmar,* AS 22 (Chicago, 1987), pp. 107–8. On Heb. *šemen ṭôb,* see L. Stager, *JSS* 28 (1983) p. 245.

10. Perhaps the designation of a container according to its form (Gordon).

11. [. . . du-ti-*n*]*i-du* (*tudinētu*); cf. iv 10. On the *tudittu,* see H. Klein, *ZA* 73 (1983) pp. 255ff.; Farber, in Rochberg-Halton, ed., *Language, Literature, and History* (see *EA* 13, n. 22), pp. 96ff.

12. Cf. i 63.

13. In line 53, perhaps Canaan is mentioned; cf. ii 26.

14. 1 *qí-iš-*⌜*šu- ú*⌝ [ša É⌝ Ì (Gordon); cf. iii 38, iv 5.

15. 1 *du-ra-ḫ*[*u i-n*]*a q*[*á*]*-ab-la-t*[*ù-u*]*š-šu*; cf. ii 9.

16. In *EA,* GAL is probably to be read *kāsu,* "cup, goblet," though this is not absolutely certain; see *CAD,* K, p. 256b. For the reading and meaning elsewhere, see K. Deller, *Baghdader Mitteilungen* 16 (1985) pp. 327ff.; J.-M. Durand, *ARMT* 21, p. 351; idem, *AÉM* 1/1, pp. 421–22; H. Limet, *ARM* 25, p. 159; *MARI,* 4, pp. 518–19; W. Mayer, *Or* n.s. 58 (1989) p. 274.

17. It is assumed that *miḫḫuṣ* = *muḫḫuṣ*; cf. *CAD,* M/2, p. 83b.

18. *mēqītu.*

19. *tatbīku.*

20. The *pwt* and *pu-wa-ti* found at Ugarit, probably "madder," are not relevant here; see Huehnergard, *Ugaritic Vocabulary,* p. 166.

21. According to *CAD,* M/2, p. 38, here and in ii 58, *mešēnu* (*ša šēpi*) is a buckle, not the sandal itself.

22. *saḫḫaru*; also ii 54, iii 70, iv 18. Cf. *sí-ḫa-ru, ARMT* 25, 818 passim and note, p. 289.

23. *qanû.*

24. ⟨⟨É⟩⟩ *mi-qí-ti*; cf. ii 3 and note É in previous line.

25. *quppû* rather than *quppu,* "chest"; cf. *AHw,* p. 928b.

26. *nalpattu,* a small (metal) bowl or ladle, used with an oil-container (ii 53) and by a barber (ii 55–56, 61; iii 6–7). Here, rather than "with claws" (*CAD,* N/1, p. 202), *AHw,* p. 724, sees the *nalpattu* used "for fingernails."

27. *ša šarri,* and *ša aššat šarri* and *ša mārti šarri* in ii 13–14, respectively, hardly means "for the king," "for the wife/daughter of the king," since everything is for the king, and additional small presents for the king's wife and daughter would not be listed here; cf. Kühne, p. 69, n. 341. Note, too, the shift in ii 13–14 to *lamassu* or *lamassatu,* a female figurine, when the gift is "of the king's wife/daughter"; cf. also *EA* 24 §25 (end); 27:19ff.

28. Following an unpublished proposal of *CAD.*

29. *šuššūgu* = *šaššūgu,* with G. Wilhelm, AOAT 9, p. 31, n. 5; see also K. Veenhof, *BiOr* 25 (1964) p. 197a.

30. 1 ^giš^MÁ *ša* ^giš^EREN . . . 6 ^giš^MÁ.ḪI.A *ru-ku-bu* . . . , with *AHw,* pp. 199, 994, and *CAD,* E, p. 276; see also Edel, *Brief,* p. 127, n. 1. *CAD*'s "which children can pull" does not translate the text, assuming *ša ṣeḫḫerūti* . . . instead of the text's *ṣeḫḫerūti ša*. . . .

31. Cf. i 74.

32. *du-ul-lu q*[*a*]*-at-nu* = *dullu* SIG (also iii 75–76, iv 1); see *CAD,* D, p. 176b.

33. *mabrû,* a West-Semitized form of *nabrû,* a type of vessel? Cf. *malbašu* for *nalbašu* in *EA* 369:9, a letter from Egypt.

34. Assuming, with *ARMT* 7, p. 308, no mistake in gender concord, and therefore taking *rabû* as a substantive. However, such a mistake seems probable in iii 62.

35. Perhaps a vessel in the shape of a donkey; for the motif, characteristic of Egyptian art, see Sally Dunham, *ZA* 75 (1985) pp. 259–60.

36. For the reading of this entry, see *CAD,* K, p. 316. The identification of ^{giš}TASKARIN as boxwood is still not universally accepted; see *Ugar.* 5, p. 319; R. Borger, *Akkadische Zeichenliste,* AOATS 6, p. 88, no. 536. On the identification of *ušû* at this period as Ethiopian ebony, see van Lerberghe, in Stol, *On Trees, Mountains, and Millstones in the Ancient Near East* (Leiden, 1979), pp. 34ff. J.-M. Durand, *ARMT* 21, p. 419, in the final clause emends the text to *ša še-er* (Durand: *šēr*)*-ṭù ikeṣṣiru ina libbišunu,* which he understands in the sense that the handles are attached by a strip of cloth. He justifies the correction of DA to DU on the mistaken assumption that *EA* 14 comes from Mittani; see ibid., n. 106.

37. *tup-ni-nu* (also iii 47, 75; iv 11); see *ARMT* 9, p. 325, n. 2; von Soden, *ZA* 67 (1977) p. 238; Edel, *Brief,* p. 128, n. 1.

38. 1 *na-*[*ma*]*-a*[*r pa-ni ša* KÙ.BABBAR N]A$_4$.⟨HI.A⟩ *s*[*úm*]*-m*[*u-ḫ*]*u,* and in the following line, 1 *na-*[*m*]*a-a*[*r pa-ni ša*] KÙ.BABBAR K[Ù.G]I; cf. ii 75, 77. The reading assumes signs that Knudtzon could see but are now no longer visible. N]A$_4$, with Gordon.

39. KAxU = *pû* (also iii 3), as at Boghazköy, Ugarit (*Ugar.* 5, p. 277), and Emar (Arnaud, *Emar* 6/4, 783 passim, for example). Here perhaps "mouth" means "setting" (for stones; cf. *AHw,* p. 874b). In line 68, ⌜*ú*⌝ with *VS* 12 rather than 14 (Knudtzon).

40. 5 G[*a*-x]-x-D*u,* with *VS* 12.

41. For the reading and interpretation of lines 11–23, see Edel, *Studien zur Altägyptischen Kultur* 1 (1974) pp. 116–25, 138–46, 295.

42. Reading ^{gada}ŠAG$_4$.DÙ-a (*šakattâ*). *AHw,* p. 1139, reads GADA instead of DÙ, and it is followed by Edel, *Studien zur Altägyptischen Kultur* 1 (1974) p. 139. M. Birot, *ARMT* 9, p. 307, suggested an undergarment; Durand, *ARMT* 21, p. 418, a belt. See now gada-šà-ga-dù = ku-ú-ša-ga-da = *né-be-ḫu* (*Emar* 6/4, 556:56′).

43. 1 ME 2[0 ^{tú}]^{g}*tu-un-zu,* and in the next line, 5 [^{túg}*tu*]*-un-zu.* On the *tunzu,* see Waetzholdt, *RLA* 6/1–2, p. 23a; cf. also *tūzu* (*AHw,* p. 1375; M. Green, *JCS* 30 [1978] p. 150).

44. Reading with Edel, *Studien zur Altägyptischen Kultur* 1 (1974) p. 125 (cf. *AHw,* p. 1308), . . . *ša pa-ni* SU GAR *ták-mu-uz-zi-e. CAD,* M/2, p. 246, sees here a colored decoration called *ša pan muṣê* but offers no explanation of the inserted KUŠ.NÍG NA$_4$ (so *CAD*).

45. *la a-*⌜mi⌝ (cf. iii 29).

46. For *amê ṣabi,* see Edel, *Studien zur Altägyptischen Kultur* 1 (1974) pp. 124–25.

47. That is, "(of) fine (threads)"; see Edel, *Brief,* p. 156. *mišlu*: gloss to ½?
48. [x ^{na_4}*k*]*i-ir-re-tu* (*AHw,* p. 484b).
49. [. . .] *kà-an-dú-ri-šu-nu* (cf. iii 64); on the reading *sabnakû,* see Rainey, AOAT 8², p. 88.
50. *CAD,* K, p. 409a, sees in the "cripple" the bowlegged god Bes. This seems very plausible, since he was extremely popular at this time, his representation serving to ward off various evils; see D. Beyer, *Miscellanea Babylonica* (see Introduction, n. 40), pp. 42–43.
51. On *šuibta,* see Rainey, AOAT 8², p. 95.
52. See above, n. 32. All the uses of SIG as predicated of fabrics in *EA* 14 should be added to *CAD,* Q, p. 174; note, too, *Emar* 6/3, 176:13, *ṣubātu* SIG.
53. The writing of *za-a* here and in iv 8, so much smaller than the other signs, is noteworthy and unexplained. It was, according to Lambdin, *Or* n.s. 22 (1953) p. 368, a small vessel; according to Edel, *Brief,* p. 128, n. 1, a type of container.
54. $^{(giš)}$ḪAŠḪUR (Gordon) = *ḫašḫuru,* "apple (tree)," on which see Å. Sjöberg, *JCS* 40 (1988) p. 174, with reference to earlier literature, and M. Civil, in Rochberg-Halton, ed., *Language, Literature, and History* (see above, n. 11), p. 45, n. 13.
55. ^{giš}GA.RÍG = *muštu/multu,* "comb"; on the Sumerogram, see Civil, AOAT 25, p. 94.
56. On the Egyptian term, besides Lambdin, *Or* n.s. 22 (1953) p. 368, see Edel, *Brief,* p. 128, n. 1.
57. Assuming *du-ša-ḫu* is an error for *du-ra-ḫu*; cf. i 62, iv 62.

EA 15

Assyria joins the international scene

TEXT: Metropolitan Museum of Art 24.2.11.

COPIES: Scheil, *Bulletin de l'Institut français d'archéologie orientale du Caire* 2 (1902) p. 114; I. Spar, ed., *Cuneiform Texts in the Metropolitan Museum of Art: Tablets, Cones, and Bricks of the Third and Second Millennia B.C.,* vol. 1 (New York, 1988), pls. 112–13.

PHOTOGRAPHS: Bull, *Bulletin of the Metropolitan Museum of Art* 21 (1926) p. 170, fig. 1 (obverse); W. C. Hayes, *The Scepter of Egypt,* 2 (Cambridge, Mass., 1959), p. 296, fig. 182 (obverse).

TRANSLITERATIONS AND TRANSLATIONS: Artzi, *Bar-Ilan Departmental Researches: Bar-Ilan Studies in History* (1978), pp. 27f.; Moran, in I. Spar, ed., *Cuneiform Texts* (see above), pp. 149f.

TRANSLATION: A. K. Grayson, *Assyrian Royal Inscriptions,* 1 (Wiesbaden, 1972), pp. 47f.

Say to the king of E[gypt]:[1] Thus Aššur-ubal[liṭ, the king of As]syria.[2] For you, your household, for your [*coun*]*try*,[3] for your chariots and your troops, may all go well. 7–15 I send my messenger to you to visit you and to visit your country.[4] Up to now,[5] my predecessors[6] have not written; today[7] I write to you. [I] send you a beautiful chariot, 2 horses, [and] 1 date-stone of genuine lapis lazuli,[8] as your greeting-gift. 16–22 Do [no]t delay[9] the messenger whom I send to you for a visit. He should visit and then leave for here. He should see what you are like and what your country is like, and then leave for here.

NOTES

1. Perhaps *m*[*i-iṣ-ṣa-ri*]; cf. *EA* 16:2, unless the spelling is tied to the language (Hurro-Akkadian).

2. For the restoration, cf. *EA* 16:3; on the emergence of the title "king of Assyria," see R. Borger, *Einleitung in die assyrischen Königsinschriften,* 1 (Leiden, 1961), p. 26.

3. [KU]R most likely (so Artzi, *Bar-Ilan Studies* [see *EA* 15 headnote]); cf. *EA* 16:5.

4. If interpreted correctly, the unusual word-order probably lays stress on the fact of sending a messenger.

5. *adi anniša*: see *Or* n.s. 53 (1984) p. 298.

6. *ab-ba-ú-ia*: following von Soden, p. 433.

7. *u_4-ma*: following Knudtzon and Artzi (see n. 3), since there is no basis in this letter for assuming the possibility of the peripheral writing of *anumma*.

8. See A. Sachs, *AfO* 12 (1937–39) p. 371, n. 1. On beads in the shape of (unripe) dates, see Artzi, p. 32, n. 15, and J. Bottéro, *RA* 43 (1949) pp. 14f. On the alleged connection between this bead and one found in Egypt bearing a cuneiform inscription, see Borger, *Einleitung* (see n. 2), pp. 20ff.

9. [*l*]*a* *tu_4-ka-as-sú*: following *CAD,* K, p. 295b, with Artzi and Grayson, *Assyrian Royal Inscriptions* (see *EA* 15 headnote). This reading is confirmed by Spar's copy (*Cuneiform Texts* [see headnote above]).

EA 16

The profit motive

TEXT: C 4746 (12209).

COPY: WA 9.

TRANSLATION: Grayson, *Assyrian Royal Inscriptions,* 1, pp. 48f.

S[ay] to ...[1] [..., Great King], king of Egypt, my brother: Thus Aššur-uballiṭ, king of [Assy]ria, Great King, your brother.

5 For you, your household and your country may all go well.

6–8 When I saw your [me]ss[en]gers, I was very happy. Certainly your messengers shall reside with me as objects of gre[at soli]citude.[2]

9–12 I send as your greeting-gift a beautiful royal chariot out[fitt]ed for me, and 2 white horses[3] also [out]fitted for me, 1 chariot not outfitted, and 1 seal of genuine lapis lazuli.[4]

13–18 Is such a present that of a Great King?[5] Gold in your country is dirt; one simply gathers it up.[6] Why are you so sparing of it?[7] I am engaged in building a new palace.[8] Send me as much gold as is needed for its adornment.

19–21 When Aššur-nadin-aḫḫe, my ancestor, wrote to Egypt, 20 talents of gold were sent to him.[9]

22–25 [W]hen the king of Ḫanigalbat [wr]ote to your father in Egy[pt], [h]e sent 20 talents of gold to him.[10]

26–31 [*Now*][11] I am the [*equal*][12] of the king of Ḫani[galba]t, but you sent me [. . .] of gold, and it is not enough [f]or the pay[13] of my messengers on the journey to and back.

32–34 If your purpose is graciously one of friendship, send me much gold. And this is your house. Write me so what you need may be fetched.

35–36 We are countries far apart. Are our messengers to be always on the march with (only) such results?[14]

37–42 As to your messengers having been delayed in reaching you, Suteans had been their *pursuers* (and) they were *in mortal danger.* [I] det[ain]ed[15] them until I could write and the *pursuing* Suteans be taken for me. Surely my messengers are not to be delayed in reaching me.

43–55 Why should messengers be made to stay constantly out in the sun and so die in the sun? If staying out in the sun means profit for the king, then let him (a messenger) stay out and let him die right there in the sun, (but) for the king himself there must be a profit.[16] Or other[wi]se, why should they [d]ie in the sun? As to the messengers we have *exch*[*anged*][17] . . . do they *keep* [*my*] messengers *alive*?[18] They are made to die in the sun!

NOTES

1. The reading of the name is uncertain. Instead of ^{m}*n*[*a-a*]*p-ḫu-*[*r*]*i-i-*x (Knudtzon, and generally accepted), Gordon read ^{m}⌜ḫu⌝-[r]u/[r]a-*ḫu-ri-i-*[tu⌝-[x-x. I thought the last sign might be *'a,* ' replacing *y* as glide. If Gordon's reading of the beginning of the name is correct, then only *ḫpr-ḫprw-rʿ,* the praenomen of Aya, seems comparable.

2. *te*⌜*k*⌝*-ni-e* is virtually certain. Reference is to the care and honors shown messengers (see *EA* 1, n. 25), concrete expressions of, and implied by, the happi-

ness just mentioned. Joy moves, almost necessarily, to external expression; cf. Moses Finley, *The World of Odysseus*, rev. ed. (New York, 1965), p. 132. See also Gary A. Anderson, *A Time to Mourn, A Time to Dance: The Expression of Grief and Joy in Israelite Religion* (University Park, Pa., 1991).

3. White horses were highly prized; see Weidner, *BiOr* 9 (1952) pp. 157ff., and *AHw*, p. 857a (add *ARM* 10, 147; *ARM* 14, 40, and 98). In the classical world, they were proverbial for their speed (*Iliad* x 437; *Aeneid* xii 84; Plautus, *Asinaria* 279; Horace, *Satires* i 7.7); see C. J. Fordyce, *Catullus* (Oxford, 1961), p. 233.

4. 1 ^{na_4}KIŠIB ZA.GÌN KUR-*e*.

5. On the sentence as question, see von Soden, p. 434. Reference is to the gifts brought by the Egyptian messengers of lines 6ff. The topic of the size of the gifts, introduced by a rhetorical question, occupies lines 13–36, concluding with another rhetorical question (*kannā́ . . . kammā́*). Lines 37–42 take up the risks of the journey between Assyria and Egypt, and the concluding section, lines 43–55, combines the two: size of gifts (profit) and risks.

6. *i-is-si-pu-uš* (*esēpu*): following von Soden, p. 434.

7. Lit. "why must it linger on in your sight (*īnē*)/presence (*pānī*)" (*AHw*, p. 1006, II, 3; *CAD*, S, p. 47a).

8. *ekalla eššeta* (Knudtzon), not *ešša* (von Soden, p. 434); note the feminine suffixes of *uḫḫuzī-ša* and *ḫišeḫtī-ša* in the following lines (Huehnergard).

9. Opinion is divided on the identification of the Assyrian king, whether the one who ruled before 1430 B.C. (so Kühne, pp. 77f., n. 387), or the one who ruled 1400–1391 (1390–1381) B.C. (so Artzi, *Bar-Ilan Studies in History*, 1978, p. 36, and others). Twenty talents is such a large sum and so much greater than the value of the gifts usually exchanged that, if the number is at all accurate, there is probably reference to bride-price gifts (Kühne, 77f., n. 387); cf. *EA* 14 ii 34 (1200 minas = 20 talents).

10. Reference here could be to the bride-price of either Tušratta's sister or daughter; see *EA* 17ff.

11. [a-nu-ma]: possible in this dialect, but perhaps [a-na-ku], "I myself," is preferable.

12. [me-eḫ-re]-*ku* (Friedrich in Kühne, p. 78, n. 389), or a virtual synonym, [ša-ni-na]-*ku* (von Soden, p. 434).

13. Sachs, *AfO* 12 (1937–39) pp. 371f.

14. See von Soden, p. 434.

15. *a⸢k-ta⸣-la-šu-nu*: following von Soden, ibid.; the reading is virtually certain. The language of lines 37ff. is ambiguous and open to several interpretations: *mītū* (line 39), as to its subject (Suteans? so generally; Egyptian messengers? so *CAD*, M/1, p. 423b) and meaning (literal? so generally, but cf. *mītu*, said of people in mortal danger, *CAD*, M/2, p. 143); *rādû*, "pursuer"? (so generally) or "guide"? (so Kupper, *Les nomades en Mésopotamie au temps des rois de Mari* [Paris, 1957], p. 100). I take *ša* in the sense of "as to" (Middle Babylonian, Aro, *StOr* 20, pp. 146f.; Old Assyrian? cf. *AHw*, p. 1118, 9b), thus making *mārū šiprīka uḫḫirūnikku* and *mārū šiprīya uḫḫarūni* parallel constructions; *uḫḫuru*, either intransitive or indefinite third plural subject (cf. *CAD*, M/1, p. 423b). Also possible: "The ones who delayed . . . were the Suteans" (so generally). If the dead or

those in mortal danger are the Egyptians rather than the Suteans, we would have a clearer connection with lines 43ff.

16. Lines 43ff. have been given many interpretations, mainly because of *ṣētu* or *ṣītu*: "pestilence" (*VAB* 2/2, p. 1587; Helck, *Beziehungen*², p. 183); "deprivation, fatigue" (Kühne, p. 83, n. 418; cf. von Soden, p. 434); "sun, open air" (*CAD*, Ṣ, p. 152; *AHw*, p. 1095b); "foreign country" (Knudtzon; Edzard, *AS* 16, p. 113). The Assyrian king probably refers to the long journeys mentioned in lines 35ff., especially the heat and other dangers of the desert (cf. *EA* 7:53ff.). Donald B. Redford, *Akhenaten, the Heretic King* (Princeton, 1984), p. 235, sees here a reference to Amenophis IV's holding audiences in the sun, thus worshipping his father.

17. *ni-i*[*l*-tap-pa-ru], or perhaps the present tense (-ta-na-ap-).

18. *ú*-⌜bal⌝-[l]a-*ṭù*-*ú* is probable; subject, indefinite third plural.

EA 17

A Mittani bid for a renewed alliance

TEXT: BM 29792.
COPY: BB 9.
TRANSLITERATION AND TRANSLATION: Adler, pp. 122–25.
PHOTOGRAPHS: Kitchen, *Suppiluliuma, I protagonisti della storia universale*, fasc. 66 (Milan, 1966), p. 260, figs. 2–3; Giles, *Ikhnaton: Legend and History*, pl. XI (obverse).

Sa[y] to Nibmuareya, the k[ing of Egypt], my brother: Thus Tuiše-ratta, the king of [M]ittani, your brother. For me all goes well. For you may all go well. For Kelu-Ḫeba may all go well. For your household, for your wives, for your sons, for your magnates, for your warriors, for your horses, for your chariots, and in your country, may all go very well.

11–20 When I sat on the throne of my father, I was young,[1] and UD-ḫi had done an unseemly thing to my country and had slain his lord. For this reason he would not permit me friendship with anyone who loved me.[2] I, in turn, was not remiss about the unseemly things that had been done in my land, and I slew the slayers of Arta[š]umara, my brother, and everyone belonging to them.[3]

21–29 Since you were friendly with my father, I have accordingly written and told you so my brother might hear of these things and rejoice. My father loved you, and you in turn loved my father. In keeping with this love, my father [g]ave you my sister. [And w]ho els[e] stood with my father [a]s you did?[4]

30–35 [*The ver*]*y next year*,[5] moreover, my brother's . . .[6] all the land of Ḫatti. When the enemy advanced against [my] country, Teššup, my lord, gave him into my hand, and I defeated him. There was [n]ot one of them who return[ed] to his own country.

36–38 I herewith send you 1 chariot, 2 horses, 1 male attendant, 1 female attendant,[7] from the booty from the land of Ḫatti.

39–40 As the greeting-gift of my brother, I send you 5 chariots, 5 teams of horses.

41–45 And as the greeting-gift of Kelu-Ḫeba, my sister, I send her 1 set of gold toggle-pins, 1 set of gold (ear)rings,[8] 1 gold *mašḫu*-ring,[9] and a scent container that is full of "sweet oil."

46–50 I herewith send Keliya, my chief minister, and Tunip-ibri. May my brother let them go promptly so they can report back to me promptly, and I hear the greeting of my brother and rejoice.

51–54 May my brother seek friendship with me, and may my brother send his messengers to me that they may bring my brother's greetings to me and I hear them.

NOTES

1. The exact implications of "young"—legally a minor or something less precise?—are not clear; see Kühne, p. 19, n. 84, and cf. RS 34.129:5–7 (*Ugar.* 7, pl. XI): "Now, there by you the king, your lord, is young (*ṣeḫer*); he knows nothing (*mimma lā īde*)," and so the correspondent writes to an official instead. On this letter, see M. Dietrich and O. Loretz, *UF* 10 (1978) pp. 53ff., and Lehmann, *UF* 11 (1979) pp. 481ff.

2. On "love," see the Introduction, sect. 4, n. 59.

3. Literally, "everything belonging to them," but the verb "to kill" argues for primary reference to persons (families and households of the traitors).

4. [*ša k*]*i-i ka-a-ša,* following Kühne, p. 18, n. 78. At the end of the previous line, *ša-n*[*u-ú*] (Knudtzon) is certain (against Adler).

5. [i-n]a TI (for MU.TI, *balāṭ*)-*ma*; [nu-kùr]-*ti-ma* (Adler) is not supported by the traces.

6. 31 ˹ki-i˺ (BB 9; Adler, despite *VAB* 2/1, p. 133, note g) is excluded.

7. On *ṣuḫāru* and *ṣuḫārtu,* see *Ugar.* 5, p. 135, n. 3; A. Finet, in D. O. Edzard, ed., *Gesellschaftsklassen im Alten Zweistromland und in den angrenzenden Gebieten,* Bayerische Akademie der Wissenschaften, Phil.-hist. Klasse, NF 75 (Munich, 1972), pp. 65ff.

8. The exact implications of "set" (pair?) are not clear; see Farber, in Rochberg-Halton, ed., *Language, Literature, and History* (see *EA* 13, n. 22), pp. 97–98.

9. According to Adler, *mašḫu* is a Kassite loanword, "god," here a representation of a god. However, the restriction of the term to a Hurrian milieu (Mittani, Alalakh, Qaṭna) argues against such a derivation.

EA 18

A lost message

TEXT: VAT 1880 (+) VAT 1879.
COPIES: *VS* 11, 8 (cf. WA 217 [+] 230 = 226).
TRANSLITERATION AND TRANSLATION: Adler, pp. 126–27.

Too fragmentary for translation.[1]

NOTE

1. The two fragments may not belong to the same letter (Michel Artzi, private communication; cf., however, *VAB* 2/1, p. 134, note b), and neither fragment has the same clay as the other Mittani letters (letter of Allan Dobel, Dec. 10, 1975; cf. A. Dobel, F. Asaro, and H. V. Michel, *Or* n.s. 46 [1977] pp. 375ff., and *AfO* 25 [1974–77] p. 259). It is questionable, therefore, whether they belong to the Mittani archive.

EA 19

Love and gold

TEXT: BM 29791.
COPY: BB 8.
PHOTOGRAPHS: E. Budge and L. King, *A Guide to the Babylonian and Assyrian Antiquities* (London, 1900), pl. XXVI; in 2d ed. (1908), pl. XXXIX (obverse).
TRANSLITERATION AND TRANSLATION: Adler, pp. 128–35.

Say to Nimmureya, Great King, the king of Egypt, [my] brother, my son-in-law, who loves me, and whom I lov[e]: Message[1] of Tušratta, Great King, [your] father-in-law, who loves you, the king of Mittani, your brother. For me all goes well. For you may all go well. For your household, for my sister, for the rest of your wives, for your sons, for your chariots, for your horses, for your *warriors,*[2] for your country, and for whatever else belongs to you, may all go very, very well.

9–16 As far back as the time of your ancestors, they always showed love to my ancestors.[3] You yourself went even further and showed very great love to my father. Now, in keeping with our constant and mutual love,[4] you have made it ten times greater than the love shown my father. May the gods grant it, and may Teššup, my lord, and Aman make *flour*[*ish*][5] for evermore, just as it is now, this mutual love of ours.

17–24 When my brother sent Mane, his messenger, saying, "Send your daughter here to be my wife and the mistress of Egypt," I caused my brother no distress and *immediately*[6] I said, "Of course!" The one whom my brother requested I showed to Mane, and he saw her. When he saw her, he praised her greatly. I will *l*[*ea*]*d* her[7] in safety to my brother's country. May Šauška and Aman make her the image of my brother's desire.[8]

25–29 Keliya, my messenger, *brou*[*ght*][9] my brother's words to me, and when I heard (them), they were very pleasing, and I rejoiced very, very much, saying, "*Certainly* there is this between us: we love each other." Now, with such words let us love (each other) forevermore.

30–33 When I wrote to my brother, I said, "Let us love (each other) very, very much, and between us let there be friendship." I also said to my brother, "May my brother treat me ten times better than he did my father."

34–38 I also asked my brother for much gold, saying, "May my brother grant me more than he did to my father and send it to me. You sent my father much gold. You sent him large gold jars and gold jugs.[10] You se[nt him] gold bricks as if they *were* (*just*) *the equivalent of* copper."[11]

39–42 When I sent Keliya to my brother, I asked for [much] gold, saying, "May my brother treat me [ten times] better than he did my father, and may he send much gold that has not been worked."[12]

43–48 May my brother send me much more than he did to my father. Thus did I say to my brother: "I am going to build a *mausoleum* for my grandfather."[13] I also said, "In accordance with a favorable *answer,*[14] I am going to make the paraphernalia." And thus did I also say: "The gold that my brother sends me may he send for the bride-price as well."[15]

49–53 Now my brother has sent the gold. I say, "It may be little or not, not a little but much. Still, it has been worked. But though it has been worked, I rejoiced over it much, and whatever it was my brother sent, I am happy about it."[16]

54–58 I now hereby write to my brother, and may my brother show me much more love than he did to my father. I hereby ask for gold from my brother, and the gold that I ask for from my brother is meant for a double purpose: one, for the *mausoleum,* and the other, for the bride-price.

59–70 May my brother send me in very great quantities gold that has not been worked, and may my brother send me much more gold than he did to my father. In my brother's country, gold is as plentiful as dirt. May the gods grant that, just as now gold is plentiful in my brother's country, he[17] make it even ten times more plentiful than now. May the gold that I ask for not become a source of distress to my brother, and may my brother not cause me distress. May my brother send me in very large quantities gold that has not been worked. Whatever my brother needs for his house, let him write and take (it). I will give ten times more than what my brother asks for. This country is my brother's country, and this house is my brother's house.

71–79 I herewith send my messenger, Keliya, to my brother, and may my brother not detain him. May he let him go promptly so that he may be on his way and I hear my brother's greeting and rejoice exceedingly. Forevermore may I constantly hear the greeting of my brother. May Teššup, my lord, and Aman grant that these words that we shall be constantly writing achieve their *purpose,* and may they be, as long as they exist,[18] just as they are now. Just as we love (each other) now, exactly as now, so may we love (each other) forevermore.

80–85 I herewith send as my brother's greeting-gift: 1 gold goblet, with inlays of genuine lapis lazuli in its handle;[19] 1 *maninnu*-necklace, with a *counterweight,* 20 pieces of genuine lapis lazuli, and 19 pieces of gold, its centerpiece[20] being of genuine lapis lazuli set in gold; 1 *maninnu*-necklace, with a *counterweight,* 42 genuine *ḫulalu*-stones, and 40 pieces of gold shaped like *arzallu*-stones,[21] its centerpiece being of genuine *ḫulalu*-stone set in gold; 10 teams of horses; 10 wooden-chariots[22] along with everything belonging to them; and 30 women (and) men.[23]

NOTES

1. On *umma,* "message," see Introduction, n. 52.
2. ÉRIN.GAL(.MEŠ, *EA* 20:6): logogram for *ḫurādu* (*CAD,* Ṣ, p. 50a)?
3. On lines 9–13, see A. Poebel, *AS* 9, pp. 29–30.
4. *inanna atta kī it-ti-⟨⟨ia⟩⟩ a-ḫa-meš nirtana' 'amu*: if the suffix is retained, the syntax is extremely difficult; besides, in the Amarna letters *aḫāmiš* is never used independently (except *EA* 29:48?), but only with a preposition: *ana* (*EA* 4, 7, and 9, all Babylonia); *itti* (*EA* 6, 8–10, Babylonia; 162, Egypt; 19:28, a line closely parallel to 19:12).
5. *li-né-ep-pí*-[šu]: against the reading *li-né-eb-bi*-[ú] (Knudtzon, followed by Adler) are the implicit assumption of an uncontracted form (an Assyrianism? cf. *EA* 25 ii 41) and the meaning of *nubbû,* which, except perhaps at Emar, does not mean "to proclaim," but "to lament." *nuppušu,* "to broaden, expand," seems plausible.
6. *ina pānâtim-ma,* lit. "among the very first things"; hardly "previously, on an earlier occasion" (Adler), which ill accords with the context; cf. *EA* 29:22. On the particle *-maku* (*annī-maku*), here and elsewhere in *EA,* I follow Kühne, p. 24, n. 111.

7. *lu-ú*-x-*ši*: x = [b]a (Knudtzon; Winckler, KB 5, p. 34); du (BB); is (Adler, *is-lim*); [r]u (Gordon). The traces are extremely faint; I follow Gordon.

8. Cf. *EA* 20:25ff.

9. *it-ta*-š[e-m]a: *it-ta*-š[a]r (Knudtzon), as if from *muššuru*, would be an unparalleled form. Against simply *it-ta*-š[e] (Adler) is the probable trace of a vertical (see *VAB* 2/1, p. 1001, no. 20, which also argues against *it-ta*-b[a]l; cf. Kühne, p. 26, n. 117).

10. gišKIRI$_6$ is a play-writing for *kirrēt* (*CAD*, K, p. 410b; Adler, p. 130, n. 4). A pin or the like (*kirissu*), a typically female adornment, does not seem a likely gift for a king (against *AHw*, p. 484).

11. *kīma ša erê ma-ṣú-ú*: cf. *maṣû* with the accusative (number of times), "reach, come to." Perhaps *ma-sú-ú*, "as if they were (only) refined copper" (*CAD*, M/2, p. 30); "when ones of copper would have sufficed" (Adler) seems much too free.

12. *ša šipra lā epšu* does not mean "that cannot be counted" (Knudtzon, followed by Zaccagnini, *Lo scambio dei doni nel Vicino Oriente durante i secoli XV–XIII* (Rome, 1973), p. 85, and Pintore, *Matrimonio*, p. 148, n. 43); see *AHw*, pp. 1245f., esp. 1246, 9a. On this passage, see also von Schuler, *ZA* 53 (1961) pp. 190f., and Kühne, p. 25, n. 115. Note, too, that earlier, at Mari, metals are given *ana šiprim*, "for working" (Limet, *MARI* 4, p. 512).

13. On *karašku*, "mausoleum," see Kühne, p. 25, n. 114. (However, *HSS* 13, 165, does not refer to cremation; see Diakonoff and Jankowska, *AoF* 2 [1975] pp. 131f.).

14. Following Kühne, p. 24, n. 111. Against taking *a-aš-ni* as if from *šanû*, "to do a second time" (Pintore, *Matrimonio*, p. 148, n. 45; Adler), is the restriction in the Mittani letters of initial V-VC writings to verbs primae aleph and primae waw (Adler, pp. 10f.).

15. *ana terḫatim-ma*: *-ma*, "also, likewise"; cf. *EA* 19:58.

16. For slightly different versions of lines 49–53, see Kühne, p. 24, n. 111, and Adler, who thinks that the entire passage is ironic.

17. The subject in the singular is surprising and probably an error; one expects a plural referring to "the gods" (Adler).

18. *adi šunū-ma* (independent pronoun).

19. On *šakru*, "handle," see *EA* 22 i 33.

20. On *qablu* in a necklace referring to the centerpiece, the part lying lowest on the breast, see Durand, *ARMT* 21, p. 242.

21. *sú-uḫ-sí*-dINANNA: following *AHw*, p. 1054; for the equivalence, *arzallu*, see also *CAD*, A/2, p. 324. Cf. *arzallu* as a piece of jewelry in Neo-Babylonian times, when apparently it was also made of gold.

22. See *EA* 3, n. 17.

23. In *HSS* 16, 10:75, SAL.NITA.MEŠ means "women (and) men," a usage, as noted by Wilhelm, *Das Archiv des Šilwa-Teššup*, 2 (Wiesbaden, 1980), p. 73, that seems pertinent here. In *Emar* 6/3, 217:8 and 256:8, 11, the logogram refers to children, female and male; see Durand, *NABU*, 1989, no. 55. Perhaps the common denominator was "subordinate members of a household." See also the discussion of SAL.UŠ(NITA) in *CAD*, S, pp. 216f.

EA 20

Humiliation and wounded feelings

TEXT: VAT 191 (not collated).
COPIES: WA 22; *VS* 11, 9.
TRANSLITERATION AND TRANSLATION: Adler, pp. 136–43.

Say [to Nim]mureya, the king of [Egypt], my brother, my son-in-law, [whom I l]ove and who love[s me: Thus T]ušratta, the king of Mitt[ani], your father-in-law, [who l]oves you, your brother. [Fo]r me all goes well. For you [may a]ll go well. For your household, for [your] wives, for your [s]ons, for your magnates, [for] your [ch]ariots, for your horses, for your *warriors*,[1] [f]or your country and whatever else belongs to you, may all go very, very well.

8–13 In view of friendly relations, Mane, my brother's messenger, came to take my brother's wife to become the mistress of Egypt.[2] I read and reread the tablet that he brought to me, and I listened to its words. Very pleasing indeed were the words of my brother. I rejoiced on that day as if I had seen my brother in person. I made that day and night a [fes]tive occasion.

14–17 I will carry out my brother's eve[ry] word [t]hat Mane brought to me. I will now, t[hi]s year, del[iver] my brother's wife, the mistress of Egypt, and they will bring her to my brother. On t[hat] day shall Ḫanigalbat and Egypt be [*one*].[3]

18–22 For this reason, Ma[n]e [*has been detained he*]*re a while*.[4] [*I was going to* se]nd Keliya and Mane promptly, but I *had* not *finished. They should be of delicate workmanship.*[5] *It* [th]us (*came*) to letting the w[or]k go, and I did not do the work, *in order to d*[*o*][6] ten times (*more*) for my brother's wife. But now I will do the work.

23–27 Within six months, I will send Keliya, my messenger, and Mane my brother's mes[senger]. I will deli[ver] my brother's wife and they will bring her to my brother. May Šauška, my mistress, the mi[stress *of all lands and* of m]y [*brother*],[7] and Aman, the god of my brother, make her the ima[ge] of [my brother's desire].

28–32 They will bring [hi]s [*wife*] to my brother, and whe[n *they show her to*] my brother, [*he will no*]*te* this:[8] she has become very mature, and . . . [. . . *She*] has been fashioned according to my brother's desire. And, *furthermore*], my brother [*will note* th]at [the *greeting-gi*]*ft* that I shall present [*is greater*] than *any* before.

33–38 *I herewit*]*h* [*send*] Ḫaaramašš[i, w]hom my brother [*sent*] to

[*me*]. I have entrusted him with a tablet. [*May my brother* read and] reread *my*] *re*[*port*] and hear its words. I *herewith*] send [Ḫaara]maššì to my brother . . . [. . .], my brother, did I not tre[at] his troops well? [. . .] . . .

39–45 . . .

46–59 [*And with regard to the gold*] that my brother sent [. . .], I gathered together all my [*foreign-gu*]*ests*. [My] brother, before all of them, [*the gold that he sent*] *has now been cu*[*t o*]*pe*[*n*[9] . . .a]ll of them. *They were* sealed, but the gold [. . .]. They were full of [. . .], and they wept very much, saying, "Are all of these gold? They do not *lo*[*ok* (like gold)]." They said, "In Egypt, gold is more plent[iful] than dirt. Besides, my brother[10] loves you very much. (But) *if there be someone*[11] whom he loves, then he would not giv[e] such things *to him*.[12] [*What*]*ever* is needed is in Egypt more plentiful than dirt, [and] anyone can give anyone[13] (else) so many things [that] they are beyond calculation." I said, "I cannot say [be]fore you, as I am used to sa[ying], 'My [brother], the king of Egypt, loves me very, very much.'"

60–63 My brother will consider whether I was somewhat distressed or not. *May he forgive me*![14] Never again may Teššup, my lord, permit me to complain against my brother. Thus have I spoken to my brother that my brother might know.

64–70 I have honored Mane, my brother's messenger, [and] all my brother's [tr]oo[ps] who accompanied Mane, and I have treated them with great distinction. Mane will indeed arrive, and my brother should [in]quire carefully from him whether I showed him very great honors. He will tell my brother, and my brother will hear from all of them whether I treated them just as was required. Mane is not dying. *Truly*, he is just the same, and he is not ill.[15]

71–79 May my brother send me much gold that has not been worked, and may my brother treat me even better than he did my father. May Teššup and Aman grant that my brother show his love for me, that my brother greatly *glorify* me before my country and before my foreign guests.[16] Forever will I do what my brother wants, and my brother shall do what I want. Just as men love the Sun, so may we as now—may the gods grant us!—forever maintain love [in] our [heart]s.

80–84 [I herewit]h send to my brother as my brother's greeting-gift 1 *rope-lock*,[17] [the . . . of which is of . . .] and its base of *ḫiliba*-stone set in gold; [. . . *that*] holds in its hand [. . .]; [. . .] with beads of genuine *ḫulalu*-stone set in gold, that *is meant for the hand* [. . .] . . .

NOTES

1. See *EA* 19:7.

2. Tušratta's daughter was not going to replace Teye (cf. *EA* 26), and Tušratta certainly knew it; see Kühne, p. 27, n. 120. In line 8, *it-ta-*[*a*]*l-ka,* following Adler.

3. [l-en a-mi]-lu-*ú*-t[u], lit. "one man(hood)," following Adler.

4. i[k-ka-la-a] *ú-ba-an*: cf. Knudtzon's [. . .]-*a*; adverbial *ubān* (see *AHw,* p. 1399a), if correct, is perhaps better taken with what follows ("I was just about to send . . .").

5. ⸢ú⸣-[ma-aš-š]ar-*šu-nu-ti* (Kühne, p. 28, n. 127) *ù la aq-ti lu qat-nu*: Knudtzon translated as if the text read *akalla-šunu*; Kühne emends to *ak-ta*[!]*-lu-šu-nu,* but the apparent subjunctive remains unexplained; *AHw,* p. 918 (hesitantly), and Adler emend to *aq-ti-ip*[!]*-šu-nu,* but neither "I did not trust them" nor "I did not trust (her) to them" (Adler) seems likely in context. Against my version is the absence of any parallel for the use of *qatû* (*uqatti* expected) and the failure to indicate the subject of *qatnū.* On *qatnu* said of work (*dullu,* lines 20ff.), cf. *EA* 14, n. 32.

6. *a-na* [e-pé-eš].

7. *be-el-ti be-l*[*e*-et KUR.KUR ù] 26 [ŠEŠ]-ia: cf. *EA* 23:13, 31f. Other interpretations: *bēlti be-l*[*e-ti*], "mistress of mistresses" (Ungnad, *OLZ,* 1916, col. 183; Schroeder, *OLZ,* 1917, col. 105; Kühne, p. 30, n. 136); and *bēltī be-e*[*l-tu ša*] 26 [KUR-*i*]*a,* "my mistress, the mistress of my land" (Adler, despite *VAB* 2/1, p. 146, note 3). In line 26, Kühne restores [DINGIR-*i*]*a,* "my god(dess)," but as subject and in the nominative case *ilī,*, not *ilīya,* is expected (cf. *EA* 23:31, and Adler, p. 26, on pronominal suffixes); cf. also "Teššup, my lord" (*bēlī, EA* 19:15; 20:61).

8. *ki-*[*i* ú-kál-la-mu-ši] 29 [i-im]-*ma-ar-šu*: on the sequence *kullumu-amāru,* cf. *EA* 19:21f., and on the writing of the latter form see Adler, pp. 10f. Free restorations: [ap-pu-na-ma] (line 30), [i-im-ma-ar] (31), [ra-bi] (32).

9. Reading and restoring (freely): 46 [ù aš-šum KÙ.GI] . . . 47 [ú-ba-ru-*t*]u_4*-ia* (cf. lines 73ff.) . . . ŠE[Š-*ia* KÙ.GI] 48 [ša ú-še-bi-lu] . . . *is-sal-*[tu] (Kühne, p. 28, n. 126).

10. A mistake for "your brother"?

11. *awīlūtu,* "anyone"?

12. *a-na áš-šu*: a mistake for *ana ša-šu*? Adler: *ana* ÁŠ (*ḫišeḫti*)*-šu,* "for his need."

13. Cf. use of *mannu* at Nuzi as indefinite pronoun (Wilhelm, AOAT 9, p. 82). See also the different interpretations by Adler and Kühne of the entire passage.

14. *lu-ú pa-aš-ra* (*napšuru,* "to forgive"). For other interpretations, see Adler and Kühne, p. 29, n. 129; also *Ugar.* 5, p. 73, n. 11.

15. This translation, rather than "he is/will be falling ill," seems required by context.

16. On *ubāru,* "foreign guest," see Kühne, p. 29, n. 128. The verb, *ú-bar-ra-ḫa-an-ni,* is probably a mistake for *ú-ša-aš-ra-ḫa-an-ni* (*CAD,* B, p. 101; J. Fin-

kelstein, *JAOS* 90 [1970] p. 253, n. 48); otherwise, Adler and G. Driver, *JSS* 12 (1967) p. 106.

17. ^{giš}ÉŠ.SAG.KUL (*ebel sikkūri*), with Adler; correct *CAD*, K, p. 56b.

EA 21

A necklace for 100,000 years

TEXT: VAT 190.

COPIES: WA 21; *VS* 11, 10.

TRANSLITERATION AND TRANSLATION: Adler, pp. 144–47.

Say to Nimmureya, Great King, king of Egypt, my brother, my son-in-law, whom I love and who loves me: Thus Tušratta, Great King, the king of Mittani, your brother, your father-in-law, and one who loves you. For me all goes well. For my brother and my son-in-law, may all go well. For your household, for your wives, for your sons, for your men, for your chariots, for your horses, for your country, and for whatever else belongs to you, may all go very well.

13–23 I have given him my daughter to be the wife of my brother, whom I love. May Šimige and Šauška go before her. May they m[ake he]r the image of my brother's desire. May my brother rejoice on *t*[*hat*] day. May Šimige and Šau[ška] grant my brother a *gre*[*at*] blessing, exquisi[te] joy. *M*[*ay they bless him*] and may *you*, my brother, *li*[*ve*] forever.[1]

24–32 Mane, [my brother's] messenger, and Ḫane, my brother's interpre[ter], I have *ex*[*alted*] like gods. I have given [them] many presents and treated them very kindly, for their report was excellent. In everything about them, I have never seen men with such an appearance. May my gods and the gods of my brother protect them.

33–41 I herewith dispatch to my brother Naḫramašši to carry out . . . ,[2] and I send 1 *maninnu*-necklace of genuine lapis lazuli and gold as the greeting-gift of my brother. May it rest on the neck of my brother for 100,000 years.

NOTES

1. 21 . . . l[ik-ru-bu-šu] 22 . . . *lu-ú bal*-ṭ[á-ta].

2. 34 *ša ta am ra*: Kühne, p. 31, n. 143, emended the text to read *ta-aš*!-*pu*!-*ra* ⟨(a-na) x-x⟩ *ana epēši*, "whom you have sent to me, I have sent to my brother to do ⟨x x⟩." Did the jargon of diplomacy develop in the periphery a word *šatamru*, "personal report," from frequently used (introductory) *ša ātamru*, "what I saw (was . . .)?" Cf. the use of *amāru* in *EA* 15. Edel, *JNES* 7 (1948) p. 24, has questioned the personal name; rather, "1 *naḫra* (made of) *mašši*."

EA 22

Inventory of gifts from Tušratta

TEXT: VAT 395.
COPIES: WA 26; *VS* 12, 199.
TRANSLITERATION AND TRANSLATION: Adler, pp. 148–69.

I

4 beautiful horses that run (swiftly).

2–3 1 chariot, its *tulemus,* its *thongs,* its covering, all of gold.[1] It is 320 shekels of gold that have been used on it (the chariot).

4–6 1 whip of *pišaiš,* overlaid with gold; its *parattitinu,* of genuine *ḫulalu*-stone; 1 seal of genuine *ḫulalu*-stone is strung on it. 5 shekels of gold have been used on it.

7–8 2 *ša burḫi,* overlaid with gold. 6 shekels of gold and 4 shekels of silver have been used on them.

9–11 2 (leather) *uḫatati,* overlaid with gold and silver; their center is made of lapis lazuli. 10 shekels of gold and 20 shekels of silver have been used on them.

12–14 2 *maninnu*-necklaces, for horses; genuine *ḫulalu*-stone mounted on gold; 88 (stones) per string. It is 44 shekels that have been used on them.

15–20 1 set of bridles; their *bl*[*ink*]*ers,*[2] of *gilamu*-ivory; their "thorns,"[3] of go[ld; . . .] . . . , and . . . [. . . o]f alabaster; [. . .] . . . their *kuštappanni*; [. . .] . . . [. . .] of *gilamu*-ivory; and their [. . .], of gold *with a reddish tinge.*

21–22 2 leather *nattullu,*[4] which are variegated like a wild dove.

23 1 set of torques, of bronze.

24–30 1 (set of) reins; its base and *straps,* overlaid with silver; the *tašli,*[5] of gold *with a reddish tinge*; its entire upper part is a gold figure [. . .] . . . ; the *opening* . . . *its surface* . . . [. . .]; it is studded with *dardaraḫ*-ornaments of gold; and the "house" . . . is studded with *dardaraḫ*-ornaments, also of gold. 60 shekels (of gold) were used on it.

31 [x] good, sharp[6] arrows.

32–35 [1] dagger, the blade of which is of i[r]on;[7] its guard,[8] of gold, with designs; its haft,[9] of ebony with calf figurines; overlaid with gold; its [pomm]el is of . . .-stone; its [. . .] . . . , overlaid with gold, with designs. 6 shekels of go[ld] have been used on it.

36–37 [1] *bow,*[10] of the *apisamuš*-type [. . .], overlaid with gold. It is 4 shekels of silver that have been used on it.

38 1 mace, of iron, overlaid with gold. 15 shekels of gold have been used on it.

39–40 1 *zallewe*-knife, of bronze; its [ha]ft, overlaid with gold. 3 shekels of gold have been used on it.

41 1 *addu*-throwstick, of *pišaiš*, overlaid with gold. 2 shekels of gold have been used on it.

42–43 1 *tilpānu*-bow, of *zamiri*;[11] 4 times overlaid with gold. 6 shekels of gold have been used on it.

44 2 multicolored *shirts*.[12]

45 1 set of snaffles, of silver; [5]0 shekels in weight.

46 1 pair of *gloves* that are trimmed with red wool.[13]

47 1 shield . . . of silver, 10 shekels in weight.

48–54 1 leather *halter*, its "flint-blade"[14] of genuine *ḫulalu*-stone; its inlay, of genuine lapis lazuli; the *tašli*, (*with*) inlay of genuine lapis lazuli. Its centerpiece is set with *ḫiliba*-stone, and (*this*) centerpiece *o*[*f ḫili*]*b*[*a-stone*] is mounted on genuine lapis lazuli. 2 genuine *ḫulalu*-stones, mounted [*on gol*]*d*, which are strung on its *straps*. 1 seal of genuine lapis lazuli, mounted on gold. 1 *ḫulalu*-stone, a *counterweight*, which is strung on its rear. 10 shekels of gold have been used on it.

55–57 1 bottle, horse-*shaped*, of *amutu*-metal, with eagles of gold as inlay; and (*also*) its inlay, genuine lapis lazuli. 300 shekels in weight.

58–59 1 fly whisk, of gold, along with its linen cloth. 3 shekels in weight.

60 [1] *counterweight*, 10 shekels in weight.

61 [1 *si*]*eve*,[15] of gold, 20 shekels in weight.

62–66 [. . .], *of* stone; its top, of *muš*[*šaru*]-stone; [. . .] its haft, overlaid with gold; 2 times [. . .]; its [. . .] . . . , of *pendu*-stone[16] [. . .]; [. . .], of gold, . . . [. . . x] shekels of gold have been [used] on it.

II

1–2 1 ha[nd-brac]elet, of i[ro]n, [*overlaid with gol*]*d*; its *mesukku*-birds (have) an inlay of genuine lapis lazuli. 6 shekels of gold have been used on it.

3–4 1 hand-bracelet, of iron, overlaid with gold; its *mesukku*-birds (have) an inlay of genuine lapis lazuli. 5 shekels of gold have been used on it.

5 1 foot-bracelet, of gold, inlaid. 5 shekels of gold have been used on it.

6–8 1 *maninnu*-necklace, cut from 35 genuine lapis lazuli stones,

35 *ḫiliba*-stones; in the center, a genuine *ḫulalu*-stone, mounted on gold *with a reddish tinge.*

9–10 1 set for the hand, beads of genuine lapis lazuli, 6 per string, mounted on gold. 6 shekels of gold have been used on it.

11 1 set of *karatnannu,* of gold, 2 shekels in weight.

12–13 1 head-binding, of gold, twisted like a torque, 14 shekels in weight.

14–15 1 set of *arapšanna,* 6 *iduzzarra,* of gold *with a reddish tinge.* 12 shekels in weight.

16–19 1 dagger, the blade of which is of iron; the haft has an inlay of . . .-st[one], overlaid with gold; its pommel, of . . .-stone; its . . ., mounted on gold; its *maṭru,* (with) variegated trim of blue-purple wool, 2 times overlaid with gold. 14 shekels have been used on it.

20–22 1 *zallulu,* its *rettu* overlaid with *ḫiliba*-stones and genuine lapis lazuli; the handle, the figure of a woman, of alabaster; the inlay, of genuine lapis lazuli.

23–26 1 pair of shoes, of *dušu*-color (leather), and studded with *dardaraḫ*-ornaments of gold; their buttons, of *ḫiliba*-stone; with *karatnannalla*-ornaments, of genuine lapis lazuli, *set here and* [*there*]. 13 shekels of gold have been used on them. 1 pair of leggings, o[f *shaggy wool*].[17]

27–28 1 pair of *betatu*-shoes, richly provided with *dardaraḫ*-ornaments of gold. 6 shekels of gold have been used on them.

29–32 1 pair of shoes, of blue-purple wool; their . . . [. . .][18] and their . . . [. . .], of gold; their buttons, of *ḫiliba*-stone; the center, an inlay of genuine lapis lazuli. 4 shekels of gold have been used on them. 1 pair of *leggings,* of *shaggy* [*wool*].

33–34 1 pair of shoes, of colored linen, which *have iduzzarri.* 1 pair of *leggings,* of *shaggy wool.*

35 1 pair of shoes, of colored linen. 1 pair of *leggings,* of *shaggy wool.*

36 1 garment of blue-purple wool. 1 pair of shirts, Hurrian-style, [*for*] *the city.*[19]

37–38 1 *city*-shirt, Tukriš-style.[20] 1 pair of s[as]hes, of red wool, adorned.[21]

39–40 1 linen garment, *aššianni*-type. 1 pair of shirts, Hur⟨rian⟩-style, of linen. 1 *city*-shirt, of linen. 1 robe,[22] of linen.

41–42 1 garment, Hazor-style. 1 pair of shirts, Hurrian-style, of linen. 1 pair of *city*-shirts. 1 robe and 1 cap, of blue-purple wool.

43–47 1 fly-whisk.[23] Its *rettu* (has) an *in*[*lay*] of genuine lapis lazuli . . . *ḫiliba*-stone. [Its] haft, [overlaid with go]ld, 3 times; its inlay, of genuine lapis lazuli; its base, of [genuine l]apis lazu[li]. Its *cloth streamers* (held by) wire [. . .] 25 shekels of gold have been used on it.

48–50 A *mumerritu*-scraper, of . . . ,[24] a[nd] it is studded [with *dardaraḫ*-ornaments] of gold. Its haft, of ebony [. . .]. 6 shekels of gold hav[e been used] on it.

51 1 wash-basin, of silver, 140 shekels in weight.

52 1 stone-. . . , (with) *gilamu*-ivory, 70 shekels in weight.

53 1 silver tube, (with) *gilamu*-ivory, 77½ shekels in weight.

54–56 2 *bows* . . . ;[25] their astragal-ornaments overlaid with gold, and on 1 of them is the gold-*o*[*ver*]*lay* double. 10 shekels of gold have been used on them.

57–58 1 spear, of bronze, with a double overlay of gold. 6 shekels of gold have been used on it.

59–60 1 *makkasu*-axe,[26] of bronze, its handle 2 times overlaid with gold. 3 shekels of silver have been used on it.

61 10 large combs, of (various) stones.

62–64 1 bottle, of stone. 1 helmet-container,[27] of alabaster, (with) an inlay of genuine lapis lazuli, the rim of which is overlaid with gold. 3 shekels of gold have been used on it.

65–66 1 helmet-container, of *malachite,* overlaid with gold. 4 [shekels] of gold have been used on it.

67–68 [. . .] of *marḫallu*-stone. 1 *kuninnu*-bowl, of *marḫallu*-stone. [. . .], of *ḫulalu*-stone. 1 *counterweight,* of stone.

69–73 [. . .], of ebony; its center and [its] rungs,[28] [*overlaid with gold*; *abov*]*e* and below [. . .], and ivory [mounted on] go[ld . . .].

III

1 [. . .] . . .

2–4 . . . [. . .] their rungs [overlaid with] gold, [above and] below[29] overlaid with silver. 60 shekels of gold, 40 shekels of silver, have been used on them.

5–6 1 plaque with winged disks and Deluge monster(s), of ebony, overlaid with gold.[30] 30 shekels of gold have been used on it.

7–9 1 dagger, the blade, of iron; its guard, of gold, with designs; its haft, of . . . ; an inlay of genuine lapis lazuli; its pommel, of *ḫiliba*-stone. 5 shekels of gold have been used on it.

10 1 set of salt (containers, in the form) of bull-calves and lions, of *ḫiliba*-stone.

11 1 *tr⟨a⟩y,*[31] overlaid with silver. 60 shekels of silver have been used on it.

12 1 small trough,[32] overlaid with silver. 40 shekels of silver have been used on it.

13–15 1 bowl, of gold, 10 shekels in weight. 10 bowls, of gold; 1 bowl, of silver, 10 shekels in weight. 1 small trough of silver, 10 shekels in weight.

16–17 1 bread shovel; its *rettu,* of . . .-stone; its hilt, overlaid with gold, its pommel, a *mesukku*-bird, of . . .-stone. 2 shekels of gold have been used on it.

18 1 bread shovel, of gold, 5 shekels in weight. 1 bread shovel, of silver, [x sh]ekels in weight.

19–20 1 bread shovel, of ebony. 1 bread shovel, of ivory. 1 bread shovel, of *boxwood.* 1 *awatamulušḫe,* of ivory.

21 1 *brazier,* of silver, 66 shekels in weight.

22–23 1 *chest,* without a cover, of ebony, with a winged disk, overlaid with gold and silver. It is 2 shekels of gold, 40 shekels of silver, that have been used on it.

24–25 10 bright garments; 10 pairs of shirts, Hurrian-style; 10 pairs of *city* shirts, 10 robes, 10 pairs of boots.

26 10 pairs of *leggings;* 10 pairs of *betatu*-shoes.

27 1 loincloth, of colored material. 1 *šusuppu*-cloth, of linen, trimmed with colored cloth.[33]

28 1 *šusuppu*-cloth, trimmed with colored cloth.

29–35 1 scent container, with myrrh-scented oil. 1 scent container with *sikil*-oil.[34] 1 scent container with *iaruttu*-oil. 1 scent container with myrtle oil. 1 scent container with *kanatku*-oil. 1 scent container with *elder*-oil. 1 scent container with *styrax*-oil.[35] 1 scent container with *peršanti*-oil. 1 scent container . . . 1 scent container with a *mixture* (of various oils).

36 10 *kirru*-pots, full of "sweet oil."

37–41 1 cuirass set, of bronze. 1 helmet, of bronze, [f]or a man. 1 cuirass set, of leather. 1 helmet, [of br]onze, for the *sarku*-soldiers.[36] 1 cuirass set, of leather, for horses, set with *ri*[*ng*]*s* of bronze.[37] 2 helmets, of bronze, f[or ho]rses.

42–43 1 shield, its *urukmannu* overlaid with silver. 10 shekels of silver have been used on it.

44 9 shields, their *urukmannu,* of bronze.

45–46 100 *bows,* of the *apisamuš*-type, of gold . . . [. . .]

47 1000 arrows, sharp. 2000 arrows [. . .]

48 3000 arrows [. . .].

49 10 *javelins,* with *ir*[*on*] tips.

50 10 *javelins,* with [bro]nze tips.

51 20 *arrows* . . . [. . .] . . .[38]

52 20 *arrows,* with "thor[ns" . . .].[39]

53 20 arrows, *šuku*[*du*-type].[40]

54 20 arrows (to be shot) flaming. 20 arrows . . . [. . .].

55 10 maces of [. . .].

56 10 *zallewe*-knives, of b[ronze].

57–59 10 "bull-toes," *bound together,*[41] of br[onze, and 1 bo]w 2 times overlaid with silver. It is 2 shekels of silver that have been used on it.

60 10 spears [. . .].

IV

1 [. . .] *of* . . . [. . .].

2–3 [x] small [. . .] *o*[*f* . . .] . . . [. . .].

4–5 [. . . *fo*]*r* a man; its *erattinnu,* of gold [. . .] . . . 8 shekels in weight.

6 1 spoon, of *elammakku*-wood. 1 *sumbiru,* of jasper.

7–8 1 set of *telannu,* of alabaster. 5 dogs, of gold, 5 shekels in weight.

9 5 dogs, of silver, 5 shekels in weight.

10 6 *sarra,* of alabaster.

11 1 (fabric) with *cording* above and below.[42]

12 3 large blankets.[43]

13 1 long spread,[44] for beds.

14 1 short spread, of which the trimmings are many-colored,[45] for a bed.

15 1 blanket, for the head. 1 blanket, for the foot.

16 1 bronze helmet as a *brazier.* 1 set of . . . , of wood.[46]

17 1 ewer, together with its cover, of bronze.

18 1 kettle, of bronze. 1 water-dipper, of bronze.

19 10 jars, of bronze, 10 stands, of bronze.

20 1 brazier, of bronze. 10 *wutru,* of bronze.

21 10 "spears,"[47] of bronze. 10 bowls, of bronze.

22 10 washbasins, of bronze. 10 braziers, of bronze.

23 2 bolts, of bronze. 30 *sakku,*[48] of bronze.

24 10 kettles,[49] of bronze. 10 sets of *angurinnu,* of bronze.

25 [. . .], of bronze. 10 *appanannu,* of bronze.
26 [x] . . . , of bronze. 5 sprinklers, of bronze.
27 1 washing-bowl, of bronze. 1 *pulluštu,*[50] of bronze.
28 [. . .] . . .-vessels, of bronze, along with a brazier, of bronze.
29 [. . .] . . .-vessels, of bronze. 1 incense bowl.
30 [. . .] . . .-vessels, of bronze. 1 pot-stand, of bronze.
31 [. . .] . . .-vessels, of bronze. 1 chest, of bronze.
32 10 [. . .], of bronze. 6 *gungubu,* overlaid with bronze.
33 For 10 teams: [x] coverings of a chariot.[51]
34 4 small troughs of *elammakku*-wood, 1 small trough of *boxwood.*
35 5 spoons.[52] 500 large *gunte memetu.*
36 5000 small *gunte memetu fr*[*om the tr*]*easury.*
37 10 *chariot-poles.* 10 chariot-frames.[53]
38 [x y]okes[54] [for a ch]ariot, . . . the chariot-platform,[55]
39 along with their [. . .]. *12* yokes [(. . .)].
40 10 teams [. . .] . . . [. . .].
41 10 teams . . . [. . .] of *kiškanu*-wood.
42 400 [(. . .)] . . . [. . .].

43–49 It is all of these *wedding-gifts,*[56] of every sort, that Tušratta, the king of Mittani, gave to Nimmureya, the king of Egypt, his brother and his son-in-law. He gave them at the same time that he gave Tadu-Ḫeba, his daughter, to Egypt and to Nimmureya to be his wife.

NOTES

1. On *siḫpu* as "cover(ing)," see *CAD,* S, p. 239.

2. 1 ŠU ^{kuš}KA.TAB.ANŠE (*katappû*) *nap*-⌈la-sà⌉-[a]-*ti-šu-nu*. The reading of the logogram, the standard form at Boghazköy and attested in an Old Babylonian forerunner to ḪAR-*ra* (*CAD,* K, p. 303a), follows *AHw,* p. 465, and *CAD,* G, p. 71. The reading ^{kuš}KA.TAB KU[NGI] (*CAD,* K, p. 303, followed by Adler), "bridles for mules," must assume an unparalleled ^{kuš}KA.TAB and at least one, probably two, mistakes in the writing of KUNGI: ⟨ŠÚ⟩ + NAB (rather than MUL). If my reading is correct, it would suggest that the blinkers were in some way attached to the bridle, or perhaps the meaning here is an extended one, applied to a part of the bridle.

3. *pu-uq-dá-a-ti-šu-nu* (*AHw,* p. 880).

4. Perhaps related to the *na-tu-la-te* in a letter found at Kumidu; see G. Wilhelm, *ZA* 63 (1973) p. 19, line 19; see also M. Görg, *ZA* 76 (1986) p. 303.

5. On a possible earlier form of *tašli* (*ti-sa-la*), see M. Civil, in L. Cagni, ed., *Ebla, 1975–1985* (Naples, 1987), p. 156.

6. *šarmu,* "cut," but probably to be understood of sharpening the tips.

7. On *ḫabalkinnu,* see M. Hoffner, *JCS* 22 (1968) pp. 42–43; J. Postgate, *BSOAS* 34 (1971) pp. 13ff. In *EA* 22 and 25, AN.BAR is perhaps to be read *ḫabalkinnu,* not *parzillu.*

8. On *gumūru*, "guard," see Salonen, *StOr* 33, p. 57.

9. KIN = *šakru*, as long established by Knudtzon, *VAB* 2/1, p. 158, note f, and now made explicit by ḪAR-*ra* forerunner, *Emar* 6/4, p. 77: 437ff.: kin = *ša-ak-ru*, kin-gír = *ša-kar pa-at-ri*, etc. How *šakru* (Middle Assyrian, Mittani, Emar)/*šikru* differs from *rettu* (*AHw*, p. 990b), with which it is also found (lines ii 21, 44; iii 16; *EA* 25 ii 43; etc.), is not clear. Is the *rettu* the lower part of the handle that fits into the palm? Cf. at Ebla, Sumerian šu-šà, "inside of the hand" = *la-'à-tum* (raḫatum) (G. Pettinato, *Materiali epigrafici di Ebla* [Naples, 1982], p. 256:516).

10. BAN (not ^{giš}BAN; also lines ii 54; iii 45, 48) = *qaštu* (*CAD*, A/2, p. 170b)?

11. On the *tilpānu*-bow, see B. Groneberg, *RA* 81 (1987) pp. 115–24. On p. 117, n. 21, Groneberg speculates that here the bow may be a musical instrument.

12. *sà-di-in-nu*; see also *EA* 266:32.

13. 1 ŠU *pí-ti-in-ka-ak* ^{síg}ḪÉ.ME.TÁ *ṣú-up-pu-ru*. On the logogram, see Goetze, *JCS* 10 (1956) p. 34, n. 19, and Landsberger, *JCS* 21 (1967) p. 168; on the reading *tabarru* rather than *nabāsu*, see *CAD*, N/1, p. 22a. *pitinkak*, "glove" (*AHw*, p. 869), though doubtful, seems more likely, in view of the trimming, than a part of the snaffle (Adler, following A. Salonen, *Die Landfahrzeuge des Alten Mesopotamien* [Helsinki, 1956], p. 57).

14. Assuming ^{na_4}GÍR.ZÚ = ^{na_4}GÍR.ZÚ.GAL, *ṣurru*; cf. ^{na_4}ZU = *ṣurru*? (*EA* 13:17).

15. [1 *ma-aš*]-*ḫa-lu* (*AHw*, p. 625; *CAD*, M/1, p. 365).

16. Assuming ^{na_4}ŠI.TIR = ^{na_4}ŠE.TIR. See *PRU* 3, p. 184:21 and note; *AHw*, p. 854b, which also refers tentatively to *LTBA* 1, 71:9 (but cf. *MSL* 10, p. 13:330).

17. *kaballu š*[*a i-li*] (cf. lines ii 32, 34–35), the last term taken as *i'lu* = ^{túg}SIG$_4$.ZA; see iv 12. Durand, *ARMT* 21, p. 423, sees in *kaballu* a special fabric for sandals or leggings.

18. *CAD*, K, p. 375a, proposes *k*[*i*-in]-*ṣí-šu-nu*, "their leggings."

19. 1 ŠU ^{túg}GÚ *ḫur-ri* [ša] URU: ^{túg}GÚ (also lines ii 39, 41, and iii 24 in this inventory; *EA* 27:110; and see ^{túg}GÚ URU in the next line) is an abbreviated ^{túg}GÚ.È(.A), *naḫlaptu* (cf. *EA* 14 iii 15, 18, 22). The same abbreviation is found at Boghazköy, and the Hurrian-style *naḫlaptu* is known from roughly contemporary documents from Alalakh, Boghazköy, and perhaps Ugarit; see Goetze, *Corolla Linguistica* (Wiesbaden, 1965), pp. 52ff.; *CAD*, N/1, p. 139b; *ARMT* 21, p. 402; S. Dalley et al., *The Old Babylonian Tablets from Tell al Rimah*, British School of Archaeology in Iraq (Hertford, Eng., 1976), pp. 59f. If the qualification is to be understood as [ša] URU = *āli*, "for the city" (longer? fuller? more elaborate?), this garment is perhaps opposed to the type of shirt worn by the military (Waetzoldt, *RLA* 6/1–2, p. 25b). The article of apparel called URU (*ālu*), if a mural crown (*PRU* 3, p. 182, note to line 4; *ARMT* 7, p. 309; Hoffner, *IEJ* 19 [1969] pp. 178ff.), hardly appears here. *alu*, a type of jewelry (*ARMT* 18, p. 169; *ARMT* 21, p. 250, n. 10), also seems excluded.

20. 1 ^{túg}GÚ URU (also ii 40, 41; iii 24; and *EA* 27:110) = *naḫlapti āli*? (See

previous line.) Tukriš (also *EA* 25 iv 25) was in Luristan and gave its name to metal objects and garments (see *tukrišû, AHw,* p. 1367).

21. 1 ŠU [túg]Í[B].LÁ (*nēbeḫu*) . . . *malû*: "full" recalls the contrast in Hittite texts of "full-empty," presumably "ornamented, non-ornamented"; see Goetze, *Corolla Linguistica,* p. 48, n. 2; cf. also ii 27.

22. 1 [túg]BAR.DUL = *kusītu* (also ii 42; iii 25; *EA* 25 iv 48), which is to be added to the references in *AHw* and *CAD* (*CAD,* K, p. 485b, misreads ii 42 as [túg]BAR.SI); cf. [túg]BAR.DUL_5/DUL, Practical Vocabulary of Assur 237f. (Landsberger and Gurney, *AfO* 18 [1957–58] p. 330), cited *CAD,* K, p. 585.

23. *ša zubbī kuššudi* (*AHw,* p. 461a; *CAD,* Z, p. 156a) is not an instrument for catching flies (Knudtzon, Adler). The difference between this whisk (also *EA* 25 iii 52) and *ša zubbī šūlî* (i 58) is not clear.

24. *ša per$_6$-a-zi* (also *EA* 25 i 27; *AHw,* p. 855): the qualification seems paralleled at Mari by *ša pí-(iḫ)-ḫa-zi(-im)*, which Durand, *AÉM* 1/1, p. 120, interprets as "having a mouse" (*piazu, pur'asu*), i.e., a part for gnawing, tearing.

25. The garment *ša-bá-at-ti* (*EA* 120:21) does not seem likely in this context; cf. *PRU* 3, p. 183, note to line 11.

26. The reference to a handle favors taking *makkasu* as a cutting instrument (*AHw,* p. 589, "an axe"; Adler) rather than as a bowl (*CAD,* M/1, p. 132). Note also 2 GÍR *ma-ka-su* (*ARMT* 21, no. 219:31), which indicates a knifelike *makkasu* as well as an axe (TÙN).

27. "Helmet" is more probably a designation of shape (also ii 65; iv 16) than a display helmet; see Wilcke, *RLA* 4/4–5, p. 312.

28. *gi$_5$-il-tù* (also iii 2): see *CAD,* K, p. 357a.

29. On *ištu,* "on, around," not "from," see N. Illingworth, *Iraq* 50 (1988) p. 103.

30. On ALAM as "winged disk" here, in line iii 22, and perhaps in line i 26, see Dalley, *Iraq* 48 (1986) pp. 94f.

31. *pa-aš-⟨šu⟩-ru,* following Adler, since *pasru,* "pole," is never found in a gift list.

32. 1 [giš]BUGIN.TUR (*buginnu ṣehru? sussullu?*): the difference between BUGIN (LAGABxA) and BÚGIN (LAGABxNINDA) is that the former was used for liquids, the latter for kneading dough; see *CAD,* B, pp. 306f., and H. Güterbock, *Otten Festschrift* (see Introduction, n. 37), p. 80.

33. On *šusuppu,* originally a cloth for wiping and later (as here) a kind of undergarment worn around the hips; see K. Deller and K. Watanabe, *ZA* 70 (1981) pp. 218f., and M. Mallul, *BiOr* 43 (1986) p. 29, n. 61.

34. Perhaps SÍ(.IK).KÍL (*EA* 25 iv 52) is a phonetic writing of Ì.SIKIL, *ellu/ ullu,* "(sesame?) oil." On these oils as cosmetics and their containers, see Helck, *Beziehungen,* pp. 399ff.

35. Contrary to *CAD,* B, p. 64, neither here nor in *EA* 25 iv 51 is the reading ŠIM.BAL; here it is ŠIM.BÚLUG (*ballukku*), and in the latter, ŠIM.GIG (*kanatku*).

36. On the *sarku,* see *Ugar.* 5, p. 98, n. 1, and I. Singer, *Tel Aviv* 10 (1983) p. 8, n. 11.

37. On *gurpisu,* "helmet," see Timothy Kendall, in M. A. Morrison and

D. T. Owen, eds., *Studies on the Civilization and Culture of Nuzi and the Hurrians* (Winona Lake, Ind., 1981), pp. 201ff. On leather cuirasses for horses, see Edel, *Brief,* pp. 151f.

38. There is not enough room for ^{gi}[*ia-ka*]*-a-tu*$_4$ (*CAD,* H, p. 264a, followed by Adler). Lines 51–54 seem to list special types of arrows.

39. *pu-uq-*⌜da-t⌝[u$_4$] (cf. i 16).

40. *šu-ku-ú-*[*du*] (Gordon).

41. 10 ŠU.SI (*ubānātu*) *ka-sà-tu*$_4$ ša GUD.MEŠ: obscure (see *AHw,* p. 1309a). Context seems to argue against interpreting ŠU.SI as *šūšī* and rendering "600 goblets (in the form of) oxen."

42. *ṭe*$_4$*-mu-ú*; see also *EA* 25 iv 48, and cf. ^{túg}GADA *ṭe*$_4$*-me-ta* (RS 34.134: 10, *Ugar.* 7, pl. XV–XVI).

43. 3 ^{túg}TUNANIBA (SIG$_4$.ZA, *i'lu*).MEŠ (omitted by Adler): on the fabric as hairy or shaggy and the logogram in peripheral texts, see Waetzoldt, *RLA* 6/1–2, pp. 21f.; Dalley, *Iraq* 42 (1980) p. 73. The *i'lu* was highly esteemed (Durand, *ARMT* 21, p. 407, n. 3).

44. TÚG.GÍD.DA: reading uncertain, but if TÚG = *ṣubātu,* then GÍD.DA = *arku* (not *ariktu,* Adler). Similarly, in the next line, GUD$_x$(PU).DA = *kurû,* not *kurītu.* Cf. perhaps *ARMT* 22, no. 164 r. 2–3, 1 TÚG GUZ.ZA BU.A, and see comments of J. Kupper, *ARMT* 22/2, p. 614.

45. *AHw,* p. 367, and *CAD,* I/J, p. 46, agree in reading UGUN (U + GUN) *iḫzetu* (a kind of special trimming) here and in *EA* 25 iv 50 (cf. iv 45ff.). As noted, however, by Knudtzon (*VAB* 2/1, p. 162, note h), the same sign is found in ii 18, 33, 35, and iii 27, and it is GÚN.A, usually *burrumu,* "variegated." On *sūnu,* "hem, trim," see Landsberger, *JCS* 21 (1967) p. 160, n. 105; Dalley, *Iraq* 42 (1980) p. 72; Moran, *RA* 77 (1983) pp. 93f.

46. *ša* GIŠ (not IZI [Adler]).

47. Among so many household objects, "spears" must be a kind of poker.

48. Cf. *sakku* II (*AHw,* p. 1012); *CAD,* S, p. 78 (perhaps *zakku*). Adler interprets ZA.AG.GI as a phonetic writing of SAG.GI = *pīḫu,* "lock," but though SAG.GI = *peḫû,* "to stop up, block," it is never a logogram for *pīḫu,* and *pīḫu* is not a lock.

49. 10 ⌜ŠEN⌝ (*ruqqu*? *šannu*? also Gordon).

50. The form (*purrusu*) and the reduplication in the corresponding Sumerian term (dug-bùr-bùr-ru) indicates a vessel with many "breaches," that is, with a strainer or sieve attachment (cf. Adler).

51. Line 33 seems out of place and looks like a heading for 37ff.

52. ^{giš}BÚGIN.TUR (see n. 32) and *itquru,* "spoon," are joined here, as in *EA* 25 iv 63–64, and the correspondence of the numbers suggests that for each ^{giš}BÚGIN.TUR there was one *itquru.*

53. 10 NÍG.GÍD.DA (*mašaddu*: *AHw,* p. 622; *CAD,* M/1, p. 351; níg-gíd-da apin = *ma-ša-ad-du, Emar* 6/4, p. 70:166′) 10 [^{gi}]^{š}*bu-bu-*[*t*]*u*$_4$ GIGIR: there is no reason to read [^{ní}]^{g} (Knudtzon, *CAD,* B, p. 302; Adler); for the determinative, note especially the Akkadogram at Boghazköy, ^{giš}BU-BU-TÙ/TI. On *bubūtu* as the main beam on either side of the chariot, not the axle, see Civil, *JAOS* 88 (1968) p. 10. Cf. also the plural *bubātim,* along with poles, for a cart (*AbB* 3, 73:7).

54. If [*ṣ*]*imittu* is the correct reading, it would refer to a part of the chariot,

and it is not clear how it should be distinguished from *nīru* in the following line. On the difficulty in general of distinguishing the two, see Civil, *JAOS* 88 (1968) pp. 9f.

55. x-y-z [^{gi}]$^{š?}$ KI.KAL.GIGIR = *sassu* (*AHw*, p. 1032; *CAD*, S, p. 195).

56. The reading of NÍG.BA.MEŠ SAL.UŠ.MEŠ remains uncertain, and *terḫatu* in the sense of "dowry" (Knudtzon, tentatively; Pintore, *Matrimonio*, p. 149, n. 53) seems excluded by the logogram and the almost exclusively masculine character of the gifts; see Kühne, pp. 34f. Were these gifts originally the bride-price or part of it and then returned to the Egyptian king as a kind of indirect dowry? On the indirect dowry in the Hurrian milieu of Nuzi, see Katarzyna Grosz, in Morrison and Owen, eds., *Studies on the Civilization and Culture of Nuzi and the Hurrians* (see n. 37), pp. 170ff.

EA 23

A goddess travels to Egypt

TEXT: BM 29793.

COPY: BB 10.

PHOTOGRAPHS: BB, pl. 23; L. Waterman, *Royal Correspondence of the Assyrian Empire*, vol. 4 (Ann Arbor, 1930), pl. 4, no. 11; H. Saggs, *The Greatness That Was Babylon* (paperback; New York and Toronto, 1968), illus. 30 (reverse only).

TRANSLITERATION AND TRANSLATION: Adler, pp. 170–73.

TRANSLATION: Ebeling, pp. 372–73.

Say to Nimmureya, the king of Egypt, my brother, my son-in-law, whom I love and who loves me: Thus Tušratta, the king of Mittani, who loves you, your father-in-law. For me all goes well. For you may all go well. For your household, for Tadu-Ḫeba, my daughter, your wife, whom you love, may all go well. For your wives, for your sons, for your magnates, for your chariots, for your horses, for your troops, for your country and for whatever else belongs to you, may all go very, very well.

13–17 Thus Šauška of Nineveh, mistress of all lands: "I wish to go[1] to Egypt, a country that I love, and then return." Now I herewith send her, and she is on her way.[2]

18–25 Now, in the time, too, of my father . . .[3] went to this country, and just as earlier she dwelt there and they honored her, may my brother now honor her 10 times more than before.[4] May my brother honor her, (then) at (his) pleasure let her go so that she may come back.

26–30 May Šauška, the mistress of heaven, protect us, my brother and me, 100,000 years, and may our mistress[5] grant both of us great joy. And let us act as friends.

31–32 Is Šauška for me alone my god(dess), and for my brother not his god(dess)?[6]

NOTES

1. *lu-ul-lik-ma-me* (Adler, also Gordon).

2. The statue sent by Tušratta need not have been the statue worshipped in the temple in Nineveh; see Kühne, p. 37, nn. 176–77.

One explanation of the goddess's visit is that she was to heal the aged and ailing Egyptian king, but this explanation rests purely on analogy and finds no support in this letter, contrary to what Ilse Wegner, *Gestalt und Kult der Ištar-Šawuška in Kleinasien,* AOAT 36 (1981) p. 65, declares. More likely, it seems, is a connection with the solemnities associated with the marriage of Tušratta's daughter; cf. the previous visit mentioned in lines 18f., perhaps on the occasion of the marriage of Kelu-Ḫeba (see *EA* 19:6), and note, too, Šauška's role, along with Aman, of making Tadu-Ḫeba answer to the king's desires (*EA* 19:24; 20:25ff.; 21:16).

3. A reading I-*en-nu-tu*$_4$, "the first time" (Adler; cf. *EA* 1:72), would make perfect sense, but it is not supported by collation, either Gordon's or my own. x-y-BE/nu (possible, against Knudtzon)-*tu*$_4$; x = DINGIR? y = IŠ?

4. *pa-na-a-nu* (Gordon).

5. NIN-*ni*$_5$ (Adler).

6. These lines are hardly an affirmation (so Knudtzon; cf. Weber, *VAB* 2/2, p. 1050; Adler, p. 173, n. 1) to support Tušratta's request that the statue be returned. It may be doubted that Tušratta would say anything so obvious, or that, if he did, he would say it here and not five lines earlier when the return of the statue is mentioned (lines 24f.). The writing *ia-ši-ma-a* indicates a question, and the implied negative answer explains why the Pharaoh may expect to share with Tušratta in the protection and blessings of the goddess. She is "our mistress" (line 28) and, therefore, our goddess.

Following lines 31f., there are three lines of Egyptian, written in black ink and the hieratic script, the reading of part of which remains uncertain. This much seems clear: "Year 36, 4th month of winter, day 1. One (the king) was in the southern villa (of) the House of Rejoicing." See Kühne, p. 37, n. 178. It is uncertain whether this letter is referred to as a "copy" (Egyptian *myt.t*); on the implications of the term, see *EA* 27, n. 20.

EA 24

A letter in Hurrian about marriage and friendship

TEXT: VAT 422.
COPIES: WA 27; *VS* 12, 200.
TRANSLITERATION: J. Friedrich, *Kleinasiatische Sprachdenkmäler* (Berlin, 1932), pp. 8–32; improved readings, Otten in Farber, *Or* n.s. 40 (1971) pp. 65–66.[1]

§1

I 1–2 [Say to Nim]murey[a, the king of Egypt, my brother, my son-in-law], wh[om I love (and) who loves me: 3 Thus (speaks) Tu]šra[tt]a, the ki[ng of the land of Mittani, your father-in-law, 4 who loves you, your brother]. All goes well with me. 5 [May all] go we[ll with you]. For m[y so]n-in-law, your wives, 6 [your children, your] magnates, your [hor]ses, your war chariots, 7 yo[ur troops], your land and your [pos]sessions, may all go very well.

§§2–4
(badly damaged)

§5

47 . . . my father Šuttarna's daughter . . . 48 . . . from the . . . of my grandfather . . . 49 . . . two . . . my brother 50 . . . he sent to me 51 . . . And give me your daughter as my wife! 52 . . . Aššutemiwuya. And I did not express 53 . . . to Mane, your envoy, 54 . . . of the (genitive plural) . . . of my brother . . . which 55 . . . graciously 56 . . . everything [ve]ry, very 57 . . . all that 58 . . . I did graciously.

§6

59 . . . Mane, your envoy, 60 . . . fine oil(?) for his head, good . . . 61 . . . fine oil(?) for his head; 62 my brother's [*wife*], the mistress of the land of Egypt 63–64 (destroyed or unintelligible).

§7

65 . . . *now* my brother has sent. And earlier 66 . . . and my entire . . . 67 my brother *us*(?) very, very 68 . . . totally, my entire land very, very 69 . . . and I did all that totally 70 . . . very, very graciously, 71 with my [. . .] . . . (and) with those whom I love. Mane, 72 your envoy, 73 saw all the things that I did.

§8

74 As now my brother loves me, 75 as now I love my brother, 76 so may Teššup, Šauška, Amanu, 77 Šimige, Ea-šarri and all 78 the gods love us in their hearts very, very much. 79 For *long* years *may* [w]e(!) *with great joy* very, very much 80 *rejoice.* And the things that we wish for ourselves, 81 may one for the other, between us, generously, 82 most graciously do.

§9

83 And Keliya, my(!) envoy, delivered ... message, 84 and he reported as follows: "Your brother Nimmureya, 85 the lord of Egypt, made a ... gift. 86 And from Iḫibe, the city of Šimige, he had it come, 87 and to Šimige, his god, his father, he conducted (it). 88 And all the gifts of his forefathers 89 were very, very *delightful,* and *the pieces of booty left* your brother's 90 country *amazed.* So the gift went off, 91 and your brother *himself,* in consideration of the gift, was 92 *amazed.*" And Keliya *expressly announced* the gift's departure, 93 and he reported as follows: "He has ... 10,000 ... the way 94 ... So he has ... that of Šimige ... 95 ... I ... very much." Thus 96 ... did he speak. The ... 97 ... of the land of my brother, 98 which are made *for him,* the 99 ... objects that my brother 100 made for the gift, these may 101 Šimige and Aman and Ea-šarri 102 for my brother and his land ... in a favorable way, 103 ... 104 The things that my brother in connection with the gift 105 did for Šimige, his god, 106 his father, these will Šimige give to my brother, 107 and all the things that my brother 108 wishes in (his) heart, 109 he will make. So shall it be (lit., so they are).

§10

110 And may my brother not distress himself about that matter. 111 My brother's envoys whom 112 I allowed to depart(?) (and whom) I sent, those ... 113 ..., and may my brother hear them ... 114 Keliya, my envoy, and Mane, your envoy, I have allowed to depart, and they are coming to my brother.

II 1–2 (destroyed) 3 ... 4 And my brother has ... them 5 ... very correctly. And when about all I had not done 6 for my brother's wife 7 I heard from Keliya and Mane, when they left, 8 I was/did ... and ... 9 to the dowry for my brother's wife ... 10 very, very much, in a way according to my brother's heart 11 ... we might ... from our ...

§11

12 And I want just (lit., one thing) to say something to my brother, and may my brother 13 heed it. And Mane, my brother's 14 envoy, comes. When a dowry is *brought*(?), 15–16 and when earlier Mane *br*[*ought*(?)] what my brother had dispatched [as] my gift, 17 I assembled my entire land 18 and my nobles, as many as there are . . . And I addressed 19 Mane: "All . . . that my brother 20 dispatched, all 21 . . . that my brother 22 dispatched are . . . 23 . . . they may all . . . , 24 they may . . . , they may be *satisfactory* . . .

§12

25 And he did . . . them very much, in . . . fashion 26 . . . and I addressed (them): "My land 27 will . . . me; my nobles will . . . me. 28–33 (badly damaged)

§13

34–49 (badly damaged) 50 . . . And my brother will inform me . . . 51 . . . , 52 may the gods not ordain . . . distressed . . . 53–54 If . . . my brother will dispatch a shipment of gold as my gift, and over that 55 I would rejoice in my heart exceedingly, totally. 56 And so I have said them (these words) now to my brother. Know (this)!

§14

57–58 And now may my brother send Mane, my brother's envoy. If the . . . 59 four . . . , two . . . of ivory, . . . 60 golden . . . Just as I 61 . . . over the one large dowry . . . 62 rejoiced exceedingly, {I will} in view of 63 what my brother dispatches, 64 [rejoice] exceedingly.

§15

65 And the things which in our midst Teššup and Amanu 66 . . . have done, . . . *Just as* . . . 67 loves, so shall we together [in ou]r midst . . . 68 and we, between us, are one, the Hurrian land 69 and the land of Egypt. From *that* . . . they 70 among them are also of one mind. 71 I am the k[ing] of the land of Egypt, 72 and my brother is the ki[ng] of the Hurrian land (sic). 73 And what both these lands do not want . . . , 74 and we together do not want . . . , 75 if those great things . . . 76 in our *marriage alliance* our gods . . . 77 and(?) we(!) do not(!) guide well the . . . of our gods, of Teššup (and) Amanu. 78–79 Whosoever did not carry on a relationship full of love in the manner of my forefathers (and) my own (manner), another matter that . . . 80 all things for us . . . 81 So shall it be (lit., so they are). . . . Land . . . 82 For us may they . . . 83 all . . . other lands, which my

brother 84–85 . . . , in view of his/her/its matter, I will have with my brother a relationship full of love. So shall it be (lit., so am I).

§16

86 May my brother send off Mane. If 87 . . . *I* have proper*ly* given, the other 88 lands, all envoys are present, 89 and all other lands, my *servants,* are present. 90 If I to my head . . . , if 91 Mane is not, . . . 92 the others that I make, *where are they*? So 93 may my brother carry on with me a relationship full of love. . . . 94 all lands . . .

§17

95 Mane, your envoy, is very good; there does not exist 96 a man(!) like [him] in all the world . . . 97 Thus my brother in my land . . . 98 . . . that I saw . . . 99 . . . *in* my land . . . that he made . . . does not exist. 100 My brother did . . . Mane . . . From this . . . 101 . . . does not exist. The word that 102 Mane will communicate to my brother is graci[ous] and 103 true. And may my brother . . . it. It is not evil 104 (and) *hostile* towards my brother. 105 Towards his affairs it is not hostile, and he tells me (that) my affairs . . . 106 . . .

§18

107–8 But now [m]y brother [*has* s]ent, and it is [M]ane [my bro]ther has sent. And guards has [my] brother . . . 109 sent . . . 110 And he has come . . . and my brother . . . him . . . 111 And Mane . . . my brot[her . . .] land . . . 112 exceedingly . . . 113–15 (badly damaged)

§19

116 The other . . . of my brother, who come with Mane, 117 have . . . in a brilliant way very much . . . 118–24 (badly damaged) 125 Just as . . .

III 1 And my brother wanted a wife . . . 2 and now I have given her, and she has gone [to my] broth[er]. 3 Just as that entire . . . is pleasant, . . . 4 that entire . . . 5 So shall it be (lit., so it is). What the 6 Hurrian land does not want at all, what the 7 land of Egypt does not want at all, all that my brother's wife *shows* 8 to my brother, is not . . . 9 . . . sees . . . not. So 10 shall it be (lit., so it is), . . . so shall it be (lit., so it is).

§20

11 And now I have given my brother's wife, and she has gone 12 to my brother. When she comes, 13 my brother will see her . . . And she comes 14 to my brother; she is *pleasing,* according to my brother's

heart. 15 And again my brother will see a dowry 16 ... We ... from our ... 17 and we are not ... 18 (The things) that I have dispatched to my brother I have dispatched, and my brother will see them. 19 They come 20 to my brother, and they are ... and they are ...

§21

21 And now when the wife of my brother comes, 22 when she shows herself to my brother, 23 may my ... belonging to me, ... and my ... 24 they may show. And the entire land may my brother 25 assemble, and may all other lands 26 and the nobles (and) all envoys be present. 27 And they may show his dowry to my brother, 28 and they may spread out everything in the view of my brother. 29 If it is spread out in the view of my brother, 30 *on/from* the earth may ... And may my brother take 31 all the nobles and all the envoys 32 and all other lands and the war charioteers 33 whom my brother desires, and may my brother go. 34 And may he spread out the dowry and may it be *pleasing.*

§22

35 And there is ... my father's daughter, my sister. 36 And the tablet of her dowry is available. 37 And there is ... my grandfather's daughter, my father's sister. 38 And the tablet of her dowry ... 39 again is available. May my brother have their tablets given to him 40 and may he hear (the words of) both their (tablets). And the tablet(!) 41 of the dowry from me, which I gave, may he have given to him, 42 and may my brother hear that the dowry is very extensive, 43 that it is splendid, that it is befitting my brother.

§23

44 If ... the tablets of the dowries of my marriage alliance (through sister and father's sister) are not available, 45—my brother 46 ... *in view of that* not(!?), and there is nobody who does not know it. 47 And my brother knows *in their regard* 48 that they exist(ed), *which* the kings (also) know.

§24

49 I just (lit., one thing) want to say something to my brother, and may my brother heed it. 50 I have ... my brother much more than my forefathers. ... 51 *in great love,* and so I have ... And I wish to say: 52–53 The things that Artatama, my grandfather, did for your father are ... 54 And with just a single dispatch of mine I have done

ten times as much. 55–57 Similarly, the things that my father did for you, (well,) with just a single dispatch of mine I have done ten times as much. The gifts that 58–59 my grandfather (and) father dispatched to your father (and) to you, thus they are ..., 60 and they ..., in comparison with mine they are not *equivalent.* 61 And now my brother is going to see (the things) that I 62–63 have dispatched to my brother. Thus I will dispatch to my brother (gifts). So shall it be (lit., so am I). 64 Thus will I *deal loyally* with my brother, thus 65 will I be most loving. So shall it be (lit., so am I).

§25

66–67 And for the *horses* my brother did not *reward* me with gold the way my forefathers (were *rewarded*). The golden ... that your father to my grandfather 68 earlier dispatched—what you to my father 69 earlier dispatched was much more than that of your father. 70 And my brother has not *given* to me *the equivalent* 71 of what he dispatched to my father. And may my brother 72 *make* me *rich* in respect to the kings, my *vassals*(?) 73 (and) the other lands. *With* much gold 74 may my brother *have me provided.* And I ... And may my brother 75 also ... *carry out* my business. And my heart 76 may he not distress. Of my sister, the wife of my brother, 77–78 may m[y brothe]r erect a mo[lt]en gold image ... 79–85 (badly damaged) And may he not distress my heart! And may my brother give, 86 in the manner desired, accor[ding to] my heart, *pleasing* (things). 87 And my brother has ... me much, much more than my forefathers. 88 And may my brother *make* me *rich* in respect to my land. 89 And may my brother not distress my heart! *For that* ... 90–92 I have requested from my brother a molten gold image of my daughter. I know that my brother loves me exceedingly, from the heart, 93 but I also know that for my brother, in his land, gold ... 94 much. And in respect to my brother ... And may my brother 95 not ...; may he not distress my heart! And *in the measure in which it appears,* 96 ... may my brother give *pleasing* (things). And *next,* 97 may my brother give an ivory image. As 98–99 I shall speak to my goddess, Šauška of Niniveh, that a gold image for me might 100 ... So shall it be (lit., so it is), Before earth 101 (and) before the heavens *are the words spoken. As* 102 *they should be spoken,* so shall it be (lit., so they are): "This 103 molten gold image is Tadu-Ḫeba, the daughter of Tušratta, 104 the lord of Mittani, whom he gave as wife of Immureya, 105 the lord of Egypt. 106 And Immureya made a molten gold image, 107 and full of love dispatched it to Tušratta."

§26

108 And because of all this we both are of one mind and love one another ... 109 exceedingly. And in our lands 110 *peace prevails.* If only an enemy of my brother 111 did not exist! But should in the future an enemy 112 *invade* my brother's land, (then) my brother writes 113 to me, and the Hurrian land, armor, arms, 114 ... and everything concerning the enemy of my brother 115 will be at his disposition. But should, on the other hand, there be for me an ene[my] 116—if only he did not exist!—I will write to my brother, 117–18 and my brother will dispatch to the land of Egypt, armor, arms, ... and everything concerning my(!) enemy. 119–24 (unintelligible)

§27

IV 1 And I want to say something (lit., one thing) more to my brother: 2 In my brother's presence *there are* not many evil words *spoken.* 3 Those do not come into the presence of the Great ... lord/king. 4 An evil word ... to my brother. 5 And *for the satisfaction* of my person he has spoken to me, 6–7 and *with satisfaction* have I again heard him. That my brother has made the ..., my brother has ... *to the* great ... 8 And for (or: among) the people of Awar he has made provision, and he has ... 9 I heard this and I rejoiced. If, however, 10 my brother had not done them this way, then I would be very distressed. 11 And now again a ... *has reported* 12 and Parattu ... *informs me*(?). My brother is brotherly (minded). 13 That word comes, that ... has thus 14 been actually expressed. This word is in ... way *spoken,* and may my brother 15 ... *it* before his land regarding the great ... 16–18 ... they could ... And evil words are not spoken to my brother. And an evil word that anyone may say about me (or) about my land, 19—may my brother 20 not hear those words if Mane and Keliya 21 do not say them. But the (words) that Mane and Keliya say 22 about me (or) about my land, 23 they are true and right, and may my brother hear them. 24–25 That too that anyone might express to me about my brother (or) about his land, 26–27 those (words) I will not hear if Keliya and Mane do not say them. But what Keliya and Mane will say 28–29 about my brother (or) about his land, they (the words) are true and right, and I will hear them.

§28

30 And now, all the things 31 that my brother has named (and) wants, these 32–33 have I done tenfold. And with not a single word have I distressed my brother's heart. My brother's wife 34 I have

given, who is *pleasing* to my brother's heart. 35–39 I have sent off Mane, my brother's envoy, most magnificently. Now, too, (I have sent off) Keliya and Ar-Teššup and Asali, my envoys—Keliya is a magnate, and Asali is ... as my clay-tablet scribe—to my brother, and my brother will see them.

§29

40 And may my brother not detain my envoys, may he not ... (them). 41 And may my brother not ... me. And my envoys 42 may my brother let go as fast as possible. And I would ... for a word. 43 And I would like to hear (about the) well-being (and the) *favorable situation* of my brother, 44 and I will rejoice very much over the well-being of my brother.

§30

45 My brother may say: "You *yourself* have also detained my envoys." 46 No, I have not detained them. And you ... me 47 to the dowry for the wife of my brother, and my brother will see 48 what I have given as the dowry for the wife of my brother. 49 It is ... It is ... And it (the dowry) is coming. 50 In the view of my brother may it be *satisfactory.*

§31

51 May my brother let my envoys go as soon as possible 52 so they can leave. And may my brother send Mane along, 53 so he can leave together with my envoy! Any other envoy 54 may my brother not send. May he send only Mane. If 55 my brother does not send Mane and sends someone else, 56 I do not want him, and my brother should know it. 57 No! May my brother send Mane!

§32

58 And this wife of my brother whom I have given, this (woman) is *pure* (a virgin?). 59 And may my brother know it. If she ... 60 ..., she will speak. And she is *pure.* 61 And ... are available, and as my ... she my ... 62 both of them, and my mother has ... both of them. 63 ... And I have ... them ... And ... threefold 64 ... And may my gods know, 65 and may the gods of my brother know! If 66–68 (unintelligible)

§§33–34

(badly damaged)

107 to my [brother] it is ... And that is the thing 108 that has [been demanded]. And may my brother know it. As 109 ... speaks in some

other way, 110 may [my br]other not hear the (things) that (in reality)
are not [said].

§35

111 In my heart I wish to be on the best of terms with my brother
112 and to love one another. And *may* my brother keep faith
113 perfectly. And we wish to be friendly (to each other), and in our
hearts *we wish to love one another* 114–15 (destroyed or unintelligible) As
by Šeri 116 (and) your god our life (and) our fate *are determined,*
117 may the gods guide both of us together, 118 Teššup and Amanu,
our lords, our fathers. 119 And may we be protected. So shall it be
(lit., so we are). And may we . . . , 120 and may we . . . Thus . . . us.
And between us 121 we wish to love one another in brotherly fashion
and *close attachment.* As 122 man loves Šimige on seeing him, so do we
want, between us, 123 to love one another. And in our relationship
one will wish for 124 the *good fate*(!?) of the other. And all the lands
that 125 exist *on* the earth, that Šimige *shines upon,* 126 . . . all for us
. . . And so . . . they 127 . . . Tušratta is the Hurrian king, 128 . . .
Immureya is the Egyptian king, and if they . . . 129 . . . between them
. . . they 130 love . . . one another exceedingly.

NOTE

[The translation and note for *EA* 24 are by Gernot Wilhelm.—WLM]

1. The "Mittani letter" is the only document in the Amarna archives written in the Hurrian language, and since this language is quite inadequately understood, the translation must be provisional and tentative. The content is often obscure even where the text is not damaged. The Staatliche Museen zu Berlin very generously made photos available, and these were consulted in numerous instances. The interpretation of the text is associated especially with the names of Messerschmidt, Friedrich, Goetze, Speiser, and Bush; the relevant literature may be found in the extensive bibliography in the appendix to the latest comprehensive grammar of Hurrian, F. W. Bush, "A Grammar of the Hurrian Language" (Ph.D. diss., Brandeis University, 1964). For the grammar also to be noted are I. M. Diakonoff, *Hurrisch und Urartäisch* (Munich, 1971), and H. J. Thiel, *Phonematik und grammatische Struktur des Hurrischen,* in V. Haas, H.-J. Thiel et al., *Das Hurritologische Archiv . . . des Altorientalischen Seminars der Freien Universität Berlin* (Berlin, [1975]), pp. 98–239. E. Laroche has published a lexicon, *Glossaire de la langue hourrite, RHA* 34 (1976) and 35 (1977), reprinted as a monograph in the series Études et Commentaires, 93 (1980). For a new interpretation of several passages, see G. Wilhelm, *ZA* 73 (1983) pp. 96–113; idem, SMEA 24 (1984) pp. 215–22; idem, *Or* n.s. 54 (1985) pp. 487–96; and C. Girbal, *ZA* 78 (1988) pp. 122–36. The Hurrian-Hittite bilinguals discovered at Boghazköy (see H. Otten, *Archäologischer Anzeiger* [1984] pp. 372–75) have been used for this preliminary translation only to the extent that parts of them have been discussed in various articles of H. Otten and E. Neu prior to July 1990.

EA 25

Inventory of gifts from Tušratta

TEXT: VAT 340 (+) fragments 2191 a–c, no. 2.
COPIES: WA 25 (without fragments); *VS* 12, 201.
TRANSLITERATION AND TRANSLATION: Adler, pp. 174–205.

i

1–15 [. . .] . . .[1]

16 1 set [of earrings, of gold]; their [cones] of genuine lapis lazuli, and their *kukkubu* of genuine *ḫulalu*-stone.

17 1 set of ear[rings, of g]old; their [cones] of genuine *ḫulalu*-stone, and their *kukkubu* of genuine lapis lazuli.

18–19 1 set of earrings, of gold; their cones of genuine lapis lazuli, 4 on each; their *kukkubu* of genuine *ḫulalu*-stone.

20–21 1 set of earrings, of gold; their c[o]nes of genuine lapis lazuli, . . . ;[2] their *kukkubu* of genuine *ḫulalu*-stone.

22 1 set of toggle pins, (with) inlay;[3] their inlay of genuine lapis lazuli; their top of genuine *ḫiliba*-stone.

23 1 set of toggle pins, (with) inlay; their inlay of genuine lapis lazuli; their top of genuine *ḫulalu*-stone.

24 1 set of toggle pins, (with) inlay; their inlay of genuine lapis lazuli; their top of genuine *ḫulalu*-stone.

25 1 set of toggle pins, (with) inlay; their inlay of genuine lapis lazuli; their top of genuine *ḫulalu*-stone.

26 1 set of toggle pins, (with) inlay; their inlay of genuine lapis lazuli; their top of *ḫiliba*-stone.

27 1 set of toggle pins, of gold *with a reddish tinge* (and) *of* . . . ; their top of *ḫiliba*-stone.

28 1 set of toggle pins, of genuine *ḫulalu*-stone; their top of genuine *ḫulalu*-stone.

29 1 set of toggle pins, of genuine *ḫu*[*la*]*lu*-stone; their top of *ḫiliba*-stone.

30 [1 se]t of toggle pins, of genuine [. . .]; their top of *ḫiliba*-stone.

31 1 set of toggle pins, of *solid* gold; their top of genuine lapis lazuli.

32 [1 se]t of toggle pins, of *solid* gold; their top of genuine *ḫulalu*-stone.

33–34 1 "weave": 6 genuine lapis lazuli stones, 7 *ḫiliba*-stones, 14 *bikru*-gems of gold, 72 strings of genuine lapis lazuli and gold, 40 strings of gold.

35–36 1 "weave": 9 genuine lapis lazuli stones, 10 *ḫiliba*-stones, 20 *bikru*-gems of gold, [x] strings of lapis lazuli, 38 strings of gold.

37 [1 "wea]ve," of gold: 1 *ḫiliba*-stone, 4 genuine lapis lazuli stones, 4 . . . of gold.

38 [1 *mani*]*nnu*-necklace, of seal-shaped stones of lapis lazuli; 13 per string, mounted on gold.

39 [1 *mani*]*nnu*-necklace, of seal-shaped stones; 13 seal-shaped stones of genuine lapis lazuli, mounted on gold; 2 seal-shaped stones of genuine *ḫulalu*-stone, mounted on gold.

40 [1 *mani*]*nnu*-necklace (*with*) a *counterweight*: 28 genuine lapis lazuli stones, 28 *ḫiliba*-stones; the centerpiece a genuine *ḫulalu*-stone mounted on gold.

41 [1 *man*]*innu*-necklace, cut: 25 genuine lapis lazuli stones, 25 *ḫiliba*-stones; the centerpiece a genuine lapis lazuli stone mounted on gold.

42 [1 *mani*]*nnu*-necklace, cut: 26 genuine lapis lazuli stones, 26 *ḫiliba*-stones; the centerpiece a genuine lapis lazuli stone mounted on gold.

43 [1] *maninnu*-necklace, cut: 37 genuine lapis lazuli stones, 39 (*pieces of*) gold *leaf*;[4] the centerpiece a genuine *ḫulalu*-stone mounted on gold.

44 1 *maninnu*-necklace, cut: 38 genuine lapis lazuli stones, 38 (*pieces of*) gold *leaf*; the centerpiece a genuine *ḫulalu*-stone mounted on gold.

45 1 *maninnu*-necklace, cut: 26 genuine lapis lazuli stones, 28 *ḫiliba*-stones; the centerpiece a genuine lapis lazuli stone mounted on gold.

46 [1] *maninnu*-necklace, cut: 38 [genuine lapis lazuli stone]s, 38 (*pieces of*) gold; its centerpiece a genuine *ḫulalu*-stone mounted on gold.

47 [1] *maninnu*-necklace, cut: 43 [genuine lapis lazuli stones], x *ḫiliba*-stones; [the centerpiece] a *sankallu*-stone mounted on gold.

48 1 *maninnu*-necklace, cut: 32 [genuine lapis lazuli stones, x *ḫil*]*iba*-stones; the centerpiece a genuine *ḫulalu*-stone mounted on gold.

49 [1] *maninnu*-necklace, cut: 30 genuine lapis lazuli stones, 28 *ḫi*[*liba*-stones]; the centerpiece a [. . .-stone] mounted on gold.

50 1 *maninnu*-necklace, cut: 34 genuine *ḫulalu*-stones, 35 [. . .]-stones; the center[piece] a genuine *ḫulalu*-stone mounted on gold.

51 1 *maninnu*-necklace, cut: 17 genuine lapis lazuli stones, 16 *sankallu*-stones, 35 (*pieces of*) gold; the centerpiece a *sankallu*-stone mounted on gold.

52–53 1 *maninnu*-necklace, cut: 23 genuine lapis lazuli stones, 25 *Marḫaši*-stones;[5] 48 (*pieces of*) gold *leaf*; the centerpiece a genuine lapis lazuli stone mounted on gold.

54 1 *maninnu*-necklace, cut: 34 obsidian stones; 33 (*pieces of*) gold; the centerpiece a genuine lapis lazuli stone mounted on gold.

55–56 1 *maninnu*-necklace (*with*) *counterweight*: 14 genuine lapis lazuli stones, 25 genuine *ḫulalu*-stones, 17 *ḫiliba*-stones; [the centerpiece] a genuine lapis lazuli stone mounted on gold.

57–58 [1 *mani*]*nnu*-necklace (*with*) *counterweight*: 14 genuine lapis lazuli stones, 16 genuine *ḫulalu*-stones; 30 (*pieces of*) gold [*leaf*; the centerpiece a . . .-stone] mounted on gold.

59–60 [1 *maninnu*-necklace . . . x] genuine *ḫulalu*-stones; 24 (*pieces of*) gold *leaf*; [the centerpiece, a . . .-stone] mounted on gold.

61 [. . .] genuine *ḫulalu*-stone; 26 gold *k*[*ama*]*ru*;[6] the centerpiece a genuine *ḫulalu*-stone mounted on gold.

62 [. . .] 24 gold *kamaru*; the centerpiece a genuine lapis lazuli stone mounted on gold.

63–64 [. . .] genuine lapis lazuli stones; 24 genuine *ḫulalu*-stones; [. . . the centerpiece] a genuine lapis lazuli stone mounted on gold.

65–66 [. . .] . . . *sankallu*-stones, 16 carnelian stones; [. . . the centerpiece a ge]nuine [. . .-stone] mounted on gold.

67–68 [. . .], mounted on gold.

69 [. . . "*cricket*]*s*," of [*genuine*] *l*[*apis lazuli*]; 10 "cr[icke]ts" of *ḫiliba-stone.*

70 [. . .] . . .

71–72 [. . .], along with their [co]vers, of gold; their tops [. . .] of genuine lapis lazuli; [. . .] are strung [on] gold wire.

ii

1–2 [x *a*]*škiruš ḫu*-vessels, along with their covers [. . .] . . . gazelle [. . .].

3–4 [x] *utuppu*:[7] 60 genuine lapis lazuli stones, 63 genuine *ḫulalu* stones, 8 *ḫu*[*lalu*-stones . . . (x +)] 5 "worms" of gold, 10 pomegranates of carnelian, 5 pomegranates of *sankallu*-stone.

5–6 [. . .] . . . : 122 genuine lapis lazuli stones, [x +] 6 *ḫulalu*-stones, 180 "worms" of genuine *ḫulalu*-stone, a thin (*band*) overlaid with gold, 3 seal-shaped stones of genuine *ḫulalu*-stone, mounted on gold.

7–8 [. . .] new-moon crescents of genuine *ḫulalu*-stone, 13 per string, of gold *tinged with red* [. . .] . . . 14 seal-shaped stones of genuine *ḫulalu*-stone, mounted on gold.

9–10 [x] large [. . .] . . . of gold *tinged with red,* 11 per string, set [in] genuine [lapis lazu]li, 12 *bikru*-gems and a seal-shaped stone of genuine *ḫulalu*-stone.

11–12 [. . .] . . . 1 new-moon crescent of [genuine] *ḫulalu*-stone, mounted on gold; 2 new-moon crescents of genuine lapis lazuli, mounted on gold [. . .] 3 genuine *ḫulalu*-stones (*for a*) *counterweight*; 4 . . . , ⟨mounted⟩ on gold.

13–14 1 set of large *agarḫu*-jewels, of genuine lapis lazuli, genuine *ḫulalu*-stone, genuine obsidian, *mu*[*ššaru*]-stone; the centerpiece a genuine lapis lazuli stone mounted on gold; their *ulluru* of *ḫiliba*-stone, not mounted.

15–17 3 sets of small *agarḫu*-jewels, of genuine lapis lazuli, genuine *ḫulalu*-stone, genuine obsidian, *muššaru*-stone; their centerpiece a genuine *ḫulalu*-stone mounted on gold; 1 *ulluru* of *ḫiliba*-stone, not mounted; 4 *bikru*-gems of gold.

18 2 "eye"-stones, of genuine *ḫulalu*-stone, mounted on gold, for the hand.[8]

19 13 "eye"-stones, of *muššaru*-stone, mounted on gold, for the hand.

20 219 "crickets," of genuine lapis lazuli, not mounted, for the hand.

21–23 3 finger-rings, of genuine *ḫulalu*-stone; 2 finger-rings, of genuine lapis lazuli; 2 finger-rings, of *ḫiliba*-stone; 1 finger-ring, of *malachite*; 2 finger-rings, (with) inlay;[9] 3 finger-rings, of *ir*[*on*]; 5 finger-rings, of *solid* gold.

24–25 14 hand-bracelets, of *solid* gold; 2 foot-bracelets, of *solid* gold. 390 shekels in weight.

26–27 2 hand-bracelets, of gold, one attached to the other, (with) *mesukku*-birds; the *mesukku*-birds (have) an inlay of genuine lapis lazuli. 30 shekels in weight.

28 10 thin bracelets, of iron, overlaid with gold; 30 shekels of gold [have been used] on them.

29–31 1 small torque, for a seal-shaped stone, of gold. 1 seal-shaped stone of genuine lapis lazuli mounted on gold. 1 . . .-stone mounted on gold. 1 seal-shaped stone of *pendu* mounted on gold. 2

genuine lapis lazuli stones (*to serve as*) *counterweights,* mounted on gold. 2 genuine *ḫulalu*-stones (*to serve as*) *counterweights,* ⟨mounted⟩ on gold. 4 . . . mo[unted on] gold.

32–33 1 pin, of genuine *ḫulalu*-stone; its top of genuine lapis lazuli mounted on gold. 1 pin, of genuine *ḫulalu*-stone; its top of *ḫiliba*-stone mounted on gold. 3½ shekels of gold have been u[sed] on them.

34–35 1 *ḫarušḫu,* of genuine *ḫulalu*-stone; its top of *ḫiliba*-stone mounted on gold. 1 *ḫarušḫu,* overlaid with gold. 1 *ḫarušḫu,* overlaid with ivory and gold. 3 shekels of gold have been [used] on them.

36–40 1 [*bunc*]*h of grapes,*[10] of gold. 1 *parakkatanu,* of gold. 1 *ussabnannu,* of gold. 6 [. . .] . . . , of gold. 1 *ḫuzunu,* of gold. 3 . . . , of *gold.* 1 *ḫarušḫu,* of gold. 7 small pomegranates, of gold. 6 "weaves," of gold. 11 "worms," of gold. 13 shekels in weight. This jewelry is *for keeping* [*girded*].[11]

41–42 10 pairs of boots and . . .[12] of gol[d . . .] Their b[ut]tons[13] are of *ḫiliba*-stone. 100 shekels of gold ha[ve been used] o[n them].

43–44 1 ointment receptacle; its *rettu* of . . .-stone; the handle a figure of alabaster.

45–46 1 ointment receptacle;[14] its *rettu* of alabaster; its handle a . . . [. . . , overlaid with g]ol[d];[15] 2 genuine lapis lazuli stones [are set][16] in the center.

47–48 1 ointment receptacle; its *rettu* of *abašmu*-stone; its handle a s[wal]low[17] overlaid with gold; one genuine lapis lazuli stone [is set] in the center.

49–50 1 ointment receptacle; its *rettu* of *marḫallu*-stone; its handle [a pan]ther [overlaid with] gold. It *is set here* [*and there*] with lapis lazuli and alabaster.

51 1 oin⟨t⟩ment receptacle; its *ret*⟨*tu*⟩ overlaid with gold; its handle a Delugue-monster overlaid with gold.

52 30 shekels of silver ⟨we⟩re overl[aid][18] on them.

53 1 wa[shba]sin, of gold; 123 shekels in weight. 1 washbasin of silver; 80 shekels in weight.

54–55 1 water-dip⟨per⟩, of gold; 30 shekels in weight. 1 alkali container of gold; 14 shekels in weight. 1 alkali container of silver; 20 shekels in weight.[19]

56–57 1 mirror, of silver; 40 shekels in weight; its handle a figure of a woman, of ivory. 1¾ shekels of silver have been overlaid on them.

58–59 1 mirror, of silver; 40 shekels in weight; its handle a figure of a woman, of ebony. 1¾ shekels of gold have been overlaid on them.

60–61 1 *kuninnu*-bowl, of stone; its *inside* and its base have been overlaid with gold; 1 genuine lapis lazuli stone is set in it.

62 1 *kuninnu*-bowl, of gold; 20 shekels in weight. 1 comb of mol[ten] glass.[20]

63 1 heart, of gold; the inlay, genuine lapis lazuli; 30 shekels in weight.[21]

64 30 hearts, of gold; (with) inlay; 900 shekels i[n weight].

65 20 combs, of silver [(. . .)] . . . [(. . .)].

66 10 combs, of silver. *10* [. . .] . . . [(. . .)].

67 10 combs, of silver [. . .] . . . [. . .].

68 10 combs, of silver [. . .] . . . [. . .].

69 10 combs, of silver [. . .] . . . [. . .].

70 [10 co]mbs, of silver [. . .].

71 10 combs, of silver [. . .].

72 10 combs, of silver [. . .].

73 10 combs, of silver [. . .].

iii

1–11 [. . .]

12 *1* [. . ., of sil]ver, 2000 [. . .].

13 [. . .], of silver. 1 set of . . . [. . .].

14 [. . .], of silver. 300 shekels [. . .].

15 1 set of *angurbinnu,*[22] of silver. 1 [. . .].

16–17 1 set of *flasks,*[23] along with their covers [. . . *ḫu*]*lalu*-stone [. . .] strung. 10 shekels of gold, 30 sh[ekels of silver . . . ala]baster.

18–19 25 sets of *flasks,* along with [their] co[vers . . .]. 42¾ shekels of gol[d have been used on the]m.

20–21 26 sets of *fla⟨sks⟩,* along with [their] c[overs . . . *eb*]*ony* [. . .]. 42⅔[4 shekels of silver have been used on the]m.

22–23 [x] sets of *flas*[*ks,* along with their covers, am]ong whi[ch] 1 of [. . .]-stone.

24–25 [. . .], overlaid with gold. 30 [. . .].

26 [. . . o]f the *country* . . . [. . .].

27–28 25 sets of *aškuruš*[*ḫu*-vessels . . .] 20 shekels of gold [. . .].

29 25 sets of *aškuru*[*šḫu*-vessels . . .].

30–31 [. . . have been used o]n them.

32 [x sets of *aškuruš*]*ḫu*-vessels, along with [their] ⟨c⟩ov[ers . . .].

33–34 1 set[24] of [. . .] their [. . .] . . . of ram-horn [. . . st]rung on a w[ire of gold]. 16 shekels of gold [have been used on them].

35 25 *ho*[*rn-rhytons*[25] . . .] overlaid with gold. 12 shekels of [gold have been used on them].

36 [x *horn-rhytons* . . .] overlaid [with gold]. 12 shekels of [gold have been used o]n t[hem].

37–38 [. . .] overlaid [with gol]d . . . [. . .] . . . [have been used o]n t[hem].

39–40 5 horn-rhytons . . . [. . .] overlaid [with go]ld. 18 [shekels] of gold [have been used on them]. Among [which] 1 [. . .].

41 5 small horn-rhytons, of ivory [. . .] their [. . .] overlaid with gold. 16 shekels [of gold have been used on them].

42 1 aurochs horn-rhyton, overlaid with gold 3 times; inlay, [. . .]; its *rettu* of [. . .]-stone.

43 1 aurochs horn-rhyton, overlaid with gold 2 times; inlay of [genuine] lapis lazuli; its *rettu* of [. . .]-stone.

44 1 mountain-ox horn-rhyton, overlaid with gold, and [its] *stand*[26] *is se*[*t here and there with* . . .].

45 1 aurochs horn-rhyton, overlaid with gold 3 times; inlay and [its] *re*[*ttu*] of alabaster.

46 1 *lulutu* (animal) horn-rhyton, overlaid with gold; its *rettu* of ebony. It [*is set*] *here and* [*there*] *with* genuine lapis lazuli [. . .].

47 1 *lulutu* (animal) horn-rhyton, overlaid with gold, its *rettu* of ivory. [*It is se*]*t here and there* with lapis lazuli (and) . . .-stone [. . .].

48 90 shekels of gold have been used on them.

49–50 20 *ayigalluḫu* (animals) horn-rhytons, overlaid with gold; their *rettu* of ivory; on one of which the *rettu* is of ebony. 35 shekels of gold [have been used] on them.

51 14 giant aurochs horn-rhytons, overlaid with gold; their *rettu* of ivory. 42 shekels of gold [have been used] on [them].

52–54 1 fly whisk, overlaid with gold; its *rettu* and its handle . . . [. . .] its [*p*]*arattatinu,* of *ḫiliba*-stone, strung on a wire of gold; and its wire strung with genuine *ḫulalu*-stones, genuine lapis lazuli stones, carnelian stones. 30 shekels of gold [have been used] on [them].

55–58 2 sets of *kapissuḫḫu*-ornaments, of gold. 2 sets of earrings, of gold; their cones, of *ḫiliba*-stone; their *kukkubu,* of *ḫulalu*-stone. 2 sets of toggle pins, of gold; their top of lapis lazuli. 2 "weaves," [of . . .] and *ḫili*[*ba*]-stone . . . 9 *maninnu*-necklaces, of lapis lazuli, *with* a gold *knob.*[27] 12 hand-bracelets, of gold. 8 foot-bracelets, of gold. This jewelry is for the 2 principal ladies-in-waiting.[28] 313 [shekels of gold].

59–62 2 sets of earrings, of gold; their cones of *ḫiliba*-stone; their . . . of *ḫula*[*lu*]-stone. 2 *s*[*ets of toggle pins*], of gold; their top of *ḫulalu*-

stone. 2 "weaves," of lapis lazuli and *ḫiliba*-stone. . . . [. . . x *maninnu-necklaces*], of lapis lazuli, *with* a gold *knob*. 12 hand-bracelets, of gold. 8 foot-bracelets, of gold. [This] jewe[lry] is for the 2 principal ladies-in-waiting. It is 208 shekels of gold that [have been used] on [them].

63 10 hand-bracelets, of gold. 10 foot-bracelets, of gold, for 10 pages.[29] 74 shekels in wei[ght].

64–67 *4*[0]0 foot-bracelets, of silver, for women. 100 sets of toggle pins, of silver, their top [. . .], for 100 dowry-women.[30] 1440 shekels of silver [have been used] on th[em]. 30 sets of earrings, of gold; their cones of lapis-lazuli, for 30 [dowry]-women. 60 shekels of silver have been used on them. 30 hand-bracelets, of go[ld, for *3*]0 [me]n.[31] 40 she[kels of silver have been used on them].

68 [1 *plaque*], with *kaziru*-figures, of gold and silver.[32] 10 shekels of go[ld] have been used on them.

69 [1 *plaqu*]*e*, with *kaziru*-figures, of gold and silver. 36 shekels of silver have been us[ed] on them.

70–72 [x spindles, of gol]d, 8 shekels in weight. 26 spindles, of silver, 10 shekels in weight. [x spindles, of . . .] 10 spindles, of lapis lazuli. 16 spindles, of al[abas]ter. [x spindles, of . . .] . . . 11 spindles, of . . . [. . .]-stone. 33 spindles, of horn.

73–75 [1 . . ., *with figures o*]*f apsasu*-animals,[33] [ov]erlaid with gol[d]. 100 shekels of gold have been used on it. [. . .] 15 (shekels) have been used o[n it. . . .] of blue-purple wool.

76–77 [. . .] goblets [. . .], of gold. 47 [. . .].

iv

1–3 [. . .], of *dušu*-stone, overlaid with [sil]ver. [. . .] . . . , overlaid with gold and silver. 15 shekels of gold, 38 shekels of silver, [have been used on it/them]. 1 *šubtu*-garment, of blue-purple wool.

4–5 [1 *plaque, with figure*]*s* of Deluge-monsters, overlaid with gold and silver. [x shekels of gold, x shekels of silver], hav[e been used o]n it.

6 [. . .] *tallu*-jars, overlaid with gold. 15 shekels of gold have been used on them.

7 [. . .] shekels of gold.

8 [. . .].

9 [. . .] 6 shekels of [si]lver [. . .].

10–11 [. . . shekels of . . . in] weight. [x shekels of . . .] have been us[ed on them].

12–13 [. . .] . . . is set. Its front [. . . x shekels of . . .] have been used on them.

14–16 [. . . *with figure*]*s of* deer[34] . . . [. . .] . . . *with figures o*]*f* lions [. . . x shekels of . . .] have been used [on them].

17 [. . .], overlaid with gold. 2 shekels [of gold] hav[e been used o]n them.

18–20 [. . .] its side-board[35] [. . .] . . . [. . .].

21–22 [. . .] lapis lazuli, its side-board [. . .] of lapis lazuli, overlaid with gold and silver. 6 shekels of gold, 26 shekels of silver, [have been used o]n [it].

23–24 [. . . , of *bo*]*xwood,* overlaid with gold and silver. 12 shekels of gold, 30 shekels of silver, have been used on them. [A *figure*], of ivory.

25–26 [. . .], of *boxwood,* overlaid with silver. 16 shekels of silver have been used on them. [*A figure*], of ivory.

27 [. . . , *of sil*]*ver,* 380 shekels in weight.

28–31 [x ches]ts, of [. . .]; their *f*[*ig*]*ures,* of iv[ory . . . x *c*]*he*[*sts,* of . . . e]bony; [*their*] *bot*[*tom* . . .] . . . [. . .] over[laid] with gold. [x] *che*[*sts* . . .] of *elammakku*-wood, overlaid with gold and silver. [. . .] 3 shekels of gold, 64 [shekels of silver], have been used [on] it.

32–44 [. . .] . . .[36]

45 4 [sh]irt[s], of many-colored cloth.[37] 1 garment, Tukriš-style, of many-colored cloth.

46 1 . . . [. . .], of many-colored cloth. [1]0 *šušinnu*-garments, of many-colored cloth.[38]

47 40 [. . .] . . .-garments, of many-colored cloth, for women.

48 41 r[*obes*]. *1*[0 fabri]cs, with *cording* above and below.[39]

49 30 large blankets. 4 long spreads, for a bed.

50 2 sh[or]t spreads, of which the trimmings are many-colored, for a bed. 4 blankets, for the feet. 4 blankets, for the head.[40]

51 1 scent container, with myrrh-scented oil. 1 scent container, with *kanatku*-oil.[41]

52 2 scent containers, with *sikil*-oil. 1 scent container, with *elder*-oil.

53 2 scent containers, with myrtle oil. 1 scent container, with *peršantu*-oil.

54 1 scent container, with *elder*-oil. 1 ⟨scent container⟩, with myrtle oil.

55 10 *kirru*-pots that are full of "sweet oil."

56 1 ewer, of bronze. [1] kettle, of bronze.

57 [x] large [jar]s, of bronze. [x] small [j]ars, of br[onze].

58 [. . .], of bronze. [. . .] pots [. . .].

59 [. . .] . . . , of bronze. [. . .].

60 [. . .] . . . , of bronze. 10 wash[basins, of bronze].[42]

61 [*10* bra]ziers, of bronze. 10 sets of *angurin*[*nu*, of bronze].

62 [1 *water-dip*]*per*, of bronze.[43] 1[44] container for alkali, of bronze. 20 knives, [of bronze].

63 [x] small troughs, of *boxwood.* 20 small troughs, of *elammakku*-wood.

64 [20 + x s]poons,[45] of *elammakku*-wood. 270 women, 30 men, are the dowry-personnel.[46]

65–67 It is all these [ob]jects (and) dowry-personnel t[hat Tu]šratta, the king of Mittani, [. . .] *her* [. . .] ga[ve . . .].[47] . . .

NOTES

1. Lines 1–5 are broken; 6–15 have only ends of lines, probably mostly concerning earrings.

2. *ša-Za-tu*$_4$: probably the same as *ša-an-Za-*[*t*]*i* in line iii 57 (Adler, p. 327), and *ša-*⟨*Za*⟩*-a-tu*$_4$, iii 60. With the second, Landsberger in Gordon tentatively compared *šamšāti*, "disks."

3. One expects here, as in i 27–32, identification of the material. Was *tamlû* also the name of a material? See below, ii 21–23.

4. See *EA* 13:14 and note.

5. Knudtzon read ^{na_4}*mar-ḫa-lim*, the last sign becoming *li* for Adler. Against *marḫallu*, however, are the absence of doubling and the apparent genitive; contrast *mar-ḫal-lu* (*EA* 22 ii 67, twice) and ^{na_4}*mar-ḫal-lu* (below, ii 49), which is also the regular writing elsewhere. For stones and other objects from the country Marḫaši, see *CAD*, M/1, p. 281, and note *mar-ḫa-šu* at Ugarit rather than the usual *marḫušu*.

6. *ka-ma-ru* (also i 62) is found at Mari (first pointed out to me by S. J. Lieberman) as a kind of ornamentation on a necklace(?), a chair, and a vase; see the discussion of Durand, *ARMT* 21, pp. 241–42, and Limet, *ARMT* 25, p. 279 on 230, and p. 283 on 445.

7. See Civil, *Ebla, 1975–1985* (see *EA* 22, n. 5), p. 149.

8. According to Landsberger in Gordon, *ša qāti*, "for the hand," means "loose, unattached."

9. See note 3 above.

10. [i]š-*ḫu-un-na-tu*$_4$ (Gordon); *CAD*, S, p. 242, retains Knudtzon's z[i-ḫ]u-[*u*]*n-na-tum*. Cf. *KUB* 22, 70:20, "a bunch of grapes made of precious stones" (*CAD*, I/J, p. 190).

11. *ša šu-ur*-k[u$_8$-si] (Landsberger in Gordon). From iii 59, 61, however, one would expect a designation of personnel, not of function.

12. The assumption of an uncontracted form, *ku*$_8$*-dup-pi-a-na* (*AHw*, p. 499, followed by Salonen, *Die Fussbekleidung der Alten Mesopotamien* [Helsinki, 1969], p. 61, and Adler), is difficult (an Assyrianism?), and there is no other evidence that *kuduppānu* derives from contraction. I follow *CAD*, K, p. 494 (reading *gumbu* or *guduppu*; relation to *kuduppānu* unclear).

13. p[u]-*ti-in-na-šu-nu* (Gordon); cf. *EA* 22 ii 24, 30.

14. *pí-iš-ša-tu* (*AHw*, p. 869).

15. Since in ii 43–44, 47–51, the handle has some sort of a figure, I assume the same feature here.

16. [GAR-*nu*]: cf. ii 61; similarly in ii 47, [GAR-*in*].

17. *s*[*i-nu*]-*un-t*[u_4] (Gordon). On the *abašmû*-stone, see *MSL* 10, p. 9:175f. and commentary p. 21.

18. *u*⟨*ḫ*⟩-*ḫu*-[*zu*] (Adler).

19. The alkali (*uḫūlu*; Sumerian naga) was used for bathing, and hence its mention here with a dipper; cf. iv 62.

20. NA_4 *bu-u*[*š-lu*] (*CAD*, M/2, p. 291a).

21. Cf. the heart-shaped cup at Mari (*ARM* 9, 268:5) and the Neo-Babylonian "hearts," which are always associated with *šulāpu*, "knife-blade(s)" (?).

22. Note the writing of *angurinnu*.

23. See *EA* 13, note 22.

24. Following *VS* 12; *VAB* 2/1, "2 sets" (not collated).

25. "Horn-rhyton" (SI, *qarnu*) as distinguished from the simple rhyton (*bibru*, *EA* 41:39f.).

26. Taking *i-ša-as*-[su . . .] as an Assyrianism.

27. Probably some kind of a clasp (Reiner, *AfO*, Beiheft 11, p. 58, on line 57; *ARMT* 7, p. 320).

28. EME(for ÉME).DA = *tārītu*; cf. the *tārītu*, a sort of nurse or governess who accompanies a young woman (*nadītu*) entering the "cloister" (*ARM* 10, 43, 92), and the nurse (*ummu*, lit. "mother") who raised Queen Beltum and accompanied her from Qaṭna to Mari, where she remained (*AÉM* 1/2, no. 298:29ff.). The two women are referred to again in iii 62, and since the numbers mentioned elsewhere are large, round numbers (100 in iii 65; 30 in iii 66; 270 in iv 64), these two women are certainly not included in the 270 women in iv 64. They were probably members of a noble family, companions to the princess far from her native land. Cf. the request in *AÉM* 1/2, no. 298:13ff. for 4 or 5 duennas (*puršumātum*, lit. "old women") familiar with the customs of the palace, to keep Queen Beltum in line.

29. Since reference here is to function rather than to age, *ṣuḫārī* seems the more likely reading (*AHw*, p. 1089, has *ṣeḫrūti*; Adler, *ṣeḫḫerūti*). Like the ladies-in-waiting of the previous paragraphs, these men, who are almost certainly not included in the 30 in iv 64, were probably of high social standing (see *EA* 17, note 7).

30. If in iv 65 *mulūgī* qualifies *udê*, and hence all the objects listed in *EA* 25 are to be understood as *m.*, as the text is generally taken, then the occasional use of *m.* in the list itself (iii 65; almost certainly iii 66, 30 MUNUS.[MEŠ *mu-lu-ki*]; iv 64) seems pointless—that is, if it is to be understood, not of the persons immediately preceding, but of the objects named (so *AHw*, *CAD*, Adler). The position, too, of *m.* is definitely, if not decisively, against the latter interpretation. As a designation of persons, *m.* is attested earlier (Nuzi) and later (Neo-Babylonian).

31. In view of the correspondence between the numbers of objects and those of persons in iii 64 (100) and iii 66 (30), 3]0 seems fairly certain. [LÚ].MEŠ, rather than [lú]TUR].MEŠ (Knudtzon, Adler), in view of 30 LÚ.MEŠ in iv 64; cf. MUNUS.MEŠ in iii 64, 66, and iv 64.

32. Cf. the following line, [1 GIŠ.DUB-p]u, and *EA* 22 iii 5. If *gištuppu* is correct, then the *kazīrū* are hardly curls on figurines (*CAD,* K, p. 310), but more likely the entire object represented, perhaps the *kazīru*-plant itself.

33. [... ALAM.MEŠ *š*]*a ap-sà-a-*⟨⟨*ab*⟩⟩*-sà-ti.*MEŠ (Landsberger, *Die Fauna des Alten Mesopotamien* ... [Leipzig, 1934], p. 88). R. M. Boehmer, *ZA* 66 (1975) pp. 18f., proposes "water-buffalo."

34. D⌜ÀR⌝A.MAŠ.MEŠ (*ayalī*): also Gordon. I could see less than Knudtzon (*VAB* 2/1, p. 1001, no. 35) but more than *VS* 12. Representations of deer (stags) were common.

35. Cf. *EA* 13, rev. 1–4 and note 14.

36. [... gu$_5$-ḫa]-*aṣ-ṣí* (iv 32); [... ku-ur]-*si-i-in-ni,* "ankles" (iv 33; Gordon); ...[ḫ]a-[z]u-[r]a (iv 40, if correct, cf. *EA* 22 ii 41); 2 TÚG.MEŠ [ša ka-*p*]*í-iz-zu-uḫ-ḫu* (iv 40; Landsberger in Gordon, and cf. iii 55); 10 *pé-pa-*[*wa-ši*] 11 x [*p*]*é-pa-wa-ši ur-ra-še-na* (iv 44; 1100 would not be written 11 ME; on the last word, *AHw,* p. 1433, "objects of desire?").

37. Cf. *EA* 22 iv 14.

38. M. Dietrich and O. Loretz, *BiOr* 23 (1966) p. 133, explains *šušinnu* as Egyptian *šus,* "byssos," plus Hurrian adjectival ending *-alenni*(*lu*).

39. Cf. *EA* 22 iv 11. At the beginning of the line, 41 TÚG.MEŠ [BAR.DUL]? (Cf. *EA* 22 ii 40.)

40. For iv 49–50, cf. *EA* 22 iv 12–15.

41. [šim]GIG (*kanaktu, kanatku* [*EA* 22 iii 32]; also Gordon: the sign in question is definitely not one of the BULUG-signs. For iv 51–55, cf. *EA* 22 iii 29–36.

42. NÍĜ.ŠU.L[UḪ.ḪA] (*namsû*): the apparent middle horizontal may be only a scratch. Cf. the sequence in *EA* 22 iv 22—*namsû* and *ša* NE—and the next entry here.

43. [1 ša me-e šu-l]i: cf. ii 54–55.

44. 1-*en,* with *VS* 12.

45. [x [gi]]š[DÍLIM.MEŠ (*itqurāti*): also Gordon. Despite Knudtzon's autograph (*VAB* 2/1, p. 1001, no. 43), apparently confirmed by the copy of *VS* 12, there are traces of only one horizontal followed by only *one* vertical and possibly a small scratch. My reading yields the same sequence in lines iv 63–64 as in *EA* 22 iv 34–35. For the assumption of the same number of spoons as troughs, see *EA* 22 iv 34–35 and note 52.

46. *mu-lu-gu*$_5$.[MEŠ] (cf. iv 65); on the interpretation, see iii 64 and note 30. The numbers seem to be totals. For the 30 men, cf. iii 66. Besides the 100 (130?) women referred to in iii 64ff., either the other 170 (140?) were also mentioned in the breaks, or, as seems more likely, no objects being assigned to them, they were simply added in here.

47. [*ú*]-*de*$_4$-*e*: following Kühne, p. 35, n. 164; cf. *EA* 7:81. The usual interpretation of this entry is that *mulūgī* qualifies *udê,* which are therefore all designated as *m.*-gifts. However, within the list itself only people seem to be called *m.* (see iii 64), and in iv 64 these people seem to form a special category, i.e., personnel as opposed to the objects with which the list had been concerned up to this point. A distinction, therefore, between *udê* and *mulūgī* as two separate categories of gifts comprising the dowry seems more probable. It is not clear, as

Pintore, *Matrimonio,* p. 118, maintains, that *m.*, like later Aramaic *m^e lūg* in pre- and early-Talmudic times (B. Levine, *JAOS* 88 [1968] pp. 271ff.), was already at this period distinguished as that part of the dowry over which the wife retained some control.

EA 26

To the Queen Mother: some missing gold statues

TEXT: BM 29794 (+) A 9356 (Oriental Institute).
COPIES: BB 11 (+) Luckenbill, *AJSL* 33 (1916) pp. 7f. Earlier copies of A 9356: Abel, *ZA* 7 (1892) p. 118; Scheil, *Mémoires,* p. 310.
PHOTOGRAPHS: BB, pl. 9 (BM 29794); E. Chiera, *They Wrote on Clay* (Chicago, 1938), p. 203 (A 9356).
TRANSLITERATION AND TRANSLATION: Adler, pp. 206–11.

[Say] t[o Teye], the mistress of Egy[pt]: T[hus Tuš]ratta, the king of [Mittani. For me] all goes well. For you may all go w[ell. For *your household,* for] your son, may all go well. For Tadu-Ḫeba, [my daughter], your daughter-in-law, may all go well. For your countries, fo[r your *troops*], and for whatever else belongs to you, may all go very, very [well].

7–18 You are the one that knows that I [myself] always showed love [to] Mimmureya, your husband, and that Mimmureya, [your] husba[nd], on the other hand, always showed love to me. A[nd *the things*] that I wou[ld write and] say [t]o Mimmureya, your husband, and the things that Mimmureya, your husband, [on the ot]her hand, [would alwa]ys write and say to me, you, [Keli]ya, and Mane know. But you are the on[e, *on the other ha*]*nd,* who knows much better than all others the things [that] we said [to one an]other. No one [el]se knows them (as well).

19–29 [And n]ow, you yourself [sai]d to Keliya, "Say to your lord: 'Mi[m]mureya,[1] my husband, always showed love to yo[ur] father, and maintained (it) for you;[2] he did not forge[t][3] his love for your father, and he did not cut o[ff][4] the [em]bassies that he had been accustomed to sending, one after the other. And now you are the one that must not forget your [l]ove[5] for Mimmu[reya], your brother. Increase (it) f[or] Napḫurre[y]a and maintain (it) for hi[m]. You must keep on send[ing] embassies of joy,[6] one after the other. Do not cut [them] off.' "[7]

30–48 I will [not] fo[rget][8] the love for Mimmureya, your husband. More than ever be[fo]re,[9] at this very moment, I show 10 times—much, much—more love to Napḫurreya, your son. [*You are the one who knows*] the words of Mimmureya, [your] husb[and, *but*] you did not *s*[*end*][10] all of my greeting-gift[11] that [*your husband ordered*] to [*be sent*]. I had asked[12] [your husband] for [statues] of sol[id] cast [gold], saying, "[*May my brother send me*] *a*[*s my greeting-gift,*[13] *statues of solid cast gold and . . . of gold*] and genuine lapis lazuli." But now Nap[ḫurreya, your son], has plated [statues] of wood. With gold being the dirt [in your son's country, w]hy have they been a source of such dist[ress] to your son that he has not given them to me?[14] Furthermore, I asked . . . [. . . t]o give *th*[*is*].[15] Is this love? I had sa[id], "Napḫurre[ya, *my brother*], is going to treat me 10 times better than his father did." But now he has not [given me] even what his father was accustomed to give.

49–57 Wh[y] have you [no]t exposed before Napḫ[urreya] the words t[hat you your]self, and with your own mouth, said to [me]? If [you] do not expose them before him, and *y*[*ou keep silent*],[16] *can anyone* [*el*]*se know?* Let [Nap]ḫurreya give me statues of sol[id] gold! He must cause me no [dis]tress whatsoever, nor [. . .]. Let him treat m[e] 10 times better [th]an his father did, [wi]th love and evidence of es[teem].

58–63 May your own messengers g[o] regularly with the messen[gers o]f Napḫurreya, with 5 [. . . t]o Yuni, my wife, and may the messen[gers o]f Yuni, my wife, [g]o regula[rly] to [you].

64–66 I [her]ewith [send] as your greeting-gift [x] scent containers[17] [filled] with "sweet oil," (and) 1 set of stones [*set in gold*].

NOTES

1. A 9356 begins here (line 21) and would join BM 29794 down through line 53.

2. *it-ta-ṣa-ar-k*[*a*]: so Knudtzon, and correctly; Adler has -[ku]. As the immediately preceding *akkâša* makes clear, the verbal suffix is dative case, not accusative, and therefore the verb in this instance does not mean "to protect"; similarly, *uṣurš*[*u*] in line 27, and here note that *rubbi,* "increase," also has no direct object expressed. Artzi, in Durand, *La femme dans le Proche-Orient antique* (see Introduction, n. 62), p. 24, is of a different opinion.

3. *im-š*[*e*]: so Knudtzon, and correctly; -[*ši*] in Adler.

4. *ip-r*[*u-us*]: so Knudtzon, and correctly; Adler has -[*ru-us*].

5. [*r*]*a-'a-mu-ut-ka*: the small oblique wedge suggesting [*r*]*u* or [*r*]*i* may be only a scratch (also Gordon).

6. Artzi, in Durand, *La femme dans le Proche-Orient antique,* p. 26, sees in the (literally) "journey of joy" reference to the royal procession conducting a bride to Egypt. In context, however, where there is no reference to marriage, this seems

most unlikely. The joy that qualifies the journey refers to the pleasure at hearing the brother's greeting and at seeing the gifts that accompany it; cf. *EA* 27:7–8.

7. *ta-pa-ar-ra-as*-[*si*-(*me*)]. Kühne, p. 39, n. 190, reads -[(*ma-a*?)-*me*] and rejects Knudtzon's *taparras*-[*si*] on the grounds that the form should be 2d masculine singular—which it is: *taparras* + suffix referring to *ḫarrāna* (line 28, feminine). There is room for at least one more sign; simple *taparras* (Adler) is certainly wrong.

8. *ra-'a-mu-ut*-t[a la] 32 *a*-⸢*ma-aš-ši*⸣: t[a, "not likely" (Gordon). If there is not enough room for [la], then we must assume a rhetorical question. In line 31, *a*-r[a-a]m-*me* (Knudtzon, retained by Adler) is certainly wrong; the correct reading was given by Winckler, *KB* 5, p. 66.

9. Read *pa-n*[*a*]-*nu* or *pa-n*[*a*]-⸢*a*⸣-*nu* (Gordon).

10. If the subject is second feminine singular, *tu*-š[e-(e)-bi-li]; if plural, *tu*-š[e-(e)-bi-la]; cf. Kühne, p. 39, n. 190.

11. *šulmānī,* "my gift" (Kühne, ibid.), but consisting of more than one piece, as *mitḫāriš* shows; cf. *EA* 27:41f.

12. *e-te-ti* (for *ri*)-*iš.*

13. *a*-[na šulmānīya (line 39; line 38 is free restoration).

14. *i-na* Š[À-*šu* 43 *ša* DUMU-*ka im-tar-ṣú-ma.* On the end of line 42, see Kühne, p. 39, n. 190; *ina libbi marāṣu,* see *EA* 19:64f.; 27:50f.; 29:139.

15. *an-ni*-t[a] (Adler); not *an-ni*-⸢i⸣ (Gordon). 44 . . . x [. . .] y: x, not š[a (so Knudtzon); y, probably not n]a (Gordon).

16. *ù* t[a-sa-ku-ti]: only a guess, but not m[a (Gordon).

17. The number is uncertain, but certainly more than 1: the head of vertical just visible is to the right both of the broken-away [a] above in line 64, and of the "1" just below in line 66 (Gordon: 3 or 5?).

Following line 66 are probably two lines of Egyptian, written in hieratic, and another line continued on the left edge, from the upper edge downwards. The end of the line reads "(. . .) the wife of the king of Upper Egypt."

EA 27

The missing gold statues again

TEXT: VAT 233 (+) 2197, no. 1; 2193.
COPIES: WA 23 (only VAT 233); *VS* 11, 11.
TRANSLITERATION AND TRANSLATION: Adler, pp. 212–25; Pintore, *Matrimonio,* p. 21 (lines 13–31).

[Say to Napḫurreya, the king of Egy]pt,[1] my brother, my son-in-law, whom [I love and who loves me: Thus T]ušratta, Great King, the king of Mi[ttani, your father-in-law, who loves you, your brother]. For me all goes well. For you m[ay all go well. For Teye, your mother, for] your [house]hold, may all go [well. Fo]r Tadu-Ḫeba, [m]y daug[hter, your wife, for the rest of your wives], for [your] sons, [for] your [mag]nates, for your chariots, [for] your [hor]ses, f[or your troops, for your country, and] for [whatever else belongs to you], may all go [ve]ry, very well.

7–8 [Ma]ne, my brother's messenger, [came and][2] I heard the [gr]eeting o[f my brother] and I [r]ejoiced greatly. I saw the goods that my brother [sen]t and I re[jo]iced greatly.

9–12 My brother said this: "Ju[st] as you always showed love to my father, Mimmureya, so now show love [to me." Af]ter my brother is desirous of my love, shall I not be desirous of my brother's lo[ve]?[3] At this very moment I show you 10 times more l[ov]e than I did to your father!

13–18 And your father, Mimmureya, s[aid] this on his tablet. When Mane brought the bride-price, thus spo[k]e my brother, Mimmureya: "These goods[4] that I have now sent are nothing, and my brother is not to complain. I have sent nothing. These goods that I have now sent to you, I have sent to you with this understanding[5] that, when my brother hands over my wife whom I have asked for, and they bring her here and I see her, then I will send you 10 times more than this."

19–27 I also asked your father, Mimmureya, for statues of solid cast gold, one *of* myself and a second statue, a statue *of* Tadu-Ḫeba, my daughter,[6] and your father said, "Don't talk[7] of giving statues just of solid cast gold. I will give you ones made also of lapis lazuli. I will give you, too, along with the statues, much additional gold and (other) goods beyond measure." Every one of my messengers that were staying in Egypt saw the gold for the statues with their own eyes. Your father himself recast the statues [i]n the presence of my messengers, and he made them entirely of pure gold.[8] [M]y messengers saw with their own eyes that they were recast, and they saw with their own eyes that they were entirely of pure gold.

28–31 He showed much additional gold, which was beyond measure and which he was sen[d]ing to me. He said to my messengers, "See with your own eyes, here the statues, there much gold and goods beyond measure, which I am sending to my brother." And my messengers did see with their own eyes!

32–34 But my brother has not sent the solid (gold) statues that your father was going to send. You have sent plated ones of wood. Nor have you sent me the goods that your father was going to send me, but you have reduced (them) greatly.[9]

35–36 Yet there is nothing I know of in which I have failed my brother. Any day that I hear the greetings of my brother, that day I make a festive occasion.

37–40 When [Ḫa]amašši, my brother's messenger, came to me, reported my brother's words, and I heard them, I spoke as follows: "Just as I always showed love to Mimmureya, your father, I will now show 10 times—much—more love to Napḫurreya." Thus did I speak to Ḫaamašši, your messenger.[10]

41–42 But now my brother has not sent me the statues of solid gold, nor has my brother sent all the additional goods that your father o[rde]red sent.

43–44 May my brother now give me the statues of solid gold that I a[sk]ed your father for, and may he not hold them back.

45–51 . . . And [*with gold being the dirt*] in [my] brother's country, [*why*] have [*the statues*] been a source of such distr[ess] to my brother[11] that he has not [given them to me . . .] . . .

52–54 . . .

55–58 [*I sent Ḫaamašši*] posth[aste *t*]*o* [*Mimmureya, my brother, and within 3 months*] he sent back [*Ḫaamašši*] po[sthas]te. [Your father] sent me [*much gold*]; there were four sacks [full of gold *that he sent me*]. May my brother ask [Ḫaa]mašši, his messenger.[12]

59–62, 63–68 . . .[13]

69–73 [*The wor*]*ds* that [*I used to speak*] *t*[*o your father*], and that [*your fa*]*ther* [*used to speak to* m]e, no one [*knows. Teye, your mother*], K[el]i[y]a, [*and Mane know th*]*em,* [but] no one else knows [them. My brother's] mother [*knows everythi*]*ng,* how your father [would speak] with me [*and did not forget* his lo]ve [*for my father*], and how [*I*] would speak with your father and [*maintained*] the lo[ve *that he had from my father*].[14]

74–78 [And n]ow my brother h[as sai]d: "Ju[st] as you [*always showed love*] to my fa[th]er, so s[how love t[o me]." My brother will see th[at] I *sh*[*all show great love to my brother. I have*] said, "My brother *m*[*ust* a]s[k][15] his mother [. . .] . . . He wi[ll s]ee that [. . .].

79–82 [M]a[ne, m]y brother's [messenger, . . .] . . . [*I heard*] my [bro]ther's words and I rejoi[ced] gre[atly].

83–88 . . .[16]

89–92 I herewith [send post]has[te] Piriss[i *and Tulubri, with a small escort, and have told them to hurry*]. May [m]y brother not [*detain them,* (*but*) *release them so*] they can report back to me, [*I may he*]*ar* [*my brother's greeting*], and *re*[*joice*].[17]

93–98 [*May*] my brother's [messengers] come to me [*wi*]*th* Pirissi, [*according*] *to the custom* [*of kings*],[18] posthaste [. . .]. . . . [. . . *the messengers of each*] *one* will turn ba[ck]. Accordingly, I will let [Mane], my [brothe]r's [messenger], go, and m[y] mes[seng]ers [*my brother shall let go*]. Gladly shall I send Mane to . . . [. . .] of my brother.

99–103 [W]h[en] my brother's [mes]sengers [arrive] a[long wi]th [Pirissi . . . *I shall invite them*] *t*[*o celebrate*] a great feast, the *kimru*-feast. [So] may they arrive [. . .], and if they do so [*arri*]*v*[*e*] *f*[*or* . . . , then h]ow will I treat them! . . . the feast.[19]

104–109 May my bro[ther] send me much gold. [*At*] the *kim*[*ru*-fe]ast, . . . [. . . *with*] many goods [*may* my] brother [*honor me.* I]n my brother's [countr]y g[ol]d is as plen[tiful a]s dirt. [May] my brother [cause me no dis]tress. May he send me [m]uch [gold in or]der that my brother, [*with the gold* and m]any [good]s, may honor me. [*May*] my [bro]ther [. . .] more than his father did. May they bring back to me [*muc*]*h* [*gold*].

110–111 [*Herewith, as your greeting-gift*: 1] shirt, Hurrian-style; 1 [*c*]*ity*-shirt; 1 r[ob]e; 1 [. . .]-stone; [. . .] pair(s?) fo[r the h]and; "eye-stones" of genuine *ḫulalu*-stone, 5 per string, mount[ed] on gold.

112 [1 scent container] fil[led] with "sweet [o]il"; 1 set of stones mount[ed] on gold—for Teye, your mother.

113 I send [1 scent container fil]led [with "sweet oil"]; 1 s[et] of stones [mounted] on gold—[for] Tadu-Ḫeba, [my daughter, y]our wife.[20]

NOTES

1. Following Knudtzon, because of considerations of space, I do not restore LUGAL GAL, "Great King," and in the omission see no implications of hostility (see *EA* 1, n. 2); Adler argues otherwise.

2. [*it-tal-ka ù*]: following Kühne, p. 39, n. 191.

3. Or: "[Af]ter my brother is desirous of friendship with me, shall I not be desirous of friend[ship] with my brother?"

4. *an-nu-ú ú-nu-t*⸢*a*⸣ (also line 6): in view of *mala annî*, "as much as this" (line 18), *annû* seems to be the demonstrative pronoun rather than an interjection or adverb, as Kühne, ibid., has suggested.

5. On the division of clauses, see Ungnad, *OLZ* 1916, col. 183, followed by Kühne, p. 39, n. 191, and Adler. For a different opinion see Knudtzon, followed by Zaccagnini, *Lo scambio dei doni durante i secoli XV–XIII* (*EA* 19, n. 12), p. 24, n. 56, and Pintore, *Matrimonio,* p. 21. Against the latter, *šūbulu* does not mean "to send back."

6. Both statues were for Tušratta's possession (cf. the plated ones in lines 32ff.), and therefore *ana iyāši* hardly means "for me." If the second statue were *for* Tadu-Ḫeba, the scribe would hardly have written *ana ṣalam Taduḫeba*. Cf. *EA* 14 ii 11–15; *EA* 24, §25 (end).

7. On *muššer,* lit. "let go," see Kühne, p. 38, n. 181.

8. See *AHw,* p. 277a, and *CAD,* Z, pp. 24b, 31b. Pintore, *Matrimonio,* p.

150, n. 66, took *zukkû* to mean "to (re)polish (after casting)," but this meaning is otherwise unattested, and it does not fit the context well.

9. *tultemīṣ*: this reading is certain (add to *CAD,* M/1, p. 350), and cf. *šulmānāti . . . mīṣā,* "the greeting-gifts . . . were meager" (RS 34.136:8, 11; *Ugar.* 7, pl. XVIII).

10. For the correction of the copy in *VS* 11, see Schroeder, *OLZ* 1917, col. 105.

11. [. . . *i-na* ŠÀ-*šu š*]*a* ŠEŠ-[*ia* ALAM.MEŠ] *im-tar-ṣa-a-ma,* and see *EA* 26:42f. For the feminine gender of *ṣalmu,* note *šanītu ṣalmu* in line 19, probably *šapikta uppuqta* in line 21.

12. On lines 55–58, see Kühne, p. 31, n. 145 (end).

13. Mention of Keliya (line 59) and Tulubri (line 60); reference to a shipment of gold (line 63).

14. Lines 69–73, cf. *EA* 26:7–18, 22–27.

15. l[u-(ú) *i-š*]*a-'a-*[*al-*(ši) . . .]: *l*[*i-iš-t*]*a-'-*[*al-ši*] (Adler) is certainly wrong.

16. Mention of Mane (line 83), probably about letting him go (cf. lines 93–98); the detention of his own messengers in Egypt (line 84); perhaps a festival (line 87, cf. lines 99–109); and Teššup and Amon (line 87).

17. On lines 89–92, see Adler, but in line 92 [. . .lu-uš]-*me-e-ma* ⌜lu⌝-[uḫ-du] seems more probable.

18. Cf. *parṣu ša šarrānī, KBo* 1, 14, rev. 6.

19. Lines 99–103 are free restorations. The festival is to be understood as celebrated in the Mittani capital, not in Egypt, and it has nothing to do with funeral rites for Amenophis III or with *sd*-festivals, as D. Redford, *The Akhenaten Temple Project,* 1 (Warminster, 1976), p. 86, n. 80, has proposed; see Kühne, pp. 43f., n. 205.

20. On the left edge, beginning at the bottom of the tablet, a hieratic docket: "[ye]ar 2, first month of winter, [day . . .], when one was in the southern city, in the castle of *Ḫ*ʿ*-m-ꜣḫt*; copy of the Naharin letter that the messenger Pirissi and the messenger [Tulubri] brought." See the Introduction, sect. 6 and note 135.

EA 28

Messengers detained and a protest

TEXT: BM 37645.

COPY: Scheil, *Mémoires,* p. 302.

TRANSLITERATION AND TRANSLATION: Adler, pp. 226–29.

Say to Napḫurereya,[1] the king of Egyp[t], my brother, my son-in-law, who lo[ves me] and whom I love: Thus Tušratta, the king of Mittan[i], your father-in-law, who loves you, your brother. For me all goes well. For you may all go well. For your household, for Teye, your mother, the mistress of Egypt, for Tadu-Ḫeba, my daughter,[2] your wife, for the rest of your wives, for your sons, for your magnates, for your chariots, for your horses, for your troops, for your country, and for whatever else belongs to you, may all go very, very well.

12–19 Pirissi and Tulubri, [m]y messengers, I sent posthaste to my brother, and having told them[3] to hurry very, very much, I sent them[4] *with a very small escort.*[5] Earlier, I had said this to my brother: "I am going to detain Mane, [my brother's] messenger, until [my] brother lets my messengers go and they come to m[e]."

20–28 And now my brother has *absolutely*[6] refused to let them go, and he has put them under very strict detention. What are messengers? Unless they are birds, are they going to fly and go away? Why does my brother suffer so[7] about the messengers? Why can't one [*sim*]*ply* go[8] into the presence of the other and hea[r] [the ot]her's greeting, [and] both of us rejoice very, very much every day?[9]

29–36 May my [brother] let my messengers go promptly so I [m]ay hear the greeting [of] my [broth]er ...

37–41 I want to let [*Mane*] go[10] and I want to send [my] mess[engers to m]y [brother] as in the past, [that] I may *h*[*ear*] my brother's *former* [. . .] . . . He went to my brother, and may my brother do absolutely everything I want and not cause me dist[ress].[11]

42–49 Teye, your mother, knows all the words that I spoke with yo[ur] father. No one else knows them. You must ask Teye, your mother, about them so she can tell you. Just as your father always showed love to me, so now may my brother always show love to me. And may my brother listen to nothing from anyone else.

NOTES

1. Determinative omitted in copy; similarly, *an* omitted in *mi-it-ta-a-an-n*[*i*] (line 4).
2. Written I.MUNUS (Gordon).
3. *aq-ta-bá-a-šu-nu*-t[i] (Gordon).
4. *altaparšun*[*ū-ti*]?
5. *mīṣūtamma*: since (*m*)*īṣu* most often refers to numbers, with Adler I follow Knudtzon. Other renderings: "at least" (Tušratta sends messengers, whereas the Egyptian king remains completely silent; Kühne, p. 45, n. 210); "at once" (*CAD*, M/2, p. 116).
6. *ana gamrātimma*: following Kühne, p. 45, n. 210; Artzi, *Actes du XXIX*[e] *Congrès international des Orientalistes*, Section organisée par Daniel Arnaud (Paris, 1975), p. 3, "finally, after all."
7. *libbašu ikkalšu*, lit. "his heart eats him." The expression, which Adler misunderstood, is elsewhere used of abdominal pains, but here clearly is figurative; cf. *CAD*, A/1, p. 255a; *AHw*, p. 549a.
8. [e-še]-*ru* or [ne-šu]-*ru lā innešer*: following Kühne, p. 45, n. 210, who understands the expression to mean "to be successful," i.e., why can't one have

success with (lit. "before") the other. The notion, however, of easy access to each other (through one's messengers), with its implication of the quick dismissal and return of the messengers, perhaps fits the context better.

9. *u₄-mi-šà*[*m-ma*] (Gordon).

10. [. . . *l*]*u-meš-š*[*è*]*r-šu*: Adler's reading, *a-ra-am-šu*, following Scheil's copy, is disproved by collation.

11. *ú-š*[*e-em-ra-aṣ*] (Gordon).

EA 29

A long review of Mittanian-Egyptian relations

TEXT: VAT 271 + fragments: 1600, 1618–20, 2195–96 nos. 3–4, 2197 nos. 3–5, and two unnumbered.
COPIES: WA 24 (without the fragments); *VS* 11, 12.
PHOTOGRAPH: WA, pl. 2 (obverse).
TRANSLITERATION AND TRANSLATION: Adler, pp. 230–51.

[Say to Napḫureya, the king of Egypt, m]y [brother], my son-in-law, whom I [lo]ve and who lo[ves me: Message of[1] Tušratta], Great [King], kin[g of Mittan]i, your brother, your father-in-law, who loves you. For me all goes we[ll. For you may all go well. For] Teye ma[y all go w]el[l. F]or Tadu-Ḫeba, [m]y daughter, may all go we[ll. For the *r*]*est* [*of your wives*] may all go well. For your sons, for your magnates, for your chariots, for [your] hors[es, for your troops, for] your [country], and for whatever else belongs to you, may all go very, very well.

6–10 [*From the beginning*] of my [king]ship on,[2] as long as Nimmureya, your father, went on writing to me, [*he wrote over and over*] about peace. There was nothing el[se][3] whatsoever that he wrote about over and over to me. T[ey]e, the principal [and favorite] wife of Nimmureya, your father, knows all the words of Nimmureya, your father, tha[t] he would write [to] me over and 〈ov〉er.[4] It is Teye, your mother, whom you must ask about all of them: [*what*] your father [*would write over and over*],[5] the words that he would speak with me over and over.

11–15 [*My love for*] my [*brother*][6] is 10 times greater than what we always had with Nimmureya, your father. [But whatever] Nimmureya, your father, would constantly discuss with me, in absolutely not[hing] did he ever cause me distress. Whatever I might say, on that very day [he did][7] it. I, too, in absolutely nothing did I ever cause him distress, and what[ever he might say] to me, on that very day I di[d] it.

16–27 When [. . .],[8] the father of Nimmureya, wrote to Artatama, my grandfather, he asked for the daughter of [my grandfather, the sister] of my father. He wrote 5, 6 times, but he did not give her. When he wrote my grandfather 7 times, then only under such pressure did he g[iv]e her. When Nimmureya, your father, [wro]te to Šutt[arna], m[y] father, and asked for my father's daughter, my own sister, he wr[ote] 3, 4 times, but [he did not giv]e her. When he wrote 5, 6 times, only under such pressure did he g[iv]e [her].[9] W[hen] Nimmureya, [yo]ur [fa]ther, wrote to me and asked for my daughter, I did [*not*] say *n*[*o*].[10] *The* [*very*] *first ti*[*me*] I said [to] his messenger, "Of course I will give her." [When] your messenger came *the sec*[*ond time*],[11] o[il] was poured [on][12] her head, and when I received her bride-price, I ga[ve her.[13] And the br]ide-price that Nimmur[eya], your [father, sen]t, was beyond measure, ri[v]alling in height heaven and earth. I did not [say], "I will [no]t give her." I sent posthaste Ḫaamašš[i], m[y] brother's [. . .] . . .[14] to Nimmureya, [and with]in 3 months, [w]ith extreme promptness, [he sen]t [him back]. He *se*[*nt along*] 4 sac[ks[15] f]ull [of] gol[d, *not to me*]*ntion*[16] the jewelry [. . .] . . . , which he se[nt] separately.

28–54 [Wh]en I gave my [daug]hter and she was brought[17] and Nimmureya, your father, saw her, [he] re[joiced]. [*Was there anything*][18] he did [no]t rejoice about? He rejoiced *v*[*ery*], very much! My brother spoke as follows: "[*My brother* g]ave [*his daughter*] *in perfect fait*[*h*]."[19] He made that day a festive occasion along, too, with his country. Because of my messenger (32–37) [. . . J]ust as when one sees [his] pee[r], he shows him respect, so Nimmureya showed respect to [my messengers as p]eers and as [f]rie[nds].[20] He sent back all my messengers that were in residence *in* (*to*?) the quarters that [*were established*] for Tadu-Ḫeba, and there was not [*a single one*] among them who went in and [*to whom he did not* g]ive [*something*].[21] He gave Keliya's [in]got of gold weighing 1000 shekels, and Nimmureya gave [. . . *sacks* fu]ll of [gold] to Tadu-Ḫeba.[22] Tadu-Ḫeba *lai*[*d*] them [*all*] *out* [*before*] my [*messengers*]. *As fa*[*r as*] my [messe]ngers [*were concerned*], Nimmureya showed them respect with love [*and evidence of esteem*].[23] (37–44) [Nimm]ureya sent Niyu, his messenger, [. . .], which belonged to me, and he *br*[*ought them* post]haste.[24] Before me [*he laid out*] 7 sacks [*full of*] gold, [*and* 1 i]ngot[25] of gold [weigh]ing [1000 shekels] for Keliya. And thus[26] [*Nimmureya, your father*], made [. . .] . . . exceed, [out of l]ove. Before my messengers [. . .] . . . he had that brought to me posthaste [. . .] and he instructed [him], "*Like* [. . . y]ou shall *eat*."[27] Because he sent him posthaste, he did not have [*the statues*] brought to me, but *every*[*thing else, wh*]*atever* he did have brought, was limitless. And thus [Nimmu]-reya, your father, did not permit that in any mat[ter, *even o*]*ne,* distress be caused. (45–50) [And with regard to] all [the things] that I say, I call no one [el]se[28] as witness. It is Teye—she is your [mother]![29]—that I call. Inquire carefully of Teye, your [mother], if in the things that I say there is [ev]en a single word of [un]truth; i[f there is a wo]rd that is not that of Nimmureya, your father; if [Ni]mmureya, your father, together with me, did not make [*mutual love fl*]*ourish*;[30] if Nimmureya, your father, [did n]ot say: "When I see to it that there is sufficient [Eg]yptian gold in Ḫanigalbat, I *certainly* will not send [. . .] . . ." (50–54) I asked for [2] statues of so⟨l⟩id chased gold from Nimmureya, your [father], and Nimmureya, [your] fat[her], said: "[W]hat are statues of just gold with nothing else [that] my [brot]her has asked for? Don't talk of just go[ld] ones! I will make o[nes with genu]ine lapis lazuli (too), and send them to you."[31] [And] thus Nimmureya, your [fat]her, in no matter whatsoever, ever rejected what I said, [or] in any matter whatsoever caused me distress.

55–60 When [m]y [brother], Nimmureya, went to his fate it was reported. [*When I heard*] what was reported, [*nothing*] was allowed to be cooked in a pot.[32] On that day I myself wept, [*and* I] sat [. . .]. On that day I t[ook] neither food nor water. I grieved, [*saying, "Let* ev]en me [*be dead*],[33] or let 10,000 be dead in my country, and in my [brother]'s [country] 10,000 as well, [*but*] let [my brother, whom I lov]e and who loves me, be alive as long as heaven and ear[th." *T*]*hat* we love [. . .] that [*love*] was in our hearts, [and] we indeed did make (it) last.

61–64 [*But when they said,* "Na]p[ḫurey]a, the oldest son of Nimmureya and Teye, his [principal] wife, is exercising the [king]ship [*in his place*], then I spoke as follows: "Nimmureya, [my brother], is not dead. [Napḫure]ya, his oldest son, [*now exercises the kingship*] in his place. Not[hing whatso]ever is going to be cha[ng]ed[34] from the way it was before."

65–68 [*Now* I went o]n *reflecting, thinking,* "Napḫureya is my brother. That we love, [*that*] is in our hearts. It is going to become 10 times gr[ea]ter [th]an what there was with Nimmureya, his father, for Teye, his mother, the [prin]cipal and favorite wife of [Nimmureya], is alive, and she will expose before Napḫureya, [the son of Nim]mureya, her husband, the fact that we always loved (each other) very, very much."

69–79 [*But at the time*] when [*my brother*] first wrote [to me], when he let Keliya go and [*my brother*] sent Mane, my brother sent me statues (made) of wood. W[hen I *sa*]*w* the gold [that Nimmure]ya himself [*had prom*]*ised*,[35] that it was not gold and that it was not solid, that [. . .] . . . , then I *w*[*as in*] even greater [*pai*]*n*[36] than befo[re]. [. . .] Moreover, [the goods] that Nimmur[e]ya, my brother, gave me, my brother [*great*]*ly* [*reduced*]. So I became angry, [*as*] *was* [*only r*]*ight*. I became extremely hostile. [. . .] . . . *As to what was from* Napḫureya, my [br]other, he added *nothi*[*ng*] *more* to [it]. [. . .] . . . [⟨He ca⟩used] me [dis]tress. [. . .] . . . Before Mane came, [I caus]ed [*you*] no distress [what]soever.

80–90 . . . [*I addressed*] my magnates as f[oll]ows: "With my brother, *in perfect* [*faith*, . . .]. My [anc]estors, moreover, [*always showed great love*] to his ancestors." [. . .] The presents that my brother sent to me and [. . .] we rejoiced greatly and we indeed made the day a festive occasion. [. . .] *He* was delaying, and I rejoiced on that day [. . .] with the foreign guests.[37] Mane, too, my brother's messenger, [*greatly*] rejoiced. Let him tell [you] (about it).

91–99, 100–107 . . .[38]

108–118 [. . .] . . . And *ri*[*ght*] now [*inquire carefully of your mother about*] the words that your mother [*spo*]*ke* to Keli[ya]. I asked for [statues] of solid chased gold, and the obj[ects of] my desire [*that I asked your father for, you have not sent. Should I*] *be confident*? My brother has not let my messengers go, and [*he*] has not [. . .]. He has not sent him back, and he has not informed me. The statues o[f solid chased gold that I asked Nimmureya fo]r, I have now asked [y]ou for, but you have not given them. And the objects of [my desire] . . . you have not [infor]med me. My messengers, since 4 years ago, . . .

119–135 . . .[39] One must not change another's words. [*Whatever be the things that I say*], my brother [*should*] *do*, and whatever the things be that my brother [*says, I will do*]. One [*shall not cause*] *distress* to the ot[her] in anything whatsoever. [. . .] We [must] love and we must rejoice as long as we live. It will make [*o*]*ur* [*countries*] happier [*than all other countries*], and they will say, "How [*the kings of Ḫanigalbat and Egy*]*pt* [*love (one another)*]." If in this way [*it makes our countries so very*] much [*more happy*] than all other countries, all other countries [*will see this, and*] they will speak of *y*[*ou*].

136–147 [. . .] . . . [Sta]tues of s⟨o⟩lid chased gold I asked for from Nimmureya, your father, and I most urgently asked for much [go]ld that had [not] been work[ed]. Now, may my brother give me the statues of [solid ch]ased [gold]; [*may*] my brother [*give me*] promptly much gold that has not been [wo]rked. Your father himself *gra*[*nted me sta*]*tues* of gold. [W]hy is it for [you] a source of distress,[40] and (why) has he not *in*[*quired*] if [I did n]ot ask [*your father*] and if, moreover, your father did not grant them to me. [. . .] . . . *They* (the words?) *are not at all t*[*r*]*ue.* If not, (*say that*) your father also gave me the statues I asked for and now [I] have asked [*my brother for other ones*]. Would my brother not make other ones? Would he not give them to me? Would he cause me distress? [. . .] . . . of the entire matter. (143–147) Teye is your mother, and it is of Teye, your mother, that you must in[quire], [if I did not a]sk for [statues of go]ld [and] much other [gol]d from [your] father, and if your father did not grant them to me. May my brother give me [statues of] solid [ch]ased [gold] and [much] other gold, and may my brother not cause me dis[tress. In my brother's country gol]d is as plentiful as [dir]t, and I have not caused [my brother dis]tress. If I cannot build a *mausoleum* [*for my ancestors*], what can I do for them?

148–154 [*I reflected*],[41] "Keliya should return to my brother. Shall I cause [my] brother distress? I will send Keliya back to him!" [*I spoke to my brother* a]s follows: "My brother, I would like to send back [*your*] messengers promptly, but as long as my brother [has detained] my messengers, I have detained these men her[e]." I also s[ai]d:[42] "As soon as he lets my messengers go, [. . .] . . . and present their report to me, I will let Ma[ne] go and [I will send] Keliya [ba]ck to my brother as before. As long as my brother detains m[y] messengers like *somethi*[*ng for*]*gotten,* I [*will do*] as I have planned." Furthermore, the *affair* of my brother has now become a matter *for some kind of de*[*nuncia*]*tion.*[43] For what reason [*has*] my brother's [. . .]. He is a man, and he has taken his seat on the throne of his father *no*[*w become a g*]*od.* Let my brother do as he pleases.

155–161 I [*hereby*] declare: "My brother has indeed not let my messengers go, and he inde[ed] detains them a long time. I certainly *de*[*noun*]*ce* [*this*],[44] my brother, I indeed *de*[*nou*]*nce* (it). [I sent] Masibadli, my messenger, (who is) also Keliya's uncle, to [my] brot[her], and I sent him [to] my [brot]her with friendly intentions. My brother must not complain that I have not se[nt] Keliya, or have not *s*[*en*]*t* him [*with friendly intentio*]*ns.* That other messenger of mine whom I sent to my brother is the brother of Keliya, son of the same mother, [. . . and] I sent him posthaste to my brother. Because my brother has not let him go promptly so he might return here, and because my brother has given me no information [*with regard to* the re]quests that I have made, for this reason I have not sent Keliya. [*Nor* is my *brother*] to *tur*[*n*] this into a matter of complaint or anything else.

162–165 [Masiba]dli, whom I sent to my brother, is Keliya's uncle. [*May my brother give*] the statues of solid ch[as]ed gold, and may my brother give me much gold that has not been worked for the *mausoleum*, as I have requested of my brother. May [my brother n]ot cause me [dis]tress and not hold back, for in my [bro]ther's country go[ld] is as plentiful as dirt. [Nor will I myself] cause my brother [dis]tress.

166–172 May [my brother] treat me with 10 times greater love and brotherliness than his father did, and we will al[ways sh]ow very, very much love t[o] my [brother]. May my brother let [m]y [mes]sengers go pr[omp]tly, and may he send Mane along with my messengers so that they may co[me . . .] . . . If my brother grants this, then I will send Keliya to my [brothe]r, (and) [*I will pro*]*vide*[45] a large expedition f[or] my [brothe]r. I will do absolutely [every]thing that my brother says. [. . .] . . . I will do [an]d they are done. I have not written as before. It is like this (now) s[o *I can write*] and my brother *understand me.* My brother is not to complain. [*I will send*] a lar[ge] mission. [I will se]nd Keliya, and I will send a large mission to my [bro]ther.

173–181 [*My brother*] spoke [*about* Art]ašuba and Asali, declaring, "They broke the law in your brother's country." They were br[oug]ht in [*before*] their [. . .], and the rest of my servants who had been living in Egypt were brought in. Ma[ne, *too,* en]tered my presence, and they were convicted in [m]y pre[sence. *Mane*] spoke [*of their reputation*], and I said in their presence, "Why [. . .] . . . your reputation?" [*My brother,* a]sk [*Mane*] how I treated them. *I p*[*ut them*] in chains and [*fetter*]*s.*[46] I had [both of] them, one alongside the other, tra[nspor]ted to a town of mine on the border. But [*my brother had said nothing*] more, and for this reason I did not execute them. My brother, *how* [*was I to know* t]heir [*crime? Since*] my [brother] did not say, [I, *for my part*], did not ask. Now, may my brother esta[bl]ish *the natu*[*re of their crime*],[47] and I will treat [them] j[ust a]s my brother wants them treated.

182–185 [A]s [my brother's] greeting-gift: 1 gold comb, inlaid with . . . , with the head of a *yak*; 1 *ḫuppalu*-mace[48] [. . .]; [. . .] lapis lazuli [. . .], 1 pair for the hands, of *šada*⟨*nu*⟩-stone; 1 . . .[49] overlaid with gold; 3 garments; 3 pairs of [. . .]-garments; [. . .] *city*-shirts; [*3*] bows; 3 quivers overlaid with gold; 9[0 ar]rows of bronze;[50] . . . [. . .]; [. . .] fine [. . .]; 3 *ma*[*ces*—I [herewith] send [a]s my brother's greeting-gift.

186–187 [. . .] of gold; 1 pair for the hands, of *šada*[*nu*]-stone; [1 pair] of earrings of [. . .]-stone; [. . .]; 2 garments—I [herewith] send as the greeting-gi[ft of Te]ye, your mother.

188–189 [. . .]; 1 pair for the hands of [*šadanu*-sto]ne; [1 pair of e]arrings [of . . .-stone; . . .]; 4 garments—[I herewith] se[nd] a[s the gre]eting-gift o[f Tadu-Ḫeba], my [dau]ghter.

NOTES

1. On *umma,* "message," see the Introduction, n. 52.

2. [*ištu rēš* LUG]AL-*ru-ti-ia*: following Kühne, p. 46, n. 212.

3. *mimma ša-n*[*u-ú*]: following Kühne, ibid.

4. *il-ta-nap-*⟨*pa*⟩*-ru*: following Adler.

5. [ša il-ta-nap-pa-ru].

6. [ra-'a-mu-ti ša it-ti ŠEŠ]-*ia.*

7. As lines 12–15 make clear, the subject here must be "he," and therefore 14 [*i-te-pu-uš*]; cf. *EA* 17:13; *EA* 29:30.

8. The praenomen of Thutmosis IV (*mn-ḫprw-r*ᶜ) may have appeared in the break. Extended negotiations seem to have been the rule in interdynastic marriages (Pintore, *Matrimonio,* pp. 16, 54), and therefore one may not infer a certain hostility towards Thutmosis IV (so D. Lorton, *The Juridical Terminology of International Relations in Egyptian Texts through Dynasty XVIII* [Baltimore, 1974], p. 172, n. 11).

9. Cf. *EA* 17:26ff.

10. *ù ú*-[ul-la] 22 [la-a] *aq-bi.* Kühne, p. 24, n. 111, proposed *ù ú*-[ul] 22 [ul-la] *aq-bi,* but this yields an unusual position for the negative and does not adequately fill the space at the end of line 21. The writing *ú-ul-la* could be due to the influence of *ú-ul* and perhaps *a-an-na* (cf. *EA* 19:20).

11. *ina ma-aḫ*-[ri-im-ma a-na (lú)] . . . *ina* ša (text: bi)-*nu-ut-t*[*im-ma*]: following Landsberger, *Symbolae . . . Martino David dedicatae* (see *EA* 11, n. 7), pp. 79f., n. 4; so also Adler in Kühne, p. 30, n. 138, but Adler retracted this reading in AOAT 201, pp. 232f. Cf. *EA* 19:58.

12. *it-ta-ab-k*[*u*]: following Landsberger, *Symbolae . . . Martino David dedicatae,* pp. 79f., n. 4.

13. *at-ta-d*[*in-ši*]: see *VAB* 2/2, p. 1588.

14. [NIM]GIR: very dubious. Pintore, *Matrimonio,* p. 150, n. 71, takes it as *susapinnu,* "attendant to the groom," "garçon d'honneur" (*PRU* 3, p. 147:15).

15. 4 K[UŠ.MEŠ]: following Kühne, p. 31, n. 145.

16. [*muš-š*]*ir* (cf. line 52) would maintain the rhetorical tone of the passage better than "I/he sent" (Kühne, p. 32, n. 146).

17. Grammar unclear, but hardly "I brought her." Subject omitted?

18. [mi-im-ma *ú-u*]*l.*

19. *ina* ku_8*-ú-ul libbīšu,* lit. "with all his heart," i.e., without duplicity, keeping his part of the agreement perfectly. Other opinions: (1) Knudtzon, followed by Adler, "joy," comparing Hebrew (and Ugaritic) *gyl,* but there is no evidence for this word elsewhere in (peripheral) Akkadian, and a Canaanitism in Tušratta's language is not likely; (2) *AHw,* p. 927b, "quiet, peace," but this does not make very good sense here, and as said of soldiers fighting (see Boghazköy references) it makes no sense at all. For fighting with all one's heart, i.e., undivided loyalty, cf. *ina gammurti libbi* in Assyrian treaties (Wiseman, *Iraq* 20 [1958] p. 41 iii 169; ibid., p. 51 v 10; cf. ibid., p. 33 i 52–53).

20. 31 [. . . *kī*]*mē amēlūtu me-ḫé-e*[*r-šu*] . . . 32 [lúDUMU.MEŠ KIN-*ia ki-i*] *meḫrūti u kī* [*i*]*t-ba-a-ru-ti*: following Kühne, p. 46, n. 212. Instead of *itbarūti*, *AHw*, p. 1399b, reads *ubārūti*.

21. The entrance probably is to the Pharaoh's presence (cf. "residing," *ašābu*, and "entering, *erēbu*," in line 174), though perhaps entering Egypt is meant (cf. *EA* 30:9f.).

22. Cf. lines 27 and 38f.

23. Cf. *EA* 26:57.

24. *it-t*[*a*-bal-šu-nu *a-n*]*a* (cf. line 41).

25. [*ma-lu-ú* it-ta-ta-ad-di ù 1 *l*]*i-ša-nu* (cf. line 36).

26. *ù* ⸢*a*⸣*-ka-an-na*: following Adler; only two heads of verticals are visible.

27. *takkal*: hardly from *ekēlu*, "to become dark" (Knudtzon, followed by Ebeling, *VAB* 2/2, p. 1365), and *akālu* does not mean "to be angry" (Adler, who correctly rejects a derivation from *nagālu*).

28. *mam*[*ma ša-na*]*-am-ma*: following Ungnad, *OLZ*, 1916, col. 184.

29. *Teyēma* [*umma*]*k*[*a*] *šīt*: Adler in Kühne, p. 46, n. 212, correctly identified *šīt* as the personal pronoun, but in AOAT 201, p. 271, he returns to the proposal of Ungnad, *OLZ*, 1916, col. 184, *ši-i-it* < *ši-i i-de*, "she knows."

30. *a-ḫa*-m[iš ra-a-ma ú-ul ú]*-ne-ep-pi-iš* (cf. *EA* 19, note 5).

31. Cf. *EA* 27:21.

32. [lā mimma] (Berger in Kühne, p. 40, n. 194) or the like seems required by context.

33. [um-ma-a lu-ú mi-ta-ku *a*]*-na-ku-ma*. On the rest of the passage see Kühne, p. 40, n. 194, who suggests that the second number be read as 60 (×) 10,000. Perhaps, as he also suggests, the direct quotation extends through line 60.

34. *ú-še-*⸢*en*⸣*-nu-ú*: following Adler.

35. 71 [ša m*nimmur*]*eya-*[*m*]*a* [iq-*b*]*u*-[šu-*n*]*u* k[i-i a-ta-m]a[r]-*šu*-[nu] . . . (not confirmed by collation). On lines 69–79, cf. *EA* 26:30ff.; *EA* 27:32ff. Tušratta seems to say that though offended and very angry, he did not show it in the presence of the Egyptian messenger.

36. *am*-[ta-ra-aṣ]: following Adler.

37. [l]ú.meš[*ú*]*-ba-r*[*u-t*]*i*: following Kühne, p. 46, n. 212; confirmed by collation.

38. On line 106, see *VAB* 2/2, p. 1588.

39. Line 122 refers to an oath by "my brother" (Amenophis III or IV?).

40. [im]*-mar-ṣa* (cf. *EA* 19:65?).

41. On lines 148–53, see Kühne, p. 24, n. 111; p. 41, n. 199.

42. *u*[*m-ma l*]*u-ú anākū-ma*: following Adler.

43. *a-na* k[a-ar-ṣ]i: see line 156.

44. [ka-ar/kar-ṣí-(šu)]: on the following *u*, after a direct object, see Wilhelm, AOAT 9, pp. 54f.

45. [lu-ú ú-ki]*-il*.

46. ù [i]z-[Š]U.[MEŠ] (*izqātī*) *aš*-[ta-ka-an-šu-nu].

47. *né-e-pé-el*-t[i *ḫiṭīšunu*]: following Kühne, p. 46, n. 212.

48. 1 gišTUKUL SAG NA_4: following Adler.

49. 1 ŠU (pair) *ru-uḫ-tu*$_4$ or *šuruḫtu* (*AHw*, p. 1287)?

50. See Eheloff, *ZA* 45 (1939) pp. 70f.

EA 30

A passport

TEXT: BM 29841.
COPY: BB 58.
PHOTOGRAPH: BB, pl. 15.
TRANSLITERATION AND TRANSLATION: Adler, pp. 252–53.
TRANSLITERATION: Artzi, *Actes* (see *EA* 28, n. 6), p. 7.
TRANSLATION: Oppenheim, *LFM,* p. 134.

To the kings of Canaan, servants of my brother: Thus the king.[1] I herewith send Akiya, my messenger, to speed posthaste to the king of Egypt, my brother. No one is to hold him up. Provide him with safe entry into Egypt and *hand* (him) *over*[2] to the fortress commander of Egypt.[3] Let [him] go on[4] immediately, and *as far as his pre⟨sents⟩ are concerned,*[5] he is to owe nothing.

NOTES

1. The "brother" is the Egyptian king, and the "king" is almost certainly the ruler of Mittani, probably Tušratta. Similar passports, though directed to one place, are *EA* 39–40; *PRU* 3, pp. 12–13, 15–16; *PRU* 4, pp. 193, 196–97.

2. *id-na*-x (Gordon): x is certainly not *šu,* perhaps *ni.*

3. G. del Monte, *OA* 22 (1983) p. 309, thinks that *ḫalzuḫlu,* "fortress commander," refers to the highest Egyptian official, usually called *rābiṣu* (see Introduction, n. 70), but Elmar Edel, *Festschrift Alt: Geschichte und Altes Testament Beiträge zur historischen Theologie* (Tübingen, 1953), p. 51, is certainly right in identifying him with the "fortress commander of Silu" (Egyptian *mr ḫtm n ṯr*), at the Egyptian frontier.

4. *li-il-l*⌈*i*⌉-[*i*]*k* (also Gordon).

5. kad-⟨ru⟩-*sú*: for the confusion of *sú* and *šu* in Mittani letters, see Kühne, p. 28, n. 126. For the sense, cf. the request for freedom from various taxes and tolls in *ARM* 5, 11; *EA* 39–40; *PRU* 3, pp. 15–16; *PRU* 4, pp. 196–97; *Ugar.* 5, no. 26. That "hand" should be written *qàt* (so Oppenheim and Artzi) does not seem likely. Gordon thought that the first sign might be *ši-ib* rather than *ù,* the next sign possibly erased or ma[r]. *ši-ib-sú* = *šibšu?*

On the seal impression on this tablet, see E. Porada, *AfO* 25 (1974–77) pp. 132ff.

EA 31

Marriage negotiations, in Hittite

TEXT: C 4741 (12208).
COPIES: WA 10; *VBoT,* no. 1; J. Friedrich, *Hethitisches Keilschriftlesebuch,* pt. 1 (Heidelberg, 1960), no. 7a.
TRANSLITERATION AND TRANSLATION: L. Rost, *MIO* 4 (1956) pp. 334ff.

Nimuwa⟨r⟩eya,[1] Great King, king of Egypt, (speaks) as follows: Say to Tarḫundaradu, the king of Arzawa:[2] By me all is well. For my houses, my wives, my children, my magnates, my troops, my chariot-fighters, all my *property*[3] in my countries, all is well.

7–10 By you (too) may all be well. For your houses, your wives, your children, your magnates, your troops, your chariot-fighters, your *property* in your countries, may all be very well.

11–16 Behold, I have sent to you Iršappa,[4] my messenger, (with the instruction): "Let us see the daughter whom they will offer to my majesty in marriage." And he will pour oil on her head.[5] Behold, I have sent to you a *sack*[6] of gold; it is (of) excellent (quality).

17–21 As to the things to be done that you wrote me about (with the words), "Send it here to me!"—now, I will send it (soon) to you, (but) later. (First) send back quickly your messenger and the messenger from me, and they must come.

22–26 Then they will come (back) to you (and) bring along the bride-price for the daughter. My messenger and your messenger who came, who . . .[7] And send to me too . . . people of the country Kaška. I have heard that everything is finished,

27–38 and that the country Ḫattuša is shattered.[8] And behold, I have sent to you as a greeting-gift a consignment in the charge of my messenger, Iršappa:[9] a *sack* of gold, weighing 20 minas of gold; 3 light linen garments; 3 light linen ⟨ma⟩ntles;[10] 3 linen *ḫuzzi*; 8 linen *kušitti*; 100 linen *šawalga*; 100 linen *ḫapp*[*a* . . .]; 100 linen *mutalliyašša*;[11] 4 large *kukkubu*-containers of "sweet oil"; 6 [*small*] *kukkubu*-containers of "sweet oil"; 3 chairs of ebony overlaid with beautiful *šarpa* [*and gol*]*d*;[12] 10 chairs of ebony [*inlaid*] with ivory; 100 (beams of) ebony, as a greeting-gift.

NOTES

[The translations and notes for *EA* 31–32 are by Volkert Haas. — WLM]

1. Reading ^{m}*ni-mu-wa-*⟨*r*⟩*e-ia,* with Albright, *JEA* 23 (1937) p. 195, n. 1,

and Edel, *Studien zur Altägyptischen Kultur* 1 (1974) p. 135; cf. *VAB* 2/1, p. 270, note e. The horizontal wedge that is missing is that of the *re,* not of the *wa* (Gordon). On paleographic and linguistic grounds, this and the following letter are to be dated in the period between the Hittite kings Arnuwanda I and Šuppiluliuma I. According to the paleographic criteria elaborated in *StBoT* 21 and 22, they approximate the script of the chancery of Arnuwanda I; cf. the signs AK, AL, DU, LI, and ŠAR. This fits too with the correct distinction between the plural determinatives MEŠ and ḪI.A, the frequent use of enclitic pronouns (note especially the use of the enclitic pronominal stem of the plural, -e, *EA* 31:18), the verb form *a-ú-ma-ni* (otherwise, in Old Hittite, *ú-me-ni, StBoT* 8, p. 78), and the plene writings such as *ḫu-u-da-a-ak* (*EA* 31:20) and *aš-šu-ú-li* (*EA* 32:18, 20, 21); cf. also *CHD* 3, pp. 254, 268 MH/MS.

2. On the location of Arzawa somewhere to the west of Cilicia, its history, and *EA* 31–32, see Heinhold-Krahmer, *Arzawa: Untersuchungen zu seiner Geschichte nach den hethitischen Quellen, THeth* 8 (1977) pp. 3–4, 50–55. Through a marriage with a daughter of the most powerful ruler among the various principalities that were found in Arzawa before Šuppiluliuma I, Egypt believed that it could assure the loyalty of the country and thus help impede the resurgence of the Hittites. Arzawa's previous isolation may be reflected in the fact that correspondence with it was carried on in Hittite and not, as was customary, in Akkadian. (The view of J. Friedrich, *Or* n.s. 8 [1939] p. 310, n. 1, that in this letter are to be found several "violations of normal Hittite speech" may be questioned. The position, however, of EGIRanda at the end of a sentence, after the verb, is a difficulty; cf. L. Rost, *MIO* 4 [1956] p. 336.)

3. The term *pippit,* "all of one's possessions," is attested only here, and it is certain that similar forms—*pí-pí-it-hi* ^{d}*a-dam-ma* (*KBo* XVII 103 rev. i 18′); *pí-pí-pí-tar*$^{S[AR]}$ *KBo* XIII 248 rev. i 9′)—have nothing to do with *pippit.* H. Kronasser, "Hethitisch *pippit* existiert nicht," *Die Sprache* 7 (1961) pp. 168–69, believes that it is a mistake for *upessar* to be equated with Akkadian *šūbultu.*

4. The name of the Egyptian messenger appears with the same writing among Hurrian gods: see *KUB* XXXIV 102 ii 13 (^{d}*ir-ša-ap-pa dam-ki-ra-a-ši*), and *KUB* XXVII 1 rev. ii 23 (*ir-šap-pí-ni-iš* DAM.GÀR-*ra-a-ši*). He is, therefore, a god of commerce; on *tamgar-(š)še,* "commerce," see I. M. Diakonoff, *Hurrisch und Urartäisch* (Munich, 1971), p. 69. The god Iršappa is the Canaanite Resheph; see E. Laroche, *RHA* 34 (1976) pp. 124f.; *Or* n.s. 45 (1976) p. 97; *Ugar.* 5, p. 521. Note, too, at Emar Nergal, the Babylonian Resheph as EN KI.LAM, *bēl maḫīri,* "lord of the marketplace, commerce," *Emar* 6/3 373:74′; 378:10.

5. On lines 11–14, see Güterbock in Landsberger, *Symbolae . . . Martino David dedicatae* (see *EA* 11, n. 7), pp. 79f., n. 4. On the rite, see *EA* 11, n. 7.

6. On the noun *zuḫalaliya,* see Otten, *StBoT* 15 (1971) p. 1, and Haas, *Kratylos* 16 (1973) p. 162. According to Gordon, here and in line 30 the first sign is SU and not ZU. See also Frank Starke, "Ein Amarna Beleg für *nbw nfr* 'gutes Gold,'" *GM* 53 (1981) pp. 55ff.

7. On the verb *aggaš,* of obscure meaning (perhaps "he is dead"), see Kühne, pp. 96f., n. 481.

8. Starke, "Zur Deutung der Arzawa-Briefstelle *VBoT* I, 25–27," *ZA* 71 (1981) pp. 221–31, interprets differently: "I have heard all that you said. And also

the land of Ḫattuša is at peace." This ingenious interpretation is based on an Egyptian parallel(?), but if one takes into consideration the historical implications, it falls short of conviction; see A. Hagenbucher, *THeth* 16 (1989) pp. 362f.

9. On lines 28–29, with their parallels in the letters of Ramesses II, see Edel, *Studien zur Altägyptischen Kultur* 1 (1974) p. 135.

10. With Edel, ibid., pp. 135–37, I read 3 GADA SIG (see *EA* 14 iii 11) 3 GADA ⟨GÚ⟩.È.A S[IG].

11. Gordon: either B/PU over an erasure, or else AŠ-B/PU, but not MU-AŠ (cf. MU in lines 1, 17, 18, 25).

12. The occurrences of *šarpa-*, *šarpašši*, have been collected by Rost, *MIO* 4 (1956) pp. 338ff. (Gordon: GIŠ.KAL clear; [KÙ.G]I GAR.RA.)

EA 32

Reply to EA 31

TEXT: VAT 342.

COPIES: WA 238; *VS* 12, 202; *VBoT,* no. 2.

TRANSLITERATION AND TRANSLATION: Rost, *MIO* 4 (1956) pp. 328ff.

Behold, (concerning the fact) that Kalbaya has spoken this word to me, "Let us establish a blood-relationship,"[1]

4–6 in this matter I do not trust Kalbaya. He has (indeed) spoken it as a word, but it was not confirmed on the tablet.

7–9 If you really desire my daughter, (how) should I not give her to you? I give her to you!

10–13 See to it now that Kalbaya returns quickly with my messenger, and write back to me on a tablet concerning this matter.

14–20 May Nabu, the king of wisdom, (and) Ištanuš of the Gateway graciously protect the scribe who reads this tablet, and around you may they graciously hold the(ir) hands.[2]

21–23 You, scribe, write well to me; put down, moreover, your name.

24–25 The tablets that are brought here always write in Hittite!

NOTES

1. This tablet is the end of a longer but only partially preserved communication replying to *EA* 31.

2. Before line 14 there is a double dividing-line. On lines 14–23, which are directed to the scribe at the Egyptian court, see Otten, *MIO* 4 (1956) pp. 179ff., esp. p. 185. See also the Introduction, sect. 4.

EA 33

An alliance in the making

TEXT: VAT 1654.
COPIES: WA 15; *VS* 11, 13.
PHOTOGRAPH: L. Hellbing, *Alasia Problems*, Studies in Mediterranean Archaeology 57 (Güteborg, 1979), p. 100 (obverse only).

To the king of Egypt, my brother: Message of the king of Alašiya, your brother.[1] For me all goes well. For you may all go we⟨ll⟩. For your household, your wives, your sons, your horses, your chariots,[2] and in your country, may all go [ve]ry well.

9–18 [*More*]*over,* I have heard [*t*]*hat*[3] you are seated on [the th]rone of your father's house. (*You said*), "[*Let us have*] *transported* (*back and forth*) [*gift*(*s*) *of p*]*eace.*"[4] [I have he]ard the greeting [*of*] my [*brother*], and I . . . [. . .] . . . [*You wr*]*ote,* "[*Have transported to me*] 200 (*talents*) of copper,"[5] [*and I* (*herewith*) *have*] *transported* to you . . . [. . .] . . . 10 talents [of *fine copper*].[6]

19–26 [The mes]senger [*that your father us*]*ed to se*[*nd* t]o [me] *I* [*let go* immedia]tely.[7] So wri[te *to me, and*] may my [bro]ther not *de*[*lay*] my [m]an that . . . [. . .] . . .[8] Let him g⟨o⟩ [imme]diately.

27–32 [A]nd[9] year by ye[ar] let my messenger go [into your presence], and, on you[r part], year by year, your messenger should come *from* [*your*] *pre*[*sence*] into my presence.[10]

NOTES

1. The king addressed was probably Amenophis IV, but neither Smenkhkare nor Tutankhamun may be excluded; see Kühne, p. 86. Perhaps, too, the entire Alašia correspondence is to be put in the reign of Amenophis IV, over a period of about a decade or so; for opinions, see Hellbing, *Alasia Problems* (see headnote), p. 47, n. 19, and *EA* 34, n. 11.

2. There is no plural marker with "chariots" or the three preceding nouns (also *EA* 37:6; 39:6), but plurals are the rule in the various forms of the formulaic greeting, and the unmarked logogram is also used for the plural in *EA* 34:44–45; 39:10–20; 40:16–28; perhaps 37:39 and 38:25.

3. In lines 1–8 the left margin moves inward, to the right (see photo), whereas Knudtzon's restorations [šá]-ni-ta$_5$ and [*a-n*]*u-ma* at the beginning of lines 9–10, respectively, assume the margin of line 8. On the other hand, the assumption of a broken sign seems inescapable. In line 10 [e/i-*n*]*u-ma* seems preferable (Kühne, p. 86, n. 427).

4. A change of rulers required allies to restate their expressions of friend-

ship; cf. *EA* 6:8ff.; 8:8ff.; 9:7ff.; 17:51ff.; 41:7ff. See also Goetze, *Kleinasien*² (Munich, 1957), p. 98; Otten, *AfO*, Beiheft 12, p. 65.

The following restoration of lines 12–13 is most uncertain: [nu-u]š-*te-bi-ri-mi* 13 [NÍG.BA š]a-*la-mi*. The first word, as if from *ebēru* (also line 17), is regularly used of crossing bodies of water and would be appropriate in a letter from an island; for overhanging *i*-vowel, cf. *li-li-ki*, lines 29, 32; for the form, probably Š-perfect, cf. *ultebilakku*, *EA* 35:10; *-mi* is a mark of direct quotation.

5. End of line 16: [šu-bi-ra-(mi)]. The measure is also absent in *EA* 35:10; 36:6; 40:7, 13; understand "talent(s)" or perhaps "bars, ingots" (Kühne, p. 86, n. 422). On the Cypriote talent of 28.2 kg or 35.25 kg, roughly the same weight of the ingots found at Cyprus, see Arnaud, *RA* 61 (1967) p. 168. Neither the gift requested nor the one sent is necessarily a coronation gift (Redford, *History and Chronology of the Eighteenth Dynasty of Egypt* [see Introduction, n. 119], p. 126).

6. Line 17: [ù u]š-*te-bi-ra-ku* x [x x]. What was actually sent seems to have been less than what was asked for, but the difference was perhaps compensated for by adding (line 18), [x-x]-AM 10 GÚ.UN [URUDU DÙG]; cf. *EA* 40:13.

7. Lines 19–22: [ù DUM]U *ši-ip-r*[*i*-šu] 20 [ša AD-ka *i*]*š-ta*-n[a-pa-ar] 21 [*a*]-*na mu-ḫi*-[ia *ki-ma*] 22 *ar-ḫi-iš* ⸢ú⸣-[wa-aš-ši-ir-(šu)]. Comparison of previous relations with the addressee's predecessor is frequent; cf. *EA* 8:8ff.; 9:6ff.; 10:8ff.; 15:7ff.; 17:21ff.; 27–29 passim.

8. Line 25: *ú*-[uḫ-ḫar/ḫa-ar-(šu)]; with the exception of *EA* 108:48, the D-conjugation of *kalû* (Knudtzon) is unattested in *EA*.

9. On the apparent *la* of the copy, see Schroeder, *OLZ*, 1917, col. 105.

10. *ip*-p[a-ni-ka]; cf. *i-pa-ni-ia* in the following line. That *in*(*a*) should mean both "from" and "to" in the same sentence, in the same expression, is not very likely. *ip*-p[a-ṭi-ka], "from your territory"?

EA 34

The Pharaoh's reproach answered

TEXT: BM 29789.
COPY: BB 6.
PHOTOGRAPH: Hellbing, *Alasia Problems*, p. 100 (obverse only, illegible).

Message of the king of Alašiya to the king of Egypt, my brother:[1] Be informed that I prosper and my country prospers. And *as to* your own prosperity, may your prosperity and the prosperity of your household, your sons, your wives, your horses, your chariots, your country, be very great. 7–15 Look, yo⟨u⟩ are my brother. As to your having written me, "Why did you not send your messenger to me?", the fact is that I had not heard that you were going to perform a sacrifice.[2] Do not ta[k]e this at all seriously.[3] Since I have (now) heard (about it), I herewith send my messenger to you. 16–25 And behold, I (also) send to you with my messen⟨g⟩er 100 talents of copper. Moreover, may your messengers now bring some goods: 1 ebony bed, gold-(*trimmed*), . . . ;[4] and a chariot, *šuḫītu*,[5] *with* gold; 2 horses; 2 pieces of linen; 50 linen *shawls*;[6] 2 linen robes; 14 (beams of) ebony;[7] 17 *ḫabannatu*-jars of "sweet oil." [*And*] *as to* byssos,[8] 4 pieces and 4 *shawls*. 26–31 [*And as*] *to* goods that are not *available* [*in your country*], I am sending [*in the charge of*] my [mess]enger a donkey-hide [. . .] of a bed, and [*ḫab*]*annatu*-jars that are not *available* [. . .] 32–41 . . .[9] 42–49 So an alliance should [be ma]de between the two of us, and my messen⟨g⟩ers should go to you and your messengers should come to me. Moreover, why have you not sent me oil and linen? *As far as I am* [*concer*]*ned*,[10] what you yourself request *I* will give. 50–53 I herewith send a *ḫabannatu*-jar [*that*] is full of "sweet oil" to be poured on your head, seeing that you have sat down on your royal throne.[11]

NOTES

1. On the writer's referring to himself first, see the Introduction, n. 53.

2. The festival cannot be identified (Campbell, *Chronology*, p. 42); for possibilities within the reign of Amenophis IV, see Kühne, pp. 86f. Cf. the coronation referred to in lines 50–53.

3. The reading *ti-š*⌜*a*⌝*-kán* is certain. The expression (*mimma*) *ina libbi šakānu* occurs also in *EA* 35:12, 15, 35 (all passive); 38:30; 170:7f.

4. *šu*-x-*a*: x is neither *ḫi* (BB, but rejected in *VAB* 2/1, p. 281, note d), nor *ḫa* (Ungnad, *OLZ*, 1916, col. 183); *u* over an erasure (or *nu*, Gordon) is possible. *šu"a*, "provided with mattress(es)"? Cf. *šē'u ša erši*; on the disagreement in gender, cf. *šalim* in line 4.

5. Mayer, *UF* 8 (1976) pp. 212f., compares Nuzi *šukītu*, (a type of) chariot.

6. GÚ.GADA (also line 25), to be added to *kišādu* (*CAD*, K, p. 449b, "scarf worn around the neck"; *AHw*, p. 490a, "Halstuch").

7. See *EA* 31:38, where Edel, *Brief*, p. 152, assumes ⟨GIŠ⟩, "⟨beams⟩," but perhaps repetition of logogram/determinative avoided.

8. See *EA* 14 iii 11.

9. At the end of line 32, ŠE.MEŠ (Gordon). Lines 39–40: ". . . my merchants and 20 merchants of yours" (⌜*ù* 20⌝, Gordon).

10. *a-na-ku*-[t]e: on the enclitic, see Krahmalkov, *JSS* 14 (1969) pp. 203f.; for the construction *anāku* . . . *anāku* (line 49?), cf. *EA* 35:21–22, 50–52. The assumption of a West Semitism is especially plausible in this letter. Among the Alašia letters it is the most strongly influenced by the West Semitized language found elsewhere in the Amarna letters from southern Syria and further south; see Kühne, p. 11, n. 47. To his observations add the use of the Akkadian subjunctive as West Semitic indicative: *tinaqqu* (line 12), *tuwašširuni* (line 48), *tērišu* (*terrišu*?) (line 49), *iddinu* (line 49). Note, too, the anomalous form of the dual pronominal suffix in *bi-*⌜*ri*⌝*-ku-ni* (line 48), paralleled only by *be-ri-ku-ni* in *EA* 113:18 and 116:33, both letters from Byblos (see *EA* 113, n. 5).

11. In a different context, "when you sit . . ." would also be possible. The language seems to imply a recent enthronement, and in both this and the arrangement for the exchange of messengers (lines 42–46) this letter is much like *EA* 33. It may be doubted that two such letters would be sent to the same king.

EA 35

The hand of Nergal

TEXT: BM 29788.

COPY: BB 5.

PHOTOGRAPH: Hellbing, *Alasia Problems,* p. 100 (obverse only, illegible).

TRANSLATION: Oppenheim, *LFM,* pp. 122f.

S[ay to the k]ing of Egypt, my brother: [Message] of the king of Alašiya, your brother. [F]or me all goes well. For my household, my wives,[1] my sons, my magnates, my horses, my chariots, and in my country, all goes very well. For my brother

6–9 may all go well. For your household, your wives, your sons, your magnates, your horses, your chariots, and in your country, may all go very well. My brother, I herewith send my messenger with your messenger to Egypt.

10–15 I herewith send to you 500 (*talents*) of copper.[2] As my brother's greeting-gift I send it to you. My brother, do not be concerned that the amount of copper is small. Behold, the hand of Nergal[3] is now in my country; he has slain all the men of my country, and there is not a (single) copper-worker.[4] So, my brother, do not be concerned.

16–18 Send your messenger with my messenger immediately, and I will send you whatever copper you, my brother, request.

19–22 You are my brother. May he send me silver in very great quantities. My brother, give me the *very best* silver, and then I will send you, my brother, whatever you, my brother, request.

23–26 Moreover, my brother, give me the ox that my messenger requests,[5] my brother, and send me, my brother, 2 *kukkubu*-containers of "sweet oil," my brother, and send me one of the experts in vulture augury.[6]

27–29 Moreover, my brother, men of my country keep speaking with m[e] about my timber that the king of Egypt receives from me. My brother, [*give me*] the payment due.[7]

30–34 Moreover, here is the situation: a man from [Alašiya] has died in Egypt, and [his] thing[s] are in your country, though his son and wife are with me. So, my brother, *loo*[*k to*][8] the things of the Alašiya people and hand them over, my brother, to the charge of my messenger.

35–39 My brother, do not be concerned that your messenger has stayed 3 years in my country, for the hand of Nergal is in my country and in my own house. There was a young wife of mine that now, my brother, is dead.[9]

40–42 Send your messenger immediately along with my messenger, with safe passage, and then I will send my brother's greeting-gift to you.

43–48 Moreover, may my brother send to me in very great quantities the silver that I have asked you for. Send, my brother, the things that I asked you for. My brother should do quite everything, and then whatever things you say I will do.

49–53 You have not been put (on the same level) with the king of Ḫatti or the king of Šanḫar.[10] Whatever greeting-gift he (my brother) sends me, I for my part send back to you double.

54–55 May your messenger come to me *as of o*[*ld, and*] may my messenger go to you *as of ol*[*d*].[11]

NOTES

1. On the absence of the plural marker, see *EA* 33, n. 2.

2. *enūma,* as if *anumma* (cf. *EA* 38:10; 40:12; and see the comments of Huehnergard, *Akkadian,* pp. 196f.). To apologize for sending only 500 talents (?—see *EA* 33, n. 5), the largest amount mentioned in the entire correspondence, is somewhat curious. Oppenheim ("pounds," "minas" understood?) reduces the amount, but consistency is required, and this solution alleviates only somewhat the difficulty. Georgiou, *Levant* 11 (1979) p. 96, thinks of irony and (more plausibly) suggests a prior request from the Pharaoh for much more. The amount would support the claim of lines 49–53. On Egyptian-Alašian trade relations in this period, see Y. Holmes, AOAT 22, pp. 96ff.

3. Whether dMAŠ.MAŠ is here to be read Nergal, or West Semitic Rašpu (Resheph; see *EA* 31, n. 4), or even the name of a native Cypriote god of pestilence, remains uncertain; see Hellbing, pp. 21ff. On *šumma,* "behold," see *JCS* 7 (1953) pp. 79ff.; also *AbB* 9, 253:13 and comment. Rainey, *Particles,* rejects this meaning of *šumma,* pointing to parallels where *inūma* replaces *šumma.* Note also in line 37 *aššum.* It does not follow, however, that *šumma* means "since, because," which would otherwise be without parallel and without explanation. As a deictic particle reflecting West Semitic *'im/hm, šumma* stresses the here-and-nowness of the situation.

4. Whether the "worker" (*ēpiš*) is here to be understood as merely mining the copper (*AHw,* p. 227a, "acquire"), or also refining, etc., is not clear; cf. *EA* 36:5, 12, 14.

5. *te-ri-iš-šu,* mistake for *e-ri-iš-šu* (*VAB* 2/1, p. 285). The ox is probably an ox-shaped object or figurine; live bovines are unattested among the gifts of this period.

6. Or "eagle-augury." The sudden request for a very specialized diviner, along with an ox and "sweet oil," is surprising, the more so since nothing is known of such a form of divination in Egypt (Brunner, *GM,* 25 [1977] pp. 45f.). Ornithomancy, as Artzi, *BiOr* 41 (1984) p. 212 has stressed, is of western origin; for the Mari evidence, see Durand, *AÉM* 1/1, pp. 38, 386f. McEwan, *ZA* 70 (1981) p. 62, n. 29, has suggested that *erû* refers here to the Neophron percnopterus (Egyptian vulture), which flies over Cyprus (Alašia) on migrations to and from Egypt. He sees the request as reflecting the cosmopolitan character of the Egyptian court, not as evidence of a native tradition.

7. ŠÀM.MEŠ (*šīmāti*), rather than ŠÁM, as not infrequently in Middle Assyrian and at Ugarit (*AHw,* p. 1240; Huehnergard, *Akkadian,* p. 373, no. 178aa).

8. Certainly MAŠK[IM], but the reading is unknown.

9. This interpretation assumes *mīt* for correct *mītat*; cf. *EA* 34, n. 4. The alternative, "a son or child has died," has other grammatical difficulties.

10. I agree with Vincentelli, *RSO* 46 (1973) pp. 143ff., that the usual version of these lines, "Do not make an alliance with . . . ," does not fit the context, and that such a request, if made, would require explanation. However, her own version, "Do not compare (me) with . . . ," has its own difficulties: *taššakin* is in form passive, and the alleged object—the crucial word—is unexpressed. Cf. *iššakin* (line 12) alternating with stative *šakin* (lines 15, 35).

11. *qad-mi-i*[*š*] (line 54), *qad-mi-*⸢is⸣ (line 55): ŠU-mi-⸢e⸣-[iš] (Knudtzon) is extremely doubtful, because for *e* there is no trace of a second vertical, and spacing favors only one sign. Interpretation is also extremely doubtful (Maynard, *JSOR* 8 [1924] p. 76). For *illik* as injunctive, cf. the injunctive use of the Š-perfect (*ultēbilanni,* line 20), Š-preterite (*ušēbila,* line 44), and N-preterite (*iššakin,* line 12).

EA 36

More about copper

TEXT: C 4750 (12187).

COPY: WA 19 + WA 20.

PHOTOGRAPH: Hellbing, *Alasia Problems,* p. 100.

Too fragmentary for translation.[1]

NOTE

1. *EA* 36 is the middle of a rather large tablet concerned with the exchange of goods. There are several references to "doing" copper (lines 4?, 5, 12, 14; see *EA* 35, n. 4). Line 6: "[*Now*] I am sending (sent?) to my brother 120 (+ x?, Gordon) (talents) [of cop]per; 70 (talents) remain . . ." Lines 9–10: "[. . .] . . . what I sent you was little. Now I have looked for (more) [*and*] I will se⟨n⟩d you [*as much a*]*s*

your heart desires. [*And* w]hat I ask [*yo*]*u* for (*e-ri-šu*-[k]a) send me." In line 6 (end), AŠ G[Ú.UN], "1 ta[lent]"; the conventional use of the horizontal wedge for the numbers 1–9 with *biltu* is also found in *EA* 37:9. In line 15, p]i-*ḫa-ti,* while paleographically possible, is questionable because of considerations of syllabary and perhaps history (Na'aman, *Political Disposition,* p. 2*, n. 19). Also dubious: *ki-na-ḫi* = Canaan.

EA 37

More about silver

TEXT: BM 29790.
COPY: BB 7.
PHOTOGRAPH: Hellbing, *Alasia Problems,* p. 100 (obverse only, illegible).

[Sa]y [t]o the k[in]g [of Egypt], m[y brother]: Message [of the king] of Alašiya,[1] your [brot]her. For me all goes well. [F]or my brother may all go well. For his household, for his wives, [f]or his sons, for the horses, his chariots,[2] and in his country, may all go ve⟨ry⟩[3] well. 8–12 [*I have he*]*ard* the greeting of my brother. [The gree]ting-gift for my brother is 5 talents (*of copper*), 5 *teams of horses.*[4] I (herewith) promptly dispatch the messenger of my brother. 13–20 Now may my brother promptly let my . . . go;[5] let me inquire about [m]y bro[the]r's health,[6] and whatever [yo]u n[ee]d[7] put down on a tablet so I can send (it) to you.[8] Send me pure silver. May my brother dispatch my messenger without delay.[9] 21–29 Pa-x-*tum*-x-*e,* ^{m}*Ku-ni-e-a,* ^{m}*E-tel-lu-na may the cit*[*y*] *expel,* and then may my brother let go x-*uš*-bar-*ra* (and) ^{m}[*B*]*e*-[*e*]*l*-x-y-z, wh[o] with . . .[10]

NOTES

1. Written *a-la-si-ia.*
2. On the absence of the plural marker, see *EA* 33, n. 2.
3. *dan* (over an erasure)-⟨*niš*⟩.
4. If the 5 talents are of copper, then of course the gift is for the Egyptian king, not from him. A gift of 5 talents of gold or silver (Weber, *VAB* 2/2, p. 1083; Georgiou, *Levant* 11 [1979] p. 97) seems out of the question, and if horses are also part of the gift—the reading cannot be confirmed—then this also argues against the gift's coming from Egypt; see Zaccagnini, *Lo scambio dei doni durante i secoli XV–XIII* (see Introduction, n. 60), p. 122, n. 1.
5. ŠEŠ-*ia* x-y-*ia* (Gordon). Note that ŠEŠ is never used alone in this letter.
6. *šulmāna ša'ālu* = *šulma ša'ālu.*
7. *ḫa*-⌜*áš*⌝-*ḫ*[*a-t*]*a* (also Gordon); see *VAB* 2/1, p. 291, note g.
8. *lu-še-bíl*-⌜*ak-ku*⌝ (Gordon).

9. *lā ikalla li-iš-pur* (completely visible), hendiadys (cf. *CAD,* K, p. 102b).

10. The names in lines 21ff. have been studied to determine the ethnic composition of Alašiya, but with little evident awareness of the epigraphic difficulties; see Astour, *JAOS* 84 (1964) pp. 240ff.; Carruba, *Studi classici e orientali* 17 (1968) pp. 25ff. Line 21: probably no personal name determinative; second sign, *pa* more likely than *áš*; fourth sign, *ni* more likely than *me.* Line 23: last sign, *na* unlikely, UR[U] more likely (?—possible?). Line 24: ⌜li-iṭ-*ru*-d⌝am-*ma* (Gordon); if correct and not an archaism, *ṭarādu* must at this period mean "drive off, expel." Line 25: x-*uš*-bar(pa?)-*ra*; x may be a personal name determinative; Gordon has Ku-*uš*-par/pa-*ra*. Line 26: ᵐB/Pel-x = *ša* or *ta*; the next two signs are illegible.

EA 38

A brotherly quarrel

TEXT: VAT 153.
COPIES: WA 11; *VS* 11, 14.
PHOTOGRAPH: Hellbing, *Alasia Problems,* p. 100 (obverse only).

Say to the king of Egypt, my brother: Message of the king of Alašiya, your brother. For me all goes well, and for you may all go well. For your household, your chief wives,[1] your sons, your horses, your chariots, among your numerous troops, in your country, among your magnates, may all go very well.

7–12 Why, my brother, do you say such a thing to me, "Does my brother not know this?" As far as I am concerned, I have done nothing of the sort. Indeed,[2] men of Lukki, year by year, seize villages in my own country.

13–18 My brother, you say to me, "Men from your country were with them." My brother, I myself do not know that they were with them. If men from my country were (with them), send (them back) and I will act as I see fit.

19–22 You yourself do not know men from my country. *They* would not do such a thing.[3] But if men from my country did do this, then you yourself do as you see fit.

23–26 Now, my brother, since you have not sent back my messenger, for this tablet it is the king's brother (as messenger). L[et] him write. Your messengers must tell me what I am to do.[4]

27–30 Furthermore, which ancestors of yours did such a thin⟨g⟩ to my ancestors? So no, my brother, do not be concerned.

NOTES

1. NÍTLAM (SAL.UŠ), distinguished from DAM (*aššatu*) in *EA* 39:6–7 and also at Alalakh (Goetze, *JCS* 13 [1959] p. 98); see also *PRU* 3, p. 4:6; ibid., p. 5:6; *PRU* 4, p. 232:11 (?—cf. *EA* 19:85?); *Ugar.* 5, no. 21:4, and no. 24:7. The reading is *ḫīrtu* or *marḫītu* (*CAD*, M/1, p. 281); *sekretu* (*CAD*, S, pp. 216f.) seems less likely. See also *EA* 49, n. 2.

2. *enūma* for *anumma*; see *EA* 35, n. 2.

3. Against copy, read *la-a e-pu-uš* (Schroeder, *OLZ*, 1917, col. 105). The context favors understanding the subject as the accused Alašians. A singular verb with a plural subject is not without parallel (*EA* 170:23; *Ugar.* 5, p. 128, n. 1).

4. The writing is so inept in this paragraph that my version is only one of several possibilities.

EA 39

Duty-free

TEXT: C 4748 (12206).

COPY: WA 12.

PHOTOGRAPHS: Hellbing, *Alasia Problems*, p. 101; catalogue of the exhibition, "Toutankhamoun et son temps," in the Petit Palais (reference from Kühne, p. 87, n. 436).

Say to the king of Egypt, my [broth]er: Message of the king of Alašiya, your brother. For me all goes well, and for you may all go well. For your household, your chief wives, your sons,[1] your wives, your chariots, your many horses, and in Egypt, your country, may all go very well.

10–13 My brother, let my messengers go promptly and safely so that I may hear my brother's greeting.

14–20 These men are my merchants. My brother, let them go safely and prom[pt]ly. No one making a claim in your name is to approach my merchants or my ship.[2]

NOTES

1. On the absence of a plural marker, see *EA* 33, n. 2, and on the plurals in lines 10ff. see *VAB* 2/1, p. 295, note *.

2. For the request of safe passage and exemption from impost, cf. *EA* 30. On the reverse, in hieratic script, "letter of the prince of Alasa." On Egyptian *wr*, "prince," as a designation of foreign rulers, see the Introduction, n. 73.

EA 40

Duty-free, governor to governor

TEXT: C 4749 (12190).
COPY: WA 13 + 14.
PHOTOGRAPH: Hellbing, *Alasia Problems,* p. 101.

Say [to the go]vernor of Eg[ypt, *my brother*]: Messa[ge of *the governor* o]f Ala[šiya, *your brother*].[1] For . . . [. . .][2] all goes well, and fo[r you] may all go well.

6–11 My brother, *before the* ar[*rival* of *Šu*]mitti,[3] I sent *t*[*o him*] 9 (*talents*) of copper, 2 pieces of i[vor]y, 1 beam for [a ship], but *h*[*e*] gave[4] [no]thing to me, and *y*[*ou* se]nt[5] (only some) ivor[y], my brother.

12–15 I herewith[6] send as your greeting-gift 5 (*talents*) of copper, 3 talents of fine copper, 1 piece of ivory, 1 (beam) of *boxwood,* 1 (beam) for a ship.

16–20 [Mo]reover, my brother, these men[7] [and] this ship belong to the king, my lord. So send [me] (back) the ship [*of the king, my lord*], promptly and [saf]ely.

21–23 [And as for y]ou, my brother, [wh]atever you ask for according to [*your fancy*], I will give it to y[ou].

24–28 These men are servants of the king, [my] lo[rd], and no one making a claim in your name is to approach them. My brother, send (them back) to me safely and promptly.

NOTES

1. This letter was written by the same scribe as that of *EA* 39, probably one after the other, and probably delivered at the same time, perhaps by the same messenger. (On messengers carrying several letters, see Edel, *Brief,* pp. 145f.) MAŠKIM (*rābiṣu*), as here said of the Egyptian official, probably refers to the high office of vizier (Helck, *Beziehungen*², p. 248), and as probably said of the Alašian official it is to be compared with LÚ.MAŠKIM.GAL, the title of the official in Alašia who sent *Ugar.* 5, no. 22, perhaps native *pidduri* (Steiner, *Kadmos* 1 [1963] pp. 130f.; Otten, *MDOG* 94 [1963] p. 15; *Ugar.* 5, p. 341, n. 2).

2. Traces fit neither *i*[*yāši* nor *m*[*aḫrīya* nor U[GU-*ia*. In the next line, *ana* [UGU-*ka*]; cf. *EA* 39:5.

3. Reading *ana* [p]a-n[i] (Knudtzon), but perhaps *ana* [m]aḫ-r[i] (Gordon). The name, which is not Egyptian, is restored on the basis of *EA* 57:13; cf. also *Ugar.* 5, no. 20:2.

4. *i-din*-n[a] seems the most likely reading (Gordon).

5. t[a]-aš-*pu-ra-am-ma* (Gordon).

6. See *EA* 35, n. 2 (read i/e-*nu-ma*?).

7. On the plural, see *EA* 33, n. 2, and *VAB* 2/1, p. 297, note ***.

EA 41

Of Egyptian-Hittite relations

TEXT: C 4747 (122–7).
COPY: WA 18.

[Thus the Sun],[1] Šuppiluliumaš, G[reat] King, [king of Ḫat]ti. Say to Ḫuriy[a, the king of Eg]ypt, my brother:[2]

4–6 [For me all goes w]ell. For you may all go wel[l. For yo]ur [*wives*], your sons, your household, your troops, your chario[ts, and i]n your country, may all go very well.

7–13 Neither my messengers, whom I sent to your father, nor the request that your father made, saying, "Let us establish only the most friendly relations between us," did I *indeed* re[fus]e.[3] Whatsoever your father said to me, I *indeed* did absolutely eve[ry]thing. And my own request, *indeed,* that I made to your father, he never refused; he gave me absolutely everything.

14–15 Why, my brother, have you held back the presents that your father made to me when he was al[iv]e?

16–22 Now, my brother, [yo]u have ascended the throne of your father, and just as your father and I were desirous of peace between us, so now too should you and I be friendly with one another. The request ⟨that⟩ I[4] expressed to your father [*I shall express*] to my brother, too. Let us be *helpful* to each other.[5]

23–28 My brother, do not hold back anything that [I asked] of your father. [*As to the* 2 st]atues of gold, one [should be *standing*], one should be seated. And, my brother, [*send me*][6] the 2 [*silve*]*r* statues of women, and a large piece of lapis lazuli, and a large stand for [. . .].

29–38 [. . .] . . . If my brother [wants *to give them*], let my [broth]er give the[m.[7] But i]f my brother does not want to give them,[8] when my chariots ha[*ve been r*]*eadied* for . . . linen *ḫuzzi,*[9] I will return them to my brother. Whatever you want, my brother, write to me so I can send it to you.

39–43 I herewith send you as your greeting-gift:[10] 1 silver rhyton, a *stag,*[11] 5 minas its weight; 1 silver rhyton, a young ram,[12] 3 minas its weight; 2 silver disks, 10 minas their weight, *as*[13] 2 large *nikiptu*-trees.

NOTES

1. [*um-ma* ^{d}UTU-*ši*]: cf. *umma* ^{d}*šamšī* RN *šarru rabû* introducing Hittite letters and decrees (*PRU* 4, passim). On the form of introduction, see the Introduction, sect. 4.

2. The Egyptian king could be either Amenophis IV, Tutankhamun, or Smenkhkare; see the Introduction, sect. 6, nn. 125 and 138. Philologically, the arguments of Wilhelm and Boese in favor of the last named are very strong.

3. Line 9: *at-te-ru-tam-*⌜*ma*⌝ (Gordon). The particle *-mi* (*nippuš-mi*) indicates direct discourse. The syntax of lines 7–10 is rather confused. The reading of the sign at the end of line 9, at the beginning of line 11, and perhaps also at the end (*mi-ri-iš-ta-ia* x-y, Gordon), is quite uncertain. Tentatively I follow Kühne's reading, LUGAL, and his suggestion of a rebus-writing for *šalurru*(*mma*); see AOAT 17, p. 101, n. 500.

4. *a-na-*⌜*ku*⌝: virtually certain (Gordon).

5. 22 [a-qab-bi] *us-sà-ta* (*usātu*): favoring *aqabbi* is the enclitic *-ma*, "my brother, *too*." Gordon also restored a-ḫu]-*uz-za-ta*, "let's make a marriage between us," but a break of five signs seems excluded. Whether a proposal of marriage would be made so laconically may also be doubted.

6. [šu-bi-la], at the end of line 28.

7. *li-it-ti-in-šu-nu-ti-*(*ma*) (also Gordon).

8. Suffix is *-šunu*, not *šunūti*. Line 34: [*la*]-⌜*a*⌝ [*ḫ*]*a-šiḫ*.

9. The reading *i*-gam-ma-*ru-ma* is very questionable. Gordon read GADA *ḫu-uz-ḫu-še*.

10. On lines 30–41, see Eheloff, *ZA* 45 (1939) pp. 71f.

11. See *CAD*, A/1, p. 375a (LU.LIM$_4$ = *lulīmu*). Cf., at Mari, rhytons in animal form, the head being specified (vessel, "head of a gazelle," etc.); see *ARMT* 25, p. 275 on no. 82.

12. UDU.DAG + KISIM$_5$xIR(?), followed by a "Glossenkeil," which is not attached to the previous wedge (against *VAB* 2/1, p. 1003, no. 60).

13. Either *-ma* over an erasure (meaning?), or ŠÈ = *ana*, as elsewhere at Boghazköy. The matching numbers suggest the possibility that the *nikiptu*-tree was depicted on the disks.

EA 42

A question of honor

TEXT: VAT 1655.
COPIES: WA 16; *VS* 11, 16.

[. . .] may all go well. For [. . .], your magnates, for [your] tro[ops, your horses], your chariots, and i[n your country, may all go very well.][1]

8–14 . . .[2]

15–26 And now, as to the tablet that [*you sent me*], why [did you *put*] your name over my name?[3] And who (now) is the one who upsets the good relations [*between us*], and is su[ch *conduct*] the accepted practice?[4] My brother, did you write [*to me*] with peace in mind? And if [*you are my brother*], why have you exalted [*your name*], while *I*, *for* [*my part*], *am tho*[*ught of as*] a [co]rpse. [*I have writ*]*ten* [*the names* . . .] . . . but your name [. . . *I will bl*]*ot out.*[5] . . . [. . .]

27–28 [*Thu*]*s*[6] the scribe . . . [. . .] Do not . . . [. . .].

NOTES

1. The Hittite provenience of *EA* 42 is virtually certain; see the remarks of Knudtzon, *VAB* 2/2, p. 1093f. Note, too, KUR URU before geographical names (KUR URU *ḫu*[*r-ri*, line 10), typical of Hittite scribes. If the restoration in line 2 is correct, it is possible we shoul ! render by "chariot-fighters" rather than "horses"; see the Introduction, n. 54.

2. The addressee is aske l, it seems, to recall the history of the two countries, going back to the time ol their grandfathers. Perhaps a defense is offered of Hittite attacks on "Ḫurri-country" (line 10), i.e., Mittani.

3. This is usually understood of the form of the introduction to letters between equals or from superior to inferior, according to which the addressor names himself first (Introduction, sect. 4); thus *VAB* 2/2, p. 1094; Edel, *Jahrbuch für kleinasiatische Forschung* 2 (1952–53) p. 265; Helck, *Beziehungen*, p. 475, n. 3. If this interpretation is correct, we must assume an addressee quite unfamiliar with standard Hittite practice. Perhaps we should think rather of a list of names in hierarchical order; cf. the list of names at the end and the possible threat not to put the Hittite on the list at all.

4. Cf. *EA* 27, n. 18.

5. 19 ŠEŠ-*ia aš-šum-ma sú-lum-me-e* [a-na ia-ši] 20 *ta-aš-pu-u-ra-a ù šum-ma* [ŠEŠ-ia at-ta šum-ka] 21 *am-mi-nim tu-ra-ab-bi ù a*-[na-ku ki-ma] 22 [*n*]*a-bu-ul-tim ki-a-am ḫa-as*-[sa-ku šu-mi ša] 23 [ᵐ(x)]-x-SAR ᵐ*ru-mi-in*-x [. . .] 24 [aš]-*ṭur ù šum-ka* [. . .] 25 [a-pa-*a*]*š-ši-iṭ ù* . . . Lines 21–22, perhaps better: "*I am like* a corpse (and) thus *am I thought of.*"

6. [um-ma]-*a*. If correct, a message from the scribe of *EA* 42.

EA 43

Of malice and murder

TEXT: Ash 1207.

COPY: Sayce, *Tell el Amarna*, pl. XXXI (obverse only).

PHOTOGRAPH: P. S. Moorey, *Archaeology, Artefacts, and the Bible* (Oxford, 1969), p. 43 (obverse only; erroneously identified as a letter from Byblos).

Too fragmentary for translation.[1]

NOTE

1. The correspondents are of equal rank ("brothers"), probably kings, and Hittite provenience of the letter is virtually certain because of the sign-forms of NI, UŠ, DAM, LA, AZ; see also *VAB* 2/2, p. 1094. The letter refers to malicious men and someone's murder.

EA 44

From a Hittite prince

TEXT: VAT 1656.
COPIES: WA 29; *VS* 11, 16.

Say to the lord, the king of Egypt, my father: Thus Zi[t]a, the king's son, your son.[1]

5–6 May all go well with the lord, my father.

7–13 On an earlier embassy of any of your messengers, they came to Ḫatti, and when they went back to you, then it was I that sent greetings to you and had a present brought to you.

14–17 . . .[2]

18–24 [. . .][3] Herewith [*I send on*] to you your messengers (coming) [from] Ḫatti,[4] and I also send to my father my own messengers along with your messengers, and I send as your greeting-gift a present of 16 men.

25–29 I myself am desirous of gold. [M]y father, send me gold. Whatever you, the lord, my father, are desirous of, write me so I can send it to you.

NOTES

1. If the title "father" implies difference of age, Amenophis III would be the addressee of this letter (Kühne, p. 102, n. 508). The writer seems not to have been in the Hittite capital at the time of writing, but his scribe was either trained there or under its influence (cf. forms of AK, AZ, and, to some extent, NI).
2. Perhaps Zita wrote in this paragraph about his new station.
3. New paragraph uncertain.
4. On lines 18–20, see Kühne, p. 103, n. 512.

EA 45

Friendly Ugarit

TEXT: 1692 (smaller of two fragments not collated).
COPIES: WA 177; *VS* 11, 17.

[*Say* to *the king*], the Sun,[1] [*my lord*: Message of Amm]istam[ru, your servant.[2] I fall at] your [feet] 7 times [and 7 times. May all go well f]o[r the king, the Sun, my lord, for your household, your chief wife, for your (other) wives, for your sons, for your archer]s, [for whatever else belongs to the king, the Sun, my lord], m[ay all go very, very well].[3]

8–21 [. . . *And*] I myself [*said* a]s follows:[4] "These men are [*Egyptians*]. Why should I *ha*[*nd them over to you?*"] I shall *prepare* [. . .] and he will acquire [. . .]. I hand them over *t*[*o the Sun, my lord*], and [*I send*] my messenger to the Sun, my lord, [*promptly*]. I now *ha*[*nd them over to the Sun, my lord*].

22–29 Moreover, the king of [. . .][5] wrote: "Why . . . [. . . *and*] do you seize [. . ."]. A second time he wrote [*to me*], and thus he sp[oke: ". . .] and to Egypt [. . .]. If you *sen*[*d*[6] . . . , *I will* . . .] Indee[d, *I am a servant*] to the Su[n, *my lord.*"]

30–35 Moreover, heaven forb[id][7] that [*the Sun, my lord*], turn against me. [*May he send me*] the life of [*my* spirit, *and*] may [*his mouth*] speak the life of [*my*] spirit.[8] [*And*] may [*the Sun, my lord*], know (this): if . . . to Ugarit [. . .]. . . .[9]

NOTES

1. *EA* 45 and 49, and almost certainly 46–48, are from Ugarit (Albright, *BASOR* 95 [1944] pp. 30ff.); the king addressed in *EA* 45 is probably Amenophis III (H. Klengel, *Geschichte Syriens*, pt. 2, p. 340; M. Drower, *CAH*³, 2/2, p. 133). On Ugarit's relationship with Egypt, see A. Altman, *Bar Ilan*, Annual of Bar Ilan University, Judaica and Humanities Series, 13 (1976) pp. 1ff. (in Hebrew; English summary, p. 17). Egyptian and, through borrowing, Hittite kings were called, literally, "My Sun," as the embodiments of royalty, which was also symbolized by the winged sun-disk (I. Winter, *Iraq* 38 [1976] p. 4f.).

2. 2 [*um-ma* ᵐ*a*l*am-m*]*i-is-tam-*[*ri* ÌR-*ka*] (Nougayrol, *PRU* 3, p. xxxvii).

3. 3 [*a-na* GÌR.MEŠ]-*ka* 7 [*ù* 7 *am-qut* 4 *lu-ú šul-mu a-na*] UG[U . . .] 6 [ÉRIN.MEŠ *pí-ṭá-t*]*i-*[*ka* . . .] (cf. *EA* 49:6). 7 [. . .] *l*[*u-ú* . . .]

4. [ù (a)-*k*]*án*ᵃⁿ*-na-am* (perhaps -⟨*ma*⟩) *a-na-ku* [aq-bi]: cf. *kán-na-am-ma* in *EA* 46:5 and (*a*)-*kán*ᵃⁿ*-na-ma* at Boghazköy (*CAD*, A/1, p. 262).

5. Whether this was the Hittite king, as is usually held, remains uncertain (Klengel, *Geschichte Syriens*, pt. 2, p. 340 and p. 480, n. 6).

6. *tu-še-bá-*[al . . .] (Huehnergard, *Akkadian*, p. 254, n. 199).

7. *as-sú-ri-im-*[*ma* . . .] (ibid., p. 195).

8. Free restorations; on the life-giving breath and speech of the king, cf. *EA* 100:36ff.; 137:71f.; 141 passim; 144:6ff.; 145:20; 146–47 passim; etc.

9. More than 10 lines missing, with traces of a few signs.

EA 46

Ongoing loyalty

TEXT: VAT 1694.
COPIES: WA 179; *VS* 11, 18.

Too fragmentary for translation.[1]

NOTE

1. References to "my ancestors" (lines 1, 9, 23; read [lú]*ab-ba-e-ia,* and cf. *EA* 47) and declarations of loyalty equal to theirs (lines 22–26).

EA 47

Loyalty unrewarded

TEXT: VAT 1693.
COPIES: WA 176; *VS* 11, 19.

[. . .] . . . My ancestors[1] did service [for] your [ancestor]s, [*and* n]ow I am truly a servant too to the king, the Sun, [m]y [lord].[2]

12–21 [*Moreover,* I sen]t[3] my messenger to my lord, but my lord did not question him. [*And to* a]ll the messengers of [*other*][4] kings [you gi]ve your tablet. You send (them), [*but*] your own messenger(s) [you (also) *sen*]*d to* them.[5] To me, however, [*and to*] my messenger(s) [*you have not giv*]*en* your tablet, and your own messenger you have not sent [*to m*]*e*. [*Am I treated in accordance*] *with* the loyal⟨ty⟩ of my heart?[6]

22–30 [*Moreover,* w]hy do you listen [to *all* the wor]ds of [Ḫa]nya?[7] [. . .] . . . *Ask someone able*[8] [. . .] . . .

NOTES

1. In view of *EA* 46:1, 9, 23, probably AB.BA.MEŠ = *abbā'ē* (all cases, Assyrianism).

2. On this clause see Huehnergard, *Akkadian,* p. 203; in the enclitic of *ardum-ma,* however, I see the meaning "also" rather than a marker of the predicate (ibid., p. 205).

3. Line 13: [*al-ta-p*]*ar* (ibid., p. 218, n. 31). Line 15: *tanandin,* not *lū tanandin* (Knudtzon).

4. [ša-nu-ti]: enough room? Huehnergard, ibid., p. 219, [ÌR.MEŠ-*ka*], "your servants," has the same problem.

5. Since we must read *i*]*a* in line 20 (see copy), and very probably [*it-ti-i*]*a*, *ittīšunu* probably means, not "with them" (the messengers), but "to them" (the kings). This West Semitism, attested elsewhere (see *EA* 167:31), is otherwise unknown at Ugarit.

6. [ep-še-ku-ú ki]-*ma ki-it-*⟨*ti*?⟩. . . . Huehnergard, ibid., p. 95 and n. 216, sees the short form *kit* as a possible option.

7. [gab-ba *a*]-*wa-te.*MEŠ, following Huehnergard, ibid., p. 219.

8. [. . .] x *ša-al le-'a*; certainly not *y*]*išāl,* the preformative *y* being unknown at Ugarit.

EA 48

A jar of balsam for my lady

TEXT: VAT 1690.
COPIES: WA 181; *VS* 11, 20.

[To . . .], my mistress. [Message of . . .-Ḫ]eba, your maidservant.[1] I fall [at the feet of] my [mist]ress. [For] my mistress may all go well.

5–8 You have given [*your maidservant* . . .]. [*I* he]rewith [*send* t]o my mistress [. . . *and*] a jar of aromatics: *ṣú-ur-wa* (balsam).[2]

NOTES

1. Probably from the queen of Ugarit to the queen of Egypt. Liverani, *Storia di Ugarit* (see Introduction, n. 128), pp. 51f., has proposed to identify the former as the Pudu-Ḫeba (*Pdǵb*) who wrote to king Niqmadda of Ugarit, thereby implying that this letter belongs in the time of Niqmadda II.

2. On the form of the gloss, see Huehnergard, *Ugaritic*, pp. 131f.; on the meaning, see M. Stol, *On Trees, Mountains, and Millstones in the Ancient Near East*, (Leiden, 1979), pp. 50ff.

EA 49

A request for a physician

TEXT: C 4783 (12238).
COPY: WA 204 + 180.

To the king, the Sun, my lord. Message of Niqm-Adda,[1] your servant: I fall at the feet of the king, the Sun, my lord. May all go well for the king, the Sun, my lord, [h]is househ[old], his ch[ief wife],[2] for his (other) wives, for [*his sons*, . . . the ar]chers, for [*everything else belonging to the king*],[3] the Sun, my lord. [. . .] 17–26 [. . .] . . . Previously [*he gave* . . . *to*] my [fa]ther's house. May my lord give me 2 attendant[s], palace ⟨attendants⟩[4] from Cush. Give me, too, a palace attendant that is a physician.[5] Here there is no physician. Look, ask [*Ḫa*]*ramassa*.[6] And here[with] ⟨I send⟩[7] as your greeting-[gift . . .] and one-hundred [. . .].

NOTES

1. ^{m}*níq-ma-*^{d}IM, following Albright, *BASOR* 95 (1944) pp. 31f. Undoubtedly, Niqm-Adda II, the successor of Ammistamru I (*EA* 45), writing probably to Amenophis IV (Klengel, *Geschichte Syriens*, pt. 2, p. 344).

2. S[AL.UŠ]-*šu*: K[UR.MEŠ] (Knudtzon) is excluded, since if it occurs at all in the greeting, it does so towards the end; cf. *EA* 38. Note that in the other

letters of the kings of Ugarit in which they wish well to the correspondent's wives, NÍTLAM (see *EA* 38, n. 1), never DAM, is used; cf. *PRU* 3, p. 4:7f.; *Ugar.* 5, no. 21:6'f.; no. 24:8f.; no. 28:7f.; no. 29:5f.; note also *PRU* 3, p. 5:7f. This seems to be a later practice; cf. Huehnergard, *Akkadian,* p. 329.

3. [gáb-bi mim-mu-ú ša LUGAL]: see the letters referred to in n. 2.

4. 2 DUMU *ṣú-ḫa-*[*ri*] 20 [lú]⟨DUMU⟩ É.GAL (cf. line 22): at the beginning of line 20, the head of one horizontal is visible, and this is not compatible with D[UMU] (*AHw,* p. 616a).

5. On the fame of Egyptian medicine, see Edel, *Ägyptische Ärzte und ägyptische Medizin am hethitischen Königshof: Neue Funde von Keilschriftbriefen Ramses' II aus Boğazköy* (Opladen, 1976). According to Homer (*Odyssey* IV 231f.), Egypt was so rich in medicines that everyone was a physician, wise above all others.

6. [mḫa]-*ra-ma-sa*: in line 26, *sa-al-m*[*i* (*-mi* is not confined to direct discourse; see Huehnergard, *Akkadian,* p. 210), or simply *sa-al* (according to Gordon, probably only erasures follow), "ask" (on the confusion of sibilants, see Huehnergard, ibid., pp. 111ff.). This fits the context—i.e., a statement about the local situation, then an appeal to testimony (cf. *EA* 69:28f.; 89:41f.; 256:16ff.; 264:11f.; etc.). It follows, almost necessarily, that]*-ra-ma-sa* is a personal name; assuming the confusion of sibilants again, cf. the Egyptian messenger in *EA* 20:33ff.

7. The scribe seems to have erased the verb, probably to correct an error, and then to have forgotten to restore it; cf. *VAB* 2/1, p. 318, note a.

EA 50

Maidservant to her mistress

TEXT: VAT 1594.

COPIES: WA 191; *VS* 11, 21.

[Say] to . . . [. . .],[1] my mistress: Message of the daughter of [. . . , your] maidservant. [I] fall at the feet [of] my mistress 7 times and 7 tim[es]. [. . .] . . . my mistress.

NOTE

1. Perhaps the queen, mft[a-ḫa-mu-un-šu], "The King's Wife"; on this title and its appearance in cuneiform, see Federn, *JCS* 14 (1960) p. 33. The provenience of the tablet is unknown. If *al*[lu-mi] (Knudtzon) in line 7 is correct, note its use, with the exception of *EA* 34:16, 50, only at Byblos and farther south.

EA 51

Loyalty tempted and preserved

TEXT: VAT 559.
COPIES: WA 30; *VS* 11, 22.

[T]o the Sun, the king, my lord, the king of Egypt: Message of Addunirari, your servant. I fall at the feet of my lord. [*No*]*t*[*e*] (that) when Manaḫpiya, the king of Egypt, your ancestor,[1] made [T]a[ku], my ancestor, a king in Nuḫašše, he put oil on his head and [s]poke as follows: "Whom the king of Egypt has made a king, [*and on whose head*] he has put [*oil*], [no] one [shall . . .]." He gave . . . [. . .]. Now, [. . .].

Rev. 1–6 And [. . .] Taku, [my] ances[tor . . .]. And now, my lord, . . . [. . .]. And the king of Ḫatti [*wrote to me about an alliance*]. My lord, [*I rejected*] (the offer of) tablets of treaty obli[gations],[2] and [*I am* (*still*) *a servant of*] the king of Egypt, [my lord].

7–17 And now, [*may*] our lord[3] [*come forth*] t[o *us*], and into [*h*]*is* power [*we will*] *in*[*deed restore the lands*], and indeed [. . .] . . . to our lord. [And] may our lord *come forth*[4] (this) year.[5] Do not be negligent. You will see that they are loyal to the service of the king, my lord. And if my lord is not [w]illing to come forth himself, may my lord send one of his advisors[6] [to]gether with his troops and chariots. [. . .] . . .

NOTES

1. Since Thutmosis III (Manaḫpiya) was not the grandfather of any of the kings possibly addressed in this letter, Akkadian *ab*(*i*) *abi*, "grandfather," must have here a more general meaning, undoubtedly through the influence of Hurrian *ammati*, "grandfather, ancestor" (Laroche, *RHA* 34 [1976] p. 47); see *EA* 59:11 and Campbell, *Chronology*, pp. 68f. Nougayrol, *PRU* 4, p. 33, n. 1, held to "grandfather."

2. *tuppāte u ri-ik-*[*ṣa-te* . . .]: cf. *tuppi riksi*/*rikilti*, etc., at Alalakh, Boghazköy, and Ugarit (*AHw*, pp. 984f.); in view of the plural, probably *riksāte*. The Hittite king (Šuppiluliumaš) hardly sent the tablets (so Altman, *Shnaton, Annual for Biblical and Ancient Near Eastern Studies*, 2 [1977] p. 30); he would have done so only as a final formality of the alliance, perhaps as a reward for demonstrated loyalty (*PRU* 4, p. 37:51f.). The rest of the restorations in this paragraph are free.

3. The shift to the first plural, "*our* lord," is perhaps because the writer thinks of his allies. Cf. below: "*they* are loyal."

4. *li-iṣ-ṣí-*⌜ma⌝: cf. rev. 13, *ana a-ṣi-i-im*, but note *ṣi*, not *ṣí*.

5. I assume otiose MEŠ.

6. Perhaps "advisor" (*milku*) refers to one of the commissioners (*rābiṣu*) of Syro-Palestine; cf. *EA* 131:15, where "commissioners" is glossed by *ma-lik*.MEŠ.

EA 52

The loyalty of Qaṭna

TEXT: C 4759 (12197, with join to former VAT 1596).
COPY: WA 196 (before join; no published copy of join).

Say[1] to the king of Egypt: Message of Akizzi, your servant. I fall at the feet of my lord, my Storm-god,[2] 7 times.

5–7 Inspect, my lord, his tablets.[3] [*He/you will find*] the houses of Qaṭna belong to my lord *a*[*lone*].[4]

8–26, 27–31, 32–35 . . .[5]

36–41 [*Fo*]*r* 3 years,[6] my lord, when *I wanted* [*to set out*][7] for my lord, *the messengers did not know of a caravan (going to Egypt). They did not know of* : *am-mu-li*(?) . . . to my [*lo*]*rd. Le*[*t* them] come in [*your*] caravan.

42–43 Come, my [. . .] has abandoned me. : *pu-ru* x *nu la-aš-ti-na-an.*

44–46 I will [cert]ainly not rebel agai[nst] the . . . of my lord or against Bir[u]aza.[8]

NOTES

1. *qí-bí-ma,* at the end of line 1, is omitted in the copy and overlooked by Knudtzon.

2. ^{d}IM: reading certain, and cf. ^{d}IM-^{d}IM, also written *Ad-di*-^{d}IM, "My Addu is Addu" (D. Charpin, *AÉM* 1/2, no. 303, note b). In this instance we perhaps have an adaptation, in local terms, of the usual title or epithet "My Sun" (*EA* 45, n. 1); cf. *EA* 53:6.

3. An unusually abrupt shift from second to third person in addressing the Pharaoh.

4. Interpreting the *u* as "resumptive" after direct object; see Wilhelm, AOAT 9 pp. 54ff. In É.HI.A the plural marker is probably otiose, and "house" is to be understood of the ruling dynasty; cf. *EA* 74:10; 89:48. End of line 6: [. . . im/ta-am-ma]r.

5. At the end of line 31, *išriqšunu,* "he stole them," is probably a charge against the Hittite king (cf. *EA* 55:53ff.?).

6. [š]a KAM.3.MU?

7. a[t]-*ta-nam*-[mu-uš]: instead of *at, ta* or x-*na* is also possible (Gordon). In the rest of the paragraph, the language is most obscure. Glosses are Hurrian; word division is uncertain.

8. 46 [*lu*]-⌜*ú*⌝ *lā ipaṭṭar* (Gordon).

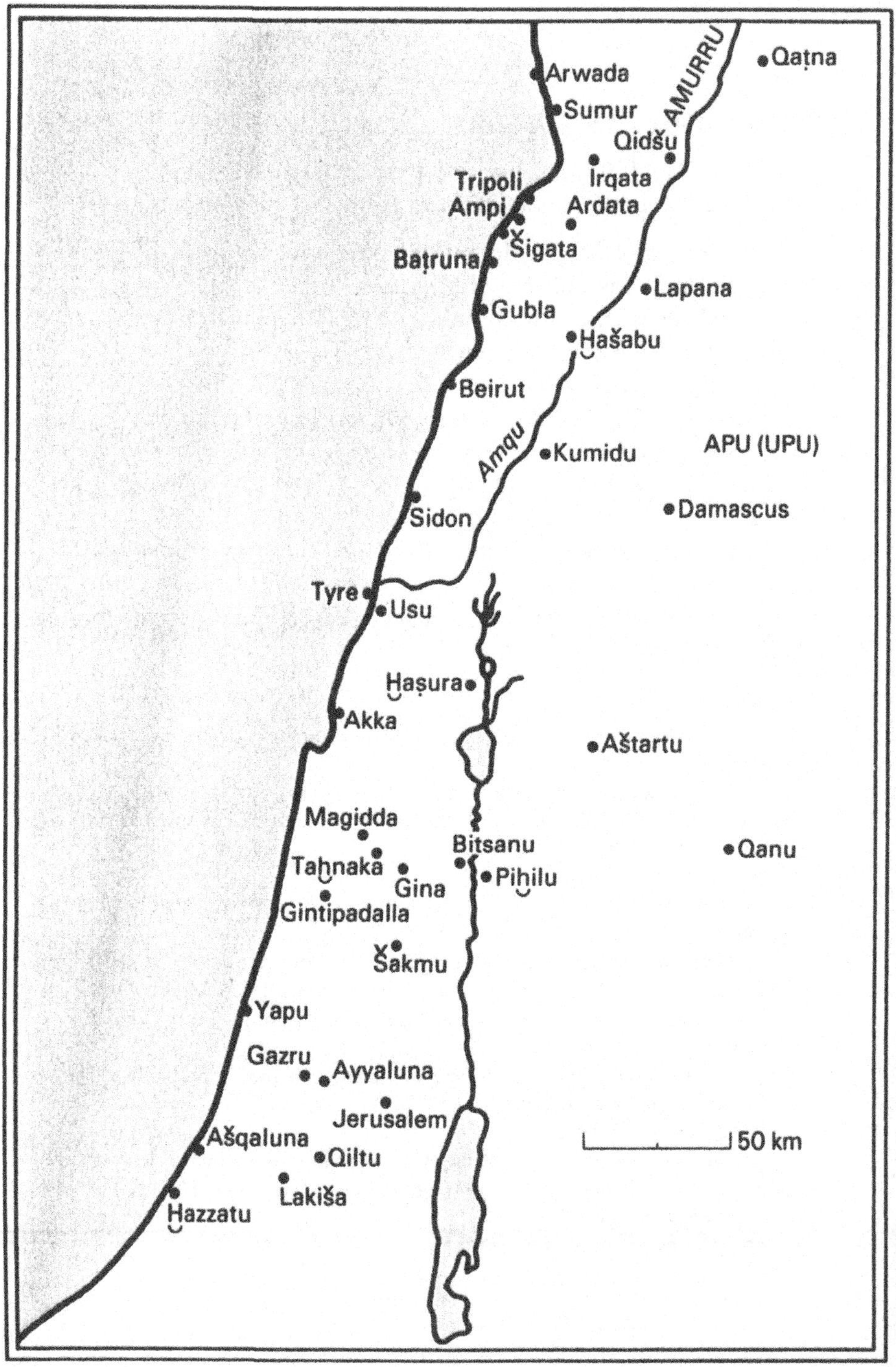

Vassal Cities and Egyptian Administrative Centers

EA 53

Of the villain Aitukama

TEXT: BM 29820.
COPY: BB 37.

To N[am]ḫ[ury]a, so[n] of the Sun, my lord: Me[ssa]ge of [A]k[i]zz[i], your servant. I fall [a]t the feet of the king, my lord, 7 times and [7 times].

4–10 [My] lor[d, . . .] . . . *has survived,* and *I will not de*[*sert*].[1] [*I belong*] to my lord.[2] [*And n*]*ow, m*[*y lo*]*rd,* of my lord alone [*am I the serv*]*ant* in the place, *the l*[*and of*] *Te*[*ššup*]. [. . .] . . . now [*in*] the place *of* the god . . . [. . .]. And now, the king of Ḫat[ti] ⟨*has*⟩ [*s*]*ent*[3] Aitukama *out* [*against*] *me,* and he seeks [my] li[fe].

11–16 And now [*Aitukam*]*a* has written me and said, "[*Come*] with me to the king of Ḫa[tti." I s]aid, "How *could* [*I go*[4] to the ki]ng of Ḫatti? I *am* [*a ser*]*vant* of the king, my lord, the king of Egypt." I wrote and [. . .] to the king of Ḫatti.

17–23 . . . May my lord send him (it?) . . . [. . .] that he (it?) may come ag[ainst Ai]tukama so that my lord [. . .] he may fear your presence.

24–34 . . . My lord, Aitukama came and [*he sent Up*]*u,* the land of [m]y lord, [*up*] i[n *flames*]. He took the (ruler's) house [. . .], and he took 200 *d*[*isks* . . .], and he took 3 [d]is[ks . . .], and he took [1 d]isk [. . .] from the house o[f] Birwaza.

35–39 My [l]ord, Teu[w]atti of L[apa]na and [A]rsawuya of Ruḫizzi place themselves at the disposition of Aitukama, and he sends [U]pu, the land of my lord, up in flames.

40–44 My lord, just as I love the king, m[y] lord, so too the king of Nuḫašše, the king of Nii, the king of Zinzar, and the king of Tunanab; all of these kings are my lord's servants.

45–51 As far as the king, my lord, can, he co[mes forth. But] it is being said, "The king, my lord, will not come forth." [*And so*] may the king, my lord, send archers [that] they may co[me] to this country. [Si]nce, my lord, these kings are ones who *l*[*ov*]*e* him, let a magnate of the king, my lord, just name their gifts so they can give them.

52–55 My lord, if he makes this land a matter of concern to my lord, then may my lord send archers that they may come here. (Only) messengers of my lord have arrived here.

56–62 My lord, if Arsawuya of Ruḫizzi and Teuwatti of Lapana remain in Upu, and Tašša remains in the Am[q], my lord should also know about them that Upu will not belong to my lord. Daily they write to Aitukama and say as follows: "Come, tak[e] Upu in its entirety."

63–70 My lord, just as Dimaški in Upu : *ka₄-di-ḫi* (*falls*) at your feet, so *may* Qaṭna : *ka₄-di-ḫu-li-eš* (*fall*) at your feet.[5] My lord, one asks for life before my messenger.[6] I do not fear [*at al*]*l*[7] in the presence of the archers of my lord, *since* the archers belong to my lord. If he sends (them) to me, they will en[ter] Qaṭna.

NOTES

1. *la a-pat*-[ṭar-(me)]: cf. *EA* 55:6. If Knudtzon's "not dead" is correct, a syllabic writing is unlikely; read, rather, *la-a* UG$_6$ [(:) mi-it].

The obverse of this tablet is extremely difficult, the traces are very faint, and therefore the translations are often extremely dubious.

2. [a-na-ku] *a-na* [*š*]*a be-lí-ia*: cf. *EA* 55:9.

3. ⟨ú⟩-š[e]-*eṣ-ṣí*: the West Semitic preformative is not used in this dialect, and therefore y[i]-*iṣ-ṣí* (Knudtzon) is excluded; besides, the form would be *yuṣṣi* (see *EA* 362:30).

4. *ki-i a*-[na-ku al-la-ak . . .].

5. On the Hurrian glosses, see Goetze, *RHA* 5 (1939) pp. 109f., and Friedrich, *WZKM* 47 (1951) p. 213.

6. Obscure; perhaps "life" is the favorable reply of the king, declared in the messenger's presence or leading him, as it were, back to Qaṭna.

7. [mi-nu-m]e-*e*.

EA 54

More about Aitukama

TEXT: VAT 1868 + 1869 + 1721.
COPIES: WA 229 + 232 + 233; *VS* 11, 23.

Too badly preserved for translation.[1]

NOTE

1. This letter is over 50 lines but, except for the greeting, very poorly preserved. Akizzi seems to repeat the charges of *EA* 53 against Aitukama and his allies, Teuwatti and Arsawuya. In line 51, perhaps Carchemish is mentioned.

EA 55

A plea for troops

TEXT: BM 29819.
COPY: BB 36.

Say to Namḫurya,[1] the son of the Sun, my lord: Message of Akizzi, your servant. I fall at the feet of my lord 7 times.

4–6 My lord, I am your servant in this place. I seek the path to my lord. I do not desert my lord.

7–9 From the time my ancestors were your servants, this country has been your country, Qaṭna has been your city, (and) I belong to my lord.

10–15 My lord, when the troops and chariots of my lord have come here, food, strong drink, oxen, sheep, and goats,[2] honey and oil, were produced for the troops and chariots of my lord. Look, there are my lord's magnates; my lord should ask them.

16–24 My lord, the whole country is in fear[3] of your troops and chariots. If my lord would take this country for his own country, then let my lord send this year his troops and his chariots so that they may come out here and all of Nuḫašše belong to my lord. If, my lord, the troops [c]ome [out], *stay for* 6 days in ... [...], then they would certainly take Aziru.[4]

25–27 If the troops and chariots of my lord do not come forth this year and do not *fi*[*ght*],[5] it (the country) will be in fear of Aziru.

28–37 ...

38–43 My lord knows it. My lord [...] his ancestors [...]. But now the king of Ḫa[tti] has sent them up in flames. The king of Ḫatti has taken his gods and the fighting men of Qaṭna.[6]

44–52 My lord, Aziru took men of Qaṭna, my servants, and has *le*[*d*] *them away*[7] out of the country of my lord. They now *d*[*wel*]*l* outside of the country of my lord. If it *ple*[*ases*] him, may my lord send [(*the ransom*) *money*] for the men of Qaṭna, and may my lord ransom them. ... [...], my lord, the money for their ransom, as much as it may be, so I can hand over the money.

53–66 My lord, your ancestors made (a statue of) Šimigi, the god of my father, and because of him became famous.[8] Now the king of Ḫatti has taken[9] (the statue of) Šimigi, the god of my father. My lord knows what the fashioning of divine statues is like. Now that Šimigi, the god of my father, has been reconciled to me, if, my lord, it *pleases* him, may he give (me) a *sack* of gold,[10] just as much as is needed,[11] for (the statue of) Šimigi, the god of my father, so they can fashion it for me. Then my lord will become, because of Šimigi, *more* famous than before.

NOTES

1. Despite the form (more like EN.ḪÉ), *nam* must be the sign intended.

2. Read ÙZ: so also, independently, Gordon and Na'aman, *Political Disposition*, p. 54*, n. 47. Since it regularly follows "oxen" (GUD.MEŠ: see *EA* 124:50; 125:20; 161:21; 324:14; 325:16), it seems to be a replacive of "sheep and goats" (UDU.MEŠ = *ṣēnu*; cf. *EA* 193:20). In comparable Egyptian texts the sequence is oxen, goats, sheep, with an alternative "sheep and goats" ("Kleinvieh"); see Edel, *Geschichte und Altes Testament* (see *EA* 30, n. 3), p. 52, n. 1.

3. *i-pal-la*-ḫé.

4. The reading in the break is most uncertain. The context seems to require that here there be a promise of victory over Aziru, followed in the next paragraph by a threat of the consequences if troops are not forthcoming. If so, then the construction is under Hurrian influence, *ilteqe* understood as passive, the subject Aziru, with the suffix *-šunu* expressive of ergative; see Kilmer, *JAOS* 94 (1974) p. 179; cf. lines 53ff.

5. *iq*-[te-ri-ib].

6. Perhaps "the god" (otiose MEŠ), since the next paragraphs seem to take up, in reverse order, the missing men and the missing god.

7. *ip*-⌈pa⌉-*šu-nu*: from *nepû*, "to distrain"?

8. On the syntax of the passage, see above, n. 4.

9. *il-te-qè-šu*-⟨⟨*nu*⟩⟩ (influence of line 43).

10. KUŠ? Cf. *EA* 29:26.

11. Von Soden, *OLZ*, 1968, col. 458, reads *ba-aṣ-ṣi-im-ma*, "like the very sand," but the *ma-* is certain and *kī maṣî(mma)* is well attested (*CAD*, M/1, p. 347a).

EA 56

A declaration of trust

TEXT: VAT 1714.
COPIES: WA 173; *VS* 11, 24 (corrections in Schroeder, *OLZ*, 1917, col. 105).

[*Say to the king, my lord: Message of . . . , your servant. I fall at the feet of*] my [*lord*].[1]

4–8 [*Look, the ene*]*my* has . . . [*Did I not write*] *th*[*is*][2] to my lord, the king of [Egypt. And] my [lord] said, "You did not write [to m]e *about* (*their*) *num*[*bers*],"[3] and my [lo]rd did not come forth.

9–13 I am your servant, and, my lord, you must not let [me] go

[from] your hand. I, for my part, will not [desert] my lord. I have put my trust [i]n my lord, his troops, [*and in*] his chariots.

14–22, 23–28, 29–35 . . .[4]

36–42 My lord's messenger came to me and said as follows: "I [*journeyed about*] in Mittani, and there were 3 or 4 kings who were host[ile to] the king of Ḫatti, al[l of whom] were [*at*] *my disposal.*"

43–51 . . .[5]

NOTES

1. Provenience unknown, but lines 36–42 = *EA* 54:38–43, and therefore *EA* 56 must be closely associated with the Akizzi correspondence; see *VAB* 2/2, p. 1121.

2. *an-ni*-[ta$_5$] 5 [la aš-pu]r.

3. *i-na* [mi-ni]: traces of possible m[i, visible to Knudtzon, have disappeared.

4. References to Taššu (line 17; cf. *EA* 53:58), Atakkama (?—lines 23, 27), and the town Ruḫizzi (line 26).

5. Reference to Ḫurri-land (line 44).

EA 57

Of kings and Tunip

TEXT: VAT 1738.
COPY: *VS* 11, 25.

Too fragmentary for translation.[1]

NOTE

1. Only the ends of lines are preserved. There are references to "Akizzi, king of Qaṭna" (line 2), "the king of Barga" (line 3), Puḫuru (line 10), Šumitta (line 13), and the city Tunip (line 12; rev. 1). See Klengel, *Or* n.s. 32 (1963) p. 45, n. 3.

EA 58

Of the king of Mittani

TEXT: VAT 1716.
COPIES: WA 214; *VS* 11, 26.

Sa[y to the *Gre*]*at* [*King*],[1] my lord: [Message of] Teḫu-Teššup,[2] [*your*] *ser*[*vant*]. I fal[l at] the feet of my lord.

4–10 [Mo]reover, be informed tha[t] the king of Mittani came forth together [with *chariots*] and together with an *expedition*[*ary force*],[3] and we heard, "At the *waters*[4] [. . .]." . . .[5]

NOTES

1. Perhaps addressed to an official ("magnate"; cf. *EA* 95, 238), but the "Great King" is more likely (*VAB* 2/1, p. 341, note h). Besides the script and the clay, this would indicate a northern provenience, for only *EA* 160–61 (Amurru), 260, and 317–18 (see below) begin with this title.

2. For Knudtzon's Qatiḫušupa, which rests partly on a misunderstanding of the glosses in *EA* 53:64–65, there is not sufficient space.

3. ÉRIN.MEŠ KASKAL + ?.[BAD?]; see *EA* 106, n. 10.

4. *a-na-mi* (*-mi* is a marker of direct discourse) *me-e* [. . .].

5. Rev. 3: reference to ʿAbdi-Aširta or his son. Line 6: perhaps [iq-b]i *ḫa-ia-mi lu* x, "he (the king) said, 'Alive . . .'" (Na'aman, *Political Disposition*, p. 17*, n. 49).

EA 59

From the citizens of Tunip

TEXT: BM 29824.
COPY: BB 41.

To the king of Egypt, our lord: Message of the citizens of Tunip, your servant.[1] For you may all go well. And we fall at the feet of my lord.

5–8 My lord, thus says Tunip, your servant: Tunip—who *ruled* it in the past?[2] Did not Manaḫpirya : *am-ma-ti-wu-uš* (*your* ancestor) *rule* it?[3]

9–12 The gods and the . . . : *na-ab-ri-il-la-an* (?)[4] of the king of Egypt, our lord, dwell in Tunip, and he should inquire of his ancients : *am-ma-ti* (ancient) when we did not belong to our lord, the king of Egypt.

13–17 And now, for 20 years,[5] we have gone on writing to the king, our lord, but our messengers have stayed on with the king, our lord. And now, our lord, we ask for the son of Aki-Teššup from the king, our lord.[6] May our lord give him.

18–20 My lord, *if* the king of Egypt has given the son of Aki-Teššup, why does the king, our lord, call him back from the journey?

21–24 And now Aziru is going to hear that in Hittite territory a hostile fate has overtaken your servant, *a ruler* (and) your gardener.[7]

25–28 Should his (the king's) troops and his chariots be delayed, Aziru will do to us just as he did to Nii.

29–33 If we ourselves are negligent and the king of Egypt does nothing about these things that Aziru is doing, then he will *surely* direct his hand against our lord.

34–38 When Aziru entered Ṣumur, he did to them as he pleased, in the house of the king, our lord. But our lord did nothing about the⟨s⟩e things.

39–42 And now Tunip, your city, weeps, and its tears flow, and there is no grasping of our hand.

43–46 We have gone on writing to the king, our lord, the king of Egypt, for 20 years, and not a single word of our lord has reached us.[8]

NOTES

1. Probably, just as the city Irqata and its elders wrote to the king because their own king had been killed (*EA* 100; 75:25f.), so too Tunip (see lines 13–20). If one may speak of its "republican" organization (Landsberger, *JCS* 8 [1954] p. 61, n. 134), the temporary character of this arrangement should also be recognized.

2. The verb is not clear; it is taken here as *ašābu,* "to sit, dwell," but as said of kings, with the implication of occupying as sovereign, as in Northwest Semitic languages (O'Connor, *BASOR* 226 [1977] p. 22) and in the Old Syrian *koine* (*ARMT* 13, 144:5 and note; 14, 69:25 and note).

3. Thutmosis III (see *EA* 51:4) took Tunip in his forty-second year.

4. The Hurrian gloss is unexplained; the word glossed is equally uncertain.

5. The 20 years here and in line 44 are round numbers meaning nothing more than "a long/considerable time" (Liverani, *OA* 10 [1971] p. 254, n. 2, also in *Three Amarna Essays,* p. 3; Wilhelm and Boese, *High, Middle, or Low?* pp. 90f.).

6. Aki-Teššup, probably the last king of Tunip, now dead, whose son had been taken to the Egyptian court for the training given to vassal princes; see Helck, *Beziehungen,* p. 155.

7. 24 NAM (*šimtu*) *sar-ra-tu*$_4$: apparently a reference to a recent Egyptian defeat. What follows is very obscure. Ruler and gardener, high and low? one and all?

8. Note the framing of the complaint, "20 years ... 20 years" (lines 13, 44), after the declaration of loyalty (lines 5–12). Lines 13–46 encompass four sections, each introduced by *u inanna*: the complaint (13–14); the request (15–20); the grounds for the request, the danger of Aziru (21–38); the complaint (39–46).

EA 60

Loyal ʿAbdi-Aširta

TEXT: VAT 343.

COPIES: WA 93; *VS* 11, 27.

TRANSLITERATION AND TRANSLATION: Izre'el, *Amurru,* pp. 7ff.

[T]o the king, the Sun, my lord: [Mess]age of ʿAbdi-Ašratu,[1] your [ser]vant, the dirt under your feet. I fall at the feet of the king, my lord,

7 times and 7 times. 6–9 As I am a servant of the king and a dog of his house, I guard all Amurru for the king, my lord.[2] 10–13 I have repeatedly said to Paḫanate, my commissioner, "Take auxiliary forces to guard the lan[ds] of the king."[3] 13–19 Indeed, all the [k]ing[s] under the king of the Ḫurri forces[4] seek to wrest the lands from my [. . .] and . . . [. . . *o*]*f*[5] the king, [my] lord, [*but* I g]uard th[em]. 19–29 [*Look*],[6] there is [Pa]ḫanate, [my] commissioner. May the king, the [Su]n, ask him if I do not guard Ṣumur and Ullassa. When my commissioner is on a mission of the king, the Sun, then I am the one who guards the harvest of the grain of Ṣumur and all the lands for the king, my Sun, my lord.[7] 30–32 May the king, [m]y lord, know me and entrust [m]e to the charge of Paḫanate, my commissioner.[8]

NOTES

1. The name of the goddess appears more frequently as Aširti/a; for a comparable fluctuation in the Old Babylonian period, see Kupper, *L'iconographie du dieu Amurru dans la glyptique de la Ire dynastie babylonienne* (Bruxelles, 1961), p. 62, n. 1. In *Ugar.* 5, no. 9:20, read ^{m}ÌR-*a-šir*$_9$*-ti*. Note, too, the fluctuation in the same letter (*EA* 137).

2. With Izre'el, *Amurru*, "zero-forms" (see the Introduction, n. 50) are not taken as preterites, though context does not rule out such an interpretation (Rainey, *UF* 7 [1975] p. 410f.).

3. The quotation may extend into the following lines.

4. The king of Mittani; on the expression, see Carruba, *Or* n.s. 40 (1971) pp. 212f.

5. [Š]U (*qāti*)*-ia* at the beginning of line 17 is improbable; space requires one large or two small signs. At the end of line 16, traces of ⌜lìb⌝-[b]i? Restore ù at the end of line 18? According to *AHw*, p. 1557, not *ḫa-ba-lim*, but *ḫa-ba-ši* = *ḫabāṯi*. Izre'el, *Amurru*, compares *ḥābal* in *Ezekiel* 18:16.

6. [*a-n*]*a-ṣa-ar-š*[*u-*(*nu*) a-mur]: following Rainey, *UF* 7 (1975) p. 411, n. 133.

7. Since logograms of verbs are extremely rare in *EA*, it is better to read the logogram as noun (infinitive) *eṣēd*, and therefore as object (*CAD*, E, p. 340; Rainey, *UF* 7 [1975] p. 411). Despite the singular suffix on the verb, "all the lands" is perhaps also the object of the verb. The temporal clause "when my commissioner . . ." Izre'el, *Amurru*, joins with what precedes.

8. "Knowing" here and in similar passages implies taking cognizance of, showing concern for, someone, much as gods know their clients (*CAD*, I/J, pp. 27f., sects. 1e and 2a 2'; Dalley et al., *The Old Babylonian Tablets from Tell Al Rimah* (see *EA* 22, n. 19), no. 118:11, "the god who knows the house of your father"; see also Whiting, *Old Babylonian Letters from Tell Asmar* (see *EA* 14, n. 9), no. 11:54 and commentary, p. 51; in Old Assyrian, cf. Veenhof, *JCS* 30 [1978] p. 188). For a different view, according to which "to know" means "to acknowledge as a vassal," see Campbell, in Frank Moore Cross et al., eds., *The Mighty Acts of God: In Memoriam G. Ernest Wright* (Garden City, 1976), p. 50, and the literature cited

there. On the Hittite evidence, see Goetze, *JCS* 22 (1968) pp. 7f. With the request to be turned over to a commissioner, cf. *EA* 253:32ff.; it is perhaps a formulaic expression of loyalty, a renunciation of autonomy.

EA 61

A lost message

TEXT: Ash 1893.1–41:410.
COPY: Sayce, *Tell el Amarna,* no. 3.
TRANSLITERATION AND TRANSLATION: Izre'el, *Amurru,* pp. 9f.

[To the k]ing, the Sun, my lord: [Mes]sage of ʿAbdi-Aširti, [your] ser[vant, *and*] the mud under your f[ee]t, a do[g o]f the house of the king, my lord. A[t . . .] . . .[1]

NOTE

1. One more line of illegible traces on obverse, and nine fragmentary lines on the reverse. Reference to Ullassa (?—[URU u]l-⌜la-zi⌝ki, rev. 3), Ṣumur, and Amurru; request for a reply (8–9, end of letter?).

EA 62

ʿAbdi-Aširta to the rescue

TEXT: VAT 1680.
COPIES: WA 158; *VS* 11, 28.
TRANSLITERATION AND TRANSLATION: Izre'el, *Amurru,* pp. 10ff.

[To P]aḫanate, [my l]or[d: Message of ʿAbd]i-Aširti, [your] s[ervant. I fall at the fe]et of my lord. 4–10 [*Wh*]*at do* your words, [my lord, *that you sp*]*eak, mean?* . . . [. . .] my lord, [*you spea*]*k* [*like th*]*is*: "*Y*[*ou are an enemy of* E]gypt, [and] you [*committed a crime against* Eg]yptians."[1] [*May my lord listen. There were n*]*o* men in Ṣumur [to gua]rd it [*as he had ord*]*ered,*[2] 10–20 and [Ṣum]ur [*was afraid of*][3] the tr[oo]ps of Šeḫl[al]; there were no m[en i]n it to [gua]rd it. [So] I myself [has]tened to the rescue from Ir[qat], and I myself [*c*]*ame* [*before*] Ṣumur[4] and . . . your [. . .] from the hand of the troops of Š[eḫ]lal. If I had not been staying in [*Irqat*], if I had been staying where life was peaceful, then the troops of Šeḫlal [would *certainly* have s]ent Ṣumur and the palace up in *fl*[*am*]*es.*[5] 21–34 When I myself hastened to the rescue from Irqat and arrived in Ṣumur, there were no men that had stayed on in the palace. Here are the (only) ones that had stayed on in the palace: Šab-Ilu, Bišitanu, Maya, Arsawa.[6] There were (only) 4 men that had stayed on in the palace, and they said to me, "Save us from the hand of the troops of Šeḫlal." And so I sav[ed t]hem from the hand of the troops of Šeḫlal. [Of 4 per]sons I saved the lives.[7] 25 (was the number of those) whom [the troops of Še]ḫlal killed. 34–36 And when ... [...] 37–45 [*t*]*hey* [*fl*]*ed*[8] from Ṣumur. I did not expel (them) [...] ...[9] the mayors lie to you, [*and* y]ou keep on listening to them? [And *Y*]*a*maya,[10] when he writes [...], lies [t]o you, and you keep on listening [to] his [wor]ds. 45–55 *As for Ya*maya, ⟨the troops⟩ of Šeḫlal [*came* wi]th him. [*They cam*]*e* to seize [Ṣumu]r. *He too*[*k* ... *t*]*o* seize the city itself ...[11]

NOTES

1. Free restoration: [at-t]a-[mi LÚ.KÚR] 7 [ša KUR *mi*]-*iṣ-r*[*i*ᵏ]ⁱ *te*-[pu-uš lum-na] 8 [a-na LÚ].MEŠ ... (cf. *EA* 106:32).

2. [li-iš-me] 9 [be-li ia]-*nu* ... 10 [*a-na na-ṣ*]*a-ri-š*[*i* ki-ma qa]-*be-šu*. Cf. *kīma qabê šarri* (*EA* 144:21, etc.); *kīma qabêka* (193:22); *kīma ša qabêšu* (302:18; 329:20).

3. [pal-ḫa-at] (beginning of line 12).

4. [*i*/*a-pan*-ni-m]a (BAN clear to Knudtzon); cf. *panû* (*AHw*, p. 822). An image of ʿAbdi-Aširta placing himself between the troops of Šeḫlal and the besieged city? For a different reading and interpretation, see Izre'el, *Amurru*.

5. ⌜i-na⌝ [I]⌜ZI⌝-*te*.MEŠ: contrary to Knudtzon (*VAB* 2/2, p. 351, note c), *i-na* fits the traces very well (*na* like the *na* at the end of line 50 and on line 52), but the writing of *išāti* is unparalleled.

6. Reading of the first two names uncertain.

7. *ú-wi*(*wa*?)-*i-mi*: following Izre'el, *Amurru*.

8. [x-x in-na]-*be*-t[u-m]a.

9. Beginning of line 40: traces do not favor [mi-ni]m.

10. [ù ᵐi]a-*ma-a-ia* (Albright, *JNES* 5 [1946] p. 13, no. 15). In line 45, collation is not decisive, but I could not see the vertical nor the heads of all three horizontals, all of which are so clear in *VS* 11 and would confirm Knudtzon's TUR.

11. Lines 50–55: very poorly preserved, with several very obscure forms.

EA 63

Orders obeyed

TEXT: BM 29817.
COPY: BB 34.
PHOTOGRAPH: BB, pl. 15.

Say [t]o the king, my lord: Message of ʿAbdi-Ašta⟨r⟩ti, servant of the king.[1] I fall at the feet of my king, my lord, 7 times and 7 times. I fall at the feet of the kin[g, my] lord.[2] 7–9 The king, [the lo]rd, has given orders [t]o me, and I heed the [or]ders of the king, [my] lord. 10–16 [I h]eed (them), and so [may] the k[ing, m]y l[or]d, heed my [wor]ds, [*for* the wa]r again[st me] is s[ev]ere. *May the k*[*in*]*g* [*kn*]*ow* [*and be in*]*formed.*

NOTES

1. Na'aman, *UF* 11 (1979) pp. 676f., has demonstrated that *EA* 63–65 and 335 were all sent by ʿAbdi-Aštarti, and all from the same place where Šuwardata resided. Schroeder, *OLZ,* 1915, cols. 293f., linked *EA* 65 and 335, and Na'aman shows the common scribal background of *EA* 63–65, 282–84, and 335: cf. *VS* 12, p. 74. Note also: the form of TU in *EA* 283:24 as well as 65 and 335; the form of GÌR in 63–65 and 283; the writing *da-na-at* in 63:13; 64:9; 283:22, 31 (elsewhere: 144:23, 178:9; 271:10); the writing 1 GÌR.MEŠ in 63:5; 64:3; 65:4. Na'aman makes ʿAbdi-Aštarti the successor of Šuwardata.

2. *a-na* GÌR.MEŠ ⌜ša⌝ ᵐLUG[AL] EN-[*ia* . . .].

EA 64

Women for the king

TEXT: BM 29816.
COPY: BB 33.
PHOTOGRAPH: BB, pl. 11.

Say to the king, my lord: Message of ʿAbdi-Aštarti, servant of the king. I fall at the feet of the king, my lord, 7 times ⟨⟨the feet of the king, my lord⟩⟩ and 7 times, *here and now,*[1] both on the stomach and on the back. 8–13 May the king, my lord, be informed that the war against me is severe, and may it seem good to the king, my lord, to send a magnate to protect me. 14–23 Moreover, the king, my lord, has sent orders to me and I am heeding (them). I heed all the orders of the king, my lord. I herewith : *ia-pa-aq-ti* (*send on*) 10 women . . .[2]

NOTES

1. The meaning of *mila* (*mili, milanna*—or *mila anna*?), which with only two exceptions (*EA* 225:6; 330:7) is confined to *EA* 64–65, 282–84, is proposed on the basis of 283:15.

2. Things requested by the king, as the ten women seem to have been, are either readied (*šūšuru*: *EA* 99, 316, 325), brought (*abālu*: *EA* 327), sent (*uššuru*: *EA* 314), or given (*nadānu*: *EA* 242, 301), and hence the meaning assigned to *yapaqtī* (Krahmalkov, *JNES* 30 [1971] pp. 22f.; idem, *BASOR* 223 [1976] pp. 78f.; Rainey, *UF* 6 [1974] p. 300). The meaning of *mi-Ki-tu* remains obscure. If

an adjective, then it should refer to some favorable quality of the women (Loretz and Mayer, *UF* 6 [1974] pp. 493f.), but the gloss marker in front of it may simply be an indication of a runover line (cf. the marker before EN at the end of line 16). Read $^{munus.meš}$*mi*-K*i*-*tu*?

EA 65

Preparations for Egyptian troops

TEXT: VAT 1685.
COPIES: WA 175; *VS* 11, 29.

[Sa]y [to the king, my lord]: Me[ssage of ʿAb]di-Aštarti,[1] your serva[nt]. I fall at the feet of my lord 7 times and 7 times, *here and now*, both on the stomach and on the back, at the feet of the king, my lord. 7–10 Since the king, my lord, has sent me orders, I am heeding (them). All the orders of [m]y king I *h*[*ee*]*d*. The cities of the king by ⟨me⟩ I guard, 11–15 and ⟨I⟩ prepare before the arrival of the arch[ers of the kin]g, my lord, [. . .].[2]

NOTES

1. Whatever the explanation of the writing, the sender of the letter must be the ʿAbdi-Aštarti of *EA* 63–64. Instead of ^{m}[a]d-[r]a-INANNA, ^{m}⌜ab⌝-[d]i + ^{d}INANNA; for the assumed ligature of *di* and dingir, cf. the extraordinary ligature of LUGAL + *ri* in line 6.

2. Only one line missing. Line 11: ⟨*i*⟩-*šu*-*ši*-*ru*, a well-attested form, rather than an otherwise unattested infinitive *šu*-*ši*-*ru* (*VAB* 2/2, p. 1383). Line 12: [*a*]-*na pa*-*ni* . . . (see Introduction, n. 100).

EA 66

A lost message

TEXT: VAT 1702.
COPY: *VS* 11, 30.

Too fragmentary for translation.[1]

NOTE

1. Reference to Ḫaya (line 4).

EA 67

A plea for a reckoning

TEXT: VAT 1591.
COPIES: WA 186; *VS* 11, 31.

1–6 . . .   6–13 [. . .] He resides i[n *Ṣumur along with*] his [*troops*] (and) along with [*his*] *c*[*hariots. Now may the Sun call*] *to account* [Ṣ]umur, [the ci]ty of the Su[n], my lord, [*and*] may the [S]un *k*[*now*] (the facts).[1] *Is it pleasing? A*[*l*]*l the E*[*gyptians* wh]o had resided in Ṣumur, the city of the Su[n, my lord, ca]me out and are residing in my land, [*m*]*y* [*lord*]. 13–18 *He* made a [tr]eaty[2] [wi]th the ruler of Gubla and with the ru[ler of . . . , *and*] all the fortress commanders of your land . . . [. . .] became friendly[3] with him, my lord. Now he is *l*[*ike*] the ʿApiru, a runaway dog, and he has seized [Ṣu]mur, the city of the Sun, my lord. . . .[4]

NOTES

1. Free restoration. Line 8: [ù i-na-an-na ᵈUTU-ši li-iš]-*al-mi.*

2. The subject of the verb is not clear; it could even be first person. Most likely, it seems, is Aziru of Amurru; then the ruler of Byblos would be the perfidious brother of Rib-Hadda (cf. *EA* 137–38; see *VAB* 2/2, pp. 1144 ff.; Greenberg, *Ḫab/piru,* p. 41). The identity of the writer of the letter cannot be determined. The designation *ḫalzuḫlu,* "fortress commander," and the epithet "(my) Sun," written ᵈUTU-*ši* (elsewhere in *EA,* only in letters from Ugarit, *EA* 45, 46, 49, and from Nuḫašše, *EA* 51; regularly at Boghazköy), give the language and writing a northern cast.

3. DÙG.GA-*nim* = *ṭābūni* (see Introduction, n. 59).

4. Of the obverse there are preserved only three fragmentary lines; the entire reverse, except for a few signs and traces, is completely lost.

EA 68

Byblos under attack

TEXT: VAT 1239.
COPIES: WA 80; *VS* 11, 32.
TRANSLITERATION AND TRANSLATION: Youngblood, *Amarna Correspondence,* pp. 1ff.
TRANSLATION: Ebeling, p. 373.

[R]ib-Hadd[a[1] sa]ys to his lord, [king] of all countries, Great King: May the Lady of Gubla grant power to the king, my lord.   7–11 I fall at the feet of my lord, my Sun, 7 times and 7 times. May the king, my lord, know that Gubla, the loyal maidservant of the king, is safe and sound. 12–18 The war, however, [o]f the ʿApiru forces [aga]inst me is extremely severe, and so may the king, my lord, not ⟨ne⟩glect[2] Ṣumur lest ever[yo]ne be joined to the ʿApiru forces. 19–26 Through the king's commissioner who is in Ṣumur, Gubla is alive. Paḫa[mna]ta, the commissioner of the king who is in Ṣumur, knows the straits : *ma-na-*AŠ (?)[3] that Gubla is in. 27–32 It is from the land of Yarimuta that we have acquired provisions. The w[a]r [agai]nst us is extremely severe, and so may the king not [ne]glect his [ci]ties.

NOTES

1. [ᵐ*ri*]-*ib-ḫa-ad-d*[*a*]: last sign, *d*[*u*] possible, but not *d*[*i*]. On *iqbi,* see *EA* 74, n. 1.

2. *la-a* ⟨*i*⟩*a-qúl-me*: *a* written over an erased *i*.

3. Gloss (read *ma-na-rù*?) unexplained (cf. *ARMT* 7, p. 320); the first sign is more like IZ than in the copy of *VS*. Youngblood, p. 37, proposes West Semitic *mānaš* < *ma'naš* (*'nš*), "trouble," which leaves the bound form before *ša* unexplained.

EA 69

Report to an official

TEXT: BM 29856.

COPY: BB 73.

TRANSLITERATION AND TRANSLATION: Youngblood, *Amarna Correspondence,* pp. 41ff.

[*Say* to . . . : Message of Rib-Hadda. I fall at *your* feet. *May the Lady of Gubla, the goddess of the king, my lord, establish your honor*] *in the pr*[*esence of the king, my lord, my god*], my Sun.[1] . . . 10–14 [*I*] said repeatedly, "They have a[ll] *agr*[*eed*] among themselves against [me]."[2] Moreover, look, they have now attacked day and ni[ght] in the war against ⟨me⟩. 15–18 Mor[eo]ver, you yourself know that my towns are threatening me,[3] [*and*] *I* have [*no*]*t* been able to make [*pe*]*ace wi*[*t*]*h* the[m].[4] 19–24 [*M*]*ore*[*ov*]*er,* [. . .] . . . [*o*]*f* Magdalu, and the forces of Kuaṣbat are at war with me, and there is no one who can rescue me from them. 24–30 Moreover, on Appiḫa's re⟨ac⟩hing me, there was an outcry against me, and, *as for* all my gates, the bronze : *nu-ḫu-uš-tu₄ was taken.*[5] As[k] Appiḫa about the w[hole] affair. 30–39 Moreover, urge with lo[ud cries][6] the king, [*your*] lor[d, *and*] *if* [*archers*] come out [*this year*][7] [. . .] . . . [*I will be able to mak*]*e pe*[*ac*]*e.*

NOTES

1. Addressed to an Egyptian official.

2. *gá*[*b-bu* a-wa-ti]: for *gabbu*, cf. *EA* 82:32; 102:25; 106:49; 114:14. For the expression *awata leqû*, see *EA* 116:51.

3. *dannū elīya*, perhaps "are stronger than I," or "are too strong for me."

4. *i-pi-iš* 17 [SIG$_5$]-q[a]: cf. line 39. If this is the correct reading, then the context argues that *dumqa epēšu* (*itti*) is "to make friendship"; cf. *damqātu*, "friendly relations," and *bēl dumqi*/*damiqti*, "friend" (as political terms, see *JNES* 22 [1963] p. 175; Weinfeld, *JAOS* 93 [1973] pp. 191ff.).

5. Syntax obscure; reading *ti-ul*$_{11}$*-qé* as third singular feminine passive (gender from *nuḫuštu*), since the context suggests no other singular subject, and note also *nuḫuštu*, nominative case.

6. See *EA* 87:25 and note.

7. See *EA* 129:40–42.

EA 70

Request for Nubian troops

TEXT: Golenischeff (see Introduction, sect. 1).
COPY: WA 67.
TRANSLITERATION AND TRANSLATION: Youngblood, *Amarna Correspondence*, pp. 61ff.

...[1] 17–23 [*And*] send me [x Eg]yptians and [x me]n from Meluḫḫa,[2] [*just*] *as* (you did to) the kings [*to wh*]*om* you [*ga*]*ve c*[*hariots*],[3] so they can *gu*[*ar*]*d* [until the coming] forth of the archers. 24–31 [And] may the king, my lord, know [that] the land of Amurru longs[4] day and [night] for the coming forth of the archers. [The d]ay the [arc]hers arri[v]e, the land of Am[urru] will [*certainly*] be join[ed ... t]o the king, [my lord]. ...[5]

NOTES

1. Lines 1–7 (greeting): only a few signs preserved. Lines 8–16: reference to Magdalu (?—line 9), "to his son [...] ... between the two of us" (15f.; *be-ri-ku-ni*, see *EA* 113:18).

2. "Meluḫḫa" designated Nubia, and Nubians and Nubian troops are mentioned frequently as part of the Egyptian army (*EA* 95:39f.; 108:67; 112:20; 117:81ff.; 132:56). They are also called men or troops of Kaši (Cush), and Meluḫḫa is probably identified as Kaši (*EA* 127:36; 132:56; 133:17). On the evidence of the Amarna letters, see Pintore, *OA* 11 (1972) p. 105; for other evidence on Nubians in the Egyptian army, see Schulman, *Military Rank, Titles, and Organization in the Egyptian New Kingdom*, Münchener ägyptologische Studien 6 (Berlin, 1964), pp. 22ff., 127ff.

3. 20 [ki-i]-*ma* LUGAL.MEŠ 21 [ša na-a]d-na-ta [giš][GIGIR.MEŠ]: cf. Na'aman, *Political Disposition*, p. 22*, n. 100; "wood" (GIŠ, *iṣu*) hardly stood alone (GIGIR.MEŠ at the beginning of the next line, narkabātī-š]u-*nu*?).

4. *tu-ba-*⟨*ú*⟩ would be more in accord with established usage (Rainey, *UF* 6 [1974] p. 302).

5. One line; rest of tablet lost.

EA 71

To a wise man

TEXT: VAT 1632.
COPIES: WA 72; *VS* 11, 33.
TRANSLITERATION AND TRANSLATION: Youngblood, *Amarna Correspondence*, pp. 78ff.

[To] Ḫaya, the *vizi*[*er*]:[1] Message of Rib-Hadda. I fal[l] at your feet. May Aman, the god of the king, [y]our lord, establish[2] your honor in the presence of the king, your lord. 7–16 You are a wise man; the king knows (this) and because of your wis⟨d⟩om[3] he sent you as commissioner. Why have you been negligent, not speaking to the king so he will send archers to take Ṣumur? 16–22 What is ʿAbdi-Aširta, servant and dog, that he takes the land of the king for himself? What is his auxiliary force that it is strong? Through the ʿApiru his auxiliary force is strong![4] 23–27 So send me 50 pairs of horses and 200 infantry[5] that I may resist him in Šigata until the coming forth of the archers. 28–35 Let him not gather together all the ʿApiru so he can take Šigat[a] and Ampi, and [*seize* . . .] . . .[6] What shall I be able to d[o]? There will be no place where [*men*] can enter against [him].[7]

NOTES

1. *pa-sí-*t[e]: a reading MAŠ[KIM] (Kestemont in Kühne, p. 145) is excluded, unless one assumes an aberrant form that also differs from MAŠKIM as written in line 10. The traces of *te* as described in *VAB* 2/2, p. 366, note c, are still visible, the *VS* 11 copy notwithstanding. For the title, see Albright, *JNES* 5 (1946) p. 12.

2. On *ti-di-nu* as plural (*tiddinū*), see *JCS* 5 (1951) p. 35; *Biblica* 45 (1963) pp. 80f.

3. *im-*⟨*qú*⟩*-ti-ka*: following Albright, *JNES* 5 (1946) p. 12, n. 8.

4. Lines 20–22, with Ebeling, *VAB* 2/2, p. 1591.

5. ÉRIN.MEŠ GÌR.MEŠ: the expression is also found in *EA* 149:62; 170:22; at Boghazköy (*AHw,* p. 1072b); in an Old Babylonian letter (*AbB* 10, 150:11) and

in unpublished Neo-Assyrian copy of an Old Babylonian *tamītu* (ND 4401; courtesy W. G. Lambert).

6. See *EA* 76:23 and note.

7. *mu-ḫi-*[*šu* LÚ.MEŠ]: cf. *EA* 76:22.

EA 72

Message lost

TEXT: VAT 1712.

COPY: *VS* 11, 34.

TRANSLITERATION AND TRANSLATION: Youngblood, *Amarna Correspondence,* pp. 100f.

Too fragmentary for translation.[1]

NOTE

1. A letter to the king, perhaps repeating the request of *EA* 71 to Ḫaya (Pintore, *OA* 11 [1972] p. 102, n. 10). Lines 14 (obv.) and 6 (rev.) are fragmentary, with references to Irqata(?), Ardata(?), Gubla, Ampi, Ṣumur, and ʿApiru.

EA 73

Of ambivalent Amurru

TEXT: BM 29798.

COPY: BB 15.

TRANSLITERATION AND TRANSLATION: Youngblood, *Amarna Correspondence,* pp. 106ff.

To Amanappa, my father: Message of Rib-Hadda, your son. I fall at the feet of my father. May the Lady of Gubla establish your honor in the presence of the king, your lord. 6–11 Why have you been negligent, not speaking to the king, your lord, so that you may come out together with archers and fall upon the land of Amurru? 11–16 If they hear of archers coming out, they will abandon their cities and desert. Do not you yourself know that the land of Amurru follows the stronger party? 17–25 Look, they are not now being friendly to ʿAbdi-Aširta. What will he do to them?[1] [And so] they are longing[2] day and night for the coming out of the archers, and ⟨they say⟩, "Let us join them!" All the mayors long for this to be done to ʿAbdi-Aširta,[3] 26–33 since he sent a message to the men of Ammiya, "Kill your lord and join the ʿApiru."[4] Accordingly, the mayors say, "He will do the same thing to us, and all the lands will be joined to the ʿApiru." 33–38 Report this matter in the presence of the king, your lord, for you are father and lord to me, and to you I have turned. 39–45 You know my conduct when you were in [Ṣ]umur; I am your [l]oyal servant. So speak to the king, [your] lord, that an auxiliary force be [s]en⟨t⟩[5] t[o] me with all speed.

NOTES

1. Perhaps "they are not friendly to (lit., love) ʿAbdi-Aširta (because of) what he does to them."

2. *tu-*⌜*ba*⌝*-ú-na*: following Rainey, *UF* 6 (1974) p. 302. Traces of only one horizontal are visible, but *ba* fits the space better, and *bu''û* is rather common in the Byblos letters (cf. esp. *EA* 70:26f.), whereas *qu''û*, "to wait for," is otherwise unattested.

3. Though the language, *ipēš* (*ipiš*?) *annûtu*, "to do/the doing of these things," is ambiguous, the mayors need not be the agents of the actions longed for, and the passage hardly speaks of their joining ʿAbdi-Aširta (Weber, *VAB* 2/2, p. 1158; Greenberg, *Ḫab/piru*, p. 34; Liverani, *RSO* 40 [1965] p. 274, as if synonymous with *nenpušu ana*, "to be joined to"). Neither here nor in *EA* 74:26ff., 36ff.—a letter probably sent at the same time as *EA* 73 (note the reference to Amanappa in *EA* 74:51)—is there any suggestion that the local rulers had or foresaw any alternative to their death or expulsion. Recognizing, rather, that ʿAbdi-Aširta had the same designs on them as on the ruler of Ammiya, they too desired a show of force by the Egyptians and an insurrection in Amurru.

4. Or " 'Kill your lord,' and then they were joined to the ʿApiru." See also *EA* 74:26 and note.

5. [*t*]*u-wa-ša-*⟨*ar/ra*⟩ *til-la-tu*.

EA 74

Like a bird in a trap

TEXT: BM 29795.
COPY: BB 12.
PHOTOGRAPH: BB, pl. 20.
TRANSLITERATION AND TRANSLATION: Youngblood, *Amarna Correspondence,* pp. 122ff.

Rib-Hadda says[1] to [his] lord, king of all countries, Great King, King of Battle:[2] May [the Lady] of Gubla grant power to the king, my lord. I fall at the feet of my lord, my Sun, 7 times and 7 times. 5–10 May the king, the lord, know that Gubla, the loyal maidservant of the king since the days of his ancestors, is safe and sound. The king, however, has now withdrawn his support of his loyal city. 10–12 May the king inspect the tablets of his father's house (for the time) when the ruler in

Gubla was not a loyal servant.[3] 13–19 Do not be negligent of your servant. Behold,[4] the war of the ʿApiru against ⟨me⟩ is severe and, as the gods of *y*[*our*] land [*are ali*]*ve*, our sons and daughters (*as well as we ourselves*)[5] are gone since they have been sold in the land of Yarimuta for provisions to keep us alive. "For lack of a cultivator, my field is like a woman without a husband."[6] 19–22 All my villages that are in the mountains : *ḫa-ar-ri* or along the sea have been joined to the ʿApiru. Left to me are Gubla and two towns. 23–30 After taking Šigata for himself, ʿAbdi-Aširta said to the men of Ammiya, "Kill your *leader*[7] and then you will be like us and at peace." They were won over, following his message, and they are like ʿApiru.[8] 30–38 So now ʿAbdi-Aširta has written to the troops:[9] "Assemble in the temple of NINURTA,[10] and then let us fall upon Gubla. Look,[11] there is no one that will save it from u[s]. Then let us drive out the mayors from the country that the entire country be joined to the ʿApiru, . . .[12] to the entire country. Then will (our) sons and daughters be at peace forever. 39–45 Should even so the king come out, the entire country will be against him and what will he do to us?" Accordingly, they have made an alliance[13] among themselves and, accordingly, I am very, very afraid, since [in] fact there is no one who will save me from them. 45–50 Like a bird in a trap : *ki-lu-bi* (cage), so am I in Gubla. Why have you neglected your country? I have written like this to the palace, but you do not heed my words. 51–57 Look, Amanappa is with you. Ask him. He is the one that knows and has experienced the stra[its] I am in. May the king heed the words of his servant. May he grant provisions for his servant and keep his servant alive so I may guard his [lo]yal [city], *along with our L*[*ad*]*y* (and) our gods, *f*[*or you*].[14] 57–62 May [*the king*] *vis*[*it*] his [land] and [*his servant*].[15] [May he] give thought to his land. *Pac*[*ify yo*]*ur* [*land*]! May it seem go[od] in the sight of the k[ing], my [lo]rd. May he send a [*ma*]*n* of his to stay this time so I may arri[ve] in the presence of the king, my lord. 62–65 It is good for me to be with you. What can I do by [my]self? This is what I long for day and night.

NOTES

1. On *iqbi* (*ištapar, ištappar*) as "Koinzidenzfall," see Introduction, sect. 5 and n. 81.

2. This epithet of the Egyptian king is confined to the letters of Rib-Hadda and appears only with the introductory form "Rib-Hadda speaks/writes." It was probably drawn from the epic, known by this name and attested at Amarna (*EA* 359), about the legendary Sargon of Akkad; see M.-J. Seux, *Épithètes royales akkadiennes et sumériennes* (see *EA* 1, n. 2), pp. 319f.

3. Or "whether the ruler in Gubla has not been a loyal servant."

4. *šumma*; see *EA* 35, n. 3.

5. *qa-du-nu,* meaning uncertain. If the preposition *qadu,* then it occurs only here in *EA* with a pronominal suffix (D. O. Edzard, in B. Hruška and G. Komoróczy, eds., *Festschrift L. Matouš* [Budapest, 1978], p. 86, n. 17); perhaps "together with some of our number" (the older generation; cf. Weber, *VAB* 2/2, p. 1159, "fellow-citizens")? In the parallel passages (*EA* 75:12; 81:39; 85:12; 90:37), the sequence is sons-daughters-wood (furnishings) of houses. Is *qad(d)u* the corresponding Canaanite word? S. Smith's idiosyncratic version of *EA* 74:13–17 (*The Statue of Idri-mi* [London, 1949], p. 34) is, as the parallels make perfectly clear, wrong. *ARMT* 22, 143:2, perhaps attests to a noun *qadu* (*i-mi-i*G *qa-di-im*), but its meaning is quite unclear.

6. On this proverb (also *EA* 75:15–17; 81:37f.; 90:42f.), with Mesopotamian and other parallels, see D. Marcus, *JANES* 5 (1973) pp. 281ff.; see also Lieberman, *Hebrew Union College Annual* 58 (1987) p. 162, nn. 20–21. On "plowing the field" in Sumerian literature see Sjöberg, *JCS* 29 (1977) p. 24, and on *ittû,* "seeder-plow," as a metaphor for father see Lambert, *RA* 76 (1982) p. 84. Later, in Greece, the metaphor belonged not only to literature (J. M. Edmonds, *Elegy and Iambus,* vol. 1, Loeb Classical Library, p. 427) but also to legal language (see the dictionaries under *arotos, aroura, speirō*).

7. The use of *eṭlu,* "(young, adult) male," if it is the correct reading ([E]N *-la-ku-nu*?), is without parallel in related or similar passages. It appears elsewhere in *EA* letters only in 29:154, probably as a distinction of age (cf. Ugaritic *baḥḥūru* = *eṭlu, Ugar.* 5, no. 137 ii 24′); for the reading, see Rainey, *IEJ* 19 (1969) p. 107, and Blau and Greenfield, *BASOR* 200 (1970) p. 17. Undoubtedly there is reference here to the murder of the ruler of Ammiya, who in *EA* 73:27 and 75:34 is called *bēlu,* "lord" (EN; cf. also *EA* 81:12), and, probably, in 140:11 is called *šarru,* "king." Unless, therefore, *eṭlu* implies here a certain sarcasm ("your young fellow"), it is probably meant to suggest authority. There is no evidence that the term could be used as a collective ("princes," Knudtzon; "chiefs," Greenberg, *Ḫab/piru,* p. 34, and Liverani, *Rivista Storica Italiana* 57 [1965] p. 324; "seigneurs" [also of *EA* 73:27; 81:12], Liverani, in Garelli, ed., *Le Palais et la Royauté,* p. 354).

8. With the possible exception of *EA* 67:16f., "like an/the ʿApiru," does not occur elsewhere. It is the narrative version of "like us" in ʿAbdi-Aširta's speech, and it implies that, for Rib-Hadda, the followers of ʿAbdi-Aširta and the ʿApiru were virtually indistinguishable (Greenberg, *Ḫab/piru,* p. 34).

9. On lines 30–41, see G. Mendenhall, *JNES* 6 (1947) pp. 123f.; see also *JCS* 7 (1953) p. 78, n. 4.

10. The absence of URU (*ālu*), "city, town," before É NIN.URTA, or of the determinative KI after it, argues against a place-name Bīt-NIN.URTA (cf. *EA* 290:16). The temple was presumably the scene of the oath mentioned in line 42. The Canaanite god referred to by Sumero-Akkadian NIN.URTA is not known; at Ugarit, Ninurta = Gašaru (*JCS* 31 [1979] p. 72, n. 23).

11. See n. 4.

12. *ù* [k]i-*tu ti-in*-⟨ni-pu-uš⟩-*ma,* "and let an alliance be made (for all the lands)": Albright in Mendenhall (see n. 9).

13. Lit. "placed an oath." NAM.RU, *māmītu,* "oath" (*JCS* 7 [1953] p. 78, n. 5), but perhaps not a mistake for NAM.⟨NE⟩.RU; cf. NAM.RU.MA$_4$, *PBS* 1/2, 72:25; Nougayrol, *JCS* 1 (1947) p. 334, n. 28; Falkenstein, *Das Sumerische* (Leiden, 1964), p. 26, 4.b; Krecher, AOAT 1, pp. 193f.

14. *a*-[na ka-ta$_5$]: following Rainey, *UF* 7 (1975) p. 414. Note that *adi* in the meaning "(along) with" occurs elsewhere in *EA* only in the Jerusalem letters (but see *EA* 92:42 and note).

15. *yi-da*-ga[l LUGAL] 58 [KUR]-*šu ù* [ÌR-šu]: cf. *EA* 85:61ff.; 116:62f. The form *yidaggalu* (Knudtzon) may not serve as an injunctive, which would be *yidaggal* or *yidaggala.*

EA 75

Political chaos

TEXT: C 4757 (12191).
COPY: WA 79.
TRANSLITERATION AND TRANSLATION: Youngblood, *Amarna Correspondence,* pp. 155ff.

Rib-Hadda [says t]o his lord, k[ing of all countries]: May the Lady of [Gubla] grant power t[o my lord]. I fall at the feet of my lord, my Sun, [7] times and 7 times. 6–14 [May][1] the king, my lord, know th[at] Gubla, the maidserva[nt of the king] from ancient times, is safe and sound. The war, however, of the ʿApiru agai[nst] me is severe. (Our) sons and daughters and the furnishings of the houses are gone, since they have been sold [in] the land of Yarimuta for ou[r] provisions to keep us alive. 15–21 "For the lack of a cultivator, my field is like a woman without a husband." I have written repeatedly to the palace because of the *illness*[2] afflicting me, [*but there is no one*] who has looked at the words that [*keep arr*]*iving.*[3] [May the king] give heed [to] the words of [his] servant. 22–25 ... 25–29 The ʿ*Apiru* killed[4] Ad[una, the king] of Irqata, *but* there was no one who ⟨s⟩aid[5] anything to ʿAbdi-Aširta, and so they go on *tak*[*in*]*g* (territory for themselves).[6] 30–34 Miya, the ruler of Araš*ni,* seized Ar[d]ata, and just now the men of Ammiy⟨a⟩ have killed the⟨ir⟩ lord. I am afraid. 35–48 May the king be informed that the king of Ḫatti has seized all the countries *that were vassals*[7] of the king of Mitta⟨ni⟩.[8] *Behold,* [*he*] is king of Naḫ⟨ri⟩ma [*and*] the land of the *Gre*[*at*] Kings, [*and*] ʿAbdi-Aširta, [*the servant*] and dog, is tak[ing *the land of the king*]. Send *arc*[*hers*]. Severe is ... 49–50 [and sen]d a man to [Gubla] that I may [...] ... *his* word[s].

NOTES

1. *amqu*[*t lu-ú*]: following Youngblood, *Amarna Correspondence,* p. 160; Rainey, *UF* 5 (1973) p. 241, n. 41.

2. Perhaps "the distress"; cf. *mariṣ* (*ana*) *iyāši* (*EA* 103:7; 362:59), *marṣāku* (*EA* 106:23), and *EA* 95, n. 4.

3. 19 [ia-nu]; 20 [ti-ik-šu]-*du-na.* Cf. *kašādu* said of words (*EA* 59:46; 136:22; 221:14), of requests (*EA* 82:16), of the breath of the king (*EA* 100:40; 145:19; 146:12), and of tablets (*EA* 100:24; 155:55?).

4. [L]Ú.MEŠ GA⌜Z⌝(?).ZA(?).ME[Š] (cf. *EA* 67:17); *i-du-ku*-š[u], last sign either *šu* or *na,* but a preterite is expected (cf. *VAB* 2/1, p. 1519).

5. ⟨*ia*⟩-*aq-bi.*

6. *ti-il*-q[ú-n]a: cf. *EA* 90:15; 104:22, 25, 32; 126:13; 117:64; 131:17.

7. The context requires that the lands be associated in some way with Mittani(?); cf. Goetze, *CAH* 2/2, p. 8, "all the lands affiliated(?) with the king of the Mita(nni) land." Very hesitantly, it is proposed that KU.TI.TI is a syllabic writing for GÚ.(UN).DI_6.DI_6, *ābilāt bilti,* lit. "bearers of tribute."

8. If KUR *mi-it-ta* refers to Mittani, note not only the omission of ⟨*na*⟩ or ⟨*ni*⟩, but also the writing with double *t,* unparalleled in nine other writings of the name in the Byblos letters. See Wilhelm, *ZA* 63 (1973) p. 71, line 16, KUR *me-t*[*a.*K]I, and commentary pp. 73f.; Görg, *ZA* 76 (1986) p. 308.

EA 76

Of ambition and arrogance

TEXT: VAT 324.
COPIES: WA 74; *VS* 11, 35.
TRANSLITERATION AND TRANSLATION: Youngblood, *Amarna Correspondence,* pp. 168ff.

Rib-Hadda says to the king of all countries, Great King, King of Battle: May the Lady of Gubla grant power to the king, my lord. I fall at the feet of my lord, my Sun, 7 times and 7 times. 7–16 May the king, my lord, know that the war of ʿAbdi-Aširta against me is severe. [H]e wants to take [*for himself*][1] the two cities that have remained to me. [Mo]reover, what is ʿA[bdi]-Aš[ir]ta, the dog, that he strives to [ta]ke all the cities of the king, the Sun, [fo]r himself? Is he the king of Mittana, or the king of Kaššu, that [h]e strives to take the land of the king for himself? 17–29 He has just gathered together all the ʿApiru against Šigata [and] Ampi, and [h]e himself has taken these two cities. [*I s*]*aid,* "There is no place where [*me*]*n*[2] can enter against him. He has seized [. . .] . . . ,[3] [so] send me [a garris]on of 400 men *a*[*nd* x pairs of h]orses [*with all speed." It*] *is* [*thus that I keep writing to the pal*]*ace, but* [*you do not rep*]*ly* [*to m*]*e.*[4] 30–37 [. . .] . . . For years archers would come out to inspect [the coun]try, and yet now that the land of the king and Ṣumur, your[5] garrison-city, have been joined to the ʿApiru, you have done nothing. 38–46 Send a large force of archers that it[6] may drive out the king's enemies and all lands be joined to the king. Moreover, you are a great lord. You must not neglect this message.

NOTES

1. [a-na ša-a-šu]: contrary to Knudtzon (*VAB* 2/1, p. 380, note h) and Schroeder's copy, I could see no *certain* traces of *signs* that exclude this obvious restoration (lines 14, 16; *EA* 71:19; 74:24; 81:9; etc.).

2. [LÚ.ME]S-*tu*$_4$: for this writing see *EA* 106:39.

3. [x-S]AG : *ša* PI-x-*Za*: x = BAR, not at all certain. Is this the name of a hill or mountain ([ḪUR.S]AG) the capture of which has made ʿAbdi-Aširta inaccessible? Cf. also *EA* 71:31ff.

4. [ki-ma ar-ḫi-iš *a-n*]*u-ma* [ki-a-ma] 28 [aš-tap-ru a-na] ⌜É⌝.[GA]L *ù* [la-a] 29 [tu-te-ru-n]a [a]-wa(text:UD)-t[a$_5$ a-na ia]-*ši*: for the restorations, see the following: *kīma arḫiš*—*EA* 73:45; 88:25; 112:22f.; etc.; *anumma* . . . *ana ekalli*—*EA* 74:49f.; 85:6; 89:7f.; 118:8f.; 122:53f.; 132:51; *u lā tuterruna* . . . —*EA* 81:22f.; 83:7f., 47f. See also Youngblood, *Amarna Correspondence*, pp. 174f.

5. The pronominal suffix is *-kunu*, probably a plural of majesty.

6. I assume that ÉRIN.MEŠ *piṭāti* is the subject, construed as third feminine singular (cf. *EA* 103:55f.; 127:38f.; 129:33ff.; 131:40; see also *JCS* 6 [1952] p. 78), with a shift from masculine singular (*rabâ*, line 39; cf. also *EA* 77:27). Also possible is "that you may drive out," the writer shifting between second and third person in addressing the king.

EA 77

A rebellious peasantry

TEXT: VAT 1635 + 1700.
COPIES: WA 81 (only 1635); *VS* 11, 36.
TRANSLITERATION AND TRANSLATION: Youngblood, *Amarna Correspondence*, pp. 178ff.

To *Ama*[*nappa, my father*]: Message of [Rib-Hadda, *your son*]. I fall [at your feet]. May [*Aman, the god of* the king], your lord, and [the Lady of Gu]b[la] establi⟨sh⟩[1] your hon[or] in the presence of the king, [your] lord. As to 7–15 your writing me f[or] copper and for *sinnu*,[2] may the Lady of Gubla *be witness*:[3] there is no copper or *šinnu* of [*cop*]*per* available to me or [*to*] *her unjustly treated ones.*[4] *Milkayu*[5] overlaid one with . . . [. . .], but I gave his *šinnu* to [*the ruler*] of Tyr[e f]or [my] provisions. 15–25 [Y]ou yourself [*should*] know [*the straits I am i*]*n*[6] . . . Wh[y have you been *neg*]*ligent?* . . . who [m]oves [agains]t the country. You do not spe[ak[7] t]o your lord so he will send you at the head of the archers to drive off the ʿApiru from the [m]ayors. 26–37 If t[hi]s year no [ar]chers come out, then all lands will be joi[ne]d t[o the ʿApir]u. If [*the king, my lor*]*d*, is neg[ligent] and there are no [*archers*], then *let* a ship [*fetch*] the men [of *Gubla*], your [*me*]*n*, (and) the g[ods] (to bring them) *all the wa*[*y to you so I can abandon Gubla. Look*],[8] I am afraid the peasa[ntry] will strike m[e] down.

NOTES

1. 3 *amqut* ᵈ[a-ma-na DINGIR ša LUGAL] 4 EN-*ka* ù ᵈN[IN ša URU g]*ub*ᵘᵇ-[la] 5 *ti-di-⟨nu⟩-mi*: cf. *EA* 71:4f.; 87:5f.; 95:3ff. The clear *gub-*⌜*la*⌝ of Schroeder's copy agrees neither with Knudtzon's collation nor with mine.

2. *sinnu*, despite *šinnu* in lines 10 and 13, is hardly ivory (*SSDB*, p. 154; *Or* n.s. 29 [1960] p. 17; Youngblood, p. 183, followed by Rainey, *UF* 5 [1973] p. 243, n. 49). Ivory was readily available in Egypt from the south and was not likely to have been the object of a special request. Besides, if at the end of line 11 the correct reading is [UR]UDU (*erû*), "copper," then ivory is excluded. For *sinnu*, see *AHw*, p. 1048.

3. x-[(ti)]-⌜*i*⌝-*de*: x, not *mi* (see *VAB* 2/1, p. 385, note d), and not *ul* (Rainey, *UF* 5 [1973] p. 243; besides, the negative *ul* is always written *ú-ul* in the Byblos letters); *lut*ₓ(LID), for *lū tīde*?

4. [a-na] *ḫab-*⌜*l*⌝*i-še*: the residents of Byblos? reference to Milkayu?

5. ⟨ᵐ⟩*mil-ka-yú*? x-*ti maḫaṣ*?

6. [pu-uš-q]a-*ia*: cf. *EA* 68:24f.; 74:52.

7. *ta-aq-*[*bu*]: see *Or* n.s. 29 (1960) p. 10, n. 3.

8. 31 *ù ia-nu* [ÉRIN.MEŠ pí-ṭá-ti ù] 32 ᵍⁱˢMÁ LÚ.M[EŠ URU gub-la] 33 [L]Ú.MEŠ-*ka* DIN[GIR.MES ti-ìl-qé] 34 *a-di mu-*[ḫi-ka ù i-te-zi-ib] 35 URU [gub-la a-mur]: cf. *EA* 82:42f.; 83:45ff.; 84:31ff.; 129:49ff.; 132:53ff.

EA 78

Request for a garrison

TEXT: VAT 1282.

COPIES: WA 84; *VS* 11, 37.

TRANSLITERATION AND TRANSLATION: Youngblood, *Amarna Correspondence*, pp. 191ff.

[Rib]-Hadda says [to] his lord, king of all countries, [Grea]t [King]: May the Lady of [Gubla gr]ant power to [the king, my lord], my [S]un. I fa[ll] at the feet of [my] lord, my Sun, 7 times and 7 times. 7–16 [M]ay the king, my lord, know [that] the war of [ʿAb]di-Aširta against m[e is se]vere, [and he has tak]en all [my] cit[ies. N]ow only two towns remain [to] me, and even these he s[trives to ta]ke. Like a bird in a trap, so am [I] in Gub[la]. 17–19 May my lord heed the w[ords of] his [servant]. I have just b[e]en in Baṭruna. 20–37 ...[1] m[y ...] send me [imm]ediately, 37–41 and [*send*] a ga[rr]ison, 3[0 pairs of hors]es [i]n the char[ge of][2] ...[3]

NOTES

1. In line 30, probably a reference to *kunāšu*, "emmer," written ŠE.ZÍZ.ḪI.A and the only mention of emmer in *EA*.

2. 3[0 ta-pal] 40 [ANŠE.KUR].⌜RA⌝.[M]EŠ [*i*]-*na qa*-[*at* ...]: cf. *EA* 83:21f.; 85:20; 103:43; 112:21; 119:12f.

3. Six to ten lines missing.

EA 79

At the brink

TEXT: VAT 1634.

COPIES: WA 75; *VS* 11, 38.

TRANSLITERATION AND TRANSLATION: Youngblood, *Amarna Correspondence,* pp. 197ff.

[Ri]b-Hadda says [to] his [lord], king of all countries, Great King, [King of Ba]ttle: May the Lady [of] Gubla grant [pow]er to the king, my lord. 6–12 I fall [at] the feet of my lord, my Sun, 7 times and 7 times. Be informed that since Amanappa reached me, all the ʿApiru have at the urging of ʿAbdi-Aširta turned against me. 13–17 May my lord heed the words of his servant. Send me a garrison t[o] guard the city of the king un[til] the archers [co]me out. 18–26 [I]f there are no ar[chers], then al[l la]nds will be joined to the [ʿApi]ru. Listen! [Si]nce Bit-Ar[ḫa] was seized [at] the urging of ʿAbdi-Aširta, they have as a result been striving to [ta]ke over[1] Gubla and Baṭruna, and thus all lands would be joi[ned] to the ʿApiru. 27–33 There are two towns that remain to [me], and they want to take th[em] from the king. May my lord sen[d] a garrison to his two towns until the archers come out, and may something be given[2] to me for their food. 34–47 I have nothing at all. Like a bird in a trap : *ki-lu-bi* (cage), so am I in Gubla. Moreover, [*i*]*f* [*the kin*]*g* is unable to save me fr[om] his enemies, [then al]l lands will be [j]oined [to ʿAbd]i-Aširta. [What is h]e, the dog, that [he ta]kes[3] the lands of the king for [him]self?

NOTES

1. Whatever the meaning of the expression "to do/make a city" elsewhere, here "to fortify" seems clearly excluded.

2. *yú-da-na-ni*: Canaanite Qal passive *yuddan* + injunctive {*a*} + pro. suff. {*ni*}; cf. *yuddana* in *EA* 85:34, 37; 86:32, 47; and see *SSDB*, p. 155, and Rainey, *UF* 7 (1975) p. 404.

3. [*yi-il*]-*qú*: cf. *EA* 71:16ff.; 75:41f.; 91:4; and the corresponding plural *tilqūna* in *EA* 104:17ff.

EA 80

A lost message

TEXT: VAT 1711.
COPY: *VS* 11, 39.
TRANSLITERATION AND TRANSLATION: Youngblood, *Amarna Correspondence*, pp. 205ff.

Too fragmentary for translation.

EA 81

An attempted assassination

TEXT: VAT 1318.
COPIES: WA 89; *VS* 11, 40.
TRANSLITERATION AND TRANSLATION: Youngblood, *Amarna Correspondence*, pp. 210ff.

[Rib-Hadda say]s to [his] lord, [king of all countries, Great King, K]ing of Battle: May the Lady of Gubla grant power [to the kin]g, [my lord]. I fa[l]l [at the feet] of my lord, my [Sun], 7 times and 7 times. 6–13 [May] the king, my lord, know that the war of ʿAbdi-Aširta is [se]vere, [and] he has taken all my cities [for] himself. Gubla and Baṭru[na re]main to me, and he strives to take the two towns. He said to the men [of *Gubl*]*a*,[1] "[Ki]ll your lord and be join[ed] to the ʿApiru like Amm[iya]." 14–24 [And so] they became trait⟨ors⟩[2] to me. A man with a bronze dagger : ⌜*pat*⌝-[*r*]*a* [at]tacked m[e],[3] but I ki[ll]ed him. A *šírdanu* [*wh*]*om I know g*[*ot away t*]*o* ʿAbdi-Aširta.[4] At his order was this [de]ed done! I have stayed [*like th*]*is* [in] my city and done nothing. I am unable to go out [into the countryside,[5] and] I have written to the palace, [but you do not re]ply [to me]. I was struck [9 ti]mes.[6] 25–33 [According]ly, I f[ear for] my life.[7] [*And I have writt*]*en re*[*peatedly to the palace*], "*Do not* [*be negligent. Why are you ne*]*gligent o*[*f the distress afflicting me?*[8] I]f within *these* two months there are no archers, then [. . .] May he not fall [upon] my [city] and take me. I *h*[*ave written to* the pal]ace.[9] What ⟨am I to say⟩[10] to my pea[santry]? 34–41 Like a bird in a [tr]ap : *ki-lu-bi* (cage), so are they in [Gubl]a. "[Fo]r l[ac]k of a cultivator their [field] is [li]ke a woman without a husband." [Their sons, their] dau[gh]ters, [the fur]nishings of their houses are gone, [since they have been s]old [i]n the land of [Ya]rimuta [for] provisions to keep them alive. 41–47 [*I*] was the one that said to them, "My god [*is send*]*ing*[11] archers." Since they (now) kno[w[12] that] there are none, they have *tu*[*rned against*] ⟨u⟩s. If within two months archers do not come ou[t], then [ʿAb]di-Aširta will certainly come up and take the two t[owns. 48–51 Pre]viously Ṣumur and [its] men were [st]rong, and there was a [gar]rison with us. Wh[at] can I [d]o by my[sel]f? 52–59 . . .

NOTES

1. Paleographically, [URU gub-l]a is the more probable reading; see Knudtzon's remarks, *VAB* 2/1, p. 393, note d). Certainly the "lord" to be killed is Rib-Hadda; cf. *EA* 74:26 and n. 7.

2. *ar-*⟨*nu*⟩, or perhaps an abbreviation (*CAD*, A/2, p. 299). For *arnu*, "traitor, criminal," cf. LÚ-*lu ar-nu* (*EA* 138:104), *ar*(-⟨*na*⟩?) LUGAL (*EA* 138:21), and *ar*(-⟨*nu*⟩?) LUGAL (*EA* 139:40). The translation follows Rainey, *UF* 5 (1973) p. 252.

3. For the confusion of logograms and the somewhat obscure syntax, cf. *EA* 82:37ff., and see *JCS* 2 (1948) pp. 247f. Read GÍR : ⌜*pat*⌝-[*r*]*a*.

4. 17 [š]a-*a i-de* p[a-ṭá-ar a-n]a *ma-ḫar* : *ša-a* instead of *ša* occurs sporadically; see *VAB* 2/2, p. 1506.

5. [*a-na* EDIN.MEŠ]: cf. *EA* 88:20f.

6. See *EA* 82:39. The expression "9 times" means "over and over" or "once and for all": Naram-Sin fights nine battles in one year (*YOS* 1, 10, and duplicates); nine times he was warred against, nine times he defeated and freed his enemies, only at the tenth attack inflicting final defeat (*VS* 17, 42; see also *Sumer* 32 [1976] pp. 63ff.); nine times Sargon captures men and animals (*TIM* 9, 48 rev. i 14f.; see also *JCS* 2 [1948] p. 248). Note, too, the nine peoples that divide the world and the nine chambers on each level of Utnapištim's ark; see J. Glassner, *Akkadica* 40 (1984) p. 19.

7. [*ki-na-an-n*]*a*: cf. *EA* 90:53, with Youngblood, *Amarna Correspondence*, p. 220.

8. Free restoration: [ù aš-ta-pa-a]r *ù aš*-[ta-ni 27 [a-na É.GAL] *ú-ul ta*-[qa-al-mi] 28 [a-na mi-nim qa]-*la-ta aš*-[šum mur-ṣi] 29 [UGU-ia *šu*]*m-ma*. Cf. *EA* 75:17f.

9. a[š-tap-par a-na].

10. ⟨*a-qa-bu-na*⟩.

11. [yú-ši-r]u: enough space?

12. *ti-du*-[ú]: cf. *EA* 105:36.

EA 82

A threat to abandon Byblos

TEXT: BM 37648.
COPY: Scheil, *Mémoires,* p. 306.
TRANSLITERATION AND TRANSLATION: *JCS* 2 (1948) pp. 241f.; Youngblood, *Amarna Correspondence,* pp. 224ff.

Say to Am[a]nappa, my father: Message of Rib-Hadda, your son. I fall at the feet of my father. 5–13 I have said to you again and again, "Are you unable to rescue me from ʿAbdi-Aširta? All the ʿApiru are on his side, and as soon as the mayors hear anything, they write to him. Accordingly, he is strong." 14–22 You ordered me again and again, "Send your man to me at the palace, and as soon as the request arrives, I will send him along with an auxiliary force, until the archers come out, to protect your life." But I told you, "I am unable to send ⟨him⟩. 23–30 Let not ʿAbdi-Aši[rta] hear[1] about it, or who would rescue m[e] from him?" You sa[id][2] to me, "Do not fea[r]!" You ordered me again and again, "Send a ship to the land of Yarimuta so silver and clothing *can get out*[3] to you from them." 31–41 All the men whom you gave me have run off. The (legal) violence done to me is your responsibility,[4] if you neglect me. Now I have obeyed. Is it not a fact that I sent my man to the palace, and he gave orders to a man and he attacked me with a bronze dagger. I was stabbed 9 times![5] He is strong through this crime, and from another crime what could rescue me? 41–46 If within two months there are no archers, then I will abandon the city, go off, and my life will be safe *while* I do what I want to do. 47–52 Moreover, do not you yourself know that the land of Amurru longs day and night for the archers? Has it not been distressed[6] : *na-aq-ṣa-pu* (have they not been angry)? So tell the king, "Come with all haste."

NOTES

1. On the form *yi-iš-ma,* see *Or* n.s. 29 (1960) p. 4, n. 4.
2. Perhaps *ta-a*[*q-bu*], "you keep saying to me."
3. Otherwise, *JCS* 2 (1948) p. 247.
4. *ḫabālīya elīka* is very reminiscent of Sarah's reproach to Abraham, *ḥᵃmāsî ʿālêkā* (*Gen.* 16:5), of which it could be the literal translation. Perhaps Rib-Hadda used an expression of contemporary customary law.
5. See *EA* 81:24. Rib-Hadda thinks that it is self-evident that ʿAbdi-Aširta is the villain; cf. *EA* 85:8 and n. 1.
6. The reading *ú-ul ta-ša-aš* must be retained, and *ú-ul-ta-ša-aš* (*CAD,* A/2, p. 424b) rejected for three reasons: (1) there is not a single instance of the first

syllable in polysyllabic words written V-VC in the Byblos letters; (2) there are only two quite dubious examples of *št* > *lt* in the Byblos letters (*EA* 92:39; 130:41); (3) if *māt amurri* is singular, then it is feminine and the form would be *tu-ul-ta-ša-aš*.

EA 83

Pleas and threats

TEXT: BM 29797.
COPY: BB 14.
PHOTOGRAPH: BB, pl. 13.
TRANSLITERATION AND TRANSLATION: Youngblood, *Amarna Correspondence,* pp. 237ff.
TRANSLATION: Ebeling, pp. 373f.

[R]ib-[Hadda sa]ys to his [lord], king of all countries, Great King: May the [L]ady of Gubla grant p[owe]r to the king, my lord. I fall at the feet of my lord, my Sun, 7 times and 7 times. 7–14 Why do you not send back word to me that I may know what I should d[o]? I sent a man of mine to my lord, and both his horses were taken. A second man—a man of his—was taken, [*and*] a tablet of the king was not put [i]n my man's hand. Listen t[o m]e! 15–20 Wh⟨y⟩ are you negligent so that your land is being taken? Let it not be said in the days of the commissioners, "The ʿApiru have taken the entire country!" Not so shall it be said in the days ⟨of the commissioners⟩, or you will not be able to take it back.[1] 21–29 Moreover, I have written for a garrison and horses, but they are not given. Send back word to me, or like Yapaḫ-Hadda and Zimredda I will make an alliance with ʿAbdi-Aširta and stay alive. Moreover, now that over and above everything else *Ṣumur* and Bit-Arḫa have defected, 30–37 may [*yo*]*u* put me[2] in Yanḫamu's charge so he will give me grain to eat th⟨at⟩[3] I may guard for him the king's city. May the king also give the order and release my man. His family are very upset with me, (saying) day and night, "You gave our son to the king." So release him, especially him.[4] 38–42 (The *other* is a citizen of Ibirta.) He is, I assure you,[5] in Yanḫamu's house. Moreover, tell Ya⟨n⟩ḫamu, "I declare Rib-Hadda to be in your charge and whatever ⟨ha⟩ppens[6] to him to be yo[ur] responsibility." 43–51 May the troops on campaign not fall upon me. And so I write, "If you do not tell him this,[7] I will abandon the city and go off. Moreover, if you do not send word back to me, I will abandon the city and go off, together with the men who are loyal to me."[8] 51–57 Also for your information:

Ummaḫnu (along with Milkuru, her husband), the maidservant of the Lady [of] Gu[bl]a, . . . *p*[*ow*]*erful* [*pray*]*s* [t]o the *L*[*ady of Gubla for the king, my lord*].[9]

NOTES

1. Perhaps the quotation begins with "in the days of the commissioners" (Knudtzon; Greenberg, *Ḫab/piru,* p. 36). The context seems to require that with the second "in the days" we supply "of the commissioners" (lost by vertical haplography?) or perhaps "in ⟨their⟩ days." There is no evidence that the phrase of itself might mean "in (future) days" (Knudtzon, followed by Greenberg). Line 20: *û*, "or," as in line 24; *ti-li-ú*, second singular (Knudtzon), not third plural (*Or* n.s. 29 [1960] p. 4, as if *ti-li-ú-na*).

2. [t]a$_5$-*din-ni*: very probable reading; certainly not [*t*]*a* (*Or* n.s. 29 [1960] p. 6, n. 3). Considerations of form (cf. *ta-di-en, EA* 91:17) and the Byblos syllabary rule out [*t*]*ú*.

3. Read *ana a-ka-li-ia* ŠI (beginning of a partially written *ù*): cf. the pronominal suffixes in *EA* 79:33; 105:85; 109:41; 125:18, 26, 30.

4. *šūt* emphasizes the pronominal suffix of *ušširšu* (*SSDB*, p. 22). Perhaps "release him, too," for if I understand the following lines, reference is to the man whose detention is mentioned in line 12 and who has made his way to Yanḫamu's house.

5. *alla-mi* (and variant forms) must begin a sentence or be preceded only by *u*, "and." On this particle see Rainey, *UF* 20 (1988) pp. 214ff. For a possible occurrence in Old Babylonian, see Durand, *RA* 82 (1988) p. 106:40 (*a-li*, "certes").

6. ⟨*en*⟩-*ni-ip-šu*: following Rainey, *UF* 5 (1973) p. 252.

7. *ana šâšu*, at the end of line 44, is written slightly smaller and higher than the rest of the line. It was probably inserted later where it could fit, and not at the end of line 45, where it belongs and alone makes sense. Reference is back to lines 39–40, "Say to Yanḫamu."

8. Lit. "who love me."

9. Ummaḫnu, who also appears in the next three letters, is always identified as the maidservant of the goddess and was probably a priestess. This is the basis for my very tentative reconstruction of her activities in this and the following letters. In line 55 I assume some form of *karābu*, "to pray" ([ti-ik-tar]-*ra*-b[u]?).

EA 84

Outrage upon outrage

TEXT: VAT 1633.

COPIES: WA 73; *VS* 11, 41.

TRANSLITERATION AND TRANSLATION: Youngblood, *Amarna Correspondence*, pp. 264ff.

[S]ay [to] the king, my lord, Sun of all countries: Message of Rib-Hadda, your servant, [fo]otstool for your feet. I fall at the feet of the Sun, my lord, 7 times and 7 times.[1] Furthermore, is the activity of ʿAbdi-Aširta, the dog, with the result that the lands of the king are joined to him, pleasing in the sight of the king, my lord, and so he has done nothing for his lands?[2] 11–21 Now, indeed, Ṣumur, my lord's court and [h]is bedchamber, has been joined to h[i]m. He has slept in the bedcha[mber of] my [lord],[3] and opened the *tre[asure]* room of my [lo]rd, and yet he (the king) has done nothing. Who is he, the *traitor*[4] and dog, [*that* he is s]trong? Moreover, as to men's [say]ing *in the pre[sence of m]y* [*lord*], "Gubla [*has been seiz*]*ed;* [*its ruler is distr*]*aught,*"[5] 21–31 my lord[6] should know (that) they have [*not tak*]*en* Gubla. *Those in authority* [*have gone off* . . .] and the situation of the lands of my lord is ve[ry] bad.[7] Moreover, may the king, [m]y lord, send his commissioner, who is strong, *al*[*ong with troops*],[8] to guard the city of my lord so that I for my part may (re)build the *brickwork*[9] and serve my lord, the Sun of all countries. 31–38 May my lord send men to take the possessions of my Adonis[10] to the king, my lord, lest that dog take the possessions of your god.[11] [*Or*] would it be pleasing that he had seized Gubla? [*Loo*]*k,* Gubla is like Ḫikuptaḫ to my lord![12] 38–44 Moreover, as ʿAbdi-NINURTA, the man I sent[13] with Puheya, is . . . Send him (back) to yo[ur] servant. [*Moreover*], Umm[aḫn]u, the maidservant of [the Lady of Gubla, and] her husband, Milkur[u[14] . . .] . . .[15] send . . .

NOTES

1. "All countries," written KUR.KI.DIDLI.ḪI.A; KUR.KI.DIDLI occurs elsewhere only in *EA* 106. Note also: (1) *gištappu,* "footstool," in the Byblos letters only in *EA* 84 and 106; (2) the only precative forms of *uššuru* in these letters, *lu-wa-ši/si-ra(-am),* in *EA* 84:26, 31; 106:26, 36, 42; (3) *īde* with precative force, in these letters only in *EA* 84:21 and 106:47.

2. KUR.KUR.KI-*šu*: following Youngblood, *Amarna Correspondence,* p. 257; for the writing, see *EA* 121, n. 4.

3. É(*bīt*)-u[r-ši BE]-*ia*: following Youngblood. *bīt urši,* also *PRU* 4, p. 109:5; Nougayrol, "maison privée." The sleeping quarters and the treasury were areas reserved to those most intimate and/or most trusted.

4. LÚ.LUL remains the most likely reading. LÚ.LUL = *sarru* (*AHw,* p. 1030; *CAD,* S, p. 180), which at Byblos (also *EA* 185–86) seems to be replaced by *šâru.* Perhaps LÚ.LUL = *narru*; cf. *narru* = *sarru,* and *EA* 94:60, 63.

5. 20 [ṣa-ab-ta]-*at-mi* (cf. line 36); 21 [LÚ-(šu) ma-an]-*ga* (cf. *EA* 106:15).

6. *be-lí-i*[*a*].

7. [paṭ(a)ru/paṭ(a)rat] *qí-ip-tu*; cf. *qīptu* = *qīpu* at Boghazköy (*AHw,* p. 922). The authorities would be the Egyptian officials in Ṣumur. End of line 24:

ma-ri-iṣ ma-g[*al*]: following Youngblood (cf. *EA* 95:41; 103:7; 114:50; 116:54).

8. *qa*-d[u ÉRIN.MEŠ]: following Youngblood.

9. SIG_4 (*libittu*)?

10. The pronominal suffix (*my* Adonis) perhaps reflects Byblian *'adônai* (suggestion of Frank M. Cross).

11. DINGIR.MEŠ very often has a singular referent and here seems best referred to Adonis.

12. This may be a saying (also *EA* 139:8) going back to much earlier times when Byblos was a very important port for the Egyptians and Memphis was the capital of Egypt.

13. *uš-šir*$_4$*-ti*.

14. ^{m}*mil-kur*-r[u].

15. x SAR *yi-ni*, "... of *wine*"?

EA 85

Nothing to eat

TEXT: VAT 1626.

COPIES: WA 48; *VS* 11, 42.

TRANSLITERATION AND TRANSLATION: Youngblood, *Amarna Correspondence*, pp. 264ff.

Sa[y to the king], my lord, the Sun: [Mes]sage of Rib-Hadda, your servant. I fal[l] at the feet of my lord 7 times and 7 times. May [the Lad]y of Gubla grant [pow]er to the king, my lord. 6–15 Though I keep writing like this to the king, my lord, he does not heed my words. Since he has attacked me[1] 3 times this year, and for two years I have been repeatedly robbed of my grain, we have no grain to eat. What can I say to my peasantry? Their sons, their daughters, the furnishings of their houses are gone, since they have been sold in the land of Yarimuta for provisions to keep us alive. 16–22 May the king, my lord, heed the words of his loyal servant, and may he send grain in ships in order to keep his servant and his city alive.[2] May he grant 400 men and 30 pair[s of h]orses, as were given to Su[r]a[t]a,[3] that they may guard the city for you. 22–32 As to Yanḫamu's having said, "I [ga]ve grain to Rib-Hadda, [and *I would g*]*ive* [...] ... : *ḫu-ta-ri-ma* (?) [...] *g*[*rai*]*n* for 40 men." W[ha]t did *he* give m⟨e⟩? I deposited the payment for them with[4] Yapaḫ-Hadda. Look, P[uḫ]eya is with[5] you; ask him to tell the whole story in your presence. 33–39 May it be pleasing in the sight of the king, my lord, and may he give grain that is pro[du]ced in the land of Yarimuta. What used to be given in Ṣumur, may it now be [g]iven in Gubla, [so that] we may have provisions until you *gi*[*ve thou*]*ght*[6] to your city. 39–50 Moreover, [as the kin]g, my lord, li[ves], *truly* my men *are lo[yal to me.*[7] ʿAbdi]-Aširta and *the* ʿ*Api[ru have gone t]o* Yapaḫ-Hadda in [*Beiru*]*t* so [*an alliance*] might be formed.[8] [As][9] there is no one in [your] city, send a garrison [to pro]tect [y]our land, lest your [*city*] be seized. Listen to me. [Te]ll Yanḫamu to [*tak*]*e* the money [. . .] . . . for the people of [Gu]bla in the land of Yarimuta. 51–63 Moreover, the king of ⟨Mi⟩ttana came out as far as Ṣumur, and though wanting to mar[ch] as far as Gubla, he returned to [h]is own land, as there wa[s n]o water for him to drink. I keep writing like this t[o] the palace for what [I] need. [*Wh*]*y* do you not reply, "What my servant [re]quests is available," or "is not avail[able],"[10] so I may know [wh]at I should do [un]til the king ar[riv]es and visits his loyal servant? 63–74 Who is ʿAbdi-Aširta, the servant and dog, that they [men]tion his name in the presence of the king, my lord? Just let there be one man[11] whose heart is one with my heart, and I would drive ʿAbdi-Aširta from the land of Amurru. Moreover, since your father's return from Sidon, from that time the lands have been joined to the ʿApiru. Accordingly, I have nothing. 75–87 May the king heed the words of his servant; may he [g]ive men to guard his [c]ity, lest he gather together all the ʿApiru and they *seize* [the city]. At [*thi*]*s* time send a [*large*][12] force that they may drive him f[rom the land of Amur]ru. When the commissioner of the k[ing was *wi*]*th* us, it was to hi[m] that [*we used to writ*]*e; we cannot write t*[*o hi*]*m* (now). Umma[ḫnu—along with] her [hus]band Milkuru—the maidservant of the La[dy] of Gub[la], as truly as the king [li]ves, i[n . . .] . . . *from* the hand of the magna[te, *to*] the Lad[y . . .].

NOTES

1. The subject is, of course, ʿAbdi-Aširta; see *EA* 82:37 and n. 5.

2. Instead of ÌR-*šu ù* URU-*šu*, Knudtzon's reading, which makes sense and is followed here, the copy of *VS* 11 offers ÌR-*šu a-na ia-šu*, which makes no sense. Not collated.

3. Undoubtedly the ruler of Akka; see *EA* 232 and cf. *EA* 88:46ff.

4. Rainey, *UF* 20 (1988) p. 213, proposes *i-na* ⟨*qa-at*⟩, but an underlying Byblian *bi* of proximity or accompaniment ("using the services of") could explain the use of *ina*.

5. On *it* (also *EA* 114:46; 130:24) as an abbreviation of *itti*, not a reflex of Northwest Semitic *'et*, see Huehnergard, *Ugaritic Vocabulary*, p. 111.

6. *ti*-m[a-la-k]u (Knudtzon) is without parallel (cf. *EA* 94:12; 104:16; 114:48), and for *ti*-m[a-li-k]u (*VAB* 2/2, p. 1591) there probably is not enough room. Read *ti*-š[a-i-l]u, "you inquire (about)"? (Cf. *EA* 89:40.)

7. It is doubtful that Rib-Hadda would admit that those he identifies as "my men" are all loyal to ʿAbdi-Aširta (so Knudtzon); cf. *EA* 83:50f.; 137:46ff.

Hence *ra*-[i-mu-ni/ia]. On *adi,* "truly," see *AHw,* p. 13a, and *ARMT* 13, p. 165, commentary on 44:8.

8. Very tentatively, 41 . . . LÚ.MEŠ G[AZ al-ku] 42 [a-na ma-ḫa]r ^{m}*ia-pa-aḫ*-^{d}IM *i-na* 43 [URU be-ru]-*ta ù tu-pa-šu* [ki-tu]; cf. *EA* 83:24.

9. [a-nu-ma]; end of line, URU-[ka ù].

10. 57 [a-na mi]-ni l[a-a *t*]*u-te-ru* 58 [a-wa-ta$_5$] *i-ba-ši-mi ù i-ia*-n[u]: l[a, in view of parallels (*EA* 81:23; 83:7, 45f.), despite Knudtzon's legitimate doubts. If the traces (missing in *VS* 11 copy, but still visible) described by Knudtzon are not *n*[*u* and do not belong to the end of line 58, I cannot explain them.

11. Probably in the sense of "ruler"; cf. *EA* 74:12.

12. Room for only one (fairly large) sign: cf. *EA* 76:39.

EA 86

Complaint to an official

TEXT: BM 29804.

COPY: BB 21.

TRANSLITERATION AND TRANSLATION: Youngblood, *Amarna Correspondence,* pp. 283ff.

[*Say to*] Ama[nappa]: Message of Rib-Had[da]. I fall [at your feet]. May Aman, [the god of the king], your lord, establish yo[ur] honor [in the presence] of the king, your lord. Listen to m[e![1] The war] 6–12 is severe, and so come w[ith] archers that you may take the land of Amurru. Day and ni[ght it has *cri*]*ed*[2] to you [*and* they s]ay (that) what is taken f[rom t]hem to Mittan[a] is very much. 13–17 [S]o now you [*yourself*] must not [*say*], "Why should . . . [. . .] come out?"[3] You have said [*ind*]*eed,* "Yanḫamu sent yo[u] grain."[4] Have you not heard? A servant . . . [. . .] 17–22 . . .[5] 23–30 [*And* be in]form[ed *that* Um]maḫ[nu—along with her husband, Milku]ru—the ma[idservant of the Lady] of Gub[la . . .] . . . [*S*]*o* speak to the king [*that*] *it* may be presented to the Lady.[6] Do [n]ot hold *an*[*ything*] back. 31–40 Moreover, speak to [*the king*] so that [grain], the product of the land of Ya[*rmuta*], be given t[o his servant], just as it was [formerly] given to Ṣumur, so we may keep alive until the king *g*[*ives thought*] to his city. For 3 years I have been constantly pl[undered] of our grain; there is no[thing] to pay for h[orses].[7] 41–50 Why should the king *g*[*rant*] 30 pairs of [horses] and you *your*[*self*] take 10 pairs? If *you t*[*ake*],[8] take al[l *of them*], but from the land of Y[arimuta] let grain be given for [*us*] to eat. [*Or*] sen[d *ships so I myself*] *can get* [*out*].

NOTES

1. *i*[*a-ši*]: following Youngblood, *Amarna Correspondence,* p. 287.

2. [ta/ti-š]a-si_{17}: as if from *šasû*; if from *ašāšu* (Knudtzon), the final vowel is a difficulty, as is the unparalleled use of *ana* (cf. *EA* 82:50; 83:23; 93:4; 122:39). Perhaps also to be considered is [ta/ti-t]a-*ši* ⟨IGI⟩ (haplography), "it has lifted (its) face to you (in hope)."

3. *la-a ta-*[aq-bu] 14 [at-ta] *a-mi-ni tu-ṣa-na* x [x]: perhaps not enough room for *attā*; x is not ÉR[IN] (as copied in BB).

4. Knudtzon's suggestion that in ḪI ŠE.ḪI.A the first ḪI anticipates the second one seems the most plausible explanation (*VAB* 2/1, p. 413, note m).

5. Line 19: [KU]Š? : *ma-aš-ka,* "hide"?

6. [t]u-*da-na*: "that she?/you? may be presented. . . ."

7. *ana nadāni ana* A[NŠE.KUR.RA: following Youngblood, p. 292. An exact parallel is *EA* 107:37f., and note the following lines.

8. *šumma* t[i-ìl-qé].

EA 87

Broken promises

TEXT: BM 29805.

COPY: BB 22.

PHOTOGRAPH: BB, pl. 5.

TRANSLITERATION AND TRANSLATION: Youngblood, *Amarna Correspondence,* pp. 294ff.

[To] Amanappa, m[y] l[or]d: Message of Rib-Hadda, your servant. I fall at the feet of my lord. May Aman and the Lady of Gubla establish your honor in the presence of the king, your lord. 8–14 Why did you *lead me astray,* saying, "Send your messenger here to me before the king so he may give you troops and chariots as a help to you to guard the city"? 15–24 So I listened to your words, and I sen[t (him)],[1] and he came out empty-handed. Then he heard that[2] there were no troops with him, and as a result Baṭruna was join[ed] to him. He has stationed the ʿApiru and chariots there, and they have not[3] moved [f]rom the entrance of the gate of Gub⟨la⟩. 25–31 [*Loo*]*k,* urge the king, my lord, with loud cries![4] Let an elite force, [*together with*] chariots, [*advan*]*ce*[5] with you that *I* may . . . [. . . the *ʿApir*]*u from it* (the gate). [*So*] *come out,* but *be on your gua*[*rd,*[6] *for if*] you die, [*then I too*] must die.

NOTES

1. *ú-wa-š*[ir_4]: *SSDB,* p. 159; perhaps, with Youngblood, *Amarna Correspondence,* p. 298, *-šu* is to be added. On lines 15–24, see Rainey, *UF* 7 (1975) pp. 424f.

2. *e-nu-ú*: following Albright in *SSDB*, p. 159.

3. *la*: following Albright, ibid.; cf. *Or* n.s. 29 (1960) p. 17, n. 2.

4. The reading *ku-ru-ub* (*JNES* 8 [1949] p. 124) is wrong, and Knudtzon's *qú-ru-ud* (also *EA* 69:30) is right. For the meaning, cf. *qardu*, "one who shouts, is noisy," and see the remarks of Civil, *JNES* 43 (1984) pp. 294f.

5. [*a-ṣa-a*]*m* (*JNES* 8 [1949] p. 125) is almost certainly wrong.

6. Not enough room for *uṣur ramānka*, "guard yourself," but the following lines favor such a meaning here; cf. Youngblood, p. 304.

EA 88

Blockaded

TEXT: BM 29800.

COPY: BB 17.

TRANSLITERATION AND TRANSLATION: Youngblood, *Amarna Correspondence*, pp. 305ff.

[Ri]b-Had[da s]ay[s *to his lord*: Be]fore the king of all countries, [Great King],[1] a[t the feet of my lord], my Sun, I fall [7] times and 7 times. I have w[ritten] 5–12 repeatedly to y[ou, "The *war* is against] Ardat, against Irqat, and agai[nst . . ., an]d Am⟨mi⟩y[a and *Šigat*]*a*, loyal [ci]ties of the king," [but the king], my lord, [*has done nothing*]. Moreover, what is [he, ʿA]bdi-Aširati, the servant (and) dog, that he has a[ct]ed as he pleased in the lands of my lord, [and yet] the king, my lord, has done nothing for [his] servant? 13–21 [Moreov]er, I sent my messenger (each time) that [he too]k my cities and moved u[p aga]inst me.[2] [N]ow he has taken Baṭruna, and he has moved up against me. [Beh]old the city! He has . . . the *entrance* of the gate of Gubla.[3] How long has he not moved from the gate, and so we are unable to go out into the countryside.[4] 21–28 Moreover, look,[5] he strives to seize Gubla![6] And [. . . *and*] may the king, my lord, give heed t[o the words of] his [ser]vant, and [may] he hasten[7] [with] all speed chariots and [troops][8] that they may gu[ard[9] the city of the king], my lord, and [. . . until] the arr[iva]l of the king, [my] lor[d]. 28–39 For my part,[10] I will [no]t neglect the word of [my] lord. But i[f the k]ing, my lord, does [not give heed] to the words of [his] ser[vant], then Gubla will be joined to him, and all the lands of the king, as far as Egypt, will be joined to the ʿApiru. Moreover, should my lord not have wor[d] brought to *hi*[*s*] *serv*⟨*ant*⟩[11] by tablet, with all speed, then . . . the city to him and I will request a town from him to stay in, and so I will stay al⟨iv⟩e.[12] 40–51 [Moreov]er, may the king, my lord, hasten the troops (and) chariots that they may guard[13] the city of the king, my lord. Look, Gubla is not like the [*other*] cities; Gubla is a loyal city of the king, [my] lo[rd], from most ancient times. Still, the messenger of the king of Akka is honored more than [my] messeng[er], *f*[*or* they fur]nished [h]im with a horse. [*May he furn*]*ish him* (my messenger) . . . with 2 horses. May he not come out [*empty-handed*].[14]

NOTES

1. LUGAL KUR.[KI.ḪI.A LUGAL GAL]: cf. KUR.KI.ḪI.A in line 11, and see Youngblood, *Amarna Correspondence,* p. 310. Knudtzon's restoration assumes a form of greeting found in no Byblos letter.

2. Lines 13–21: see Rainey, *UF* 7 (1975) p. 425. Line 14: [*ìl-q*]*é,* following Youngblood, p. 312; cf. line 16.

3. [*a*]-*mur* URU UD (virtually certain) ŠI x *pí* (Rainey) KÁ.GAL; x, possibly KAB (Knudtzon), iD? *ta*₅-*ši-it,* "the city has *kept away from the entrance* of the city-gate" (*šêtu, AHw,* p. 1221?)?

4. *ma-ni* UD.KÁM.MEŠ-*ti la yi-na-mu-uš* (*Or* n.s. 29 [1960] p. 17, n. 2) . . . 21 *a-ṣa-am a-na* EDIN.MEŠ (*RA* 69 [1975] pp. 156f.).

5. There can hardly be any doubt that ʿAbdi-Aširta wishes to capture Byblos, and hence *šumma,* "look, behold" (see *EA* 35, n. 3).

6. Departing from normal word order and fronting the object Byblos, Rib-Hadda stresses that now his very own city is under attack.

7. [*ù lu*]-*ḫa-mu-uṭ*: following Rainey, *UF* 7 (1975) p. 415, but perhaps -*ṭám* rather than -*uṭ* (cf. *ḫu-mi-ṭám, EA* 102:29); also line 40.

8. [ÉRIN.MEŠ], without *piṭāti,* as in line 41. Furthermore, archers are never requested for purposes of defense; see Pintore, *OA* 11 (1972) pp. 106ff.

9. *ti*-[*ṣú-ru*] (also line 41): as required by the rules of modal sequence; see also Rainey, *UF* 7 (1975) p. 415.

10. On the use of *anāku,* which sets up a contrast with "the king, my lord" and what is expected of him (lines 23ff.), see Agustinus Gianto, *Word Order Variation in the Akkadian of Byblos,* Studia Pohl 15 (Rome, 1990), p. 85. The following sequence of object-verb emphasizes Rib-Hadda's fidelity to the word of his master. *izzib*: injunctive? zero = preterite? (See Introduction, n. 50.)

11. *a-na* Ì⟨R⟩-Š[u]: a reading that Knudtzon rejected (*VAB* 2/1, p. 420, note b), but note (1) the ligature of the alleged *aš-šad*; (2) that the postulated *šu* is identical with the last sign of *EA* 87:28 (Knudtzon, *šu*?); and (3) sense. The construction, however, that is assumed here—an unmarked protasis of a conditional sentence—is without certain parallel in the Byblos corpus.

12. *ú bal*-⟨*ṭá*⟩-*ti*: cf. *EA* 82:45; 83:27; 123:35; *ú,* "and," lines 10, 22; 84:32; non-Byblos occurrences in *EA* 62, 260, 317, and 337. Lines 34–39 seem to be a threat, especially comparable to *EA* 83:47ff., so that "him" must refer to ʿAbdi-Aširta and *ù na-ri*-x at the end of line 36 must be an expression for surrendering Byblos, perhaps first plural (i.e., a common action of Rib-Hadda and fellow citizens; cf. line 20, "we are not able"); x = *i*G or *šu. na-re-eq,* "we will distance ourselves from the city for him" (*rêqu*?)?

13. See n. 9.

14. 49 [ia-d]i-na ... 50 [x x] x ... 51 [ù ri-qú-t]a$_5$: cf. *EA* 87:17. Kühne, p. 107, n. 525, offers a different interpretation: Rib-Hadda's messenger was deprived of two horses.

EA 89

Events in Tyre

TEXT: VAT 1627.
COPIES: WA 49; *VS* 11, 43.
TRANSLITERATION AND TRANSLATION: *JCS* 4 (1950) pp. 164f.; Youngblood, *Amarna Correspondence,* pp. 322ff.

[Rib]-Hadda say[s to his lord, k]ing of all countries, Gre[at] King: [May the Lady] of Gubla [grant power t]o the king, [my] lord. I fall [at the fee]t of my lord, [m]y Su[n, 7 times and 7] times. 7–14 [Though] I keep writing like this [*to the pala*]*ce,* my words are not [taken to he]art, and they go utterly un[hee]ded. Look at the deed in Tyre. On this account I am afraid. Even now the king makes no inquiry about his mayor, my brother. May the king h⟨eed⟩ my words. Their *words* are not *true.* 15–29 "If the king makes inquiry, we will devote ourselves to your service." I made connubium with Tyre; they were on good terms with me. (But now) they have, I assure you, killed their mayor,[1] together with my sister and her sons. My sis⟨te⟩r's daughters I had sent to Ty[re], away from ʿAbdi-A[širta. *They killed*] *him al*[*ong with my sister* ...] ... 30–39 [*If*] the king [*makes inquiry about my brother*], then all lands [*will be joined to the king, my lord. But*] if the king does [*not*] make inquiry about [my] brother, [*then*] ... [...] He wrote again and again to the king, [but h]is words went unheeded. And so he died. I know it! 39–47 But if you make inquiry about my brother, then the city will say, "This man is not the mayor! Inquire, O king, about him! We are unable to do anything." They are afraid. Will the king not make inquiry about the mayor of Tyre? For his property is as great as the sea. I know it! 48–57 Look, there is no mayor's residence like that of the residence in Tyre. It is like the residence in Ugarit. Exceedingly [gr]eat is the wealth [i]n it. May the king heed [the word]s of ⟨his⟩ servant. May he send [...] ... that he may stay [in the l]and and [*be concerned*] for the mayors. 58–67 May [*no*] property be handed [over to] them.[2] G[*ive thought to* the com]missioner of the king. He[3] is *t*[*aking* fr]om the king [*all*] the lands [*of the king*]. I know (it)! Does the king like it [*that* ʿAbdi-A]širta has taken the *sea* [*in*] *front of* them, and so they are at peace? May the king [*ter*]*rify* them! Do I not continue to write of ⟨*the*⟩*ir* crime to the king?

NOTES

1. After the asseverative particle *allû,* the word order, object-verb, stresses the object and underscores the enormity of the crime.

2. Lines 58–67 follow Knudtzon's restorations with one exception and these additions: 59 [qa-ti]-*šu-nu* (the rebels in Tyre); 60 *i*-[le-qú]; 61 [iš-tu] . . . k[a-li]; 64 . . . *a-ia-ab* š[a]; 65 [i-na]; 66 [yú/yi-pa-l]i-*iḫ-šu-nu*; 67 *ar-na*-⟨šu⟩-*nu.* Rib-Hadda seems to say that ʿAbdi-Aširta controls the sea around the island town of Tyre, thus rendering the rebels secure. For a discussion and commentary on the entire letter, see *JCS* 4 (1950) pp. 163ff.

3. Probably ʿAbdi-Aširta.

EA 90

Alone and unheeded

TEXT: VAT 1661.

COPIES: WA 53; *VS* 11, 44.

TRANSLITERATION AND TRANSLATION: Youngblood, *Amarna Correspondence,* pp. 337ff.

[S]ay [t]o the king, my lord: Message of Rib-Hadda, [your] se[rvant]. I fall at the feet of my lord, [my] Su[n, 7 times and 7 times]. Be informed [that] the war aga[inst me] is severe. [He has taken][1] all my cities; [Gubla] alone rem[ains] 8–12 to me. I was in Šigata and I wr[ote] to [y]ou, "Give thought to [your] city lest ʿAbdi-Aširta take it." 13–19 [But] you did not listen to m[e. Then fr]om Baṭruna I wr[ote to yo]u, "Send men to ta[ke[2] the ci]ty for you." [My] words went [u]nheeded, [and][3] they were [no]t taken to heart. Now they have [*ta*]*k*[*en*] my cities. 19–28 Moreover, that [*do*]*g*[4] is [i]n Mittana, but his eye is on [Gu]bla. What can I do by myself? You yourself have been [neg]ligent of your cities so that the ʿApiru [*dog*] takes them.[5] It is to you that I have tu[rn]ed.[6] Moreover, all the [*mayors*][7] are at peace with ʿAbdi-A[širta]. 29–35 . . . 36–47 [Ou]r [sons], [our daughters, the furnishings] of the houses are gone, since they have been so[ld in the land] of Yarimuta ⟨⟨[fo]r⟩⟩ for provisions to keep [u]s alive. Li[k]e [a bird] in a tr[ap], s[o am I] in [Gub]la. "For lack of a cultivator my fie[ld] is [l]ike a woman without a [hus]band." Moreover, . . . [. . .], and send [x m]en and 30 pairs of [h]ors[es] that [I] may g[ua]rd the city for yo[u].[8] 48–56 [And] *yo*[*ur*] me[ss]engers send . . . , and if you do not send a garrison, [then] . . . I am afrai[d] for my life. [And] al[l] messenger[s *that*] were *b*[*ou*]*nd have been rele*[*ased*].[9] . . . 57–62 Do not be negligent. Send ar[chers that they may ta]ke the land of [Amurru].[10] Day and night [*everyone awaits the coming forth of the ar*]*ch*[*ers*].[11] I have been plundered of [my grain, *and*] it is [to you] that I have tur[ned].[12]

NOTES

1. [*ìl-qé*]: cf. *EA* 91:19ff., an exact parallel to *EA* 90:6ff.

2. *ti-*[*ìl-qú*] or *ti-*[*ìl-ti-qú*]: according to the rule of modal sequence.

3. Probably room only for *ù*; I could not see traces corresponding to Knudtzon's [la-q]a.

4. [UR.K]U: cf. esp. *kalbu šūt* (*EA* 84:35).

5. If plural, then [*ti-ìl*]*-ti-qú-šu-nu*, "when the ʿApiru took . . ." In *EA* 91:5, however, LÚ.GAZ.MEŠ UR.KU is singular, and it also suggests the restoration 26 [UR.KU]; hence [*yi-ìl*]*-ti-qú-šu-nu*, with Knudtzon (*yi-ìl-ti-qú*, also *EA* 109:17, 19), but singular, not plural (Knudtzon, followed by Ebeling, *VAB* 2/2, p. 1453).

6. 27 [*pa-ni-i*]*a*: see *VAB* 2/2, p. 1591.

7. The restoration of *bēl ālānī*, "lord(s) of the cities," on the basis of *EA* 102:23, is, statistically, less probable than some reference to the mayors (cf. esp. *EA* 114:14; 126:11), and also, it would seem, less likely in a context speaking of many cities; hence [*ḫa-za-nu*]. Perhaps *sal-mu* (*AHw*, p. 1014), not *šal-mu*.

8. The reading *yi-ì*[*š*]*-mi* at the end of line 44 (Youngblood, *Amarna Correspondence*, p. 346, followed by Rainey, *UF* 7 [1975] p. 414) seems excluded, though the sign is not clearly *aš* as in the copy of *VS* 11. On *ušširū* in line 45 as plural of "majesty," and ⌜*a-na-ṣa-r*⌝*a* in line 47 (collated), see Youngblood, p. 346.

9. 54 . . . ⌜gáb⌝-[bu ša] 55 ḫ[a]r-*šu ut-ta-*[ša/ši-ru]: readings dubious and context unclear.

10. 61 [*ù ti*]-⌜*el*⌝*-qé* KUR [a-mur-ri]: cf. *EA* 91:38, 45; 94:11; 107:30; 121:48; 123:42.

11. 62 [*u*]*r-ra mu-ša* p[a-nu ka-li a-na a-ṣí ÉRIN.MEŠ pí-ṭ]á-[ti]: cf. *EA* 91:39–41.

12. Cf. *EA* 85:9f.; 86:35f.; 90:26f.; 91:16.

EA 91

A plea for a payoff

TEXT: VAT 931.

COPIES: WA 56; *VS* 11, 45.

TRANSLITERATION AND TRANSLATION: Youngblood, *Amarna Correspondence*, pp. 351ff.

[Rib-Hadda says to] h[is] lord: I fall [at the feet of my lord 7 times and 7 times. *I wrote to you,* "*W*]*hy* have you sat idly by [and] done nothing, so that the ʿApiru dog[1] tak[es *you*]*r cities*?" 6–13 [*When*] he took Ṣumur, [I wr]ote to you, "Why *do you* [*do noth*]*ing*?" (Then B[it]-ar*q*[*a*] was taken.) [Wh]en he saw [that] there was no one [t]hat said anything [to h]im about Ṣumur, his intentions were re[in]forced,[2] so that he strives to take Gubla. 14–23 *He* has attacked me[3] (and) my orchards, [*and*] my own [me]n have become hostile. I have been plundered of my [grain]. [May] you pay a thousand (*shekels of*) silver and 100 (*shekels* of) gold,[4] so he will go away [fr]om me. He has taken [al]l my cities; Gubla alone remains [t]o me, and he strives to take it. 23–30 I have just heard (that) he has gathered together [a]ll the ʿApiru [t]o attack me. What can I [d]o by myself? I go on writing like this for archers and an auxiliary force, but my words go unheeded. 31–36 [Mo]reover, *give* [*thought your*]*se*[*lf t*]*o* your lands.[5] [. . .] . . . Moreover, [*listen to me, and i*]*f* there are no [archers] and auxiliary force, [*then there will be no* . . .] for Gubla, [*and it will be*] *joined* [*to the ʿApiru*]. 36–41 O king, [*listen to me, and* s]end ar[chers t]o take the land of Amurru. [*Now indeed*] everyone *aw*[*aits day and nigh*]*t* [*the coming forth of the arch*]*ers.*[6] 42–49 [*And may*] the king, my lord, [. . .] . . .

NOTES

1. The forms of the verb, *yi-ìl-qú* (line 4) and *yi-ìl-qa* (line 6), are singular, and therefore LÚ.GAZ.MEŠ is also singular (Knudtzon; Greenberg, *Ḫab/piru,* p. 38).

2. *yi-*⌜da⌝*-ni-en*: following Greenberg, ibid., though the sign seems a little larger than *da. šab* (Knudtzon) is certainly wrong.

3. *am-ma-qú-ut*: contamination by *ammaššaḫ* (line 16)? The grammar of line 14 is obscure.

4. Unless emphasis is intended through gross exaggeration, the numbers hardly refer to minas (Knudtzon; Helck, *Beziehungen,* pp. 382, 384).

5. *mi-*[li-ik at]-t[a a-n]a KUR.MEŠ-*ka*: cf. *EA* 133:2.

6. Free restoration: 33 [ši-mi a-na ia-ši ù šum-m]a *ia-nu* 34 [ÉRIN.MEŠ pí-ṭá-ti] *ù til-la-ta* 35 [ù ia-nu x x (x)] *a-na* URU *gub-la* 36 [ù a-na LÚ. MEŠ.GAZ.MEŠ ti-ni]*-ip-šu* LUGAL 37 [ši-mi a-na ia-ši ù *uš*]*-ši-ra* ÉRIN.MEŠ 38 [pí-ṭá-ti ù *t*]*i-il-qé* KUR *a-mur-*[*r*]*i* 39 [a-nu-ma i-na-an-na] *pa-nu ka-li* 40 [ur-ra ù mu-s]a 41[a-na a-ṣí ÉRIN.MEŠ pí-ṭ]á-*ti.*

EA 92

Some help from the Pharaoh

TEXT: VAT 868.
COPIES: WA 50; *VS* 11, 46.
TRANSLITERATION AND TRANSLATION: Youngblood, *Amarna Correspondence,* pp. 360ff.

Rib-Hadda says to the king, his lord, the Sun of [all countries]: I fall at the feet of my lord, [my] S[un], 7 times and 7 times. May the Lady of Gub[la] g[rant powe]r to the king, my lord, [m]y [Sun]. 7–15 [Moreov]er, ˁAbdi-A[šrati . . .] . . . If he *had* made inquiry . . . [. . .], *he would* [*no*]*t have taken up residence in them.*[1] A[n]d[2] now an evil war has been waged against [me], and I sent my tablet and [m]y [messenger] to the king, my lord, but the *k*[*ing*] paid no attention to the words of my tablet and [*my*] *me*[*ssenger*]. So what am [I t]o do? 16–24 I sent my messenger to the king, [m]y lord, [in regard to] my cities that ˁAbdi-Ašrati had taken. ˁAbdi-Ašrati hea[rd] that my man had arrived from the king, my lord, and he heard that there was nothing (with him). Since there was no auxiliary force that [cam]e out to me, he has [n]ow *mo*[*ved*] *up*[3] against me. 25–29 . . . 29–40 And what could I say? Moreover, it was a gracious deed of the king, my lord, that the king [wr]ote to the king of Beirut, to the king of Sidon, and to the king of T[y]re, [*sa*]*ying,*[4] "Rib-Hadda will be writing to you for an auxiliary force, and all of [y]ou are to go."[5] This *pl*[*eased*] *me,*[6] [and so] I sent my messenger, but they have [no]t come, and *they* [*have*] not *s*[*en*]*t* their messenger(s) to *gre*[*et*] us.[7] 41–48 Moreover, who[8] is he, that he [*has taken*][9] the men *to*[*gether wi*]*th* the oxen with *th*[*em*]?[10] What did he give for t[h]em? As the three of us are brothers, I wrote to them for help.[11] May it seem right in the sight of the king, my lord, that [they should s]end[12] soldiers of an expeditionary force[13] . . . 48–57 . . .[14]

NOTES

1. Reference to ˁAbdi-Aširta's occupation of cities?
2. *ù*: sign extended because of continuation on edge.
3. *i-ti-*˹el˺-[l]a: cf. *EA* 81:46; 88:14, 17.
4. [u]m-˹ma˺-*mi*: if the correct reading, it would reflect Egyptian usage (*EA* 1:26, 37). *VS* 11, 46: [al-l]u-*mi*.
5. *ù* ˹*a*˺*t*-[*la*]-*ku gáb-bu*-[*k*]*u-nu*. Rib-Hadda alludes to this order in line 39.
6. DÙG.[GA] (*ṭāb*) 38 *elīya*.
7. *a-na ša-al* š[u]l-[mi]-*nu*: *šulma šâlu*/*ša'ālu* as in *EA* 96:5f.; 97:3.
8. *mi*-˹*ia*˺-*mi*: following Youngblood, *Amarna Correspondence,* p. 370.

9. *il*-[qé]: cf. line 17 and *EA* 88:14, 16; 91:19.

10. *a*-[di] GUD.M[EŠ] *it-ti*-š[u-nu]: *adi,* following a private communication of N. Na'aman; see also *EA* 74:56 and n. 13.

11. One expects "the four of us." The sign gives evidence of hesitation or correction; see Knudtzon's note.

12. The singular injunctive is incompatible with the "indicative" marker, and therefore the form is plural. Read [*tu-wa*]-*ši-r*[*u*]; also possible but less likely is [*lu-wa*]-*ši-r*[*u*] (see *EA* 84, n. 1).

13. ÉRIN.MEŠ KAL.BAD.KASKAL + ?: see *EA* 109, n. 10.

14. Lines 52–55: perhaps "If the king, my lord, does not send troops . . . , I will abandon the city of my lord." Cf. *EA* 82:43; 83:46, 49.

EA 93

An angry vassal

TEXT: VAT 1663.
COPIES: WA 55; *VS* 11, 47.
TRANSLITERATION AND TRANSLATION: Youngblood, *Amarna Correspondence,* pp. 372ff.

[To Am]anappa: [Message of R]ib-Hadda. I fall [at] your [f]eet. [Look, I] was distressed :[1] *na-aq-ṣa-ap-ti* (angry) [a]t your words, "I am [on my] way to y[o]u." **8–18** You are always writing [li]ke this to me! Listen to me. Tell the king to give you 300 men so we can visit[2] the city and regain (it) [*for the king*]. Do not the [com]missioners *lo*[*ng for*][3] the coming out of the archers? He is stronger than the king![4] **19–28** Moreover, if we are able to [se]ize Baṭrun[a] fo]r you, then[5] the men will abandon ʿAbdi-Aširta. Things are [n]ot as they were previously. [I]f this year there are no archers, [then] he will be strong forever.

NOTES

1. [*a-mur a*]-*ta-ša-aš*: following Youngblood, p. 375. On [*ul*]-*ta-ša-aš* (*CAD,* A/2, p. 424), see *EA* 82, n. 6.

2. Perhaps "to visit" (*dagālu,* "to look at") is used to suggest that a mere show of power will suffice to regain Baṭruna.

3. ti-b[a-u-na]: *ti* is quite probable.

4. Perhaps this is to be understood as a quotation citing the commissioners' fears.

5. On the confusion in lines 18–21 of *šanīta* and *u,* see Youngblood, p. 376.

EA 94

Treachery everywhere

TEXT: C 4756.
COPY: WA 78.
TRANSLITERATION AND TRANSLATION: Youngblood, *Amarna Correspondence,* pp. 377ff.

Rib-Hadda [wri]tes[1] to the king, [the kin]g of [all cou]ntries,[2] the ki[ng, *his*] lord, his [*god*]: I fall at the feet of my lord 7 times and 7 times. 4–18 Why has my lord not heeded the word of his servant? My lord should know that there is no evil in the words of his servant. I do not speak any treacherous word to the king, my l[ord]. The king, my lord, has examined the words and has *heard*[3] the words! I said to the king, my lord, "Send archers to take[4] ʿAbdi-Ašrata." Who would advise, "He would resist (successfully) the archers of the king, my lord"? ... Treacherous men say [trea]cherous [things] t[o the king], my lord. [...] archers [...] 19–58 [...] 59–64 ...[5] 65–78 he has brought them *water,*[6] and he is the one who has given them provisions. Since I am the one who *checked* the ʿApiru,[7] there are hostilities against me. He is the one who has given them provisions, and so may the king give thought ⟨to⟩ his servant. May the king send his commissioner. [Le]t him advise on the spot itself. That fellow is [*no*]*t* to make a raid. [*Ear*]*lier* the king ordered [*with regard*] *to* the asses[8] that they be g[ive]n to [*his loyal*] servant [...] ...

NOTES

1. [*i*]*š*-[*t*]*a-par*: cf. *EA* 108:1; 116:1; 119:1; 123:1; form of *ta,* slightly aberrant.

2. [LUG]AL [KU]R.⌜KUR.KI⌝: cf. the parallel passages cited in n. 1.

3. *iš-mi* ⟨⟨IG⟩⟩: perhaps unerased beginning of *iq-bi*/*bu,* but hardly an attempt to reproduce a form of *šmʿ* (*VAB* 2/2, p. 1592).

4. *te-el-*⌜*qé*⌝: quite clear and as expected (*Or* n.s. 29 [1960] p. 12, n. 1). Knudtzon's *qú* is undoubtedly a misprint.

5. LÚ *na-a-ru* (line 60; also 63?), "treacherous person" (cf. *EA* 84, n. 4). Reference to a "singer" (*nāru*) does not seem likely.

6. *A mi-e*: perhaps *amê*-red (cloth) should not be ruled out; see *EA* 14, n. 46. End of line 64: *ša-na* = *šanna,* "kettle"?

7. LÚ.MEŠ GAZ: reading virtually certain; cf. GAZ in *EA* 179:22.

8. Cf. *EA* 96?

EA 95

Men from Meluḫḫa

TEXT: VAT 1668.
COPIES: WA 70; *VS* 11, 48.
TRANSLITERATION AND TRANSLATION: Youngblood, *Amarna Correspondence,* pp. 388ff.

Say [to] the magnate: [M]essage of Rib-Hadda. I fall at [your] feet. May Aman and the Lady of Gubla establish your honor in the presence of the king, your lord. 7–26 [A]s to your wr[it]ing me, . . .[1] 27–33 . . . The king of Mitta[ni] visited the land of Amurru itself, and he said, "How great is this land! Your land is extensive." May the [*kin*]*g* of Egypt [sen]d[2] me his commissioner that he may take it for him. 34–43 [Mor]eover, come yourself with all speed, and *t*[*ake*] everything. Then return to get the archer[s] later on. [Mo]reover, get [. . .][3] (and) get, too, 200 [men] of Meluḫḫa [. . .] ʿAbdi-Aširta is very *ill.*[4] [*Wh*]*o* knows, when he dies, [w]hat . . . 44–53 . . .[5]

NOTES

1. The dubious (*VAB* 2/1, p. 998) [*y*]*ú* before *ku-uš-da* in line 17 must be an incomplete *ù* ([Š]I + ⟨LU⟩). Line 20: ⌜*ú*⌝-*š*[*i*]-⌜*ru-bu*⌝-*ka*, "*I will* get you into the land of Amurru"; cf. *īrub,* "he entered," in line 25.

2. *yú-wa-š*[*i-r*]*a*: there is no reason to read -*r*]*u* (see copy of *VS* 11, which is accurate), and strong reasons against it; see *EA* 92, n. 12.

3. Since Nubian troops, with the single exception of *EA* 133:16f., always appear in conjunction with Egyptians (*EA* 70:18f.; 108:67; 112:19f.), or simply with soldiers (*EA* 127:36; 131:11ff.; 132:56), or finally with a garrison (*EA* 117:78ff.; see Pintore, *OA* 11 [1972] p. 105), we should undoubtedly restore 39 [x LÚ.MEŠ]. Since they are also regularly associated with protection, at the end of line 40 we should probably restore something like [*anaṣṣar*(*a*)/*tinaṣṣarū āla*], "that I/they may guard the city."

4. Of the eight other occurrences of *marāṣu*/*marṣu* in the letters from Byblos, not one clearly refers to physical illness, and several clearly refer to distress caused by enemies and the political situation (*EA* 103:7, 15, 49; 114:50; 116:54; 131:26; 362:59). Of the four occurrences of *murṣu,* two clearly refer to physical illness (*EA* 137:29, 32), two not clearly at all (*EA* 75:18; 116:58; see *EA* 75, n. 2). Therefore, ʿAbdi-Aširta may simply be under severe distress, especially since it is not clear who is the subject of BA.ÚŠ, *mâtu,* "to die," in the next line.

5. Line 44: after Šigata, probably URU [am-pí]; cf. *EA* 71:30f.; 76:19; 98:11f., 40f.

EA 96

The king's asses

TEXT: VAT 1238.
COPIES: WA 82; *VS* 11, 49.
TRANSLITERATION AND TRANSLATION: Youngblood, *BASOR* 168 (1962) pp. 24ff.

Say to Rib-Hadda, my son: Message of the general, your father. May (your personal) god show concern for you and your household. As to[1] your saying, "I will not permit men from Ṣumur to enter my city. There is a pestilence in Ṣumur," 12–27 is it a pestilence affect[ing] men or one affect[ing] asses? What pes[til]ence affects asses so that they cannot walk?[2] But *watch* [*out*]![3] Do the asses belong to the king or not? Properties of the king are not lost; indeed, their owner seeks them out. If the king is the owner of the asses, then look for the king's asses. Why do you act so towards servants of the king? 28–33 Send men [t]o guard the city. [And] at the same time I am writing [t]o the king about you. He is to [r]eply to me by tablet about the whole af[fair].

NOTES

1. *i*-[*n*]*u-ma* (text: GIŠ).

2. *ta-la-ku*-[*na*]: the writer seems to anticipate Rib-Hadda's claiming that the asses are unable to leave Byblos because they can no longer walk, or (cf. lines 20ff.) that they are lost.

3. *ú*-ṣ[ú-ur]: see *EA* 87, n. 6.

EA 97

A bad reputation

TEXT: VAT 1598.
COPIES: WA 183; *VS* 11, 50.

To Šumu-Hadd[i (. . .): Mes]sage of Yap*pa*[*ḫ-Hadda*]. May (your personal) god show concern for you. [*I* kn]ow that your reputation with the king is [b]ad, and so you cannot leave Egypt. 9–11 You did [n]ot cause the loss of [*the king's lands*; *ʿAbdi-Aširta* c]aused the loss.[1] 12–21 . . .

NOTE

1. 10 [mātāt šarri] ⌜*ú*⌝-*hal-li-iq* 11 [^{m}ÌR-a-ši-ir-ta . . .]. Cf. line 21, which mentions ʿAbdi-Aširta or perhaps "the son of ʿAbdi-Aširta." In *EA*, *ḫulluqu* always

has a place as object, and "destruction" is not necessarily physical, but rather (Egyptian) loss of political control. And the same is true of *ḫalāqu* with a place as subject; see Greenberg, *Ḫab/piru*, p. 44.

EA 98

Losses from Byblos to Ugarit

TEXT: VAT 1675.
COPIES: WA 128; *VS* 11, 15.

[S]ay [t]o Yanḫamu: Message of Yapaḫ-Hadda. Why have you been neglectful of Ṣumur so that all lands from Gubla to Ugarit have become enemies in the service of Aziru? 10–18 Šigata and Ampi are enemies. He has now [st]ationed ships of Arw[ad]a[1] [i]n Ampi and in Šigata so grain cannot be brought into Ṣumur. 19–26 Nor are we able to enter Ṣumur, and so what can we ourselves do? Write to the palace about this [mat]ter. It is good [tha]t you are inf⟨or⟩med.[2]

NOTES

1. [URU] *ar-w*[*a-d*]*a*: so also Na'aman, *Political Disposition*, p. 60*, n. 7.
2. *lum-*⟨*mu*⟩*-da-ta*: following *AHw*, p. 532, but perhaps better -⟨*mi*⟩- in view of the widespread use of *purris* as stative/perfect in *EA*. We should probably also allow for lam_x (LUM).

EA 99

From the Pharaoh to a vassal

TEXT: C 4742 (12196).
COPY: WA 202.
TRANSLATION: Oppenheim, *LFM*, p. 120.

[S]ay [to . . .] . . . , [*the ruler of* . . .] . . . :[1] Thus the king. *He* herewith sends this tablet to you, saying to you:[2] Be on your guard. You are to guard the place of the king where you are.[3] 10–20 Prepare your daughter for the king, your lord, and prepa⟨re⟩ the contributions:[4] [2]0 first-class slaves, silver,[5] chariots, first-class horses. And so let the king, your lord, say to you, "This is excellent,"[6] what you have given as contributions to the king to accompany your daughter. 21–26 And know that the king is hale like the Sun in the sky. For his troops and chariots in multitude all goes very well.[7]

NOTES

1. What Knudtzon read as *ma* in line 1 may not be a sign at all; indeed, it is not certain that there was anything inscribed on this "line." On this hypothesis, Gordon considered reading line 2 as line 1, and thus: [a-na ᵐz]i-[i]⌜r⌝-d⌜am⌝-*ia* -⌜aš-da⌝ (cf. *EA* 234:11). The traces, however, are extremely faint, and this reading would leave the addressee without indication of his place of residence, which would be unparalleled in the letters to vassals.

2. *u⌜š-t⌝e-bi-la-ku*: following Thureau-Dangin, *RA* 19 (1921) p. 100.

3. *uṣ-ṣur lu-ú* 8 *na-ṣa-ra-ta*: see Introduction, sect. 5.

4. On the girl as being given in marriage, and the translation of *šūšir* and *tāmarātu,* see Pintore, *Matrimonio,* p. 146, n. 21.

5. Not "silver-coated chariots" (Oppenheim).

6. *ši-ia-tù ba-an-tù*: as in *EA* 369:21.

7. Formulaic short form (see Introduction, sect. 5). *ma-a-du* (line 26, and regularly in both long and short forms) is probably not a predicate; cf. *mād* (*EA* 1:9) and perhaps *mādu* (*EA* 5:10), both from Egypt; *ina ma-a-du* ÉRIN.MEŠ-*ka* (*EA* 38:5) and *ma-du* ANŠE.KUR.RA.MEŠ-*ka* (*EA* 39:7), both from Alašia; and indeclinable *ma-a-ad* (*EA* 367:16f., also from Egypt).

EA 100

The city of Irqata to the king

TEXT: BM 29825.
COPY: BB 42.
PHOTOGRAPH: BB, pl. 4.

This tablet is a tablet from Irqata. To the king, our lord: Message from Irqata and its el⟨d⟩ers.[1] We fall at the feet of the king, our lord, 7 times and 7 times. To our lord, the Sun: Message from Irqata. May the heart of the king, (our) lord, know[2] that we guard Irqata for him. 11–19 When the [ki]ng, our lord, sent D[UMU]-*Bi-ḫa-a,* he said to [u]s, "Message of the king: Guard Irqata!"[3] The sons of the traitor to the king seek our harm;[4] Irqata see[ks][5] loyalty to the king. 20–32 As to [*silver*] having been given to S[u]baru al[ong with] 30 horses and cha[riots], may you know the mind of Irqata. When a tablet from the king arrived (saying) to *ra*[*id*] the land that the ʿA[*piru*] had taken [from] the king, *they wa*[*ged*] war with us against the enemy of our lord, the man whom you pla[ced] over us.[6] Truly we are guarding the *l*[*and*].[7] May the king, our lord, heed the words of his loyal servants. 33–44 May he grant a gift to his servant(s) so our enemies will see this and eat dirt.[8] May the breath of the king not depart from us.[9] We shall keep the city gate barred until the breath of the king reaches us. Severe is the war against us—terribly, terribly!

NOTES

1. *ši-b⟨u⟩-ti-ši*: following Albright, *JNES* 5 (1946) p. 23.

2. At the beginning of a letter, where *lū īde* is so common, *īde* probably has the force of a precative, as occasionally elsewhere (*EA* 84:21; 106:47; 137:30?; 144:18; etc.).

3. ⌜*ú*⌝*-ṣa-ru-mi,* though an anomalous form, must be the imperative of *naṣāru.* The king's order to guard the city was standard in letters to vassals (Introduction, sect. 5). Moreover, the writers here have just assured the king that they are guarding the city, and they go on to assert their loyalty, which their actions prove.

4. For *bu''û,* "to seek someone," in the sense of seeking his harm, cf. *EA* 125:38. Perhaps, however, we should not exclude *tuba''ūna* NU.⟨KÚR⟩, "in the king's regard, they are intent upon war, (but) Irqata is intent upon loyalty." This yields better parallelism.

5. *tu-b*[*a-ú*], since this letter has the same verbal system as the Byblos letters.

6. I understand this very difficult passage as follows: the loyalty of Irqata had been questioned by the king, who had learned of the city's giving gifts to Mittani. The writers defend themselves by pointing out that Mittani had cooperated in the war against ʿAbdi-Aširta and his ʿApiru followers, the very ones responsible for killing their own king whom the Pharaoh had placed over them (cf. *EA* 75:26f.; 139:15; 140:10). In other words, the gifts were only right and proper. Readings: Line 25: *ana ša*-[ḫa-aṭ] (*šaḫāṭu,* "to raid," fairly common in *EA*). Lines 26f.: LÚ.MEŠ G[AZ iš-tu]. Line 27: LUGAL-*ri* (enough room in 26?). Line 28: K[Ú]R is virtually certain. Line 29: "our lord" is not the Egyptian king, but the Irqata king who had been killed; *ti-eš-ta-*[*kán-*(*šu*)] (in *EA, šapāru eli/muḫḫi,* which Knudtzon restores here, means only "to write about"; *šitkunu eli/muḫḫi,* said of royal appointments, see *EA* 101:30). If my understanding of this passage is at all correct, then the attack on Amurru may have contributed to the capture of ʿAbdi-Aširta (cf. *EA* 108:28ff.; 117:24ff.).

7. Instead of K[UR] (*māta*), "land," perhaps K[I] (*ašru*), "place"; cf. the frequent expression *ašar šarri ša ittīka naṣāru.*

8. "To eat dirt" means "to be defeated" (*CAD,* A/1, p. 256).

9. On the "breath" (*šāru*) of the king, which is his message and gives life to his vassal, see esp. *EA* 141, 143–45, and also the same use of the synonymous *šēḫu* in the letters of Abi-Milku (*EA* 146–55). On the Egyptian background, see Lorton, *The Juridical Terminology of International Relations in Egyptian Texts through Dynasty XVIII* (see Introduction, n. 4), pp. 136ff. Though the conception as it appears in *EA* is undoubtedly of Egyptian origin, the influence of the West Semitic substratum is probably to be seen in the feminine gender agreement (*EA* 100:37; 141:15; 297:18; cf. Hebrew *rûaḥ,* "breath," fem.).

EA 101

The death of ʿAbdi-Aširta

TEXT: BM 29827.
COPY: BB 44.

Moreover,[1] why[2] is there war [*against*] the king? Is it not Ḫaya?[3] [*No*]*w*, the ships of the army are not to enter the land of Amurru, for they have killed ʿAbdi-Aširta,[4] since they had no wool and he had no garments of lapis lazuli or MAR-stone color : *bu-bu-mar*(?) to give as tribute[5] to the land of Mittana. 11–18 Moreover, whose ships have attacked me? Is it not the men of Arwada? Indeed, they are now with you. Seize the ships of the men of Arwada that are with you in Egypt. 18–25 Moreover, though Ḫaya [s]ays, "[. . .] . . . If *we* [do] not [*give*][6] (it) to the land of Amurru, then [*the men*] of *Tyre*[7] and the men of Sidon and the men of Beirut will furnish (it)," 25–31 to whom do these cities belong? Is it not to the king? Put a man in each city and let him not allow a ship from the land of Amurru (to enter), for they have killed ʿAbdi-Aširta.[8] It was the king that placed him over them, not they! 32–38 Let the king tell the 3 cities and the ships of the army not to go to the land of Amurru. *If* a servant seize a *bo*[*a*]*t*,[9] let him give it to you. Be informed of the affairs of your loyal servant.

NOTES

1. This is the second of a two-tablet letter, like *EA* 113, 245, 251, and Wilhelm, *ZA* 63 (1973) pp. 69ff. It is almost certainly addressed to the king, and very probably by Rib-Hadda; see *Eretz Israel* 9 (1969) p. 94, n. 1; Altman, *UF* 9 (1977) p. 8.

2. *mīnu*, "why," as in *EA* 126:14, 19; 138:138.

3. Perhaps Ḫaya is here absolved of responsibility, so that this should be read, "Not (because of) Ḫaya" (Na'aman, *Political Disposition*, p. 63*, n. 33). If, however, I understand the thrust of lines 18ff., Ḫaya is criticized for the advice he gives the king, and therefore I assume that he is also criticized here.

4. For another interpretation of these lines ("if/when the ships of the army do not enter . . . , then they will kill . . .") and its implications, see Altman, *UF* 9 (1977) pp. 7f.

5. GÚ.UN: see *RA* 69 (1975) p. 158; so also, independently, Na'aman, *Political Disposition*, p. 10.

6. [na-ad-nu] ⸢ni⸣-*nu*: for the form, cf. *na-ad-na* (*EA* 89:16).

7. [U]RU ṣur-*ri*: following Na'aman, ibid., p. 63*, n. 33.

8. See n. 4.

9. The reading ᵐÌR-*a*-⟨*ši*⟩-*ir*-[*t*]*a* (*Or* n.s. 29 [1960] p. 11, n. 3) is quite wrong, and Knudtzon's description (*VAB* 2/1, pp. 454f., notes c and e) is exact. The last sign could not possibly be [*t*]*a*, as the space is much too small, and of

course we may not assume a writing of the name with one sign omitted and an unparalleled [*t*]*a*₅. Very tentatively, *u ṣabāt* (for the use of the infinitive, see *JCS* 4 [1950] pp. 169ff.) ᵐÌR (for the determinative with common nouns, see Böhl, *Sprache*, pp. 9f.) *a*-ni-[t]a₅ (cf. *a-na-yi, EA* 245:28; Hebrew *'ᵒniyyā*). Any Amurru ship intercepted is to be turned over to the king.

EA 102

An empty house

TEXT: BM 29806.
COPY: BB 23.

[S]ay [to . . .] . . . [. . .]:[1] Message of Rib-Hadda. I fall at your feet. May the Lady of Gubla, the goddess of the king, my lord, establish your honor in the presence of the king, your lord, the Sun of all countries. 8–19 Moreover, you know that, though informed, you have delayed coming out. Why did you write?[2] Now you are going to come into an empty house.[3] Everything is gone. *I am utterly ruined.* Moreover, as to your writing me, "Go, stay in Ṣumur until I arrive," know[4] that the war against me is very severe and I have been unable to go. 20–28 Now Ampi is at war with me. Know t⟨hat⟩ the magnate and the lords[5] of the city are at peace with the sons of ʿAbdi-Aširta, and accordingly I am unable to go. Know that all are traitors, and you must not inquire about me from my enemies. Now, because of the situation, I am afraid. 28–38 Moreover, listen to me. Hasten your arrival with all speed, and go in there. Know that they are traitors. Moreover, do not [*del*]*ay* your arrival, [and *send*] archers [*to capture the city of the king*], *your* [*lord.*[6] *Go*] *in.* Do *not be* afraid. [*As soon as* you *en*]*ter*[7] the city, it is from there that you must write [*me*].

NOTES

1. Perhaps addressed to [ᵐia-an-ḫa]-m[i] (Knudtzon).

2. The analysis of *tašapparta* and the even more difficult *ti-iḫ-ta-ti* (line 13) remains uncertain; see Rainey, *UF* 5 (1973) pp. 257f. The same letter is referred to in lines 14ff.

3. An "empty house" seems to have been a popular image of destitution and desolation: cf. *EA* 316:16ff.; "you left me in an empty house" (Old Assyrian; K. Balkan, *Letter of King Anum-ḫirbi of Mama to King Warshama of Kanish* (Ankara, 1957), p. 16, n. 20); "I am desolate in an empty [house]" (Taanach Letter, no. 2:6, trans. of Albert E. Glock, *Berytus* 31 [1983] p. 60, n. 27); "I have entered an empty house, an empty ruin" (A. 818, cited by *AÉM* 1/1, no. 234, note a).

4. In this and the following lines *ti-di* seems best taken as an injunctive.

5. The property owners (also *EA* 138:49). Cf. the similar use of *baʿal* in

Hebrew and Ugaritic (*b ʿl ḫlb,* "the lords of Ḫalba," *Ugar.* 7, p. 143); see Reviv, *IEJ* 16 (1966) pp. 252f.

6. Free restoration.

7. [ù ir]-*ba-ta*: the word order, with the adverbial phrase fronted, stresses where the letter should be written.

EA 103

Critical days for Ṣumur

TEXT: VAT 1208.
COPY: WA 77; *VS* 11, 52.

[T]o the king, my lord, my Sun: Message of Rib-Hadda, your servant. I fall at the feet of my lord, my Sun, 7 times and 7 times. 5–19 May the king, my lord, heed the words of his loyal servant. My situation is very difficult. The war of the sons of ʿAbdi-Aširta against me is severe. They have occupied the land of Amurru, and the entire country is theirs. Ṣumur and Irqata remain to the magnate. I *have* now *been*[1] in Ṣumur because the magnate is in difficulty due to the war. I left Gubla, but Zimredda and Yapaḫ-Hadda were no[t wi]th me.[2] 20–29 So the [mag]nate keeps writing [t]o them, but they pay n[o] attention to him. May the king, my lord, heed the [w]ords of his loyal servant. [S]end an auxiliary force with all speed to Ṣumur in order to guard [i]t [un]til the arrival of the archers of the king, the Sun. 30–39 May the king, the Sun, expel the traitors from his land. Moreover, may the king, my lord, heed the words of his loyal servant. Sen⟨d⟩ a garrison to Ṣumur and to [I]rqata. As the entire garrison has fled from Ṣumur, 40–49 may it seem right in the s[igh]t of the lord, the Sun of all countries, and give me 20 pairs of horses, and send an auxiliary force with all speed to Ṣumur in order to guard it. Whatever is left of the garrison is in difficulty,[3] 50–57 and few people are still in the city. If you do not ⟨⟨not⟩⟩ se⟨n⟩d archers, then there will not be a city remaining to you. But if arch[ers] are on hand, we will take all the lands for the king.

NOTES

1. Perhaps "I am now in Ṣumur," and therefore *EA* 103 would have been written from there. The siege of Ṣumur, which begins to be mentioned in *EA* 104, had apparently not yet begun.

2. *ia*-[nu], "were not with me," i.e., did not assist? Cf. *VAB* 2/2, p. 1201, n. 1.

3. Probably *ma-ar-ṣa-⟨at⟩*: following Rainey, *UF* 5 (1973) p. 256; see *EA* 114, n. 5.

EA 104

Ullassa taken

TEXT: C 4751 (not collated).
COPY: WA 60.

Say to the king, my lord, my Sun: Message of Rib-Hadda, your servant. I fall at the feet of my lord, my Sun 7 times and 7 times. 6–13 May the king, my lord, know that Pu-Baḫla, the son of ʿAbdi-Aširta, has occupied Ullassa. Theirs are Ardata, Waḫliya, Ampi, Šigata. All the cities are theirs. 14–26 So may the king send an auxiliary force to Ṣumur until the king gives thought to his land. Who are the sons of ʿAbdi-Aširta, the servant and dog? Are they the king of Kaššu or the king of Mittani that they take the land of the king for themselves? Previously, they would t[ak]e cities of your mayors, and you did nothing. 27–39 Now they have driv[en] out your commissioner and have taken his cities for themselves. They have taken Ullassa. If in these circumstances you do nothing, then they are certainly going to take Ṣumur and kill the commissioner and the auxiliary force[1] in Ṣumur. What am I to do? I cannot go personally to Ṣumur; 40–48 the cities of Ampi, Šigata, Ullassa, Erwada,[2] are at war with me. Should they ⟨⟨they⟩⟩ hear[3] that I was entering Ṣumur, there would be these cities with ships, and the sons of ʿAbdi-Aširta in the countryside.[4] 49–54 They would attack ⟨me⟩, and I would be unable to get out, and Gubla would be joined [t]o the ʿApiru. They have gone to Ibirta, and an agreement has been made with the ʿApiru.[5]

NOTES

1. ÉRIN.MEŠ BI-*la-ti*: either BI = til_x or probably simply a mistake for *til* (BE). The phrase is more probably the object of *tidūkūna*, "they will kill" (so also Ebeling, *VAB* 2/2, p. 1402; Greenberg, *Ḫab/piru*, p. 38) than the subject of *i-pu-šu-na*, "what will the auxiliary forces do?" (Knudtzon, followed by Liverani, *AoF* 1 [1974] p. 186). Against the latter view are several considerations: (1) the assumed position of the interrogative pronoun (unparalleled in the Byblos letters); (2) attested usage, *i-pu-šu-na*, 10 times first person, never third (on *EA* 119:18, see below); (3) *mīna īpušuna/ippušuna*, "what shall I do?," is a stock phrase of the Byblos letters. See also Izre'el, *UF* 19 (1987) pp. 79ff.

2. URU er_4*-wa-da*, or perhaps simply a mistake, but certainly Arwada is the city in question; see *RA* 69 (1975) p. 157, n. 4.

3. *šamâ-ma*, third plural feminine; so also *izzizā* (line 49), *alkā* (line 52), perhaps *ennepšā* (line 52), agreement with "cities" understood, *ālu* being regularly construed as feminine in Canaanite *EA*. See *SSDB*, p. 164; Greenberg, *Ḫab/piru*, p. 38.

4. See *RA* 69 (1975) p. 157.

5. So *CAD,* E, p. 216. Less likely from the viewpoint of attested usage, though perhaps yielding better sense, in "and (t)here (too) (the city) has gone over to the ʿApiru" (Greenberg, *Ḫab/piru,* p. 38; cf. Bottéro, *Ḫabiru,* p. 92). *pu-ú* = Canaanite *pô,* "here, in this place" (Böhl, *Sprache,* p. 71); *en-ni-ip-ša-⟨at⟩*.

EA 105

Ṣumur under siege

TEXT: VAT 1628.

COPIES: WA 51; *VS* 11, 53.

Rib-Hadda says to [his] lord, Great King, king of all countries, the King of Batt[le]: May the Lady of Gubla grant power to the king, my lord. I fall at the feet of my lord, my Sun, 7 times and 7 times. 6–13 Moreover, may the king give thought to Ṣumur. Look at Ṣumur! Like a bird in a trap : *ki-lu-bi* (cage), so is Ṣumur; the sons of ʿAbdi-Aširta by land, the people of Arwada by sea, are agai[nst it] day and night. 14–21 I se⟨n⟩t 3 *s[hi]ps* to Yanḫamu, [*but ships*] of the people of Arwada were (there) to intercept *th[em]*, and out they came! Consider the case of the people of Arwada. When the archers came out, all the proper⟨ty⟩ of ʿAbdi-Aširta in their possession was not taken away, and their ships, by an agreement, left Egypt. 21–33 Accordingly, they are not afraid. Now they have taken Ullassa, and they strive to take Ṣumur. Everything belonging to ʿAbdi-Aširta they gave to the [so]ns, and so now they are strong. They have taken the army ships together with everything belonging to them, and I am unable to go to the aid of Ṣumur. Yapaḫ-Hadda is at war with me because of [my] property in his possession. 33–45 Let us put the case before Aman-... and DUMU-B*i-ḫa-a* and before Yanḫamu, for they are the ones that know what is my due[1] concerning [...]. Because my property in his possession is considerable, he has accordingly waged war against me. When I heard of the *ca[ptu]re*[2] of Ullassa, I wro[te *repeatedly*][3] [...] ... to him, but he [*r*]*aide[d* ...] and too[k ...]. He has wa[ged *war* agai]nst me. 46–78 ...[4] 79–88 [*May he* s]end [... that w]e may put the case be[fore them].[5] May [*an*]y property of mine in his possession be taken for the king, and let the faithful servant live for the king. The Egyptians that got out of Ullassa are now with me, but there is no [gr]ain for them to eat. Yapaḫ-Hadda does not let my ships [in]to Yarimuta, and I cannot send them to Ṣumur because of the ships of Arwada. Look, he says, "Rib-[Hadda *to*]*ok* [*i*]*t, a*[*nd s*]*o* he is against *m*[*e*]." [...]

NOTES

1. See *EA* 118, n. 1.
2. ṣ[a-ba]t.
3. "Repeatedly," if with Knudtzon one reads *aš-*[*t*]*a-pa-*[*ru*]; otherwise, *aš-*[*t*]*a-pa-*[*ar*] (cf. *EA* 74:49; 75:17; 132:12), and simply "I wrote."
4. Line 76, end: [. . . *mi*]*-im-mi-ia* (cf. lines 32, 38, 81); in the last sign, the wedges are very compressed.
5. *ina* [*pa-ni-šu-nu*].

EA 106

Ṣumur holding out

TEXT: VAT 344.
COPIES: WA 43; *VS* 11, 52.

Rib-Hadda says t[o his lord, Great King], the king[1] of all countries: I fall at the feet [of my lord, *the kin*]*g*, 7 times and 7 times. Gubla is [from] ancient times the loyal city of my lord, the Sun of all countries, and I am a footstool for the feet of the king, my lord, and his loyal servant. 8–13 Now as for Ṣumur, the war against it is severe, and it is severe against me. Ṣumur is now raided up to its city gate. They have been able to raid it, but they have not been able to capture it. 13–22 Moreover, "Why does Rib-Hadda keep sending a tablet this way to the palace?"[2] He is more *distraught*[3] than his brothers about Ṣumur. Look, in my case, there has been war against me for 5 years.[4] Accordingly, I keep writing to my lord. Look, I am not like Yapaḫ-Hadda, and I am not like Zimredda. All brothers have des[erted] me. There is war against Ṣumur, and now its commissioner is dead. 23–29 Indeed, I myself am now in distress. I was in [Ṣumur], and all its people f[led]. May my lord [s]end [a commissioner and troop]s with him with al[l speed that he may g]uard it.[5] I myself *can*[*not get out*].[6] [*Let* him] move in between the two of them th[at *are against it*].[7] 30–40 How can the king say, "Why does Rib-Hadda keep sending a tablet to his lord?" Because of the evil that was do[ne][8] before, and especially so nothing like this will be done to me now! Moreover, may it seem right in the sight of [my] lor[d], and may he send Yanḫamu as its commissioner, Yanḫamu the parasol-bearer[9] of the king, my lord. I have heard it reported that he is a wise man and (that) everyone loves him. 41–49 Moreover, may it seem rig⟨h⟩t to my lord, and may he send 20 pairs of first-class horses to his servant—there are many men on my side—so that I can march against the enemies of the king, my lord.

Moreover, as for all my cities that I have reported on to the king, my lord, as my lord is witness, they have not returned. The day the troops of my lord's expeditionary force[10] left, all became enemies.

NOTES

1. LUGAL-*ri*: the apparent NUN, which would be unparalleled, is a carelessly formed *ri*; cf. LUGAL-*ri* KUR.KUR.KI in *EA* 123:3. Line 2: . . . GÌR.M[EŠ BE-*ia* LUGAL?-r]i.

2. This seems to be a quotation from a letter of the king, as in lines 30ff. The king found Rib-Hadda an excessively diligent correspondent (see the Introduction, sect. 5).

3. *ma-an-ga*: following Thureau-Dangin, *RA* 19 (1922) p. 92, n. 3; see also Rainey, AOAT², p. 80. I. Kottsieper, *UF* 20 (1988) pp. 125ff., argues in favor of a Northwest Semitic root *mgg*, "to war, to fight."

4. For the syntax, see Gianto, *Word Order Variation in the Akkadian of Byblos* (see *EA* 88, n. 10), p. 51.

5. [*li-iṣ*]-*ṣur-ši*: as in *EA* 84:28 (on the scribe of *EA* 84 and 106, see 84, n. 1), though [(*ù*) *yi-na*]-*ṣár-ši* is possible. In any case, an injunctive is required.

6. *u*-[ṣú-ú/na]: the form is unattested.

7. *bi-ri-šu-ni š*[*a* UGU-ši]: the dual pronominal suffix (*BASOR* 211 [1973] pp. 50ff.; see also Na'aman, *Political Disposition,* p. 19*, n. 6) probably refers to the forces, sea and land, that surround Ṣumur (*EA* 104:46ff.; 105:11ff.).

8. *i-ni-pu-*[*uš*].

9. Following Helck, *Beziehungen,* p. 249, who sees here a reflection of Egyptian *ḫbśw bh*(*.t*). Albright, *JNES* 5 (1946) p. 13, "fan-bearer," follows Ranke in Weber, *VAB* 2/2, p. 1173, and he is followed by *AHw,* p. 1110, and *CAD,* Ṣ, p. 240.

10. ÉRIN.MEŠ KI.KAL.KASKAL + ?.BAD: cf. ÉRIN.MEŠ KAL.KASKAL + ?.[BAD?] (*EA* 58, n. 3) and KAL.BAD.KASKAL + ? (*EA* 92, n. 13). I interpret the logograms as variants and the equivalent of KI.KAL.BAD/KALxBAD, *karašu,* "camp, expeditionary force"; cf. ÉRIN.MEŠ *ka-ra-*[*š*]*i* (*EA* 83:43) and [ÉRIN.MEŠ *k*]*a-ra-š*[*u* (*EA* 134:39). The unidentified sign, given the likely meaning, is probably formed with KASKAL. P. Steinkeller suggests KASxŠUDUN (private communication).

EA 107

Charioteers but no horses

TEXT: VAT 346.

COPIES: WA 41; *VS* 11, 55.

Rib-Hadda says to ⟨his⟩ lord, king of all countries, Great King, King of Battle: May the Lady of Gubla grant power to the king, my lord. I fall at the feet of my lord, my Sun, 7 times and 7 times. Being a loyal servant of the king, the Sun, 10–19 with my mouth I speak words to the king that are nothing but the truth. May the king, my lord, heed the words of his loyal servant. May the archer-commander[1] stay in Ṣumur, but fetch Ḫa'ip to yourself, examine him, and find out about [his] affai[rs]. 20–28 Then if it pleas[es] you, appoint as its commissioner someone respected by the kin[g's] mayors.[2] May my lord heed my words. Seeing that Aziru, the son of ʿAbdi-Aširta, is in Damascus along with his brothers, 29–36 send archers that they might take him, and the land of the king be at peace. If things go as they are now, Ṣumur will not stand. Moreover, may the king, my lord, heed the words of his loyal servant. 37–48 There is no money to pay for horses; everything is gone so that we might stay alive. So give me 30 pairs of horses along with chariots. I have *charioteers* [:] *mar-ia-nu-ma,*[3] but I do not have a horse to march against the enemies of the king. Accordingly, I am afraid, and accordingly, I have not gone to Ṣumur.

NOTES

1. ᵐ*iḫ-ri-pí-ṭa*: Egyptian *ḥry-pḏt,* with Albright, *JNES* 5 (1946) p. 14.

2. Read *šukun ina rābiṣi-ši* DUGUD (*kabta*) *ina* . . . ; see *RA* 69 (1975) pp. 155f., and cf. also *EA* 129:15f.

3. The sign(s) at the end of line 42 are still unidentified; see *EA* 108, n. 2. On the gloss, with its Canaanite plural formation, see Schroeder, *OLZ*, 1918, cols. 125ff., and Helck, *Beziehungen*, p. 483.

EA 108

Unheard-of deeds

TEXT: VAT 345.
COPIES: WA 42; *VS* 11, 56.

Rib-Hadda writes to his lord, king of all countries, Great King, King of Battle: May the Lady of Gubla grant power to the king, my lord. 6–17 I fall at the feet of my lord, my Sun, 7 times and 7 times. Moreover, is it pleasing in the sight of the king, who is like Baal and Šamaš in the sky,[1] that the sons of ʿAbdi-Aširta do as they please? They have taken the king's horses and chariots, and they have sold *into captivity charioteers* : *ši*-x-y(?)[2] and soldiers to ⟨⟨to⟩⟩ the land of Su⟨ba⟩ru.[3] 18–25 In whose lifetime has such a deed been done? False words are now being spoken in the presence of the king, the Sun. I am your loyal servant, and whatever I know or have heard I write to the king, my lord. 25–33 Wh[o] are they, the dogs, that they could *res*[*ist*][4] the archers of the king, the Sun? I wrote t[o] ⟨⟨to⟩⟩ your father, and he he[eded] my wor[d]s, and he sent ar[ch]ers. Did he not take ʿAbdi-Aširta for *h*[*imself*]?[5] 34–45 Moreover, since the mayors have not oppo[sed] th[em], they are stron[g].[6] The army furnishes whatever they ne[ed], and so they are not afra[id] of the magnate. Because they have taken the hors[es], they are bold.[7] Because we know that they are strong, we have *to*⟨*ld*⟩ the king, "They are strong."[8] Truly, they will not prevail. 46–58 When I sent 2 messengers to Ṣumur, I retained this man in order to report to the king. Moreover, why do you listen to other men? The king's messengers must bring (news) by night and bring (it) back by night because of the dog. If the king, the Sun, desires, they will be taken in a day.[9] 59–69 Moreover, has he [n]o[t] *plotted* evils [*upon evils a*]*gainst* you,[10] and *rev*[*olted*? A]nd as for the man of [*my*] *god,* ʿApiru came from Ṣumur to take him prisoner, but I did not give him up. May the [k]ing he[ed] the words of his servant. Send me [2]0 men from Meluḫḫa and 20 men from Egypt to guard the city for the king, the Sun, my lord. ⟨I am⟩ your loyal se[rvan]t.

NOTES

1. The storm god (perhaps Haddu rather than Baal) and the sun god; cf. *EA* 147:14.

2. The same logogram as *EA* 107:42; the gloss (second and third signs ni/ir?-ba/ma, respectively) remains unexplained. The reading of the logogram as KEŠDA and the explanation of the gloss as identification of the sign (ŠÌR; so *SSDB,* p. 166) are to be rejected.

3. Cf. *EA* 109:40.

4. *ti*-z[*i*-zu-na].

5. š[a-šu]: perhaps, with Rainey, *UF* 7 (1975) p. 400, n. 56, "was not ʿAbdi-Aširta taken to *him?*" Rib-Hadda returns to this event (*EA* 117:27f.; 132:16ff.; 138:33f.; 362:20).

6. On lines 34–38, see *JCS* 7 (1953) p. 79.

7. KALAG.GA (*dannū*) *ina pānīšunu,* lit. "they are strong in their face," reflects Canaanite idiom; cf. *Proverbs* 7:13, *hēʿēzā pānêhā,* "she 'strengthens' her face," i.e., "she acts boldly"; 21:29, *hēʿēz 'îš rāšāʿ bᵉpānau,* "a wicked man 'shows strong' in his face; *Qohelet* 8:1, *ʿoz pānîm*; *Deuteronomy* 28:50, *ʿaz pānîm.*

8. If *ni-iq*-⟨bi⟩, then the enclitic in KALAG.GA (*dannū*)*-me* marks direct quotation.

9. On UD.KAM.MEŠ as singular, see *EA* 109:16ff. Total victory in a single day, which is also promised in *EA* 109:16ff., 117:60ff., and 132:10ff. (cf. 70:27ff.), was of course a display of power and something to boast about; see the texts cited by Stuart, *BASOR* 211 (1976) pp. 161ff., and Sollberger-Kupper, *Inscriptions royales sumériennes et akkadiennes* (Paris, 1971), pp. 157f., III A5b–c; *RLA* 5, p. 6b.

10. *ul yaškun* 60 *lum-ni* [lum-ni-ma *i*]*-na lìb-bi* [U]GU?*-ka* 61 *ù pa*-[ṭa-ar] ⌜*ù*⌝ LÚ DINGIR-[ia]: cf. *lumna lumna-ma šakānu* in *EA* 113:12f. (with *ana*) and 116:41f. (with UGU, *eli*/*muḫḫi*); after *libbi,* possibly traces (*šu*?).

EA 109

Then and now

TEXT: VAT 1629.
COPIES: WA 52; *VS* 11, 57.

Rib-Hadda [says] to his lord, king of all lands, [Great] King: May the Lady of Gubla grant power to the king, my lord. I fall at the feet of my lord, my Sun, 7 times and 7 times. In times past, 6–14 whenever the [ki]ng of Mittana was at war with your ancestors, your ancestors did not deser[t my] ance[stors]. Now the sons of ʿAbdi-Aširta, the [servan]t and dog, have t[aken] the cities of the king and the [ci]ties of his mayor, just as they please; they are the ones that [took] *A*[*rdat*]*a* for themselves. And you did nothing [about t]heir [actions] when you heard (of them). 15–25 [*And so*][1] they have taken [Ull]assa. For my part, I keep saying, "[If] the king gives heed for a [d]ay, in (that) day the king will take them. [And i]f he gives heed for a night, [in (that) n]ight he will take them."[2] Accordingly, I *am* [*fi*]*rm*[3] in my resolve. They have taken [*the treas*]*ures*[4] of your mayors, and [*they have tak*]*en* the [*charioteers*], your chariots, and soldiers, [but] you have done nothing. Accordingly, they *are fi*[*rm*][5] in their [resol]ve, and they intend crime upon cri[me]. 25–29 [Being at war] with me, they seized [12 men of mine];[6] they bound ⟨th⟩em,[7] (and) they are *in pri*[*son*].[8] The rans[om price] between us they have set as 50 (shekels of) silver,[9] and [. . .] 30–34 . . . 35–46 They go about and [. . .]. They are the ones who have *kidnapped,*[10] and [. . .] Yanḫamu knows. The king [. . .] a man. They put him in [. . .] : *tu-uḫ-nu*(?), and they sold a soldier *into captivity* in Subaru for their food. Look, I am a loyal servant of the king, [and] the king has no servant like me. Previously, on seeing a man from Egypt, the kings of Canaan fled bef[ore him, 47–55 but] now the sons of ʿAbdi-Aširta make men from Egypt prowl about [*like do*]*gs.*[11] Death would be sweet t[o m]e.[12] Let them [*not*] be *arrogant* towards my lord and [*towards*] my [li]fe.[13] As all our gods [*and the Lady o*]*f* Gubla *live,* ⟨*tr*⟩*uly*[14] [*h*]*e* is a man that intends evil fo[r h]is [lord]. (But) note well,[15] it is power, only power, that I intend for my lord. 56–69 Moreover, I am una[ble] to [g]et this man of yours into Ṣ[um]ur. All my towns are at war with me, on the side of the sons of ʿAbdi-Aširta. Accordingly, they are strong. The mayors are not just to me. [W]hen Ḫa[ya and A]manap[pa de]parted fro[m Ṣu]mur, along with the copper [*and*] his [. . . t]hey sai[d that] I [was your loyal servant].

NOTES

1. [ù URU *ul-l*]*a-sà*.

2. 16 [*šum-ma* UD.K]AM.MEŠ *yišmu šarru* 17 [*ù* UD].KAM.MEŠ *yi-ìl-ti-qú-šu-nu*. The parallelism with the singular *mūša*, "night," in the following lines, and the absence of MEŠ in the roughly parallel *EA* 117:63 (*ina* UD.KAM), favor taking the logogram as singular and another example of otiose MEŠ.

3. [ka-i]a$_8$-*a-na-ku*, and in line 23, *ka*-i[a$_8$-nu]: the assumed syllabary (*ia*$_8$) and the absence of parallels make these readings very tentative.

4. [NÍG.G]A (*makkūru*): *makkūru* is otherwise unattested in the Middle Babylonian periphery, with the possible exception of *EA* 138:106.

5. See n. 3.

6. [12 LÚ.MEŠ-*ia*]: cf. *EA* 114:8; if not enough room, then probably the number was omitted.

7. *ra-ak-šu-⟨šu⟩-nu*.

8. É [ki-li]: *bīt kīli* is well attested in the Western Periphery.

9. A ransom price of 50 minas (Knudtzon; *CAD*, I/J, p. 172), even if the ransom of all twelve men, would come to 250 shekels a person, an improbably high price. In *EA* 292, 100 shekels are considered outrageously high. Therefore, 50 shekels per person; cf. *EA* 91, n. 4.

10. *ša-ra-qú-ma*: interpreted as Canaanite perfect and translated according to context, but perhaps better *šarrāqū-ma*, "they are thieves" (*AHw*, p. 1188; Rainey, AOAT², p. 93).

11. *māt mi-iṣ-r*[*i* ki-ma] 49 [UR].KU.MEŠ: the verb must be *dâlu* (also *EA* 114:65, and perhaps 110:54); the assumption of scribal error both here and in *EA* 114 (*CAD*, D, p. 59b) is most implausible. The meaning is clearly transitive, and therefore we must assume either a confusion of the G and D conjugations, or another example of the sporadic replacement of *ul/tu*-person marker by *i/ti*. Perhaps *dâlu* contrasts with the proper orderly advance of troops; it is an action typical of dogs (see the dictionaries). *AÉM* 1/2, no. 391:50–52 suggests hesitant or evasive action ("tergiverser"; see note k), which would also fit here and in *EA* 114.

12. *damiq mūtu a*-[na ia]-*ši*: against [giš].TUKUL.MEŠ (*kakkī*) *da-mi iq-mu-dú*, "they laid hold of weapons of blood" (*AHw*, p. 896), apart from the unusually vivid language, are the following: (1) GIŠ is too small a sign for the space (as Knudtzon already noted in *VAB* 2/1, p. 484, note b); (2) *kakku* is attested only once in *EA*, and then in a literary text (*EA* 359:4; on 20:80, see above, *EA* 20, n. 17), and is extremely rare in the Middle Babylonian western periphery (*CAD*, K, lists under *kakku* three occurrences, deleting reference to *EA* 20:80; and under *bēl kakki* three occurrences at Alalaḫ, plus its use as a Sumero-Akkadogram at Boghazköy); (3) the value *dú* is not expected in the Byblos syllabary; and (4) the verb is extremely rare and the sense otherwise unattested.

13. [la t]i-*iš-mu-ḫu*$_5$: the assumption of *ḫu*$_5$ is difficult; cf. the Old Assyrian meaning of the verb, "to act independently(?)" (*AHw*, p. 1153b).

14. 53 [T]I.LA ⟨a⟩-d[i šu-u]t: for the assumed *liblutu*, cf. TI (*liblut*), *EA* 74:15; *liblut šarru*, *EA* 85:39, 86; 256:10f.; 289:37; for ⟨*a*⟩*di*, cf. *adi* introducing the object of an oath in *EA* 85:40, 86 (see n. 7) and its use elsewhere as an asseverative particle.

15. *šumma*: see *EA* 35, n. 3.

EA 110

The army's ships

TEXT: VAT 1666.

COPIES: WA 64 (a.e.b.c.); *VS* 11, 58.

. . .[1] 48–54 [*N*]*o* ship of the [ar]my [*is*] *to lea*[*ve*] *Can*[*aan*].[2] [W]hy does he not giv[e *me*] (some of) the royal [*pro*]*perty* that the ships of the army *tr*[*ansport*,[3] *and then*][4] the mayors a[nd . . . *trans*]*port*[5] to [*Aziru*]. 55–end . . .

NOTES

1. Letter to the king; references to Aziru. 40 [. . . mi]-*i-na la-a yú-ṣú*, "Why does he not come out?"

2. KUR ⌜ki⌝-n[a-aḫ-ni]: so also Na'aman, *Political Disposition*, p. 1*, n. 14; cf. *EA* 101:3f.

3. *t*[*u*-ba-lu-na]: cf. *EA* 108:39, and below, line 54; also *EA* 111:23.

4. 52 . . . LÚ.MEŠ *mi-š*[*i* ù].

5. [tu-ba]-*lu-na*.

EA 111

Army activities

TEXT: VAT 1631.

COPIES: WA 68; *VS* 11, 59.

. . .[1] 17–24 [If] this [year] there [are no a]rchers, then all lands [will be joined] to "the ʿApi]ru. Look, members of the ar[my] have en[ter]ed Akka [*in*] *or*[*der to tr*]*ansport*[2] . . . [. . .] [*nee*]*ded* by the king. 25–end . . .

NOTES

1. Letter to the king, which probably began by recalling how often Rib-Hadda had written in vain for a garrison and then renewing the request. At the beginning of line 17, : *ba-lu*, or does the *Glossenkeil* indicate a runover line? tu]- : *ba-lu*?

2. 22 *i*[*r-ru*]-*bu*: perhaps, following Na'aman, *Political Disposition*, p. 48. 23 [aš]-šu[m a]-*ba-li* x-[. . .]: cf. *ḫišiḫta abālu*, *EA* 108:39. Na'aman, ibid., proposes *aššum ba-li*-i[ṭ ù], *baliṭ* being either stative or a noun and variant of *balāṭu*, "provisions."

EA 112

Questions for the king

TEXT: VAT 1664.
COPIES: WA 57; *VS* 11, 61.

Rib-[Hadda says t]o his lord, ki[ng of all lands], Great [K]ing: [I] fall at the feet of [my] lord, my Sun, 7 times and 7 times. Why does the king, my lord, write to me, 9–15 "Guard! Be on your guard!" With what[1] shall I guard? With my enemies, or with my peasantry? Who would guard me? If the king guards his servant, [then I will survi]ve. 16–24 [But i]f the [ki]ng does not [gu]ard me, who will guard me? If the king sends men from Egypt and Meluḫḫa, and horses in the charge of this man of mine, with all speed, then I will survive to serve the king, my lord. 25–39 [No]te well,[2] I have nothing with which to acquire horses. Every[thing of] mine [is gon]e through being sol[d i]n the land of Yarimuta for provisions to keep me alive. I[f] the king wants his servant and his city to survive, then send a [g]arrison to guard your city and your servant until the king is (really) concerned for his lands, sends his archers, and brings peace to his lands. 40–50 Thus was it pleasing in the si[ght] of the king when you wrote to [your ser]vant, "Get Ḫaya into Ṣumur." I paid 13 (shekels of) silver and a pair of mantles as the hire[3] of the ʿApiru when he brou⟨gh⟩t the tablet into Ṣumur.[4] Look, ask Ḫaya. Truly it was by night that he got (him) into ⟨⟨into⟩⟩ Ṣumur. 50–56 Previously, provisions from the king were at [m]y disposal, and we could pay the hi⟨r⟩e of a man whom we sent. But [lo]ok, now there are n[o prov]isions from the king, [and there is no garri]son [at my disposal]. . . . 57–59 . . .

NOTES

1. Or "with whom." Though *ištu*, "from," rather than the much rarer equivalent of *itti*, here yields good sense, this is not true in parallel passages, which do not refer to the enemies and peasantry. It is quite clear, in general, from Rib-Hadda's letters *from* whom or what he must protect himself and the king's city. In *EA* 123:31, note the sequence: the need of the three men to guard the city (lines 23–28), then the question to the king's order to guard himself, and finally back to the need of the three men; here "from whom" makes little sense. In *EA* 125:11ff., Rib-Hadda shifts immediately from the question of from whom or with whom to guard himself, to the absence of manpower; again, "with whom" obviously makes better sense. Cf. also in *EA* 119:9ff. and 122:10ff. the transition from the king's command to the absence of manpower. In *EA* 126:33, *ištu manni* is replaced by *kī*, "how." We must, therefore, take the question "With my enemies,

or with my peasantry?" as ironical. On *ištu* = *itti*, see *EA* 145:6; 166, n. 1; 170:5, 15; *Jerusalem Scribe*, p. 165, n. 68.

2. *šumma*: see *EA* 35, n. 3.

3. *agrūtu*. On shekels rather than minas, see *EA* 109, n. 9; here again, even though the word order (initial position) stresses the size of the pay, minas would yield an excessively high figure.

4. Getting the tablet in and getting Ḫaya in, who should probably be thought of as bearing a tablet with the king's orders, were probably the same thing. That Rib-Hadda is himself in Ṣumur is not clear; otherwise, Greenberg, *Ḫab/piru*, p. 39.

EA 113

War and peace

TEXT: C 4753.
COPY: WA 63.

Moreover,[1] [. . .] . . . 4–10 *Inquire from*[2] another may[or]. Is he not [always] c[ommitting][3] or plotting a crime? Look, Yapaḫ-Hadda has commit[ted] a crime. Be informed! [*What*] has the king done to hi[m]? 11–18 Moreover, what have I done t[o] Yapaḫ-Hadda that he plo[ts] evil upon evil against m[e]? As he has plundered two of my ships and my sheep and goats[4] so that the amount of my property in his possession is very large, may the king [se]nd his commissioner [to de]cide between the two of us.[5] 19–28 [Everything] that [is ta]ken from him [*may he* (the king) *take*].[6] Concerning [my] property [that] is in [his] possession [*he should inquire of*] my [*m*]*en*[7] . . . [. . . fr]om Rib-Hadda [*and*] for the ʿApiru has [all of it] *be*[*en acquired*],[8] but there is no one that [*can ta*]*ke* anything belonging to him from my [*hand*]. 28–35 Why am [I] not able like my associates to send a man to the palace?[9] Their cities are theirs, [and] they are at peace. May the Sun establish [my] honor in your presence so that you bring peace to [*your servant*],[10] and then he will never leave your side. 36–48 Tell Amanmašša to sta[y] with me so he can brin[g] my tablet to yo[u. For] once he goes off, there will be no one to bring [my tablet] to you. So may the [k]ing be con[cerned] about Amanmašša [so] he sta[ys with me] . . . and Yapaḫ-Hadda . . . [*So send*] provisions for the cities *t*[*hat* have *not*] turned *again*[*st you*].

NOTES

1. *EA* 113 is a two-tablet letter; cf. *EA* 101. The addressee is not clear, but the king seems likely.

2. Occasionally *aššum* means "from" in *EA* (VAB 2/2, p. 1385), and this

sense seems to fit the context better than "about, with regard to." Rib-Hadda says that, on inquiry, any other ruler will confirm the criminal activities of Yapaḫ-Hadda.

3. *y*[*i-pu-šu*]: as required by the parallelism with the indicative *yaškunu.*

4. See *EA* 55, n. 2.

5. Not "the two of you" (*BASOR* 211 [1973] p. 52), which is forced. Note, however, that, when the litigants are three, then *ina berīnu* replaces *ina berīkunī* (cf. *EA* 117:64ff.). Whatever then the explanation, {*kunī*} is first person dual pronominal suffix. Cf. also *EA* 34:33; 116:33.

6. The beginning of lines 19–21: [ka-li]; [yú-ul]-qú; [yi-ìl-qé]. For the restorations, cf. *EA* 116:34ff.; 117:67ff. Contrary to Knudtzon (*VAB* 2/1, p. 494, note h), there is ample room for *yi-ìl* or *yú-ul* at the beginning of line 20; elsewhere on the tablet the space corresponds to three or four signs.

7. Free restoration: 22 [ša-a] *it-ti*-[šu yi-ša-al] 23 [a-na L]Ú.MEŠ-*ia.*

8. Free restoration: *ip*-[pu-šu] 26 [gáb-ba].

9. The question was probably asked by the addressee, whom Rib-Hadda now quotes; cf. *EA* 106, n. 2. The other mayors, here called "associates" (cf. *EA* 120:45), are "friends" in *EA* 126:16. Both terms seem to imply equality of rank, rights, and obligations.

10. The use here of the expression *bašta nadānu* is unusual.

EA 114

Loyalty and its rewards

TEXT: BM 29796.
COPY: BB 13.

[Rib-Hadda says] to [his] lord, [king of all countries, Great King, King of B]attle: May the La[dy o]f [Gu]bla grant power to the king, my lord. I fall at the feet of my lord, my Sun, 7 times and 7 times. May the king, my lord, know 7–17 that Aziru is at war with me. He has seized 12 men of mine, and the ransom price between us he has set at 50 (shekels of) silver.[1] It was the men whom I sent to Ṣumur that he has seized.[2] In Waḫliya are the ships of the rulers[3] of Tyre, Beirut, and Sidon. Everyone in the land of Amurru is at peace with them; I am the enemy. As Yapaḫ-Hadda is now on the side of Aziru against me, he has, I assure you, seized a ship of mine, 18–26 and he has, I assure you, for this very reason been going to sea to seize my ships. May the king give thought to his city and his servant; my peas⟨an⟩try long only to desert. If you are unable to rescue m[e][4] from my enemies, then send back word so I can know what action I am to take. 26–34 Look, I (must) keep writing like ⟨th⟩is to you about Ṣumur.[5] Look, I did go and I strongly urged the troops to [*guard* i]t, but now they have abandoned it, [and] the garrison [*has deserted*].[6] And [*for this reason I keep wr*]*iting*.[7] I have sent [. . .][8] a messenger of mine time and again. 35–43 How often did I send him and he was unable to get into Ṣumur! They have blocked all the roads against him.[9] That fellow looks with pleasure on the war against me and against Ṣumur. For 2 months he has been encamped against me. For what reason is your loyal servant so treated? For service to you! 44–50 If you are unable to fetch you[r] servant, then send archers to fetch me. It would be good to be with you.[10] The enemies of the king are at war with me, as are his mayors, to whom he gives thought.[11] For this reason my situation is extremely grave. 51–59 Look, ask the other Amanmašša if it was not ⟨from⟩ Alašiya that I sent him to you.[12] Give thought to your loyal servant. Pre[vi]ously, my peasantry got provisions from the land of Yarimuta, but now, now Yapaḫ-Hadda does not let them go. 59–69 *W*[*hy are you negl*]*igent?*[13] [*The king must*] send a garrison [*to protect*] yo[ur *loya*]*l* [*servant*. . . .] . . . the enemies of the king, for they *make* a mayor who serves you with loyalty *prowl about*.[14] Moreover, give thought to me. Who will be loyal were I to die? Look, Yapaḫ-Hadda is on the side of Aziru.

NOTES

1. See *EA* 109, n. 9.

2. The unusual absence of coordinating conjunctions and clause-markers in lines 10ff., along with our ignorance of the location of Waḫliya, makes the division of clauses and the interpretation of these lines quite difficult. I reject Knudtzon's version, according to which the ships of the three cities capture the men sent to Ṣumur, for this results in a construction without parallel in the Byblos corpus (feminine plural subject, masculine singular verb; in *EA* 105:20f., the same subject, "ships" [*eleppētu*], has a third feminine plural verb, *aṣâ*). I take *u* . . . *ṣab(b)at* as an explanatory clause, with inversion of word order stressing the identity of the men who were seized, though it might refer to another crime. Perhaps "in Waḫliya" belongs with this clause, but whether ships might as a result be at peace with the people of Amurru is not clear. Of course, if Waḫliya was not on the coast, then it could not serve as a port. I take the remark on the ships as intended to show the friendship of the three cities to Aziru, who now holds Waḫliya (*EA* 104:11).

3. On "men" in the sense of "rulers," see Introduction, nn. 73–74.

4. *la-qa-i*[*a*]: cf. *EA* 79:40; 82:7.

5. *ki-*⟨*a*⟩*-ma,* rather than *ki-ma,* for the following reasons: (1) *kīma* as a conjunction occurs only once in the Byblos corpus (*EA* 127:31), whereas *anumma ki'amma* followed by *šapāru,* usually in the indicative, is quite common (*EA* 74:49; 85:6, 55; 89:7; 91:27; 103:20; 118:8; 119:10f.; 122:53f.; 132:51); (2) *anumma* never introduces a subordinate clause; (3) *anumma* . . . *anumma* not infrequently introduces coordinate clauses (*EA* 78:1ff.; 85:6ff.; 90:18ff.; 106:8ff.; 362:21ff.). Occasionally, and perhaps here, *kī'amma,* usually "thus, like this," shades over into

the illative, "so, this being the case" (cf. *EA* 91:27; 103;20, "in these circumstances" [Knudtzon]; 119:11).

6. Except for the curious *marṣa* (*EA* 103:49), (ÉRIN.MEŠ/LÚ.MEŠ) *maṣṣartu* is in all clear cases construed *ad sensum* as masculine plural: cf. *EA* 79:30 / 125:14 (referred to by plural pronominal suffix in lines 33/18, respectively); 103:37, 49; 112:34; 130:37 (*maṣṣartu* subject, verbs in the plural). In *EA* 126:25, the agreement with ÉRIN.MEŠ *maṣṣartu* is probably therefore plural (*tuššarūna*), though feminine singular (*tuššaru*) is also possible; see *EA* 116, n. 1. Cf. also LÚ.MEŠ *maṣṣārū*, also referred to by plural pronominal suffix (*EA* 117:79, 81); on 117:50, see below. Therefore, the subject of *ītezib* (line 30) is not *maṣṣartu*, and it can only be ÉRIN.MEŠ (*ṣābu*) understood; cf. ÉRIN.MEŠ as masculine singular in *EA* 76:38f.; 117:24, 27; 124:12; 126:40. Both *ṣābu* and *maṣṣartu* must refer to the same troops; cf. *EA* 126:25, where ÉRIN.MEŠ is immediately followed by ÉRIN.MEŠ *maṣṣartu* as synonymous. Line 31: [ù pa-aṭ-ru]: cf. the sequence *ezēbu-paṭāru* in *EA* 73:13f.; 82:42f.; 83:46ff., 49f.; 118:34f.); perhaps [ù en-na-bi-tu] (cf. *EA* 103:37).

7. [ki-na-na iš-tap]-*ru*: cf. *EA* 106:17f.

8. Probably a personal name in the break.

9. Perhaps "to it" (Ṣumur).

10. Cf. *EA* 74:62f.

11. Cf. line 54, "Give thought to your loyal servant." The king is concerned for those who are disloyal to him, while he is unconcerned for the loyal Rib-Hadda.

12. The word order puts stress on the place, but how or why Rib-Hadda should send anyone from or via Alašia remains obscure. The translation of lines 52f. by Smith in G. F. Hill, *History of Cyprus*, vol. 1 (Cambridge, 1940), p. 43, n. 2, has Rib-Hadda freeing Alašia.

13. *a*-[na] 60 [mi-ni qa-l]a-ta: the space seems too large to be filled by either *ba* ([ba-l]a-aṭ/ṭá) or TI (TI.L[A-ṭá). Besides, why "provisions for the garrison," since at this time there was no longer a garrison at Byblos, in contrast, as Rib-Hadda notes so often, to earlier and better days?

14. Free restoration: 61 [LUGAL-ru yú]-*wa-ši-ru-na* 62 [a-na na-ṣa-ar ÌR ki-t]i-k[a .... Cf. *EA* 117:76ff. On *ti-da-lu-na* (line 65), see *EA* 109, n. 11.

EA 115

Message lost

TEXT: VAT 1630.
COPIES: WA 69; *VS* 11, 60.

Too fragmentary for translation.[1]

NOTE

1. A letter to the king of which 14 lines on the obverse and 9 on the reverse, all of them fragmentary, are preserved. There are references to Aziru, Ṣumur, Amurru, and perhaps the difficulties of rescuing Ṣumur. Lines 5, 7–9: 5 [...

i]-*na ṣé*-[ri], "in the countryside" (cf. *EA* 104:48) 7 [. . . *šu*]*m-ma i-ia-nu* š[a-a] 8 [ú-še-zi-bu UR]U *i-na qa-ti*-[šu ù] 9 [ki-na-na i-ia-n]u *lìb-ba a-na* UR[U ṣu-mu-ri, "Note well, there is no one that can save the city from him, and so Ṣumur is disheartened."

EA 116

Who do they think they are?

TEXT: C 4752 (not collated).
COPY: WA 61.

[Rib-Had]da writes t[o his lord], Great [Kin]g, king of all countries, King of [Ba]ttle: May the Lady of Gub[la gr]ant power to the king, my [lord]. I fall at the feet of [m]y lord, the Sun, [7 times] and 7 times. 6–16 May the king, my lord, know that the war [again]st us is very severe. As to its being told to you, "Ṣumur belongs to the king," may the [ki]ng know that *there was an attack on our garrison,*[1] and the sons of ʿAbdi-Aširta seized it. And so there has been no one to carry wor[d t]o the king. But give thought to the fact that I am your loyal servant, and whatever I hear I write to [my] lord. 17–24 Moreover, give thought to Ṣumu[r]. It is like a bird in a t[rap] : *ki-lu*-[*bi*] (cage). [The war] is very severe, and the messengers that [*came*] from the palace were [u]nab[le] to get [in]to Ṣumur. It was by nig[ht] that I got them in. 25–33 And here is how Yapaḫ-Hadda is not just in my regard: when my man arrived, he bound him.[2] May *what is due to me* [*be gi*]*ven*;[3] it is very much.[4] Now as the king is going to send the royal commissioners, may the king tell them to decide between us. 34–44 If the king gives (the property) to his servant, well and good! Or, on the other hand, let the king take everything for himself.[5] Moreover, all my towns have been joined to the ʿApi[ru], and all of them [*are extremely hostile*] to me, for [Yapaḫ-Hadda keeps devising][6] evil upon evil against me. They have no[th]ing, having paid ransom money, some twice, some three times.[7] 44–55 May the king heed the words of his loyal servant and give provisions to his servant and his maidservant, Gubla. Moreover, it would please me were I with you and so at peace. Look, Aziru and Yapaḫ-Hadda have made an agreement against me,[8] and I am unable [to d]o anything. Their actions [*are hosti*]*le*[9] to me. Accordingly, my situation is [ext]remely gra[ve]. 55–69 Moreover, note that we have been loyal servants of the king from ancie[nt ti]mes. Moreover, note that I am [your] loyal servant, but I have nothing but distress.[10] No[te] this matter. Note that I am the dirt at your feet, O king! Note: did not your father come out and visit (his) lands and his mayors?[11] And now the gods and the Sun and the Lady of Gubla have granted that you be seated on the throne of your father's house (to rule) your land. Who are they, the sons of ʿAbdi-Aširta, that they have [t]aken the lands of the king for themselves? 70–74 The king of Mittani? The king of Kaššu? The king of Ḫatti? May the king send archers (and) Yanḫa⟨mu⟩ along with [*the prefec*]*ts*[12] from the land of Yarimuta. 75–80 The commissioner from Kumidu [. . .] . . .

NOTES

1. Line 8: *yú-qa-bu-na*, following Izre'el, *UF* 19 (1987) p. 86. Lines 11f.: *ma-qa-ti-ma a-*⟨na⟩ UN-*nu*: narrative infinitive; UN = *maṣṣartu*, as in *EA* 114:31, 136:18, 234:15(?), and probably several times at Ugarit (Rainey, *IOS* 3 [1973] p. 44); *ṣabtū-še*, suffix referring to *maṣṣartu* (see *EA* 103, n. 3; 114, n. 6; 117, n. 10). Difficulties: (1) in *EA*, *eli/muḫḫi* is expected rather than *ana*; (2) it is assumed that there is a sign omitted (but cf. esp. *EA* 74:13; 103;10; 125:31; 138:135); (3) the motivation for "*our* garrison" is not clear. Both *AHw*, pp. 591 and 637, and *CAD*, M/1, pp. 140 and 437 (though on p. 333 UN is taken as *maṣṣartu*) agree in reading *ma-ka*$_4$*-ti ma-a-un-nu*, "I lack a dwelling." The difficulties with this reading: (1) *ka*$_4$ occurs only once in the Byblos corpus (*ka*$_4$*-bi-it*, *EA* 88:17); (2) of a third weak verb the form expected here is *makīti* (at Byblos, *qabīti*, *laqīti*, *šamīti*, and the same rule elsewhere; *ibaššâti*, *ibaššâtunu*, etc., is a special development); (3) this assumes the sudden intrusion of Canaanite and necessitates postulating, against the available evidence (Hebrew), that **maʿônu* was of feminine gender, in order to explain the suffix on *ṣabtū-še*; (4) in context, the statement makes little sense.

2. On the construction, see *JCS* 4 (1950) p. 169; *rakša-šu* is a verb (cf. *rakšū-*⟨*šu*⟩*nu*, *EA* 109:27), not an adjective (*AHw*, p. 948).

3. [tu]-*ta-na*, probably the passive form (*tuttana/tuddana*, third feminine singular) of *yad(d)ina kittīya ina qātīya* in *EA* 118:16f., which also refers to the litigation between Rib-Hadda and Yapaḫ-Hadda.

4. *ma'id* is predicated of *mimmīya*, "my property," or something similar, understood (cf. *EA* 105:38). The subject is not *kittīya* (*CAD*, K, p. 471), which would have required *ma'idat*.

5. Cf. *EA* 118:16ff. The syntax is not clear.

6. The context seems to require an iterative (*yaškunu*, *yīpušu*).

7. Perhaps "some for two (persons), some for three." I read *apil* (active? passive?), stative of *apālu*. Were it not for the resulting very low sums, one might also consider "Some fetched (*abil*) two (shekels), some three, as ransom money" (cf. *CAD*, A/1, p. 20b).

8. For *awata leqû ina birī*, cf. *EA* 69, n. 2, and *alkamma awatam ina birītīni i nilqe*, "Come so we can reach an agreement between us" (Dalley et al., *The Old Babylonian Tablets from Tell al Rimah* [see *EA* 22, n. 19], no. 15:8ff.).

9. [KÚR-nu-t]um: cf. *EA* 103:8.

10. *mar*$_x$*-ṣa-ma*? Error for *mur-ṣu-ma*?

11. The sequence in lines 55–61 of *šanīta amur . . . šanīta amur . . . amur . . .*

amur . . . amur is without close parallel and seems to be extraordinarily emotional language.

12. [qí]-p[a]-*ni*: see *VAB* 2/2, p. 1593.

EA 117

A lesson from the past

TEXT: VAT 350.
COPIES: WA 45; *VS* 11, 62.

Rib-Hadda [writes to his lord], Great [Kin]g, King of [Battle]; May the Lady of G[ubl]a gr[ant pow]er to the king, my lord, [m]y [Sun]. I fall at the feet of my lord, [m]y Sun, [7] times and 7 times. Indeed the king, my lord, keeps saying, "Why do you alone keep writing to me?" Here is my situation: there is not 10–21 a mayor from Ṣumur (southward) that supports me, and indeed, everyone is turned against me. And the two men from Egypt whom I sent to the palace have not come out. Did I not write to the king, "There is no one to bring my tablet to the palace. It is these two men that must bring a tablet to the king." And ⟨n⟩ow,[1] as they have not come out, I am accordingly afraid and I have turned to my lord. 21–28 Moreover, I sent a ma[n][2] to your father. When Amarnappa ca[me][3] with a small force, I wrote to the palace that the king should s[en]d ⟨⟨should send⟩⟩ a large force. Did he not take ʿAbdi-Aširta along with everything belonging to him, just as I said? 29–34 Had I been writing treacherous words to my lord? And you say, "Why do you write treacherous words?" If my words are heeded, Azaru will certainly be taken like [hi]s f[ather]. Look, I am *the strong one* of the king, [my] l[ord].[4] 35–43 Moreover, just who are they, the sons of ʿAbdi-Aširta, the servant (and) dog, [that they have tak]en[5] the cities of the king's mayors for [themselves]? They are with you? The cities are in Aziru's *se*[*rvice*].[6] May the king not en[ter] their cities. They are not at peace (with you) from . . . [. . .[7] *as far as*] Ullassa, the city where he has been sen[ding][8] chariots. 43–52 Previously, I would desire to send a man [. . .] . . .[9] I [*sent*] men to Egypt an[d] ⟨⟨and⟩⟩ a *g*[*ar*]*ri*[*so*]*n was* sent[10] to me in their charge. Accordingly, I have sent this man. 53–64 Moreover, did I not write to the king, "The two men from Egypt must now come out to me. There is *treachery*[11] *against* me." But they have not come out. If th[is] year there are no archers, all the lands will belong to the ʿApiru. And if the king does not want to sen[d] archers, may he write to Yanḫamu and Piḫura, "March along with your mayors. Take the land of Amurru." In a day they will take it. 64–71 Moreover, I have litigation with Yapaḫ-Hadda and Ḫa'⟨ip⟩. May the king send a com[missioner to] de[ci]de between us. Everything that is taken from them belongs to the king. Let no one else take it for himself. May it please the king. 71–82 Moreover, may the king send horses to ⟨⟨to⟩⟩ his servant that I may guard the city of the king. I have nothing. Everything is gone, having been sold for provisions to keep me alive. May the king send this man of mine with all speed and give a garrison to guard his loyal servant and his city, and along with them men from Meluḫḫa, according to the practice of your ancestors. 83–94 Moreover, as to the king's saying, "Guard! Be on your guar[d],"[12] [wh]at i[s to guard me? Look, *in*] the days of [my] an[cestors, there was property of the king at their disposal, and] a garri[son of the king] was with them.[13] [But now], as for me, the wa[r is severe again]st me. I [have become af]raid of my peasantry. Thus must I be the one that keeps writing [to] the palace fo[r] a garrison and men from Meluḫḫa. But you have not wri⟨tt⟩en. Only one is *st*[*ro*]*ng*.[14] What am I to do? May the king se⟨n⟩d a gar[ri]son and men from Meluḫḫa to guard me. May the city not be joined to the ʿApiru.

NOTES

1. ⟨*i-na*⟩*-an-na*.

2. L[Ú]: certain.

3. *yi-la-*[*ak*]: if *yi-la-*[*ku-na*] (Knudtzon, and see copy of *VS* 11), then "when he was coming." On *laqi* in line 27, see *EA* 108, n. 5.

4. If KALAG.GA corresponds to *dannu,* "strong (one)," or to *dunnu,* "strength," as always elsewhere in the Byblos letters, the context suggests that strength is used here as implying trustworthiness. Or perhaps the reference is to the future, the situation after Aziru is taken, and the strong one then will be, not Aziru, but Rib-Hadda.

5. [*ù la*]*-qú*: cf. *EA* 116:68f.; 123:39. The present-future form corresponding to singular *yilqu* (*EA* 71:18; 75:42; 91:4) is *tilqūna* (*EA* 104:22).

6. *šunu ittīka*: whether *šunu* refers to the mayors or the sons of ʿAbdi-Aširta, it is hardly a simple statement of fact. It may be simply a rhetorical question, but the context suggests that Rib-Hadda here alludes to the letter of the king just mentioned, in which, in answer perhaps to one of Rib-Hadda's charges, the king claimed that those referred to were really "with him," on his side. To this Rib-Hadda replies, quoting the king in a tone either of shock and sheer disbelief or perhaps of bitter sarcasm.

Instead of Knudtzon's d[a-gi-il], which is followed here, Greenberg, *Ḫab/piru,* p. 39, proposed *i*[*t-ti*], "the cities are with Aziru." Attractive as this reading is, it seems excluded by comparison with *it* in the same line and in lines 65 and 81 (the broken sign lacks the two verticals at the beginning).

7. Kestemont proposed the reading URU N[IN.URTA] (Kestemont, *Berytus* 20 [1971] p. 49).

8. Against (URU *ša*) *ia*$_8$-d[i-nu], "the city which gave" (Knudtzon) are the following: (1) the verbal prefix written with *ia*$_8$ (*ia*$_8$*-am-li-ik*, *EA* 105:6, is the only certain example); (2) the assumption of *ālu* as masculine (prefix {ia}, not {ta}), whereas the noun is regularly feminine (exception, *ennepša*, *EA* 88:31? *en-ni-ip-ša-⟨at⟩*?). Hence, *yú-w*[*a-ši-ru*], "he has been sending"; for sending chariots, said of the king, see *EA* 131:12; 132:56 (?) [both from Byblos]; 180:6, 10, 21; 270:24; and 271:18. For the absence here of a resumptive pronoun or an adverb, I can offer no parallels—the evidence is extremely meager—except the general ones of Akkadian (*GAG* §165d, §166c) and Hebrew (P. Joüon, *Grammaire de l'hébreu biblique* [Rome, 1948], pp. 484f.), the use of the relative pronoun in reference to nouns of place.

9. References to Ṣumur, to the official Pawuru (line 47, [^{m}*pa*]-*wu-ra*; *pawuru* as a common noun is found only in letters from Tyre, *EA* 149:30; 151:59; so also Na'aman, *Political Disposition,* p. 159), and perhaps to Aziru (line 47; the absence of a determinative is not decisive).

10. The assumed passive meaning of the verb is unusual, and if *ma-ṣa-ar* is the correct reading, it is almost certainly an error for *maṣṣartu.* On the gender agreement, see *EA* 116, n. 1.

11. *šâri*: narrative infinitive (cf. *EA* 116, n. 1). Cf. *šāru,* "treacherous, enemy," and *šâru,* "to lie, charge falsely" (*VAB* 2/2, p. 1518), and perhaps *šārum* at Mari (*AÉM* 1/1, no. 199, note e).

12. *lu na-ṣa-ra-*[*ta*]: cf. *EA* 99:8; 112:9; 367:4; 370:5.

13. 85 [a-mur *i-na*] 86 UD].MEŠ *a-b*[*u*]-⌜*t*⌝[*i-ia mi-im-mi* LUGAL-*ri* UGU-*šu-nu*] 87 [ù] *ma-ṣa-ar-*[⟨*ti*⟩ LUGAL-*ri*]. Cf. *EA* 121:11ff.; 122:11ff.; 125:14ff.; 130:21ff. In line 86, *balāṭ šarri,* "provisions of the king," is also possible. Against this as the reading at the end of line 87 (Knudtzon), *itti,* "with," is said only of a garrison, whereas *eli/muḫḫi* is used with *balāṭu* and *mimmû.* In line 87 I assume a reduction in number of signs in the line; note the following line.

14. 1 d[a-a]n-*na*: perhaps "Is a single (person) strong?" (Rib-Hadda referring to himself).

EA 118

Not like other mayors

TEXT: BM 29808 + VAT 1662.

COPIES: BB 25 + WA 54; *VS* 11, 54.

Say to the king, my lord: Message of Rib-Hadda, your servant. I fall at the feet of my lord 7 times and 7 times. 6–15 May the Lady of Gubla grant power to the king, my lord. I keep writing like this to the pala[ce], . . . [. . .] the war against me, and so may the king give a garrison to his servant. Moreover, I have litigation. Send the commissioner, let him hear my case, 16–23 and give me [*m*]*y due,*[1] or, on the other hand, let the king take from the mayors anything of mine for himself. Moreover, the war [again]st me is severe, and so there are no provisions [for] the peasantry. 24–33 Look, [*th*]*ey* have [*gone off*][2] to the sons of ʿAbdi-Aširta, to Si⟨do⟩n and Beirut. As the sons of ʿAbdi-Aširta are hostile to the king, and Sidon a⟨nd⟩ Beirut do not belong (any longer) to the king, send the commissioner to take them, 34–44 lest I abandon the city and go off to you.[3] Look, if the peasantry goes off, the ʿApiru will seize the city.[4] Seeing that my only purpose is to serve the king in accordance with the practice of my ancestors, may the king send archers and pacify them. 45–56 As for the mayors,[5] since the cities are theirs and they are at peace, they do not keep writing to the king. It is against me and against Yanḫamu that there is war. Look,[6] previously the commissioner at Ṣumur would [d]ecide[7] between us, but now no mayor listens to hi[m]! The king has no servant like Yanḫamu—a loyal servant!

NOTES

1. The usual meanings of *kittu,* "justice, loyalty, truth," do not fit this passage; see also *EA* 116:29. Context requires "right" (Knudtzon), "vindication," or, even more concretely, "due." Cf. Hebrew *ṣedeq* and *ṣᵉdāqā,* both of similar semantic range.

2. If [p]a-*ṭ*[*á*-ru] is the correct reading, then we must understand the desertion to have been only partial; cf. lines 39ff.

3. Against the reading *ú-ul* 1 (Knudtzon) are the position of the numeral and the considerations that support our version: as the sequence *āla ezēbu-paṭāru* is used in the Byblos letters, the subject is first person and *paṭāru* means "to go away"; cf. *EA* 82:43f.; 83:46f., 49f.; perhaps 114:30f. The difference between *paṭrātī* in the other passages and *ipaṭṭara* here is the explicit marking for mode in the latter.

4. Lines 36–39; see *JCS* 4 (1950) pp. 169f.

5. As the clear parallels in *EA* 124:35ff. (39) and 125:34f. make evident, either we must delete *ana* at the beginning of line 45 (anticipation of *ana* at the beginning of line 46 and failure to erase?), which seems preferable, both because of *EA* 125:34f. and because of the unusual type of error in the use of case endings (*ana ḫazānūtu*), or we must take *ana* in the sense of "as to, concerning" (*VAB* 2/2, p. 1374f.).

6. *a*-⟨⟨*na*⟩⟩-[*m*]*ur*: cf. *EA* 122:11; 130:21.

7. [*yú*]-*pa-ri-šu*: taking the form as singular, despite MASKIM.MEŠ, for the passage is concerned with customary action in the past, and the expected plural form would be *tuparrišūna*. Cf. *tilqūna, EA* 104:25; *tuballiṭūna,* 114:56; and *tīpušūna,* 131:31.

EA 119

Recalling past kindnesses

TEXT: VAT 349.
COPIES: WA 44; *VS* 11, 64.

Rib-Hadda writes to his lord, Great King, King of Batt⟨le⟩: May the Lady of Gubla grant power to the king, my lord. 6–13 I fall at the feet of my lord, my Sun, 7 times and 7 times. As to the king, my lord's having written me, "Guard yourself," [wh]at is to guard me? Indeed, I keep writing like this to the palace ⟨for⟩ a [g]ar[ri]son and for horses in order that I may gu[ard][1] his [city]. 14–21 What am I to do? While alive I shall guard the king's city for him, but if I die, what can I ⟨d⟩o? As to its having been said to the king, "Rib-Hadda has caused the death of (some) royal archers,"[2] 21–32 since the commissioners are alive, let me tell about all their deeds so the king will know that I am a loyal servant of his. May the king pay [n]o attention to the slanders against his loyal [ser]vant that [*a treacherous man*] may *utt*⟨e⟩r[3] before [*the king, m*]*y* [*lord*]. . . . 33–42 Rib-Hadda, is[ol]ated, is a servant of the king. [There is n]o one that has report[ed] my loyalty before the king, my lord. He knows my loyalty! The king knows how often he has done some kindness to me because I am without duplicity. 43–52 My only purpose is to serve the king, my lord. Now this case is a case concerning my loyalty, which I have declared.[4] Everything (belonging to me)—may the king, my lord, take [*all of it*][5] for himself. [O]r my lord may give the small(er) [*things*] to ʿAbdi-Ha[dda].[6] Or 53–59 *this may not be acceptable.*[7] What more shall I say? There is still a second tablet, and it is this that will lay before the king all my things that are in Yapaḫ-Hadda's possession.

NOTES

1. [*i-n*]*a-ṣa-*[*ru*]: according to the rule of modal sequence; perhaps trace of *ru* as in copy of *VS* 11.

2. The grounds of the charge are not clear; see *EA* 124:51ff. Nor, in my opinion, is there evident a connection between *EA* 119 and 122–24 (Pintore, *OA* 12 [1973] p. 304, n. 29). The following clause does not make much sense if included in the charge (Knudtzon; *Or* n.s. 29 [1960] p. 15). The clause is understood here as the reason why Rib-Hadda is prepared to attack his accusers: the commissioners (?) (officials? officers?) associated with the events in question are alive and would support Rib-Hadda's version of what actually happened.

3. **28** [i]-d[a]-*bu*-⟨bu⟩: a verb of speaking seems required, but no form of *qabû* is compatible with the traces; cf. *adabbuba* in line 23.

4. Cf. *kitta qabû* in lines 36f. That a relative clause (*ša qabītī*) should begin a sentence would be unparalleled. The declaration probably refers to the immediately preceding lines, but it might also be understood of what follows. The case concerns Rib-Hadda's loyalty probably in the sense of demonstrating it, for he is willing to give to the king all his stolen possessions. We may not exclude *kittīya*, "my due" (*EA* 118:16ff.), though it does not seem as likely an object of *qabû*.

5. Perhaps at the end of line 48 [gáb-ba], reemphasizing the extent of the offer.

6. 49 . . . ⌜ù⌝ 50 [ú-nu-te/ta$_5$: following Rainey, *UF* 7 (1975) p. 400, n. 54. *ʿAbdi-ḫe-[ba]* (Rainey, ibid., n. 55) is not a likely reading. Knudtzon saw a whole IM; cf., too, *EA* 120:31.

7. *annû lā laqê*: cf. Rainey, ibid., p. 400. This proposal is here understood to mean that the king may want to give something to ʿAbdi-Hadda, which only here is joined to the proposal that the king take everything. The assumed construction with the infinitive is not attested elsewhere in the Byblos corpus.

EA 120

Stolen goods

TEXT: VAT 1636.
COPIES: WA 85; *VS* 11, 65.

[These are] the things that are wi[th]
[Yapaḫ]-Hadda[1] *and I clai*[*m*]:[2]

[. . .] . . . 2000 *each*
[th]eir [wei]ght. 10 (leather-) . . . , *braided,*[3]
[*1*]000 *each* their weight.
100 swords. 100 dag[gers]. *80 šubūbu.*[4]
1 (leather-) . . . , *braided.* 4 [. . .] . . .
1 (reed-) . . . 4 [. . .] . . .
1 (reed-) *ku-ku-tu.* 4 ([re]ed-) . . .
1 (reed-) . . . 4 [. . .].
[1] hammer.[5] [. . .].
[1] *washbasin.*[6] [. . .] . . .
[*1*]1 . . . [. . .] . . .
*1*0[00 . . .]. [. . .].
[. . .] . . . [. . .].
. . . [. . .].
[1] bed. 2,[7] over[laid] with gold.
1 chair[8] ove[rlaid] with gold.
All of them *pertain to* . . . [. . .].[9]

[*10 k*]*ipa*[*l*]*allu* of *bo*[*xwood*].[10] 100 chairs. 100 ... [...].
15 *šabattu*-garments. 15 blank[ets].[11]
90–100 maidservants (and) manservants.[12]
...[13]
...
...
100 (shekels?) of gold. *With regard to* ...

They have acted unjustly. ... [...]. Her brother [... He is po]werful, and so there is no [*one*] 30–34 who will take *ac*[*tion*] *against* him. The king sent ʿAbdi-Hadda and Bin-aZimi to fetch her. *They have waited.* 35–39 And to ʿAbdi-Hadda the king said, "Send her things *for* her." And [...] ... the king. When the [*message*] was heard, no decision was *announced.* 40–45 I herewith [s]end to the kin[g] all the things [o]n a tablet. May [the king *inquire*] *about* him. [*He is hostile*] to my lord. He has acted kindly towards my partner.[14]

NOTES

1. See *EA* 119:55ff. The inventory form, which I retain, is abandoned at the end (lines 26ff.?).

2. *u* a-*ša-lu*; or "10 *ašallu*-bowls"; or "12 *šalu*" (Knudtzon).

3. KUŠ LAGABx? *ze-ru-tu*; see *CAD*, Z, p. 89. The same word appears in line 7.

4. Perhaps a kind of weapon; see E. Salonen, *Die Waffen der Alten Mesopotamier* (Helsinki, 1965), p. 56. The reading is doubtful.

5. *ma-qí-bu*: see Huehnergard, *Ugaritic Vocabulary,* p. 154.

6. *nam-ši-ti* for *namsītu* (*nemsētu*)?

7. "A second (bed)"?

8. 1 [G]U.ZA *ka-aḫ-šu*: see K. Bonkamp, *Die Bibel im Lichte der Keilschriftforschung* (Recklinghausen, 1939), pp. 274f.; and cf. Ugaritic *kḫṯ*, despite Friedrich, *AfO* 14 (1941–42) pp. 329f.

9. Perhaps the remark concerns only the beds and the chair just mentioned; it certainly does not refer to material or weight. It may also be a summary remark, the conclusion of the list of Rib-Hadda's possessions, with the list of "her things" (line 36) in lines 20ff. Suggesting this possibility is the fact that the litigation with Yapaḫ-Hadda, which hitherto seemed to involve only Rib-Hadda's things, now also seems somehow concerned with a woman and "her things."

10. GIŠ.TASKARIN?

11. *ma-ar-*⌜*ba*⌝*-d*[*u*]: with Rainey, AOAT², p. 81, following Bonkamp, *Die Bibel* (see n. 8), p. 274. Besides Hebrew *marbaddîm,* cf. Ugaritic *mrbd* (*PRU* 5, no. 50:9, followed by *mškbt,* "bed[s?]), *mrbdt* (*PRU* 2, no. 111:11), and the verb *rbd* in *trbd.ʿrš.pdry.bšt.mlk,* "you prepare the bed of Pidriya with royal covers" (*Ugar.* 7, p. 42:2f.). Both *ma-ar-ṣú-ú* (*AHw,* p. 617) and *ma-ar-ṣa-ú* (*CAD,* M/1, p. 290) are to be rejected; see now *AHw,* p. 1573b.

12. The reading "90 hundred" yields an absurdly high number and assumes

an unparalleled writing of 9000; for "90–100," see *EA* 132, n. 6. Until lines 22ff. are better understood, we must allow for "90–100 maidservants; of manservants there are none."

13. Lines 22–25 are extremely difficult; perhaps on line 23 a remark on the beauty of the females (UR [bāšta]-*ši*-n[a]). The woman with whom lines 28ff. are concerned must have been named at the end of line 26. The powerful man of line 29 I assume was Yapaḫ-Hadda, and if his sister was to be fetched by emissaries of the king, and if she has "things," it would seem that she was to become part of the royal harem (cf. *EA* 99). If so, Yapaḫ-Hadda had still not sent either her or the "things." All of this remains quite obscure. See the discussion of Weber, *VAB* 2/2, pp. 1220f.

14. Who the partner—that is, fellow mayor—was is not clear. The charge would seem to be that he directs his good deeds, not to the crown, but to others, from whom of course he will demand much in return. Instead of *ú-da-me-i*[*q*] (Knudtzon), *ú da-me-i*[*q*], "but he is kindly"?

EA 121

Past and present

TEXT: VAT 1665.
COPIES: WA 59; *VS* 11, 66.

Rib-Hadda w[rit]es to his lord, king of all countries, Great King: May the Lady of Gubla grant power to the king, my lord. I fall at the feet of my lord, my Sun, [7] times and 7 times. As to the king, my lord's, writing me, 8–17 "Guard yourself," what is to g[uar]d [me]? Consider that with my ancestors there was a garrison of [the king], and pro[visions from the k]ing were at th[eir] disposal, but in my case, [there are no pro]visions[1] (or) garrison of the king for [me. 18–25 And] as the war against ⟨me⟩ is very severe, the sons of ʿAbdi-Aširta have said to the ʿApiru and the men who have [jo]ined them, "What is there [wit]h Rib-Hadda?" [*So give thou*]*ght t*[*o*] your [ser]vant and let me tell my [*lord*] 26–40 . . . 41–49 [I wr]ote to [*the king, my lord,* "S]end [*archers*]." Did they [no]t take [*in a day*][2] the lands for *the k*[*ing, your father*]? Now, may the king [heed] the words of [his] serva[nt] and send archers to ⟨*t*⟩*a*[*ke*][3] the land of the king for the king, 50–53 that you may give p[ea]ce in the lands to the [king's] mayors.[4] Have they not been [*ki*]*lled* like [*do*]*gs,*[5] and you have done nothing? 54–59 Moreover, . . . 60–64 [S]end . . . [. . .] If [*the king, my lord*], love[s] his servant, [*then may he fetch his servant*] to himself [. . .].[6]

NOTES

1. *a-na-ku* [*ú-ul*] 16 [*ba*]-*la-ṭ*⌜*ú*⌝: cf. *EA* 122:28ff. If [*ia-nu*] (Knudtzon) were used, we should have the accusative *balāṭa*; see *JCS* 2 (1948) p. 248.

2. [i-na UD.KAM]: see *EA* 108, n. 9. If archers are requested, then the subject of *laqû* is indefinite third plural; cf. n. 3.

3. ERÍN.MES *pí-ṭá-ti* ⟨ti⟩-e[l-qé]: see *EA* 90, n. 10. Among the parallels note especially *EA* 107:30 and the sequence there of *leqû-pašāḫu*. Haplography explains the omission of *ti*. All the parallels have *u tilqe*, but the conjunction seems optional in general. Of course, one could partly avoid the difficulty and translate "Let it take . . ."

4. KUR.KUR.MEŠ: following Thureau-Dangin, *RA* 19 (1922) p. 93, n. 1.

5. *ú-ul* [tu]-*da-ku* 53 *ki-ma* [UR.K]U: for the passive *tudākū*, cf. *EA* 131:28; 132:50.

6. Cf. *EA* 74:60ff.; 114:45ff.; 129:50f.

EA 122

An enormity

TEXT: VAT 1625.
COPIES: WA 47; *VS* 11, 67.

Rib-Hadda writ[es t]o his lord, king of all countries, [Great] King, King of Battle: May the Lady of Gubla grant power to the king, my lord. I fall at the feet of my lord 7 times and 7 times. 9–19 As to the king's saying, "Guard yourself," consider that previously, in the days of my ancestors, there was a garrison of the king with them and property of the king was at their disposal, but as far as I am concerned, there are no provisions from the king at my dis[pos]al, and there is no garrison of the king with me. 19–31 I must guar[d mys]elf by myself.[1] . . . There *is* a garri[son] . . . of the king[2] with him, and there are pro[visi]ons from the king at his disposal, but for me there is neither garrison nor provisions from the king. 31–39 Paḫura has committed an enormity against me. He sent Suteans and they killed *širdanu*-people.[3] And he brought 3 men into Egypt.[4] How long has the city been enraged at me! 40–49 And indeed the city keeps saying, "A deed that has not been done since time immemorial has been done to us!" So may the king heed the words of his servant and send (back) the men, lest the city revolt. What am I to do? 50–55 Listen to *m*⟨*e*⟩. *For* ⟨*my*⟩ *sake,* do not *refuse*![5] [But *whether*] the men are at court o[r n]ot, listen to me. I keep writing like this to the palace, but ⟨my⟩ w⟨ords⟩ are ⟨not⟩ heeded.[6]

NOTES

1. ⌜*i*⌝-*na-ṣa-r*[*u ra-m*]*a-ni-ia*: *inaṣṣar* is also possible, but context favors the durative. *ramāna naṣāru*: besides the frequent *uṣur ramānka*, see also *EA* 125:12f.; 126:33.

2. In lines 24f., *maṣṣar*[*ti* LU]GAL-*ti* LUGAL-*ri* is hardly right, since *šarrūtu* is unknown in the vassal letters, and the repetition of "royal" makes no sense.

3. Cf. *EA* 81:16. The same charge, in almost the same words, is repeated in *EA* 123, which clearly was written about the same time as *EA* 122. The use of Suteans probably implies a raid, killing, and kidnapping.

4. The word order emphasizes the object. It is these three men that are the pressing concern of Rib-Hadda and have aroused Byblos.

5. *ši-mi* ⟨ia⟩-*ši* UGU (*eli*)-⟨ia⟩: cf. the omission in line 55. On *ti-im-i*, see *EA* 136, n. 2.

6. *a*-⟨*wa-tu-ia ú-ul*⟩ *tu-uš-mu-na*: cf. *EA* 74:49f.; 89:7ff.; 103:20ff.; 132: 51ff.

EA 123

An enormity: another version

TEXT: BM 29803.
COPY: BB 20.

Rib-Hadda writes to his lord, Great King, king of all countries, King of Battle: May the Lady of Gubla grant power to the king, my lord. I fa⟨ll⟩ at the feet of my lord, ⟨my⟩ Sun, 7 times and 7 times. 9–15 A deed that has not been done from time immemorial has been done to Gubla.[1] Piḫura [s]ent Suteans; they kill[ed] *širdanu*-people, 16–21 [t]ook 3 men, and brought them in[to] Egypt. 22–28 [If] the king, [my] lord, does not se[nd] them (back), there is [su]rely going to be a revolt against m[e. I]f the ki[ng], my [lor]d, loves [his] loya[l] servant, [then] send (back) the [3] men that I may live and guard the city for the king. 29–37 As to the king's writing, "Guard yourself," with what am I to guard? Send the 3 men whom Piḫura brought in and then I will survive: ʿAbdi-Rama, Yattin-Hadda, ʿAbd⟨i⟩-Milki. 38–43 [Wh]at are the sons of ʿAbdi-Aširta that they have taken the land of the king for themselves? May the king send archers to [take][2] them.

NOTES

1. Cf. *Ea* 122:31ff.

2. ⌜*ù*⌝ [*ti-ìl/el-qé*]: see *EA* 121, n. 3.

EA 124

The tireless correspondent

TEXT: C 4755 (12188).
COPY: WA 62 + WA 64d + WA 65.

[To the k]ing, my lord, [my Sun: Mess]age of Rib-Hadda, [your] ser[vant. May the La]dy of Gubla [grant po]wer to the king, [my] lord. I fall [at the fe]et of my lord, my Sun, [7 times and 7] times. Ri[b-Hadda] 7–13 writes to his lord, "Aziru has taken all my cities. Gubla alone remains to me. So give thought to your loyal servant." Now, should troops advance against Gubla, they will take it. 14–19 He is now in fact gathering together all the cities in order to take it. Where am I to make a stand? Loo[k], he now speaks as follows: "The cities of Ri[b-Hadd]a have been taken [*and*] Ṣumu[r . . .]." 20–26 Who is t[his fellow, servant (and) dog], that he has taken the ci[ties of the king for himself], and (even) mayor[s *has killed.*[1] And so] may the king make inquiry [. . .] *whether* [*things are*] like th[is]. May the king [give thought] to guard[ing *his city* . . .] 26–31 . . . [. . .] 32–40 [. . .] he sent troo[ps to se]ize Gubla [and to se]ize Baṭruna. *It* [*is true*], you keep talking [li]ke this, "Yo⟨u⟩ are the one that writes to me more tha[n a]ll the (other) mayors."[2] Why should the[y be the ones] to write [t]o you? Th[ey] have (their) cities,[3] (but) my [ci]ties Aziru has taken! 41–52 In fact, he has returned in order to [se]ize Gubla. *In view of the mur*[*der*[4] of ʿAbdi]-Aširta [and] Paw[ura], *h*[*e n*]*ow* [*says*] to me, "No[w], the king will [*not*] come out."[5] So [may *the king come out*], as your ancestors did. The traitors [*have rebelled*] agai[nst *the king*].[6] As far as I am concerned, there are no oxen nor any sheep and goats.[7] Why has the king ⟨*not*⟩ sent [*chari*]*oteers* (*and*) archers to take the ci[ties]?[8] 53–60 If he[9] is unable to take [them, then] he will also take Gubla [fr]om you. [*You will*] not [*ta*]*ke* it ev[er] (again).[10] If the king's desire is to ⟨*gu*⟩*ar*[*d his city, gr*]*ant*[11] and send [a gar]rison [with all s]peed in[to . . .] 61–67 . . .[12]

NOTES

1. 20 *mi-ia-*[*mi*] *š*[*u-ut* ÌR UR.KU] 21 *ù la-qa* U[RU.MEŠ LUGAL *a-na ša-šu*] 22 *ù ḫa-za-nu-*[*ti* da-ka/ak]: for lines 21f., cf. *EA* 71:16ff.; 75:41ff.; 76:12ff.; 79:45ff.; for end of line 22, cf. *EA* 139:14; 140:11, 13, 26.

2. *at-*⟨*ta*⟩*-m*[*a*]: cf. *at-ta-ma tištapruna* (*EA* 117:8) in a virtually identical context.

3. *ālānū ana š*[*a-šu-nu*]: cf. *EA* 125:33f.

4. *di*-[ik-ti/ka-at]: though *dīktu* occurs only once in peripheral Akkadian (S. Lackenbacher, *RA* 76 [1982] p. 145:37), still the proposed restoration seems worthy of consideration, seeing that the verb *dâku*, "to kill," is used of both ʿAbdi-Aširta and Pawuru; see *EA* 101:5, 29; 131:22; 362:69; cf. 132:45.

5. Another possibility: "If at the death of ʿAbdi-Aširta and Pawuru the king did not come out, he will not come out now." Cf. *Or* n.s. 29 (1960) pp. 14f.

6. 47 ... [na-ak-ru] 48 LÚ.MEŠ *ša-ru-tu iš-t*[*u* LUGAL]: cf. *EA* 113.49.

7. *ú-ul* GUD.MEŠ 50 *ù la-a* ÙZ.MEŠ: on the writing of *ul*, see *EA* 118, n. 3, and note the absence of "one" before ÙZ.MEŠ (*EA* 55, n. 2).

8. As the text stands, Rib-Hadda asks why the king sent *charioteers* (and? or?) archers, as if they could not be expected to be successful (Weber, *VAB* 2/2, p. 1206), and they were not. These archers could then be connected with those for whose death Rib-Hadda has been accused of being responsible (*EA* 119:18ff.; Pintore, *OA* 12 [1973] pp. 304f., n. 29). There are, however, no other clear links between *EA* 119 and *EA* 122–24, and in an unemended text there seems to be no grammatically and stylistically acceptable way of reading lines 54ff. that also makes sense.

9. I assume a shift of persons in referring to the king in lines 53–55. Also possible: "He will not be able ..., and then. ..."

10. 55 ... *la-a*-[(mi)] 56 [ti-ìl-q]ú-*še*: probably not enough room for [yi-ìl-q]ú-*še*.

11. 57 ... *a-na* ⟨na⟩-ṣ[a-ar URU-šu] 58 [id]-*na* ...: cf. *EA* 127:26–29. A garrison (line 59) is not used for offensive purposes, and hence *ana* ṣ[*abāt*] is excluded.

12. Another reference to the three Byblos citizens detained in Egypt; see *EA* 122f.

EA 125

A study in contrasts

TEXT: BM 29802.

COPY: BB 19.

TRANSLATION: Oppenheim, *LFM*, pp. 130f.

To the king, [my] lord: Message of Rib-Hadda, [your] ser[vant]. I fall at the feet of my lord, my S[un], 7 times and 7 times. 5–13 May the Lady of Gubla grant power to the king, my lord. As to the king, my lord's, saying, "Guard yourself and guard the city of the king where you are,"[1] with what shall I guard myself and the city of [the king]? 14–24 Previously, there was a garrison of the king with me, and the king was accustomed to give grain for their food from the land of Yarimuta. But now Aziru has repeatedly raided me. I have neither oxen nor sheep and goats.[2] Aziru has taken everything. 25–32 And there is no grain for my food, and the peasantry has gone off to towns where there is grain for their food. Moreover, why does the king compare[3] me with the (other) mayors? 33–40 The mayors have their towns, and their pea⟨sant⟩ry[4] is in their control. But Aziru has my cities, and he seeks my life.[5] Why shall I make an alliance with him? 40–45 What are the dogs, the sons of ʿAbdi-Aširta, that ⟨⟨that⟩⟩ they do as they please and set fire to the cities of the king?

NOTES

1. *ša ittīka*: see Introduction, sect. 5.

2. See *EA* 55, n. 2.

3. *yištak(k?)anu-ni*: durative, not punctive (Oppenheim), and *šakānu*/*šitkunu kīma* means "to compare"; see Liverani, *RA* 61 (1967) p. 8, n. 1; *OA* 10 (1971) p. 264, n. 61 (also in *Three Amarna Essays*, p. 11).

4. The first sign seems to be *ḫu* rather than *ri*, for the damage is such that, were the sign *ri*, one would expect to see some trace of the missing vertical. A reference here to the peasantry of the other mayors would also yield a more complete contrast with Rib-Hadda's plight; see lines 27ff. Against the alternative reading *rēšušunu* (Knudtzon; Liverani, ibid.) is also the fact that *rēšu* as the designation of a person does not appear in *EA*. Oppenheim's version, "The regents of the other towns, however, belong from head to toe to them (i.e., the tribe of ʿAbdi-Aširti)," is without foundation in either grammar or context. See also *EA* 113:30f.; 118:45f.; 124:39.

5. Cf. *EA* 100, n. 4.

EA 126

Rejection of Byblos or Rib-Hadda?

TEXT: VAT 1183.
COPIES: WA 76; *VS* 11, 68.

Rib-Eddi.[1] Say to the king, my lord: I fall beneath the feet of my lord 7 times and 7 times. As for my lord's having written for *bo*[*xwood*],[2] it is taken from the lands of Salḫi and from Ugarit. 7–13 I am unable to send my ships there, since Aziru is at war with me, and all the mayors are at peace[3] with him. Their ships go about as they please, and they get what they need. 14–23 Moreover, why does the king give the mayors, my friends,[4] every sort of provision, but to me not give anything? Previously, money and everything for the⟨ir⟩ provisions were sent from the palace to my ancestors, and my lord would send troops to them. 23–33 But now I write for troops, but a garrison is not sent,[5] and nothing at all is given [to m]e. A[s for] the king, my lord's, [having said], "Gua[rd yourself] and [the city of the king where you are]," how am I to guar[d *myself*]?[6] 34–42 I wrote t[o the king, my lord], "They have taken a[ll] m[y cities]; the son of ʿAbdi-Aširta is their [*master*]. Gub[la is the only c]ity I have." I have ind[eed sen]t my mes⟨sen⟩ger t[o the king], my [lo]rd, but troops are not sen[t], and [my] messenger you do not allow to come out. 43–52 So send him along with rescue forces. If the king hates his city, then let him abandon it; but if me, then let him dismiss me.[7] Send a man of yours to g[uar]d it. Why is nothing given to me from the palace? . . .[8] the Hittite troops and they have set fire to the country. 53–60 I have written repeatedly, but no word comes back to me. They have seized all the lands of the king, my lord, but my lord has done nothing to them.[9] Now they are mobilizing[10] the troops of the Hittite countries to seize Gubla. 61–66 So give thought to [your] city. And may the [k]ing pay no atten[tion] to the men of the army.[11] They give all the silver and gold of the king to the sons of ʿAbdi-Aširta, and the sons of ʿAbdi-Aširta give this to the strong king,[12] and accordingly they are strong.

NOTES

1. A number of distinctive features associate *EA* 126, 129, 137(?), and 362, indicating that they were written by the same scribe, about the same time: (1) the greeting formula of *EA* 126 and 362, identical and unparalleled except perhaps in *EA* 129; (2) the writing *am-qut*^{ut}, in *EA*, only 126:3, 362:4, and possibly 128:23 (x-*qut*^{ut}); (3) fluctuation between {*ūna*} and {*ūni*} only in *EA* 126 and 362 (*EA* 126: *tu-ba-lu-na* in lines 58–59, but *ta-di-nu-ni* in lines 64–65; *EA* 362: *te-eq-bu-ni* in lines 17 and 25, but *te-eq-bu-na* in line 21; see also lines 24, 35, 44, and n. 12 below); (4) Hittites referred to as a threat only in *EA* 75:35ff., 126:50ff., and probably 129:76ff.; (5) *te/i-ba-ú-na* only in *EA* 129 and 362, perhaps 93:15, instead of normal *tu-ba-ú-na*; (6) *kazbūtu*, "lies," only in *EA* 129:37 and 362:53, besides 138:119; (7) *EA* 129:32f. = 362:25f., and 129:29 = 362:45; (8) *ḫummuṭu*, "to send (troops) quickly," only in *EA* 129:78 and 362:7, besides 102:29 (see also *EA* 88, n. 7); (9) the Egyptian official, whose name is written in several ways, appearing as ^{m}*pí-wu-ri* only in *EA* 129, 131, and 362.

2. In view of *tu-ul*$_{11}$*-qú-na* in line 6, the logogram is to be read as feminine singular or common plural. The latter seems more likely ("logs," "beams," being understood). If the correct reading is ^{giš}⌜TASKARIN⌝-*ma*, the force of the enclitic escapes me.

3. See *EA* 90, n. 7.

4. See *EA* 113, n. 9.

5. *tu-š*[*a-ru*] or *tu-š*[*a-ru-na*]: see *EA* 114, n. 6, and cf. *yú-ša-ru*, line 40.

6. *a-na-ṣa-r*[*u* ra-ma-ni-ia]: see *EA* 122, n. 1.

7. I read *ia-ti-ia* ⌜*ù*⌝, though Knudtzon's *ši*-b[a], "old man," is possible. Nothing requires it, however, and the parallelism of the two sentences favors the introduction of both apodoses by *u*. In support of taking *i-zi-ba-ši* in the sense of "(then) I will abandon it," *EA* 82:41ff. and 83:45ff. have been cited as parallels, and it has also been argued that the king would not be asked to send a replacement

if he were being told to abandon Byblos (Liverani, *RA* 61 [1967] p. 13, n. 4). The latter argument ignores the fact that the replacement is called for only under the *second* condition. My interpretation, in which, depending on whether the king rejects the city itself or its ruler, the king has two possible courses of action, seems clearer and more forceful. Note, too, how frequently, if one hates, one also flees (*nābutu*) or abandons (*ezēbu*); see the passages cited in *CAD*, Z, pp. 97f.

8. Knudtzon's description of the sign(s?) is exact; *aš-šu* is excluded. *la*(?), "Are there not the Hittite troops . . . ?"

9. *iš*(text:*tu*)-*tu*.

10. See M. Lichtenstein, *JANES* 2 (1970) p. 100, n. 49.

11. See *EA* 101, n. 4.

12. In *ta-di-nu-ni* I take {*ūni*} as a free variant of {*ūna*} and a peculiarity of this scribe. *Izre'el, UF* 16 (1987) p. 91, n. 37, has challenged this view and would translate the forms with {*ūni*} as preterites. In *EA* 362:21–25, however, the time reference of *teqbūna* and *teqbūni* is almost certainly the same; note also the parallelism of *teba'ūna* and *teqbūni*. Decisive, however, is the fact that in the strictly parallel passages *EA* 129:32–33 = 362:25–26, the *teqbūna* of the first is replaced in the latter by *teqbūni*.

The "strong king" was probably the Hittite ruler (Murnane, *The Road to Kadesh* [see Introduction, n. 119], p. 206) rather than the king of Mittani (G. Bunnens, *AIPHOS* 20 [1968–72] p. 150).

EA 127

Alone against the world

TEXT: VAT 1687.
COPIES: WA 184; *VS* 11, 69.

. . .[1] **12–22** Let *the arch*[*ers*] come out [*an*]*d* fetch us.[2] Cry out, *"On to Gubla*!"[3] For who—seeing that everyone is against me—who is to rescue me? [*I assure yo*]*u*, upon the taking of Gubla[4] there will be no men from Egypt [*who*] will get in here. Should Gubla be [jo]ined[5] [to] the [ʿAp]iru, then there will be no [*soldiers from Ka*]*ša* who will get in. **23–29** [*Certai*]*nly*, Yanḫamu being [*with you*], the king should inquire from him [*about the sl*]*anders*.[6] Gubla is a loyal city. If it is the desire of the king, my lord, to guard his city, then may my lord give a garrison of . . . [. . .], and it will be guarded. **30–41** And now I declare, my lord: when[7] previously ʿAbdi-Aširatu used to come up against me, *I w*[*as str*]*ong*, but now *there has been a controversy among* my men, and *it is different*.[8] *I am being hard-pressed* : *ṣí-ir-ti* (I am besieged).[9] May my lord grant 100 men and 100 soldiers from Kaši, and 30 chariots, that I may guard the land of my lord until a large force of archers comes out, [and] my lord [ta]kes the land of Amurru [fo]r himself, [and it h]as peace. [. . .] . . .[10]

NOTES

1. Line 8: *ù qé-bi-ir qa-al,* "and he *was buried.* [The king] did nothing." Line 12: [. . . ᵐia-ab-*n*]*i*-ᵈIM (Hadda/Baʿal).

2. If ÉRIN.MEŠ *piṭāti* is the subject of both verbs, *tuṣṣi* and *tilqe* are expected; cf. the feminine singular adjective *rabīti* in line 39.

3. "(Let us set) our faces upon Gubla," (*nad/tna*) pa-*ni-nu eli/muḫḫi* U[R]U *gub-la.*

4. [al-lu]-*mi la-qé*: infinitive rather than stative *laqat*; for the construction, with loss of voice distinction, see *JCS* 4 (1950) pp. 169ff.

5. [ti-ni-*i*]*p-ša-mi*: lit. "let Gubla be joined" (*yaqtula*); cf., however, *EA* 88:31 (*en-ni-ip-ša-⟨at⟩*?).

6. [a-na k]a-*ar-ṣí*: cf. *EA* 119:26; perhaps "the slanders against Gubla, the loyal city."

7. *kīma,* "when," is without parallel in the Byblos corpus.

8. If Durand's analysis of *riḫṣu* in *AÉM* 1/1, pp. 181ff., is correct, and if it is pertinent here, then the context suggests that the controversy or palaver concerned their loyalty to Rib-Hadda. *šani,* "another" (palaver)?

9. I read *is-sà-qú* : *ṣí-ir-ti*; Akkadian *siāqu,* "to become narrow, straitened" = Canaanite *ṣûr,* "to confine, besiege." The Akkadian form seems to be an erroneous perfect, *issāq*(for *issīq*) + {u} of Canaanite durative.

10. Five lines, with a reference to the ʿApiru. Last words: "[*then I will*] die."

EA 128

Message lost

TEXT: VAT 1873 (not collated).
COPIES: WA 227; *VS* 11, 71.

Too fragmentary for translation; addressed to the king.[1]

NOTE

1. A few signs preserved on the obverse, and 13 very fragmentary lines on the reverse. Lines 21ff. may contain a postscript of the future ruler of Byblos (cf. *EA* 140), written by the same scribe as that of *EA* 126: 21 [um-ma] ᵐ*i-li-ra*-[pí-iḫ] 22 [a-na KI].TA GÌR.MEŠ LUGAL E[N-*ia*] 23 [7 ù 7 am]-*qut*ᵘᵗ-*ma,* "Message of Ili-rapiḫ: I fall 7 times and 7 times beneath the feet of the king, my lord. And may the king, my lord, hear about the deed of (that) criminal . . ." On postscripts, see Introduction, sect. 4.

EA 129

A long review of the situation

TEXT: VAT 1637 + 1638.
COPIES: WA 86 + WA 87; *VS* 11, 70.

[Rib]-Add[i. Say t]o the [ki]ng, [my] lord: [I fall beneath the fee]t ⟨of my lord⟩ 7 times and 7 [times].[1] 4–12 May the king, my lord, inq⟨ui⟩re[2] abo[ut the s]on[s] of ʿAbdi-Aširt[a, f]or they *d*[*o*][3] as they please. Who are they, the dogs[4] [. . .] that they should *acquire fo*[*r themselves* a]nything? *They have piled up prop*[*erty of*] the lands of the king in [*their own*] *han*[*ds*].[5] The mayors of the king . . . [. . .] soldiers and [. . .] 13–21 Now what they *too*[*k ha*]*d been i*[*n the charge of*][6] the commissioners of the king, [my] lord, and the (*last*) commissioner [was] a *wi*[*se*] man who was highly respected,[7] b[ut *they have killed him*].[8] All my cities belong to ⟨t⟩hem.[9] Baṭruna remai[ns *to me*],[10] and they strive to ta[ke] it. On its being [ta]ken [*Gubla* (itself)] they will [t]ake.[11] 22–25 . . . 26–34 greatly. Truly, they have *long*[*ed*][12] to commit a great [crime]. Since a tablet to the mayors is [not *pro*]*duced,*[13] they are intent on committing [a crime].[14] If there are no archers, [then] their aim will be to seize [Gubla]. They say, "If w[e] seize Gubla,[15] what will the archers do?" 34–54 L[ook],[16] as to the king, my lord's, having written, "Troops have indeed come out," you spo[ke] lies : *ka-ma-mi*(?).[17] There are no archers; they do not come out. And they are stronger[18] than we are. [Look],[19] unless archers come out within this year, they will [tak]e[20] Gubla. If Gubla [*is taken, then they will be strong.*[21] W]hat will the troops do [*for your servant*], Rib-Hadda? *Fo*[*r my ancesto*]*rs,* earlier kings guard[ed][22] Gubla, and you yourself must not abandon it. If there are no archers this year, then send ships to fetch me, along with (my) living god,[23] to my lord. May the king, my lord, not say, "Surely it cannot be seized. It is *at pe*[*ace*]."[24] And now . . .[25] [. . .] . . . 55–74 . . . 75–89 the king of [. . . *and*] the king of the Hittite countries,[26] *so that* [*the lands of the king belong*] to the sons of ʿAbdi-Aširta, servants (and) dogs.[27] Accordingly, may the king hasten the sending of the archers so he may take them, and the lands be joined to the king, m[y l]ord. Who are they, the dogs? If Biryawaza *is afraid* ⟨*o*⟩*f* the king, my lord, he has not taken them.[28] If the king, my lord, keeps telling the magnate of . . . [. . .][29] and the magnate of Kumidu, "*Ta*[*ke* (*them*)],"[30] they have not taken them. [*They have committed*] *a cri*[*me.*[31] Th]ey are against me; they *have won* [*the lands*] for the ʿApiru.

90–94 ... 94–98 Since there are n[o arc]hers, *th*[*ey are str*]*ong*.[32] They took Pewur[u and ki]lled him. *They are* [*against me*]; they took the *territo*⟨ry⟩ of Ṣ[umu]r for themselves,[33] and [*they killed the commissioner of the king*], Pewuru. If [*the king*] is not going to list[en to *his servant, then may he se*]*nd* ships.

NOTES

1. 1 [^{m}*ri-ib*]-*ad-d*[*i qí-bi*/*bí-mi*] 2 [*a-n*]*a* [LUG]AL *be-li*-[*ia a-na* KI.TA] 3 [G]Ì[R].MEŠ 7 *u* ⸢7⸣ [*am-qut*^{ut}]: cf. *EA* 126:1–3; 362:1–4, and see *EA* 126, n. 1, on the scribe of *EA* 129.

2. ⸢*y*⸣*i*-⟨ša⟩-*al*: cf. *EA* 124:23. The reading and interpretation of lines 4–21 are extremely difficult, and so the translation is here often extremely tentative.

3. *ti*-⸢i⸣-[pu-šu-na]: cf. *ti-e-te-pu-šu* in line 88.

4. UR.MEŠ-⸢*ka*⸣-*b*[*u*]: as in line 81, for *ka*-UR.MEŠ-*bu* (*kalbū*), which is comparable to KÚR-*nu* (originally for *nukurtu*, passim), TÉŠ-*ba* (for *bāšta*, *EA* 102:7), and perhaps [SA]G?-*q*[*à*]-*di* (for *qaqqadī*, *EA* 209:16). Better, *ka*-⟨*al*⟩-*bu*?

5. 8 *tīpušūna a-n*[*a* ša-šu-nu] 9 [*m*]*a-am-ma ku-mi-ru mi*-a[m-ma ša] 10 [K]UR.MEŠ LUGAL *a-na* UZ[U.M]EŠ *qa*-[ti-šu-nu]: *kummirū* (*kamāru*, "to pile up"), like *uššir, puḫḫir,* etc.; *mi-am-ma,* as elsewhere in the Byblos letters (*VAB* 2/2, p. 1469).

6. ⸢a⸣-[n]a [qa-at].

7. LÚ e[m-qu šu-ut] 16 *ša ka-bu-ut ma-gal*: cf. *EA* 106:39 and 107:23, assuming here a sporadic Assyrianism (*kabbut*).

8. ⸢*ù*⸣ [da-ku-šu]: cf. line 96 and *EA* 362:69.

9. *ana* ⟨ša⟩-*šu*-[nu].

10. *irtīḫa*[*t* a-na ia-ši]: enough room?

11. [URU.KI gub-la]: enough room?

12. *ti-iṣ-b*[*u* ar-na]: *ṣabû,* "to desire, long for," is otherwise unattested in the periphery.

13. *i-nu*-[*ma* la-a] 28 š[u-*l*]*i*: the king's silence shows indifference and encourages the rebels.

14. *i-pi-iš* [*ar-ni*]: *EA* 129:29 = 362:45.

15. *ṣa-bat-mi ni*-[*nu*]: *EA* 129:32 = 362f.; see *JCS* 4 (1950) p. 170. In *EA* 129 and 362, the MEŠ in URU.(KI).MEŠ is either otiose or carries with it the connotation of "all/greater Gubla" (or the like); see also Thureau-Dangin's translation, *RA* 19 (1922) pp. 91ff. Cf. URU.KI in line 31, but here URU.KI.MEŠ; similarly, *EA* 362:26 has URU.MEŠ, but 362:28 URU.KI. That Byblos, and not the outlying villages, is intended throughout is also required by context. Only the city of Baṭruna remains, and the prize sought by the enemy and feared by Rib-Hadda is the capture of Byblos itself (*EA* 362:12f.). Note, too, that in *EA* 129:53, where the hope is expressed that the king will not dismiss the threats expressed by Rib-Hadda, only one city is referred to.

16. Cf. *amur-mi* in *EA* 362:27, which follows immediately after the sentence beginning, "If we seize ..."

17. Artzi, *Bar-Ilan* 1 (1963) pp. 38f., explains the gloss as Akkadian

kâmma-mi, "thus," whereby the scribe emphasizes that it is right to call what the king wrote lies. I do not accept the alleged parallel in *PRU* 3, p. 48:16.

18. Perhaps better: "(If) there are no archers (and) they do not come out, they will be stronger. . . ." Cf. *EA* 362:27 and line 44 below.

19. [a-mur-*m*]*i*: cf. *EA* 362:27, and see n. 16 above.

20. [ù la]-*qú-mi*.

21. [ù da-nu *m*]*i-na* . . . 45 [a-na ÌR-ka ᵐ]*rib-hadda*: cf. *u dannū* in *EA* 362:28; Knudtzon's restoration is grammatically unacceptable (*tiqbūna* required). In line 45, the parallel in line 34 suggests a restoration of [*pí-ṭá-tu*], which would also fit the break perfectly. But this would leave the personal name hanging in the air. Perhaps Rib-Hadda refers to himself by name because he is implicitly citing the words of his enemy.

22. *ti-n*[*a-ṣa-ru-n*]*a*.

23. If the ships were to fetch "me alive" (Knudtzon), we should expect *balṭa*, not *balṭi*, and right after *tilqūni*; see *Or* n.s. 29 (1960) p. 4, n. 3. The "living god" is very likely the same god that is mentioned in *EA* 84:35.

24. *mi-di la ṣa-ab-ta-at pa*-[aš-ḫa-at]: see *JCS* 31 (1979) p. 94, n. 46.

25. *tu*-⸢iṣ⸣-*ba*-t[u-na], "your messengers are being seized"?

26. Perhaps, 74ff., "Who are they? the king of Mittani? the king of Kaššu? the king of Hittite countries?" Cf. *EA* 116:70f.

27. See n. 4.

28. *pal-ḫa* ⟨iš⟩-*tu* LUGAL BE-[*ia*]: cf. Hebrew *yārēʾ min*. If Biryawaza is afraid of the king (as the king says he is), he is not showing it and attacking the king's enemies.

29. The most likely reading seems to be URU.KI a[z-za-ti], Gaza; see Na'aman, *Political Disposition*, p. 170; Helck, *Beziehungen*, p. 249.

30. *le*-[qú-mi]: again (see n. 28) Rib-Hadda seems to refer to a letter from the king.

31. a[r-na] 87 [ep-šu]: despite Knudtzon's objections, *VAB* 2/1, p. 552, note a.

32. ⸢dan⸣-*nu*.

33. The scribe of *EA* 126, 129, and 362 never introduces a city simply by URU, but by URU.MEŠ or URU.KI(.MEŠ), and so it is unlikely that URU *ṣ*[*u-mu-r*]*i* is correct. I propose *i-pi*-⟨ri⟩ KI.URU (logogram reversed) *ṣ*[*u-mu-r*]*i*; cf. *eperū*, "territory," which is attested in Alalakh, Aleppo, and Boghazköy (Šunaššura treaty).

EA 130

Life among the ʿApiru

TEXT: VAT 1624.

COPIES: WA 46; *VS* 11, 72.

Say [t]o the king, my lord: Message of Rib-Hadda, your servant. May the Lady of Gubla grant power to the king, my lord. I fall at the feet of the king, my lord, my Sun, 7 times and 7 times. 9–14 As to the king's having written to me, "Irimayašša is coming to you," he has not come to me. 14–20 As to the king's having written me, "Guard yourself and guard the city of the king where you are," who can guard me? 21–31 Look, formerly my ancestors [were str]ong. There was war against the[m, but] a garrison [of the king] was wi⟨t⟩h them. There were provisions from the king at their disposal. [*Though the war against me*] is seve[re], I have [n]o [provision]s [from the king or gar]ri[son of the king]. Wh[at shall I] do? 32–42 As for the mayors, [the]y are the ones who strik[e][1] our city. They are like dogs, and there is no one who wants to serve them. What am I, who live among ʿApiru, to do? If now there are no provisions from the king for me, my peasantry is going to *fi*[*gh*]*t* (against me).[2] 43–52 A⟨ll⟩ lands are at war against me. If the desire of the king is to guard his city and his servant, send a garrison to guard the city. [I] will guard it while I am [a]live. When [I] die, who is going to [gu]ard it?

NOTES

1. *ti-du-ku-*[*na šu*]*-nu*.

2. If the verb in question is *šanānu,* perhaps "will become hostile"; see Liverani, in Garelli, ed., *Le Palais et la Royauté* (see Introduction, n. 73), p. 188, n. 111, who notes the parallelism in Ugaritic of *nkr̠* and *t̠n*.

EA 131

A commissioner killed

TEXT: BM 29807.
COPY: BB 24.

[. . .] 6–14 My lord [*us*]*ed to send*[1] a garri[son] to Gubla. Ṣumur has now been seized; troops from Gubla have been killed. If the desire of the king, my lord, is (to guard) Gubla, then may my lord send 300 soldiers, 30 chariots, and 100 men from Kaši, that they may guard Gubla, the city of my lord. 15–20 If the king does not send the *summer-grain,*[2] *should* troops *a*[*dv*]*an*[*ce*][3] on Gubla, they will s[ur]ely take it, and *m*[*e, your servant*],[4] they will kill. . . . 21–30 They have attacked[5] commissioners : *ma-lik.*MEŠ (counselors) of the king. When Pewuru, the king's counselor, was killed, he was placed in . . . We are servants of the king, and it is distressing for us to see that w⟨e⟩ *are going to be taken.*[6] I myself am afraid I will be *kil*[*led.*[7] *The corps*]*e was cas*[*t aw*]*ay; i*[*t*] *had no one for fu*[*nerary offerin*]*gs.*[8] 30–40 [*Form*]*erly,*[9] this is the way they acted: the king, [*your*] *fath*[*er*], did [not][10] send a small archer force, and he *t*[*ook*] everything. Paḫamnata would not listen to me, and he went on with his tr[eacher]ous activities. Now his son has *plund*[*ered*][11] Ṣumur. If [the king] heeds the words of his servant and [sends] a large archer force, he (the king) *wil*[*l take everyt*]*hing*.[12] 41–47 As to its being said[13] be[fore] the king, "There is no grain (or) food [*for*] the archers to eat," wherever are all the cities of the king food and grain [*may be found*].... 48–56 [...] 57–62 [... *arch*]*ers* and auxiliary forces [...][14] He must not *ne*[*glec*]*t* [*his city*.[15] If] he does not send (them) [*to Gubl*]*a*, they will take it, and [...]. The lands of Canaan will not belong to the king. [May the king ask] Yanḫamu about th⟨ese⟩ ma⟨tt⟩ers.[16]

NOTES

1. [yú-š]i-*ru*: cf. *yú-ši-ra* (line 12) and *yú-ši-ru* (line 15); [uš-š]i-*ru* (Knudtzon) must assume an extremely rare plural of majesty.

2. The difficulties with ŠE.MEŠ *qè-e-ṣí* are (1) ŠE is not completely certain; (2) *qè* (GI) is otherwise unknown in the Byblos corpus; and (3) the subject of supplies is introduced suddenly and in an unparalleled manner.

3. ⌜yi-ṣa⌝-[ba]-*ta*$_5$ *a-na* URU.KI *gub-l*[*a* KASKAL$^?$ (ḫarrāna)]: if *yiṣabbata* is the correct reading, note the change in number in *tilqūnaši*, which is perhaps to be taken as an indefinite plural. The final {*a*} is probably a fossilized ventive, not modal. Also possible (Knudtzon): "If ..., then troops will advance ..."

4. *ia*-[a]-t[i ÌR-ka]: cf. line 28. The tablet is badly damaged or eroded here, and the interpretation of traces is extremely difficult and subjective.

5. The context suggests that *qerēbu*, "to approach," here implies hostility; cf. *qitrubu* and *taqrubtu*, Hebrew *qᵉrāb*.

6. *ni*-⟨nu⟩ *na-lá-qú*: very tentatively taken as passive of *leqû* (*nuiaqqu* or *nulqu* expected); *alāqu* = *ḫalāqu*, "to perish"?

7. *ú-da-a*-k[a]: the reading is almost certain; on the syntax, see *Or* n.s. 29 (1960) p. 14.

8. 28 ... *udāk*[a LÚ.Ú]Š 29 *yú-n*[*a-d*]*a* LÚ KI.[SÈ.GA]-*pí* 30 *ia-nu a-na ša-a*-[*šu* ...]: quite conjectural. Reference to Pewuru's body? Another possibility: "Should a corpse be laid to rest, there is no one...."

9. 30 ... *ana ša-a*-[*šu* pa-na]-*nu-ma*: elsewhere in the Byblos corpus, *pānānu*, not *pānānumma*.

10. Unless this passage contradicts *EA* 117:23ff., either a negative is to be restored or the sentence must be read as a question; note, too, the request for a large force in lines 38ff. Beginning of line 32: read probably *yú-šìr* or *yú*-⟨*wa*⟩-*šìr*; see *VAB* 2/2, p. 1594. End of line 32: if *ab-b*[*u-ka*] is the correct reading, the doubling must be ignored. Read AD-*b*[*u-ka*] = *abūka*?

11. Na'aman, *Political Disposition*, pp. 166f., proposes *yu-ḫa*-[*li-iq*], but it is questionable whether there is enough room.

12. In view of *yišmu* (line 38), probably [y]ú-[ši-ru] (line 39) and *yi*-[ìl-qú] (line 40).

13. *yú-qa-bu*: following Izre'el, *UF* 19 (1987) p. 86.

14. If archers are mentioned in line 57, then a form of *naṣāru*, "to guard," is not to be restored in the break; see *EA* 88, n. 8. Parallels (*EA* 112:33ff.; 132:56ff.) suggest a form of *pašāḫu* (*u pašḫat āl gubla*, "then Gubla will be at peace"?).

15. *lāmi* [i-m]a-a[k]-*ki* 59 [ana URU.KI-šu].

16. 62 [yi-ša-al ᵐ]*ia-an-ḫa-ma a-na a-*⟨*wa*⟩*-te.* MEŠ *an-*⟨*nu-tu*⟩: cf. *EA* 132:29ff.

EA 132

The hope for peace

TEXT: BM 29801.
COPY: BB 18.

[S]ay [to] the king, my lord, m[y] Sun: Message of Rib-Hadda, your [ser]vant. May the Lady of Gubla grant power to the king, my lord. I fall at the feet of my lord 7 times and 7 times. 8–18 Moreover, give thought to Gubla, your loyal city. Earlier, ʿAbdi-Aširta attacked me, and I wrote to your father, "Send the royal archers, and the entire land will be taken in a day."[1] Did he not take[2] fo[r himself] ʿAbdi-Aširt[a], together with his possessions? 19–23 Now Aziru has gathered a[ll] the ʿApiru and has said to them, "If Gubla *is* not ... [...]"[3] 24–28 [...] ... 29–37 [L]ook, Yanḫamu being with you, a[sk him] if I did not say to him, "If you make an alliance ... [...] with the sons of ʿAbdi-Aširta, they will take you prisoner."[4] He listened t[o me], and he guarded the c[ities] of the king, his lord. 37–50 I said the same thing to Pawuru so he would not listen to the words of Ḫa'i[p], whose father turned the citi[es] into enemies.[5] Now Ḫa'ip has hand[ed over] Ṣumur. May the king not neglect this deed, since a commissioner was killed. If now you are negligent, then Piḫura will not stay in Kumidu, and all your [ma]yors will be killed. 51–59 I keep ⟨wr⟩iting like this to the *pa*[*lac*]*e*, [but] no attention is paid [t]o me. Send ships to fetch the Lady's property and me. [Sen]d 50–100 men and 50–100 *m*[*en fro*]*m* [Meluḫ]ḫa, 50 chariots, [to g]uard [*the city*] for you.[6] Se[nd] archers and bring peace to the land.

NOTES

1. On the otiose MEŠ in UD.KAM.MEŠ, see *EA* 109, n. 2.

2. On *laqi*, see *EA* 108, n. 5.

3. Perhaps ni-x-[x] (line 23); the third vertical of *ir* (Knudtzon, BB) is not clear. "If *we* do not ... Gubla, then ..."?

4. *a-pa-ši* x-[x-x] *at-ta ki-ta it-*[*ti* DUMU.M]EŠ ᵐÌR-*a-ši-ir-ta ù la-qú-ka ša-ma a-na* [*ia-ši*]: see *JCS* 4 (1950) p. 170; *Or* n.s. 29 (1960) p. 10, n. 1. In my opinion, MEŠ definitely belongs on line 33; on line 32, the vertical after ŠI in BB is certain, but a plausible restoration escapes me.

5. On lines 37ff., see *Or* n.s. 29 (1960) p. 10, n. 1; for a somewhat different version, see Na'aman, *Political Disposition,* p. 167.

6. Line 57: [(*ù*) *ti-n*]*a-ṣí-r*[*u*]. If there is not enough room for the conjunction, the construction is asyndetic, for which see *EA* 121, n. 3. Rules of modal sequence exclude *anaṣṣiru* (Knudtzon). On the reading of the numbers, see Pintore, *OA* 11 (1972) p. 103, n. 9.

EA 133

Some advice for the king

TEXT: VAT 1667 (not collated).
COPIES: WA 66; *VS,* 11, 74.

[. . . the kin]g, [my] lord. [. . . *Moreov*]*er,* give thought your[self t]o your servant and to Gubla. . . . [. . .] 5–11 Ṣumur [. . .]. The sons of ʿAbdi-Aši[rta *have taken*] all [your] cities. They [ar]e at war wi[th *me.* A]s Ḫa'ip is [*with you*], ask him. And [may it seem right] in your sight, and then 12–19 send a [garrison] to your cities with all [sp]eed. [I ke]ep writing like [this] to the king, [my lord]: [Se⟨n⟩]d me 10 [*men from Meluḫ*]ḫa : *ka-*[ši *that I may gua*]*rd* [. . .][1]

NOTE

1. On the gloss, see Pintore, *OA* 11 (1973) p. 105, n. 24.

EA 134

Departure of the gods

TEXT: C 4754 (12189).
COPY: WA 83.

[*Sen*]*d* [*troops to Gu*]*bla,*[1] lest Azi[ru ta]ke it. From time im[memorial] the g[ods] have not *gone aw*[*ay*][2] from Gubla. 7–14 [N]ow Aziru has sen[t] troops t[o sei]ze it, so that *we must* give up[3] our gods, a[nd *they have gone for*]*th.* And there being no [troops i]n the city to smit[e *the servant*], *the evil dog,*[4] 15–22 they can[not] return. [Wh]at am I to do [b]y myself? [The people w]ho were i[n the cit]y have deserted *i*[*n order to g*]*et provis*[*ions fo*]*r th*[*emselves*]. . . . 23–29 [*and he* s]ends a [*garris*]*on* to [*his*] *ci*[*ty*]. [*I*] and Gubla, the king's loyal city [. . .]. As I have sent a man of mine to the palace, why has the ki[ng] not written? 29–38 . . . and *I* wrote. *N*[*ow*] the war against me is severe, and I am afraid. He has, I ass[ure you], taken Ṣumur. Who has said anything to him? *This being true,* he has turned again[st Gub]la . . . 38–41 [. . .] . . .

NOTES

1. [uš-ši-ra]-*mi* [ÉRIN.MEŠ]: cf. *EA* 82:15; 90:15; 94:10; 132:13.

2. If read correctly, lit. "have not gone up" (*elû*). To their heavenly dwellings, abandoning their earthly ones in Byblos?

3. *nad/tnu*: taken as first plural (cf. *nad/tna* in *EA* 89:16); perhaps *nadnū,* "have been given up."

4. [ÌR] ⌜LÚ⌝? UR.RI (*kalbi*)? In the break there is room for an average-size sign, followed by a somewhat oblique wedge, under which traces of a horizontal, possibly crossed by two or three verticals; then the erasure. Cf. LÚ UR.KU (*EA* 84:35; 320:22; 322:17), UR (*kalbu, EA* 129:7, 77, 81; 137:26), and UR.KI, genitive of UR.KU (*EA* 138:96).

EA 135

Message lost

TEXT: Ash 1893. 1–41: 409.
COPY: Sayce, *Tell el Amarna,* no. 2.

Too fragmentary for translation.[1]

NOTE

1. This tablet no longer exists; see Introduction, n. 9.

EA 136

Rib-Hadda from Beirut

TEXT: BM 29799.
COPY: BB 16.
PHOTOGRAPH: BB, pl. 20.

[T]o the king, my lord: Message of Rib-Hadda, your servant, the dirt at your feet. I fall at the feet of the king, my lord, 7 times and 7 times. 6–15 May the king, my lord, heed the words of his servant. Men of Gubla, my own household, and my wife, kept saying to me,

"Ally yourself with the son of ʿAbdi-Aširta so we can make peace[1] between us." But I refused.[2] I did not listen to them.

16–23 Moreover, I repeatedly wrote to the king, my lord, "Send *immediately*[3] a garrison to your servant that they may guard the city for the king, ⟨my⟩ lord." No word, however, from the king, my lord, has reached his servant.

24–36 Moreover, when I was *hard pressed,*[4] I thought to myself, "Come! I must mak⟨e⟩ an alliance of friendship : TU.KA[5] with Ammunira." So I went to his house in order to make an alliance of friendship between ⟨us⟩. Then I returned to my own house, but he barred the house against me.[6] May the king, my lord, give thought to his servant.

37–46 I am now awaiting day and night the archers of the king, my lord. May the king, my lord, give thought to his servant. If the king, my lord, does not have a change of heart, then I will die.[7] May the king, my lord, give life to his servant. Moreover, they have given two of my sons and two of my wives to the rebel against the king.

NOTES

1. *šalma epēšu,* for *salīma epēšu* (*AHw,* p. 1149b), or perhaps *šul*$_x$*-ma epēšu.*

2. Cf. *ma'û,* "to push away, repel" (*AHw,* pp. 637, 1574; von Soden, *OLZ* 76 [1971] cols. 246f.); see also *EA* 122, n. 5.

3. BIL? *ḫamāṭu,* "to burn," confused with *ḫamāṭu,* "to hasten"? *uššira ḫumṭa* (imperative), hendiadys? Cf. *EA* 137:79.

4. Following *CAD,* Ṣ, p. 123.

5. DÙG.GA : TU.KA: the gloss is a syllabic writing of the Sumerogram DÙG.GA. The Akkadian equivalent—if there was one and the expression was not simply "to make *tuka*"—was probably *ṭābūtu* (*JNES* 22 [1963] pp. 173ff.; *AHw,* p. 1378); see also *EA* 302, n. 2, and Introduction, n. 59.

6. The form *id-du-ul* is more easily explained as active; the unnamed subject would be Rib-Hadda's brother (cf. *EA* 137:14ff. and *EA* 82, n. 5). If it is passive (*CAD,* E, p. 26b), *eddul,* an Assyrianism?

Locked out of his own house and driven from his city (*EA* 137:24f.), Rib-Hadda writes this letter and *EA* 137–38 from Beirut. The format (crude paragraphings) and some features of the language (e.g., *šanīta u* and *endu(m)* in line 24; *ittīšu ša* PN in line 29) distinguish *EA* 136 from the letters written at Byblos.

7. Perhaps better: "Look, there is no divided loyalty. For the king, my lord, I would die." On *šumma,* "look," see *EA* 35, n. 3; on *libbu šanû,* "divided loyalty," lit. "another heart," cf. *EA* 119:42; 169, n. 2; 371:18; and "another face" in *EA* 253:27.

EA 137

An old man in exile

TEXT: Golenischeff (see Introduction, sect. 1).
COPY: WA 71.
TRANSLATIONS: Oppenheim, *LFM,* pp. 132ff.; Albright, *ANET,* pp. 483f.; Seux, *Textes du Proche Orient,* pp. 48ff.

Rib-Ad[di says][1] to the king, [his] lord, [the Sun of all countries]: [I fall] beneath the feet [of the king, my lord], 7 times and 7 tim[es]. 5–14 I wrote repeatedly fo[r a garrison], but it was not granted, [and] the king, my lord, did [not] heed the word[s of his servant]. I sent a mess[enger of mine] to the palace, but he *re[turned]* empty-handed; he had no garri[son]. The men of my [*house*] saw that no money had been given, and so, like the mayors, my brothers, they *did me injustice*[2] and despised me. 14–26 Moreover, when I had gone to Ḫammuniri, my younger brother turned Gubla into an enemy in order to give the city to the sons of ʿAbdi-Aširta. When my brother saw that my mess⟨en⟩ger had come out empty-handed and that there was no garrison with him, he despised me. Accordingly, he committed a crime and drove me from the city. May the king, my lord, not neglect the deed of this dog. 27–35 I personally am unable to enter the land of Egypt. I am old and there is a serious illness in my body. The king, my lord, knows that the gods of Gubla are *holy,* and *the pains are severe,*[3] *for* I *com⟨mit⟩ted* sins against the gods.[4] Accordingly, I shall not enter the presence of the king, my lord. 36–51 So I herewith send my own son,[5] a servant of the king, my lord, into the presence of the king, my lord. May the king heed the wo⟨r⟩ds of his servant, and may the king, my lord, grant archers so they may se[ize][6] Gubla, and traitor⟨ous⟩ troops and the sons of ʿA[bdi]-Aširti not [en]ter it,[7] and the archers of the king, m[y] lord, be too few[8] to take it. As there are many that are loyal to me in the city (and) few the traitors in it, when the archers come forth and they hear (of it),[9] as soon as they arrive, the city will return to the king, my lord. 52–58 The king, my lord, knows that I will die for him. When I was in the city, I guarded it for my lord, a⟨nd⟩ I was dedicated to the king, my lord. I did not give the city to the sons of ʿAbdi-Ašrati.[10] Accordingly, my brother turned the city into an enemy in order to give it to the sons of ʿAbdi-Ašrati. 59–65 May the king, my lord, not neglect the city. Note, there is much silver and gold in it, and much is the property belonging to its temples.[11] If the king, my lord, seizes it, let him do to his servant as he will, but may he give⟨e⟩ Burusilim for me to live in.[12] 65–77 I am now with Ḫammuniri. *When the cities became hostile,* Burusilim *became hostile,* being in fear of the sons of ʿAbdi-Aširta.[13] When I came to Ḫammuniri because of the sons of ʿAbdi-Ašrati, seeing they were stronger than I and there was no breath from the mouth of the king for me, I said to my lord, "*If* Gubla *becomes their* city,[14] there is much property of the king in it, possessions of our an⟨ces⟩tors in the past. If the king neglects the city, of all the cities of Canaan not one will be his. May the king not neglect this matter." 78–89 I herewith send your servant, my son, to the king, my lord, and may the king send him quickly along with troops that they may take the city. If the king, my lord, shows me favor and returns me to the city, then I will guard i[t[15] . . .] as before for the king, my lord. If the king, my lord, [*does not return me*] to it, then [. . .] the city from *B*[*ur*]*us*[*ilim*. *May the king, my lord,* d]o as he wi[ll *to his servant, but let him not*] *ab*[*andon me. I am with*] Ḫammun[iri . . .]. *How lo*[*ng am I to stay with him*]? 90–104 May [*the king, my lord*], heed [the words] of his servant . . . [. . .], and may he send troops quickly to take the city. May the king, my lord, not neglect this painful deed that has been done to the lands of the king, [my lord]. May the king, [my] lord, rush[16] archers to seize the city as quickly as possible. Should it be said to the king about the city, "It is a strong city," it will not be strong before the troops of the king, my lord.

NOTES

1. Perhaps ᵐ*ri-ib-ad-*[*di qí-bí-ma*/*mi*], "Rib-Addi. Say . . ."; see *EA* 126 and n. 1.

2. *ti-iš-la-u₅*: *šalā'u* (*AHw*, p. 1147; only Old Assyrian)? Knudtzon and Ebeling translate as "inveigh against," Oppenheim, *LFM*, pp. 132ff., as "insult," and Albright, *ANET*, pp. 483f., as "ridicule," all apparently only from context; no etymology is proposed.

3. *mur-ṣú-ú* (cf. *mur-ṣí-i, EA* 75:18?) *magal*: since *magal* elsewhere never serves as an adjective, perhaps better, *murṣu-ma* GAL (*rabi*/*rabû*), "the pain/pains, too(?), is/are great." Albright, "the illness is severe"; Oppenheim, "my disease has become chronic" (too free).

4. *ep-*⟨*ša*⟩*-ti*: cf. *EA* 89:17; 113:11. Against the reading *ep-ti*, "I confessed" (Knudtzon; Oppenheim, *LFM*, pp. 132ff.; *AHw*, p. 860b) is that neither Akkadian *petû* nor the related root *ptḥ* in West Semitic languages ever means "to confess." The attested meaning of "to reveal" does not fit the context; Rib-Hadda's sins were presumably no secret to the gods. Furthermore, unless one assumes either a parenthetical remark or an unparalleled construction (Oppenheim: "although I confessed . . ."), the clause enunciates one more reason why Rib-Hadda cannot go to Egypt, and this can hardly be because he confessed his sins.

Mutatis mutandis, *ep-dì*, "I have redeemed (by a vow)" (Albright), suffers from the same difficulties: the assumed meaning is without parallel in Akkadian or West Semitic. It could explain Rib-Hadda's not going to Egypt only on the assumption that he had vowed not to go.

ḫīṭa epēšu: Standard Babylonian, Ugarit, Egypt (*EA* 162:9). *ḫīṭīṭa epēšu*: Boghazköy. On a causal clause introduced by *u*, cf. *EA* 101:3ff., 29f.; 104:36ff.; 105:36f.; 139:11f. The word order (object-verb) stresses the object: Rib-Hadda *sinned* against the gods.

5. The word order (object-verb) emphasizes the fact that Rib-Hadda is sending his own son, a measure of the gravity of the whole situation.

6. *te-iṣ-*[*ba-at*]: third feminine singular required in view of *timtaṭi* in line 44 (see n. 8) and *ana ūmi kašādi-ši*, "on *its* [feminine] arrival." The plural *tiṣbatū* in line 98 is probably due to confusion with simple ÉRIN.MEŠ, which is treated as plural in lines 42(?), 80, and 93.

7. If [ti-*r*]*i-bu-mi* (Knudtzon) is correct, then the apparent accusative *šara* should probably be *ša-ra-*⟨*tu*/*te*⟩.

8. The generally accepted reading *ti-*[i]ḫ-[š]a-[*ḫ*]*i* (Knudtzon) suffers from several difficulties: (1) the wrong thematic vowel in Babylonian; (2) an overhanging vowel; and (3) interpretation (unidentified object, Knudtzon; passive sense, Oppenheim; unparalleled sense, with key words supplied, Albright). The reading *ti-*[*i*]*m-*[*t*]*a-*[*ṭ*]*í*, which fits well with what Knudtzon seems to have seen, makes sense and is unobjectionable. The assumed leveling through of the perfect for all functions of the volitive has many parallels (*ezēbu*, *leqû*, *šemû*, etc.), and for *ṭí* see *ḫé-e-ṭí* in line 33. Rib-Hadda's advice to the king is to send forces now to take the city from his brother before the Amurru forces occupy it, for then, the troops that the king might be expected to send would be too few to capture the city.

9. Lit. "when the archers come out, then they will hear (of it)."

10. *kīnanna*, "accordingly," in line 57 indicates that lines 53–56 are the explanation of the perfidious brother's activity, which is more likely, it seems, to lie in the past (Knudtzon, Oppenheim) than in the future (Albright).

11. On *šumma* in this sentence, see *EA* 35, n. 3. It does not introduce an oath (Oppenheim). Perhaps there is reference to only one temple.

12. In line 62, *yi-iṣ-ba-tu-ši* is always interpreted as plural, "If they take it, . . . ," but against this is the fact that the plural throughout this letter has the {t}-preformative (*tuddanū*, line 6; *tīmurū*, 11; *tišlaḫū*, 12; *tina''iṣū-ni*, 14; *tilqū*, 80, 93; *tiṣbatū*, 98; [ti-*r*]*i-bu-mi*, 42?). Moreover, when *šarru* and/or *bēlī* function as subject of the verb, they always appear right after the verb (lines 7, 26, 31, 38, 39, 52, 59, 75, 77, 84?, 90?, 94, 97), with only two exceptions (80–81), neither of them comparable to the word order assumed here. For *šumma* with the indicative, see lines 81f.

Rib-Hadda does not assume he will be restored to his city (cf. 81ff.), and he expresses his willingness to accept any decision of the king, only adding a request to be allowed to live in a place apparently dear to him.

13. Lines 67f. are extremely difficult. I follow Oppenheim, except that I take *pal-ḫa-tu* as feminine singular participle, not as first singular "stative" (so also Albright) because I doubt the existence of the {ātu}-ending (see *EA* 138, n. 28). We must thus take NA.KÚR.RU, originally no doubt a writing of *nakrū*, as

simply logographic for any form of *nakāru,* here *nakrat.* In line 67, perhaps NA.KAR$_5$-*ra-at* (*nakrat*). Instead of a singular verb with plural subject (*EA* 85:72f.?; 129:80?), perhaps the plural marker DIDLI should be ignored. The city, of course, would be Byblos. Albright renders this, "since *there is left but one city,* namely, Burusilim," reading *ña-šá-ra-at* URU.KI I URU . . . ; see *BASOR* 95 (1944) p. 31, n. 4. The writing hardly reflects assumed Canaanite *naš'arat,* the numeral would not be written with a horizontal wedge, and Knudtzon saw two wedges (DIDLI).

14. The assumed feminine plural pronominal suffix is very difficult. If it refers to the sons of ʿAbdi-Aširta, then Rib-Hadda could not have said that they actually hold the city (Knudtzon, Oppenheim). "Behold our city Byblos" (Albright) takes the *na* of the suffix as first plural (cf. *kaspu-na, EA* 138:38) and ignores the *ši.*

15. *a-na-ṣár-š*[*i*]: cf. *a-na-an-ṣár* (*EA* 147:61; 151:6; 153:15); see also *EA* 235, n. 2, and von Soden-Röllig, *Das akkadische Syllabar*², Analecta Orientalia 42 (Rome, 1967), p. 50, no. 255; idem, *Ergänzungsheft zum akkadischen Syllabar,* Analecta Orientalia 42A (Rome, 1976), p. 7*; Gelb, *Or* n.s. 39 (1970) p. 536. *anaṣṣar*: volitive, following Rainey, *UF* 5 (1973) p. 413.

16. Or, "may he get the troops moving" (*AHw,* p. 943). On *tiṣbatū* (line 98), see n. 6.

EA 138

De profundis

TEXT: VAT 351.
COPIES: WA 58; *VS* 11, 73.

To the king, [my] lord, [the Su]n of all countries: Message of Rib-Ad[d]i, your [ser]vant. I fall beneath the feet of the king, [m]y lord, 7 times and 7 times. **5–18** As to its being said to the king, "He (*should be*) *in* Yapu. *He is exh*[*austed; he should*] *get* strong and *be* like *th*[*em*]." I have not [go]ne to Ap[i].[1] Just now people from Gubla have written me, "Do not leave Beirut since we . . . and we will come in to you."[2] Look at their treacherous [*words*] . . . **19–25** for my entrance into [. . .],[3] *After the re*[*vol*]*t of my territory,*[4] *s*[*in*]*ce* [*1*]2 *mo*[*nth*]*s ago,* have I not lived in Beirut? . . . I sent a tablet [to] the [pala]ce of the king. Now [. . .] *has come out* to me [*since*] *4* months ago. Thus *does* my lord [. . .] for his servant. I am a servant of the king. **26–38** The king has no royal mayor l[ike m]e who will die [for] my [lo]rd. When ʿAbdi-Ašrati seized Ṣumur, I guarded the city by ⟨my⟩self.[5] There was no garrison with ⟨me⟩, and so I wrote to the king, my lord. Troops came out [and] took Ṣumur and [ʿAbdi-Aš]irti.[6] Now Aziru *has ta*[*ken*][7] Ṣum[ur], and when the people of Gubla saw this, (they said), "How long shall we *contain* the son of ʿAbdi-Aširti. *Our*[8] money is completely gone for the war." 39–50 Then they moved against me, but I killed them. They said, "How long can you go on killing us? Where will you get people to live[9] in the city?" So I wrote to the palace for troops, but no troops were given ⟨to⟩ me. Then the city said, "Abandon him.[10] Let's join Aziru!" I said, "How could I join him and abandon the king, my lord?" Then my brother spoke and [*sw*]*ore*[11] to the city. They had a discussion *a*[*n*]*d* the lords of the city [were jo]ined to the sons of ʿAbdi-Ašrati.[12] 51–70 I myse⟨lf⟩ [w]ent to Beirut for a dis[cuss]ion with Ḫammuni[ri], and we ma[de an al]liance so that Ḫa[mmuniri], when . . . [. . .], then [. . .] . . . We went, [. . .] and I, t[o the cit]y. They did not pe[rm]it me to enter. The rebel *against the ki*[ng had taken [*troop*]*s*[13] of Aziru; he had stationed (them) in the city, and the city saw[14] that there were foreign troops in the city. So the *residents* favored my entering the city, and they said to him, "(You say), 'Behold, our lord is dead.' How can you say, 'Rib-Addi is dead, *and so we are* out of his control?' Let him not write to Egypt or he will take us and our children." So they drove the troops of Aziru fro[m] the city.[15] 71–80 Half of the city is on the side of the sons of ʿAbdi-Aširti, and half of it is on the side of my lord, and just as is done to a ruler that resides in his own city should be done to me.[16] Though I sent my son to the palace of the king seconds after[17] I arrived in Beirut, he has not had an audience with the king for four months. My man reports, "I have reached him at Taḫda." 80–93 Why is my man whom I se[nt *t*]*o the p*[*alac*]*e of the k*[*ing*] detained?[18] For my part, I keep saying to [. . .] Why do *you* [. . .] the lands of Yapu? Wh[y do *you* . . .] to me, since [*you know that Gubla has been*] a loy⟨al⟩ city? And . . . [. . .] Though I am living in [Beirut], there has been no man of the king who *ha*[*s come*]. The city has said, "Look, [Rib-Addi] is living in Beirut. Where is a man who has come to him from Egypt?"[19] And so they are being joined to Aziru. 94–109 Previously I would write to the king; he would not heed my word. Now I am living in Beirut like a dog,[20] and my word is (still) unheeded. If the king listened to his servant and troops were given to me, the city [*would return*][21] to the king. So [*may the king give troo*]*ps* that we may seize the cit[y. *Let*] *n*[*ot*] the troops of the sons of ʿAbdi-Ašrati [*take it*][22] for [themselves] and its people revol[t].[23] He is a rebel. In order to give (it)[24] to ⟨⟨to⟩⟩ Aziru, he committed a [great] crime; he took the ⟨*trea*⟩*sures*[25] and then drove [m]e away, and [*he has sh*]*own contempt* for [*A*]*pi along wi*[*th* . . .][26] 109–21 May the king, my lord, [not ne]glect his city so that the city says, "Rib-Addi is dead, *and s*[*o we are* out of] hi[s control. *Let's be* joined t]o Aziru."[27] . . . [. . .]

Against [*the men*] he a[c]ted treache[rous]ly. At the urging of the sons of ʿAbdi-Aširati he committed *that* cri⟨me⟩. Moreover, look, I myself *did* [*n*]*o*[*t tel*]*l lie*[*s to the king, my lord*]. Fearful [. . .] . . . **122–30** Look, the people of Gubla keep writing, "Where are the days when the king, your lord, used to writ[e t]o you? Where are the troops of the days [wh]en they were sent to you?" A nice thing : *ḫa-mu-du* (desirable) that was sent from the king, ⟨my⟩ lord, has not been given to me. Gra[in] for my city is held back : *ḫa-ṣí-ri.* **131–38** And what is Ḫammu[ni]ri goi[ng to s]ay? How long I have sta[ye]d with him! May the king give troops lest the sons of [⟨ʿAbdi⟩-Aš]eratu enter[28] the city. Should they seize Beirut, then the king, my lord, will have no lands. Moreover, is this the sort of treatment that is to be given to [m]e whom the king, my lord, should be concerned about? And why should we . . . another man? When I am dead[29] but my sons, servants of the king, are alive, they will write to the king, "Please, restore us to our city." Why has my lord neglect⟨ed⟩ me?

NOTES

1. Line 7: g[a-m]i-[ir lu] *da-an-na,* assuming that apparent traces before *da* may be ignored. It seems that one view at court was that Rib-Hadda should leave Beirut and go to Joppa, there to regain his strength and also to meet Api, apparently an Egyptian official. Rib-Hadda does not agree, and he points to a loyal faction in Byblos that shares his view. Cf. Na'aman, *Political Disposition,* p. 71*, n. 40.

2. To join forces with him? It would make even better sense if we could render "we will get you in (to Gubla)"—that is, restore him to his throne—but usage does not support such a rendering. The treachery mentioned in the next line is presumably that of a different faction, the one against Rib-Hadda (see lines 71ff.).

3. URU.[K]I x [. . .] seems a possible reading, and the city, of course, is Byblos, which is frequently so designated in this letter.

4. ḪI.G[A.R]I K[I]-*ia*: for *bārti ašrīya* (*ittīya,* "against me"?), ḪI.GAR being pronounced and declined (cf. n. 20 and *EA* 75, n. 7)? Very dubious.

5. *i-di-*⟨*ni*⟩*-ia*: more likely than an unattested use of *idu,* "arm, strength"; with *ana* in *EA* 91:26.

6. For the restoration, see *Eretz Israel* 9 (1969) p. 98. The questionable sign is almost certainly *ni* rather than *ir,* but note *ga-mi-ni* for *gamir* in line 38.

7. *l*[*a-qí*/*qa*].

8. If a pronominal suffix is intended, then *na* is certainly a mistake for *nu*; cf. lines 41, 65, 68f., and 138, as regularly in the southern tradition. Perhaps better, KÙ.BABBAR-*pu* ⟨⟨na⟩⟩, simply a mistake prompted perhaps by the following *a-na.*

9. The vertical after *a-ša-bi* in line 41 is perhaps the unerased beginning of an *a*; note *a-na* at the beginning of the next line.

10. Imperative rather than indicative: following Rainey, *UF* 5 (1973) p. 254.

11. y[i]-it-*mi*: following Rainey, ibid.

12. Discussion, with perhaps the connotation of plotting (Rainey, ibid.), or formal declaration (see *EA* 8:12); see also line 52. On the lords of the city, see *EA* 102, n. 5. Line 50: [*ti-t*]*e-pu-šu-mi*.

13. L[UGAL ÉRIN.M]EŠ: the first sign may be LÚ (Na'aman, *Political Disposition*, pp. 186ff.).

14. The translation assumes that city is construed *ad sensum* as plural; cf. *tiqbu*, line 90 (but here an iterative is quite possible—"the city [feminine] keeps saying"), and contrast *taqbi* in line 111. Perhaps better, "They saw (the situation in) the city, (namely), that there were foreign troops in the city."

15. Lines 62–70 are very difficult. In view of the lines that immediately follow, it seems likely that Rib-Hadda in lines 62–70 gives evidence of the loyalty he is about to claim. Line 62: *aššābu*, "residents," perhaps of inferior status, in contrast with "the lords of the city" who have sided with Rib-Hadda's brother; cf. *CAD*, A/2, p. 461b. The "death" of Rib-Hadda is probably the legal one of loss of office and royal support. The answer to this false claim is that he need only write to the king and he would have the support to capture all of them; for the construction, cf. *EA* 362:22f.

16. *awīlu* seems better taken as "ruler" rather than simply "man" (Introduction, nn. 73–74).

17. *iš-tu* 10 ŠE-*ti* (*uṭṭāti*): lit. "after 10 grains." The reference is to a clock, probably a water-clock (Akkadian *dibdibbu*; see Thureau-Dangin, *RA* 30 [1933] pp. 51f.; O. Neugebauer, *Isis* 37 [1947] pp. 37ff.) rather than a sand-clock (Akkadian *maltaktu*). In the Babylonian system of weights (180 grains = 1 shekel, 60 shekels = 1 mina), if 1 mina = 4 hours (see dictionaries, also Neugebauer), then 10 grains is little more than 10 seconds. Reckoning according to the lighter Syrian mina (50 shekels) would mean only a slight modification. The expression seems idiomatic for "immediately."

18. *ḫa-ṣí-ri*, also the gloss in line 130: probably *ʿaṣiri*; see *VAB* 2/2, p. 1416, and cf. Hebrew *ʿāṣar*, "to confine, stay, restrain." The final vowel is probably simply a question of writing; cf. *di-ki*, *EA* 131:23.

19. Rather than assume an omission here, *maḫ-*⟨*ri*⟩*-šu*, and in line 124, *maḫ-*⟨*ri*⟩*-ka* (perhaps also *EA* 140:25), I take MAḪ as a logogram for *ṣēru*, assuming confusion of virtual homonyms, *ṣīru*, "high," and *ṣēru*, "back" (as used in prepositional phrases). In view of the durative in line 93, probably better, "The city keeps saying . . . they keep being joined. . . ."

20. *kī* UR.KI: logogram UR.KU, properly UR.GI_7, to be explained either as a declension of the logogram, UR.KI being genitive, or syllabic writing, UR.GI_5.

21. [ù ta-ra-at]-*mi*: cf. *EA* 137:51.

22. In view of ÉRIN.MEŠ as feminine singular in lines 98 and 125, l[a-a ti-ìl-qí-ši].

23. *ti-bal-ki-*⌜*tu*⌝.

24. *a-na na-da-*⟨⟨*na*⟩⟩*-n*[*i*] *a-na* ⟨⟨*a-na*⟩⟩.

25. ⟨NÍG⟩.GA.MEŠ (*makkūrī*): cf. *EA* 109:21 and n. 4. A reference to the

treasures of Byblos (cf. *EA* 137:60ff. 74f.) fits the context better than oxen (GUD.MEŠ, Knudtzon).

26. ⸢*ù*⸣ [ṭ]á-*pí-il*: as preserved, the dubious sign looks more like *ša* (Knudtzon). In line 8, ᵐ*a-p*[*í*]; here ᵐ*a-pí*, or ᵐ*a-bi*-[x] and a different person.

27. ⸢*a*⸣-*na* 113 ᵐ*a-zi-ri* [ni-te-pu-uš . . .]: cf. line 45.

28. Distinctive of *EA* 137–38 and the letters from Ḫasi, *EA* 185–86, are forms of *erēbu* with *i* as thematic vowel, which appears elsewhere in *EA* only in 127:19; see *EA* 137:34, 42; 138:12, 134; 185:20, 36, 40; 186:26, 50, 57. It may not be simply a provincial aberration; note [*i-t*]*e-ri-ib* in Whiting, *Letters from Tell Asmar, AS* 22, no. 2:6.

29. The value *tú* is so rare in *EA* (never occurring in a letter from Byblos or Beirut), and the other evidence for {*ātu*} so uncertain (*pal-ḫa-tu, EA* 129:82; 137:68; 138:120), that we must consider *mi-ta-tú* simply a mistake, or possibly an unfinished *te*.

EA 139

A new voice, an old story

TEXT: BM 29828.
COPY: BB 45.
PHOTOGRAPH: BB, pl. 4.

To the king, [my] lo[rd, my Sun]: Message of Ili-ra[piḫ, your servant]; message of Gu⟨b⟩la,[1] [your maidservant. I fall at] the feet of the lord, the Sun, 7 times and [7 times]. 5–12 Do not neglec[t Gu⟨b⟩la], your city and the city of [your] ancesto[rs] from most ancient times. Moreover, behold Gu⟨b⟩la! Just as Ḫikuptaḫ, so is Gu⟨b⟩la to the king, my lord.[2] Do not neglect *the delicts* of *a serva*[*nt*],[3] for he acted as he pleased in the lands of the king. 12–17 Here is the crime that Aziru . . .[4] against the king: [he kill]ed the king of Ammiya, and [the king of E]ldata, and the king of Ir⟨qata⟩, [and a co]mmissioner of the king, my lord.[5] He also broke into Ṣumur.

18–29 [And indeed] he is now intent on [*committing*] a cri⟨me⟩ against the king.[6] Moreover, . . .[7] 29–40 May the king, ⟨my⟩ lord, know [I] am his loyal servant. And so let him send a garrison to his city—30 to 50 men—as far as Gubla. The king is to take ⟨n⟩o account of[8] whatever Aziru sends him. *Where* were the things that he sends *coveted*?[9] It is property belonging to a royal mayor whom he has killed that he sends to you.[10] Look, Aziru is a reb⟨el⟩ against the king, my lord.

NOTES

1. The writing *gu-la* is so frequent that it should probably be considered a conscious abbreviation. Line 34: conventional URU *gub-la.*

2. See *EA* 84, n. 12.

3. *a-na-a-me sú-ri* ì[R]: very tentative; cf. *a-na-me* in *EA* 197:6, and see *surru* (*AHw,* p. 1063; *CAD,* S, p. 413, but no longer attested only in Old Assyrian; see *AÉM* 1/2, 436:43). Apart from the unlikelihood of "one that sits on the back of a servant" (Knudtzon), note that the value *šib* is not attested in the southern tradition.

4. Between *a* and *aš* undeciphered traces but certainly not *pa* (*apaš,* "committed").

5. Aziru is charged with his father's crimes; cf. *EA* 75:25ff. Eldata is the same as Ardata (cf. *EA* 140:12), and the commissioner is undoubtedly Pawuru (cf. *EA* 129:95ff.; 362:69).

6. 19 [i-pí-iš] *ar*-⟨ni/na⟩: cf. lines 22 and 40.

7. Line 23: *yi-de.* Line 27: probably *š*]*a-ra*-[*q*]*í* (cf. *EA* 109:36).

8. *libba šakānu* does not mean here "to encourage," as in Akkadian, but "to consider, pay attention" (cf. Hebrew *śîm lēb*). The king is to disregard Aziru's payments of tribute as expressions of apparent fealty, for it is all stolen goods.

9. *a*-ia$_8$-*ti*: like *ayya-mi.* On the enclitic, see *EA* 34, n. 10.

10. We see here a general charge rather than a reference to an unnamed mayor (Weber, *VAB* 2/2, p. 1241).

EA 140

Again the crimes of Aziru

TEXT: VAT 1639.
COPIES: WA 91; *VS* 11, 75.

[To] the king, the lord, my Sun: Message of Gubla, your maidservant; message of Ili-rapiḫ, your servant. I fall at the feet of my lord, the Sun, 7 times and 7 times. 5–16 The king, my lord, shall not neglect Gubla, his maidservant, a city of the king from most ancient times. Moreover, why did the king *communicate through* Aziru? He does as he pleases. Aziru killed Aduna, the king of Irqata; he killed the king of Ammiya, the king of Ardata, and a magnate.[1] He took their cities. To him belongs Ṣumur; to him belong the cities of the king. 16–33 Gubla alone is a . . . of the king. Moreover, he broke into Ṣumur and Ullassa. Moreover, Aziru even [com]mitted a crime [wh]en he was brought [in]to you. The crime [*was against*] us. He sent [*his*] men [*t*]*o*[2] Itakkama [and] he smote all the lands of Amqu, lands of the king. Now he has sent his men to seize the lands of Amqu and (their) territories. Moreover, is not the king of Ḫatta active, and the king of Narima and[3]

NOTES

1. Cf. *EA* 139:14ff. The commissioner of *EA* 139 is here called a magnate (Introduction, n. 70).

2. *ana ṣēr*: see *EA* 138, n. 19. Na'aman, *Political Disposition,* p. 82*, n. 15, proposes 25 [ú-sa]-*maḫ,* "he conspired with."

3. The letter breaks off here, probably to be continued on a second tablet. On *yi-pu-šu* as singular, see Izre'el, *UF* 19 (1987) p. 82. That the sentence is interrogative is not certain.

EA 141

Ammunira of Beirut

TEXT: BM 29809.
COPY: BB 26.
PHOTOGRAPH: BB, pl. 23.

Say to the king, my lord, m[y] Sun, my god, the breath of my life: Message of Ammunira, the ruler of Beirut, your servant and the dirt : *a-pa-ru*[1] at your feet.

6–17 I fall at the feet of the king, my lord, my Sun, my god, the breath of my life, 7 times and 7 times. Moreover, I have heard the words of the tablet of the king, my lord, my Sun, my god, the breath of my life, and the heart of your servant and the dirt at the feet of the king, my lord, my Sun and my god, the breath of ⟨my⟩ life, has rejoiced very, very much that the breath of the king, my lord, my Sun, my god, has come forth to his servant and the dirt at his feet.

18–35 Moreover, as to the king, my lord, my Sun's, having written to his servant and the dirt at his feet, "Make preparations before the arrival of the archers of the king, your lord," I listened very, very carefully, and I have indeed made preparations,[2] including my horses and my chariots and everything of mine that is available to the servant of the king, my lord, before the arrival of the archers of the king, ⟨my⟩ lord. And may the arch⟨e⟩rs of the king, my lord, my Sun, my god, smash[3] the heads of his enemies, and may the eyes of your servant look with pleasure[4] on life from the king, my lord.

36–48 Moreover, may the 2 . . . of the king, my lord, my Sun, my god, the breath of my life, aven[g]e his servant.[5] I am indeed a servant of the king, ⟨my⟩ lord, and a footstool for his feet. I will indeed guard the city of the king, my lord, my Sun, the breath of my life, and its wall : *ḫu-mi-tu,* until I see[6] the eyes of the archers of the king, my lord, and . . . the servant of the king . . .

NOTES

1. Read SAḪAR.RA, a frozen context form ("in the dust"), rather than SAHAR-*ra* (*epera*), an erroneous accusative; cf. *CAD,* A/2, p. 166. On the breath of the king, see *EA* 100, n. 9.

2. *šūširāku,* with no object expressed, corresponds to the absolute use of the imperative in line 21, and it has other parallels in the absolute use of the infinitive (*ana šūširi,* 8x) and of first singular durative (*išūširu, EA* 65:11 and 216:10; *ušēširu,* 329:19). These parallels, especially the latter, argue against "I am (prepared and) ready" (*CAD,* A/2, pp. 132a, 148a; see also *EA* 144, n. 1). This version is also rejected by Pintore, *OA* 11 (1972) p. 119, n. 97.

3. *ti-ra-'a*$_4$*-as*: *râsu*; see *AHw,* p. 959.

4. *amāru ina,* "to look upon," with the connotation of pleasure, is a West Semitism; cf. Hebrew *rā'ā bᵉ*.

5. In the context of the immediately preceding lines and lines 45ff., Ammunira probably states a wish rather than a fact (Knudtzon, tentatively). The subject, 2 ḪAR or A.ḪAR, remains unexplained. Or should we read *a-mur,* "behold," and assume that the subject has been omitted?

6. Not "until the eyes see the archers" (Knudtzon), which would require *tīmurūna*; cf. *lū tīmurū* in line 34. For "to see the eyes," see *EA* 237:16.

EA 142

News about Byblos

TEXT: BM 29810.
COPY: BB 27.
PHOTOGRAPH: BB, pl. 2.

[To the king, my lord, the breath] of my life: [Message of Ammuni]ra, your servant [and the dir]t at your feet. [I fall at the feet] of the king, my lord, 7 times and 7 times. Moreover,[1]

6–10 [*I have hea*]*rd* the words of the tablet that the king, my lord, *sent* ⟨*thr*⟩*ough* [*Ḫan*]*i,*[2] and when I [he]ard the words of the tablet of the king, my lord, my heart rejoiced and my eyes [sh]one brightly.

11–14 Moreover, I am indeed very much on my guard, and I shall guard Beirut for the king, my lord, until the arrival of the archers of the king, my lord.

15–24 Moreover, as to the ruler of Gubla, who is here with me, I shall indeed guard him until the king gives thought to his servant. Moreover, may the king, my lord, be informed of the deed of his brother, who is in Gubla, (namely) that he has g[i]v[en] the sons of Rib-Hadda, wh⟨o⟩ is here with me, to the rebel[s] again[st] the king who are in A[mu]rr[u].[3]

25–31 Moreover, I have indeed made preparations, including my horses and ⟨⟨and⟩⟩ chariots and everything that is available to me, before the arrival of the archers of the king, my lord.

32–33 Moreover, I fall at the feet of the king, my lord, [7] times and 7 times.

NOTES

1. Misplaced; intended to introduce the following paragraph: cf. lines 11, 15, 25, 32.

2. *uš-ti-šir* ⟨i-na⟩ ŠU (*qāt*) 7 [^{m}ḫa-n]i: cf. *EA* 145:11.

3. KUR *a*-[*mu*]*r*-*r*[*i*]: reading certain.

EA 143

Egyptian ships in Beirut

TEXT: VAT 1584 (+) C 4764.

COPIES: WA 211; *VS* 11, 79 (see *VS* 12, p. 95) (+) WA 203.

[Say] to the king, my lord, the br[eath] of my life: [Mes]sage of Ammunir[a, your servant and] the dirt at [your] feet. [I fall at the fee]t of the king, [my] l[ord, 7 times and 7 times. ... the breath] of my [lif]e.

10–17 The king, my lord, [*wrote*] to his servant and to the dirt : *ḫa-pa-ru*[1] at his feet. As to his order, wherever what was ordered by the king, my lord, the breath of my life, is, I shall search it o[ut] and then send it on to the king, my lord, the breath of my life.

18–31 [M]ore[ove]r, note how, as soon as ships of the king, my lord, [th]at have been sailed[2] into Beirut, come in, I relea[se] (them).[3] As to the maidservant of the king, my lord, just as ...,[4] so is Beirut for the king, my lord. And I am like a *warmer*[5] of the horses of the king, my lord, [...] ... to the king, my lord.

32–35 [...] ... [i]n *sh*[*ips of* the king], my lord, *I ha*[*ve sent*].

36–38 Moreover, may [the king, my lord], be info[rmed] that the [...] of the king, my lord, are used [up ...].

39–41 Moreover, may [the king, my lord], be inform[ed] that *powerful*[6] are the [... *fo*]*r* his servant.

NOTES

1. See *EA* 141, n. 1.

2. *sí-ki-pu*: following *ARMT* 3, p. 115; see also *CAD*, S, p. 73b.

3. Perhaps we should not exclude another version: "as soon as the ships ... that are under sail for Beirut come in, I will send (it)," that is, what has been searched out and is ready for delivery.

4. Lines 23f. remain hopelessly obscure. Line 23: instead of *iḫ* (Knudtzon), perhaps DI. Line 24: za-*ta*, also possible.

5. *ta-a*[*ṣ-r*]*a-ḫi*: following *AHw*, p. 1337.

6. Cf. *da-at-nu* = *qar-ra-*[*du*] (*CAD*, D, p. 122). The relevance of EZEN *da-a*D-*na-ti*, "feast of the . . ." (*Emar* 6.1, 369:48), is unclear.

EA 144

Zimreddi of Sidon

TEXT: VAT 323.
COPIES: WA 90; *VS* 11, 76.
TRANSLATION: Oppenheim, *LFM*, pp. 126f.

Say to the king, my lord, my god, my Sun, the breath of my life: Thus[1] Zimreddi, the mayor of Sidon. 6–12 I fall at the feet of my lord, god, Sun, breath of my life, ⟨⟨at the feet of my lord, my god, my Sun, the breath of my life⟩⟩ 7 times and 7 times. May the king, my lord, know that Sidon, the maidservant of the king, my lord, which he put in my charge, is safe and sound. 13–21 And when I heard the words of the king, my lord, when he wrote to his servant, then my heart rejoiced, and my head went [h]igh, and my eyes shone, at hearing the words of the king, my lord. May the king know that I have made preparations[2] before the arrival of the archers of the king, my lord. I have prepared everything in accordance with the command of the king, my lord. 22–30 May the king, my lord, know that the war against me is very severe. All the cit[i]es that the king put in [m]y ch[ar]ge, have been joined to the ʿAp[ir]u. May the king put me in the charge of a man that will lead the archers of the king to call to account the cities that have been joined to the ʿApiru, so *you* can restore[3] them to my charge that I may be able to serve the king, my lord, as our ancestors (did) before.

NOTES

1. As the following ^{lú}*ḫa-za-nu* (nominative) indicates, *umma* here probably does not mean "message of"; similarly, *EA* 232:3; 253:2//254:3; 255:3 (note *ṭiṭṭu* in line 5); 366:6 (*qaqqaru*). See R. Marcus, *JCS* 2 (1948) p. 223; as a gloss, however, *a-pa-ru* in *EA* 141:4 proves nothing; cf. *ana* SAḪAR.RA : *ḫa-pa-ru* in *EA* 143:11.

2. Oppenheim, "I am in readiness"; line 21, "I am ready." See *EA* 141, n. 2.

3. Reading *tú-ta-ri-ši-na*: cf. *tú-ti-ra-an-ni, EA* 145:10; *tú-te-ra-am,* 145:26. The alternative, *ut-ta-ri-ši-na,* understood of the king or the leader of the troops, lacks the expected {*yu*}, and in context first person is not likely. In my reading, third feminine, agreement with ÉRIN.MEŠ *piṭāt šarri* is possible, but, in my

opinion, less likely than second masculine. Form: D of *târu, tutâr* + epenthetic vowel (sporadic and typical feature of the periphery; see Kühne, *UF* 3 (1971) p. 370, n. 14) + pronominal suffix.

EA 145

Word on Amurru

TEXT: VAT 1695.
COPIES: WA 182; *VS* 11, 77.

[Sa]y [to . . .] . . .[1] [my *lord*: Message of Z]imre[ddi]. I fall [at ⟨your⟩ fee]t. [May][2] you know that I am safe and sound, and with your greeting from the presence of the king, my lord, you yourself brought back to me the breath of *his* mouth.[3] **11–22** I have heard your words that you sent me through . . . [. . .]. The war is very severe. [. . .] . . . The king, our lord, *has* indeed *been ea*[*rnestly ad*]*dressed*[4] from his lands, but the breath of his mouth does not reach his servants that are in the *hinterlands*.[5] **22–29** Moreover, as to your ordering with regard to the lands of Amurru, "The word you hear from ther[e] you must report to me,"[6] *everyone* [has] heard (that) [. . .] . . . : *ia-aq-wu-un-ka* (*he awaits you*).[7] [. . .] . . .

NOTES

1. Someone other than the king. This is the only letter in which a vassal reports in the introduction of his letter on his own well-being; see Introduction, n. 54. The message referred to in lines 6ff. seems to have implied an exception would be in place.

2. [*lu-ú*] *ti-*⌈*i*⌉*-de*: cf. *EA* 144:10; *lū īde inūma šalmat* . . . , passim in the Byblos letters; *lū tīde inūma* . . . , *EA* 333:4.

3. On *ištu*, "with," see *EA* 112, n. 1. ^{uzu}KA : *pí-šu* (text, *ka*): the messenger brought the breath of the *king* back to the vassal (see esp. *EA* 147:17ff.), and the only breath that is of any importance and is ever mentioned elsewhere is the breath of the king, "the breath of his mouth" (line 20), "the breath of the mouth of the king" (*EA* 137:7). The assumed error might easily have been occasioned by the logogram KA just before.

The addressee, in person or by letter, brought along with his own greeting word from the king. The conjunction probably does not introduce a second clause dependent on *inūma*, but, rather, a virtual causal clause in which the pronoun *attā* emphasizes the contribution of the addressee: "I am well, for it was you who . . ."

4. u[p-ti-*i*]*g-gi*: up, less clear than in *VS* 11 copy; *pagû* (*AHw*, p. 809; cf. *mupeggû*?).

5. Despite *EA* 334:3, hardly a place-name. Read *ṣú-uḫ-ri* (*ṣuḫri*), West Semitic "back" (cf. *ṣuḫru* in the greeting-formula)? Are the "back-lands" simply the provinces?

6. In favor of the direct quotation are the enclitic, which is regularly attached to the first word of a direct quotation (*awat-mi*), and the parallels in *EA* 149:55ff.; 151:49ff.; cf. also the conclusion of a letter in Ugaritic, *w.mnm rgm.d.tšmᶜ ṯmt.w.št b.spr.ᶜmy*, "And whatever word you hear there, put in a letter to me" (A. Herdner, *Corpus des tablettes en cunéiformes alphabétiques découvertes à Ras-Shamra-Ugarit de* 1929 *à* 1939, Mission de Ras Shamra 10 [Paris, 1963], no. 53). Rainey, *Particles*, cites *u awata mimma ša tešme ištu ašrānum šupram itya*, "whatever word that you have heard from there put in writing to me" (Taanach Letter 1:15–18).

7. *iaqwu* + *n*(*a*) + *ka*: Akkadian *qu''û*, Hebrew *qiwwā*?

EA 146

Abi-Milku of Tyre

TEXT: VAT 1871.

COPIES: WA 231; *VS* 11, 78 (see *VS* 12, p. 95).

[To the king, my l]o[rd, my *Sun*: Message of A]bi-M[ilku, your servant. I fall a]t the feet [of the king, my lord, 7 times and 7 times. I am the di]rt under the feet (and) sandals of the king, my lord. 6–13 You [*are the Eternal Sun*]. The sweet breath [*of life belongs* t]o my lord, [*my Sun, and I*], your servant, *am guar*[*ding* Tyr]e, the city of the king, [my] lor[d, and *waiting f*]*or*[1] the brea[t]h of [*the king. For m*]*e* [*there is to be hostility*] until [*the breath*] of the king com[es] to m[e] with power. 14–22 [*No*]*w*, indeed, the ruler of [Sidon, Z]imredda, *is ho*[*stile* to m]e. *Dai*[*ly*] he does not [*per*]*mit* [*me to fetch water* : *m*]*i-ma*.[2] [*I cry*] *out*.[3] . . . [. . .] take me [. . .] . . . [*There is no*] water : *m*[*i-m*]*a* [for] them [*to drin*]*k*.[4] . . . [. . .] ᶜApiru . . . [. . .].[5]

NOTES

1. [ú-qa-(am)]-*ma*.

2. *i-na* u_4-*m*[*i*-ša-ma la-qé] 17 [A? : *m*]*i-ma la-a i*-[n]a-[din-ni]: cf. *EA* 148:24; 154:13ff.

3. [a-ša-*a*]*s-sí*: enough room?

4. . . . *mīma* [ia-nu] 21 [a-na ši-*t*]*i-šu-nu*: cf. *EA* 148:13; 154:18.

5. More than 30 lines missing.

EA 147

A hymn to the Pharaoh

TEXT: BM 29812.
COPY: BB, pl. 11.
TRANSLATIONS: Oppenheim, *LFM*, pp. 123ff.; Albright, *ANET*, p. 484.

To the king, my lord, my god, my Sun: Message of Abi-Milku, your servant. I fall at the feet of the king, my lord, 7 times and 7 times. I am the dirt under the sandals of the king, my lord. My lord is the Sun who comes forth over all lands day by day,[1] according to the way (of being) of the Sun, his gracious father, 9–15 who gives life by his sweet breath and returns with his north wind;[2] who establishes the entire land in peace, by the power of his arm : *ḫa-ap-ši*; who gives forth his cry in the sky like Baal,[3] and all the land is frightened[4] at his cry. 16–21 The servant herewith writes to his lord that he heard the gracious messenger of the king who came to his servant, and the sweet breath that came forth from the mouth of the king, my lord, to his servant—his breath came back! 22–28 Before the arrival of the messenger of the king, my lord, breath had not come back; my nose was blocked.[5] Now that the breath of the king has come forth to me, I am very happy and : *a-ru-u* (he is satisfied), day by day.[6] 29–38 Because I am happy, does the earth not *pr*[*osp*]*er*?[7] When I heard the gracious me[sse]nger from my lord, all the land was in fear of my lord, when I heard the sweet breath and the gracious messenger who came to me. When the king, my lord, said : *ku-na* "(Prepare)[8] before the arrival of a large army," then the servant said to his lord : *ia-a-ia-ia* ("*Yes, yes, yes!*")[9] 39–51 On my front and on : *ṣú-ri-ia* (my back) I carry the word of the king, my lord. Whoever gives heed to the king, his lord, and serves him in his place, the Sun com⟨e⟩s forth over him, and the sweet breath comes back from the mouth of his lord. If he does not heed the word of the king, his lord, his city is destroyed, his house is destroyed, never (again) does his name exist in all the land. (But) look at the servant who gives heed to ⟨⟨to⟩⟩ his lord. His city prospers, his house prospers, his name exists forever. 52–60 You are the Sun who comes forth over me, and a brazen wall set up for him,[10] and because of the powerful arm : *nu-uḫ-ti* (I am at rest) : *ba-ṭì-i-ti* (I am confident). I indeed said to the Sun, the father of the king, my lord, "When shall I see the face of the king, my lord?" 61–71 I am indeed guarding Tyre, the principal city,[11] for the king, my lord, until the powerful arm of the king comes forth over me, to give me water to drink and wood to warm myself. Moreover, Zimredda, the king of Sidon, writes daily to the rebel Aziru, the son of ʿAbdi-Ašratu, about every word he has heard from Egypt. I herewith write to my lord, and it is good that he knows.[12]

NOTES

1. According to Assmann, *Liturgische Lieder an den Sonnengott: Untersuchungen zur altägyptischen Hymnik,* vol. 1 (Berlin, 1969), p. 119, n. 22, "day by day" reflects Egyptian *rʿ nb* and implies the days of all eternity. On the hymn in lines 5–15 and its Egyptian background, see Albright, *JEA* 23 (1937) pp. 197ff.

2. See C. Grave, *Or* n.s. 51 (1982) pp. 161ff.

3. See *EA* 108, n. 1. On *ḫapšu* as the designation of a part of the body rather than the name of a weapon, see Knudtzon's note, *VAB* 2/1, p. 608, note d, which is still relevant; Peterson, *BiOr* (1966) p. 151a; and Lipiński, *RSO* 44 (1969) pp. 89f. For a different view, see Durand, *ARMT* 21, p. 344.

4. *t*[*a*]*r-gu*$_5$*-ub*: following de Moor, *UF* 1 (1969) p. 188; cf. also the personal name *yrgbbʿl* (*Ugar.* 7, p. 6, RS 24.246:16).

5. An Egyptianism meaning "I was distressed," as demonstrated by Grave, *OA* 19 (1980) pp. 205ff., in a discussion of lines 16–27. Read *i-sà-kir* KA.MES *ap-pí-ia.*

6. On the Egyptian gloss, see Albright, *JEA* 23 (1937) p. 197, n. 3. According to Na'aman, *Lingering over Words,* pp. 401ff., the source of the writer's joy is not simply his receiving a message from the king, but the content of the message—namely, that the king is coming at the head of his troops. Similarly, in *EA* 141:8ff.; 142:5ff.; 144:13ff.; 195:16ff.; 227:5ff.; 292:8ff., he thinks the writers rejoice because troops or the king himself (*EA* 227) are soon to arrive. See also the Introduction, nn. 117–18.

7. *ti*-[ši-i]r: from *ešēru*? Perhaps better, with Na'aman, *Lingering over Words,* p. 402: "Did not the (entire) land prosper? (*ti*-[*ši-i*]*r*) since it has heard of the gracious messenger from my lord?"

8. Since one of the most frequent orders of the king in the *EA* correspondence is to make preparations before the arrival (*ana pānī*) of the Egyptian army (Introduction, sect. 5), cf. Hebrew **kūn*: Niphal, "prepare (intransitive), be ready" Hiphil, "prepare (transitive), make ready." So also, independently, Na'aman, *Lingering over Words,* p. 402, n. 25. *kūna*: imperative singular + {*a*} as in Hebrew *lᵉkā,* etc. See also *EA* 154, n. 1. For other versions, see Albright and Oppenheim.

9. See Albright, *JEA* 23 (1937) p. 197.

10. See Alt, *ZDMG* 86 (1933) pp. 33ff.; Auelette, *RB* 80 (1973) pp. 321ff. Here, as so often in this letter, the author speaks of himself in both the first and the third person.

11. As opposed to mainland Tyre, the city of Usu; cf. *rabītu,* "capital," in a Tell al Rimah inscription (Walker, *Iraq* 32 [1970] pp. 27ff., who compares *EA* 147:62).

12. Eyre, *JEA* 62 (1976) pp. 183f., considers *u damiq inūma* another Egyptianism.

EA 148

The need for mainland Tyre

TEXT: C 4765.
COPY: WA 99.

To the king, my lord, [m]y god, my Sun: Message of Abi-Milku, your servant. I fall at the feet of the king, my lord, 7 times and 7 times. 4–17 The king, my lord, has written for glass. I give to the king, my lord, what I have on hand—100 (units) in weight. May the king, my lord, give his attention to his servant and give Usu to his servant so he can drink a jug : *a-ku-ni* of : *mi-ma* (water). May the king, my lord, give 10 *palace attendants*[1] to guard his city in order that I may enter and see the face of the ki[ng], my lord. 18–26 My presence will be as pleasing to the king, my lord, as when the king, my lord, charged me with the guarding of his city. I write to the king, my lord, because every day the king of Sidon has captured a *palace attendant* of mine. 26–34 May the king give attention to his servant, and may he charge his commissioner to give Usu to his servant for water, for fetching wood, for straw, for clay. 34–40 Since he has acted hostilely, has he not *violated*[2] the oath? There is not another *palace attendant.* The one who rai[d]s the land of the king is the king of Sidon. 41–47 The king of Ḫaṣura has abandoned his house and has aligned himself with the ʿApiru. May the king be concerned about the *palace attendants.* These are treacherous fellows.[3] He has taken over the land of the king for the ʿApiru. May the king ask his commissioner, who is familiar with Canaan.

NOTES

1. LÚ.GÌR (also lines 26, 38, 44; and *EA* 149:18, 83; 151:60) is probably not the same as ÉRIN(MEŠ).GÌR(MEŠ) (*EA* 149:62). Very tentatively, I take it as a logogram for *girseqû.* Albright, *JEA* 23 (1937) p. 202, n. 2, thought it meant simply "man, person."

2. Albright, ibid.: "Though (he) has made war (against me) he has not returned the oath of peace (*i.e.*, he is still nominally at peace)."

3. The kings of Sidon and Ḫaṣura.

EA 149

Neither water nor wood

TEXT: BM 29811.
COPY: BB 28.
PHOTOGRAPH: BB, pl. 14.

To the king, my lord, my Sun, my god: Message of Abi-Milku, [yo]ur servant. I fall at the feet of the king, [m]y lo[rd], 7 times and 7 times. I am the dirt under the feet and sandals of the king, my lord. 6–20 O king, my lord, you are like the Sun, like Baal,[1] in the sky. May the king give thought to his servant. The king, my lord, charged me with guarding Tyre, the maidservant of the king, but after I wrote an *express* tablet to the king, my lord, he has not replied to him. I am a commissioner of the king, my lord, and I am one that brings good news and *also* bad (news) to the king, my lord. May the king send 20 *palace attendants* to guard his city in order that I may go in to the king, my lord, and see his face. 21–27 What is the life of a *palace attendant* when breath does not come forth from the mouth of the king, his lord? But he lives if the king writes [t]o his servant, and he lives [for]ever. 28–40 For my part, [si]nce last year [my intention has been] to go in [and beho]ld the face of the king, my lord, [*but Zimredda,* the p]rince, [*heard about m*]*e*. He made [*my caravan*] turn back [*fro*]*m* the king, my lord, [*saying, "Who c*]*an* get you in [*to the king*?" *Hea*]*r*,[2] my lord! Aziru, [the son of ʿAbdi]-Ašratu, [the re]bel against the king, [*has taken possession of Ṣumu*]*r*. Ḫaapi [. . .] . . . [g]ave Ṣumur [t]o Aziru. 40–54 May the king not neglect [th]is city and his land. When I hear the name of the king and the name of his army, they will be very afraid, and all the land will be afraid, that is, he who does not follow the king, my lord. The king knows whether you installed me as commissioner in Tyre. (Still), Zimredda seized Usu from ⟨his⟩ servant. I abandoned it, and so we have neither water nor wood. Nor is there a place where we can put the dead. So may the king, my lord, give thought to his servant. 54–63 The king, my lord, wrote to me on a tablet, "Write whatever you hear to the king." Zimredda of Sidon, the rebel against the king, and the men of Arwada have exchan⟨ge⟩d[3] oaths among themselves, and they have assembled their ships, chariots, and infantry,[4] to capture Tyre, the maidservant of the king. 64–73 If the powerful hand of the king comes, it will defeat them. They will not be able to capture Tyre. They captured Ṣumur through the instructions of Zimredda, who brings the word of the king to Aziru. I sent a tablet to the king, my lord, but he has not replied to his servant. 74–84 [Si]nce last year there has been wa[r a]gainst me. There is no water, [th]ere is no wood. May he send a tablet to his servant so he may go in and see his face. May the king [give thought] to his servant and to his city, and may he not [*abandon*] his city and his land. Why should [*a commissioner* of] the king, our lord, move awa[y] from the land? [*Zimredda*] knows, and the *traitor* knows, that the arm[5] of the king is absent. Now a *palace attendant* [*is bringing*] my tablet to the king, the Sun, [my] lord, and may the king reply to his servant.

NOTES

1. See *EA* 108, n. 1.

2. 28 [*pa-nu-ia* (cf. *EA* 151:8ff.)] *a-na i-ri-bi* 29 [*a-na da*]-*ga-li pa-ni* LUGAL *be-li-ia* (cf. *EA* 150:11ff.; 151:13ff.) 30 [^{m}zi-im-re-da *p*]*a-wu-ra* 31 [iš-te-mi-*n*]*i it-te-er-mi* 32 [ḫar-ra-ni iš-*t*]*u* LUGAL *be-li-ia* 33 [ma-an-nu-mi *ū*/*i*]-*še-ri-ib-ka* 34 [a-na UGU-ḫi LUGAL ši]-*ma be-li* 35 [il-qè URU ṣu-mu]-*ra* ... On the restoration of line 30, see the remarks of Krauss, *Das Ende der Amarnazeit* (see Introduction, n. 119), p. 59, n. 2; on "prince," see the Introduction, n. 73.

3. *iš-ta-*⟨*nu*⟩*-ni*: following Grave, *OA* 19 (1980) p. 207, n. 16.

4. See *EA* 71, n. 5.

5. Here Á (ID) rather than ZAG (*EA* 147:12); cf. *EA* 147, n. 3.

EA 150

Needed: just one soldier

TEXT: C 4766.

COPY: WA 98.

[To] the king, [my] lo[rd, my god, my Sun: Mes]sage of Abi-Milk[u, your servant]. I fall at the feet of the k[in]g, [my] lo[rd], 7 times and 7 times. 4–13 The king gave his attention to his servant and gave soldiers t[o] guard the city of the kin[g, m]y [lord]. I am like th[i]s *m*[*a*]*n*.[1] *Should* a single soldier guard the city of the king, my lord, then I would go in to behold the face of the king, my lord. 14–21 May the king give his attention [t]o his servant and give him Usu that he may live and [*dr*]*ink w*[*ate*]*r*. 22–32 ... [...] 32–37 [*They are wai*]*ling* (*i*)*n the str*[*eet*(*s* that) *I should*] give (them) wood. The king, my lord, [is ex]*ceeding great*. [Y]ou gave [t]o my fathers [...] ...

NOTE

1. Since Abi-Milku usually laments the absence of the Egyptian military, he probably refers here to support given to his predecessor. He says he is like him and also needs such support. Pintore, *OA* 11 (1972) p. 102, n. 5, maintains that Abi-Milku here calls himself a soldier, but Pintore does not translate the passage.

EA 151

A report on Canaan

TEXT: BM 29813.
COPY: BB 30.
PHOTOGRAPH: BB, pl. 13.

To the king, my Sun, my god, my gods: Message of Abi-Milku, your servant. I fall at the feet of the king, my lord, 7 times and 7 times. 4–11 I am the dirt under the sandals of the king, my lord. I am indeed guarding carefully the city of the king that he put in my charge. My intention has been to go to see the face of the king, my lord, but I have not been able, due to Zimredda of Sidon. 12–24 He heard that I was going to Egypt, and so he has waged war against me. May the king, my lord, give me 20 men to guard the city of the king, my lord, so I can enter before the king, my lord, to behold his gracious face. I have devoted myself to the *service* : *ú-bu-dì*[1] of the ki[ng], my lord. May the ki[ng], my lord, ask his commissioner whether I have devoted myself to the king, my lord. 25–34 I herewith send my messenger t[o the kin]g, my lord, and may [the king], my lord, send [his messenger and] his ta[bl]et t[o me], so I may enter before the king, my lord. [I] have devoted myself *to*[*tally*][2] to ⟨*the king*⟩, *t*[*o seeing*] the face of the king, [my] lord. 35–48 May [*the king, my lord*], not abandon his servant. May the king, my lord, give [his] attention and gi[ve] water for *o*[*ur*] drink and wood to his servant. The king, my lord, knows that we are situa[te]d on the sea; we have neither water nor wood. I herewith send Ilumilku as messenger to the king, my lord, and I give 5 talents of bronze, *ma*⟨*ll*⟩*ets,* (and) 1 whip.[3] 49–58 The king, my lord, wrote to me, "Write to me what you have heard in Canaan." The king of Danuna died; his brother became king after his death, and his land is at peace. Fire destroyed the palace[4] at Ugarit; (rather), it destroyed half of it and so hal⟨f⟩ of it *has disappeared.*[5] 59–70 There are no Hittite troops about. Etakkama, the prince of Qidšu, and Aziru are at war; the war is with Biryawaza.[6] I have experienced the injustices of Zimredda, for he assembled troops and ships from the cities of Aziru against me. Is it good that a *palace attendant* of my lord should become frigh[tened]? All have become frightened. May the king give his attention to his servant and return : *yú-ṣa* (come forth).

NOTES

1. With Grave, *Or* n.s. 51 (1982) p. 166, n. 30, the gloss is taken as reflecting West Semitic *ʿbd.* The preceding *mi-ru-*TI remains obscure: *a-na-mi* ⟨ur⟩*-ru-dì*? Cf. *EA* 147:42; 155:27f.

2. *ma-*[gal ma-gal].

3. ^{giš}*ma-*⟨qì⟩*-bu-ma* 1 ^{giš}ÙSAN? : *qì-na-zu* (*AHw*, p. 922; *CAD*, Q, p. 256).

4. É LUGAL: as already confirmed by Gadd in Schaeffer, *Syria* 17 (1936) pp. 146f.

5. Lit. "there is not hal⟨f⟩ of it," but the repetition is curious, and one wonders whether the meaning is not, rather, that half was destroyed, half not.

6. For Etakkama's title, see the Introduction, n. 73. For the various interpretations of lines 55–63, see Liverani, *Storia di Ugarit* (see Introduction, n. 128), pp. 28ff., and Redford, *History and Chronology of the Eighteenth Dynasty of Egypt* (see Introduction, n. 119), p. 222, n. 17.

EA 152

A demand for recognition

TEXT: VAT 1719.
COPY: *VS* 11, 80.

[T]o the k[in]g, my lord, [my] g[od, my Sun: Me]ssage of Abi-Mi[lk]u, yo[ur] servant, [the dirt und]er the sandals on the feet of [my lo]r[d. I fall] a[t the feet of the king], my l[or]d, my god, [m]y Sun, [7 times and 7 times]. 5–8 May the king, [m]y lord, [my god, my Sun], take cognizance of his city, [his maidservant. *As* Z]imre[dda, the rule]r of [Sidon, *is at war*] *with* me, 9–46 ... [...] 47–57 [and] may he give me 80 *s*[*oldiers*] to gu[ard] *h*[*is*] ...,[1] [for] the war again[st *me is sev*]*ere. In addition to the s*[*oldier*]*s*, [*wh*]*ere are*[2] the ... [...], and so may he give provisions. May the king, the Sun, my lord, know *that* Abi-Milku is a servant [...] ..., and he has dev[oted him]self to : *ú-bu-ud* (*the service*)[3] of the kin[g, his lord, *and* the ki]ng, the Sun, my l[o]rd [...] 58–66 [...] ...

NOTES

1. *ti-e-ti-*š[u]: probably a designation of Tyre; see also *EA* 295, n. 7, and Na'aman, *UF* 11 (1979) pp. 674f.

2. *a-ia*$_8$ Zu-x-[x-x]: *ayya,* however, is otherwise attested in *EA* only at Byblos.

3. See *EA* 151, n. 1.

EA 153

Ships on hold

TEXT: Metropolitan Museum of Art 24.2.12.
COPIES: Scheil, *Bulletin de l'Institut français d'archéologie orientale du Caire* 2 (1902) p. 116; I. Spar, ed., *Cuneiform Texts* (see *EA* 15), pls. 114–15.
PHOTOGRAPHS: Bull, *Bulletin of the Metropolitan Museum of Art* 21 (1926) p. 170, fig. 2 (obverse); Pritchard, *The Ancient Near East in Pictures* (see Introduction, n. 85), no. 245 (obverse).
TRANSLITERATION AND TRANSLATION: Moran, in Spar, ed., *Cuneiform Texts,* pp. 150f.

[To] the king, my lord: [Mes]sage of Abi-Milku,[1] your servant. I fall at your feet 7 times and 7 times. 4–11 I have carried out what the king, my lord, ordered. The entire land is afraid of the troops of the king, my lord. I have had my men *hold* ships *at the disposition of* the troops of the king, my lord. 12–20 Whoever has disobeyed has no family, has nothing alive. Since I gua[rd the ci]ty of the king, [my] lo[rd], *m*[*y*] *s*[*afety*] is the king's *responsibility.* [*May he take cognizance*] *of* his servant who is on his side.[2]

NOTES

1. Written *ia-bi*-LUGAL, perhaps reflecting a glide between the *a*-vowels (*um-ma a-bi* > *yabī*).

2. 17 [ù šu-u]l-m[i] 18 [m]u-*ḫi* LUGAL l[i-de$_4$] 19 *a-na* ÌR-*šu ša* 20 *it-ti-šu.* Cf. *EA* 154:27–29 and n. 2.

EA 154

Orders carried out

TEXT: VAT 1718.
COPIES: WA 162; *VS* 11, 81.

To the king, my lord: Message of Abi-Milku, [your] servant. I fall at the feet of the king, [m]y lo[rd], 7 times and 7 times. I am the d[i]rt un⟨der⟩ the sandals of the king, my lord. 5–10 I have heard what the king wrote to his servant, "*Let* my *forces* : [ia-k]u-⟨un⟩ (*be prepar⟨ed⟩*)[1] *again[st]* *Yawa.*" What the king ordered, that I have carried out with the greatest joy. 11–20 Moreover, since the departure of the troops of the king, my lord, from me, the ruler of Sidon does not allow me or my people to go to land to fetch wood or to fetch water for drinking. He has killed one man, and he has *capt[ured]* another. 21–29 [. . .] . . . May the king take cognizance of his servant.[2]

NOTES

1. See *EA* 147, n. 8. For another reading see Dossin, *RA* 30 (1933) pp. 89f.

2. 27 *šu*[*l*-mu/mi . . .] 28 *ù li-i-de*$_4$ LUGAL *a-na* 29 ÌR-*šu*.

EA 155

Servant of Mayati

TEXT: BM 29814 (+) VAT 1872.
COPIES: BB 31 (+) WA 228; *VS* 11, 82.

To the king, [the Sun, *my lord*]: Message of Abi-M[ilku, your servant. I fall] at the feet of the k[ing, my lord], 7 times and 7 times. I am the dirt under the sandals of the k[ing, my lord], and the king is the Etern[al] Sun. 7–17 The king ordered that the breath (of life) be given to his servant and to the servant of Mayati, and water : *mi-ma* be ⟨given⟩ for his drink, but they have not acted in accordance with the command of the king, my lord; they have not given (these things). So may the king give thought to the servant of Mayati, that water be given so he may live. 17–23 Moreover, O king, my lord, since there is no wo[od, n]⟨o⟩ water, no straw, no supplies, no *burial*[1] for the de[ad], may the king, my lord, take cognizance of the servant of Mayati, that life be gi[ve]n to him. 24–39 Should the king, my lord, give water to drink to the servant of Mayati, then I will devote myself to his service (and that of) Mayati, my mistress,[2] night and day. Should I en[ter] before the king, [my] lo[rd], I would be afraid : *ir*-x-[x](?), [and] unable [*to speak*], since the king, the Sun, looked on. But the commissioner has not done [*what*] the king [*commanded*]. He does [not] give [*water,* a]s the ki[ng] commanded. 40–47 So may the king take cognizance of his servant and of Tyre, the city of Mayati, for whatever command has issued from the mouth of the king to his servant, that he has done. The word of the king [g]oes : *pa-ni-mu* (*before him*).[3] 47–54 The king is the Eter[n]al Sun, and I am the loyal servant of the king, [m]y lord.

The ki[ng charged me] with guar[ding] the ci[ty] of [M]a[y]ati, my mistress.[4] . . . [. . .]. Moreover, my lord, [*since the departure*] of the troops from me, [*I can*]*not* [*go*] to land. 55–64 Should a *ta*[*bl*]*et* [*of*] the king, my lord, arrive, then I will approa[ch] the land. May the king, my lord, know the sentiments of the enti[re] land. May the king gi[ve] attention to [his] ser[vant] and to Tyre, the city of Maya[ti], so [wood and] water are given that [he] might li[ve]. 65–71 Moreover, [my] lord [. . .] the king should inquire from his commissioner whether Ṣumur is [set]tled. As the ruler of Bei[r]ut *has done service* with one ship, and the ruler of Sido[n] *is doing service* with two ships, I *will do service* with all *yo*[*ur*] ships. So may the king give thought to his servant [*and*] protect the *s*[*hips*] of the king with all my city.[5]

NOTES

1. *ša-mu,* lit. "placing," under West Semitic influence (cf. Hebrew *śîm*)?
2. BE-*ti-ia* (*bēltīya*): following Na'aman, *UF* 11 (1979) p. 675.
3. For the various possible interpretations, see Albright, *JEA* 23 (1937) p. 197, n. 2.
4. See n. 2.
5. Following Gordon's recognition that : *gáb-bi* URU-*ia* is placed with *Glossenkeil* at the end of line 70 because of insufficient room at the end of line 71.

EA 156

Aziru of Amurru

TEXT: VAT 337.
COPIES: WA 34; *VS* 11, 83.
TRANSLITERATION AND TRANSLATION: Izre'el, *Amurru,* pp. 15f.

To the king, my lord, my god, my [S]un: Message of Aziru, your servant. I fall at the feet of my lord 7 times and 7 times.

4–8 Now as to a(ny) request that the Sun, my lord, makes, I am [yo]ur servant forever, and my sons are your servants.

9–14 I herewith give [*my*] sons as 2 *att*[*endants*],[1] and they are to do what *the k*[*ing, my lord*], orders. But let him leave [me] in Amurru.[2]

NOTES

1. LÚ.T[UR.(MEŠ): following Knudtzon; on the meaning, see *EA* 17, n. 7. On the historical background of the Aziru correspondence, see most recently S. Izre'el and I. Singer, *The General's Letter from Ugarit: A Linguistic and Historical Evaluation of RS* 20.33, *Ugaritica* V, no. 20 (Tel Aviv, 1990), pp. 128ff.
2. Cf. the request of Aziru as reported by the Pharaoh in *EA* 162:42–54.

EA 157

Eager to serve

TEXT: VAT 624.
COPIES: WA 36; *VS* 11, 84.
TRANSLITERATION AND TRANSLATION: Izre'el, *Amurru,* pp. 17ff.

[S]a[y to] the king, [my] lo[rd, my god, and my Sun]: Message of Az[iru, your servant]. I f[all] at [the feet of my lord] 7 times and 7 times.

6–8 Now may the king, my lord, know that I am [your] servant forever. I do not deviate from the orders of my lord.

9–16 My lord, from the very first I have wanted (to enter) the service of the king, my lord,[1] but the magnates of Ṣumur[2] do not permit me. Now, of dereliction of duty or the slightest thing against the king I am innocent.[3] The king, my lord, knows (who the real) rebels (are).

17–19 And whatever the request o[f the king, my lord], I will gr[ant] (it).

20–24 . . .

25–33 And thus [. . .] . . . If the king of Ḫa[tti] [*advances*] for war against me, the king, my lord, should give me . . . [. . .] troops and chariots [t]o help me, and I will guard the land of the king, my lord.

34–36 Moreover, in all haste send me my messenger, and [*I wi*]*ll* [. . .].

37–41 And whatever the mayors have given, I too will give to the king, my lord, my god and my Sun. I will give forever.

NOTES

1. On LÚ.ÌR.MEŠ, *ardūtu,* "service," see *Or* n.s. 53 (1984) pp. 298f.; so also Izre'el, *Amurru.*

2. Egyptian high officials residing in, or in charge of, Ṣumur, not the city's elders (Kitchen, *Suppiluliuma and the Amarna Pharaohs* [see Introduction, n. 119], p. 17). In *EA* 171, Yanḫamu is mentioned as one of these magnates.

3. Lit. "I have not committed," and reading, with Izre'el, *Amurru, la-a ḫi-iṭ-ṭa*$_x$, not *la a-ḫi-iṭ-ṭa*$_x$. The expression *ḫīṭa epēšu* as used in *EA* 27:35 (failure to show messengers due honors) and 162:9 (failure to denounce) suggests that *ḫīṭu* refers to negligence, a dereliction of duty. This would explain why the nouns *ḫīṭu* and *ḫīṭītu* and the verb *ḫaṭû* are so rarely used in the Amarna correspondence, even though it is filled with denunciations: the acts denounced are those of commission (*arnu*). Perfect innocence is to be guilty of neither (*EA* 253:16ff.; 254:11ff.). The

distinction of "l'*arnu* faute délictuelle et le *ḫīṭu* faute contractuelle" (Kestemont, in Garelli, ed., *Le Palais et la Royauté* [see Introduction, n. 73], p. 481), whether or not it obtains elsewhere, does not seem to explain adequately the Amarna evidence. Note, for example, that at the time of *EA* 157 Aziru, as he himself laments, is not formally an Egyptian vassal, and he is therefore under no contract. The basis for Kestemont's claim (ibid., n. 46) that the case of Aziru shows how the same act could be, before a pact, *arnu,* and after a pact, *ḫīṭu,* is not clear. The contrast I postulate between *arnu* and *ḫīṭu,* etc., goes back to the Old Babylonian period; cf. *awīlum šû arnam u ḫiṭītam ul īšu,* "This man has (committed) neither sin nor fault" (*AÉM* 1/2, no. 312:11′, "péché" and "faute").

EA 158

Father and son

TEXT: C 4758 (12205).
COPY: WA 40.
TRANSLITERATION AND TRANSLATION: Izre'el, *Amurru,* pp. 20ff.

T[o] Tutu, my lord, [my] father: Message of Aziru, your son, your servant.[1] I fall at the feet of my father. For my father may all go well.

5–9 Tutu, I herewi[th gr]ant[2] the re[ques]t of the ki[ng, m]y l[or]d, [and] whatever may be the request [o]f the king, my lord, he should write and I w[ill g]rant it.

10–13 Moreover, a[s] you in that place are my father, whatever may be the request of Tutu, my f[at]her, just write and *I* will grant it.[3]

14–19 [A]s you are my father and my lord, [and] I am your son, the land of Amurru is your [lan]d, and my house is your house. [Wr]ite me any request at all of yours, and I will grant your [*eve*]*ry*[4] request.

20–26 [And] you are in the personal service [of the king], my [lord. Hea]ven forbid[5] that treacherous men have spoken maliciously [again]st me[6] in the presence of the king, my lord. And you should not permit them.

27–31 [And a]s *you are*[7] in the personal service [of the king, m]y lord, *representing me,*[8] you should not permit malicious talk [ag]ainst me.

32–35 I am the servant of the king, my lord, and I will [n]ot deviate from the orders of the king, my lord, or from the orders of Tutu, my father, forever.

36–38 [*But i*]*f* the king, my lord, does not love me and rejects me, then what a[m] I to s[a]y?

NOTES

1. *ardi-ka-*[*ma*]: as in all of Aziru's letters; Gordon saw possible traces of *ma.*

2. [*a*]*t*-[*t*]*a-din* (Gordon). Line 7: certainly *erištu-*⌜*šú*⌝.

3. Neither *i* nor *ad-din*: so also Gordon.

4. [gáb-b]á: almost certainly not [a-mu]r; so also Gordon. Cf. *EA* 160:9.

5. [*as-s*]*ur*$_x$-[*r*]*i*: the Amurru form of ZUR-sign is quite clear, and the spelling as elsewhere in Aziru's letters (*EA* 165:20, 166:23; 167:25).

6. [*a-na* UGU-*ḫ*]*i-ia*: so also Landsberger in Gordon; cf. line 31.

7. *aš*-bá-*ta*: *bá* dubious (Gordon).

8. ⌜ki-i-ma a'-ia-*ši*: Landsberger in Gordon, *ia* dubious (Gordon); lit. "in my place, instead of me."

EA 159

Nothing but the truth

TEXT: VAT 1658.

COPIES: WA 35; *VS* 11, 85.

TRANSLITERATION AND TRANSLATION: Izre'el, *Amurru,* pp. 24ff.

[T]o the king, my lord, my Sun: [Mess]age of Aziru, your servant. I fall at the feet of the king, my lord, [m]y [god] and my Sun, 7 times and 7 times.

5–10 I do not deviate [fr]om the order[s] of the king, my lord, my god [and] my [Su]n. [*As*] you are like Ba[al and y]ou are like the Sun, [*then* h]ow could (any) [*serva*]*nts* li[e][1] to my lord, [*my god*]?

11–16 [*Loo*]*k,* I am going to build Ṣumur. No[w . . .] . . .

17–28, 29–38 . . .[2]

39–42 [*And* as fa]r as the mayor[s] are concerned, [I dec]lare: they are all [tr]aitors of my lord. [Do not tr]ust them.[3]

43–46 [M]y lord, right now, [in] all haste, I am going to build Ṣumur. [N]ow, may he trust me [th]at I am going to build Ṣumur. [(. . .)].

NOTES

1. *ú-ka-az-zi-*[bu-nim]: following Nougayrol, *Ugar.* 5, p. 49, in deriving the verb from *kuzzubu.* If 10 [a-ma-t]e.MEŠ (Nougayrol), then *ukazzi-*[*ba*], "how could I tell likes . . . ," I also read 9 [ù *k*]*i-i* rather than [ki-i-k]i-*i* (Nougayrol). See also *EA* 108, n. 1.

2. Line 26: [. . . *ú*⌝*-nu-ta,* "vessels, gear" (gifts for the king?). Lines 33ff.: preparation (line 38, *ú-*[še-še-er]) of (additional?) gifts for the king(?): GIŠ.Ì.MEŠ, "oils" or *šamaššammē* (Izre'el; meaning disputed, either "sesame" or "linseed"; line

32); [x ma]-*na as-sí mi*-[. . .], "[x *mi*]*nas of myrtle*" (line 34, *assu* as at Boghazkoy?); [x KUŠ.MEŠ] SÚN.MEŠ, "[x *hides of*] wild-cows" (line 36).

3. EN-*ia-ma* [*la*-(*a*)] 42 [*ta-qí-i*]*p-šu-nu*: cf. line 45. The use of the preterite form instead of the correct present-future *taqâp* is, in this dialect, not a difficulty.

EA 160

Ships and lumber for the king

TEXT: Golenischeff (Introduction, sect. 1).
COPY: WA 34a.
TRANSLITERATION AND TRANSLATION: Izre'el, *Amurru*, pp. 28ff.

[To] the Great King, [my] l[ord, my god, my Sun: Messa]ge of Aziru, [your] serva[nt]. I fal[l] at the fee[t of my lord], my god and my Sun, 7 times and 7 times.

5–8 My lord, my god, my Sun, I am your servant, and my sons and my brothers are servants of the king, my lord, forever.

9–13 I am indeed preparing all the requests of the king, my lord, and whatever came forth from the mouth of the king, my lord, I am preparing.

14–19 I am indeed, in very truth, now [preparing] 8 ships, *box*[*wo*]*od* logs, and large logs of [. . .] . . . , everything that ca[me forth] from the mo[uth] of the king, [m]y lord, [my god, my Sun].

20–32 [And], O king, [my lord, *as to Ṣumur, about which*] he say[s, "*Why have*] *you* [*not*] buil[t *Ṣumur?*"],[1] [. . .] . . . of [my] lo[r]d, [. . .], and the kings of Nuḫa[šše] have been at war with [me], and so I have not built Ṣumur. This year I will bui[l]d Ṣumur. My lord, I am your servant forever. O king, do not listen to the treacherous men that [de]nounce me be[for]e the king, my lord.

33–37 May the king, my lord, my god and my Sun, send me his mes[sen]ger so he can fet[ch] everythi[ng] that the kin[g, *my lord*], orde[r]s.

38–40 My lord, no[w you are going to hear t]hat I am buil[ding *the city of* the king], my lord, my god, [my Sun].

41–44 [And, O k]ing, m[y] lord, send me [*your messenger* al]ong with [my] messenger [in] all haste, [and] then he can brin[g] the tribute of the king, my lord.

NOTE

1. [EN-*ia* aš-šurn URU ṣu-mu-ri] 21 [ša] *i-qá-a*[*b-bi* am-mi-(i)-ni] 22 [la *t*]*a-bá-an-*[*ni* URU ṣu-mu-ri]: cf. *EA* 161:35–40.

EA 161

An absence explained

TEXT: BM 29818.
COPY: BB 35.
PHOTOGRAPH: BB, pl. 22.
TRANSLITERATION AND TRANSLATION: Izre'el, *Amurru*, pp. 31ff.

To the Great King, my lord, my god, [my Sun]: Message of Aziru, your servant. I fall at the feet of my lord, [m]y god, my Sun, 7 times and 7 times.

4–10 My lord, I am your servant, and on my arrival in the presence of the king, my lord, I spoke[1] of all my affairs in the presence of the king, my lord. My lord, do not listen to the treacherous men that denounce me in the presence of the king, my lord. I am your servant forever.

11–22 The king, my lord, has spoken about Ḫan'i. My lord, I was residing in Tunip, and so I did not know that he had arrived. As soon as I heard, I went up after him, but I did not overtake him. May Ḫan'i arrive safe and sound so that the king, my lord, can ask him how I provided for him. My brothers and Bet-ili were at his service; they gave oxen, sheep and goats,[2] and birds,[3] his food and his strong drink.[4]

23–34 I gave horses and asses [f]or his journey. May the king, my lord, hear my words. [W]hen I come to the king, my lord, Ḫan'i will go before me; like a mother and like a father he will provide for me. And no⟨w⟩ my lord says, "You hid yourself from Ḫan'i." May your gods and the Sun be witnesses: (I swear) I was residing in Tunip.

35–40 The king, my lord, has spoken about the building of Ṣumur. The kings of Nuḫašše have been at war with me and have taken my cities at the instruction of Ḫatip. So I have not built it. Now, in all haste, I am going to build it.

41–46 And may my lord know that Ḫatip has taken half of the things that the king, my lord, gave (me). All the gold and silver[5] that the king, my lord, gave me, Ḫatip has taken. May my lord know (this).

47–53 Moreover, the king, my lord, also said, "Why did you provide for the messenger of the king of Ḫatti, but did not provide for my messenger?" But this is the land of my lord, and the king, my lord, made me one of the mayors![6]

54–56 Let my lord's messenger come to me so I can give all that I promised in the presence of the king, my lord. I will give food supplies, ships, oil, logs of *boxwood* and (other) woods.

NOTES

1. Following Izre'el, *Amurru*. Aziru refers to this occasion again at the very end of the letter, giving his message a kind of *inclusio*. It was on this occasion, too, that he was probably installed formally as a mayor; see lines 47–53.
2. See *EA* 55, n. 2.
3. Probably fowl; see Kraus, *AbB* 10, 124, note a of the translation.
4. Or "bread and beer."
5. KÙ.BABBAR-*pa*: following Izre'el, *Amurru*.
6. One of the more notable *ignorationes elenchi* in the Amarna letters.

EA 162

A letter from the Pharaoh: threats and promises

TEXT: VAT 347.
COPIES: WA 92; *VS* 11, 86.

Say [to Aziru], ruler of Amurru: [*Thu*]*s* the king, your lord, saying:[1] The ruler of Gubla, whose brother had cast him away at the gate, [sai]d to you, "[Ta]ke me and get me into my city. [*There is much silv*]*er*, and I will give it to you. Indeed, there is an abundance of everything, [*but* n]ot with me."[2] Thus did the ruler speak to you.

7–11 Do you [n]ot write to the king, my lord, [say]ing, "I am your servant like all the previous mayors in his city"? Yet you acted delinquently by taking the mayor whose brother had cast him away at the gate, from his city.[3]

12–14 He was residing in Sidon and, following your own judgment, you gave him to (some) mayors. Were you ignorant of the treacherousness of the men?

15–18 If you really are the king's servant, why did you not denounce him[4] before the king, your lord, saying, "This mayor has written me, saying, 'Take me to yourself and get me into my city' "?

19–21 And if you did a[c]t loyally, still all the things you wrote were not true. In fact, the king has reflected on them as follows, "Everything you have said is not friendly."

22–29 Now the king has heard as follows, "You are at peace with the ruler of Qidša.[5] The two of you take food and strong drink together."[6] And it is true. Why do you act so? Why are you at peace with a ruler with whom the king is fighting? And even if you did act loyally, you considered your own judgment, and his judgment did not count. You have paid no attention to the things that you did earlier.[7] What happened to you among them that you are not on the side of the king, your lord?[8]

30–32 Con[sider] the people that are [tr]aining you for their own advantage. They want to throw you into the fire. *They have lit* (*the fire*), and (still) you love everything so very much!

33–38 But if you perform your service for the king, your lord, what is there that the king will not do for you? If for any reason whatsoever you prefer to do evil,[9] and if you plot evil, treacherous things, then you, together with your entire family, shall die by the axe of the king.

39–41 So perform your service for the king, your lord, and you will live. You yourself know that the king *does* not *fail* when he rages *against* all of Canaan.[10]

42–54 And when you wrote, saying, "May the king, my lord, give me leave this year, and then I will go next year to the king, [my] l[ord]. If this is impossible, I [will *send*] my son [*in m*]*y* [*place*]"[11]—the king, your lord, let you off this year, in accordance with what you said. [Co]me yourself, or send your son, and you will see the king at whose sight all lan[ds] live. You are not to say, "May he give me this year, too." If it is impossible to go to the king, your lord, send your son to the king, your lord, in your place. If it is impossible, he is to come.

55–67 Now the king, your lord, has heard that you wrote to the king, saying, "May the king, my lord, send Ḫanni, the messenger of the king, once more, so I can have the enemies of the king delivered into his charge." He herewith goes off to you, in accordance with what you said. So have them delivered, omitting no one. The king, your lord, hereby sends you the names of the king's ene⟨mi⟩es on [this] tablet given to Ḫanni, the messenger of the king. Have the[m] delivered to the king, your lord, omitting no one. Copper fetters are to be put on their *ankles*. Here are the men whom you are to have delivered to the king, your lord:

68 Šarru along with all his sons;
Tuya;
70 Leya along with all his sons;
Pišyari along with all his sons;
72 the son-in-law of Manya, along with his sons,
along with his wives;[12]
74 the *commissioner, who is expert in sacrilege,*
that fellow ⟨*who*⟩ *has mocked a resident-alien;*[13]
76 Daašarti; Baaluma;
Nimmaḫe—he is a brigand in Amurru.[14]

78–81 And know that the king is hale like the Sun in the sky. For his troops and his chariots in multitude, from the Upper Land to the Lower Land, the rising of the sun to the setting of the sun, all goes very well.[15]

NOTES

1. [um-ma-(a)-m]i: *umma-mi* is attested in *EA* 1:26, 37 (Egypt). Whatever the correct restoration may be, it is clear that no conventional form of introduction was used. With the exception of the conclusion (lines 78ff.), *EA* 162 is in form as well as content quite unlike the Pharaoh's letters to inferiors (see Introduction, sect. 5).

2. 5 [ma-ad KÙ.BAB]BAR ... 6 [ù i]-*ia-nu*: free restorations; note the writing *i-ia-nu* in line 27 and *i-ia-nu-um-ma* in line 52. It is not clear that "take" means "take as a vassal," as proposed by K. McCarter, *OA* 12 (1973) p. 17.

3. This is a delinquency because upon receiving Rib-Hadda's communication, Aziru should have immediately denounced him to the king (lines 15ff.); see *EA* 157, n. 3.

4. *ta-a-ku-ul kar-ṣí-i-šu*: following McCarter, ibid., pp. 15ff. The reading is confirmed by collation; the copy is inexact, and there is a ligature of TE and A. The denunciation would also have required handing over the vassal to Egyptian authorities; cf. *EA* 245:1ff., and see Kühne, *Andrews University Seminary Studies* 1 (1963) pp. 71ff., and Kestemont, in Garelli, ed., *Le Palais et la Royauté* (see Introduction, n. 73), p. 477. Aziru was, therefore, doubly delinquent.

5. Etakkama.

6. See *EA* 161, n. 4. Meals sealed alliances and were shared only by allies and friends.

7. This is probably a reference to Aziru's having become a vassal-mayor.

8. This seems to be a reference to an initial contact with the Hittites, which is alluded to elsewhere, before Aziru's final capitulation as a Hittite vassal; see Klengel, *MIO* 10 (1964) pp. 72ff.

9. Instead of *lì-mu-ut-ti* here and in the following line, Gordon and *CAD*, S, p. 185a, propose *an-mu-ut-ti*, "these things"; see *anmû*, *CAD*, A/2, p. 125, and comparable forms at Alalakh and Boghazköy.

10. The language is somewhat obscure and other versions are possible.

Na'aman, *Lingering over Words*, p. 405, proposes: "And you know that the king does not want (to go) to the entire land of Canaan when he is angry."

11. *a*-[šap-pa-ra ki-mu]-⌜ú-a⌝: quite doubtful.

12. DAM.MEŠ-*ti-šu aš-ša-te-e-šu*: following Knudtzon and recognizing the Hittite-Egyptian ductus of DAM, not NIN, as proposed by Ries, *RLA* 6, p. 183b, followed by Moran, *Or* n.s. 53 (1984) p. 297.

13. "Commissioner": following Albright, *JNES* 5 (1946) p. 18; perhaps an additional identification of "the son-in-law of Manya." Instead of "commissioner," Jeffrey Zorn, *JNES* 50 (1991) pp. 129ff., argues well in favor of "the soldier." We then read: *ša ḫa-an-ni-pa i-de*$_4$*-e-i-ú* 75 *ša-šu* ⟨*ša*⟩ *u-bá-a-ra il-ta-na-aṣ* (*šanāṣu*). The charge seems to refer to a serious breach of international law involving a foreign dignitary.

14. ^{lú}*ḫa-bá-tù* (*ḫabbātu*, "robber"): following *AHw*, p. 304.

15. Long form: see the Introduction, sect. 5, and *EA* 99, n. 7.

EA 163

Message lost

TEXT: VAT 1885.
COPY: *VS* 11, 87.

Too fragmentary for translation.[1]

NOTE

1. A letter from the Pharaoh, with the same conclusion as *EA* 162:78ff.

EA 164

Coming—on condition

TEXT: VAT 249.
COPIES: 38; *VS* 11, 88.
TRANSLITERATION AND TRANSLATION: Izre'el, *Amurru*, pp. 36ff.

To Tutu, my lord, my father: Message of Aziru, your servant. I fall at the feet of my lord.

4–17 Ḫatip has come and brought the gracious and sweet words of the king, my lord, and I am quite overjoyed. My land and my brothers, the servants of the king, my lord, and the servants of Tutu, my lord, are overjoyed when the breath of the king, my lord, comes. I do not deviate from the orders of my lord, my god, my Sun, and from the orders of Tutu, my lord.

18–26 My lord, since Ḫatip is staying with me, he and I will make the journey. My lord, the king of Ḫatti has come to Nuḫašše and I cannot g[o]. Just let the king of Ḫatti depart and straightaway I will make the journey with Ḫatip.

27–34 May the king, my lord, heed my words. My lord, I am afraid of the king, my lord, and of Tutu. Here are my gods and my messenger. Tutu and the magnates of the king, my lord, I would put under oath[1] and then I will make the journey.

35–42 And thus Tutu, the king, my lord, and the magnates: "(We swear) we will not *devise*[2] anything regarding Aziru that is not good." Thus are you to be put under oath to my gods and to Aman.[3] Indeed, Ḫatip and I are servants of the gracious king.

43–44 Tutu, know [t]hat I will come to you.

NOTES

1. *lu-ú-*⌜*ta*$_5$⌝ -[*a*]*m-mi*: following Izre'el, *Amurru.*

2. *AHw,* p. 1179, proposes *ni-iš-qú-uq,* a Canaanite loanword, "to rush upon," but this leaves *mimma . . . ša lā damiq* without adequate explanation. I propose a derivation from *šakāku,* "to string together," using "devise" from context. Izre'el, *Amurru,* following Winckler's comparison with the problematic *šak* in *Jeremiah* 5:27, is in essential agreement and renders by "plot."

3. Written ^{d}A; see Schroeder, *OLZ,* 1915, cols. 326f.

EA 165

Tunip threatened

TEXT: VAT 325.
COPIES: WA 33; *VS* 11, 89.
TRANSLITERATION AND TRANSLATION: Izre'el, *Amurru,* pp. 40ff.

[T]o the k[ing, my lord, my god, my Sun]: Message of [Aziru, your servant]. [I fall at the feet of my lord] 7 times and 7 [times].

4–9 My lord, m[y] god, [my Sun], what m[ore do I *seek*]? I seek [*to see*] the gracious face of the king, m[y] lord, [*my Sun*], forever. Baaluya and [I] are [yo]ur [servants].

10–13 I am guarding the land of the king, my lord, and I am devoted to the service[1] of the king, my lord. Safe and sound,[2] I would *s*[*ee*] the gracious [f]ac[e] of the king, my lord.

14–17 My lord, Ḫatip and I are coming, and may my lord know that I will [be] there in all ha[st]e.

18–21 The king of Ḫatti is staying [in Nuḫašše], and I am afra[id of him]. Heaven forbi[d that *he come into Amurru*] and the land [*of the king, my lord*].

22–27 Because of [these] things I have been staying on. Just let him d[epart[3] and] return t[o his own land, and straightaway] I will ma[ke the journey] with Ḫatip. [*I*] am a [ser]vant of the ve[ry], ve[ry] gracious king.[4]

28–41 [*My lord,* do not wor]ry at all. I will be [th]ere! [*My only concern has been*][5] the king of Ḫatti, [*but n*]*o*[*w*] I shall b[e th]ere to *s*[*ee* the f]ace of [my] Sun, [m]y [lord]. My lord, [*when*] I was staying [i]n [. . . , the king] of Ḫa[tti] ca[me] into Amurru, the land of the k[in]g, [m]y lo[r]d, because the king, my lord, did not let me stay to guard his land. And now he is staying in Nuḫašše. It is (only) two *day-marches* to Tunip, and so I am afraid of his attacking Tunip. May he depart.

42–45 Mo[reo]ver, my lord, do not listen to the *tr*[*eacherous men*]. I, [my brothers], and my sons are [servants of the king, my lord], foreve[r].

NOTES

1. See *EA* 157, n. 1.

2. *ina šulmi*: lit. "in a state of well-being," said of arrivals (*EA* 161:18; 167:18; 168:5, 9, and cf. line 11), an event also implied here. Cf. the sequence in *EA* 167:18ff. of arrival *ina šulmi* followed by seeing the face of the king. In Old Babylonian, *ina šalimtim* was fairly common; see *AHw*, p. 1148, and add *ARM* 10, 1:9; 17:7.

3. *l*[*i-ip-ṭu*$_4$*-ur*]: cf. line 41; *EA* 164:24; 167:12ff., 24; also 166:29.

4. *banû* is said of the king's face, which is grammatically singular (*EA* 163:1) or plural (*EA* 165:7; 166:7; 167:19), of his words (*EA* 164:6), and of the king himself (*EA* 166:11). In its usage in *EA* 166:11, "all my brothers are servants *ša šarri bēlīya bá-ni*," the form is clearly genitive singular agreeing with *šarri*, and there is not the slightest reason to refer it to the brothers. Hence here, too, *bani* refers to the king, not to Aziru.

5. [pa-ni-ia-ma].

EA 166

Coming—but not yet

TEXT: VAT 250.
COPIES: WA 31; *VS* 11, 90.
TRANSLITERATION AND TRANSLATION: Izre'el, *Amurru*, pp. 43ff.

[T]o Ḫaay, my brother: Message of Aziru, your brother. For you may all go well, and for[1] the archers of the king, my lord, may all go very well.

6–11 What more do I seek? I seek the gracious face of the king, my lord. I, my sons, and my brothers are all servants of the gracious king, my lord.

12–16 Ḫatip and I are indeed coming, right now, in all haste. Ḫaay, may you be convinced that I will be there.

17–20 I do not deviate [f]rom the orders of my lord, and from your orders ⟨I do not deviate⟩. I am the servant of my lord.

21–29 The king of Ḫatti is staying in Nuḫašše, and I am afraid of him. Heaven forbid that he co⟨m⟩e into Amurru. If he attacks Tunip, then it is (only) two *day-marches* to where he is staying. So I am afraid of him, and for this reason I have been staying on until he departs.

30–32 And (then) straightaway I will come with Ḫatip.

NOTE

1. That the greeting should come *from* the archers (so Knudtzon, *VAB* 2/2, p. 1598) would be without parallel; for *ištu*, "with," see *EA* 112, n. 1.

EA 167

The constant Hittite menace

TEXT: VAT 326.
COPIES: WA 32; *VS* 11, 91.
TRANSLITERATION AND TRANSLATION: Izre'el, *Amurru*, pp. 46ff.

[. . .]

5–7 [I do not devi]ate [from the orders of my lord, and from *your* orders I do not dev]iate [*forever*].

8–10 [And wh]at m[ore do I seek? I seek] the graciou[s face of the k]in[g]. [. . .] . . . [. . .].

11–15 [The king] of Ḫatti is [sta]ying in Nuḫašše. Just let him d[epar]t, and straightaway [. . .] Ḫ[atip] and I will co[m]e [in all haste].

16–19 Do not be [wo]rried at all. *I* [*will be*] *the*[*re,* s]afe and sound, and I would see the gracious face of [my] lord.

20–24 The king of Ḫatt[i] is staying [i]n Nuḫašše, and I am afraid of [him]. It is (only) two *day-marches* fro[m] Tunip to where he is staying, and so I am afraid. Just let him depart and straightaway I will be there.

25–27 He[av]en forbid that he come he[r]e into Amurru, the land of my lord. I am afraid *for* the land of my lord.

28–34 Tutu,[1] now as my heart and my words are [in ac]cordance with[2] whatever is in [*your*] intentions, [*I will be reac*]*hing* Tutu,[3] [*my*] *lo*[*rd*]. [*My lord*], may you be happy [*since*][4] I will [*indeed*] be there, *sa*[*fe and sound, to se*]*e* the face of the king, [my] l[ord].

NOTES

1. This is probably a vocative (cf. *EA* 164:43), which would make Tutu the recipient of this letter.

2. [*a*]*m*-[*m*]*a*-⌜*la*⌝: a highly probable reading.

3. [a-kà]-*aš*-⟨ša⟩-*d*[*u* i]t-*ti* ᵐ*tù-u-tù*: Izre'el, *Amurru,* accepts my interpretation of *itti,* but considers, and rightly, West Semitized Akkadian in this dialect intrusive and improbable. That the use of *itti* is of West Semitic origin only partly alleviates the difficulty; cf. *EA* 35:54f.; 47:16; 82:15; 87:10. His own interpretation, according to which Aziru's heart and words have reached (*kašdū*) Tutu, seems somewhat obscure.

4. [i-nu-ma]: following Izre'el, *Amurru.*

EA 168

Royal cargo

TEXT: VAT 1659.

COPIES: WA 37; *VS* 11, 92.

TRANSLITERATION AND TRANSLATION: Izre'el, *Amurru,* pp. 49ff.

[T]o the king, my lord, [m]y god, [my Sun]: Message of Aziru, yo[ur] servant. I fall at the feet of [my lord, my god], my Sun, 7 times and 7 times.

4–12 O Sun, my lord, my god, I [will be th]ere, sa[fe] and soun[d, *to s*]*e*[*e*] *the f*[*ace of the king, m*]y [*lord,* and] . . . [. . . and Ḫ]atip *will ar*[*rive,* safe and s]ound. The thin[gs], too, [*for* the king], my lord, [my god, wi]ll be there [i]n ships, [*unha*]*rmed,* in the land of the king, and . . .

Reverse

1–16 [. . .] . . .

EA 169

Aziru in Egypt

TEXT: VAT 1660.
COPIES: WA 39; *VS* 11, 93.
TRANSLITERATION AND TRANSLATION: Izre'el, *Amurru,* pp. 51ff.

[. . . may all g]o well.[1]

4–15 [*In me*] there is no [*dupl*]*icity.*[2] [. . .] . . . [Y]ou may keep me alive [and] you may put me to death. To you alone do I look, and you alone are my lord. So may my lord heed his servants. Do not delay Aziru, your servant, there (any longer). Send him here immediately so he may guard the countries of the king, our lord.

16–39 Moreover, to Tutu, my lord:[3] Hear the words of the kings of Nuḫašše. They said to me: "You sold your father [t]o the king of Egypt for gold, and w[he]n will he let him go from Egypt?" All the country and all the Sutean forces said to me, also to that point, "Aziru is not going to get out of Egypt." And now the Suteans are *deserting*[4] the country [and I am] repeatedly informed, "Your father is staying [i]n Eg[yp]t, [*and so*] we are going to wage war against you." [. . .] . . . Listen, [*my lord. Tut*]*u,* my lord, [let] Aziru go [immediately. . . .] . . . Nuḫašše . . . 40–47 [. . . ". . . Let] him stay on, [*and then we will wage*] war against you." [*Now indeed ever*]*yone is d*[*eser*]*ting.*

NOTES

1. The sender of the letter is Aziru's son, perhaps DU-Teššup, the father of Aziru's successor, as Klengel, *MIO* 10 (1964) p. 75, n. 102, has proposed; see also Klengel, *Geschichte Syriens* (see Introduction, n. 127), Teil 2, p. 281. Izre'el, *Amurru,* suggests Bit-ili. If, following Izre'el, ibid., in lines 16ff. we see Tutu being addressed, then he is hardly the addressee of the preceding message. The latter must be another high Egyptian official.

2. [a-na ia-ši ŠÀ]: cf. *EA* 136, n. 7. For objections against this restoration, see Izre'el, *Amurru.*

3. See n. 1.

4. *i-pa-*ṭa*-ru-nim*: following *AHw,* p. 850, but the reading of the third sign is most uncertain.

EA 170

To Aziru in Egypt

TEXT: VAT 327.

COPIES: WA 143; *VS* 11, 94.

TRANSLITERATION AND TRANSLATION: M. Dietrich and O. Loretz, in Stiehl and Stier, eds., *Beiträge zur Alten Geschichte und deren Nachleben,* Band 1 (Berlin, 1969), pp. 16ff.; Izre'el, *Amurru,* pp. 55ff.

To the king, our lord:[1] Message of Baaluya and message of Bet-ili. We fall at the feet of our lord. For our lord may all go well. Here with[2] the lands of our lord all goes very well.

7–13 Our lord, do not worry at all. Do not trouble yourself. Our lord, as soon as you can, *meet with*[3] them : *zu-zi-la-ma-an*(?) so they will not delay you there (any longer).

14–18 Moreover, troops of Ḫatti under Lupakku have captured cities of Amqu, and with[4] the cities they captured Aaddumi. May our lord know (this).

19–35 Moreover, we have heard the following: Zitana has come and there are 90,000 infantrymen that have come with him. We have, however, not confirmed[5] the report, whether they are really there and have arrived in Nuḫašše, and so I am sending Bet-ili to him. As soon as we *meet with* them, I will immediately send my messenger so he can report to you whether or not it is so.

36–44 To Rab(i)-Ilu and ʿAbdi-ᵈURAŠ, to Bin-Ana and Rabi-ṣidqi: Message of Amur-Baʿla. For you may all go well. Do not trouble yourselves, and do not worry at all. Here with your families all goes very well. Wish Anatu well.

NOTES

1. The king is Aziru, during his stay in Egypt, and this letter seems to have been written by the same scribe as that of *EA* 169, with which it was probably delivered; see Klengel, *MIO* 10 (1964) pp. 76f., and Dietrich and Loretz, *Beiträge* (see headnote), pp. 14f.

2. See *EA* 112, n. 1.

3. In lines 30–31, *pānī ṣabātu* is achieved by a journey (what Bet-ili does, Baaluya in effect does too) and provides the necessary check on the report; there-

fore, "to meet, face to face." Here in line 11, the meeting referred to is perhaps the official audience with the king and his court, without which Aziru could not depart. The interpretation of the Hurrian gloss is uncertain.

4. See n. 2.

5. Following *AHw*, p. 1327; for *turruṣu* = *kunnu*, "to confirm," cf. *tiriṣ kussê*, "firming of the throne," in A. Abou-Assaf, P. Bordreuil, and A. Millard, *La statue de Tell Fekherye et son inscription bilingue assyro-araméenne*, Études assyriologiques, Cahier no. 7 (Paris, 1982), p. 14, line 21.

EA 171

Eager to serve

TEXT: VAT 1723.

COPIES: WA 185; *VS* 11, 95.

TRANSLITERATION AND TRANSLATION: Izre'el, *Amurru*, pp. 59ff.

[To the king . . . : Message of Aziru . . .].[1] . . . I fall a[t the fee]t of the king, the Sun, my [lord]. 3–8 [*From the very first*[2] I ch]ose to enter [the servi]ce of the ki[ng], the [Su]n, my lord, [but Ya]nḫamu would not a[ll]ow me. [*I* s]ent my mes[sen]gers [*to*][3] the king, my lord, [*but*] Yanḫamu [*stopped th*]*em*[4] on the way, and [*they have not got away.* 9–13 May][5] the gods of the king, my lord, grant that my messengers get away [fr]om Yanḫamu. I would enter the service of the king, the god, the Sun, my lord, but Yanḫamu has not allowed me. 14–21 And now, O king, my lord, [*Pu*]*wuru*, [*the archer*]-*comma*[*nder of the king, my lord, has reach*]*ed me.*[6] [*Pu*]*wuru* [*knows*] my [lo]yalty, and [*may*] the Sun, the king, my lord, [*inquire from him*] . . . [. . .] May he tell them. For I am a servant of [*the Sun, the king, my lord, and*] *wh*[*at*]*ever* the ki[ng, *the Sun, the king, my lord, orders*], I *d*[*o it . . . May*] the Sun, the king, my lord, [*know: I am a loyal servant*] of the king, my lord.

22–37 Moreover, my lord [. . .] Yanḫamu when . . . [. . .] . . . I do not deviate from [*his*] orders or from *th*[*is*][7] servant of the Sun, the king, my lord.

NOTES

1. This letter is very reminiscent of *EA* 157, but the scribe has his peculiarities: the greeting is not ruled off from the body of the letter, and "7 times and 7 times" is omitted. See also Knudtzon, *VAB* 2/2, p. 1275, n. 1.

2. [iš-tu pa-na-nu-um-ma]: following Na'aman, *Political Disposition*, p. 60*, n. 9; cf. *EA* 157:9.

3. [a-na]: despite the reservations of Knudtzon, *VAB* 2/1, p. 679, note h.

4. [ù ik-ta-la-šu-n]u.

5. [la it-ta-aṣ-ṣú-nim] 9 [lu-ú].

6. [ik-š]u-*ud-ni* 15 [^{m}pu]-*ú-wu-ru* [$^{\text{m/lú}}$iḫ-r]i-*pí*-[ṭá LUGAL be-li-ia]: that *ú*-PI-*ru* is part of a personal name seems, in context, plausible, and otherwise makes no sense. If a personal name, Pa/uwuru is the obvious choice, and if correct, then certainly the Pawuru of the Byblos letters. That he might have been the unnamed commander of *EA* 107:14 is, of course, only a guess.

The following restorations are free.

7. LÚ.ÌR *šu*-[(ú)-ut].

EA 172

Message lost

TEXT: VAT 1887.
COPIES: WA 224; *VS* 11, 96.

A small fragment.

EA 173

An attack on Amqu

TEXT: VAT 1875.
COPIES: WA 22; *VS* 11, 97.

[. . . *and*] chariots he fel[l upon] Amqu.

3–16 [An]d *I* went to the rescue . . . [. . .] . . . [*I went*] *up* to . . . [. . .] of the king, my lord, and [*defea*]*ted* them. [And I here]with send 10 *pr*[*isoners*][1] to the king, my lord. [*May*] the king, my lord, [*know about*] the *mat*[*ter*][2] of his enemies.

NOTES

1. *a*-[si-ri]: to introduce alleged *āširu*-merchants, as proposed by M. Astour, *Gesellschaftsklassen im Alten Zweistromland und in den angrenzenden Gebieten* (see *EA* 17, n. 7), p. 23, is without any support in context, which is uniquely concerned with military matters. (Contra Astour, first and third persons do not contrast as *attaššer* and *uttaššer*.)

2. *a*-b[a-at]: following Knudtzon; cf. the same Assyrianism in *EA* 211:10, 19. Another possibility is *abād,* "flight, perishing" (Akkadian *nābutu,* Hebrew *'ābad*); cf. *EA* 244:42.

EA 174

A joint report on Amqu (1)

TEXT: VAT 1585.
COPIES: WA 160; *VS* 11, 98.
TRANSLITERATION AND TRANSLATION: M. Weippert, in Kuschke and Kutsch, eds., *Archäologie und Altes Testament* (Tübingen, 1970), pp. 268f.

Say to the king, [my] lord, [my god, m]y [Sun]: Message of Bieri, [yo]ur se[rvant], the ruler of Ḫašabu. I fall down in the dir[t] under the feet of the king, my lord, 7 times and 7 times. 8–17 Look, we[1] are in Amqu, (in) cities of the king, my lord, and E[takka]ma, [the ruler] of Kinsa, assisted[2] the troops of [Ḫ]att[i] and set [the cities] of the king, my lord, on fir[e]. 18–26 May the king, my lord, take cognizance, and may the king, my lor[d], give archers that we may (re)gain the citi[es] of the king, my lord, and dwell in the cities of the king, my lord, my god, my Sun.

NOTES

1. "We" refers to his fellow mayors, who send exactly the same report to the king in *EA* 175–176 and 363.

2. *ana pānī alāku* has here been taken to mean to go "towards, to" (Knudtzon; Thureau-Dangin, *RA* 19 [1921] p. 95), which has been followed by Kitchen, *Suppiluliuma and the Amarna Pharaohs* (see *EA* 157, n. 2), p. 14, n. 4, and cf. Greenberg, *Ḫab/piru*, p. 43, on *EA* 195), or "at the head of" (Rainey, AOAT 8², p. 25; Weippert; cf. also Bottéro, *Ḫabiru*, p. 104, on *EA* 195). Neither meaning seems satisfactory. It does not seem likely that Egyptian vassals would be ordered to march at the head of Egyptian troops (cf. *EA* 191:15f., and 202:8ff.), and it is not clear why the vassal should go to meet the Egyptian troops. Having made preparations for their arrival, he would rather wait for, and then join, them, adding his forces to theirs and proceeding on the march. Furthermore, "(to be) *ana pānī* the troops wherever they go" (*EA* 203:13ff.; 204:15ff.; 205:13ff.) seems to be virtually synonymous with *ana pānī alāku*. Therefore, *ana pānī*, "for, at the disposition of"; cf. Hebrew *hālak lipnê*, "to serve," and see M. Weinfeld, *Maarav* 3/1 (1982) p. 31, n. 76.

EA 175

A joint report on Amqu (2)

TEXT: VAT 1588.
COPIES: WA 163; *VS* 11, 99.

[Sa]y [to] the king, my lord, [my] god, my [Sun: Mess]age of 'Ildayyi,[1] [your] s[ervant], the ruler of Ḫasi. I fall down in the dirt under the feet of the king, my lord, 7 times and 7 times. 7–13 Look, we are in Amqu, (in) cities of the king, my lord, and E[takkam]a, the ruler of Kinsa, assisted the troops of Ḫat[ti and s]e[t the cities of the king, my lord, on fire. 14–20 May the king, my lord, take cognizance, and may the king, my lord, give archers that we may (re)gain the cities] of the ki[ng, my lord], and [dwel]l in ⟨the cities⟩ of the ki[ng], my lo[rd].

NOTE

1. The analysis of this name as West Semitic is uncertain; for other possibilities, see Na'aman, *UF* 20 (1988) p. 188, n. 41.

EA 176

A joint report on Amqu (3)

TEXT: BM 29829.
COPY: BB 46.

[Say to the king, my lord, my god, my Sun: Message of . . . , your servant, the ruler of . . .]. I fall [down in the di]rt under the feet of the king, m[y] lord, 7 times and 7 times. 7–13 Look, we are in Amqu, (in) cities of the k[ing], my [lord], and Eta[kkama], the rul[er] of Kinsa, assisted the t[roops] of Ḫatti, [and s]et the cities of the ki[ng], my [l]ord, [o]n [f]i[r]e. 14–20 [May the king, my lord, take cognizance, and may the king, my lord, give] archers that we may (re)gain the citi[es] of the king, my lord, my god, [my Sun], and dwell in the cities of the king, my lord.

EA 177

A broken message

TEXT: VAT 1684.
COPIES: WA 170; *VS* 11, 101.

To the king, my lord, my god, my Sun: Message of Yamiuta, the ruler of Guddašuna, the servant of the king, my lord. I fall down in the dirt under the feet of the king, my lord, 7 times and 7 times. May the ki[ng], my [lord], take cognizance of his lands and the men . . . [. . .] . . .

EA 178

On grain supplies

TEXT: VAT 1677.
COPIES: WA 146; *VS* 11, 100.

[To the m]agnate, my lord: [Mess]age of Ḫibiya, your servant. I fall at the feet of my lord. 4–11 We have now moved up into the land(s) of Yatanu. We will [g]uard it [un]ti[l] the arrival of the magnate, my lord, but the war against the cities of the magnate, my lord, is severe. 12–19 Moreover, I have heeded the order, in accor[dance with the *com*]*mand* [*of the king, my lord*]. [. . .] . . . 20–26 [*He ca*]*me down* from Amurru and kept saying to me, "There will be plen[ty of g]rain in [*Amur*]*ru* [*until*] the magnate [*arri*]*ves* [*from the kin*]*g,* my lord."

EA 179

A treacherous brother

TEXT: VAT 1703.
COPIES: WA 171; *VS* 11, 103.

. . . 11–18 May [the king, my lord], my [g]od, my Sun, send back word. And *brea*[*the on me*],[1] the servant of the king, my lord, [my Sun]. Look, my brother who is in Ṭubiḫu,[2] is a . . . ,[3] and he goes about taking over cities of the king, my lord, my god, [my] Sun. 19–29 [*He has made*] Amurru an *enemy* territory, [and] has turned over[4] all the men in the cities of the king, my lord, [m]y god, [my] Sun, to the ʿApiru. And *now*[5] the god of the king, my lord, my god, my Sun, has permitted (it) and he has seized Ṭubiḫu. And so *I would* curse[6] my brother and guard Ṭubiḫu for the king, my lord, my god, [my Sun], for, consider, Ṭubiḫu is my ancestral city.

NOTES

1. *up-š*[*a* a-na ia-ši]: *napāšu* is not used elsewhere in *EA* except perhaps in *EA* 19:16 and 29:48, but the association of the king's message with his breath is quite frequent; see *EA* 100, n. 9.

2. Whether a member of his family or a fellow vassal is meant is not clear.

3. See *CAD,* S, p. 415. As used here, *sūru* seems a pejorative.

4. [ú'-*ga-mi-ir*: there is not enough room for *ù,* which was probably at the end of the previous line.

5. Following Rainey, *UF* 7 (1975) p. 413.

6. Person and mood of *e-ra-ar* are not certain. The curse seems in context to imply banishment.

EA 180

An audience with the king requested

TEXT: C 4788 (12233).
COPY: WA 198.

[. . . And behold, I] a[m a loyal servant of the king, m]y [lord, my] god, [my Sun], in thi[s] place.[1] I send (even) my own son [to] the king, my lord, my god, my Sun, and may the king, my lord, my [g]od, my Sun, send chariots along with my son, that they may guard the cities of the king, my lord, my god, my Sun. 10–20 Send chariots, O king, my lord, my god, my Sun, that they may take me to the king, my lord, my god, my Sun, and I may enter into the presence of the king, my lord, my god, my Sun, and tell what has been done against the lands. As a loyal servant of the king, my lord, my god, my Sun, I am of course slandered[2] before the king, my lord, my god, my Sun. 21–24 Send chariots [that t]hey may take me to [the king, m]y [lord], my god, [my Sun . . .]. . . .

NOTES

1. Cf. *EA* 187:9–11. In line 1, [. . .*a-n*]*a-k*[*u* . . .] (Gordon). Gordon also suggested that *EA* 180 may be the continuation of *EA* 183.

2. *ši-ir* (text *ni*)-*te*: (1) cf. *šâru ina pānī* in *EA* 252:14 (*ši-ir-ti*) and 286:6–7, 21 (cf. also 24); (2) *lemnu* (*lamnu*) is very rare in *EA*, its use as a predicate unattested, and ŠI = *lim* is extremely rare except as a writing of 1000 or in frozen phonetic complements.

EA 181

A broken message

TEXT: VAT 1623.
COPY: *VS* 11, 102.

[. . .] . . . [. . . the king, my lord, my god], my Sun, [. . .] his [m]en [. . .] . . . Sen[d, O king, my lord, m]y [god], my Sun, [. . .] that we may protect [the *cities* of the king, my lord], my god, m[y] Sun . . .[1]

NOTE

1. Lines 11–26 contain formulaic references to the king, plus other signs impossible to interpret.

EA 182

Request for a garrison

TEXT: VAT 1615.
COPIES: WA 130; *VS* 11, 104.

[To the king], m[y] lord, [my god], my Sun: Message of Šutarna, [your] serva[nt], the ru[ler] of Mušiḫuna. I fall down in the dirt at the feet of the king, my lord, my god, my Sun, 7 times and 7 times. 6–15 May the king, my lord, take cognizance of his lands, and may the king, my lord, send a garrison that we may *hol⟨d⟩*[1] the cities of the king, my lord, my god, my Sun, until the king, m[y] lord, takes cognizance of his lands.

NOTE

1. *ni-leq-⟨qé⟩*: I durative of *leqû*, very rare in *EA* (Alašia, Babylonia, Egypt, Mittani, Jerusalem; on *EA* 109:53, see ibid. n. 14), and the meaning "to hold," which seems required by context—garrison troops were not an offensive force—is also unparalleled. Note the erasure that follows.

EA 183

A lost message

TEXT: VAT 1595.
COPIES: WA 130; *VS* 11, 105.

Say to the king, m[y] lord, [my god], my Sun: Message of Šutarna, [the ruler] of Mušiḫuna, the servant of the king, my lord [(...)]. [I fall down] below, in the dirt under the feet of the king, my lord, [...] ... [...][1]

NOTE

1. See *EA* 180, n. 1.

EA 184

A lost message

TEXT: Ash 1893. 1–41: 426.
COPY: Sayce, *Tell el Amarna,* no. 18 bis.

Too fragmentary for translation.[1]

NOTE

1. From Šutarna to the king; part of prostration formula preserved.

EA 185

An Egyptian traitor

TEXT: VAT 1725.
COPIES: WA 189; *VS* 11, 106.
TRANSLITERATION AND TRANSLATION: Bottéro, *Ḫabiru,* pp. 97ff. (lines 9–63); Greenberg, *Ḫab/piru,* pp. 41f. (lines 1–64).

Say to the king, my lord, my god, [m]y Sun: Message of [*M*]*a*yarzana, the ruler of Ḫasi, your servant, the dirt under the feet of the k[in]g, my lord, my god, m[y] Sun, the groun[d h]e t[r]ea[d]s on. I fall at the feet [of the kin]g, m[y] lord, [7 times] and 7 times.

9–15 M[ay] the king, my lord, [m]y [g]o[d], my S[un], *know of*[1] the d[ee]d that Amanḫatpe, the ruler of Tušultu, committed against the [c]ities of the king, my lord, when the ʿApiru forces [w]a[ge]d[2] war against me and captured the cities of the king, my lord, my god, my Sun.

16–20 The ʿApiru captured Maḫzibtu, a city of the ki[n]g, my lord, and plundered ⟨it⟩ and sen[t] it up in flames, and then the ʿApiru took refuge[3] with Ama[nḫatp]e.

21–27 And the ʿApiru captured Gilunu, a city of the king, my lord, plundered it, sent it up in flames, and hardly one family escaped from Gilunu. Then the ʿApiru t⟨o⟩ok refuge with Amanḫatpe.

28–36 And the ʿApiru cap⟨tu⟩red [M]agd[a]lu, a [ci]ty of the king, my lord, my god, m[y] Sun, plundered it, se⟨n⟩t it up in flames, and h[a]rd[l]y [on]e family escaped from Mag[da]lu. Then the ʿApiru took refuge with Amanḫatpe.

37–41 And Uštu, a [ci]ty of the king, my lord, the ʿApi[ru] captured, plundere[d i]t, and sent it up in flames. Then the ʿApiru took refuge with Amanḫatpe.

42–75 And then the ʿApiru having raided Ḫasi, a [ci]ty of the king, my lord, we did battle with the ʿApiru, and we defeated them. Then 40 ʿApiru *w[ent]* t[o Amanḫ]atpe, and Amanḫatpe welcomed whoever had escaped. [*And*] *they were gathered* ⟨*together*⟩ [*in*] the city.[4] [Ama]nḫatpe *is an* ʿApir[u]![5] We he[ar]d [tha]t the ʿApi[ru w]ere with Amanḫatpe, so [m]y broth[ers] and my so[ns], your servants, *d[rov]e*[6] a chariot t[o] Amanḫatpe. My [br]others sa[i]d to Amanḫatpe, "Hand ov[er] the ʿApiru, traitors to the king, our lord, so we can [de]mand a reckoning of those ʿApiru that have taken re[fu]ge[7] with you, f[or having c]aptured cities of the king, my lord, and burning them down." He [a]gre[e]d to hand over the ʿApiru, but he took them in *the night*[8] and fled to the ʿApiru. Amanḫatpe being a traitor, may the king, my lord, demand a reckoning of him. He has fled from him. May the king, my lord, not be negligent, with no *reck[on]ing*[9] demanded of Amanḫatpe. (As to another ruler, traitors are not to be ⟨al⟩lowed into the loyal land of the king, my lord.)[10] When [the kin]g, my lord, has demanded a reckon[ing of] Amanḫatpe, the traitor, *he will make* (*him*) *fl[ee]* from him.[11] [And so we] (always) obey. And note: I am a loyal servant of the king, my lord.

NOTES

1. [ù l]i-⌜i⌝-d[e_4]: cf. *EA* 148:43; 248:9; 257:8, etc., for the writing, but the reading is doubtful because the horizontal at the beginning of the last sign is certain. Perhaps it was meant to be erased.

2. ⌜*i*⌝*-p*[*u-š*]*u-m*[*i*]: virtually certain.

3. Lit. "entered." Characteristic of *EA* 185–86 is *i* as thematic vowel in forms of *erēbu*: see *EA* 185:20, 26, 36, 40; 186:26, 50, 87. The only parallels are *EA* 127:19; 137:34, 42; 138:12, 134. These forms may not be provincial aberrations; note Old Babylonian [*i-t*]*e-ri-ib*, R. Whiting, Jr., *Old Babylonian Letters from Tell Asmar* (see *EA* 14, n. 9), no. 2:6.

4. [ù i-na] URU *pa-aḫ-*⟨ru⟩*-mi*: there is no reference in the parallel passage (*EA* 186:50–52) to a place called Paḫmu, which is otherwise unknown, and in context it is hard to see what role the place might have played. The scribe omitted a sign in lines 26, 28, 31, 69, and possibly 60 (*i-ša-ra-pu-ni-*⟨*ši*⟩*-na*). Throughout the letter *-mi* is regularly attached to the verb (27 times).

5. *ù* LÚ.SA.GA[Z ᵐ*a-ma-a*]*n-ḫa-at-pé*: almost certainly not enough room for GA[Z. MEŠ . . .].

6. t[i-na-am]*-mi-šu*: following Landsberger in Bottéro, *Ḫabiru*, p. 98.

7. *i-*[*ri*]*-bu-mi*: once it is recognized that *erēbu itti* can mean "to enter into (the presence)," the restoration seems virtually certain; see esp. *EA* 283:11; 286:40.

8. *a-na mu-ši* ⟨⟨*ir*⟩⟩: assuming the *ir* should have been erased like the preceding *Winckelhaken*.

9. *ba-lu* š⌜a⌝*-a-al*: the alleged *ma-ḫa* is actually written much closer than in the copies, making *ša* very probable.

10. A parenthetical remark referring to Amanḫatpe's replacement?

11. Syntax ("converted perfect"?) and meaning (banishment?) unclear.

EA 186

Another report on the Egyptian traitor

TEXT: VAT 1724.
COPIES: WA 193; *VS* 11, 107.
TRANSLITERATION AND TRANSLATION: Bottéro, *Ḫabiru*, pp. 100ff. (lines 12–69).

[To the king, my lord, my god, m]y [Sun: Message of *Ma*yarzana, the ruler of Ḫasi, your servant, the dirt beneath your feet. I fal]l [at the feet of the king, my lord, my god, my] Sun, [7 times and 7 times. A]s I a[m] a loy[al] servant of [the king], my lord, [my god], my Sun, I serve the [k]ing, [my lord, my god], my [Su]n, together with ⟨my⟩ brothers and [my] sons, lo[yal servants of the king, my lord], my god, my Sun. [*No*]*te that* [*we would*][1] die beneath the feet of the king, [my] lord, my [Sun], my god.

12–27 A[s fo]r [Am]anḫa[tp]e, the ruler of Tušul[tu, whe]n the ʿAp[ir]u captured [*Maḫzib*]*tu*,[2] a loyal city of the k[ing, my] l[ord, my god], my Sun, p[lundered] i[t, and] burned it down, they [*w*]*en*[*t*] to [Aman]ḫatpe, the r[uler of Tušultu, and Amanḫatpe, the ruler of Tušu]ltu, [kept giving food along with ... to] the ʿApir[u. *Gilunu*, too], a loyal city [of the king, my lord, my go]d, [my Sun, the ʿApiru] captur[ed, plundered it, bur]ned [it down], and then took ref[ug]e [wi]th A[manḫatpe], the ruler of T[ušultu], and [Amanḫatp]e, the ruler of T[ušultu], kept giving food a[long with ... t]o the ʿApiru.

28–34 [*Magd*]*al*[*u*,[3] too, a loyal] city of the king, [my] lord, my god, [my Sun], the ʿApiru captu[red], plundered it, [burned it down], and then they t[ook refuge wit]h [Amanḫatpe], the ruler of [Tušultu], and [Amanḫatp]e, the ruler of [Tušultu], kept gi[ving food along with ... to the ʿApiru].

35–42 ...[4]

43–85 And there was [Ḫasi, *a loyal city of the king, my lord*]. The ʿApiru r[aided Ḫasi, a loyal city] of the king, my lord, my god, [my Su]n, [*and*] the loyal servants of [the king], m[y lo]rd, my [god], my Sun, *f*[*ough*]*t*,[5] and the loyal servants of the king, my lord, my god, my Sun, *personally co*[*nquered*][6] the ʿApiru. But 40 ʿApi[ru] ⟨⟨ʿApiru⟩⟩ took refuge with A[manḫatpe], the ruler of [Tušul]tu. We he[ard] th[at] the 40 ʿApi[ru were] wi[th Amanḫatp]e, the ruler of Tu[šultu], and [my] broth[ers] and [m]y [s]on[s], servants of the king, my lord, m[y] god, m[y Su]n, *d[rov]e*[7] their chariots and en[tered] the presence of Amanḫatpe, the rule[r of T]ušultu. They said to Amanḫatpe, "[Hand over] the ʿA[pi]ru, the traitors to the king, [m]y lo[rd], [m]y god, my Sun, so we can demand a reckoning of th[em] fo[r having cap]tured cities of the king, m[y lor]d, [my go]d, my Sun, and for having raided [Ḫas]i, [a city of the kin]g, my lord, my god, my Sun." (64–85) [He ag]reed to hand over the ʿAp[iru. *I was going to r*]*emove*[8] the ʿApiru, but he to[ok] his [*servants*] and [w]ent off to the ʿApi[ru. . . .] . . . from his city. [*And*] *I* knew his crime, but he went [off to] the ʿAp[ir]u. [*What*] can *I* do?[9] [. . .] I have sent [. . . *to* the king], my lord, m[y] god, [my] S[un, . . .] . . . Like . . . [. . .] *he raised* [ag]ain[st the king, my lord], my god, [my] Sun, [*and*] against [*his lo*]*yal* land. *But* we listen t[o *the words* of the king, my lord], my [go]d, [m]y Sun [. . . *And*] as to his having said [to the king, my lord], my god, my Sun, [. . .] . . .

NOTES

1. [*šu*]*m-ma* BA.UG$_7$ [ni-mu-ut]: *Glossenkeil* before *nimūt*? Cf. *EA* 362:11.

2. URU.K[I ma-aḫ-zi-ib]-*ti*^{ki}: cf. *EA* 185:17. Against URU *t*[*u-šu-ul*]-*ti* (Knudtzon, followed by Bottéro): (1) it does not fill the break; (2) it seems highly unlikely that the ʿApiru destroyed Amanḫatpe's own city and still gained his support; (3) after their forays they seem to retreat to Tušultu (Greenberg, *Ḫab/piru*, p. 42, n. 13). Against my reading is the fact that nowhere else in *EA* 185–86 is a city name preceded by URU.KI. I assume influence of the immediately following URU.KI *kitti*.

3. URU [ma-ag-d]a-l[i]: cf. *EA* 185:29. Note, however, the absence of determinative ki at the end.

4. Pillaging of another city, presumably Uštu; cf. *EA* 185:37–41.

5. *i*-[du-k]u-*mi*: *dâku* without an object? [. . . MÈ?] 46 *i*-[pu-š]u-*mi*, "they waged war"? (Cf. *EA* 185:44–45.)

6. *i*-k[a-ša-du/da].

7. *ti*-[*na-mi-š*]*u-mi*: cf. *EA* 185:52 and n. 6.

8. [a-la]-*qa-at*.

9. [mi-na] *i-pu-šu-na*: cf. *EA* 74:63; 90:22; 91:25f.; 104:36f.; etc.

EA 187

A daughter sent to the Pharaoh

TEXT: BM 29860.
COPY: BB 77.

Sa[y to the kin]g, my lord, [my god, my Sun: Mess]age of Šatiya, the ruler of [Enišasi], your [ser]vant, the dirt und[er the f]eet of the king, my lord. I [fa]ll [a]t the feet of the king, [my] lord, my god, my Sun, 7 times and 7 times.

9–16 As I am the loya[l] servant of the king, my lord, my god, [my Sun], in this place, and Enišasi[1] is a city of the king, my lord, [my] god, my [Sun], I am guarding [*the pl*]*ace*[2] of the king, [m]y lo[rd, my god, my Sun, *where I am*]. 16–21 [. . .] 22 And I herew[ith s]end my daughter to the [pa]lace, [t]o the king, my lord, m[y] god, my Sun.

NOTES

1. URU *e-ni-ša-si*$_{29}$[(*-i*)]; see Rainey, *Tel Aviv* 2 (1975) p. 15; Na'aman, *UF* 20 (1988) pp. 188f.
2. Reading not certain; 16 [ša it-ti-ia . . .] (see Introduction, sect. 5).

EA 188

Message lost

TEXT: C 4793 (12237).
COPY: WA 208.

[. . . I fall at the fee]t of the k[ing, m]y [*god*], m[y] Sun, [7 times] and 7 times. [A]s I am . . . [. . .], and as I [a]m a l[oyal] servant of the ki[ng, *my*] g[*od,*[1] my Sun], and [. . .] . . .[2] [. . .].

NOTES

1. Sign more like DINGIR than EN (Gordon).
2. The sign in line 8 is not *a*, as it begins with two horizontals (Gordon).

EA 189

Etakkama of Qadesh

TEXT: VAT 336.
COPIES: WA 142; *VS* 11, 108.

To the king, my lord: Message of Etakkama, your servant. I fall at the feet of my lord, my Sun, 7 times plus 7. My lord, I am your servant, but the wicked Biryawaza has gone on defaming me in your sight, my lord, and when he was defaming me in your sight, *then* he took my entire paternal estate along with[1] the land of Qidšu, and sent my cities up in flames. 13–20 But, I assure you, the commissioners of the king, my lord, and his magnates know my loyalty, since I said to the magnate Puḫuru, "May the magnate Puḫuru know that [. . .] . . ."

Reverse

1–8 [. . .] . . . Biryawaza. Thus do I serve you along w[it]h all my brothers, and wherever there is war against the king, I go, together with my troops, together with my chariots, and together with all my brothers. 9–18 Since Biryawaza had allowed all of the cities of the king, my lord, to go over to the ʿApiru in Taḫši and Upu, I went, and with your gods[2] and your Sun leading me, I restored from the ʿApiru the cities to the king, my lord, for his service, and I disbanded the ʿApiru. 19–27 May the king, my lord, rejoice at Etakkama, his servant, for I serve the king, my lord, together with all my brothers. I serve the king, my lord, but Biryawaza caused the loss of all [your] lan[ds.[3] *His intention*][4] is solely injustice, but I am [your servant] forever.

NOTES

1. See *EA* 112, n. 1. Or did Biryawaza cut off the paternal estate *from* the land?
2. Perhaps "your god."
3. On the verb, see *EA* 97, n. 1.
4. [pa-nu-šu].

EA 190

A letter from Egypt

TEXT: Ash 1893. 1–41: 411.
COPY: Sayce, *Tell el Amarna*, no. 4.

[. . . *Guard*][1] the land of the king, [*your*] lord, [*and guard* Pu]ḫuru, [*your*] . . . [. . . Be on your gu]ard, and gua[rd *Qid*]šu, and guar[d . . .],[2] the garrison city [of *the king*].

6–12 . . .[3]

NOTES

1. Sign forms and formulaic expressions indicate the Egyptian origin of *EA* 190, which was sent either by the king or by a high Egyptian official. Restorations: uṣ-ṣur (lines 1–2, not uṣṣur-mi! see Rainey, *UF* 6 [1974] p. 306, on lines 3–4) and [*lu-ú na-ṣa*]-*ra-ta* (line 3), following Na'aman, *Political Disposition*, p. 73*, n. 63.
2. Na'aman, ibid., proposes [URU *ku-mi*]-*di*.

3. No connected sense: *qí-pa*, "trust" (line 9); Ḫ[UR.SAG, "mountain"(?) (line 10); [. . .]*te-eš$_{17}$-ši*(?) (line 11); [. . .]-*eš$_{17}$-ši*(?) (line 12).

EA 191

Preparations for war

TEXT: C 4760 (12192).
COPY: WA 125.

To the king, my lord: Message of Arsawuya, the ruler of Ruḫizza. I fall at the feet of the king, my lord. The king, my lord, wrote to me to make preparations before the arrival of the archers of the king, my lord, and before the arrival of his many commissioners.[1]

9–10 And could I think of not serving the king, my lord?

11–21 May I join up[2] with the archers of the king and his commissioners so that, having everything prepared, I might follow them wherever they are at war against the king, my lord, and we capture them (and) give his enemies into the hand of the king, our lord.

NOTES

1. As used here, high officials and military commanders.
2. Against Knudtzon, *lukšudam-me* is first person, not third, and singular, not plural.

EA 192

Message received

TEXT: VAT 1674.
COPIES: WA 126; *VS* 11, 109.

[Sa]y [t]o the king, my lord, both Sun and my god: Message of [A]rsawuya, the loyal servant [o]f the king, my lord, [and the di]rt at the feet of the king, my lord. I fall at the feet of the king, my lord, both Sun and my god, 7 times and 7 times.

10–17 [I have] heard the words [of the king], my lord and my god, [and here]with [. . .] . . . [the king], ⟨my⟩ lord. And the king, [m]y lord, must [not] neglect his country.

EA 193

On the alert

TEXT: VAT 1608.
COPIES: WA 161; *VS* 11, 110.

To the king, my lord: Message of Tiwati. I fall at the feet of the king, my lord, 7 times plus 7 times.

5–24 I am indeed in the city; I am very much on my guard. *M*[*y*] horses and [*my*] *t*[*roops* (*and my chariots*)[1] *are for*] *the ser*[*vice of the king, my lord*], and (*when*) the archers *c*[*ome forth*],[2] I will accompany th[em]. (The ruler [who] does not serve the king curses.)[3] I have indeed oxen and sheep and goats ready, in accordance with your command on the tablet to me.

NOTES

1. If there was writing on the edge; see *VAB* 2/1, p. 718, note b, and copy.
2. ⸢a⸣-[ṣa-at]: the assumed asyndetic construction is found on lines 17–18.
3. Or, "will curse"; perhaps not "ruler," but simply "man."

EA 194

A tradition of service

TEXT: VAT 1705.
COPY: *VS* 11, 112.

To the king, my lord: Message of Biryawaza, yo[ur] servant. I fal[l] at the feet of the king, my lord, 7 times and 7 times. 6–16 Behold, we are servants (*who*) *have* served the king from time immemorial. Like Šutarna, my father, like . . . [. . .] . . .,[1] [*my*] *grand*[*father,* . . .] . . . 17–27 . . . [. . .] to gu[ar]d the cities. And the expedition[2] that you sent to Naḫrima . . . [. . .] 28–32 [. . .] is very afraid.[3] [I] herewith [s]end[4] [m]y brother [t]o you.

NOTES

1. Collation shows only the horizontals of the fairly clear TAR of copy; Na'aman, *Political Disposition,* p. 74*, n. 65, ^{m}*ḫa*[*š*-x]-*tar.* Na'aman, *UF* 20 (1988) p. 180, sees here the beginning of Biryawaza's defense against charges by the king, perhaps of robbing a Babylonian caravan (cf. *EA* 7:75).

2. KASKAL-*na* (written *šu*). Instead of "expedition," perhaps "caravan"; see n. 1.

3. The gender (feminine) suggests that the subject is a city.

4. [ú-*w*]*a-aš-šar.*

EA 195

Waiting for the Pharaoh's words

TEXT: C 4761 (12230).
COPY: WA 96.

Say to the king, my lord: Message of Biryawaza, your servant, the dirt at your feet and the ground you tread on, the chair you sit on and the footstool[1] at your feet. I fall at the feet of the king, my lord, the Sun of the dawn (over) : *li-me-ma* (peoples),[2] 7 times plus 7 times. **16–23** My lord is the Sun in the sky, and like the coming forth of the Sun in the sky (your) servants await the coming forth of the words from the mouth of their lord. **24–32** I am indeed, together with my troops and chariots, together with my brothers, my ʿApiru and my Suteans, at the disposition[3] of the archers, wheresoever the king, my lord, shall order (me to go).

NOTES

1. GIŠ.GIR.GÙB : *giš-tap-pí.*

2. That the same scribe wrote *EA* 195 and 201–6 (so also Gordon; cf. Knudtzon, *VAB* 2/2, p. 1294, n. 2) is indicated by (1) a constellation of unusual sign-forms (note esp. *ša, ni, bi, na, i, ia*); (2) the presence only in these letters (not in *EA* 202) of 7-*šu a-na pani* 7-*ta*-(*an*)-*ni*; and (3) the appearance only in these letters of *a-nu-ma a-na-ku qa-du* ÉRIN.MEŠ-*ia ù* (*qa-du*) GIŠ.GIGIR.MEŠ-*ia.* Therefore, ^{d}UTU *li-mi-ma* in *EA* 205:6 rules out *le-la-ma* and makes *li-me-ma* certain. Following Rainey, *Particles,* chapter 1, read KIN as an abbreviation or KIN.⟨NIM⟩ *še-ri.*MEŠ, "dawn(s)." The West Semitic plural formation *lim* + *īma* argues for *li*(')*mu.* The following lines elaborate the image of the rising sun. Cf. the hymns celebrating the sun breaking over the horizon, giving life to men and arousing them from deathlike sleep and torpor (John A. Wilson, *ANET,* p. 368, Amenophis III; ibid., pp. 370a–371a, Amenophis IV).

3. See *EA* 174, n. 2.

EA 196

Unheard-of deeds

TEXT: VAT 1592 + 1710.
COPIES: WA 159 (+) 143; *VS* 11, 111.

[S]a[y to the king, m]y [lord: Message of Biry]awaza, [your] servant. I fall [a]t the feet of the k[in]g, ⟨my⟩ l[ord], 7 times pl[us] 7 times. **5–12** I obeyed when the k[ing, my] lord, sent [. . .]saya. [*I a*]*m on my* [*guard*],[1] and [*I serv*]*e* [the k]in[g, my lord], *i*[*n*] *this* [*plac*]*e.*[2] May [*a* *larg*]*e* [*force*[3] of the ki]ng, my lord, co[m]e [*immediately*][4] *aga*[*inst the king of Ḫ*]*at*[*ti*].[5] *The gar*[*rison of the king, my lord, has left* (*me*)].[6] 12–19 I [*am the servant of*] the ki[ng] that has [*o*]*pened the* ⟨*w*⟩*ays*[7] fo[r *the troops, but*] the king, my lord, [should kn]ow that [al]l the servants of the king [have *g*]*one* (*run off*)[8] [to] Ḫatti, and all the commissione[rs of the king], my [lo]rd, who *came* [*forth*],[9] 20–26 [. . .] . . . 27–33 [. . .] my wives [*and*] my [*daug*]*hter-in-law,*[10] and [*he pu*]*t* in [*his*] *lap*[11] (anyone) [*pre*]*sent.*[12] *Now* [the kin]g, [my] lord, has been informed of this affair. No one has ever done such a thi⟨ng⟩. 33–43 Moreover, may the king, [my] lord, send me 200 men to guard ⟨⟨to guard⟩⟩ the cities of the king, [my] lord, [un]til [I] see the archers [of the king], my lord. The king, my lord, must not negle[ct] this deed that Biridašwa [has] committed, for he has *moved* the land of [the king], my lord, and [his] cities *to rebellion.*

NOTES

1. [*n*]*a-a*[*ṣ*]-*r*[*a*-k]u: cf. *EA* 142:11; 193:7; 230:10.
2. *i*-n[a aš-r]i *an-ni*: cf. *EA* 55:4; 180:3; 187:11; 286:11. A vertical wedge is visible before *an-ni* (cf. *an-ni,* line 40).
3. [ar-ḫi-iš ÉRIN.GA]L: cf. *EA* 117:26; 337:10, 17, 22.
4. See note 3, and cf. *EA* 82:52; 93:35; 102:30; 367:19.
5. *a-na* m[a-ḫar . . .].
6. *ma*-⌜ṣar⌝ [LUGAL EN-ia i-pa-ṭar]: cf. *i-pa-ṭar* in *EA* 197:19. For a quite different reading of lines 10–11, see Na'aman, *UF* 20 (1988) p. 187, n. 33.
7. ⌜ip⌝-*te* ⟨ur⟩-*ḫa-te*: if *ipte* is the correct reading, then the context requires something like this; ⟨pé⟩-*ḫa-te,* "the blocked (roads)?"
8. [i]t-*ta-al-ku éb-tú*: from *abātu* (*nābutu*)? *tú* is rare but attested (*EA* 145:10).
9. [*u*]*ṣ*-ṣ[u-ni]: following Maynard, *JSOR* 9 (1925) p. 130.
10. [ù] ⌜É⌝.GI-*ia*: cf. É.GI.A = *kallātu* (Mittani, Ugarit; *CAD,* K, p. 80).
11. ÚR : su-n[i-šu]: this seems to have been the gloss, before the erasure. Appropriation(?) of wives and daughter-in-law, and/or violation of the available women, would be unusual charges.
12. [ba]-*ši-ta*$_5$.

EA 197

Biryawaza's plight

TEXT: BM 29826.
COPY: BB 43.
PHOTOGRAPH: BB, pl. 3.

[. . . he] said t[o *me when*] your servant *was* in A[*dura.*[1] . . . *They gave*] his horses and hi[s] chariot to the ʿApiru, and they did not [*give them*] to the king, my lord. 5–12 And who am I? My (only) *purpose*[2] is to be a servant. Everything belongs to the king. Biridašwa saw this deed and moved Yanuamma to rebellion[3] against me. Having barred the city gate against me, he took chariots from Aštartu but gave *both of them*[4] to the ʿApiru and did not give *both of them* to the king, my lord. 13–23 When the king of Buṣruna and the king of Ḫalunnu saw (this), they waged war with Biridašwa against me, constantly saying, "Come, let's kill Biryawaza, and we must not let him go to [. . .] . . ."[5] But I got away from them and stayed[6] in [. . .] Dimašqa, for [*by myself* h]ow can I serv[e *the king, my lord*]? 23–31 [They] keep saying,[7] "[We are servants of the king of Ḫat]ti," and I keep saying, "I am a servant of the king of Egyp[t]." Arsawuya went to Ki[ssa], took (some of) Aziru's troops, and captured Šaddu. He gave it to the ʿApiru and did not give it to the king, my lord. 31–42 Now, since Itatkama has caused the loss[8] of the land of Kissa, and since Arsawuya along with Biridašwa is causing the loss of Apu, may the king look carefully to his land lest the enemies take it. Since my brothers are at war with me, I am guarding Kumidu, the city of the king, my lord. May the king indeed *be at one*[9] with his servant. [M]ay the king [not] abandon his servant, [*and may*] the kings of [. . . (*and*) the ki]ngs of Apu see *whe*[*ther* . . .] . . . I have seen the archers.

NOTES

1. See Na'aman, *UF* 20 (1988) p. 183.
2. IGI.2?: despite the possible dual-marker *pānū*.
3. *yi*-⟨⟨*maš*⟩⟩-*na-mu-uš*: following Rainey, *UF* 6 (1974) p. 306. On the subject of the verb, see Kühne, p. 7, n. 34 (end).
4. On the pronominal suffix, see *BASOR* 211 (1973) p. 53. The implication that Biridašwa took only two chariots is somewhat surprising and perhaps not right (mistaken use of the dual suffix?).
5. [x]-x-*še*: of the second sign only one oblique wedge is visible; against Taḫše is its distance from the area that is Biryawaza's present concern, as noted by Na'aman, *UF* 20 (1988) p. 183, n. 23.
6. Perhaps "made a stand"; cf. Na'aman, ibid., p. 184.
7. 23 [LUGAL EN-ia ù *te*]-*eq-bu-na*: cf. line 16, *tilqū-še* (line 36) and *tedaggalū* (line 41).
8. See *EA* 97, n. 1.
9. *lu-ú* ⟨⟨UD⟩⟩ *ša-lim*, or perhaps *lu-ú y*⟨*i*⟩-*ša-lim*.

EA 198

From Kumidu

TEXT: C 4763 (12194).
COPY: WA 205.

Say [to the kin]g, [my] lord, [my] personal god:[1] Message of Ara[*šš*]*a*, the ruler of Kumidu, the dirt at your feet, the ground you tread on. I fall at the feet of the king, my lord, 7 times and 7 times. 10–17 I am indeed your loyal servant. May the king, my lord, inquire[2] of all of his commissioners whether I am a loyal servant of the king, my lord. May the king, my lord, inquire of Ḫamašš[a] whether I am a loyal servant of the king, my lord. 17–23 May the king, my lord, welcome (me) and give me life, for I have neither horse nor chariot. 24–31 May *it please*[3] the king, my lord, to give life to his servant. Truly, I send my own son to the king, my lord, and may the kin[g], my l[or]d, give me life.

NOTES

1. Lit. "the god of my head"; cf. in Syrian Old Babylonian *il ālim*, "city-god," and *il rēšim* (*rēšīn?*), "god of the head = personal god" (*AÉM* 1/1, p. 239, n. 43; no. 108, note a).

2. *li-eš-al$_x$*: cf. *al$_x$-lu-ú-me*, line 27.

3. *li-ut*-r[u]-*aṣ-me* = *litruṣ-me* (cf. *EA* 92:46f.; 103:40; 106:35; 286:44): the horizontal wedge is not only lower than in *ši* (Knudtzon), but somewhat longer, so that *ru* is possible. Gordon came independently to the same reading and the same interpretation.

EA 199

Caravan escort

TEXT: C 4789 (12234).
COPY: WA 205.

[To the king, *my lord, my Sun*: Message of . . . , *your servant*]. I [f]all at the feet of [my lord]. 5–14 The king, my Sun, *is a fath*[*er*][1] to me, and . . . [. . .] I heard the *con*[*sent*] *of* the king, my lord. [I *made* very] careful *preparat*[*ions*],[2] and [I *escorted*[3] a]ll the king's caravans as far as Buṣrun[a]. I heeded [*you*]. 15–21 As I am your servant [. . .] . . .

NOTES

1. *a*-⌜bu⌝-mi: Gordon thought *a-mu*[*r*]-x possible.

2. [u]š-*šu-ur*-t[e]: if the correct reading, it seems to reflect a confusion of *uššuru,* "to send," and *šūšuru,* "to prepare."

3. [ú-bi-il]: cf. *EA* 255:23.

EA 200

About Aḫlameans

TEXT: VAT 1622.
COPIES: WA 164; *VS* 11, 113.

[S]ay to the king, my lord, [my god, my Sun: Messa]ge of [your] servants.[1] We [fa]ll 7 times and 7 times [a]t the feet of the king, my lord.[2] 7–17 [*Her*]*e* is what we *hear*:[3] [. . .] . . . The Aḫlamean(s?) [. . .] the king of Karaduniaš[4] [. . .] the Aḫlamean(s?) [. . .] . . .

NOTES

1. The scribe of this letter is distinguished by less archaic writing practices: *qí-bi* (not *bí*)-*ma*; *ni*-[x *q*]*u* (not *qú*)-*ut*; distinct AḪ-sign.

2. Formulaic "the king, my lord" prevails over context.

3. *nišmu*: durative seems much more probable than punctive + subjunctive-marker, the use of the latter being virtually unknown. The peculiarities of the scribe (see n. 1), however, preclude certainty on the matter.

4. An incomplete *ra* is more likely than *ár* (Knudtzon). Perhaps, as Na'aman, *UF* 20 (1988) p. 181, n. 14, also suggests, Babylonian caravans were being harassed by the Aḫlamean(s?); cf. *EA* 16.

EA 201

Ready for marching orders (1)

TEXT: VAT 338.
COPIES: WA 132; *VS* 11, 114.

Say to the king, my lord: Message of Artamanya, the ruler of Ṣiribašani, your servant.[1] I fall at the feet of the king, my lord, 7 times plus 7 times. 9–16 As you have written me to make preparations before the arrival of the archers, who am I, a *mere* dog,[2] that I should not go?[3] 17–24 I am herewith, along with my troops and my chariots, at the disposition[4] of the archers wherever the king, my lord, orders (me to go).

NOTES

1. On the scribe of *EA* 201–6, see *EA* 195, n. 2. Probably all seven letters were written about the same time and perhaps in the same place. Another possibility is that Biryawaza sent his scribe from town to town; but see *EA* 204, n. 1.

2. *kalbu ištēn* (also *EA* 202:13; 247:15?): Pintore, *OA* 11 (1972) p. 125, n. 136, thought the phrase refers to a wild dog (wolf, jackal) cut off from the pack and living isolated and miserable; but cf. *EA* 319:19ff.

3. *al$_x$-la-ku* (also *EA* 202:14): cf. *EA* 198, n. 2.

4. See *EA* 174, n. 2.

EA 202

Ready for marching orders (2)

TEXT: VAT 331.
COPIES: WA 135; *VS* 11, 115.

Say to the king, my lord: Message of Amawaše, your servant. I fall at the feet of the king, my lord, 7 times and 7 times. 7–14 You have written me to assist the archers. Who am I, a *mere* dog, that I should not go? 15–19 I am herewith, along with my troops and my chariots, at the disposition of the archers.[1]

NOTE

1. See *EA* 201.

EA 203

Ready for marching orders (3)

TEXT: VAT 330.
COPIES: WA 134; *VS* 11, 116.

Say to the king, my lord: Message of ʿAbdi-Milki, the ruler of Šasḫimi, your servant. I fall at the feet of the king, my lord, 7 times and 7 times. 9–19 You have written me to make preparations before the arrival of the archers. I am herewith, along with my troops and my chariots, at the disposition of the troops of the king, my lord, wherever they go.[1]

NOTE

1. See *EA* 201.

EA 204

Ready for marching orders (4)

TEXT: VAT 328.
COPIES: WA 133; *VS* 11, 117.

Say the king, my lord: Message of the ruler of Qanu, your servant. I fall at the feet of the king, my lord, 7 times plus 7 times. **9–20** You have written me to make preparations before the arrival of the archers. I am herewith, along with my troops and along with my chariots, at the disposition of the troops of the king, my lord, wherever they go.[1]

NOTE

1. See *EA* 201. The fact that here and in the two following letters the ruler's name is not given suggests that it was not known to the scribe, which also suggests that he did not write on the spot.

EA 205

Ready for marching orders (5)

TEXT: BM 29861.
COPY: BB 78.
PHOTOGRAPH: BB, pl. 7; C. Pfeiffer, *Tell el Amarna and the Bible* (Grand Rapids, 1963), p. 11 (obverse only).

Say to the king, my lord: Message of the ruler of Ṭubu, your servant. I fall at the feet of the king, my lord, the Sun of (all) peoples,[1] 7 times plus 7 times. **9–18** You have written to me to make preparations before the arrival of the archers. I am herewith, along with my troops and my chariots, at the disposition of the troops of the king, my lord, wherever they go.[2]

NOTES

1. See *EA* 195, n. 2.
2. See *EA* 201.

EA 206

Ready for marching orders (6)

TEXT: C 4762 (12229).
COPY: WA 151.

Say to the king, my lord: Message of the ruler of Nazi*ba,* your servant. I fall at the feet of the king, my lord, 7 times plus 7 times. 9–17 You hav[e wr]it[ten][1] to make preparations before the arrival of the archers, and I am herewith, along with my troops and my chariots, at the disposition of the archers.[2]

NOTES

1. Gordon saw traces below the *-ra* of *ša-ap-ra* and the *ši-ri* of *šu-ši-ri,* "probably : *ta.*"

2. See *EA* 201 and 204, n. 1.

EA 207

A loyal servant

TEXT: VAT 1593.
COPIES: WA 194; *VS* 11, 118.

[S]ay to the king, my lord, [*my Sun*]: ⟨Message⟩ of Ipte[. . .], your [servant. I fall a]t the feet of m[y] lord. 4–9 I have obeyed *a*[*ll the orders of the kin*]*g* on the [*tablet*]. Look, I am a [*loyal*] servant [*that*][1] has served [*the king. Wh*]*o* [*is a loyal*] *servant* like m[e? 9–14 *As to your saying,* "*Wh*]*y*[2] must the commissioner of the king [sp]eak twice the wor[d of . . .] . . . Look, [*I* . . .] . . . 15–24 [. . .] . . . like the Sun and like [*Baal*].[3] In fact, Puḫur[4] has not protected me. Lost to the ʿApiru : *ḫa*-[. . .][5] from [my] control are all the cities of the king.

NOTES

1. ÌR [ki-it-ti] 7 [ša-a]: cf. *EA* 114:56.

2. *i-nu-ma* [ta-a]q-*bu* 10 [mi-nu]-mi . . . *a-wa*-a[t x-(x)]-x: for *taqbu,* cf. *EA* 116:8; 131:41; 145:23; for *mīnu,* "why," cf. *EA* 126:14, 49.

3. Cf. *EA* 159:5ff.

4. The reference to the commissioner Puḫur(u) locates the origin of this letter somewhere in the area of his administration; see Helck, *Beziehungen,* p. 183, n. 96.

5. Reading of the gloss is uncertain; see Bottéro, *Ḫabiru,* p. 105, and Greenberg, *Ḫab/piru,* p. 44.

EA 208

Inquiry urged

TEXT: VAT 1699.
COPY: *VS* 11, 119.

1–7 [. . .] . . . 8–14 to me and . . . [. . .], and I sent him ⟨*imme*⟩*diately.* And look, there is Puḫuru.[1] Ask him about the cities of the king, my lord, [whe]ther the cities of the king, my lord, are safe.

NOTE

1. See *EA* 207, n. 4.

EA 209

Abounding joy

TEXT: AO 2036.
COPIES: WA 149a; Thureau-Dangin, *RA* 19 (1922) p. 101.

[S]ay to the king, m[y] lord: Message of Zišamimi, yo[ur] servant. I fall at [yo]ur feet.[1] 7 times and 7 times I fall before the king, my lord. 7–11 Your cities where I am are happy.[2] Look, I am your servant forever. And look, I am your servant and your [*son*].[3] 11–16 And look, your cities where I am are cities of the king, my lord, and if I have [*n*]*ot* guarded[4] y[our] cities, may the gods where you are *smash* my [he]ad.[5]

NOTES

1. Written ANŠE.MEŠ-*pí*.

2. The joy of a subordinate usually implies a message from the king (cf. *EA* 141–42, 144, 147, 154, 362), perhaps telling of his arrival (cf. *EA* 227); see also Na'aman, *Lingering over Words*, pp. 401ff. Novel features of this letter: the place, not its ruler, is happy; the language alludes to the vassal's duty of protecting the place where he is (lines 11ff.).

3. Cf. *EA* 288:66.

4. See Rainey, *UF* 6 (1974) p. 306.

5. [S]⸢AG⸣-*ka-di* (*qaqqadī*): virtually certain.

EA 210

Message lost

TEXT: VAT 1876.
COPIES: WA 223; *VS* 11, 120.

Too fragmentary for translation.[1]

NOTE

1. Addressed to an Egyptian (see Introduction, n. 82). Line 3: "[Message of] Zišami[mi]."

EA 211

Inescapable orders

TEXT: VAT 1648.
COPIES: WA 140; *VS* 11, 121.

Say to the king, my lord: Message of Zitriyar[a], your servant. I fall at the feet of the king, my lord, 7 times and 7 times, both on the back and on the stomach. 7–15 As I am a servant of the king, my lord, he has obeyed the order that the k[ing, m]y [lord], s[e]nt [t]o hi[s] servant. I am the servant of the king, my lord. 15–25 As the king is like the Sun from the sky : *ša-mu-ma,* we are unable to ignore the order of the king, my lord, and we obey the commissioner that you have placed over me.

EA 212

Perfect obedience

TEXT: VAT 1587.
COPIES: WA 141; *VS* 11, 122.

To the king, my lord: Message of Zitriyara, your servant. I fall at the feet of my lord 7 times and 7 times. 6–14 Just as we have alw[a]ys acted—as all the mayors (have acted)[1]—*s*⟨*o*⟩[2] shall I act towards the king, my lord. I am the servant of the king, my lord. Every order of the king, m⟨y⟩ lord, I do obey.[3]

NOTES

1. Probably a reference to his predecessors; cf. *EA* 74:10ff.; 194:10ff.; 253:11ff.

2. *ki*-⟨a/ia-am⟩.

3. The word order, with the object at the beginning of the sentence, emphasizes the completeness of the obedience.

EA 213

Preparations under way

TEXT: BM 29859.
COPY: BB 76.
PHOTOGRAPH: BB, pl. 6.

Say to the king, my lord, my Sun, my god: Message of Zitriyara, your servant, the dirt under your feet, and the mire you tread on. I fall at the feet of the king, my lord, my Sun, my god, 7 times and 7 times, both on the stomach and on the back. 10–15 I have heard the message of the king, my lord, my Sun, my god, to his servant. I herewith [m]ake the preparations in accordance [w]ith the command of the king, my lord, my Sun, my go[d].

EA 214

Message lost

TEXT: VAT 1607.
COPY: *VS* 11, 123.

Too fragmentary for translation.[1]

NOTE

1. A letter to the king; possible mention of Zitriyara on line 11 (cf. *EA* 211–13).

EA 215

A warning

TEXT: BM 29843.
COPY: BB 60.
PHOTOGRAPH: BB, pl. 7.

To the king, my lord, my Sun, my god: Message of Bayawa, your servant. I fall at the feet of the king, my lord, my Sun, my god, 7 times and 7 times, on the stomach and on the back. 9–17 Should[1] Yanḫamu not be here within this [year, a]ll the lands are [lo]st to the ʿApiru. So give life to your lands.

NOTE

1. The position of *lū* at the beginning of the sentence and not before the predicate suggests Canaanite influence (cf. *AHw,* p. 560) and argues against taking *lū* as asseverative (Campbell, *Chronology,* p. 100, n. 70).

EA 216

Obedience to the commissioner

TEXT: C 4784 (12202).
COPY: WA 195.

Say t[o] the king, my lord: Message of Bayawa, your servant.[1] I fall at the fe[et] of the king, my lord, [my] Sun, 7 times and 7 times. 6–11 I have heard the message of the king, my lord, to his servant to make preparations before the arrival of the archers. [I] am now making preparations [in] accordance with the comma[nd] of the king, my lord. 12–14 I obey most carefully the words of Maya, the commissioner of the king, my lord. 15–20 May the king, my lord, send arc[hers] to his servants. To men who do not obey the king, will the king, my lord, give thought?[2]

NOTES

1. The script of *EA* 216 is quite different from that of *EA* 215. Between Yanḫamu and Maya a new scribe was employed.

2. Or, "the king, my lord, will give thought" (threat), but not "may the king . . . ," which is incompatible with the indicative *yimluku.*

EA 217

About Maya

TEXT: VAT 1604.
COPY: *VS* 11, 124.

Sa[y] to the k[in]g, m[y] lord: Message of . . . [. . .], yo[ur] servant. I fall at the feet of the king, [my] lord, [my Su]n, 7 times and [7] times. 7–12 I have heard all the words of the king, [my] l[ord], and indeed [. . . *of*] the king, [*my lord* . . .]. 13–23 And wh[o am] I that I would not obey [M]ay[a, *the commissioner of* the kin]g, [my] l[ord]? May the ki[ng], m[y lor]d, send troops to his country, *so that* [*I can g*]*uard.*[1] The men who have not *o*[*beyed*] Maya, they shall . . . [. . .]—all of ⟨*th*⟩*em.*

NOTE

1. Here and in the following lines interpretation is very dubious.

EA 218

Preparations and obedience

TEXT: VAT 1696.
COPY: *VS* 11, 125.

[*Say* t]o [the king, my lord: Message of . . .], the rul[er of . . . *I f*]*all* [*at the feet of my lord,* 7 *times*] *and* [7 *times.* **7–12** I] have he[ard a]ll the wo[rds] of the king, m[y] lord, [and n]ow *I* [*am preparing*][1] what the king, my [lo]rd, [. . .] **12–17** A[nd] I obey the wor[ds] of Maya [ve]ry caref[ully]. May the king, my lord, send troops to his countries.

NOTE

1. *e*-[šu-ši-ru]: cf. *i-šu-ši-ru* in *EA* 216:10; 226:15; 316:23.

EA 219

Message lost

TEXT: VAT 1720.
COPY: *VS* 11, 126.

Too fragmentary for translation.[1]

NOTE

1. Letter to the king; on the reverse, probably reference to gifts or tribute (25 30 GAL.[MEŠ . . .] KÙ.G[I], "30 goblet[s . . .], of gol[d]").

EA 220

Awaiting the commissioner

TEXT: C 4785 (12226).
COPY: WA 150.

Say to the king, my lord, (*my Sun*] Message of *Kurtuya,* the ruler of . . . nu, your servant, the dirt at the feet of the king, my lord, my Sun, and the mire you tread on. I fall at the feet of the king, m[y] lord, my Sun, 7 times and 7 times. 9–14 I have heard all the words of the king, my lord, my Sun. Who am I that I should not obey the commissioner of the king, my lord, my [Su]n, in accordance with the command of the [kin]g, my lord? 15–24 I am [in]deed guarding the [ci]ty of the king, my lord, my S[un], until the arrival of the commissioner of the king, my lord, my Sun. May the king, my lord, know that the city of the king, my lord, my Sun, where I am, was raided and my father struck down. 25–31 I am indeed guarding the city of the king, my lord, my Sun, where I am, until the arrival of the commissioner of the king, my lord, my Sun, to learn ab[out the la]nds of the king, my lord, [my Sun].[1]

NOTE

1. There is an Egyptian notation of some sort, in black ink, on line 2; similarly, *EA* 221, 225, 262, 294, 326.

EA 221

Message received

TEXT: VAT 341.
COPIES: WA 136; *VA* 11, 127.

Say to the king, [m]y lord, the Sun from the sky: Message of Wiktasu, your servant. I prostrate myself at the feet of the king, my lord, 7 times and 7 times. 8–10 I have heard the message of the king, my lord, to me. 11–16 I am indeed guarding the city of the king, my lord, until the word of the king, my lord, arrives (again).[1]

NOTE

1. Egyptian notation at the end of the tablet; see *EA* 220.

EA 222

Giving all

TEXT: VAT 1683.
COPY: *VS* 11, 128.

Say to the k[i]ng, [my lord]: Message of Wik[tasu, your servant]. I prostrate myself at the feet of the king, my lord, 7 times and 7 times.

6–11 A[s] to the king, my lord's, having written me, I *he[rewith]*[1] give to the king, [my] lor[d], whatever [I] have on ha[nd].

NOTE

1. *a*-[nu-ma].

EA 223

Compliance with orders

TEXT: VAT 1870.
COPIES: WA 220; *VS* 11, 129.

Say to the k[in]g, my lord, the Sun fr[om] the s[k]y: Message of En[d]a[r]u[t]a,[1] your servant. I prostrate myself at the feet of the king, my lord, 7 times and 7 times. 7–10 Whatsoever the king, my lord, orders, I shall prepare.[2]

NOTES

1. m*en-*[*d*]*a*[*r*]-*ú*-[*t*]*a*: following Thureau-Dangin, *RA* 19 (1922) p. 100, n. 1; see *EA* 367.
2. Or "I prepare."

EA 224

From ancestral days

TEXT: BM 29849.
COPY: BB 66.
PHOTOGRAPH: BB, pl. 15.

Say to the k[in]g, [my lo]r[d], my [*Sun*]: Message of Šum-Add[a], the serva[nt o]f the king, my lord. I fall at the feet of the king, my lord, 7 times and 7 times. 7–13 As to the king, my lord's, having written for grain . . . ,[1] it has been destroyed. May the king, my lord, ask his commissioners whether our ancestors, since the days of Kusuna, our ancestor, always shipped (grain).

NOTE

1. Na'aman, *Political Disposition,* p. 78*, n. 78, proposes ⟨*du*⟩-*uḫ-ni,* "millet." In the next line, despite the *Glossenkeil, mu-ḫu-ṣu* is probably not a gloss.

EA 225

Perfect obedience

TEXT: C 4787 (12222).
COPY: WA 131.

Say to the king, my lord: Message of Šamu-Adda, the ruler of Šamḫuna. I fall at the feet of my king 7 times and 7 times. 7–13 I obey all the orders of my king, and I obey all the orders of the commissioner whom my king appoints over me.[1]

NOTE

1. Egyptian notation follows (see *EA* 220).

EA 226

Cultivating and plucking

TEXT: VAT 1610.
COPIES: WA 157; *VS* 11, 130.

S[a]y t[o] the king, [my] lord: Messa[ge] of Šipṭu-riṣ[*a,* your servant], and the dirt a[t] your [feet]. I fall at the feet of the king 7 times and 7 times. 6–14 May the king, my lord, know that hi[s] city is safe and sound, and all the orders the king, my lord, has sent to his servant, I am obeying. I am indeed cultivating : *aḫ-ri-*[*šu*] and pluckin[g,[1] *and so* I] must keep going out[2] [of] my city. I am, however, preparin[g the . . .], and food and [strong drin]k[3] before the arrival of the expeditions[4] of the [k]ing, my lord, [*be*]*cause* I obey all the orders of the king, my lord.

NOTES

1. Cf. *EA* 244:8ff.
2. ù] 13 [ú]-*aṣ-ṣú-m*[*i*]: this permits a normalization *uṣṣu* conforming to established usage.
3. Cf. *EA* 55:12.
4. Perhaps "expedition."

EA 227

The happy king of Hazor

TEXT: BM 29830.
COPY: BB 47.

Say to the king, my lord: Message of the king of Ḫaṣuru. I fall at the feet of my lord. 5–13 Look, I have the cities of the king, my lord, under guard until my lord reaches [*me*].[1] And when I heard these words of yours and of the *coming forth of* the Sun *to m*[*e*],[2] *I rejoiced accordingly.*[3] I *pond*[*ered*][4] (*the news*), and my jubilation came forth.[5] *There was peace,*[6] and the gods themselves *looked* (*favorably*) on me.[7] 13–17 And I have indeed prepared everything until the arrival of the king, [my] lord. Look, whenever [*Ḫan*]*i,* your messenger, arrives,[8] the heart [*rejoic*]*es* exceedingly. 18–19 [*In*] my [*heart*] my joy [*is great*].[9] *When* ... [...] 20–28 ... [...].

NOTES

1. *an* [ia-ši]: cf. lines 9, 13; *an* for *ana,* probably an archaic survival. On lines 5–18, see Na'aman, *Lingering over Words,* p. 403.

2. *a-ṣí-ti* ^{d}UTU *an-ia-*š[i]: following Rainey, *UF* 7 (1975) p. 422, n. 35. If the writer's joy comes, not from the news of the king's journey, but simply from having heard from the king, another possibility is *a-ṣé* TI (*balāṭ*) ..., "the coming forth of the life of ..."; cf. the message (breath) of the king as life-giving, *EA* 100, n. 9.

3. *ki-ia*$_{8}$*-ša-ma*: if right, another archaism; cf. *kīašu, CAD,* K, p. 309, and *kīam* (4), *AHw,* p. 470b. The alternative, *ki yú-ša-ma,* "when it (the message?) was heard," introduces a repetition that is hard to explain.

4. *aḫ-di am-tal-*[li-ik/lik]: *aḫ-di,* with Rainey, ibid., who postulates another archaism, uncontracted *aḫdiam,* and restores *ri-*[iš-te] (cf. line 19).

5. *AHw,* p. 1563, *ellatīya,* "my band."

6. *ša-li-*mu: indefinite third plural?

7. *ip-pal-šu* (for *ippalsū*) *an ia-ši*: following Na'aman, *Political Disposition,* pp. 55f.

8. The durative *yikšudu* argues for a general statement and against "when Ḫani arrived," though it is very likely that Ḫani was in fact the bearer of the message to which *EA* 227 is the answer. See also *EA* 200, n. 3.

9. Free restorations.

EA 228

An invitation to recall the past

TEXT: BM 29831.
COPY: BB 48.
PHOTOGRAPH: BB, pl. 16.

Say [t]o the king, my lord: Message of ʿAbdi-Tirši,[1] the ruler of Ḫaṣuru, your servant. I fall at the feet of the king, my lord, 7 times and 7 times ⟨⟨at the feet of the king, my lord⟩⟩. 10–17 As I am the loyal servant of the king, my lord, I am indeed[2] guarding Ḫaṣuru together with its villages for the king, my lord. 18–25 May the king, my lord, recall : *ia-az-ku-ur-mi* whatever has been done against Ḫaṣuru, your city, and against your servant.

NOTES

1. M. Weippert, *ZDPV* 82 (1966) p. 322, proposed ÌR-*dir*$_4$-*ši*, ʿAbd(i)-Irši, and is followed by Na'aman, *UF* 20 (1988) p. 188, n. 38.

2. *a-nu-um-ma-mi*: following Gordon.

EA 229

Message lost

TEXT: VAT 1689.
COPIES: WA 178; *VS* 11, 131.

Say to the king, my lord, [my Sun]: Message of ʿAbdina, [*the ruler of* ...],[1] your servant, the [loyal] servant of the [king], my lord, the dirt [at the feet of the k]ing, [my] lord, [my Sun. I fall at the fe]et [of the king, my lord, ...].

NOTE

1. Both the reading of the personal name and the assumption of room sufficient for LÚ URU are uncertain.

EA 230

An unusual message

TEXT: BM 37646.
COPY: Scheil, *Mémoires,* p. 309.
TRANSLATION: Na'aman, *Lingering over Words,* p. 401.

Say to the king, my lord: Message of Yama,[1] your servant. I fall at your feet. 4–10 As I am your servant in the place where I am, the places where I am are all cities belonging to you. As your ⟨*lo*⟩*yal* servant,[2] I have indeed guarded your *commissioners.*[3] 11–16 If a soldier of yours comes to me, then I guard [h]im. And the cities where I am are all really guarded for you. 17–22 Just ask your *commissioners* whether they are really guarded.[4] May you know tha⟨t⟩ all your cities are safe and sound.

NOTES

1. Na'aman, *Lingering over Words,* p. 401, proposes that Yama is a mistake for Maya, the name of a well-known Egyptian commissioner (*rābiṣu*). This reading would explain the claim to offer protection to *ḫazannūtu,* a term that only very exceptionally does not refer to the local rulers, the "mayors." If Maya is the writer, *EA* 230 is the only communication of an Egyptian official written in cuneiform.

2. ÌR ⟨ki⟩-*te-ka*: cf. *VAB* 2/2, p. 1601. Na'aman, ibid., reads ÌR-di_{12}-*ka*.

3. If this letter is written by a vassal, then *ḫazannu,* as in *EA* 237 and 317, must refer to Egyptian officials, for a mayor's duty was to protect, not other mayors, but Egyptians.

4. *na-àṣ-ru*: see Otten, *MIO* 1 (1953) p. 137, n. 30. For *lū,* "really," cf. *EA* 255:25, *mādiš naṣrat,* "it is much guarded."

EA 231

Following orders

TEXT: VAT 1599.
COPIES: WA 212; *VS* 11, 132.

[Say to the king, my lord, *the Sun from the sky:* Message of . . . , the ruler of . . . , the ser]vant o[f the king, the dirt] at [his] fee[t, the ground on which] h[e] treads. [I fall at the feet] of the king, my lord, [the Sun from] the sky, 7 [times and 7 times]. 11–19 In accordance with what the king, my lord, [the Sun f]rom the sk[y], *w[rote,* "G]ua[rd] the city o[f the ki]ng where you [are]," I have [g]uarde[d] the cit[y in ac]cordance with what the king, [my] lord, [my god], my Sun, *w*[*rote*].

EA 232

Who would not obey?

TEXT: VAT 1640.
COPIES: WA 93; *VS* 11, 133.

Say to the king, my lord, the Sun from the sky: Thus Surata, the ruler of Akka, the servant of the king, the dirt at his feet and the ground on which he treads. I prostrate myself at the feet of the king, my lord, the Sun from the sky, 7 times and 7 times, on the chest : *ba-aṭ-nu-ma* (belly)[1] and on the back : *ṣú-uḫ-ru-ma.* 12–20 Who is the ruler,[2] should the king, his lord, write to hi[m], that would not ob[e]y? In accordance with what has issued from the mouth of the Sun from the sky, so is it done.

NOTES

1. On the gloss, see Rainey, *UF* 3 (1971) p. 170.
2. Or simply "the man."

EA 233

Work in progress

TEXT: C 4767 (12201).
COPY: WA 94.

Say to the king, [m]y [lord], the Sun from [the sky]: Message of Satatna, the ruler of Akka, your servant, the servant of the king and the dirt at his feet and the ground on which he treads. I prostrate myself at the feet of the king, my lord, my god, the Sun from the sky, 7 times and 7 times, both on the stomach and on the back. 16–20 He is obeying what the king, my lord, has written to his servant, and preparing everything that my lord *has order*[*ed*].[1]

NOTE

1. *yi-q*[*a*-bi]: if Knudtzon's restoration of *-bu* is correct, then lines 16–20 state a general truth: "he obeys . . . and prepares everything that my lord ord[ers]."

On line 2, Egyptian hieratic notation, in black ink, *wr*, "prince"; see Introduction, n. 73.

EA 234

Like Magdalu in Egypt

TEXT: VAT 1641.
COPIES: WA 95; *VS* 11, 134.
TRANSLATION: Albright, *ANET*, pp. 484f.

To the king, m[y] lord, the Sun from the sky: Message of Satatna, the ruler of Akka, your servant, the servant of the king, and the dirt at his feet, the ground on which he treads. [I] prostrate myself at the feet of the king, my lord, the Sun from the sky, 7 times and 7 times, both on the stomach and on the back.

10–35 May the king, my lord, heed the word of his servant. [Zir]damyašda des[er]ted [B]iryawaza. He w[as] with Šuta, a . . . [. . .] of the king, in *the gar*[*rison*] city.[1] He said [n]ot[hi]ng [t]o him. Out came[2] the troops of the king, my lord. He[3] w[as] with them in Magidd[a]. Nothing was said to hi[m].[4] Then he deserted to me, and

Šuta has just written to me, "Hand over Zirdamyašda to Biryawaza." But I have not agreed to hand him over. Akka is like Magdalu in Egypt,[5] and has the king, [*my lord*], not [h]eard *that Šuta* is *turned* against me? May the king, my lord, [sen]d his [com]missioner to fet[ch] him.

NOTES

1. URU ⌜UN⌝-[ti/šu?]: on UN = *maṣṣartu,* see *EA* 116, n. 1; *āl maṣṣarti* occurs in *EA* 76:36 (Ṣumer) and 190:5 (Kumidu?). The text does not say that the Zirdamyašda's desertion occurred in this place (so Pintore, *OA* 11 [1972] p. 307).

2. *aṣû,* "to go/come forth," as said of troops, always refers in *EA* to leaving Egypt; the text does not say that the troops have departed (so Albright).

3. Perhaps the subject is plural ("they"), referring to Šuta too. Zirdamyašda and Šuta might have joined the Egyptian forces in Gaza and marched with them as far as Megiddo.

4. Since *lā* is consistently written *la-a* (lines 16, 26, 30), we should read, with Knudtzon, *la-a qa-bi,* not *la a-qa-bi,* "I said nothing" (so Albright); note also the nominative *mi-mu.*

5. The point of the comparison is not clear: whether the thorough Egyptianization of Akka (Albright), or its loyalty (Na'aman, *Political Disposition,* p. 21*, n. 84). The reading and interpretation of what follows is also quite uncertain. In line 34, read [*yú-ši*]-*ra* (cf. *EA* 270:24), since *uššira* (Knudtzon) is always imperative.

At the end of line 10, Egyptian hieratic notation, in black ink; see *EA* 258.

EA 235 (+) 327

An order for glass

TEXT: BM 29815 (+) C 4791 + VAT 1882 (with join = C 12235).
COPIES: BB 32 (+) WA 206 (without join).[1]
PHOTOGRAPH: BB, pl. 6.

Say to the king, my lord, my Sun, my god, the Sun from the sky: Message of Sitatna, your servant, the dirt at your feet. ⟨I pr⟩ostrate myself at the feet of the king, my lord, my Sun, my god, 7 times and 7 times, ⟨⟨at the feet of the king, my lord⟩⟩. 11–21 (*EA* 327:1–11) [I] have obeyed the [or]ders of the king's comm[issioner] to me, to guard[2] the citie[s f]or the king, my lord. I have guarded very carefully. M[oreover], the king, my lord has wri[tten] to me for *glass,*[3] [and] I herewith send 50 (units),[4] [*their*] weight, to the king, my lord.

NOTES

1. The long-distance join, made without comment, is Gordon's. Apart from other considerations, Knudtzon's assumption in *EA* 235:11 of a[m-qut . . .] was in itself very improbable; *šuḫēnu* and *maqātu* in the same letter would be without parallel, and any repetition of the proskynesis is confined to the scribe who wrote *EA* 63 (probably omitted by mistake in 64–65) and 284, and to 184. A mistaken repetition of "at the feet . . ." in line 10, as in *EA* 228, is in itself most plausible.

2. *na-ṣár*; similarly, *ú-na-ṣár* (line 15 = 327:5); see *EA* 137, n. 15.

3. ^{na_4}⌜eḫ⌝*-tu-Ba-ak-ku*: almost certainly an error for *eḫlipakku* (*AHw*, p. 191); cf. *EA* 314, 323.

4. The unit of measure is not clear. "50 (pieces), (total) weighed out"? Cf. *EA* 326:16.

EA 236

Message lost

TEXT: Ash 1893 1–41: 423.
COPY: Sayce, *Tell el Amarna*, no. 16.

Too fragmentary for translation.[1]

NOTE

1. Perhaps a reference to the ruler of Akka as an enemy.

EA 237

Under fire

TEXT: VAT 1701.
COPY: *VS* 11, 135.

[. . .] . . . They have [ca]ptured La*b*['*ayu*] and attacked the citi[es] of the king, my lord. They have captured, too, the cities of the king, my lord, that the king, my lord, [*pu*]*t* in [my] charge to guard. **8–18** May the king, my lord, be informed that they have [ca]ptured the [ci]ties o[f] the king, m[y] lord, [but] the city in which I am I now keep under guard until I see the eyes of the commissioner[1] of the king, my lord. **18–24** Indeed, from the day I send this tablet to the palace, they will be attack[ing *me*], and . . . [. . .].

NOTE

1. Cf. *EA* 230:9.
EA 237 is probably from the writer of *EA* 238; see *VAB* 2/2, p. 1304.

EA 238

Absolute power

TEXT: VAT 1867.
COPIES: WA 219; *VS* 11, 136.

[To] the magnate, [my] lord: [Messa]ge of Bayadi, [your] servant. I fall [a]t the feet of the magnate, my lord. 4–14 As to the cities that the magnate, my lord, put in my charge, they have seized all the cities, and the city in which I am I cannot guard. So may the magnate, my lord, s[en]d me a 50-man garris[on] to guar[d the city] until the arr[ival] of the magnate, [my lord]. 15–21 And [. . .] 22–23 *again*[*st* . . .] and the son of *S*[*a*]*t*[*atna*][1] and Ḫagurr[u . . .] and they have captured [. . .] and attacked [*me*]. They have captured the cities of the magnate, my lord, so may the magnate, my lord, be informed. It is you who can keep us alive, and it is you who can put us to death.[2]

NOTES

1. For chronological difficulties with this reading, see Campbell, *Chronology,* p. 108.

2. An expression of apparently absolute power, which one would have expected to be ascribed only to the king; cf. Lorton, *The Juridical Terminology of International Relations in Egyptian Texts through Dynasty XVIII* (see Introduction, n. 73), p. 73, n. 25. Perhaps the fact that plural "you" is addressed implies the king as well as the magnate.

EA 239

Evil talk

TEXT: VAT 334.
COPIES: WA 139; *VS* 11, 137.

Sa[y to] the king, my [l]ord: Message of Baduza*n*[*a*], your [ser]vant. I fall at the feet of the king, my lord, 7 times and 7 times. 8–17 I will execute[1] every order of the king, my lord, until the magnate comes forth and fetches everything the king, my lord, has ordered. 18–27 As we are the servants of the king, may the magnate come forth and know our crime, [f]or in yo[ur] presence he has been speak[ing] evil of your servants.[2]

NOTES

1. *i-pá-aš-ši*: *ippaš* + *-ši* (pronominal suffix) rather than overhanging vowel; cf. *i-pa-aš* (*EA* 196:32, 41), *e-pa-aš* (*EA* 289:9).

2. The form *y*]*i-iq*-[*bu*] is singular; see Izre'el, *UF* 19 (1987) pp. 84f. If *y*]*i-iq*-[*bi*], then "has spoken."

EA 240

Message lost

TEXT: VAT 2198 + 2707.
COPY: *VS* 11, 240.

Too fragmentary for translation.[1]

NOTE

1. A promise of service to troops and chariotry.

EA 241

A servant from ancient times

TEXT: VAT 1678.
COPIES: WA 148; *VS* 11, 139.

Say to the king, my lord, my god, the Sun: Message of Rusmanya, the ruler of Šaruna, your servant, the dirt at your feet, the mire on which you tread, the footstool of the feet of my lord. ⟨I fall at the feet of the king, my lord⟩, 7 times and 7 times. 9–11 As I am a servant of the king from time immemorial, it is the king, my lord, I serve. 12–16 And here and now the king, my lord, [. . .], the king, my lord. 17–20 Another he *smo*[*te*][1] throu[gh] my se[rvic]es, for I am a loyal servant of the king, my lord.

NOTE

1. ⸢*da*⸣-k[i : perhaps infinitive + *i* (*JCS* 4 [1950] pp. 169ff.), and perhaps to be rendered as passive, "another was smitten," on the assumption of no distinction of voice in the infinitive.

EA 242

Request granted

TEXT: VAT 1670.
COPIES: WA 114; *VS* 11, 140.

Say to the king, my lord and my Sun: Message of Biridiya,[1] the ruler of Magidda, the loyal servant of the king. I prostrate myself at the feet of the king, my lord and my Sun, 7 times and 7 times. **9–17** I herewith give what the king, my lord, requested:[2] 30 oxen, [x *sheep and goats*, x *bi*]*rds*[3] [. . .] . . . [. . . *And in*]*deed,* [the . . .] . . . of *the* [*l*]*and*[4] are at peace, but I am at war.

NOTES

1. On the Biridiya in a Kamid el-Loz letter and his relationship to the ruler of Megiddo, see M. Görg, *ZA* 76 (1986) p. 308.

2. ŠU.KAM.MI (*erišti*) *šarri* [*bēlī*]*ya*: see *JCS* 31 (1979) pp. 247f.; *NABU*, 1988, no. 36.

3. 30 GUD.MEŠ 12 [x ÙZ.MEŠ x iṣ-ṣu]-*ra-te*: cf. GUD.MEŠ ÙZ.MEŠ *ù* MUŠEN.MEŠ (*EA* 161:21); after *nadnāku*, "I give," a restoration [. . . šu-ši]-*ra-te*, "I prepare" (cf. *EA* 193:21; 227:13), is not likely.

4. [K]UR.KI: following Na'aman, *Political Disposition*, p. 15*, n. 35, who also reads at the beginning of the line [a-n]a [E]N.

EA 243

Around-the-clock defense

TEXT: VAT 1669.
COPIES: WA 113; *VS* 11, 141.

[Say] to the king, [my l]ord and my Sun and [my] go[d]: Message of Biridi[ya], the loyal servant of the king. I f[a]ll at the feet of the king, [my] lord and my Sun and my god, 7 times and 7 times.

8–22 I have obeyed the orders of the king, my lord and my Sun, and I am indeed guard[ing] Magidda, the city of the king, my lord, day and night : *l*[*e-l*]*a*.[1] By day I guard (it) [f]rom the fields with chariots, and by n[ight][2] *on* the wall[s[3] of] the king, my lord. And as the warring of the ʿA[pi]ru in the land is seve[re], may the king, my lord, take cognizance of his land.

NOTES

1. GI_6-*ša* (*mūša*): there is no reason to postulate **mīšu*. The reading of the gloss follows Rainey, *UF* 7 (1975) p. 405.

2. l[e-l]a: following Rainey, ibid.

3. BÀD.M[EŠ (*ša*)]: the reading is certain; the MEŠ, perhaps otiose. I assume accusative of place, but ⟨*ištu*⟩ *dūrānī* is another possibility. Another reading that has Biridiya guarding the walls seems unlikely.

EA 244

Besieged by Lab'ayu

TEXT: C 4768 (12200).
COPY: WA 244.
TRANSLATIONS: Albright, *ANET,* p. 485; Campbell, *Shechem,* p. 193; H. Freydank in A. Jepsen, ed., *Von Sinuhe bis Nebukadnezar: Dokumente aus der Umwelt des Alten Testaments* (Stuttgart and Munich, 1975), p. 101; Seux, *Textes du Proche-Orient,* pp. 51f.

Say to the king, my lord and my Sun: Message of Biridiya, the loyal servant of the king. I fall at the feet of the king, my lord and my Sun, 7 times and 7 times. 8–17 May the king, my lord, know that since the return (to Egypt) of the archers, Lab'ayu has waged war against me. We are thus unable to do the plucking : *Ka-Zi-ra* (*harvesting*),[1] and we are unable to go out of the city gate : *ša-aḫ-ri* because of Lab'ayu. 18–24 When he learned that archers were not co[ming o]ut,[2] he immediately [de]termined[3] to take Magidda. 25–33 May the king save his city lest Lab'ayu seize it. Look,[4] the city is consumed by pestilence, by . . .[5] So may the king give a garrison of 100 men to guard his city lest Lab'ayu seize it. Look, Lab'ayu has no other purpose. He seeks simply the seizure[6] of Magidda.

NOTES

1. The gloss is difficult. That what precedes is to be read ZÚ.SI.GA *ba-qa-ni,* "plucking," must be considered certain; see Meissner, *AfO* 5 (1928–29) p. 184; Kraus, *Staatliche Viehhaltung im altbabylonischen Larsa* (Amsterdam, 1966, p. 13); Finkelstein, *RA* 63 (1969) pp. 61ff. On the left of the gloss marker, there is nothing about harvesting fields (so Campbell). Middle Babylonian *baqānu* replaces Old Babylonian *baqāmu*; the apparent genitive *baqāni* rather than the expected accusative *baqāna* remains unexplained. The gloss may not be read *ga*$_{14}$*-zi-ra* (Hebrew *gāzar,* "to cut off, divide"), which, difficulties of form aside (Piel infinitive *gazzira*?), would imply cutting up the sheep, not plucking or shearing them. Therefore, *qà-ṣí-ra,* "harvest(ing)," seems much more likely (cf. Hebrew *qāṣîr*), but not as a gloss to what precedes; rather, as another activity, the gloss marker simply indicating a non-Akkadian word. Interference in the basis of agrarian life, flocks and fields, seems to belong to the topos "under siege" (cf. *EA* 226:10ff.).

2. *ti-it-*[*ta-ṣ*]*ú-na*: following Gordon; this reading fits with the nominative *piṭātu* in the following line.

3. [š]u-*ut-ri-iṣ*: only one vertical visible. Rainey, private communication, 18 January 1981, after collation, reads [*t*]*a-ri-iṣ*.

4. On *šumma* (also line 38), see *EA* 35, n. 3.

5. The reading *u*[*p*]-*ri* has yielded no satisfactory sense. Dhorme, *RB* 33 (1924) p. 16, n. 3, also published in *Recueil Édouard Dhorme* (Paris, 1951), p. 501, n. 4, proposed "the dust (of Sheol)," but one does not die *from* the dust of the netherworld; see also *JCS* 7 (1953) p. 79, n. 8. It should be noted that neither sign is clear (so also Gordon). Albright and Campbell (see headnote) propose "*disease,*" apparently from context. Perhaps *dáb-ri* (Hebrew *deber*), a virtual gloss and synonym of Akkadian *mūtānū*, which is here treated as singular.

6. ⌜ṣa⌝-*ba-at-me*: more likely than *abātme*, "destruction" (Gordon); note *ṣabātu* in lines 18 and 37. The inverted word order, object-verb, stresses the former.

EA 245

Assignment of guilt

TEXT: BM 29855.
COPY: BB 72.
PHOTOGRAPHS: BB, pl. 3; Barnett, *Illustrations*, p. 16 (obverse).
TRANSLATIONS: Albright, *ANET*, p. 485; Campbell, *Shechem*, pp. 198f.

Moreover,[1] I urged my brothers, "If the god of the king, our lord, brings it about[2] that we overcome Lab'ayu, then we must bring him alive : *ḫa-ia-ma* to the king, our lord." 8–14 My mare, however, *having been put out of action* : *tu-ra* (*having been shot*), *I took my place behind him* : *aḫ-ru-un-ú* and rode with Yašdata.[3] But before my arrival they had struck him down : *ma-aḫ-ṣú-ú*. 15–23 Yašdata being truly your servant, he it was that entered with me into batt[le]. May . . . [. . .] the *life*[4] of the king, my [lord], that *he may br*[*ing peace to ever*]*yone*[5] in [*the lands of*] the king, [my] lord. 24–35 It had been Surata that took Lab'ayu from Magidda and said to me, "I will send him to the king by boat : *a-na-yi*."[6] Surata took him, but he sent him from Ḫinnatunu to his home, for it was Surata that had accepted from him : *ba-di-ú* his ransom. 36–47 Moreover, what have I done to the king, my lord, that he has treated me with contempt : *ia*$_8$-*qí-ìl-li-ni* and honored : *ia*$_8$-*ka-bi-id* my *less important* brothers?[7] It was Surata that let Lab'ayu go, and it was Surata that let Baʿl-meḫir go, (both) to their homes. And may the king, my lord, know.

NOTES

1. A two-tablet letter; see *EA* 101, n. 1.

2. On the singular referent of DINGIR.MEŠ and on *yi-pu-šu* as singular, see Izre'el, *UF* 19 (1987) pp. 82f.

3. On lines 8ff., see Campbell.

4. TIL.LA-*aṭ*: perhaps *balāṭ* refers to provisions rather than to a message from the king; *til-la-at*, "auxiliaries," should not be ruled out.

5. *li-pa*-a[š-ši-iḫ]: but only the base and causative conjugations are attested in *EA*: -a[l-li-iṭ] is excluded.

6. Finley, *Word Order in the Clause Structure of Syrian Akkadian* (see Introduction, n. 8), pp. 67f., shows that in lines 24–45, where the word order is subject-verb-object, Surata as the guilty one is stressed.

On the gloss, cf. Emar(?) dialect *anu*, "gear, equipment," in apin-á-kár = *ú-nu-tu* = *a-nu* (*Emar* 6/4, no. 545: 136′).

7. Biridiya's "brothers" were probably his confederates joined with him against Lab'ayu (cf. lines 1ff.), and therefore, "small" (*ṣeḫrūta*) would seem better understood in terms of rank rather than age ("younger").

EA 246

The sons of Lab'ayu

TEXT: VAT 1649.
COPIES: WA 111; *VS* 11, 142.

Say to the king, my lord and my Sun: Message of Biridiya, your loyal servant. I fall at the feet of the king, m[y] lord and my Sun, 7 times and 7 times.

8–9 I have heard the mes[sage] o[f] the ki[ng . . .] . . .

Rev. 1–11 and [. . .], and indee[d . . .] you ar[e . . .].[1] May the king, my lord, know. The two sons of Lab'ayu have indeed gi[v]en[2] their money to the ʿApiru and to the *Su*[*teans*[3] *in ord*]*er to w*[*age war again*]*st* me.[4] [*May*] the king [*take cognizance*] *of* [*his servant*].

NOTES

1. *i-ba-aš-ša-tu*-[nu . . .]: following Rainey, *UF* 5 (1973) p. 250.

2. *te-ed*-[di]n-*na*: the copy of *VS* 11 is exact.

3. LÚ.MEŠ KUR s[u-ti]: following Na'aman, *Political Disposition*, p. 40; cf. *EA* 195:27ff.; 318:11ff. For the writing, cf. *EA* 122:34; 123:14; 297:16.

4. [a-n]a *i-pé*-e[š nu-kur-te] 10 [UG]U-*ia*: cf. Greenberg, *Ḫab/piru*, p. 45.

EA 247

Who am I?

TEXT: C 4792 (12236).
COPY: WA 207.

[. . .][1] 7 times [I fall]. 8–13 As to the *me*[*ssage that* the king], my lord, sen[t] *t*[*o me*], I have obeyed very [carefully the orders] of the king, my lord. 14–21 Wh[o am] I, a [*mere*] do[g],[2] that I would not [*grant*[3] *a re*]*ques*[*t* of the king], my lord? I am in[deed] prepar[ing *for*] the king, [my lord, *what*[4] *he or*]*dered.* [. . .].

NOTES

1. The script and the clay make the provenience of this fragment clear; it was Megiddo. The character of the message favors Biridiya, the ruler, rather than Yašdata, the exile (cf. *EA* 248).

2. On *kalbu ištēn,* if the correct reading, see *EA* 201, n. 2.

3. If *erištu* occurs in the next line, then a form of *nadānu,* "to grant," not *šemû,* "to heed," seems required, for in common parlance one did not heed requests; one either granted or refused. See *JCS* 31 (1979) pp. 247f. The form should be indicative (*addinu, anaddinu*); cf. the indicative forms of *šemû* in *EA* 201–2, 319–20, 322.

4. Or *ki-ma*] 21 [*q*]*a-b*[*é* LUGAL-*ri*]: cf. *EA* 144:21; 155:12, 39; 216:11; 220:13; 323:11.

EA 248

An exiled ruler

TEXT: BM 29842.
COPY: BB 59.

Say [to] the king, my lord, Sun and god: Message of Ya[šd]ata, the loyal servant of the king and the dirt at the feet of the king. I fall at the feet of the king, my lord, Sun and god, 7 times and 7 times.

9–22 May the king, my lord, know that everything the king, my [l]ord, gave to [his] servant, the men of *Taḫn*[*ak*]*a*[1] [*have m*]*ade off with*;[2] they have slaughtered[3] my oxen and driven me away. So I am now with Biridiya. May the king, my lord, take cognizance of his servant.

NOTES

1. URU *ta-aḫ*-n[a-k]a: there seem to be traces of the beginning of one horizontal, and above these the traces of a slightly indented, slightly oblique wedge. In the letters of Biridiya and Yašdata, NA is written with rather sharply

oblique wedges, but the absence of this feature here could be due to the position of the sign on the upper corner of the reverse.

2. [*na*]*m-šu-mi*: here transitive, with *AHw*, p. 726; otherwise, *CAD*, N/1, p. 220.

3. *na-ak-šu* = *naksū*: *AHw*, p. 721; *CAD*, N/1, p. 177b.

EA 249

A desperate vassal

TEXT: VAT 1603.

COPIES: WA 149; *VS* 11, 143.

[Sa]y [to] the king, [my] lo[rd]: Message of Baᶜ[lu-UR.SAG], your servant. I fall at the feet of m[y] lord. 4–10 *As to* the king, my lord, may he know that *my m*[*en*] *are doing service in the day*(*s*) *of Mi*[lkilu].[1] What have I done to Milkilu that he should treat my men (even) *more* unjustly than his own servants? (To Tagi, his father-in-law, he has handed over his own servants!)[2] 10–17 And what can I myself do? *They have been struck down because*[3] I am a [*lo*]*yal* servant of the king. And so they can*not* [*ser*]*ve you.* [*May*] the king [*rel*]*ease* me![4] *Where* [. . .] . . . Milkilu and Lab'ayu? 17–30 [. . .] . . .

NOTES

1. L[Ú.MEŠ-*i*]*a* UD (ūm) ᵐ*mi-i*[*l-ki-li*]: first restoration with Albright, *CAH* 2/2, p. 106, and Na'aman, *Political Disposition*, p. 62, whom, however, I do not follow in the assumption of ⟨*a*⟩ by haplography and of UD by mistake for *na*, so that the men are going over *to* (*ana*) Milkilu. My own solution, perhaps hardly less desperate, is *alāku*, "to serve, do service"; see *CAD*, A/1, pp. 309f., and note its use in the periphery.

2. For a somewhat different version of the difficult lines 8–10, see Albright and Na'aman, ibid. (note 1).

3. maḫ-ṣú: the difference from Knudtzon's meaningless maḫ-ba is minimal and easily concealed in a damaged sign; UGU (*eli? muḫḫi?*), "because," as in *EA* 250:17.

4. [yi-i]p-*ṭú-ra-ni*: the petition, a measure of the vassal's desperate situation, is to be released from obligations of service and dismissed (cf. *EA* 126:47). Another proposal is Na'aman's in *Political Disposition*, p. 61: [ù i]š-*ṭú-ra-ni* . . . , "And the king wrote to me, 'What have Milkilu and Lab'ayu done?' ([*yi-pu-u*]*š-mi*)." Although this accounts for more of the text, it postulates too many features that are exceptional (*šaṭāru*; indirect personal object expressed by the accusative verbal suffix; singular verb with plural subject) or unparalleled (*ayyû-ma*, interrogative pronoun).

EA 250

A calling to account

TEXT: C 4769 (12204).
COPY: WA 154.
TRANSLATIONS: Albright, *ANET,* pp. 485f.; Campbell, *Shechem,* pp. 202ff.

Say [t]o the king, my lord: Message of Baʿlu-UR.SAG, your servant. I fall at the feet of the king, my lord, 7 times and 7 times. 4–8 May the king, my lord, know [t]hat the two sons of the rebel against the kin[g], my [l]ord, the two sons of Lab'a[y]u, have made their purpose the loss of the land of the kin[g], my lord, over and above the loss that the[ir] father caus[ed].[1] 9–14 May the king, my lord, know that—for how many days!—the two sons of Lab'ayu have been calling[2] me to account, (saying), "Why have you handed Gittipadalla [t]o the king, your lord, a city that Lab'ayu, our father, had taken?" 15–27 And the two sons of Lab'ayu keep talking to me like this, (saying), "Wage war against the people of [G]ina for having killed our father. And if you do not wage war, then we will be your enemies." I have answered the two of them, "May the god of the king, my lord, preserve me from waging war against the pe[op]le of [G]ina, servants of the king, my lord." May it seem rig[ht] in the sight of the king, my lord, and may he sen[d] one of his magnates to Biryawaza [to tel]l him, "You will ma[r]ch against the two sons of Lab'ayu or [yo]u are a rebel against the king." 28–30 After this may the king, my lord, wr[i]te t[o m]e, "*D[o]* the work of the [*kin*]*g,* your [*lo*]*rd,* against the two son[s of L]ab'ayu."[3]

31–36 [. . .] . . .[4] 37–39 . . . *in order to*[5] cause the loss, with the assistance of the two of them, of the *r*[*es*]*t*[6] of the lan[d] of the k[ing, m]y [l]ord, over and above what Milkilu and Lab'ayu caused to be lost. 40–47 And thus the two [s]on[s of L]a[b'a]yu keep saying to me, "Wage war against the king, your lord, as our father did, when he attacked Šunama, Bur[q]una, and Ḫarabu, and deported *the evil ones, li*[*fti*]*ng up the loyal.*[7] He also seized Gittirimmunima, and he *cultivated* the *fi*[*el*]*ds*[8] *of* the king, your lord." 48–54 But I have answered the two of them, "May the god of the king, my lord, preserve me from waging war against the king, my lord. It is the king, my lord, I serve, along with my brothers that give heed to me."[9] The messenger of Milkilu does not move from the two sons of Lab'ayu. 55–60 Now, Milkilu is indeed trying to cause the loss of the land of the king, my lord, but I have no other purpose: the king, my lord, I serve, and the orders that the king speaks I obey.

NOTES

1. *arki ša,* "over and above what": see *BASOR* 211 (1973) p. 51, n. 6. On *ḫulluqu,* see *EA* 99, n. 1.

2. *tu*-[*b*]*i-ḫu-na*: reading certain.

3. *i*-[pu-uš]-*mi ipši*: cf. *ipša ana muḫḫi epēšu, EA* 287:71f.

4. The reading of lines 31–36 is so difficult that it seems best to avoid even a very tentative version. The following may be noted: (1) the copy of WA omits line 31 and makes the first line of the reverse the last line of the obverse; (2) end of line 33 has *yi-e*[*n*]*-na-Bi-*⌜*il*⌝ (with copy; also Gordon); (3) any readings at the beginning of lines 34–35 must be considered extremely tentative; (4) line 35: ... *a Zi* x UZU.ZI.

5. The reading of the beginning of the line is extremely difficult, with not one sign certain. Gordon doubted *a-n*[*a*] and suggested that there was only one sign (*li*? *ta*?).

6. According to Gordon, not EGIR-*ki*-[*t*]*i,* but only EGIR-*ki,* the alleged -[*t*]*i* being in reality the *m*]*e* of the end of line 23. The meaning is deduced from context; perhaps, with Na'aman, *Political Disposition,* p. 60, "hinterland."

7. *yi-is-sú-uḫ lem-ni* : *ia*-a[n-š]u *ke-en-ni*: (1) *lemnī* (substantive, not adjective, and therefore not necessarily *lemnūti*) seems preferable to an unmotivated dual pronominal suffix (*-ši-ni*; so *BASOR* 211 [1973] p. 53); (2) the reading (-a[n-n]a is also possible, though perhaps less likely) and the interpretation of the apparent gloss are tentative in the extreme (*kennī,* for *kēnī,* like *lemnī*; *yanšu,* indicative, circumstantial clause, "lifting," i.e., "promoting, favoring"; gloss marker marking specifically non-Akkadian syntax). See also *EA* 180, n. 2.

8. *yú-pa-at-ti* : *ú*-[gàr]r-*ri*: the dubious sign is very probably ("definitely," according to Gordon) not GI or ZI; GÀR is likely. This reading guides the interpretation of *yupatti,* "he opened," i.e., loosened the earth and made the fields ready for further cultivation, as the verb was used in both Akkadian and Hebrew. If this is the correct reading, the context suggests that this action was seen as a sign of appropriation. Na'aman, in Heltzer and Lipiński, eds., *Society and Economy in the Eastern Mediterranean (c. 1500–1000 B.C.),* Orientalia Lovaniensia Analecta, 23 (Louvain, 1988), p. 185, sees here a reference to the crown lands in the Jezreel Valley. Gloss marker used to mark a quasi-logogram (Ú.GÀR-*ri*)?

9. Note that the word order—object-verb ("the king, my lord, I serve")—stresses the object of service (also lines 58–59); cf. too lines 59–60 ("the orders the king speaks I obey").

EA 251

A reckoning requested

TEXT: BM 29862.
COPY: BB 79.
PHOTOGRAPH: BB, pl. 6.

Let the king inquire of them if I have taken anything from a mayor.[1] Let him speak in the presence of the king, and let the king, my lord, demand of me a reckoning. 6–15 You have now in this way been negligent. Surely the king, my lord, is going to learn of this matter, and the king, my lord, will reply to me as he will, and the order of the king I will obey.

NOTE

1. Cf. *EA* 280:25ff. A two-tablet letter (cf. *EA* 101, n. 1), perhaps addressed to the king (so Gordon) rather than to an Egyptian official (so Knudtzon).

EA 252

Sparing one's enemies

TEXT: BM 29844.
COPY: BB 61.
PHOTOGRAPHS: BB, pl. 21; Barnett, *Illustrations*, p. 15 (obverse).
TRANSLITERATION AND TRANSLATION: Albright, *BASOR* 89 (1943) pp. 30f.; B. Halpern and J. Huehnergard, *Or* n.s. 51 (1982) pp. 227f.
TRANSLATIONS: Albright, *ANET*, p. 486; Campbell, *Shechem*, p. 195.

Say to the king, my lord: Message of Lab'ayu, your servant. I fall at the feet of the king, my lord. 5–9 As to your having written me, "Guard[1] the men who seized the city," how am I to guard (such) men? It was in war that the city was seized. 10–15 *When I had sworn my peace*—and *when I swore* the magnate *swore* with me—the city, along with my god, was seized. He has slandered me[2] : *ši-ir-ti* (I am slandered) before the king, my lord. 16–22 Moreover, when an ant is struck, does it not fight back[3] and bite the hand of the man that struck it? How *at this time* can I show deference[4] and then another city of mine will be seized? 23–31 On the other hand, if you also order, "Fall down beneath them so they can strike you," I will d⟨o⟩ (it).[5] I will guard the men that seized the city (and) my god. They are *the despoilers* of my father,[6] but I will guard them.

NOTES

1. *ú-ṣur-me*: following Rainey (private communication), confirmed by collation. My understanding of this difficult letter is that, in time of peace under oath, to which an Egyptian official was also a party (lines 10f.), certain enemies of Lab'ayu had taken his paternal city or village but had then been captured and come into his hands. On learning of this, the crown had written him, telling him to keep his prisoners in custody, presumably for investigation by Egyptian officials. Lab'ayu points out that he was not the aggressor, as he seems to have been accused (lines 13f.), and that his striking back was only natural (lines 16–19). Moreover, deference now to royal orders would only encourage further aggression (lines 20–22). Nevertheless, if ordered to do so, he would let his enemies have the upper hand, even kill him. Faithful vassal, he capitulates, and returning to the beginning of the letter, he promises to guard the prisoners.

2. The subject is the Egyptian official; see Halpern and Huehnergard (headnote), p. 229, n. 14. Cf., too, *EA* 253:16f.

3. See *RA* 69 (1975) p. 149, n. 1.

4. *i-ša-ḫa-tu*: on *šaḫātu* (properly of the *u-u* class), to renounce personal action out of deference to authority, see Durand, *AÉM* 1/1, no. 32, note c.

5. *i-pé-*⟨šu⟩: very dubious.

6. By taking the statue or image of the family god, Lab'ayu's enemies had violated his family.

EA 253

Neither rebel nor delinquent (1)

TEXT: VAT 1589.
COPIES: WA 155; *VS* 11, 144.

[To the ki]ng, [my lord] and my [Sun]: Thus [L]ab'ayu, your [servant] and the d[irt on which] you tre[ad]. I fall [a]t the feet of the k[in]g, my [l]ord, 7 times and 7 times. 7–10 I have [o]beyed the orders [th]at the king, my lord, [w]rote to m[e] on a tablet. 11–17 [*A*]*s* [*I am*] a servant of the king [*like*] my [*fathe*]*r* and my [gr]andfa[th]er, a servant [o]f the ki[n]g from *l*[*on*]g *a*[*g*]*o*, I am [n]ot a rebel [and] I am not delinquent in duty.[1] 18–25 Here is my act of rebellion and here is my delinquency: when I entered Gazru, I (spoke) as follows: "The king treats us kindly."[2] 25–31 Now there is indeed no other purpose (for me) except the service of the king, and whatever [the k]ing orders, I [o]bey. 32–35 May the king keep me in [*the char*]*ge* of my commissioner [in order to] guard the *c*[*it*]*y* [*of the king*].

NOTES

1. See *EA* 157, n. 3.

2. "The king punishes/will punish us" (Rainey, AOAT, 8², p. 70) would require a quite different and, it seems to me, quite implausible interpretation of *EA* 253–54.

EA 254

Neither rebel nor delinquent (2)

TEXT: VAT 335.
COPIES: WA 112; *VS* 11, 145.
TRANSLATIONS: Albright, *ANET,* p. 486; Campbell, *Shechem,* pp. 196f.; Oppenheim, *LFM,* p. 125; Freydank, in A. Jepsen, ed., *Von Sinuhe bis Nebukadnezar* (see *EA* 244, headnote), pp. 254f.; Seux, *Textes du Proche-Orient,* pp. 52f.

To the king, my lord and my Sun: Thus Lab'ayu, your servant and the dirt on which you tread. I fall at the feet of the king, my lord and my Sun, 7 times and 7 times. 6–10 I have obeyed the orders that the king wrote to me. Who am I that the king should lose his land on account of me? 10–15 The fact is that I am a loyal servant of the king! I am not a rebel and I am not delinquent in duty.[1] I have not held back my payments of tribute; I have not held back anything requested by my commissioner. 16–29 He denounces me unjustly,[2] but the king, my lord, does not examine my (alleged) act of rebellion. Moreover, my act of rebellion is this: when I entered Gazru, I kept on saying, "Everything of mine the king takes, but where is what belongs to Milkilu?" I know the actions[3] of Milkilu against me! 30–37 Moreover, the king wrote for my son.[4] I did not know that my son was consorting with the ʿApiru. I herewith hand him over to Addaya. 38–46 Moreover, how, if the king wrote for my wife, how could I hold her back? How, if the king wrote to me, "Put a bronze dagger into your heart and die," how could I not execute the order of the king?[5]

NOTES

1. See *EA* 253, n. 1.

2. On *yi-ka-lu* as singular, see Izre'el, *UF* 19 (1987) p. 83; on *karṣī akālu,* "to denounce," see *EA* 162, n. 4. I take *ḫa-ba-lu-ma* as an infinitive expressing circumstance; cf. the infinitive absolute in biblical Hebrew after a finite verb, and see Paul Jouon, S.J., *Grammaire de l'Hébreu Biblique* (Rome, 1947), §123r.

3. *ep-še-et-šu ša*: last two signs omitted in Knudtzon's transliteration; see Schroeder, *OLZ,* 1915, col. 175.

4. ᵐDUMU.MU-*ia* (also line 33): an unparalleled personal name, Dumuya (Knudtzon, Oppenheim, Seux), does not seem likely, and ᵐ*i-mu-ia,* "my father-in-law" (Albright, *CAH* 2/2, p. 115, n. 7), must be rejected on grounds of grammar (genitive expected in line 31) and especially paleography (the DUMU- and I-signs are quite distinct, and in both instances the sign in question is clearly the former). In view of ᵐDUMU-*a-ia*$_8$ at roughly contemporary Taanach, most probably Binaya (Glotz, *BASOR* 204 [1971] p. 20), the same name may occur here. The apparent association, however, of ideas—delivery of a son, readiness to deliver a wife—favors a common noun and a display of provincial learning: Sumerian DUMU.MU, "my son," plus Akkadian pronominal suffix. See also *EA* 3, n. 2.

5. On the Egyptian docket after the letter, see Introduction, sect. 6.

EA 255

No destination too far

TEXT: VAT 333.
COPIES: WA 144; *VS* 11, 146.
TRANSLATION: Campbell, *Shechem,* p. 205.

Say [t]o the king, [my] lord and my Sun: Thus Mut-Baḫl[u], your servant, the dirt at your feet, the mire you tread on. I fall at the feet of the king, my lord, 7 times and 7 times. 8–11 The king, my lord, sent Ḫaaya to me to say, "A caravan to Ḫanagalbat is this (man) to send on, and (all of you) send it on!"[1] 12–21 Who am I that I would not send on a caravan of the king, my lord, seeing that [*La*]*b*'ayu, my father, [*used to ser*]*ve* the king, his lord, [*and*] he [*himself*] used to send on [*all* the carav]ans [*that*] the king [would se]nd[2] to Ḫanagalbat. 21–25 Let the king, my lord, send a caravan even to Karaduniyaš.[3] I will personally conduct it under very heavy guard.[4]

NOTES

1. The position of *annû* in the sentence argues against its being the deictic particle, and *uwaššeruna* is not a plural form. The plural imperative *uššerū* is perhaps addressed to the entire local administration, but more probably, it seems to me, to all whom Ḫaaya would meet on his journey.

2. [ša *yú-wa-š*]*e-ru* or [*yú-wa-š*]*e-ru.*

3. Placed at the beginning of its clause, "to Karaduniyaš" becomes an *ultima Thule.*

4. To paraphrase: "Send a caravan even much farther, even to Babylonia, and I will not only send it on but conduct it there myself, with a large escort."

EA 256

Oaths and denials

TEXT: BM 29847.
COPY: BB 64.
PHOTOGRAPH: BB, pl. 5.
TRANSLITERATION AND TRANSLATION: Albright, *BASOR* 89 (1943) pp. 10ff.
TRANSLATION: Albright, *ANET,* p. 486.

Say to Yanḫamu, my lord: Message of Mut-Baḫlu, your servant. I fall at the feet of my lord. 4–10 How can it have been said in your presence,[1] "Mut-Baḫlu has fled. He has hidden Ayyab"? How can the king of Piḫilu flee from the commissioner : *sú-ki-ni* of the king, his lord? 10–19 As the king, my lord, lives, as the king, my lord, lives, I swear Ayyab is not in Piḫilu. In fact, he *h[as been in the fie]ld*[2] for two months. Just ask Ben-Elima. Just ask Tadua. 19–28 Just ask Yišuya whether, after *he [ro]bbed* Šulum-Marduk, I went to the aid of Aštartu, when all the cities of Garu had become hostile: Udumu, Aduru, Araru, Mešta, Magdalu, Ḫeni-anabi, Sarqu.[3] (Ḫayyunu, along with Yabiluma, has been captured.)[4] 29–35 Moreover, seeing that, after you sent me a tablet, I wrote to him, before you arrive from your journey, he will surely have arrived in Piḫilu. And I do obey [your] orders.[5]

NOTES

1. The rhetoric of defense: a rhetorical question challenging the two charges against Mut-Baḫlu (lines 4–6); another rhetorical question challenging the first charge (6–10); under oath by the life of the king, twice invoked, denial of second charge, followed by statement of the facts (10–14); invocation of possible witnesses to support denial of implied third charge (15–28); transition ("Moreover") and, by implication, return to the first two charges: assuring Ayyab's presence in Piḫilu (29–34), general statement of compliance with orders (35, as against the charge of flight?).

2. *ia*-a[r-b]i-iṣ: this reading fits the traces, which *ia*-[a-nu]-*ma* (Albright), though making very good sense ("he is not/has not been here"), does not; cf. *šurbuṣu* at Mari, said of putting troops in camps (*ARMT* 2 23:22). Ayyab, in this reading, is still engaged in stamping out the rebellion referred to later in lines 22–28. He might therefore be difficult for Yanḫamu to reach, who might then suspect Ayyab's alleged ally of hiding him.

3. This new understanding of lines 15–27 depends on Na'aman, *UF* 20 (1988) pp. 181f. Line 20: of the two readings that have been proposed—⌜gán⌝-*ba* (Knudtzon) and ⌜É⌝ *ša* (BB, followed by Albright)—only the first is possible. The reading *ša* is wrong: of the putative two oblique wedges before the last vertical,

the lower is the end of the middle horizontal in *ba,* the upper a break in the tablet and not writing at all. Besides, only most rarely are personal names written without a determinative (the final vertical of the alleged *ša*). Mut-Baḫlu wishes to deny that after Ayyab's serious crime against a Babylonian—according to Na'aman, robbing his caravan, but the usage of *gānab* in biblical Hebrew favors kidnapping (cf. *EA* 8:34ff.)—he gave any (further?) support to the ruler of Aštartu when the latter was faced with rebellion. (If the city Aštartu were the subject of *ennerir* [Albright], the form would have to be either *tennerir* or *ennerirat.*) What remains unclear in this reconstruction is how Mut-Baḫlu, having in some sense broken off relations with Ayyab, could assure Yanḫamu of Ayyab's presence soon in Piḫilu.

4. Does this mean that these cities have been retaken?

5. *ištimuna*: first person, following Rainey, AOAT, 8[2], p. 94.

EA 257

Under the yoke

TEXT: VAT 1715.

COPIES: WA 149; *VS* 11, 147.

[Sa]y [to the king], my [lor]d: [Messa]ge of Baʿlu-meḫir, your [ser]vant. I fall at the feet of the king, my lord, 7 times and 7 times. 7–11 As I am the loy[al] servant [o]f the king, may the king, my lord, know [th]at [h]is [city], along with his servant, is safe and sound. 12–19 As I have placed my [n]eck in the yoke that I carry, may the king, my lord, know that I serve him [with com]plete devotion, and [. . .i]Gmate[1] [s]erves him [with complete devotio]n.

NOTE

1. [URU x-x-*i*]*G-ma-te*: following Na'aman, *Political Disposition,* p. 34. For a different reading, see Rainey, *Biblica* 70 (1989) pp. 570f.

EA 258

Complete approval

TEXT: VAT 329.

COPIES: WA 167; *VS* 11, 148.

To the king, my lord: Message of Baʿlu-meḫir, the loyal servant of the king. I fall at the feet of the king, my lord, 7 times and 7 times.

6–9 Whatsoever the king, my[1] lord, has done to his land is very good.[2]

NOTES

1. Text: EN EN for EN-*ia*.

2. On the uninscribed reverse there appears apparently the same hieratic notation as on *EA* 234.

EA 259

All the news

TEXT: VAT 1582.

COPIES: WA 213; *VS* 11, 149.

To the k[ing], my [lord]: Message of [Baʿlu-meḫ]ir, the loyal servant of the king. I fal[l] at the feet of the king, my lord, 7 times and 7 times.

6–8 Whatsoever [*I have hear*]*d*[1] I have told (to the king], my [lor]d. [. . .].

NOTE

1. [eš/iš-m]e. A few lines are missing on the reverse.

EA 260

A plea for royal concern

TEXT: Oppert (see Introduction, sect. 1 and n. 7).

COPY: none published.

TRANSLITERATION: Artzi, *JNES* 27 (1968) p. 170.

Balu-Mer says to the Great King, my lord: I fall at the feet of the Great King, the Sun in the sky, 7 times and 7 times.[1] 6–10 As for me, when the Great King, my lord, commands, I obey the orders of the Great King, my lord, the Sun in the sky.[2] 11–16 *May*[3] the Great King take cognizance of his servant. I reside in Bit-Tenni, and *may* the Great King, my lord, take cognizance of his servant.

NOTES

1. On the northern origin of this letter, see Artzi.

2. The shift from present-future *iqabbi* to preterite *išme* cannot be interpreted with certainty; quite probable is ". . . commanded, I obeyed" (see Introduction, n. 50).

3. The marking for mood is not explicit.

EA 261

Total obedience

TEXT: BM 29858.
COPY: BB 75.
PHOTOGRAPH: BB, pl. 16.

Say to the king, my lord, my Sun: Message of Dašru, the loyal servant of the king. I f[al]l at the feet of the king, my lord and my Sun, 7 times and 7 times.

7–10 Whatsoever the king, my lord, orders, I obey.

EA 262

Total approval

TEXT: C 4786 (12220).
COPY: WA 127.

Say to the king, my lord: Message of Dašru, the loyal servant of the king. I fall at the feet of the king, my lord, 7 times and 7 times.

6–11 Whatsoever the king, my lord, does to his land is very, very good.

EA 263

Robbed of everything

TEXT: VAT 1688.
COPIES: WA 169; *VS* 11, 150.

[*Say* to my lord: Me]ssage of [. . . , your servant].[1] I fall at the feet of my lord 7 times and 7 times . . . [. . .].[2] 5–17 [*A*]*nd* may my lord listen to the wo[r]ds of his servant. When I vi[si]ted the house of my lord, everything was taken from the house of your servant. Silver was taken; men were taken; sheep and goats : *ṣú-ú-nu* were taken. The cities of my lord : *ḫa-sí-lu* (were despoiled),[3] and whatever my lord had given to his servant, this too was taken. 17–25 So may my lord give thought to his servant. I make this speech through Pawura. May my lord send a garrison and horses : *sú-ú-*[*sí-ma*]. 26–34 My lord commanded his servant [. . .] . . . [*fr*]*om* Tagi [*an*]*d from* Lab'ayu.[4]

NOTES

1. Although the addressee is never called king, the sevenfold prostration is given to the king alone.

2. Traces and a small break.

3. On *ḫasilū,* see Held, *AS* 16, pp. 398ff.; *ḫsl,* with the same meaning, is also attested in Ugaritic (*Ugar.* 7, p. 52).

4. [i-n]a ^{m}*ta-a-gi* 34 [ù" *i-na*: following Na'aman, *Political Disposition,* p. 16*, n. 36.

EA 264

The ubiquitous king

TEXT: BM 29853.
COPY: BB 70.
TRANSLATION: Oppenheim, *LFM,* p. 127.

To the king, m[y] lord: Message of Tagi, you[r] servant. I fall at the feet of the king, my lord, 7 times and 7 times. 5–10 As I am the servant of the king, I tried to assemble a caravan,[1] with my brother[2] in charge, but he barely escaped being killed. He is[3] unable to send my caravan to the king, my lord. 11–19 Ask your commissioner if my brother did not barely escape being killed. Moreover, as far as we are concerned, it is to you that my eyes (are directed).[4] Should we go up into the sky : *ša-me-ma,* or should we go down into the netherworld, our head : *ru-šu-nu* is in your hand. 20–25 So now I try herewith to send my caravan to the king, my lord, with a partner of mine in charge. May the king, my lord, be informed that I serve the king and am on my guard.

NOTES

1. It seems more likely that a vassal would be sending one caravan, not many; for otiose ḪI.A, cf. KASKAL-*ra-ni*.ḪI.A (*EA* 255:9), referred to by singular pronominal suffix (*uššeru-ši,* line 11). Organizing a caravan involved assembling the various goods requested or expected, and this could entail searching in various places (cf. *EA* 143:10ff.).

2. Or "a brother of mine." Since *tappû,* "partner" (line 22), probably always refers in *EA* to fellow mayor-vassals (*EA* 113:30; 120:45; 295 rev. 3), "brother" must mean here either a blood relation or someone of Tagi's immediate entourage.

3. "I am unable" (Knudtzon) is hard to reconcile with lines 20ff.

4. The explanation of the alternation of first person singular and plural is perhaps that "it is to you that my eyes (are directed)" is an insertion in a stock expression of the impossibility of escaping the Pharaoh's control and support.

EA 265

A gift acknowledged

TEXT: VAT 1697.
COPIES: WA 165; *VS* 11, 151.

To the king, my lord: Message of Tagi, your servant. I fall at the feet of the king, my lord. My own man I sent along[1] with [. . .] to see the face of the king, my lord. 7–15 [And] the king, my lord, [s]ent a *present* to me in the care of Taḫmaya, and Taḫmaya gave (me) a gold goblet[2] and 1[2 se]ts[3] of linen garments. For the information [of the kin]g, my lord.

NOTES

1. The word order (object-verb), which stresses the object, suggests that a vassal was not expected to send his own man (whatever that means), at least not in the writer's situation, to the court. The king acknowledged such devotion by sending back a generous gift. This report might also have served as a check on Taḫmaya's honesty.

2. GAL (*kāsu*): reading certain.

3. "Set" seems to imply that the garment consisted of more than one piece; see Oppenheim, *JCS* 21 (1969) p. 250, n. 76.

EA 266

And there was light

TEXT: VAT 1590.
COPIES: WA 156; *VS* 11, 152.

[S]ay [to] the king, [my] lo[rd], my [g]od, my [Sun]: Message of Tag[i, your servant], the dirt at [your] fe[et. I fall] at the feet of the king, [my] lor[d], my god, my Sun, 7 times and 7 times. 9–15 I looked [th]is way, and I l[oo]ked [th]at way, and there was no [li]ght. Then I looked [to]wards the king, [my lord, and the]re was light. 16–25 I am [ind]eed deter[min]ed to serve the king, my lord. A brick may move fro[m u]nder [its] par[tner]; still I will not move from [un]der the feet [of the k]in[g], my lord. 26–33 I herewith se[nd] [ha]rness(es) [*for* a pa]ir of hor[ses, *and*] a bow, and [a qu]ive[r], [a s]pea[r, *c*]*ove*[*rs*,[1] t]o the king, [my] l[ord].

NOTE

1. 27 [KUŠ].MEŠ *a-ši-ti* 28 [ša *t*]*a-pal* ANŠ[E.KUR.RA] 29 [ù G]IŠ.BAN *ù* 30 [KUŠ] É.MA[R.URU$_5$ (ù)] 31 [GIŠ] *i-mi-*[*it-ta*] 32 [TÚG] :

sà-dì-[in-ni]: for the reading of lines 27–31, see Na'aman, *JCS* 29 (1977) p. 238 (on line 30, see also Kühne in Wilhelm, *ZA* 63 [1973] p. 73); for the reading of line 32, see Na'aman, *Political Disposition,* p. 76*, n. 77. In line 28 Na'aman restores *ù,* so that a team of horses is also given, but in this case one would expect this gift to be at the head of the list. If *saddinnu* is the correct reading, it must have been some kind of cover for the horses; cf., at Nuzi, "*saddinnu* and harnesses," *CAD,* S, p. 17, citing *Joint Expedition with the Iraq Museum at Nuzi,* 588:36.

EA 267

Safe and sound

TEXT: C 4771 (12232).
COPY: WA 109.

[Sa]y [t]o the king, my lord, my [g]od, my Sun: Message of Milkilu, your servant, the dirt at your feet. I fall at the feet of the king, my lord, my god, my Sun, 7 times and 7 times. **9–14** The order the king, my lord, my god, my Sun, dispatched to me I am indeed carrying out for the king, my lord, the Sun from the sky. **15–20** May the king, my lord, my god, my Sun, know that the place of the king, my lord, where I am is safe and sound.

EA 268

A consignment of personnel

TEXT: VAT 1532.
COPIES: WA 108; *VS* 11, 153.

Say [to] the ki[n]g, my [l]ord, [m]y g[o]d, my [S]un: Message of Milkilu, your servant, the [d]i[r]t at your feet. **5–11** I fall at the feet of the king, my lord, my god, my Sun, 7 times and 7 times. May the k[ing], my [lor]d, know that [the city of the king, my lord], that [*he put*] i[n *my*] *ch*[*arge*], is safe and sound, [*and*] the word[1] **12–14** . . . [. . .]. **15–20** [*I sen*]*d*[2] [*in the care o*]*f* Ḫay[a] 46 female-. . . [. . .],[3] and 5 male-. . . [. . .],[4] and 5 *aširūma*[5] to the king, my lord.

NOTES

1. 11 *qa*-[ti-ia ù] *a-w*[*a*]-*at*. For lines 12ff., cf. *EA* 267:9ff.? Instead of only one completely destroyed line (line 14 according to Knudtzon), there are perhaps two or three.

2. 15 [ù uš-ši-ir-*t*]*i*: following Na'aman, *Political Disposition,* p. 76*, n. 73.

3. ^{sal}*ar-d*[*i-ti*], for *ardāti*, "slave-girls" (Astour, *Gesellschaftsklassen im Alten Zweistromland und in den angrenzenden Gebieten* [see *EA* 17, n. 7], p. 23), is highly unlikely. Read *ar*-k[i-ta], "a later/follow-up contingent" (cf. *CAD*, A/2, p. 288), a group to be added to a previous contingent?

4. LÚ.MEŠ DUMU.[KIN]: Rainey, *JNES* 26 (1967) p. 299, tentatively; Astour, *Gesellschaftsklassen* (see n. 3). Another possibility is TUR.[MEŠ], *ṣuḫārī*, "attendants."

5. The function of the *aširūma* is still not clear. That they were merchants (Astour, *Gesellschaftsklassen* [see n. 3]) does not seem supported by solid evidence. (*aširūma*, rather than *āširūma*, which should appear at Gezer as *ōširūma*, *ú-ši-ru-ma*. See Huehnergard, *Ugaritic Vocabulary*, p. 163.)

EA 269

Archers and myrrh

TEXT: BM 29846.
COPY: BB 63.

Say to the king, my lord, my god, my Sun: Message of Milkilu, your servant, the dirt at your feet. I fall at the feet of the king, my lord, my god, my Sun, 7 times and 7 times. 9–17 I have heard what the king, my lord, wrote to me, and so may the king, my lord, send the archers to his servants, and may the king, my lord send myrrh[1] for medication.

NOTE

1. [Š]IM.ZAR.MEŠ : *mu-ur-ra*: see *CAD*, M/2, p. 221.

EA 270

Extortion

TEXT: BM 29845.
COPY: BB 62.
PHOTOGRAPH: BB, pl. 2.
TRANSLATION: Oppenheim, *LFM*, p. 128.

Say to the king, my lord, my god, my Sun: Message of Milkilu, your servant, the dirt at your feet. I fall at the feet of the king, my lord, my god, my Sun, 7 times and 7 times. 9–16 May the king, my lord, know the deeds that Yanḫamu keeps doing to me since I left the king, my lord. 17–21 He indeed wants 2000 shekels of silver from me, and he says to me, "Hand ov[er][1] your wife and your sons, or I will kill (you)." 22–29 May the king know of this deed, and may the king, my lord, send chariots and fetch me to himself lest I perish.

NOTE

1. *id-na*-m[i]: following Izre'el, *IOS* 8 (1978) p. 59, n. 175 (and last sentence of n. 176), who claims that his collation supported this reading. My own collation was inconclusive.

EA 271

The power of the ʿApiru

TEXT: VAT 1531.
COPIES: WA 110; *VS* 11, 154.
TRANSLATIONS: Albright, *ANET,* pp. 486f.; Seux, *Textes du Proche-Orient,* p. 54.

Say to the king, my lord, my god, my Sun: Message of Milkilu, your servant, the dirt at your feet. I fall at the feet of the king, my lord, 7 times and 7 times. 9–16 May the king, my lord, know that the war against me and against Šuwardata is severe. So may the king, my lord, save his land from the power of the ʿApiru. 17–27 O[th]erwise, may the king, my lord, send chariots to fetch u[s] lest our servants kill us. Moreover, may the king, my lord, ask Yanḫamu, his servant, about what is bein[g] done in his [l]and.

EA 272

ʿApiru activity

TEXT: BM 29863.
COPY: BB 80.

[T]o the kin[g, my lord, my *Sun*: Messa]ge of *Šum*-[. . . ,[1] the *ruler of*] . . . [. . . ,[2] your servant, the dir]t a[t your feet. I fal]l [a]t the f[eet of] the k[in]g, [my] lord, [my god], my [Sun, 7 t]imes and 7 ti[mes]. 8–17 I [a]m the [lo]ya[l servan]t of the [king], my lord. [*May*] the king, my lord, [*kn*]*ow* [*tha*]*t* the mayors that were in the (major) ci[ties[3] *of my lord*] are gone,[4] and the [*entire*] land of the king, my l[or]d, [has de]serted *to*[5] the ʿApiru. 18–25 May the king, my lord, inquire of [h]is commissioner about what is b[eing d]one in the land of the k[ing], m[y l]ord, so the king, my lord, will instruct his arc[hers] in my regard.[6]

NOTES

1. Knudtzon's transliteration omits the determinative of the text, ^{m}*Šum*-[. . . .

2. Na'aman, *Political Disposition*, p. 68, proposes URU [m]a-[aḫ]-*ḫ*[*a*-zi] and would identify it with the URU *muḫḫazi* in *EA* 298:25. Though n]a (Knudtzon; Na'aman's m]a) is quite uncertain, it may be doubted that *ma-ḫa-zi* in line 13 explains the deviant spelling (so Na'aman).

3. *CAD*, M/1, p. 88, puts this use of *māḫāzu* under "town, settlement," but this seems to be a later meaning of the word, and if it had this meaning, it is hard to see why it occurs nowhere else in *EA*. If here the connotation is not of "important city" (*CAD*, M/1, p. 87), perhaps it is "harbor (city)" (ibid., p. 88, 5).

4. "Gone," not just "have gone" or "disappeared" (*ḫalqū*), but "used up, destroyed, wiped out" (*gamrū*), like the sons and daughters of Byblos (*EA* 74:15ff. and parallel passages).

5. Or, "through the activity of, abetted by" (*ina*).

6. ÉRIN.MEŠ *pí*-⌈*ṭá*⌉-[*ti*]-*šu*: following Rainey, *Lingering over Words*, p. 417, a reading tentatively noted in my collation notes.

EA 272–77 were written by the scribe of the Milkilu letters; see Knudtzon, *VAB* 2/2, p. 1329, n. 1, and *EA* 278, n. 1.

EA 273

From a queen mother

TEXT: VAT 1686.
COPIES: WA 137; *VS* 11, 155.

Say to the king, my lord, my god, my Sun: Message of ^{f}NIN-UR.MAḪ.MEŠ,[1] your handmaid. I fall at the feet of the king, my lord, 7 times and 7 times. 8–14 May the king, my lord, know that war has been waged in the land, and gone is the land of the king, my lord, by desertion *to*[2] the ʿApiru. 15–24 May the king, my lord, take cognizance of his land, and may the [k]ing, my lord, kn[ow][3] tha[t] the ʿApiru wrote to Ayyaluna and to Ṣarḫa, and the two sons of Milkilu barely escaped being killed. 25–26 May the king, my lord, know of this deed.

NOTES

1. The bearer of this name, still of uncertain interpretation, was probably ruling as queen mother; see Liverani, in Garelli, ed., *Le Palais et la Royauté* (see Introduction, n. 73), p. 336, n. 5.

2. See *EA* 272, n. 5.

3. Note the different nuances of *yīde* in this and the preceding clause; for the latter, see *EA* 60, n. 8.

EA 274

Another city lost

TEXT: C 4773 (12216).
COPY: WA 138.
TRANSLITERATION (PARTIAL) AND TRANSLATION: Albright, *BASOR* 89 (1943) p. 17.

Say to the king, my lord, my god, my Sun: Message of ^{f}NIN-UR.MAḪ.MEŠ, your handmaid, the dirt at your feet. I fall at the feet of the king, my lord, 7 times and 7 times. 10–19 May the king, my lord, save his land from the power of the ʿApiru lest it be lost. Ṣapuma has been take⟨n⟩.[1] For the information of the king, my lord.

NOTE

1. ⌜*la*⌝-⌜*q*⌝*í-ta*-⟨*at*⟩: the text reflects perhaps some confusion between Akkadian *leqû* and *laqātu,* Canaanite *lakada*; cf. *EA* 284:7. Since city names are feminine in this dialect, -⟨*at*⟩. Albright's reading, 15 URU.KI-*ka* 16 URU *ṣa-pu-na*^{ki}, must be rejected: URU in line 15 is most unlikely (the copy is exact), and *ka* is impossible (copy is exact); in line 16, the next-to-last sign is conceivably *ba,* but certainly not *na* (so also Gordon). Ṣapuna, if identified with biblical Ṣaphon in the Jordan Valley, is also open to objections on geopolitical grounds; see Na'aman, *UF* 11 (1979) p. 680, n. 33.

EA 275

As ordered (1)

TEXT: VAT 1682.
COPIES: WA 166; *VS* 11, 156.

Sa[y to the king, my lord, my g]od, [my Sun]: Message of Yaḫzib-Adda, your servant, the dirt at your feet. I fall at the feet of the king, my lord, my god, my Sun, 7 times and 7 times. 9–14 The order that the king, my lord, my [g]od, my [Sun], gave [t]o me, I am [in]deed carrying out [for] the king, my lord.

EA 276

As ordered (2)

TEXT: VAT 1706.
COPIES: WA 187; *VS* 11, 157.

[S]a[y to the king, my lord, my god, my Sun]: Message of Yaḫzib-Adda, your servant, the dirt [at] your feet. I fall at the feet of the king, my lord, my god, my Sun, 7 times and 7 times. 9–15 The order that the king, my lord, my god, my Sun, sent to me, I am [in]deed carrying out [f]or the king, my lord, the Sun from the sky.

EA 277

As ordered (3)

TEXT: BM 29864.
COPY: BB 81.

[To the king, my lord, my god, my Sun: Message of . . .], yo[ur ser]vant, [the dirt at] your [fee]t. [I fa]ll [a]t the fe[et of the king, my lord], my god, [my Sun], 7 times and 7 t[imes]. 8–16 The order that the king, my lord, my god, my Sun, sent to me, I am indeed carrying out for the king, my lord.

EA 278

As ordered (4)

TEXT: BM 29852.
COPY: BB 69.
PHOTOGRAPH: BB, pl. 5.

Say to the king, my lord, my god, my Sun: Message of Šuwardata, your servant, the dirt at your feet. I fall at the feet of the king, my lord, my god, my Sun, 7 times and 7 times. 9–15 [The or]der that [the king], my lord, the Sun [fr]om the sky, sent to me, I am [in]deed carrying out [for the kin]g, my lord, [the Sun f]rom the Sky.[1]

NOTE

1. The sign forms of *EA* 278–80 exhibit many differences from those of *EA* 281, 282–84, and are indistinguishable in script and clay from *EA* 267–77; see Knudtzon, *VAB* 2/2, p. 1329, n. 2. Note, too, the virtually identical messages of *EA* 275–78. A fourth scribe was responsible for *EA* 366. Cf. *EA* 272, n. 6.

EA 279

A wasteland

TEXT: VAT 1647.
COPIES: WA 107; *VS* 11, 158.

S[a]y [to] the king, my lord, my [god], my Sun: Mess[age] of Šuwardata, your servant, the dirt at your feet. I fall at the feet of the king, my lord, 7 times and 7 times. 9–13 May the king, my lord, know that the land of the king, my [lor]d, is [go]ne.[1] I must *dri*[*ve back*]![2] I must go fo[rt]h to Qeltu [again]st the *t*[*raitors*].[3] 14–23 May the [king] sen[d *ar*]*cher*[*s. May the king, my lord, l*]is[ten to *his*] may[ors][4] so that we may attack them and drive out the traitors from the land of the king, my lord.

NOTES

1. See *EA* 272, n. 4.
2. *i*-n[i-i]: perhaps traces of *i*; from *nê'u*?
3. LÚ.MEŠ š[a-ru-ta/ti]: cf. line 21.
4. [yi-i]š-[me LUGAL EN-ia a-na] 17 [LÚ].MEŠ *ḫa-za-nu*-[*ti*-šu].

EA 280

Lab'ayu *redivivus*

TEXT: C 4772 (12213).
COPY: WA 100.
TRANSLATION: Albright, *ANET,* p. 487; Seux, *Textes du Proche-Orient,* p. 60.

Sa[y] t[o] the king, my lord, [m]y g[od], my Sun: Mes[sage] of Šuwardata, [yo]ur servant, the dirt at your feet. I fall at the [fee]t of the king, my lord, [m]y god, my Sun, 7 [ti]mes and 7 times. 9–15 The king, my lord, permitted[1] me to wage war against Qeltu. I waged war. It is now at peace with me; my city is restored to me. 16–24 Why did ʿAbdi-Ḫe[b]a write to the men of Qeltu, "[Ac]cept silver and follow me"? 24–29 Moreover, may the king, my lord, conduct an inquiry. If I took a man, or a single ox, or an ass, from him, then he is in the right! 30–35 Moreover, Lab'ayu, who used to take our towns, is dead, but now [an]other Lab'ayu is ʿAbdi-Ḫeba, and he seizes our town. 36–40 [So] may the king take cognizance of [hi]s servant because of this deed, but I will do nothing until the king sends back[2] word to his servant.

NOTES

1. Or "sent," but in any case stressing the intervention of the crown, without which he promises (lines 36ff.) no further action (occupation of Qeltu?).

2. Instead of *yú-šu-te-ru,* perhaps *yú-na-ki-ru,* "changes," i.e., revokes an earlier decision (so Gordon).

EA 281

Rebellion

TEXT: VAT 1681.
COPIES: WA 190; *VS* 11, 159.

Say to the king, my lord, my god, ⟨my⟩ Sun,[1] [and] my breath (of life): Message of [Š]uwardata, your servant. I fall at the feet of my lord 7 times and 7 times, both on the st[oma]ch and on the b[a]ck. 8–17 May the king, [my] lord [be informed t]hat [*no*]*w* my own cities are hostile to me, and so may the king, my lord, send archers to [d]o [*to t*]*he*[*m*] as in the case of . . . ,[2] so the king, my lord, may t[a]ke them. The . . . [. . .] 18–26 and *may they writhe* [*be*]*fore* the kin[g, my] lord. The king, my lord, has *r*[*ej*]*ected my pr*[*o*]*posal,* but the king should *k*[*now* the h]ostilitie[s *again*]*st m*[*e. Wh*]*o* is [co]mmitting [*a crime*] *ag*[*ain*]*st* the king? [*Th*]*ese fellows are d*[*ogs*], and so *they have com*[*mit*]*ted* [*a crime*] *against* the king.[3] 27–31 So may the k[in]g send archers that he may ta[ke t]he[m]. May the king, my lord, be informed.

NOTES

1. ^{d}UTU.MEŠ.

2. The reading of the first two signs as UR[U ḫ]a(*-ra-bu-*WA) is extremely doubtful. Line 14: [a]-n[a ša-š]u-*nu*.

3. 23 . . . me/mi-i]a-*mi* 24 [*y*]*i-pu-šu* [ar-na] *a-na* LUGAL 25 *ù* UR.[KU.MEŠ a]n-nu-*tu* 26 ù t[i]-*pu-*[š]u [ar-na] *a-na* LUGAL: following Na'aman, *UF* 11 (1979) p. 679, n. 31.

EA 282

Alone

TEXT: BM 29851.
COPIES: BB 68; A. Millard, *Biblical Archaeologist* 45 (1981) p. 147.
PHOTOGRAPHS: M. Noth, *Die Welt des Alten Testaments* (Berlin, 1953), Tafel 3; Barnett, *Illustrations,* p. 16 (obverse only).
TRANSLITERATION AND TRANSLATION: Millard, *Biblical Archaeologist* 45 (1981) p. 146.

To the king, my lord, ⟨my⟩ god, my Sun: Message of Šuwardata, ⟨your⟩ servant. I fall at the feet of the king, my lord, 7 times and 7 times, both on the stomach and on the back. 8–16 May the king, my lord, be informed that I am alone. May the king, my lord, send a very large archer-force that it may save me : *ia-ṣí-ni* (get me out). May the king, my lord, be in⟨fo⟩rmed.

EA 283

Oh to see the king

TEXT: VAT 339.
COPIES: WA 101; *VS* 11, 160.

To the king, my lord,[1] my god, my Sun: Message of Šuwardata, your servant. I fall at the feet of the king, my lord. I fall at the feet of the king, my lord, 7 times and 7 times *more.* 7–13 The king, my lord, has written me, "Enter and pay me homage." Into the presence of the king, my lord![2] Would that it were possible[3] to enter into the presence of the king, my lord, *to*[4] receive the ... and the ...[5] of the king, my lord. 13–17 Since Yanḫamu is with you, speak with him. If there are *still* no archers available, then may the king, my lord, take me away. 18–24 May the king, my lord, be informed that 30 cities have waged war against me. I am alone! The war against me is severe. The king, my lord, has cast me[6] from his hand. 25–33 May the king, my lord, send archers. May the king, my lord, ta⟨k⟩e me away.[7] Since Yanḫamu, *that is,* the commissioner[8] of the king, my lord, is there, may the king, my lord, spea[k] with him, (asking), "Is the war against Šuwardata severe or is it not?"

NOTES

1. There is a ruling between lines 1 and 2, and two more between lines 16 and 17.

2. *du-gu-la-ni* KI (*itti*) . . . : following *AHw,* p. 576a.

3. *mīya-mi yumaggir,* lit. "who would grant"; cf. Hebrew *mî yittēn.*

4. The interpretation of line 12 is quite tentative: *ana* omitted (for the construction, see Introduction, n. 75) or ⟨*a-na*⟩; *le-qé-ma,* infinitive, but *la-qé-ma* expected (see *VAB* 2/2, p. 1452).

5. The reading of KÙ + 40 and KÙ + 40 x is as obscure as ever. If the occasion of the visit reflects the presence of a new king on the throne, there may be reference here to the renewal of the vassal oath.

6. Cf. *AHw,* p. 709, *nadû,* IV; *CAD,* N, p. 309, *nuddû.*

7. Taking Šuwardata away is the alternative to sending archers; cf. lines 15–17.

8. It does not seem likely that the commissioner in question is someone different from Yanḫamu, and so, tentatively, I take the *u* as corresponding to *waw-explicativum.*

EA 284

The powerful hand of the king

TEXT: BM 29850.
COPY: BB 67.

To the king, my lord: Message of Šuwardata, [your] servant. I fall at the feet of the king, my lord. I fall 7 times and 7 times *more,* both on the stomach and on the back. 6–12 Be informed, O king, my lord, that all the lands of the king, my lord, have been taken away.[1] I am all alone. As Ra[ḫ]manu,[2] *wh*[*o in*]*spected the lands* of the king, my lord, has departed, [th]ere is n[o] one for the king. May the king, my lord, t[a]ke m[e]. 13–16 I wrote to the king, my lord, "He knows . . . [. . .]." May the king, my lord, se[n]d 17–20 . . . [. . .] *still. May* the king, my lord, [*s*]*end* [*forth*] his power[fu]l hand.[3] 21–35 . . . [. . .].[4]

NOTES

1. See *EA* 274, n. 1.

2. ᵐ*ra-a*[*ḫ*]*-ma-nu* š[a].

3. [y]ú-u[š]-*ši*-[ra] 19 ᵐLUGAL-*ri* EN-*ia qa-ti-ḫu* 20 *da-an-na-*[*t*]*a*: following Na'aman, *Political Disposition,* p. 43*, n. 57. The feminine adjective agrees with *qāti* + *hu* (pronominal suffix); cf. *EA* 366:34, in another letter of Šuwardata, ZAG (*pāṭi*)-*ši* : *up-sí-ḫi* = *upsī* + *hi* (pronominal suffix). *qāta uššuru, EA* 299:19f.

4. Lines 21ff., except for line 22 ("I fall 7 times and 7 times") and an occasional word or phrase, are unintelligible. Because of the sevenfold prostration

formula this is not likely to be a postscript, despite the possible imperative plural [l]*imadū*, "be informed" (line 23). See also *EA* 298, n. 2.

EA 285

The soldier-ruler of Jerusalem

TEXT: VAT 1601.
COPIES: WA 174; *VS* 11, 161.
TRANSLITERATION (LINES 9–25) AND TRANSLATION: Na'aman, *Political Disposition,* pp. 97f.[1]

[Say to the kin]g, [my lord: Message] of ʿAbdi-Ḫ[eba, your servant. I fall at] the feet [of the king, my lord], 7 times and 7 ti[mes]. 5–11 I am not a [mayor]; I am a soldier fo[r the king, my lord]. Why has the ki[ng, my lord], not sent a messenger . . . [. . .] . . .[2] [Acc]ordingly, [*Enḫa*]mu se[nt] a *military* [*force*][3] here, [*and it has not vac*]*ated* the house [*that I w*]*ant.*[4] 12–19 [*And n*]*ow*[5] *as for* me, may the king [*give heed to*[6] ʿAbdi]-Ḫeba, his servant. [*If* th]ere are no[7] archers available, may the king, my lord, [sen]d [a commissione]r that he may fetch [the ma]yors to himself. 20–25 [. . .] . . . And *as for* [*the garrison*] that *belongs* [*to Adday*]*a,*[8] the commissioner of the king, [I] want their house. 26–31 So may the ki[ng] provide [f]or them, and may he send a mess[enger qu]ickly. When [*I d*]*ie, w*[*hat*[9] . . .] . . .

NOTES

1. In the summer of 1951, I prepared with Albright a transliteration and translation of the Jerusalem letters that, though often considerably modified, I here draw on.

2. Perhaps k[i-ma ar-ḫi-e]š, "with all speed" (Knudtzon), but this expression is otherwise attested only at Byblos.

3. *e*-m[u-qí/qa]: so also Na'aman, *Political Disposition,* p. 97. Though the word is attested only in *EA* 154:7, its appearance in a letter from Tyre is especially relevant because of a certain shared background of the Jerusalem and Tyrian scribes. Note also in the north *emūqa kašādu,* "to have the advantage over someone" (Nougayrol, *Ugar.* 5, no. 20: 14, 17′, 23′).

4. 10 . . . ù] 11 [la-a it/ti-*t*]*i-ṣi* É [ša a-*t*]*ar-šu*: cf. line 25; on the assumed vowel-harmony, *ittaṣi* > *ittiṣi,* see *Jerusalem Scribe,* p. 153.

5. [ù i-na]-*an-na.*

6. 13 [li-iš-m]e LUGAL-*ru* 14 [a-na ᵐÌR]-*ḫe-ba*: cf. *EA* 290:19.

7. [šum-ma *i*]*a-a-nu-mi*: cf. *EA* 286:59; 287:23; 288:57.

8. LÚ.MEŠ 23 [ma-ṣar-tu] *ša i-ba-šu-ú* 24 [a-na ᵐad-da-*i*]*a*: see Campbell, *Chronology,* p. 103, n. 75; cf. *EA* 287:46–48.

9. *m*[*i*-na: cf. *EA* 119:17f.

EA 286

A throne granted, not inherited

TEXT: VAT 1642.
COPIES: WA 102; *VS* 11, 162.
PHOTOGRAPHS: H. V. Hilprecht et al., *Explorations in Bible Lands during the Nineteenth Century* (Philadelphia, 1903), p. 621; R. W. Rogers, *Cuneiform Parallels to the Old Testament* (New York and Cincinnati, 1912), p. 529, pl. 30.
TRANSLATIONS: Ebeling, pp. 374f.; Albright, *ANET*, pp. 487f.; Borger, in Galling, ed., *Textbuch zur Geschichte Israels*[2] (Tübingen, 1968), pp. 25f.; Seux, *Textes du Proche-Orient*, pp. 54f.

Say [t]o the king, my lord: Message of ʿAbdi-Ḫeba, your servant. I fall at the feet of my lord, the king, 7 times and 7 times. 5–15 What have I done to the king, my lord? They denounce me : *ú-ša-a-ru* (I am slandered) before the king, my lord,[1] "ʿAbdi-Ḫeba has rebelled against the king, his lord." Seeing that, as far as I am concerned, neither my father nor my mother put me in this place, but the strong arm of the king[2] brought me into my father's house, why should I of all people commit a crime against the king, my lord? 16–21 As truly as the king, my lord, lives,[3] I say to the commissioner of the king, [my] lord, "Why do you love the ʿApiru but hate the mayors?" Accordingly, I am slandered before the king, my lord. 22–31 Because I say,[4] "Lost are the lands of the king, my lord," accordingly I am slandered before the king, my lord. May the king, my lord, know that (though) the king, my lord, stationed a garrison (here), Enḫamu has taken *i*[*t al*]*l* away. [. . .] . . . 32–43 [Now], O king, my lord, [there is n]o garrison, [and so] may the king provide for his land. May the king [*pro*]*vide* for his land! All the [la]nds of the king, my lord, have deserted. Ili-Milku has caused the loss of all the land of the king, and so may the king, my lord, provide for his land. For my part, I say, "I would go in to the king, my lord, and visit the king, my lord," but the war against me is severe, and so I am not able to go in to the king, my lord. 44–52 And may it seem good in the sight of the king, [and] may he send a garrison so I may go in and visit the king, my lord. *In truth*,[5] the king, my lord, lives: whenever the commissioners have come out, I would say (to them), "Lost are the lands of the king," but they did not listen to me. Lost are all the mayors; there is not a mayor remaining to the king, my lord. 53–60 May the king turn his attention to the archers so that archers of the king, my lord, come forth. The king has no lands. (That) ʿApiru[6] has plundered all the lands of the king. If there are archers this year, the lands of the king, my lord, will remain. But if there are no archers, lost are the lands of the king, my lord. 61–64 [T]o the scribe of the king, my lord: Message of ʿAbdi-Ḫeba, your [ser]vant. Present eloquent words to the king, my lord. Lost are all the lands of the king, my lord.

NOTES

1. On the gloss, see *EA* 180, n. 2. For the various explanations of EN.RI, see Schroeder, *OLZ* 1915, cols. 295f. Hurrian influence has also been suggested: EN-*ri* = Hurrian *iwri* (*ibri*); see Loretz, *UF* 6 (1974) p. 485, and *Jerusalem Scribe,* p. 163, n. 52. Rainey, in Avishur-Blau, eds., *Studies in Bible and the Ancient Near East* (Jerusalem, 1978), p. 151, prefers a mistaken transposition from LUGAL-*ri,* an error occurring three times in this letter but nowhere else in the Jerusalem correspondence, though the work of the same scribe.

2. *zu-ru-uḫ* LUGAL-*ri* KALAG.GA (*dannatu*): cf. *EA* 147:12, and see Weippert, *UF* 6 (1974) p. 415, n. 2; not "the arm of the mighty king" (Albright). See also M. Görg, *Homages à François Daumas,* Institut d'Egyptologie, Université Paul Valéry (Montpellier, 1986), pp. 323ff.

3. "As long as the king lives, I (will) say" (Knudtzon, Ebeling, Albright) does not make much sense, whereas *adi* as asseverative/conditional ("whether") particle in an oath does: ʿAbdi-Ḫeba swears that what he actually said or did, as against the charges of rebellion, was nothing more than to accuse the commissioner(s) of preferring the king's enemies to his supporters.

4. *à-qa-bi*: see *Jerusalem Scribe,* p. 161, n. 37.

5. In view of the parallelism with *adi* in line 16 (see n. 3), *enūma* reflects Canaanite asseverative *kî* (cf. Albright's translation).

6. The Ili-Milku of line 36.

EA 287

A very serious crime

TEXT: VAT 1644 (not collated).
COPIES: WA 103; *VS* 11, 163.
PHOTOGRAPH: A. Jepsen, ed., *Von Sinuhe bis Nebukadnezar* (see *EA* 244, headnote), pl. 29.
TRANSLATIONS: Ebeling, pp. 375f.; C. Mullo Weir, in D. Winton Thomas, ed., *Documents from Old Testament Times* (London, 1958), pp. 39f.; Albright, *ANET,* p. 488; Freydank, in A. Jepsen, ed., *Von Sinuhe bis Nebukadnezar,* pp. 102f.; Seux, *Textes du Proche-Orient,* pp. 55ff.

[Say to the kin]g, m[y] lord: [Message of ʿAb]di-Ḫeba, yo[ur] servant. [I fall at the feet] of my lord 7 t[imes and 7 times. 4–9 *Consider*] *the ent⟨ire⟩* affair.[1] [*Milkilu and Tagi* brou]ght [*troop*]*s* into [*Qiltu*] *against me.*[2] [Consider] the deed that they did [*to your servant*].[3] Arrow(s)[4] [. . .] . . . 10–19 [. . .] they brought into [*Qilt*]*u*. May the [kin]g know (that) all the lands are [at] peace (with one another), but I am at war. May the king provide for his land. Consider the lands of Gazru, Ašqaluna, and *L*[*akis*]*i*.[5] They have given them food, oil, and any other requirement. So may the king provide for archers and[6] send the archers against men that commit crimes against the king, my lord. 20–24 If this year there are archers, then the lands and the mayors will belong to the king, my lord. But if there are no archers, then the ki[ng] will have neither lands nor mayors. 25–32 Consider Jerusalem! This neither my father nor m[y] mother gave to me. The [str]ong hand : *zu-ru-uḫ* (arm) [of the king] gave it to me.[7] Consider the deed! This is the deed of Milkilu and the deed of the sons of Lab'ayu, who have given the land of the king ⟨to⟩ the ʿApiru. Consider, O king, my lord! *I am in the right*![8] 33–42 With regard to the Kašites, may the king make inquiry of the commissioners. Though the house is well fortified, they attempted a very serious crime. They [t]ook their tools, and *I had to seek shelter by a support*[9] for the roof : *ga-ag-gi*. *A*[*nd so i*]*f* he is going to send [*troop*]*s* into [*Jerusalem*], let them come with [*a garrision for*] (regular) *service.*[10] May the king provide for them; [*all*] of the land *might be in dire straits*[11] on their account. 43–52 May the king inquire about the[m. Let there be][12] much food, much oil, much clothing, until Pauru, the commissioner of the king, comes up to Jerusalem. Gone[13] is Addaya together with the garrison of soldiers [that] the king [pro]vided. May the king know (that) Addaya [sa]id to me, "[Beh]old, he has dismissed me."[14] Do not abandon it, [and] send this [year] a garrison, and send right here[15] the commissioner of the king. 53–59 I sent [*as gift*]*s*[16] to the king, my lord, [x] prisoners, 5000 . . . [. . .],[17] [*and*] *8 porters*[18] for the caravans of the k[ing, my lord], but they have been taken in the countryside : *ša-de₄-e* of Ayyaluna. May the king, my lord, know (that) I am unable to send a caravan to the king, my lord. For your information! 60–63 As the king has placed his name in Jerusalem forever, he cannot abandon it—the land of Jerusalem.[19]

64–70 Say to the scribe of the king, my lord: Message of ʿAbdi-Ḫeba, your servant. I fall at (your) feet. I am your servant. Present eloquent words to the king, my lord: I am a soldier of the king. I *am always yours.*[20]

71–78 And please make the Kašites responsible for the evil deed.[21] I was almost killed by the Kašites [i]n my own house. May the king [*make an inquiry*] in the[ir] regard. [May the kin]g, my lord, [*provide*] for th[em. 7 t]imes and 7 times may the king, my lord, [*provide*] for me.[22]

NOTES

1. [a-mur g]áb-⟨bi⟩ *a-wa-ta*$_5$: all the letters from Jerusalem, with the exception of *EA* 286, begin the body of the letter with *amur*; cf. Na'aman, *Political Disposition*, p. 39*, n. 37.

2. Cf. Albright (see headnote), but other restorations are of course possible; see lines 29–31. Ventive, "against me"?

3. Or "did to me"; cf. *EA* 290:5.

4. ^{urudu}GAG.Ú.TAG.GA (*mulmullu, šiltāḫu*): following A. Sachs, *AfO* 12 (1937–39) pp. 371ff.

5. Enough room? See Na'aman, *Political Disposition*, p. 40*, n. 38.

6. *pi-ṭa-ti ú*: *ú* for *u*, "and," sporadically in *EA* and elsewhere; see *JAOS* 100 (1980) p. 186; Schramm, *Einleitung in die assyrischen Königsinschriften*, pt. 2 (Leiden and Cologne, 1973), p. 2.

7. See *EA* 286, n. 2. On ^{lú}AD.DA.A.NI, logogram with frozen pronominal suffix (cf. *EA* 3, n. 2), see *Jerusalem Scribe*, p. 163, n. 52, and Huehnergard, *Ugaritic Vocabulary*, p. 48, n. 2, and his criticisms of Weippert, *UF* 6 (1974) pp. 415ff. (The DUMU.A.NI *iš-ki-ba-al*, *Iraq* 32 [1970] p. 27:2, should be read, with I. Gelb, DUMU *A-ni-iš-ki-ba-al*; private communication of C. B. F. Walker.)

8. *ṣaduq ana iyāši*: translation, with Albright, according to context (criminal charges against enemies), but the assumed impersonal subject—lit. "it is right for me"—is difficult; see Feigin, *JQR* 34 (1943–44) pp. 443ff. For a different version, "it is the king my master that is *ṣaduq* for me," *ṣaduq* = "generous," see H. Cazelles, *JANES* 5 (1973) p. 76.

9. aš-⸢ru-ú⸣: cf. *šerû* (*AHw*, p. 1220), with accusative of place, but no satisfactory explanation of the apparent durative (*yaqtulu*). For earlier proposals and various possible readings, see Feigin, *JQR* 34 (1943–44) pp. 449ff. Albright, against the copy, read *bat-⸢qú-ú⸣*, "they breached" (see already Feigin, p. 449); Na'aman, *Political Disposition*, p. 91, reads ⟨*e*⟩-*tel-⸢lu-ú⸣*, "they climbed up." As copied, the first sign is considerably larger than the BE on lines 37 and 45.

37 [*e*⸣-*mid* (*imdu*): following an earlier reading of Albright, later retracted (see *ANET*). After the gloss, ⸢ù] 38 [šum-m]a.

10. 39 ÉRIN].MEŠ *ti-ta-lu it-ti* [LÚ ma-ṣar-ti] 40 [a-na] ÌR.MEŠ: *ana ardūti*, with Albright (cf. *EA* 157, n. 1). ʿAbdi-Ḫeba asks, not for a punitive expedition, but for troops stationed permanently in Jerusalem that will give him the needed protection (cf. lines 46f.). The assumption of *ti-ta-lu* as erroneous for *ti-la-tu*, "auxiliary troops," a proposal of Na'aman, *Political Disposition*, p. 91, and Rainey, *Studies in Bible* (see *EA* 286, n. 1), p. 144, seems unnecessary and unlikely. Albright restores [^{lú}*ú-e-e*] (cf. line 47), and translates "officer." Egyptian *wʿw*, however, referred to an infantryman (lowest grade) or simply a soldier; see A. R. Schulman, *Military Rank, Title, and Organization in the Egyptian New Kingdom*,

Münchner ägyptologische Studien, vol. 6 (Berlin, 1964), pp. 36f.; *EA* 288, n. 1.

11. *ta-ṣa-qa*: cf. perhaps Hebrew *ṣûq*; form, *yaqtula* (cf. *teppaša* in line 71). A more venturesome proposal is found in Rainey, *Studies in Bible* (see *EA* 286, n. 1), p. 149.

12. *lišâl ana šâšu*[*nu lu-ú*]: *šâlu* does not mean "requisition" (Albright, Seux), and *mād* seems to be a predicate, not attributive, adjective (private communication of D. Gropp).

13. On the use of the infinitive (*paṭāri*), see *JCS* 6 (1952) p. 77.

14. Against "let me go" (Albright)—apart from the difficulties of form (*paṭranni* for expected *puṭranni*)—is the unlikelihood of a high Egyptian official's asking permission from a local ruler for anything. The subject understood is the king. The dismissal of Addaya—i.e., sending him elsewhere—arouses ʿAbdi-Ḫeba's fears that the king is going to abandon Jerusalem to its own resources.

15. *annikānu,* "here," its initial position in the sentence stressing Jerusalem as the place a commissioner should be stationed; see *Jerusalem Scribe,* p. 154.

16. [NÍG.BA].ḪI.A: following Albright; cf. *EA* 288:22.

17. Albright, "silver (shekels)," but the copy is against K[Ù.BABBAR].

18. Before "8" Knudtzon saw traces that he tentatively read as "318."

19. See *Jerusalem Scribe,* p. 162, n. 46.

20. *ma-at-ti*: a desperate crux; cf. Hebrew *tāmîd* and perhaps *md,* "to endure"(?), in Amorite personal names (see Huffmon, *APNMT,* p. 229). Albright translated as "insignificant(?)," as if *ma-ṭi-ti* (*maṭû*), and Finkelstein, *Eretz Israel* 9 (1969) pp. 33f., as "I would surely die (for you)," but the modal force of the perfect is questionable, and one may doubt whether it is possible to die "very much" (*magal, EA* 289:50).

21. On lines 71–72, see *Jerusalem Scribe,* p. 164, n. 61.

22. Restoring *liskin* in both breaks, with Na'aman, *Political Disposition,* p. 92, but understanding the first instance as provision in terms of justice for the Kašites, not of provision or concern for the garrison, which has not been mentioned for over 20 lines. Albright's "avenge" assumes [*li-iq-qí-im*] and an unsupported Canaanitism (*nqm*); see W. Pitard, *Maarav* 3/1 (1982) pp. 5ff.

On messages to the scribes of addressees, see the Introduction, sect. 4, n. 58.

EA 288

Benign neglect

TEXT: VAT 1643 (not collated).

COPIES: WA 103; *VS* 11, 164.

TRANSLATIONS: Ebeling, pp. 376f.; C. Mullo Weir, in D. Winton Thomas, ed., *Documents from Old Testament Times,* pp. 43f.; Albright, *ANET,* pp. 488f.; Freydank, in A. Jepsen, ed., *Von Sinuhe bis Nebukadnezar,* pp. 103f.

Say [t]o the king, my lord, [my Su]n: [M]essage of ʿAbdi-Ḫeba, your servant. I fall at the feet of the king, my lord, 7 times and 7 times. 5–10 Behold, the king, my lord, has placed his name at the rising of the sun and at the setting of the sun. It is, therefore, impious what they have done to me. Behold, I am not a mayor; I am a soldier of the king, my lord.[1] 11–15 Behold, I am a *friend* of the king and a tribute-bearer[2] of the king. It was neither my father nor my mother, but the strong arm of the king that [p]laced me in the house of [my] fath[er].[3] 16–22 [. . . c]ame to me. . . . [. . .]. I gave over [to *his* char]ge 10 slaves. Šuta, the commissioner of the king, ca[me t]o me; I gave over to Šuta's charge 21 girls,[4] [8]0 prisoners, as a gift for the king, my lord. 23–28 May the king give thought to his land; the land of the king is lost. *All of it has attacked* me.[5] I am at war as far as the land of Šeru and as far as Ginti-kirmil. All the mayors are at peace, but I am at war. 29–33 I am treated like an ʿApiru,[6] and I do not visit the king, my lord, since I am at war. I am situated like a ship[7] in the midst of the sea. 34–40 The strong hand (arm) of the king took the land of Naḫrima and the land of *Kasi*,[8] but now the ʿApiru have taken the very cities of the king.[9] Not a single mayor remains to the king, my lord; all are lost. 41–47 Behold, Turbazu was slain in the city gate of Silu. The king did nothing. Behold, servants who were joined to the ʿApi[r]u *smote*[10] Zimredda of Lakisu, and Yaptiḫ-Hadda was slain in the city gate of Silu. The king did nothing. [*Wh*]*y* has he not called them to account? 48–53 May the king [pro]vide for [his land] and may he [se]e to it tha[t] archers [come ou]t to h[is] land.[11] If there are no archers this year, all the lands of the king, my lord, are lost. 54–61 They have not reported to the king that the lands of the king, my lord, are lost and all the mayors lost. If there are no archers this year, may the king send a commissioner to fetch me, me along with my brothers, and then we will die near the king, our lord. 62–66 [To] the scribe of the king, my lord: [Message] of ʿAbdi-Ḫeba, (your) servant. [I fa]ll a[t (your) feet]. Present [the words that I hav]e offered[12] to [the king, my lord]: I am your servant [and] your [s]on.

NOTES

1. ʿAbdi-Ḫeba does not deny that he is a soldier (so Albright); cf. *EA* 285:5–6, and see the remarks of Liverani, *RA* 61 (1967) p. 15, n. 4. Israelit-Groll, in M. Görg, ed., *Fontes atque pontes* (see *EA* 3, n. 17), p. 238, is of the view that Egyptian *we'u* (*wʿw*) here means "post commander."

2. On ^{lú}*ru-ḫi*, "friend"(?), see Donner, *ZAW* 73 (1961) pp. 269ff. *ūbil*, "bearer," like *ūbilī* in *EA* 287:55, or "I have brought."

3. See *EA* 287, n. 7.

4. MUNUS.DUMU.MUNUS, *ṣuhārtu*?

5. Cf. *tiṣbutu*, "to seize one another, fight." The usual version, "all of it has been taken from me" (Knudtzon, followed more or less by Ebeling, Albright, et al.), has against it not only the assumption of a separative accusative (another example in *EA*?), but the fact that *all* of the king's land cannot be taken from a vassal because he never had all of it to lose.

6. *enūma* [lú]*ḫapiri*: translation with Albright, who recognized that *enūma*, used commonly as a synonym of *kīma* as conjunction, is here also given the latter's meaning as preposition.

7. *enūma eleppi*: see n. 6.

8. KUR *ka*-⟨⟨pa⟩⟩-*si*: following Rainey, AOAT², p. 105, perhaps for *ka-a-si*.

9. Though royal power is sufficient to achieve conquests far to the north and far to the south, so very close by are the conquests of the ʿApiru.

10. *ig-gi-ú-šu*: following Ebeling, *VAB* 2/2, p. 1546, for *yiggeʿū-šu*. Bottéro, *Ḫabiru*, p. 109, reads *iq-qì-ú-šu*, "slaves ... have immolated(?) him," as if from *naqû*.

11. [*u l*]*iddin šarru pānīšu* ⌜*ù*⌝ [*lu-ṣi-m*]*i* 50 [LÚ.MEŠ] ÉRIN.MEŠ *pi-ṭa-ti a-na* KUR-*š*[*u*]; cf. *li-din* LUGAL *pa-ni-šu a-na* LÚ.MEŠ *pi-ṭa-ti ù lu-ṣi-mi* LÚ.MEŠ ÉRIN *pi-ṭa-ti*, in *EA* 286:53f. The reading 49 ... ⌜*ù*⌝ [*lu-ma-še-e*]*r* 50 [LUGAL] (so Albright) accords with neither the space nor the traces. There is no reason why -*m*]*i* belongs at the end of line 50 (Knudtzon) rather than line 49.

12. 65 [*ša na*]-⌜*ad*⌝-*na-ti*: following Na'aman, *Political Disposition*, p. 37*, n. 19.

EA 289

A reckoning demanded

TEXT: VAT 1645 + 2709.
COPIES: WA 105 + WA 199; *VS* 11, 165.
TRANSLATIONS: Ebeling, pp. 377f.; Albright, *ANET*, p. 489; Campbell, *Shechem*, pp. 200f.; Seux, *Textes du Proche-Orient*, pp. 58f.

[Say t]o the king, my lord: Message of ʿAbdi-Ḫeba, your servant. I f[all] at the feet of my lord, the k[ing], 7 times and 7 times. 5–10 Milkilu does not break away from the sons of Lab'ayu and from the sons of Arsawa, as they desire the land of the king for themselves. As for a mayor who does such a deed, why does the king not ⟨c⟩all him to account? 11–17 Such was the deed that Milkilu and Tagi did: they took Rubutu. And now as for Jerusalem, if this land belongs to the king, why is it ⟨*not*⟩ *of concern*[1] to the king like Ḫazzatu? 18–24 Gintikirmil belongs to Tagi, and men of Gintu are the garrison in Bitsanu.[2] Are we to act like Lab'ayu when he was giving the land of Šakmu to the

Ḫapiru? 25–36 Milkilu has written to Tagi and the sons ⟨*of Lab'ayu*⟩, "Be *the both of you a protection.*[3] Grant all their demands to the men of Qiltu, and let us isolate Jerusalem."[4] Addaya has taken the garrison that you sent in the charge of Haya, the son of Miyare; he has stationed it in his own house in Ḫazzatu and has sent 20 men to Egypt. May the king, my lord, know (that) no garrison of the king is with me. 37–44 Accordingly, as truly as the king lives, his *irpi*-official,[5] Pu'uru, has left me and is in Ḫazzatu. (May the king *call* (*this*) *to mind when he arrives.*)[6] And so may the king send 50 men as a garrison to protect the land. The entire land of the king has deser[ted]. 45–51 Send Ye⟨⟨eh⟩⟩enḫamu that he may know about the land of the king, [my lord]. To the scribe of the king, [my lord: M]essage of ʿAbdi-Ḫeba, [your] servant. Offer eloq[uent] words to the king: *I am always, utterly yours.*[7] I am your servant.

NOTES

1. With Albright, *CAH* 2/2, p. 116; cf. *ina libbi šakānu*? On *enūma*, "like," see *EA* 288, n. 6.

2. His enemies make up the protective forces to the north. "Who will guard the guardians?"

3. *lu-ú* 2 *ṣíl-la-tu-nu*: difficult and obscure; see *Jerusalem Scribe*, p. 162, n. 42, and the remarks on the reading *lu-ú a-mi-la-tu-nu*, "be men" (*AHw*, p. 90b). Other emendations: *lu* É-*mi at-tu-nu*, "you are of my house" (Albright, *ANET*; Campbell); *lu-ú ṣa-mi at-tu-nu*, "as for you, go on" (Albright, *CAH* 2/2, p. 116, n. 6; imperative of *aṣû*?).

4. *lū nipṭur*: lit. "let us separate"; perhaps, "let us desert." By their generosity to Qiltu they would entice the city to their side and thereby isolate Jerusalem; see Na'aman, *Political Disposition*, p. 100.

5. *ir-pí*: following *AHw*, p. 386; MAŠKIM (*rābiṣu*, "commissioner" [so Albright and Campbell]) is excluded.

6. A reading *li-is-kìn* (Albright and Campbell), instead of *li-iz-kur*, is excluded because of the assumed *kìn* (a value unknown in *EA*) and the construction (all nine occurrences of *sakānu* are with *ana*, never *ina pānī*).

7. See *EA* 287, n. 20.

EA 290

Three against one

TEXT: VAT 1646.

COPIES: WA 106; *VS* 11, 166.

TRANSLATIONS: Ebeling, p. 378; Albright, *ANET*, p. 489; Seux, *Textes du Proche-Orient*, pp. 58f.

[Sa]y [t]o the king, my lord: Message of [ʿAbdi]-Ḫeba, your servant. I fall at the feet [of the kin]g, my lord, 7 times and 7 times. 5–13 Here is the deed *against the land*[1] that Milkilu and Šuardatu did: against the land of the king, my lord, they *ordered*[2] troops from Gazru, troops from Gimtu, and troops from Qiltu. They seized Rubutu. The land of the king deserted to the Ḫapiru. 14–21 And now, besides this, a town belonging to Jerusalem, Bit-^{d}NIN.URTA by name, a city of the king, has gone over to the side of the men of Qiltu. May the king give heed to ʿAbdi-Ḫeba, your servant, and send archers to restore the land of the king to the king. 22–30 If there are no archers, the land of the king will desert to the Ḫapiru. This deed *against the land*[3] was [a]t the order of Milki[lu and a]t the order[4] of [Suard]atu, [*together w*]*ith* Gint[i].[5] So may the king provide for [his] land.

NOTES

1. *ipša* KUR (*ipšu* KUR, line 25): not *ipša* gloss-marker (Knudtzon, followed by Ebeling and Albright, who ignores the KUR in line 25). Na'aman, *Political Disposition*, p. 51*, n. 19, suggests a syllabic writing, KUR = KÚR, "hostile."

2. *mu-'ì-ru*: see *Jerusalem Scribe*, p. 151. Other solutions: "they hired" (Knudtzon, Ebeling; cf. Hebrew *mohar*, "bride-price"); "they rushed" (Albright; cf. Hebrew *nimhar*, "to hasten"); "they were taken in" (*CAD*, M/1, p. 68, Akkadian *muḫḫuru*); "they assembled" (emending *mu* to *pu*, Greenberg, *Ḫab/piru*, p. 49, followed by Rainey, *Studies in Bible* [see *EA* 286, n. 1], p. 150).

3. See n. 1.

4. ⸢*a-na*⸣ KA-*i* ... 27 [*ù a*]-*na* KA-*i*: following Albright.

5. URU *gin*$_8$-*t*[*i*]: with copy and Schroeder, *OLZ*, 1915, col. 175.

EA 291

Message lost

TEXT: VAT 1713.
COPY: *VS* 11, 167.

Too fragmentary for translation.[1]

NOTE

1. A letter from Jerusalem; see *VAB* 2/2, p. 1344, n. 1; note, too, the form of *ti* and *li*, and the verbal form *lumaššer*.

EA 292

Like a pot held in pledge

TEXT: BM 37647.
COPY: Scheil, *Mémoires,* p. 298.
TRANSLATION: Albright, *ANET,* pp. 489f.

Say to the king, my lord, [my] go[d], my Sun: Message of Adda-danu,[1] your servant, the dirt at your feet. I fall at the feet of the king, my lord, my god, my Sun, 7 times and 7 times. 8–13 I looked this way, and I looked that way, and there was no light. Then I looked towards the king, my lord, and there was light. 13–17 A brick may move from under its partner, still I will not move from under the feet of the king, my lord.[2] 17–26 I have heard the orders that the king, my lord, wrote to his servant, "Guard your commissioner, and guard the cities of the king, your lord." I do indeed guard, and I do indeed obey the orders of the king, my lord, day and night. 26–40 May the king, my lord, be informed about his servant. There being war against me from the mountains, I built : *b*[*a*]-*n*[*i*]-*t*[*i*][3] a house—its (the village's) name is Manḫatu—to make preparations before the arrival of the archers of the king, my lord, and Maya has just taken it away from me and placed his commissioner in it. Enjoin Reanap, my commissioner, to restore my village to me, as I am making preparations before the arrival of the archers of the king, my lord. 41–52 Moreover, consider the deed of Peya, the son of Gulatu, against Gazru, the maidservant of the king, my lord. How long has he gone on plundering it so that it has become, thanks to him, like a pot held in pledge.[4] People are ransomed from the mountains for 30 shekels of silver, but from Peya for 100 shekels.[5] Be informed of these affairs of your servant.

NOTES

1. The reading of the name, written ^{d}IM-DI.KUD remains a matter of discussion. See *RA* 69 (1975) pp. 153f.; Izre'el, *Tel Aviv* 4 (1977) pp. 159ff.; idem, *IOS* 8 (1978) p. 15, n. 16; Na'aman, *UF* 11 (1979) p. 681, n. 38.

2. Lines 8ff.: cf. the virtually identical introductions of *EA* 266 and 296.

3. The reading of the gloss is not entirely certain.

4. Cf. *EA* 297:12ff. *ri-qi* = *riqqu,* a byform of *ruqqu* (*AHw,* p. 995, *ruqqu* I); *ḫu-bu-li,* in view of *ḫu-bu-ul-li* in *EA* 297:14, must derive from *ḫubullu,* "debt, interest," and "the pot of a debt" makes sense only as a type of security held until the debt is paid. The modesty of such a security carries with it, too, the implications of extreme poverty. This line of thought leads to the redemption in the following lines.

5. According to *PRU* 3, pp. 7f., the king of Carchemish paid a ransom of 50 shekels to get someone from the Suteans.

EA 293

Always on the watch

TEXT: C 4774 (12231).
COPY: WA 201.

[Say to the king], my [lord, my god], my [Sun: Me]ssage of A[dda-d]anu,[1] [your] ser[vant, the di]rt at your feet. I fall [at] the feet of the king, my lord, my god, my Sun, 7 times and [7] times. 8–13 [I h]ave heard[2] the order that the king, my lord, wrote to his servant, "Guard the place of the king where you are." I am indeed guarding day and night. 14–22 Since[3] ...[4] the king, my lord, ...[5]

NOTES

1. ^{md}x-⌜D⌝I.KUD: the second determinative (*deus*) is virtually certain, and is almost identical with the determinative in ^{d}UTU-*ia* (line 6) (also Gordon). The next sign is doubtful only because so little is preserved, and this is compatible with IM. In view of the otherwise (except *EA* 294) unparalleled features common to *EA* 292–93, there can be no doubt about the identity of the sender of this letter.
2. [*i*]*š-te-mi*: following Gordon.
3. *i-nu-ma*: the first sign is completely preserved (also Gordon); perhaps "when, as to the fact that."
4. Traces of LÚ?.KÚR? (Gordon).
5. Lines 16–22, too badly damaged for translation.

EA 294

Unquestioning obedience

TEXT: BM 29854.
COPY: BB 71.
PHOTOGRAPH: BB, pl. 1.

Say to the king, my lord, my god, my Sun: Message of Ad[d]a-[d]anu,[1] your servant. I fall at the feet of the king, my lord, my god, my Sun, 7 times and 7 times. 6–13 I have heard the orders that the king, my lord, wrote to his servant, "Obey your commissioner, and guard the cities of the king, your lord, where you are." I am indeed obeying the orders that the king, my lord, gave me. 14–24 May the king, my lord, be informed about his servant. Consider the deed of Peya, the son of Gulatu, [against] me. My men whom I sent to serve in Yapu and to guard the house : *šu-nu-ti* (granary)[2] of the king, my lord, Peya, the son of Gulatu, has just taken.[3] 25–35 May the king, my lord, be informed of these affairs of his servant. If the king, my lord, says this to me, "Abandon your city, (fleeing) from before Peya,"[4] then of course I will abandon it, and I will come and of course serve the king, my lord, day and night, forever.

NOTES

1. On the syllabic writing here and the contested readings, see *EA* 292, n. 1.
2. *šu-nu-ti* = Egyptian *šnwtj*: see Helck, *MDOG* 92 (1960) p. 11.
3. Cf. *EA* 292:41ff.
4. A pregnant expression very reminiscent of *Isaiah* 17:9, *ka*^{ʿa}*zûbat* . . . '^{a}*šer* ʿ*āz*^{e}*bû mipp*^{e}*nê b*^{e}*nê yiśrā'ēl,* "like the region deserted by the . . . that they deserted (fleeing) from before the sons of Israel."

EA 295

A servant from head to toe

TEXT: VAT 1650.
COPIES: WA 88; *VS* 11, 168.

[Sa]y [to the king], my lord, my Sun, my g[od: Message of . . .]-DI.KUD,[1] your servant, a loy[al] servant, [the dirt] beneath the sandals of the [ki]ng, my lord. I fall at the feet of the king, my lord, my Sun, my god, 7 [times] and 7 times. 8–11 I am indeed the servant of the king, my lord, who serves the king, my lord, [*from*] my head to my feet, just as my [an]cestors[2] (have done) since time immemori[al]. 12–15 May the king, [my] lord, be i[nformed] of the de[ed that] Yab[*ni*-. . . , *the ruler of S*]*idon*[3] [d]id to me. 15–22 . . . [. . .] Evil [*was done* . . .], and he fell [*upon* . . .], along with *the d*[*og, the ruler of* . . .],[4] along with *h*[*is*] brothers [. . .], along with *the men of the l*[*and of* . . .], and *he assemb*[*led* . . .] . . .

Reverse

[. . .] 3–10 *E*[*vi*]*l* [*has* (*also*) *b*]*een don*[*e*] to [*my*] partner.[5] May the king be informed of [*my*] *loy*[*alty*], and may the king, [my] lord, give 50 men along with the *garr*[*ison*] commander[6] to guard the city : *ti-e-ti* (. . .)[7] *f*[*or the king*]. I am indeed prepa[ring] my caravan and my intention is to go (to Egypt) to serve the king.

NOTES

1. Na'aman, *UF* 11 (1979) pp. 673ff., has shown that *EA* 295 was sent by a ruler of Tyre. He was probably the predecessor of Abi-Milku (*EA* 146–55), and the one killed in a palace revolt (see *EA* 89). The scribe of *EA* 295 is not the same as that of *EA* 146–55; perhaps he too perished with his master.

2. [*a-bu*]-*ti-ia*: so also Na'aman. The syllabic writing without the determinative LÚ is found only at Byblos and Tyre.

3. From Knudtzon's description of traces before -*du-na* (*VAB* 2/1, p. 887, note f), no longer visible even to Schroeder, Na'aman proposes [... LÚ URU ṣ]í-*du-na*; see *UF* 11 (1979) p. 673 (also Gordon).

4. *qa-du* ᵐ*ka-a*[*l*-bi LÚ URU ...]: for the determinative, see Böhl, *Sprache*, p. 9; however, a syllabic writing of ***kalbu*** is found elsewhere in *EA* only in *EA* 320:22 and 322:17.

5. [a-p]í-i[š]: if correct, this occurs elsewhere only at Byblos (*a-pí-eš*, 5 times), and always passive. Was the partner ("partners" is also possible) the ruler of Byblos? (See n. 1, and cf. *EA* 264, n. 2.)

6. LÚ.IGI.KÁR EN.[NUN/NU.UN]: in favor of EN.NUN (*maṣṣartu*), "garrison," are the task assigned to the men and the fact that 50 is a common number for manning a garrison (see *EA* 139:32; 238:11; 289:42). LÚ.IGI.KÁR, perhaps *āširu* or *pāqidu*, and *āšir*/*pāqid maṣṣarti* may correspond to Egyptian *ỉmy-r jwʿjt*, "overseer of the garrison." For further discussion, see *Acta Sumerologica Japonensia* 5 (1983) p. 176, and cf. *EA* 337, n. 1.

7. Cf. *EA* 152:48.

EA 296

Under the yoke

TEXT: BM 29840.

COPY: BB 57.

PHOTOGRAPH: Pfeiffer, *Tell el Amarna and the Bible* (see *EA* 205, headnote), p. 11 (reverse only).

TRANSLATION: Oppenheim, *LFM*, pp. 125f.

Say to the king, my lord, my god, my [Sun]: Message of Ya[ḫ]tiru, your servant, the dirt at your feet. I fall at the feet of the king, my lord, my god, my Sun, 7 times and 7 times. 9–16 Moreover, I am indeed the loyal servant of the king, my lord. I looked this way, and I looked that way, and there was no light. Then I looked towards the king, my lord, and there was light. 17–22 A brick : *la-bi-tu* may move from [un]der its partner, still I will not move from under the feet of the king, my lord.[1] 23–29 May the king, my lord, inquire of Yanḫamu, his commissioner. When I was young, he brought me into Egypt. I served the king, my lord, and I stood at the city gate of the king, my lord.

30–35 May the king, my lord, inquire of his commissioner whether I guard the city gate of Azzatu and the city gate of Yapu, and (whether) where the archers of the king, my lord, march, I *m*[*arch*][2] with them. And indeed, now that I have [*p*]*la*[*ced*] the . . .[3] of the yoke : *ḫu-ul-lu* of the king, my lord, on my neck, I carry it.

NOTES

1. Lines 9ff.: see *EA* 292, n. 2.
2. After *it-*. . . , I could see nothing.
3. Traces impossible to read.

EA 297

The sweet breath of the king

TEXT: BM 29834.
COPY: BB 51.
PHOTOGRAPH: BB, pl. 5.
TRANSLATION: Albright, *ANET,* p. 490.

Say to the king, my lord, my god, my Sun: Message of Yapaḫu, your servant, the dirt at your feet. I fall at the feet of the king, my lord, my god, my Sun, 7 times and 7 times. 8–16 Whatsoever the king, my lord, has said to me, I have listened to with the greatest care. Moreover, I have become like a (bronze) pot : *sí-ri*[1] given in pledge, because of the Suteans. 17–21 I have, however, just heard the sweet breath of the king. It has come forth to me, and my heart is very content.[2]

NOTES

1. *ki-ma ri-qí* URUDU : *sí-ri*: on *riqqi,* see *EA* 292, n. 4. To judge from the synonymous gloss *sîri,* URUDU is probably best taken as a determinative. As to the gloss, Rainey, *UF* 5 (1973) p. 251, n. 82, compared Hebrew *sîr,* but this had already been assumed by Albright, as seems clear from his translation, "an empty [*rīqi*] bronze [URUDU] cauldron [*sîri*]," and he restored the gloss in *EA* 292:46. On the position of the gloss, not in the previous line (Knudtzon), *sí-ri* is written higher than the rest of line 13, but this seems to have been occasioned by the scribe's awareness of the lack of room; *ri* is even higher than *sí,* and the writing slopes gradually upward. See also *EA* 292, n. 4.
2. See *EA* 100, n. 9.

EA 298

A perfidious younger brother

TEXT: BM 29833.
COPY: BB 50.
TRANSLATIONS: Albright, *ANET,* p. 490; Freydank, in A. Jepsen, ed., *Von Sinuhe bis Nebukadnezar,* p. 100.

[T]o the king, my lord, my god, my Sun, the Sun from the sky: Message of Yapa[ḫ]u, the ruler of Gazru, your servant, the dirt at your feet, the groom of your horses. I prostrate myself at the feet of the king, my lord, the Sun from the sky, 7 times and 7 times, both on the stomach and on the back. 14–19 Whatsoever the king, my lord, has said to me, I have listened to very carefully. I am a servant of the king and the dirt at your feet. 20–33 May the king, my lord, be informed that my younger brother, having become my enemy, entered Muḫḫazu and pledged hi⟨m⟩self to[1] the ʿApiru. As [Ti]anna[2] is at war with me, take thought for your land. May my lord write to his commissioner with regard to this deed.

NOTES

1. *qa-⟨ti⟩-šu*: "to give the hands" is understood, with Greenberg, *Ḫab/piru,* p. 49, in the light of Hebrew parallels; *CAD,* N/1, p. 54, "to join."

2. Cf. URU *t*[*i*]-i[a-n]a (*EA* 284:31) and [KUR/URU ti-a]n-*na*^{ki} (*EA* 306:34), following Na'aman, *UF* 11 (1979), p. 679, n. 28.

EA 299

A plea for help

TEXT: BM 29832.
COPY: BB 49.
PHOTOGRAPH: Barnett, *Illustrations,* p. 14.

To the king, my lord, my god, the Sun, the Sun [f]rom the sky: Message of Yapaḫu, the ruler of Gazru, your servant, the dirt at your feet, the groom of your horses. Truly I fall at the feet of the king, my lord, my god, my Sun, the Sun from the sky, 7 times and 7 times, on the stomach and on the back. 12–21 I have listened to the words of the messenger of the king, my lord, very carefully. May the king, my lord, the Sun from the sky, take thought for his land. Since the ʿApiru are stronger than we, may the king, my lord, ⟨g⟩ive[1] me his help, and may *the king*, my lord, get *me*[2] away from the ʿApiru lest the ʿApiru destroy us.

NOTES

1. ⟨*yú*⟩-*uš-ši-ra*: following Izre'el, *Tel Aviv* 4 (1977) p. 163.

2. *yi-it-ra*-⌜ni⌝: the last sign, which is more probably -*ni* than -*nu*, "us," seems to have been written over LUGAL, which should probably be ignored in the translation; cf. *EA* 298:31, *bēlīya* alone. For the reading, see Bottéro, *Ḫabiru*, p. 110; Na'aman, *UF* 11 (1979) p. 679, n. 29.

EA 300

A servant like his father

TEXT: VAT 1606.
COPY: *VS* 11, 171.

[*Say* to the king], my [lor]d, [my g]o[d, my Sun, the Su]n f[rom the sky: Message of *Yapaḫu*], *the r*[*uler of G*]*a*[*zru*], your serv[ant, the dirt at] your feet, the g[ro]o[m of] your [hor]ses. [I fa]ll at the f[ee]t [of the king, m]y lord, 7 times and 7 times. 10–14 [*May the king, my lord, m*]*y* [*god, know th*]*at the means of sub*[*sistence have disappea*]*red* [fr]om my [coun]try, and *in*⟨*d*⟩*eed* I *have* [*nothin*]*g at all.*[1] 15–22 May he send [*hi*]*s a*[*rcher*]*s*. It is they alone who [. . .] must get me back into my cities so I can serve the king, my lord, in accordance with (the practice of) my father and [*his fr*]*iendly deeds.*[2]

23–28 I have indeed o[bey]ed the or[ders] of the king, my lord, and I obey [al]l the orders of May[a, the com]mi[ssio]ner of the [k]ing, my lord, [the Sun] from the sky, the s[on] of the Sun.

NOTES

1. 10 [*am*]-*qut* [li-de-m]i [LUGAL EN-ia] 11 [DINGIR.M]E[Š-i]*a* ⌜i-n⌝[u-ma] 12 T[I.LA? ḫal]-*qa i*[*š*]-*tu* 13 KUR-*ia u a*-⟨nu⟩-ma *ia-nu* m[i-im-m]a *a-na ia-ši*: see also Izre'el, *IOS* 8 (1978) p. 14, n. 15; Na'aman, *UF* 11 (1979) p. 679, n. 30.

2. Against t[a-*p*]*á-ti*-[šu], "his (female) partner," understood either of the local queen (*VAB* 2/2, p. 1348) or of the writer of *EA* 273f. (Gordon), is the fact that *tappû* (4 times) and *tappâtu* (3 times; note that *EA* 292:14 was perhaps written by the same scribe as *EA* 300) are always written with the *tap*-sign. For ṭ[á-*b*]*a-ti*-[šu], plural of *ṭābtu*, see *EA* 136, n. 5.

EA 301

500 oxen and 20 girls

TEXT: C 4781 (12214).
COPY: WA 117.

To the [k]ing, my lord, the [Sun] fr[om] the sky: Message of Šuban[d]u, your servant, the dirt at your feet. I prostrate myself, on the stomach and on the back, at the feet of the king, my lord, my god, my Sun, the Sun from the sky, 7 times and 7 times. 12–23 The king, my lord, the Sun from the sky, sent Ḫanya to me, and I have indeed listened to the [w]ords of the king, my lord, [ve]ry carefully, and I herewith g[iv]e 500 oxen and 20 girls.[1] For the information of the king, my lord, the Sun from the sky.

NOTE

1. The position of the one clear vertical and the traces I thought I could see favor, I believe, Knudtzon's reading of "500" or "300"; Gordon could see nothing besides the single vertical. The reading "20" is virtually certain.

EA 302

Preparations as ordered

TEXT: VAT 332.
COPIES: WA 120; *VS* 11, 172.

To the king, my lord, my god, my Sun, the Sun from the [s]ky: Message of Šuban[d]u, your servant, the dirt at your feet. I prostrate myself at the feet of the king, my lord, the Sun from the sky, 7 times and 7 times. 11–18 As to the messenger whom the king, my lord, sent to me, I have listened to his words [ve]ry carefully, [and] I am indeed [ma]king the preparations j[ust as h]e commanded.

EA 303

Careful listening

TEXT: BM 29821.
COPY: BB 38.

To the king, my lord, my god, my Sun, the Sun from the sky: Message of Šubandu, your servant, and the dirt at your feet, the groom of your horses. 7–12 I prostrate myself, on the stomach and on the back, at the feet of the king, my lord, the Sun from the sky, 7 times and 7 times. 13–18 I have heard [a]ll the words of the king, my [lord], the Sun from the [s]ky, and I am indeed [g]uarding the place [of the kin]g where I am. 19–21 I have listened [t]o Taḫmašši [ve]ry carefully.

EA 304

Guarding the place of the king

TEXT: BM 29822.
COPY: BB 39.
PHOTOGRAPH: BB, pl. 12.

To the king, [my lord, my god], my Sun, the Sun from the sky: Message of Šubandu, your servant, the dirt at [your] feet, the groom of your [hor]ses. 8–14 I [p]ro[st]rate myself, on the [st]omach and on the b[a]ck, at the feet [of the king], my lord, the Sun [fr]om the sky, 7 times and 7 times. 15–24 I have heard the words of the t[ab]let of the king, my lord, that he s[e]nt me, and I am indeed [g]uarding the place of the king, my lord, where I am. May the king take cognizance [of] his lands.

EA 305

The power of the ʿApiru

TEXT: C 4780 (12215).
COPY: WA 116.

To the king, my lord, the Sun from the sky, my god, my Sun: Message of Šubandu, your servant, the dirt at your feet, the groom of your horses. 8–14 I indeed prostrate myself, on the stomach and on the back, at the feet of the king, my lord, the Sun from the sky, 7 times and 7 times. 15–24 I have heard the words of the king, my lord, that he sent me, and I am indeed guarding the place of the k[i]ng where I am. As the ʿApiru are more p[ow]erful than we, may the king take cognizance of his lands.

EA 306

Vicarious homage

TEXT: BM 29823.
COPY: BB 40.

[To the king, my lord, my god, m]y [Sun, the Sun from the sky: Mess]age of Šuban[du, your servant, the di]rt at [your] f[eet, the groo]m of [your horses]. I [in]deed prostrate myself at the feet of the king, my lord, the Sun from the sky, 7 times and 7 times, on the stomach and on the back. 12–18 As to the king, my lord's, having written, "[*Co*]*me a*[*nd pay homage to*] the king, yo[ur] lord,"[1] [*to w*]*ho*[*m*] *can I l*[*eave the king's city*]?[2] *The war is se*[*ver*]*e.* I am a servant of the king who *kn*[*ow*]*s*[3] the land of the king, my lord. 19–27 I indeed tire myself out in order to guard the land of the king. Being hard pressed,[4] I herewith send another servant of the king *to proc*[*eed*] *direc*[*tly*] (*to you*)[5] and to pay [homage] to the king, the Sun from the sky. 28–35 And may you, my lord, know that they have set fire to your cities and your places.[6] [As *Tia*]nna[7] [*is at war against you*]*r* [*servant*], [. . .] . . .[8]

NOTES

1. [a]l-*ka*-[m]e ⌜ù⌝ [du-gu-ul pa-ni] 14 LUGAL *be-lí-k*[*a*]: if Knudtzon's copy of the first sign (*VAB* 2/1, p. 1007, no. 165) is accurate, my reading is excluded; what I could see allowed for *al.* Cf. lines 26–27 below, where Šubandu sends someone else after apparently excusing himself in the previous lines; cf., too, *urruba dugulani,* "Come into (Egypt) and visit me" (*EA* 283:8f.). For a different reading, see Na'aman, *UF* 11 (1979) p. 680, n. 34.

2. 14 . . . [ù a-na] 15 [m]a-*an*-[ni] *e*-[zi-bu URU LUGAL]: cf. "leave city—go to the king" (*ezēbu—alāku, EA* 294:31ff.) and "leave city—go away (to Egypt)" (*ezēbu—paṭāru, EA* 118:34ff. and n. 3).

3. Traces suggest a final vertical, and hence ⌜de⌝ rather than m[u]r (Knudtzon). Besides, *amāru,* except as deictic imperative, is rare and northern language.

4. *marṣāku*: perhaps, "I am sick," especially after "I tire myself out," but still the context suggests that it is the current hostilities that demand his presence in the city.

5. *šu*-⌜ta⌝-*ši*-r[i]: if this is the correct reading—or Knudtzon's *šutaširu*—then the reference is hardly to making preparations, which is always expressed by *šūšuru.* Cf. *šutēšuru,* "to proceed, march on," *CAD,* E, p. 358.

6. ⌜K⌝I.UD (KISLAḪ) : *ma-aš-ka-n*[*a-ti-k*]*a*: there is no doubt about the reading of the first sign. *maškanātu* seems to replace the more usual *ašru,* "place"; cf. *EA* 315:8f., *alu–ašru,* and see Na'aman, *UF* 11 (1979) pp. 680f., n. 34.

7. See Na'aman, ibid., p. 689, and p. 679, n. 28.

8. Lines 36–41: a few legible signs.

EA 307

The power of the ʿApiru

TEXT: VAT 1586.
COPIES: WA 215; *VS* 11, 170.

[. . . I pro]strate myself [7 times and] 7 [times]. 3–10 I am indeed guarding the city of the king where I am, and may the [k]in[g], my lord, know [tha]t the [ʿApi]ru are more powerful than we. 11–12 May [the king] take cognizance of [his] lands.

EA 308

A request for horses

TEXT: VAT 1602.
COPIES: WA 172; *VS* 11, 173.

[. . . the dirt at your] f[e]et. I indeed pr[ostr]ate myself [at the f]e[e]t of the king, my lord, my [god], my [Sun], the Su[n] fr[om] the sky, [7] times [and 7 tim]es. [. . .]

Reverse

[. . .] and for the infor[matio]n of [the king], my lord, [my S]un, 4–9 so horses will be given to yo[ur] servant for keeping [*gua*]*r*[*d*] for the king, my lord, the [Su]n fr[om the s]ky, and so [. . .].

EA 309

Servants and shekels

TEXT: VAT 1874.
COPIES: WA 221; *VS* 11, 174.

To the k[in]g, [my lord], my god, [my Sun], the Sun [from the sky]: Message of [. . . , *the ruler o*]*f* [. . .]. 18–24 [. . .][1] . . . [x +] 1 *you*[*ng*] servants [. . . an]d 10[0] shekels of sil[ver *fo*]*r* the king, m[y] lord. 10 servants . . . [. . .] and 10 maidservants . . . [. . .] 25–28 For the information of the ki[ng], my lord, the Sun from the s[ky].

NOTE

1. Lines 19ff.: see Na'aman, *Political Disposition,* p. 76*, n. 74.

EA 310

Message lost

TEXT: VAT 1698.
COPY: *VS* 11, 169.

Too fragmentary for translation.

EA 311

Following orders

TEXT: VAT 1597.
COPY: *VS* 11, 175.

[To the king, my lord, my] Sun . . . [. . . the dirt at] your [feet, the groom of your] hors[es. I prostr]a[te myself at the feet] of the king, [my lord, the Sun fr]o[m the sk]y, [7 ti]mes and 7 times. 14–19 [. . .] . . . I guard the city [of the king] wh[ere I am]. [. . .].

EA 312

Message lost

TEXT: VAT 1886 + 1709.
COPY: *VS* 11, 176.

Too fragmentary for translation.

EA 313

Payment to the commissioner

TEXT: C 4782 (12228).
COPY: WA 197.

[. . .][1] 1–11 your[2] [. . .] 13 *mer*[*chants*][3] from Egypt, who were struck down in the attack of the ʿApiru. I have given 400 shekels of silver, *plus* 1000,[4] to the commissioner of the k[in]g who is over me. 11–20 And ⟨⟨and⟩⟩ the men that did this deed the Sun has given *into* the *powerful* . . .[5] of the king. And truly the 2 servants [*of* the ki]ng [*were*] not [. . .]; *they were struck* [*down*],[6] . . .

NOTES

1. To judge from the clay (grayish and filled with seashell fragments) and the script, this letter was very probably sent by Šubandu (*EA* 301–6).

2. *k*]*a* probably belongs on line 1 (Gordon) rather than on line 2 (Knudtzon).

3. LÚ.MEŠ DA[M?.GÀR?.MEŠ?]: the first questionable sign is certainly not *i*[*ḫ* (Knudtzon); the copy is accurate. Gordon saw traces following SAL that require DAM; if correct, the rest of the restoration is obvious.

4. Unless there is question of two separate payments or two separate indemnities, this is a strange way to write 1400. Or are 400 shekels paid *against* a debt of 1000?

5. x-*ri*: first sign is not [š]a (Knudtzon); unless two signs, a large sign.

6. *me-eḫ*-ṣ[ú]: last sign is hardly ḫ[a (Knudtzon); cf. line 4.

EA 314

A shipment of glass

TEXT: C 4778 (12219).
COPY: WA 153.

To the king, my lord, my god, my Sun, the Sun from the sky: Message of Pu-Baʿlu, your servant, the ruler of Yurṣa. I indeed prostrate myself at the feet of the king, my lord, my god, my Sun, the Sun from the sky, 7 times and 7 times, on the back and on the stomach. 11–16 I am indeed guarding the place of the king, ⟨my⟩ lord, my Sun, the Sun from the sky. Who is the do[g *that would not o*]*be*[*y the orders of the king, the Sun from the sk*]*y?* 17–22 [*Since the king, my lord, has ord*]*ere*[*d*] some glass, I [s]end it to the king, my lord, my god, the Sun from the sk[y].

EA 315

Like a command of the Sun

TEXT: BM 29839.
COPY: BB 56.

[To the kin]g, my lord, my god, the Sun from the sky: Message of Pu-Baʿlu, the ruler of Yurṣa, the dirt at your feet. I indeed prostrate myself at the feet of the king, my lord, 7 times and 7 times, on the back and on the sto[ma]ch.

8–12 I am indeed guard[ing] the city of the king, [my] lo[rd], and the place of the king, my lord, the Sun fr[om the sk]y. Whatever the king, my lord, has commanded—I am indeed observing, day and night, the order of the king, my lord.

13–18 As to [R]eanapa, the commissioner [of the kin]g, ⟨my⟩ lord, what the king, my lord, commanded (through him), [is *mig*]*hty* like the command of the Sun in the sky. [Wh]o is the dog[1] that would not [ob]serve[2] the orders of the king, my lord, [the Sun] f[ro]m the sky?

NOTES

1. On the logogram UŠ.GU, see Kühne, p. 145.
2. [*yi-n*]*a-ṣa-ru*: following Rainey, AOAT 8², p. 84.

EA 316

Postscript to the royal scribe

TEXT: BM 29838.
COPY: BB 55.

[To the kin]g, m[y] lord, [my] god, my Sun fr[o]m the s[ky: Mess]age of Pu-B[a]ʿlu, your servant and the dirt at your feet, the [gr]oom of your horses. I fall at the feet of the king, my lord, my god, my Sun from the sky, 7 times and [7] times, on the back and on the stomach. 10–15 I am indeed guarding the pla[ce of the kin]g carefully. And who is the [d]og that would [*ne*]*gl*[*ec*]*t*[1] [*the comma*]*nd*[2] *of* the king? I am indeed obeying the orders of [*Ta*]*ḫm*[*ay*]*a*,[3] the commissioner of the king.

16–25 To the scribe[4] of [*my lord*: Me]ssage of Pu-Baʿlu. I fal[l] at your feet. There was nothing in my h[ou]se when I [en]ter[ed] it,[5] and so I have not sent a caravan to you. I am now preparing a fine caravan for you.

NOTES

1. [i]a$_8$-a[m-*t*]*a-ku*$_8$: from *mekû*?
2. [a-n]a [IN]IM.G[AR.R]A?
3. [^{m}ta]ḫ-m[a-i]a; Albright, *JNES* 5 (1946) p. 11, rightly doubted the existence of an otherwise unknown [^{m}ḫ]a-b[a-i]a (Knudtzon), but his own reading ⌜^{m}ḫa-an-ia⌝, is unlikely; cf. *EA* 265:9.
4. For the Egyptianism, see Albright, ibid., pp. 20f.; Helck, *Beziehungen*, p. 435, n. 6; Schulman, *Journal of the American Research Center in Egypt* 3 (1964) p. 60, n 73.
5. Perhaps referring to his accession to the throne; cf. *EA* 286:13.

EA 317

A family tradition of service

TEXT: VAT 1676.
COPY: WA 129; *VS* 11, 177.
TRANSLITERATION: Artzi, *JNES* 27 (1968) p. 170.

Dagantakala, your servant, says to the Great King, my lord: I fall at the feet of the Great King, my lord, 7 times and 7 times.[1] 7–12 And now Dagantakal[a], your servant, belongs to the Great King, my lord. I have indeed listened to the orders of the Great King, my lord. 13–18 Dagantakala says, "Just as my father [and] my [gran]d-father, too, [a]cted towards the Great King, I have act[ed] towards the Great King, my lord." 19–25 The Great King, my lord, has said to me, "Obey your commissioner."[2] I have obeyed very carefully, and the commissioner is the one who knows whether I have not obeyed him.

NOTES

1. On the northern origin of *EA* 317f., see Artzi.
2. LÚ.⟨M⟩AŠKIM *ḫa-za-ni-ka*: on *ḫazannu* as the designation of an Egyptian official, see *EA* 230, n. 3.

EA 318

Save me

TEXT: BM 29857.
COPY: BB 74.
PHOTOGRAPH: BB, pl. 1.
TRANSLITERATION: Artzi, *JNES* 27 (1968) p. 170.

Dagantakala, your servant, says to the Great King, [my] lord, the Sun in the sky: I fall at the feet of the Great King, my lord, 7 times and 7 times.[1] Save me from the *powe*[*rful*] enemies, from the hand of the ʿApir[u], robbers, and Suteans. And save m[e], Great King, m[y] lord![2] And *behold! I have wr⟨it⟩ten* [*to*] *you*![3] Mo[reov]er, you G[reat] Ki[ng], my lord, save me or *I will be lo*[*st*][4] to the Great King, [my] lord!

NOTES

1. See *EA* 317, n. 1.
2. Following the proposal of Weippert, *Die Landnahme der israelitischen Stämme in der neueren wissenschaftlichen Diskussion* (Göttingen, 1967), p. 76, n. 2, to read *ù-še-zi-ba-an-ni* and to translate as if the precative does not seem probable.

3. *ù a*-⸢mu-ur-mi⸣ 17 ⸢al⸣-⟨tap⟩-*ra*-[k]a$_4$?

4. *i-na-ba-a*-a[t]: so Artzi, based on his collation, and translation on the basis of *EA* 288:52 (perhaps third person, "it will be lost," i.e., the territory). The thematic vowel, however, is puzzling, and the writing *ba-a* is also unexpected. Simply *i-na-ma-a,* "it will become a wasteland"?

EA 319

An obedient dog

TEXT: VAT 1722.
COPIES: WA 145; *VS* 11, 178.

[To the king], my lord, my god, [my Sun], the Sun from the [sk]y: Message of Ṣur-Ašar, the ruler of A[ḫ]tiašna,[1] your servant, the dirt at your feet, the groom of your horses. I indeed pros[tr]ate myself at the feet of the king, my lord, my god, my Sun, the Sun from the sky, 7 times and 7 times, on the stom[ach and on] the back. 15–23 I have indeed listened to the orders of the com[mi]ssioner of the king, my [lo]rd, very carefully. Who is the [d]⟨og⟩ that would not obey the orders of the king, his lord, the Sun from the sky, the son of the Sun?

NOTE

1. Or A[ḫ]tirumna, A[ḫ]tiruna: following Knudtzon's reading and the arguments of Na'aman, in E. Stern and D. Urman, eds., *Man and Environment in the Southern Shephelah: Studies in Regional Geography and History* (Massada, 1988), sect. 98, n. 19, against Gi[n]tiašna.

EA 320

Listening carefully (1)

TEXT: C 4777 (12218).
COPY: WA 121.
TRANSLATION: Albright, *ANET,* p. 490.

[T]o the king, my lord, my god, my Sun, the Sun from the sky: Message of Yidya, the ruler of Ašqaluna, your servant, the dirt at your feet, the groom of your horses. 10–15 I indeed prostrate myself, on the stomach and on the back, at the feet of the king, my lord, 7 times and 7 times. 16–21 I am indeed guard[ing] the place of the king where I am. Whatever the k[ing], my lord, has written me, I have listened to very carefully. 22–25 Who is the dog that would not obey the orders of the king, his lord, the son of the Sun?

EA 321

Listening carefully (2)

TEXT: VAT 1671.
COPIES: WA 119; *VS* 11, 182.

To the king, my lord, my god, my Sun, the Sun from the sky: [Mes]sage of Yidya, the ruler of Ašqaluna, your servant, the dirt at your feet, the [gr]oom of your hors[e]s. 10–14 I indeed prostrate myself at the feet of the king, my lord, the Sun from the sky, 7 times and 7 times. 15–23 As to the commissioner of the king, my lord, whom the king, my lord, the Sun from the sky, sent to me, I have listened to his orders [ver]y carefully.

24–26 [And] I am indeed guarding the [pla]ce of the king whe[re] I am.

EA 322

Listening carefully (3)

TEXT: C 4776 (12217).
COPY: WA 118.

To the k[ing], my [lor]d, [m]y g[od], [m]y Sun, the Sun fr[om] the sky: Mess[age] of Y[i]dya, the ruler of A[šq]aluna, y[our] servant, the [di]rt at [y]our f[eet], the g[roo]m of your horses. 9–14 I [in]deed prostrate myself, on the stomach and on the back, at the f[eet of the k]ing, my lord, the Sun from the sky, 7 times and 7 times. 15–19 I am indeed guarding the place of the king where I am. Who is the dog that would not obey the commissioner of the king? 20–24 I have indeed listened very carefully to the commissioner of the king, my lord, the son of the Sun from the sky.

EA 323

A royal order for glass

TEXT: BM 29836.
COPY: BB 53.

To the king, my lord, my god, my Sun, the Sun from the sky: Message of Yidya, your servant, the dirt at your feet, the groom of your horses. 6–13 I indeed prostrate myself, on the back and on the stomach, at the feet of the king, my lord, 7 times and 7 times. I am indeed guarding the [pl]ace of the king, my lord, and the city of the king, in accordance with the command of the king, my lord, the Sun from the sky. 13–16 As to the king, my lord's, having ordered some glass, I [her]ewith send to the k[ing], my [l]ord, *30* (*pieces*) of glass. 17–23 Moreover, who is the dog that would not obey the orders of the king, my lord, the Sun fr[o]m the sky, the son of the Sun, [wh]om the Sun loves?

EA 324

Preparations completed (1)

TEXT: BM 29837.
COPY: BB 54.
PHOTOGRAPH: BB, pl. 21.

To the king, my lord, my Sun, my god, the Sun from the sky: Message of Yidya, [y]our servant, the dirt at your feet, the groom of your horses. I indeed prostrate myself, on the back and on the stomach, at the feet of the king, my lord, 7 times and 7 times. 10–15 I am indeed observing the orders of the king, my lord, the son of the Sun, and I have indeed prepared food, strong drink, oil, grain, oxen, sheep and goats,[1] before the arrival of the troops of the king, my lord. I have [*st*]*ored*[2] everything for the troops of the king, my lord. 16–19 Who is the dog that would not obey the orders of the king, my lord, the son of the Sun?

NOTES

1. See *EA* 55, n. 2. Yidya may be here replying to the demands of *EA* 370.
2. [*b*]*e-it-ti*: the reading is virtually certain; the translation assumes derivation from *biātu,* as if "to house." It may also be an aberrant form of *bu''ītī,* "I have searched out"; cf. *EA* 143:15; 264:6, 20.

EA 325

Preparations completed (2)

TEXT: BM 29835.
COPY: BB 52.
PHOTOGRAPHS: BB, pl. 14; Barnett, *Illustrations,* p. 15.

[To] the king, my lord, my god, my Sun, the Sun fr[om the s]ky: Message of Yidya, your servant, the dirt at your feet, the groom of

[yo]ur horses. I indeed prostrate myself, on the back and on the stomach, at the feet of the king, my lord, 7 times and 7 times.

10–14 I am indeed guarding the place of the king, my lord, and the city of the king, my lord, [w]here I am. Who is the dog that would not obey the orders of the king, the Sun from the sky?

15–19 I have indeed prepared absolutely everything—[f]ood, strong drink, oxen, sheep and goats,[1] grain, straw, absolutely everything that the king, my lord, commanded. I have indeed prepared it.

20–22 And I am indeed *p[reparing]* the tribute of the Sun, in accordance with the comma[nd] of the king, my lord, the Sun fr[om the sky].

NOTE

1. See *EA* 55, n. 2. This letter is hardly more than a restatement of *EA* 324, and like *EA* 324, it may be an answer to *EA* 370.

EA 326

A new commissioner

TEXT: VAT 1672.
COPIES: WA 122; *VS* 11, 183.

To the king, my lord, my god, [my] Sun, the Sun from the sky: Message of Yidya, your servant, the dirt at your feet, the groom of your horses. I indeed prostrate myself, on the [back] and on the stomach, at the feet of the king, my lord, 7 times and 7 times.

9–12 I am indeed guarding the city of the king, my lord. May the gods of the king, my lord, [*guard*] his cities, and may the [*power*]*ful*[1] hands of the king guard his entire land.

13–19 I have heard the word of the king, my lord, to his commissioner. Since he was unable to guard the land of the king, my lord, the king, my lord, has now appointed Reanapa as [com]missioner of the king, my lord. He brings to m[e][2] whatever seems good to the king, my lord.

20–24 [Wha]tever procee[ds] from the mouth of the king, my lord, I indeed observe it day and nig⟨ht⟩.

NOTES

1. [da-an/dan]-*nu-tu-ma*: following Rainey, *UF* 7 (1975) p. 412; on the gender agreement, cf. *annûtu,* both masculine and feminine, in *EA* 101:26; 104:46; 227:9; 292:52; 294:26.

2. Lit. "to my head." On *qaqqadu,* "person, self," and its survival in the Western Periphery, see *CAD,* Q, pp. 106f.

EA 327

An order for glass

See *EA* 235.

EA 328

Obedience to the commissioner

TEXT: C 4775 (12193).
COPY: WA 124.

To the king, my lord, [my] god, my Sun, the Sun from the sky: Message of Yabni-Ilu, the ruler of Lakiša, your servant, the dirt at your feet, the groom of your horses. 10–16 I indeed prostra[te] myself at the feet of the king, my lord, my god, my Sun, the Sun from the sky, 7 times and 7 times, on the stomach and on the back. 17–26 As to the [com]missioner [of] the king, my lord, [wh]om [the k]ing, my lord, sent to m[e], I have indeed heard all the words that Maya, the kin[g's] commissioner, has spoken to me. I am indeed carrying out every one of them.

EA 329

Preparations under way

TEXT: VAT 1673.
COPIES: WA 123; *VS* 11, 181.
TRANSLATION: Freydank, in A. Jepsen, ed., *Von Sinuhe bis Nebukadnezar* (see *EA* 254, headnote), p. 100.

To the king, my lord, my god, my Sun, the Sun from the sky: Message of Zimreddi, the ruler of Lakiša, your servant, the dirt at your feet. I prostrate myself at the feet of the king, my lord, the Sun from the sky, 7 times and 7 times. 13–20 As to the messenger of the king, my lord, whom he sent to me, I have listened to his orders very carefully, and I am indeed making preparations in accordance with his order.

EA 330

Dirt at the feet of the king

TEXT: BM 29848.
COPY: BB 65.
PHOTOGRAPH: Barnett, *Illustrations,* p. 15.

Say t[o] the king, my lord: Message of Šipṭi-Baᶜlu, your servant and the dirt at the feet of the king, my lord. I fall at the feet of the king, my lord, my god, my Sun, 7 times and 7 times, at the feet of the king, my lord. 9–16 May the king, my lord, know that I have heard all the [w]ords of the king, my lord. Moreover, note, too, that Yanḫamu is the loyal servant of the king and the dirt at the feet of the king. 17–21 Moreover, may the king, my lord, know that the city of the king where I am is safe and sound.[1]

NOTE

1. *šal*$_x$ (*šul*)*-ma-at.*

EA 331

Glass for the king

TEXT: C 4779 (12221).
COPY: WA 200.

[T]o the k[in]g, [my] lord, my god, [my] Sun, the Sun from the [sk]y: Message of Šipṭi-B[aᶜ]lu, your se[rv]ant, the dir[t] at your feet, the groom of your horses. I in[de]ed pr[ostr]ate myself at the feet of the king, my lord, my god, my Sun, the Sun [f]rom the sky, 7 tim[es] and 7 times, on the sto[ma]ch and on the ba[c]k. 12–24 I am indeed gu[ar]ding the place of the king, my lord, and the city of the king where [I] am. And as to the king, my [l]ord's, [having] ordered *w[hate]ver* glass [I] may have on hand, I herewith [s]end (it) to [the kin]g, my lord, my god, my [S]un, [the S]un from the sky.

EA 332

Message lost

TEXT: VAT 1883.
COPY: *VS* 11, 184.

[To the ki]ng, ⟨my⟩ lord, [my] Su[n], my [god, the Sun fro]m the [sky: Message of] Šipṭi-Ba[ᶜlu, the ruler of L]akiša, [your servant], the dirt [at yo]ur [feet], [the groo]m o[f] your [horses . . .].

EA 333

Plots and disloyalty

TEXT: Istanbul Arkeoloji Müzeleri, Tell el-Ḥesi, Fi. 11.
COPY: *BE* 1/2, pl. LXIV, no. 147.[1]
PHOTOGRAPH: *BE* 1/2, pl. XXIV, nos. 66–67.
TRANSLITERATION AND TRANSLATION: Albright, *BASOR* 87 (1942) pp. 33ff.
TRANSLATION: Ebeling, p. 370; Albright, *ANET,* p. 490; Na'aman, in E. Stern and D. Urman, eds., *Man and Environment in the Southern Shephelah: Studies in Regional Geography and History* (Massada, 1988), sect. 94 (Hebrew).

Say [to] the magnate: [Message of P]aapu.[2] I fall [a]t your feet. 4–18 May you know that Šipṭi-Baᶜlu and Zimredda are acting disloyally[3] together, and Šipṭi-Baᶜlu said to Zimredda, "⌈*The for*⌉*ces*[4] of the town of Yaramu have written to me. Give me [x +] 11[5] bows, 3 daggers,[6] and 3 swords. Look,[7] I am about to sally forth against the land of the king, and you are in league[8] with me." 19–26 To be sure, he rejects[9] (the charge of) disloyalty to the king, (saying), "The one who is disloyal is Paapu, so send him [t]o[10] me." I [*no*]*w*[11] send Rabi-Ilu. He will [*certain*]*ly answer*[12] him [*i*]*n*[13] this matter.

NOTES

1. I have not seen the copy by Scheil (see *VAB* 2/1, p. 15).

2. [*um-ma* ᵐ*p*]*a-a-pí*: following Albright, *BASOR* 87 (1942) pp. 33ff., and cf. Knudtzon, *VAB* 2/1, p. 945, n. 1; the reading is certain.

3. This form, *tu-ša-ṭú-na, šu-uṭ* (line 20), and *ú-ša-aṭ* (line 21), are classified by *AHw,* p. 1205, as (Canaanite) passives of *šâṭu,* "to despise." Formally, this is possible, but I cannot make sense of the letter under this assumption, and so I follow Albright in taking all forms as "intensives" (ibid., p. 33, n. 8). The

absolute use in this line is comparable to *šêṭu,* "to contemn," but also "to sin," and there may have been some confusion between *šâṭu* and *šêṭu.*

4. ⌜a⌝-*bi* or ⌜ṣa⌝-*bi*: traces of two verticals, with Knudtzon and *BE* 1/2; Albright's LÚ (ibid., p. 34, n. 10) is impossible.

5. Traces favor *10* + 1, with room for another *10.* Against 6 (Knudtzon) is the fact that enough of the final vertical is visible to argue against another above it.

6. GÍR.URUDU: following Albright, ibid.

7. "If" does not seem to fit the context; on *šumma,* see *EA* 35, n. 3.

8. The erasure at the end of line 18 seems to have been of *a-na*; cf. *a-na ia-ši* in the line above.

9. *ú-ti-ru*-m⌜i⌝: following Albright, ibid., the visible horizontal is lower than one would expect if the last sign were -*ši* (Knudtzon).

10. [*i-n*]*a* (Knudtzon) fills the break better than [*a-n*]*a* (Albright).

11. [i-na-n]a.

12. [lu]-⌜ú⌝ *yi-pal-šu.*

13. [i-n]a: traces of a vertical probable (Knudtzon).

EA 334

Message lost

TEXT: VAT 1609.
COPY: *VS* 11, 185.

[Sa]y [t]o the kin[g], my lord: Message of [. . .] . . . Zuḫra.[1] [. . .] . . .

NOTE

1. [. . .] x L[Ú] URU *zu-uḫ-ra*$^{\text{k[i]}}$ seems a possible reading of the traces. For the possibility of reading *zu-uḫ-ra-t*[*a*$_5$], see Na'aman, in Stern and Urman (see *EA* 333), sects. 97–98, n. 18. The rest of the letter is too fragmentary for translation.

EA 335

All alone

TEXT: VAT 1616 + 1708.
COPY: *VS* 11, 186.
TRANSLITERATION AND TRANSLATION: Na'aman, *UF* 11 (1979) p. 677.

[Say to the king, my lord: Message of ʿAbdi-Aštarti, your servant. I fall at the feet of the king, my lord, 7 times and 7 times, both on the stomach and] on the back, [at the feet of the king], my lord.[1] 6–12 [May the kin]g, my lord, be [informed that] I am [all alone]. May [the kin]g, my lord, be in[formed] that Tu[rbazu *and*] Yaptiḫ-Hadda *h*[*ave been slai*]*n* : *mi-ḫi-ṣa,* and ... [...[2] L]akišu. May the king, my lord, *be in*[*formed*]. And [*the r*]*ebel has* [*taken*] 13–21 all my ... May the king, my lord, be informed that Lakišu is h[os]tile, Muḫraštu s[ei]zed, [*Jerusalem hos*]*tile.* [*And so may*] the king, [*my lord, sen*]*d* [*archers* ...].

NOTES

1. The lineation is Na'aman's. See also *EA* 63–65.

2. If one reads *nu*-k[i-ir] (Knudtzon, Na'aman), one must find a masculine subject. By rule, Lachish is feminine; cf. line 15.

EA 336

Message lost

TEXT: VAT 1707.
COPY: *VS* 11, 188.

[S]ay [to the kin]g, [my] lo[rd: Message of] Ḫiziru, [your] servant. [I fa]ll [at the f]eet of my lord 7 times [and 7 ti]mes. [...] ...

EA 337

Abundant supplies ready

TEXT: VAT 1679.
COPIES: WA 147; *VS* 11, 187.

Say to the king, my lord, my Sun, my god: Message of Ḫiziru, your servant. I fall at the feet of the king, my lord, 7 times and 7 times. 7–12 The king, my lord, wrote to me, "Prepare the supplies ⟨:⟩ *ma-aṭ-ni-a*[1] before the arrival of a large army *of* : *pí-ṭa-ti* (archers)[2] of the king, [m]y l[ord]. 13–23 May the god of the king, my lord, grant that the king, my lord, come forth along with his large army and learn about his lands. I have indeed prepared accordingly abundant supplies : *ma-aṭ-ni-a* before the arrival of a large army of the king, my lord.

24–30 The king, my lord, wrote to me, "Guard Maya," the commissioner of the king, my lord. Truly, I guard Maya very carefully.

NOTES

1. On IGI.KÁR, "provisions, supplies," see P. Steinkeller, *Acta Sumerologica Japonensia* 4 (1982) pp. 149ff.; on its use here and the gloss (cf. Phoenician *mṭn'*), see the Introduction, sect. 3, and n. 37, and *Acta Sumerologica Japonensia* 5 (1983) pp. 175f.

2. *pí-ṭá-ti* is perhaps simply a gloss to ÉRIN.MEŠ; note the position of the gloss in line 21, and see Introduction, n. 100.

EA 338

Message lost

TEXT: VAT 1884.
COPY: *VS* 11, 189.

Too fragmentary for translation.

EA 339

Message lost

TEXT: VAT 1887.
COPY: *VS* 11, 190.

Too fragmentary for translation.

EA 340–61

A sequence of tablets not containing letters or inventories, and therefore omitted here. See the Introduction, sect. 2.

EA 362

A commissioner murdered

TEXT: AO 7093.
COPY: Thureau-Dangin, *RA* 19 (1922) pp. 102f.
PHOTOGRAPH: "Amarna," *Dictionnaire de la Bible,* Supplément, vol. 1 (Paris, 1928), fig. 10.
TRANSLITERATION AND TRANSLATION: Thureau-Dangin, *RA* 19 (1922) pp. 91ff.; Rainey, AOAT 8^2, pp. 18ff.
TRANSLATION: Oppenheim, *LFM,* pp. 131ff.

Rib-Haddi. Say to the king, my lord: I fall beneath the feet of my lord 7 times and 7 times.[1] 5–11 I have indeed heard the words of the king, my lord, and my heart is overjoyed. May my lord hasten the sending of the archers with all speed. If the king, my lord, does not send archers, then we ourselves must die and 12–20 Gubla[2] will be taken. *He was distraught* recently; *he is* also *distraught* now.[3] Recently they were saying, "There will be no archers," but I wrote with the result that archers came out and took their father. 21–30 Now indeed they are saying, "Let him not write or we will certainly be taken."[4] They seek to capture Gubla, and they say, "If we capture Gubla, we will be strong." If they capture Gubla, they will be strong;[5] there will not be a man left, (and) they (the archers) will certainly be too few for them.[6] 31–39 I for my part have guarded Gubla, the city of the king, night (and) day. Should I move to the (outlying) territory, then the men will desert in order to take territory for themselves,[7] and there will be no men to guard Gubla, the city of the king, my lord. 40–50 So may my lord hasten the archers or we must die. Because my lord has written to me, they know indeed that they are going to die, and so they seek to commit a crime.[8] As to his having said[9] before the king, "There is a pestilence in the lands," the king, my lord, should not listen to the words of other men. There is no pestilence in the lands. It has been over for a long t⟨i⟩me.[10] 51–59 My lord knows that I do not write lies to my lord. All the mayors are not in favor of the archers' coming out, for they have peace. I am the one who wants them to come out, for I have distress. 60–65 May the king, my lord, come out, visit his lands, and take all. Look, the day you come out, all the lands will be (re)joined to the king, my lord. Who will resist the troops of the king? 66–69 May the king, my lord, not *leave this year free* for the sons of ʿAbdi-Aširta, for *you know* all their *acts of hatred*[11] against the lands of the king. Who are they that they have committed a crime and killed the commissioner : *sú-ki-na,* Pewure?

NOTES

1. See *EA* 126, n. 1.
2. On URU.MEŠ as singular, see *EA* 129, n. 33.
3. URU.MEŠ *gub*^{ub}*-li tu-ul*$_{11}$*-qu ma-a-ga-mi* . . . : *agāmi,* "today" (Thureau-Dangin, *RA* 19 [1922] p. 92, n. 1; *AHw,* p. 15; *CAD,* A/1, p. 141) must be rejected. It is neither West Semitic (*AHw, CAD*), where it is unknown and has no explanation, nor a compound of *agâ* + *ūmi* (Thureau-Dangin), since the first element is attested only in very late times. Moreover, *tulqu-ma* is improbable, since enclitic *-ma* is rare in general and does not appear once in this letter, where we find *-mi* 13 times and even *qí-bi-mi,* an extremely rare replacement of standard *qí-bí-ma.* We thus have a twofold comparison between the past and the present: *ma-a-ga-mi* in the past (*tumāl šalsâmi*), *ma-an-ga-am-mi* (also) in the present (*inanna*; on the non-initial position, cf. *EA* 101:11–18); but, in the past (*tumāl šalsâmi*) they were saying . . . (*teqbūni*; on the form see *EA* 126, n. 12), now (*inanna*) they are saying . . . (*teqbūna*). An unattested West Semitism, *mā*(*n*) "what" + *gam*

"also" (Rainey), understood to mean that what was true in the past is also true now, does not allow for the statement of contrast between the past and the present. And so I assume either a mistake (*ma-a* for *ma-an*) or *māga* = *manga*. The subject I would identify as Aziru, who reappears unnamed in line 46 (see n. 9). On the meaning of the verb, see *EA* 106, n. 3.

4. Lines 15–23: see *Or* n.s. 29 (1960) pp. 4 and 15.

5. Lines 25–29: see *JCS* 4 (1950) p. 170.

6. *ia-nu-am-mi* LÚ-*la te-i-ṣa a-na ša-šu-*[*nu*]: accusative *awīla*, governed by *iyānu*, according to rule (*JCS* 2 [1948] p. 248); *te'īṣa* is from (*w*)*iāṣu*, not from (*w*)*aṣû*, since in the latter the preformative is always *tu-* (see lines 19, 56, and 62 in this letter). On a similar warning about the archers (feminine singular, by rule; see *JCS* 6 [1952] p. 78), cf. *EA* 137:44 and n. 8.

7. Lines 33–39: see *Or* n.s. 29 (1960) p. 14.

8. Rib-Hadda seems to imply that the sons of ʿAbdi-Aširta were familiar with the Pharaoh's letter promising the arrival of archers, an event that would mean their deaths. The crime would be the capture of Byblos, an event rendering the arrival of the archers meaningless; see above, lines 25–30. Perhaps the murder of Pewure should also be included; see below, line 69.

9. *yiqbu* is in form singular, and the subject can only be Aziru, at this period at least *primus inter pares* (*fratres*); see Rainey, AOAT 8^2, p. 21.

10. Or "all is healthy for a long time" (cf. Rainey, ibid.), "all is healthier than before" (cf. Thureau-Dangin; Dhorme, *RB* 33 [1924] p. 8 [also in *Recueil É. Dhorme,* p. 492]; Oppenheim, *LFM*).

11. Line 66: following Thureau-Dangin; cf. *EA* 162:42f. Line 67: *ti-dì šu-na-i*: cf. *šannā'um*, "hater, enemy" (*AHw,* p. 1164), but the comparison is questionable, and other interpretations are possible (Thureau-Dangin, Oppenheim, Rainey).

EA 363

A joint report on Amqu (4)

TEXT: AO 7097.

COPY: Thureau-Dangin, *RA* 19 (1922) p. 107.

TRANSLITERATION AND TRANSLATION: Thureau-Dangin, *RA* 19 (1922) pp. 94f.; Rainey AOAT 8^2, pp. 24f.

Say to the king, my lord, my god, my Sun:[1] Message of ʿAbdi-Riša,[2] your servant, the ruler of E⟨ni⟩šasi.[3] I fall in the dirt under the feet of the king, my lord, 7 times and 7 times. 7–14 Look, we ar⟨e⟩ in Amqu, in cities of the king, my lord, and Etakkama, the ruler of Qinsa, assisted the troops of Ḫatta and set the cities of the king, my lord, on fire. 15–23 May the king, my lord, take cognizance, and may the king, my lord, give archers that we may (re)gain the cities of the king, my lord, and dwell in the cities of the king, my lord, my god, my Sun.

NOTES

1. ^{d}UTU-*ia,* written on the reverse, was omitted in the copy; see *RA* 69 (1975) p. 155, n. 1. On this letter, see *EA* 174, n. 1. Joint reports 1–3 are *EA* 174–76.

2. Na'aman, *UF* 20 (1988) pp. 187f., suggests that *-ri-ša* is a mistaken metathesis for *-ša-ri,* an element well known in Hurrian names. Against this proposal is the fact that "servant of . . ." is a type of name unattested among the Hurrians (Gernot Wilhelm, private communication).

3. See *EA* 187, n. 1.

EA 364

Justified war

TEXT: AO 7094.
COPY: Thureau-Dangin, *RA* 19 (1922) p. 104.
TRANSLITERATION AND TRANSLATION: Thureau-Dangin, ibid., pp. 95f.; Rainey, AOAT 8^2, pp. 26f.

To the king, my lord: Message of Ayyab, your servant. I fall at the feet of my lord 7 times and 7 times. I am the servant of the king, my lord, the dirt at his feet. 10–16 I have heard what the king, my lord, wrote to me through Ataḫmaya. Truly, I have guarded[1] very carefully [the *citie*]*s*[2] of the king, my lord. 17–28 Moreover, note that it is the ruler of Ḫaṣura who has taken 3 cities from me. From the time I heard and verified this,[3] there has been waging of war against him. Truly, may the king, my lord, take cognizance, and may the king, my lord, give thought to his servant.

NOTES

1. *aṣ-ṣur-*⌜*mi*⌝: following Thureau-Dangin; if *aṣ-ṣur-*⌜*ru*⌝ is the reading (Rainey), "I am guarding."

2. Though [KUR].MEŠ seems required by the space, KUR is only very rarely the object of *naṣāru,* and never with plural determinative, whereas URU + plural marker is quite common.

3. In lines 18f., the word order, subject-verb, stresses the identity of the one who took the cities. In line 21, the sequence *šemû-amāru,* "hear-see," brings out the fact of personal verification. Perhaps *a-ma-ru* is best taken as an infinitive, "I heard and then there was verification." Rainey postulates a West Semitism, "I commanded (the waging of war)."

EA 365

Furnishing corvée workers

TEXT: AO 7098.

COPY: Thureau-Dangin, *RA* 19 (1922) p. 108.

TRANSLITERATION AND TRANSLATION: Thureau-Dangin, ibid., pp. 97f.; Rainey, AOAT 8^2, pp. 28f.

TRANSLATIONS: Ebeling, p. 378; Alt, *Kleine Schriften zur Geschichte des Volkes Israel,* vol. 3 (Munich, 1959), pp. 169ff.; Albright, *ANET,* p. 485; Borger, in Galling, ed., *Textbuch zur Geschichte Israels*[2] (Tübingen, 1968), p. 28; Na'aman, in M. Heltzer and E. Lipiński, eds., *Society and Economy in the Eastern Mediterranean (ca. 1500–1000 B.C.), Orientalia Lovaniensia Analecta* 23, pp. 180f.

Say [to the ki]ng, my lord and my [Su]n: Message of Biridiya, the loyal servant of the king. I fall at the feet of the king, my lord and my Sun, 7 times and 7 times.

8–14 May the king, my lord, take cognizance of his servant and his city. In fact, only I am cultivating : *aḫ-ri-šu* in Šunama, and only I am furnishing corvée workers. 15–23 But consider the mayors that are near me. They do not act as I do. They do not cultivate in Šunama, and they do not furnish corvée workers. 24–31 Only I : *ia*$_8$*-ḫu-du-un-ni* (by myself) furnish corvée workers. From Yapu they come, from [*my*] *resources* here, (and) from Nuribta.[1] And may the king, my lord, take cognizance of his city.

NOTE

1. Lines 26–29: the language is quite ambiguous, and various translations have been proposed. Line 27: *yi-la-ku,* singular, subject *massu,* a collective; *ištu* ŠU-[ti/ia]. The restoration *istu šu*-[*na-ma*$^{(ki?)}$] (Albright, *CAH* 2/2, p. 106) is highly improbable, since throughout this letter, city names are preceded by URU. Na'aman reads "from [your?] hand," i.e., by the Pharaoh's authority they come to Megiddo ("here") from Yapu, an Egyptian garrison-city; whether, however, *ištu qātīka* can have this meaning is not clear.

EA 366

A rescue operation

TEXT: AO 7096 (not collated).
COPY: Thureau-Dangin, *RA* 19 (1922) p. 106.
TRANSLITERATION AND TRANSLATION: Thureau-Dangin, ibid., pp. 98f.; Rainey, AOAT², pp. 32f.
TRANSLATIONS: Ebeling, pp. 378f.; Alt, *Kleine Schriften zur Geschichte des Volkes Israel,* vol. 3, pp. 162ff.; Albright, *ANET,* p. 487; Borger, in Galling, ed., *Textbuch zur Geschichte Israels²*, p. 27; Seux, *Textes du Proche-Orient,* p. 59.

Say to the king, my lord, my Sun, my god: Message of Šuwardata, your servant, the servant of the king and the dirt at your feet, the ground you tread on. I prostrate myself at the feet of the king, my lord, the Sun from the sky, 7 times and 7 times, both on the stomach and on the back.

11–19 May the king, my lord, be informed that the ʿApiru that rose up : *na-aš-ša-a* against the lands, the god of the king, my lord, gave to me,[1] and I smote him. And may the king, my lord, be informed that all my brothers have abandoned me. 20–28 Only ʿAbdi-Ḫeba and I have been at war with (that) ʿApiru. Surata, the ruler of Akka, and Endaruta, the ruler of Akšapa, (these) two also[2] have come to my aid : *na-az-a-qú* (have been summoned to help)[3] with 50 chariots, and now they are on my side in the war. 28–34 So may it seem right in the sight of the king, my lord, and may he send Yanḫamu so that we may all wage war and you restore the land of the king, my lord, to its borders : *up-sí-ḫi.*[4]

NOTES

1. Lines 11–15: with Na'aman, *Political Disposition,* p. 120.
2. On the dual pronoun *šunī* (-ma, "also"), see *BASOR* 211 (1973) p. 51. For another interpretation of these lines, see Albright, *CAH* 2/2, pp. 114f.
3. On the gloss *naz/ṣʿaqū,* see Finkelstein, *Eretz Israel* 9 (1969) p. 33.
4. See *EA* 284, n. 3.

EA 367

From the Pharaoh to a vassal

TEXT: AO 7095.

COPY: Thureau-Dangin, *RA* 19 (1922) p. 105; idem, *Recueil d'études égyptologiques dédiées à la mémoire de Jean-François Champollion* (Paris, 1922), pp. 377ff.; Rainey, AOAT 8^2, pp. 36f.

TRANSLATION: Albright, *ANET,* p. 484.

Say to Endaruta, the ruler of Akšapa: Thus the king. He herewith dispatches to you this tablet, saying to you, Be on your guard. You are to guard the place of the king where you are.

6–21 The king herewith sends[1] to you Ḫanni, the son of Maireya, the stable overseer[2] of the king in Canaan. And what he tells you heed very carefully lest the king find fault in you. Every word that he tells you heed very carefully and carry out very carefully. And be on your guard! Be on your guard! Do not be negligent! And may you prepare before the arrival of the archers of the king food in abundance, wine (and) everything else in abundance. Indeed he is going to reach you very quickly, and he will cut off the heads of the enemies of the king.

22–25 And know that the king is hale like the Sun in the sky. For his troops and his chariots in multitude all goes very well.

NOTES

1. Liverani, *Lingering over Words,* pp. 341ff., maintains that the king here and in *EA* 369–70 announces an event of the future, "will send," but this is incompatible with the form of the verb, *umteššer,* which is clearly a perfect. It no more has future reference than *uštēbilakku* in line 3. In lines 18–20 the subject is the king, not Ḫanni. See also Introduction, n. 78.

2. *akil tarbaṣi* renders Egyptian *ḥry ỉḥw*; see Helck, *Beziehungen,* p. 438. For the rest of the letter, see the Introduction, sect. 5, and *EA* 99, n. 7.

EA 368

A list of Egyptian words written in syllabic cuneiform, and therefore omitted here. See Introduction, sect. 2.

EA 369

From the Pharaoh to a vassal

TEXT: Musées Royaux d'Art et d'Histoire (Brussels) E. 6753.
COPY: G. Dossin, *RA* 31 (1934) p. 127.
PHOTOGRAPH: Dossin, *Académie Royale de Belgique, Bulletin de la Classes des Lettres et des Sciences Morales et Philosophiques* 20 (1934), facing p. 86.
TRANSLITERATION AND TRANSLATION: Dossin, *RA* 31 (1934) pp. 126, 128; Rainey, AOAT 8², pp. 40ff.
TRANSLATIONS: Dossin, *Académie*, pp. 87f.; Albright, *ANET*, p. 487; Borger, in Galling, ed., *Textbuch zur Geschichte Israels²*, pp. 24f.; Seux, *Textes du Proche-Orient*, p. 53.

To Milkilu, the ruler of Gazru: Thus the king. He herewith dispatches to you this[1] tablet, saying to you, He herewith sends to you Hanya, the stable ⟨overseer⟩ of the archers, along with everything for the acquisition of beautiful female cupbearers:[2] 9–14 silver, gold, linen garments : *ma-al-ba-ši*, carnelian, all sorts of (precious) stones, an ebony chair; all alike, fine things. Total (value): 160 *diban*.[3] Total: 40 female cupbearers, 40 (shekels of) silver being the price of a female cupbearer. 15–23 Send extremely beautiful female cupbearers in whom there is no defect, so the king, your lord, will say to you, "This is excellent, in accordance with the order[4] he sent to you." 24–32 And know that the king is hale like the Sun. For his troops, his ch[ariot]s, his horses, all goes very well. Aman has indeed put the Upper Land, the Lower Land, where the sun rises, where the sun sets, under the feet of the king.

NOTES

1. *an-⌜na-am⌝*: see *RA* 69 (1975) p. 151, n. 2. This (elsewhere *an-na-a*) is one of several features that set *EA* 369 apart from the other letters to vassals (Introduction, sect. 5): (1) non-Hittite ductus; (2) *ultēbilakku* (elsewhere *uštēbilakku*); (3) *ana qabê* (elsewhere *qabê*); (4) omission of *qibīma*; (5) conclusion of letter without parallel.

2. *ša-qí-tu*: see *RA* 69 (1975) p. 151, n. 2.

3. *ṭì-ba-an*: Egyptian *dbn*; on the reading, see Edel, *GM* 15 (1975) p. 12. The *dbn* weighed ca. 91 grams, and therefore the shekel here (10 shekels = 1 *dbn*) is not the Babylonian shekel (8.416 g) but the slightly heavier Syrian one (ca. 9 g).

4. KA (*pî*) *ši-pir₆-ti*: see *RA* 69 (1975) pp. 151ff.

EA 370

From the Pharaoh to a vassal

TEXT: BM 134870.
COPY: Gordon, *Or* n.s. 16 (1947) p. 15.
TRANSLITERATION AND TRANSLATION: Gordon, ibid., p. 5; Rainey, AOAT 8^2, pp. 44f.

Say to Idiya, the ruler of Ašqaluna: Thus the king. He herewith dispatches to you this tablet, saying to you, Be on your guard. You are to guard the place of the king where you are.

7–8 The king herewith sends to you Irimayašša,[1] 9–22 ... [...]. 23–29 And know that the king is hale like the Sun in the sky. For his troops and his chariots in multitude, from the Upper Land to the Lower Land, the rising of the sun to the setting of the sun, all goes very well.[2]

NOTES

1. Gordon, followed by Rainey, would make Irimayašša a commissioner (LÚ.MAŠKIM = *rābiṣu*), whereas Na'aman has him a stable overseer (LÚ PA.TÙR), a parallel to *EA* 367:8 (*Lingering over Words*, p. 400, n. 16).
2. The long form; see Introduction, sect. 5, and *EA* 99, n. 7.

EA 371

Smitten, smitten!

TEXT: BM 134868.
COPY: Gordon, *Or* n.s. 16 (1947) pp. 16f.
TRANSLITERATION AND TRANSLATION: Gordon, ibid., pp. 8f.; Rainey, AOAT 8^2, pp. 46f.; Izre'el, *Amurru,* pp. 62ff.

[...] 10–18 [...] ... I guard them [...] ... until the king, the Sun, [*gives tho*]*ught*[1] to his servants. [*And hea*]*r* my lord, *truly* [*I guar*]*d* his place and [*the cit*]*y* of my lord, *a*[*s my father did*]; there is no duplici[ty]. 19–24 [*With regard t*]*o* the troops of Šeḫlalu,[2] [*may he*] *know that* [*they are*] not friendly, and they *go on* seizing [*the land*]*s* along with the men *who* [*assi*]*st them.* [*I am guard*]*ing* the commissioners[3] ... 25–33 [*and*] I went to the rescue [...] along with my chariots [*and*] my [troops], but [...] ... had been burnt down, and slain [the ...] who were in the house [*of my lord*]. The very city of the king, my lord, from [...] was smitten, smitten! And [...] ... with money [... *bef*]*ore* the kings. 34–39 [At] their orders[4] he seized[5] [. . . *of*] the city, and I was afraid.[6] [. . .] . . .

NOTES

1. [yi-ma]-*lik*: cf. *EA* 85:38; 104:16. Izre'el includes *EA* 371 in the Amurru corpus (see n. 2). His collation of the tablet also suggested to him a wider tablet than allowed for here.

2. The town of Šeḫlalu figures prominently in ʿAbdi-Aširta's adventures as told in *EA* 62.

3. 15 [ù ši-m]i EN-*ia a-di* 16 [a-na-ṣa-*a*]*r aš-ri-šu- ù* 17 [URU?.K]I?EN-*ia ki*-⸢ma⸣ [a-bi-ia] 18 *ia-nu* ŠÀ-*ba ša-na-a*[*m*] 19 [aš-šu]m . . . 20 [li]-*de i-nu-ma la-a* DÙG.GA 21 [šu-nu] . . . 22 [KUR.KUR].KI . . . 23 [a]-*la-ki a-na pa-ni-šu*-[nu] 24 [a-na-ṣa]-*ru* . . . Line 15: the imperative addressed to the king is fairly common, especially in letters from Byblos; line 16: the apparent genitive is a difficulty, and accepting Izre'el's larger format (see n. 1), one might suggest [pa-nu-ia a-na na-ṣa-*a*]*r aš-ri-šu*, "my purpose is to guard his place"; line 17: I could see only one final vertical at the beginning of the line, and the last sign is not clearly *iṣ* (Gordon); line 20: if not [li], then [yi], and at the end of the line DÙG.GA is quite clear (see copy); line 21: perhaps not enough room for [šu-nu] and not necessary for sense; line 22: the durative (?) *tiṣbatūni* (cf. *EA* 126, n. 12?) probably calls for some sort of plural object (no oblique wedge in *qa*-sign; correct copy); line 23: after -*šu* I could identify nothing as certainly traces of writing; line 24: I could not make out the last sign, but Rainey's *ti* seemed possible and Izre'el suggests ka_4 (QA).

4. [*i-na*] UZU *pí-šu-nu*: quite clear.

5. *yi-iṣ-bat*: quite clear; so already Rainey.

6. *ap-lu-*⸢*uḫ*⸣: for *aplaḫ*.

EA 372–77

Omitted; see Introduction, sect. 2.

EA 378

All orders obeyed

TEXT: BM 50745.

COPY: Millard, *PEQ* 97 (1965), pl. XXV.

TRANSLITERATION AND TRANSLATION: Millard, ibid., pp. 14ff.; Rainey, AOAT 8^2, pp. 54f.

[To] the king, my [lord], m[y] god, [my Sun], the Sun fr[om] the sky: [Mess]age of Ya[paḫu], the ruler of Gazru, [your servant], the dirt at [your] feet. 5–13 I indeed prostrate myself at the feet of the king, my lord, my god, my Sun, the Sun from the sky, 7 times and 7 times, on the stomach and on the back. I am indeed guarding the place of the king, my lord, the Sun from the sky, where I am, 14–26 and all the things the king, my lord, has written me, I am indeed carrying out—everything! Who am I, a dog, and what is my house, and what is my [...], and what is anything I have, that the orders of the king, my lord, the Sun from the sky, I should not obey constantly?

EA 379–81

Omitted; see Introduction, sect. 2.

EA 382

About greetings

TEXT: BM 58364.
COPY: Walker, *JCS* 31 (1979) p. 249.

[*Th*]*us* ... [... *To*] my [*brother*] *s*[*ay*: ...] ... [M]ay [*my brother*] *be we*[*ll*]. Why [*has he*] not [*sent me*] greetings, (saying), "May all go we[ll *with my brother*]"? Why [*has he*] not [*sent*] in *the charge of* [..., *the* ...] of the king, ... [...] and ... [...]. If ... [...] ... [...] [...] the scri[be].[1]

NOTE

1. On the assignment of this fragment to the Amarna archive, see Walker. The script, especially the forms of *la* and *ni*, argues for either Hittite or Egyptian provenience. Note, too, the form of address (see Introduction, sect. 4). The text is probably a letter, with the obverse and reverse of the *editio princeps* to be exchanged (I keep the lineation, however). If so, then it seems to be sent by one official to another, not by a king to another king. My translation is based on the following reading:

Reverse

[um]-*ma* ^{m}x [... a-na]
[ŠEŠ]-*ia qí*-b[í-ma ...]
[(x)]-x *ma a* KA[B ...]
[x] *ma a u*Z [...]
[*l*]*u-ú ša*-l[i-im ŠEŠ-ia]
am-me-ni la [iš-pu-ra]
šul-ma [(...)]
lu-ú šul-[*mu* a-na ŠEŠ-ia]
am-me-ni l[*a* išpura/ušēbila]
i-na ŠU [^{m}...]

Obverse

ša LUGAL *a* [. . .]
ù šu x [. . .]
šum-ma PA x [. . .]
[x *u*]*m ma a* x [. . .]
[. . .] ^{lú}DUB.S[AR (. . .)]

That *ana* should appear on the first line and not at the beginning of the next line would be without parallel, as far as I know.

Index of Words Discussed

The following list contains the words discussed either in the Introduction (reference by page number [roman]) or in the notes to the letters (reference by *EA* number). The order is strictly alphabetical, even of Egyptian words. Note the sequences: *d, ḏ; h, ḥ, ḫ; s, ṣ, š; t, ṭ, ṯ; z, ẓ.*

Akkadian

Sumerian (Sumerograms)

Index of Proper Names

This index includes all the ancient proper names found in the introduction, the letters, and the notes to the letters. Where possible, the language of the personal names in the letters is identified and the names translated. It should be noted that many names classified here with the remark "language uncertain" have been considered by many scholars to be of Indo-Aryan origin. The analyses of these names, however, are often so divergent, and the objections against them so serious, that the option here is on the side of caution.

Abbreviations: Akk. = Akkadian; Egy. = Egyptian; Hitt. = Hittite; Hurr. = Hurrian; hypo. = hypocoristique; Kass. = Kassite; l.u. = language uncertain; Ugar. = Ugaritic; WS = West Semitic; DN = divine name; PN = personal name

The order is strictly alphabetical. Note the sequences: *s, ṣ, š; t, ṭ, ṯ.* All references are to *EA*.

Personal names

Aaddumi (WS[?] "It is Haddu"[?]), mayor(?) captured by Hittites, 170:17

ʿAbdi-Aširta /-Aširti /-Ašratu (WS "servant of Aširtu"), Amurru leader, position in Egy. administration not clear, 58 rev. 3; 60:2; 61:2; 62:2; 71:17; 73:18, 25; 74:24, 30; 75:29, 41; 76:8, 12; 78:9; 79:12, 22, 44; 81:7, 18, 47; 82:8, 23, 25; 83:25; 84:8; 85:41, 64, 68; 88:10; 89:24, 64; 90:12, 28; 92:7, 18–19; 93:23; 94:11; 95:24, 41; 97:21; 101:6, 30; 102:23; 103:9; 104:8, 18, 47; 105:11, 19, 25; 107:27, 36; 118:26, 29; 121:20; 123:38; 124:43; 125:41; 126:36, 64–65; 127:31; 129:5; 132:11, 17, 34; 133:7; 137:19, 43, 56, 58, 68, 70; 138:29, 34, 37, 50, 52, 72, 102, 116, 134; 147:68; 362:67

ʿAbdi-Aširti. *See* ʿAbdi-Aširta

ʿAbdi-Ašratu. *See* ʿAbdi-Aširta

ʿAbdi-Aštarti (WS "servant of ʿAštartu"), mayor of Qiltu(?), 63:3; 64:3; 65:3

ʿAbdi-Hadda (Baʿla?) (WS "servant of Haddu [Baʿlu]"), messenger of the Pharaoh, 119:51; 120:31, 35

ʿAbdi-Ḫeba (WS "servant of Ḫeba"), ruler of Jerusalem, 280:17, 23, 34; 285:2, 14; 286:2, 7, 61; 287:2, 65; 288:2

ʿAbdi-Irši (WS "servant of Iršu"), mayor of Ḫaṣura, 228:3 (*see note*)

ʿAbdi-Milki (WS "servant of Milku"), 1. Citizen of Gubla (instead of ^{m}l⟨R⟩-LUGAL, perhaps ^{m}*Aš-kur*-LUGAL, "Aškur is king"), 123:37; 2. Mayor of Šasḫimi, 203.3

ʿAbdina (WS hypo. "servant" [of DN? "servant of Na-[x-x]"?]), mayor in northern Palestine? 229:3

ʿAbdi-NINURTA (WS "servant of NINURTA"), citizen of Gubla? 84:39

ʿAbdi-Rama (WS "servant of Ramu"), citizen of Gubla? 123:36

ʿAbdi-Riša (WS "servant of Rišu"), mayor of Enišasi, 363:3

ʿAbdi-Tirši (WS "servant of Tiršu"), mayor of Ḫaṣura, 228:3 (*see note*)

ʿAbdi-URAŠ (WS "servant of URAŠ"), detained in Egypt with Aziru, 170:36

Abi-Milku (WS "My father is Milku"), mayor of Tyre, 146–55:2; 152:55

Adda-danu (WS "Hadda has judged" [*see* 292 n.1]), mayor of Gazru, 292–94:3

Addaya (WS[?], hypo. "Hadda"[?]), commissioner, 254:37; 285:24; 287:47, 49; 289:32

Addu-nirari (Akk. "Addu is my rescue[r]"), a king in Nuḫašše, 51:2

Rab(i)-Ilu (*cont'd*)
[Ilu] "has pleaded" [*rab<ryb*]), 1. Detained with Aziru in Egypt, 170:36; 2. Paapu's envoy, 333:24
Rab(i)-Ṣidqu (WS "Great is Ṣidqu"), detained with Aziru in Egypt, 170:37
Raḫmanu(ma?) (WS hypo. "the merciful one"), Egy. official, 284:9
Ramesses II, Pharaoh 1279–1212 B.C.
Reanap(a) (Egy. "Reᶜ is beautiful"), commissioner, 292:36; 315:13; 326:17
Rib-Adda/i. *See* Rib-Hadda
Rib-Eddi. *See* Rib-Hadda
Rib-H/Hadda (WS "plead, Hadda" or "plea of Hadda"), mayor of Gubla, *in the beginning of* 68–71; 73–79; 81–96; 102–14; 116–19; 121–26; 129–30; 132; 136–38; 362. *Also* 83:40; 85:24; 92:35; 105:88; 106:14, 31; 113:24; 119:19, 34; 121:23; 124:18; 129:45; 138:66, 90, 111; 142:21
Rib-Haddi. *See* Rib-Hadda
Rusmanya (l.u.), mayor of Šaruna, 241:3

Satatna, Sitatna, Šutatna (l.u.), mayor of Akka, 8:19, 38; 233:4; 234:3; 235:5; 238:23
Sitatna. *See* Satatna
Sitriyara/Zitriyara (l.u.), mayor? 211–14:3
Smenkhkare, Pharaoh 1336–1334 B.C.
Surata, Šaratu (l.u.), mayor of Akka, 8:19; 85:21; 232:3; 245:31, 33, 41, 43; 366:2
Ṣalmu (Akk. "black"), Babylonian envoy to Egypt, 7:73, 80; 11 rev. 8
Ṣur-Ašar (WS[?] "The rock is Ašar"[?]), mayor of Aḫtiašna, 319:4
Šab-Ilu (WS "Ilu/the god has pardoned [lit. returned]"), saved by ᶜAbdi-Aširta, 62:26
Šamu-Adda (WS "child [lit. name] of Adda"), mayor of Šamḫuna, probably the same as Šum-Adda, 225:3
Šaratu. *See* Surata
Šarru (Egy. "prince"), Pharaoh's enemy, 162:68
Šatiya (l.u.) [cf. Ugar. *bn šty?*]), mayor of Enišasi, 187:3
Šindi-Šugab (Kass. "gift of Šugab"[?]), Babylonian envoy to Egypt, 10:37, 48
Šipṭi-Baᶜla (Hadda) (WS "judged by Baᶜla [Hadda]), mayor of Lakiša, 330:3; 331:4; 332:3; 333:5, 9
Šipṭu-riṣa (WS[?] "Šipṭu, come to the rescue"[?]), mayor? 226:3
Šuardatu. *See* Šuwardata
Šub-Andu (WS[?] "pardon [lit. return] Andu"[?]), mayor in Palestine, *in the beginning of* 301–6
Šulum-Marduk (Akk. "well-being of Marduk"), identity unknown, 256:20
Šum-Adda (WS "child [lit. name] of Adda"), son of Balume (*see* Šamu-Adda), 8:13, 35; 224:3
Šumitta/i (l.u.), Egy. agent(s) in Alašia and Syria, 40:6; 57:13
Šumu-Haddi (WS "child [lit. name] of Haddu"), mayor(?) detained in Egypt, 97:1
Šuppiluliumaš (Hitt. "he who originated in the pure pool"), Hitt. king, 41:1
Šuta (Egy. hypo., the god Seth), commissioner, 234:14, 23, 33; 288:19, 22
Šutatna. *See* Satatna
Šut(t)arna (l.u.) 1. Father of Tušratta, 24 i 47; 29:18; 2. Mayor of Mušiḫuna, 182:2; 183:3; 184:4; 3. Father of Biryawaza, 194:9
Šutti (Egy. hypo., the god Seth), Pharaoh's envoy to Babylonia, 5:19
Šuwardata, Šuardatu (l.u.), mayor of Qiltu? 271:12; *in the beginning of* 279–84; 290:6, 27; 366:3

Tadu-Ḫeba (Hurr. "beloved of Ḫeba"), daughter of Tušratta, 22 iv 46; 23:7; 24 iii 103; 24 iv 67, 89; 26:4; 27:4, 20, 113; 28:8; 29:3, 32, 35, 189
Tadua (Hurr. hypo. "beloved [of DN]"), identity unknown, 257:17
Tagi (Hurr. hypo. "beautiful"), mayor of Gintikirmil(?), father-in-law of Milk-ilu, mayor of Gazru, 249:8; 263:33; 264–65:2; 266:4; 289:11, 19, 25
Taḫmašši (Egy. "Ptaḥ is born"; hypo. is [A]taḫmaya), Egy. official, perhaps a commissioner, 265:9; 303:20; 316:15; 364:13
Taku (Tagu?) (Hurr. hypo.[?] "beautiful"[?]) ancestor of Addu-nirari, 51:5, rev. 2

Fragmentary names

Divine names outside of personal names

Ninurta, Sumero-Akk. god of war and agriculture, son of Enlil. *See* 74 n.10

Rašpu (Resheph), WS god corresponding to Nergal. *See* 31 n.4 and 35 n.3

Sun, Šamaš, Šamšu (Akk.) *See also* Ištanuš, Re^c, Šimige, and Utu, 99:23; 108:10; 147:8, 43, 52, 58; 149:6; 159:8; 162:78, 80–81; 163 rev. 2, 4–5; 207:16; 367:23; 369:25, 30–31; 370:24, 28

Šamaš, Akk. sun-god. *See* Sun

Šauška, the Hurr. Ištar. Her cult was very popular among the Phoenicians, and to be identified with the Ištar of either Nineveh or Arbail, 19:24; 20:25; 21:15, 18; 23:13, 26, 31; 24 i 76; 24 iii 98

Šeri, bull-god in the service of Teššup, 24 iv 115

Šimige, Hurr. sun-god, 21:15, 18; 24 i 77, 86–87, 94, 101; 24 iv 125; 55:53, 56, 59, 63, 66

Teššup, Hurr. storm-god. *See* Adad

Utu, Sumerian sun-god. *See* Sun

Divine names only in personal names

ʿAmmu, WS deified paternal uncle or people (tribe): Ammistamru, (H)ammunira

ʿAnatu, WS goddess of war and love: Anatu

ʿAnu, WS god known only in PN: Bin-Anu

Api, Egy. god known only in PN: Api, Appiḫa(?)

Ašar, WS god known only in PN: Ṣur-Ašar(?)

Aširtu, Ašratu, biblical Asherah, according to Ugar. myths, spouse of El, mother of the gods and creatress of mankind: ʿAbdi-Aširta

Aškur, WS god known only in PN: Aškur-milku?

Aššur, numen of the city Aššur, national god of Assyria: Aššur-nadin-aḫḫe, Aššur-uballiṭ

ʿAštartu, Ugar. *ʿṯtrt,* Astarte of the Greeks, identified with Aphrodite, the planet Venus: ʿAbdi-Aštarti

Buriyaš, Kass. storm-god: Burna-Buriyas

Dagan, perhaps originally a storm-god, known to the Akkadians, but extremely popular along the Middle Euphrates and in Syria: Dagan-takala

El(u). *See* Il(u)

Enlil, supreme god of the Sumerian pantheon: Kadašman-Enlil

Ḫaʿapi (*ḥʿpy*), Egy. god of the Nile: Ḫaapi, Ḫaip

Ḫammu. *See* ʿAmmu

Ḫeba(t), Hurr. goddess, spouse of Teššup: ʿAbdi-Ḫeba, Kelu-Ḫeba, Tadu-Ḫeba

Horus, Egy. falcon-god, lord of the sky: Ḫaramašši, Ḫaramassa

Il(u), El(u), head of Canaanite pantheon: Rab(i)-Ilu, Šab-Ilu, Yabni-Ilu

Iršu, WS god, known mainly from PN: ʿAbdi-Irši

Marduk, god of Babylon and Babylonian national god: Šulum-Marduk

Mer, Mir, Wer, storm-god, assimilated to Adad: Balu-Mir, Pirissi(?)

Mḥyt, Egy. goddess of the northwind: Pamaḫu(?)

Milku, WS god, "the king": ʿAbdi-Milki, Ili-Milku, Milk-ilu, Milkayu, Milkuru

NIN.UR.MAḪ.MEŠ. *See* Personal names

Ptaḥ, god of Memphis and, according to Memphite theology, the Creator: (A)taḫmaya, Taḫmašši

Ramu, WS, "the exalted one," known only in PN: ʿAbdi-Rama

Reʿ, Egy. sun-god: Ḫuriya, Maireya, Manaḫpirya, Napḫurureya, Nib/pḫurrereya, Nibmuareya, Reanap(a)

Rišu (WS[?], meaning uncertain [cf. Ugar. *ʿbdrš*?]): ʿAbdi-Riša

Geographical names

Names marked with *, see map of Near East (p. l); names marked with +, see map of vassal cities (p. 124); modern site identifications given in italics.

Fragmentary names

Group names

Aḫlamean (*aḫlamayyu*), in the Amarna-period a name for certain bands moving along the Middle Euphrates and in northern Mesopotamia; originally, perhaps the name of a tribe (cf. Suteans), 200:8, 10
ʿApiru, usually a pejorative term, meaning uncertain, used of those who did not accept Egy. authority or who wished to throw it off. Their identity and

Designed by Sue Bishop

Composed by Village Typographers, Inc.,
in Garamond No. 3 text and display

Printed by The Maple Press Company, Inc.,
on 50-lb. Glatfelter Eggshell Cream
and bound in Arrestox cloth

9 780801 867156

Made in the USA
Monee, IL
20 July 2021

73991911R00246